D1595341

THE
BOOKS OF
HISTORY

Old Testament Survey Series

THE
BOOKS OF
HISTORY

JAMES E. SMITH

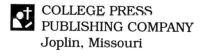
COLLEGE PRESS
PUBLISHING COMPANY
Joplin, Missouri

Library of Congress Cataloging-in-Publication Data

Smith, James E. (James Edward), 1939–
  The books of history / James E. Smith
    p.   cm. — (Old Testament survey series)
  Includes bibliographic references.
  ISBN 0-89900-424-5
  1. Bible. O.T. Historical Books—Criticism, interpretation, etc.
  2. Bible. O.T. Historical Books—History of Biblical events.
  3. Bible. O.T. Historical Books—History of contemporary events.
  I. Title. II. Series: Smith, James E. (James Edward), 1939–
  Old Testament survey series.
  BS1286.5.S65 1995
  222'.061—dc20   95-3858
                                                          CIP

DEDICATED TO

GLENN BOURNE
LYLE BUNDY
MICHAEL CHAMBERS
TWILA SIAS

MY COLLEAGUES OF MANY YEARS
AT
FLORIDA CHRISTIAN COLLEGE

CONTENTS

Part Three
The Restoration Period

Charts and Diagrams

Maps

PREFACE

Modern man views history with disdain. Many would agree with Shakespeare that history is "a tale told by an idiot, full of sound and fury, signifying nothing." Others would echo the more blunt assessment of Henry Ford: "History is bunk!" Casual students find history a dull recitation of facts and dates. Believers, however, find God in all history. It is truly HIS-story! The unshakable conviction of the Christian faith is that the Lord rules forever; his throne is from generation to generation (Lam 5:19).

The focus of the following pages is on the so-called historical books of the Old Testament. Though much biblical history is contained in the Pentateuch, the bulk of the history of Israel as a nation is contained in the twelve books beginning with Joshua. These books relate the history of God's interaction with his people from the time they entered Canaan about 1407 BC to the reforms instigated by Nehemiah about 432 BC.

This survey proceeds from the general to the specific. The opening chapter is an overview of the twelve books as a collection. The collection is then subdivided into three parts according to the period of history which each relates. The first three books (Joshua, Judges, Ruth) are the pre-monarchy books. The three double books of Samuel, Kings and Chronicles narrate the history of Israel's monarchy. The last three books (Ezra, Nehemiah, Esther) describe events following the collapse of the monarchy. Each of the three parts has its own introductory chapter.

The translation of Scripture in the following pages is that of the author unless otherwise indicated. The notes themselves have been collected over thirty years of teaching a freshman level course in the history of Israel at Cincinnati Bible College and Florida Christian College. Every effort has been made to credit secondary literature where appropriate. From time to time over the years, however, lecture notes were supplemented with citations without documentation.

In the production of this volume the encouragement and assistance of Linda Stark, Librarian of Florida Christian College, is gratefully acknowledged.

CHAPTER ONE

The Books of History
An Overview

Sunday School children memorize the divisions of the Old Testament library as five books of law, twelve books of history, five books of poetry, five major and twelve minor prophets. The second of these divisions is the focus of this volume.

THE TWELVE VOLUME COLLECTION

Actually the 5-12-5-5-12 breakdown of the thirty-nine Old Testament books is but one of several systems for organizing this material. The rabbis of old, as well as modern writers, have proposed other schemes of representing the organization of the Old Testament library.

A. Ancient Arrangements.

As early as the second century BC Jews saw their Bible as consisting of three divisions: Law (*Torah*), Prophets (*Nebhi'im*) and Writings

(*Kethubhim*). The modern Hebrew Bible follows this arrangement. The five books of Moses—the so-called Pentateuch—constitute the first division. The Prophets consists of eight books: Joshua, Judges, Samuel and Kings (the Former Prophets); Isaiah, Jeremiah, Ezekiel and the Twelve (the Latter Prophets). The remaining books are considered the Writings. In this system the books which follow the Book of the Twelve (the Minor Prophets) are: Psalms, Job, Proverbs, Ruth, Song of Solomon, Ecclesiastes, Lamentations, Esther, Daniel, Ezra-Nehemiah, and Chronicles.

Not much has been written about the twelve historical books as a collection. This is probably due to the false perception that the arrangement of books in the modern Hebrew Bible represents an ancient assessment of the Old Testament collection. The evidence, however, points in a different direction.

While it is true that the tripartite organization of the Old Testament can be traced to pre-Christian times, the present-day assignment of books to the three divisions (5-8-11) can be traced only to the fourth century AD. In the days of Josephus (c. AD 90) the second division (*Nebhi'im*) contained thirteen books. According to Josephus the third division (*Kethubhim*) consisted of four books containing "hymns to God" and "precepts for the conduct of human life" (*Against Apion* 1:8). Most likely those four books were Psalms, Proverbs, Ecclesiastes, and Song of Solomon.

The reasons for shifting Chronicles, Ezra-Nehemiah, Ruth and Esther from the *Nebhi'im* to the *Kethubhim* after the days of Josephus are obscure. The important point is, however, that the twelve historical books were considered as being "prophetic," i.e., written by prophets. These twelve books—eleven when Ruth is counted as part of Judges—were a unit even from pre-Christian times.

Whereas the tripartite arrangement of the Old Testament books is attested as early as Ben Sira (c. 280 BC), the Dead Sea Scrolls point toward a twofold breakdown, viz., the law and the prophets. Both the twofold and the threefold system are reflected in the New Testament.[1] One is therefore forced to conclude that the two ways of organizing the Old Testament books enjoy equal antiquity.[2]

Other ancient evidence regarding the organization of the Old Testament books is more difficult to assess. The earliest extant manuscripts of the Septuagint (Greek) version come from the fourth century AD and come from Christian circles. Here the books of the Apocrypha—books which never were accepted as Scripture in authoritative Jewish circles—have been mingled with the canonical books of Scripture. A discussion of the reasons for this strange circumstance lies beyond the scope of the present volume. The lists of Old Testament books which come from the early Church Fathers support the conclusion that at least the books of Joshua, Judges, 1 & 2 Samuel, 1 & 2 Kings, and 1 & 2 Chronicles were regarded as a unit. Ruth and Esther and sometimes Ezra and Nehemiah were mingled in these lists with the poetic books.[3]

B. Modern Arrangements.

J. Sidlow Baxter[4] has proposed a modern threefold breakdown of Old Testament books as they appear in the English Bible. He classifies the first seventeen books as history and the last seventeen as prophecy. Sandwiched between are the five experiential books which focus on the inner life of Old Testament believers. In detail his organizational scheme looks like this:

I. HISTORY (17)
A. Basic Law (5)
B. Pre-exilic Records (9)
C. Postexilic Records (3)
II. EXPERIENCE (5): the heart
III. PROPHECY (17)
A. Basic Prophecy (5)
B. Pre-exilic Prophets (9)
C. Postexilic Prophets (3)

Another threefold way of viewing the Old Testament library is as follows:

I. FOUNDATIONAL BOOKS (5): Genesis-Deuteronomy
II. FRAMEWORK BOOKS (12): Joshua-Nehemiah
A. Pre-monarchy (3)
B. Monarchy (3 double books)
C. Post-monarchy (3)

III. FOCUS BOOKS (22): Psalms-Malachi
    A. Focus on Individuals (5): Psalms-Song
    B. Focus on Issues (17): Isaiah-Malachi

Chart No. 1

THE CONTENTS OF THE HISTORICAL BOOKS					
PRE-CROWN		CROWN		POST-CROWN	
Joshua	Judges	1-2 Samuel	1-2 Kings	Ezra	Nehemiah
Conquest of Canaan	Unrest in Canaan	Birth & Expansion of the Kingdom	Decline & Destruction of the Kingdom	Return to Canaan	Rebuilding in Canaan
	Ruth A Family Preserved	1-2 Chronicles A Dynasty Preserved		Esther A Nation Preserved	
Settling in Canaan		**Ruling over Canaan**		**Returning to Canaan**	

In the above scheme the framework books are those which give the outline for the history of Israel from the time of the conquest through the second governorship of Nehemiah. Merely seeing these twelve books in a list, however, conveys the erroneous impression that each continues the history which was recorded in the preceding book. Actually in each of the triads of books the first two might be designated "forward motion books" because they advance the history of Israel chronologically. Thus Judges, for example, advances the history which was narrated in the Book of Joshua. Kings advances the history of Samuel and Nehemiah that of Ezra.

The third book in each triad might be labeled a "sidestep book" or "spotlight book." The Book of Ruth highlights an incident which chronologically fits somewhere into the Book of Judges, probably into chapter 10. The two books of Chronicles (considered one book in Jewish tradition) spotlight God's dealings with the Davidic dynasty. The Book of Esther fits chronologically between chapters 6 and 7 of the Book of Ezra. Ruth records the preservation of a family, Chronicles the preservation of a dynasty, and Esther the preservation of a nation. The arrangement of the historical books in the English Bible

16

moving two steps forward and one to the side creates the impression that one is virtually waltzing through a thousand years of history.

THE SCOPE OF ISRAEL'S HISTORY

History has been defined as that branch of knowledge which records and explains the past. Bible history would then be that recitation and interpretation of the past which is recorded in the Bible. Perhaps Old Testament history could be defined as that part of history in which God prepared for Christ through a specially chosen and trained people. The history of Israel should be defined still more narrowly as the history of that people which became a nation at Mt. Sinai and was subsequently known as Israel.

Those who have written in the field are not united in their understanding of the scope of the history of Israel. The *terminus a quo* for this study has been taken to be creation (Sanders, Snell, Ottley); Abraham (Payne, Bright); the Exodus (Oesterley and Robinson, Bailey and Kent); and the settlement in Palestine (Noth). The present work is not technically a history of Israel, but is a survey of the historical books of the Old Testament. Hence the starting point has been defined by the historical circumstances reflected in the first chapter of the Book of Joshua.

Scholars are also divided over the *terminus ad quem* (ending point) of the history of Israel. Should it be the second governorship of Nehemiah (Flanders, Crapps, W. Smith)? The end of the Maccabean revolt in 165 BC (Bright)? The first Roman conquest of Jerusalem in AD 70 (H. Wheeler Robinson)? Or the final revolt against Rome in AD 135 (Noth, Payne, Oesterley and Robinson)? Some would even argue that the history of Israel continues to modern times (Bailey and Kent). Because this present volume is a survey of the twelve historical books of the Old Testament the *terminus ad quem* has been defined as the conclusion of the Book of Nehemiah which relates what is chronologically the last event of the Old Testament.

THE NATURE OF BIBLICAL HISTORY

In one of the most significant studies of the past fifty years Meredith Kline[5] has proposed a revolutionary way of looking at the Old Testament canon. Building upon research into ancient treaty forms, Kline has proposed viewing the entire Old Testament as a treaty (covenant) document consisting of a basic treaty core (Genesis-Deuteronomy) and four types of related treaty documents. The core consists of a prologue (Genesis-Exodus 19) and stipulations (Exodus 20-Deuteronomy). All the other books are creative expansions of that core document.

Kline saw the Old Testament wisdom books—especially Proverbs—as an expansion of the stipulation section of the core document. These books also explore the mysteries of the government of Yahweh the Great King to whom Israel had pledged allegiance at Sinai. The Psalms expand upon the vassal ratification response of the people found in the treaties of the ancient Near East and in the core covenant document (e.g., Exod 24:1-8).[6] The role of the prophets in Israel corresponds to the role of the ambassadors of the great kings in the politics of the ancient world. Their job was to declare Yahweh's claims, enforce his will, and apply the ancient covenant sanctions in new situations.

According to Kline, the so-called historical books are an extension of the prologue in the core document. The theme of these twelve books is the covenant relationship with God. In these books Yahweh's fidelity to the covenant is placed in juxtaposition to Israel's infidelity.

The shape of all historical works is determined by the sources available to the historian and the focus which he wishes to give to the material. Thus some choose to focus on economics, others on political history, still others on social institutions. The biblical historians wrote from a prophetic point of view. They wrote sacred history which emphasizes the role of God in human events. They feature the acts of prophets like Samuel. They emphasize the great prophetic themes of the Exodus, the gift of the land of Canaan, and the covenant obligations of justice and exclusive worship of Yahweh. This, then, is sacred history. The persons, peoples, movements, institutions herein described are those which God used to fulfill his gracious and holy purpose.

THE METHOD OF BIBLICAL HISTORY

All historians are dependent on contemporary sources. The biblical books of history, with the possible exception of Joshua and Nehemiah, cover such enormous time spans that the use of earlier written sources and oral tradition was mandatory. The biblical historians often mention the sources from which they derived their information. In Chronicles, for example, some twenty-five extrabiblical documents are named.[7] Some of these sources were journals or day books in which principal events of the two kingdoms were recorded by court "remembrancers." Other sources were memoirs of various prophets. The "Book of Jasher" mentioned twice in the text (Josh 10:13; 2 Sam 1:18) appears to have been a poetic account of the battles of ancient Israel.

From these ancient sources the biblical historians selected the strands of raw material with which they wove their account of covenant history. The Holy Spirit guided in the selection process so that no erroneous material was incorporated into the text. These twelve books are part of Holy Scripture which the Lord Jesus, the Apostles and the early church regarded as inspired of God (2 Tim 3:16).The exact mechanics of the working of the Spirit cannot now be explained. What is important is that the writings of these historians are different from all other histories ever written except those which are found in the New Testament. Thus these books contain "sacred history" not only because of the facts related therein, but because this material has the imprimatur of God's Holy Spirit.

COMPOSITION OF THE BOOKS

As in the case of most of the Old Testament library, the critical and conservative explanations of the composition of the historical books are quite different.

A. Critical View.
Modern historical criticism has proposed two alternative theories to explain the composition of the historical books. The first—the so-called documentary theory—was advanced by Otto Eissfeldt. In this

theory the Book of Joshua is regarded as the concluding volume of a Hexateuch. The documentary sources (J,E,D & P) which the critics imagine they have discovered in the Pentateuch are traced through Joshua. The second theory, which was put forward by Martin Noth, envisions an independent historical work consisting of the Book of Deuteronomy followed by Joshua through Kings. This material was organized sometime after the Exile by a redactor which the critics have dubbed the "deuteronomist."

These critical theories flounder on one hard fact. Both historically and exegetically the historical books are distinct from the Pentateuch. The trend in Old Testament studies is to focus on the final shape of each of the canonical books, to appreciate each as separate and distinct from the others. While there is certainly interdependence among these books, they yet reflect a certain independence. In any case, after a century of scholarly debate agreement among the critics remains an elusive goal.[8]

Critics generally regard Esther as a literary romance, i.e., a good story with a kernel of truth. Ruth is regarded as a postexilic tract written to oppose the harsh exclusiveness of Ezra and Nehemiah.

B. Conservative View.

The authorship of the various historical books will be discussed later in this volume. Suffice it to say that conservative scholars are more open to the possibility that the traditional authors of these books did in fact author them. Tradition associates the name of Joshua with the authorship of the book that bears his name. Samuel is said to have been the author of Judges. The life of David as recorded in the books of Samuel was chronicled by the prophets Samuel, Nathan and Gad (1 Chr 29:29). Tradition assigned the authorship of Kings to Jeremiah. Chronicles and Ezra-Nehemiah may have come from the pen of Ezra. Jewish tradition is not united on the authorship of Esther. Mordecai and Ezra have both been nominated.

Each book in this collection of twelve (with the possible exception of Ruth) should be regarded as a separate entity. The authors, however, seem to have been conscious of contributing to a continuing history. By means of a literary "hook" an author would connect his work to the work which preceded. Joshua 24:26 suggests that Joshua added his work to that of Moses. His work probably begins with Deuteronomy 34 and concludes with Joshua 24:28. The author of Judges would have added the record of Joshua's death (Josh 24:29-33). The author of Kings joins his work to Samuel by opening his book with the narration of David's death.

An obvious discontinuity occurs at the conclusion of Kings. Chronicles begins with genealogies stretching back to Adam. The focus quickly moves, however, to David and his descendants. The hooking principle is again evident with the opening verses of Ezra. They repeat verbatim the concluding verses of Chronicles.[9]

CHRONOLOGICAL OVERVIEW

Chronologically speaking, Old Testament history begins with Abraham. Attempts to establish chronology prior to the call of this great patriarch are futile. In the broadest possible outline of Old Testament history, about six hundred years elapsed between Abraham and Moses. About four hundred years passed between Moses and David. Between David and the conclusion of Old Testament history (Ezra-Nehemiah) another six hundred years can be assigned. The intertestamental period lasted about four hundred years. Thus a pattern emerges which may be illustrated as follows:

Abraham to Moses	600 years.
Moses to David	400 years.
David to Nehemiah	600 years.
Nehemiah to Christ	400 years.

To fine tune this general picture, Old Testament history is frequently divided into twelve periods. Five of these periods are covered in the Pentateuch. These are:

Antediluvian	Duration unknown.
Postdiluvian	Duration unknown.
Patriarchal	215 years.
Egyptian	430 years.
Wilderness	40 years.

The history related in the framework books (Joshua-Esther) is usually divided into seven periods.

Conquest	40 years (1407-1367 BC).
Judges	324 years (1367-1043 BC).
United Monarchy	112 years (1043-930 BC).
Divided Monarchy	210 years (930-722 BC).
Judean	135 years (722-586 BC).
Exilic	48 years (586-538 BC).
Postexilic	106 years (538-432 BC).

THEOLOGICAL OVERVIEW

The faith of Israel's historians is transparent in their writings. These writers were passionately monotheistic and aniconic (worship without idols or images). Though they were aware of the existence of local "godlings" (e.g., Baal; Asherah) and even of the national gods of surrounding nations (e.g., Chemosh, Milcom), they believed that one God—Yahweh—ruled over all. All other pretenders to deity were worthless non-entities.

The biblical historians also firmly believed that the one true God had revealed himself to man. For them the primary source of this revelation was the Mosaic law. Yahweh, however, also spoke to his people through priestly oracle, the so-called Urim (1 Sam 14:41; 23:2; 30:7f.), dreams (1 Kgs 3:5), and prophets both named (e.g., Micaiah in 1 Kgs 22) and unnamed (e.g., 1 Sam 2:27). In 1 Samuel 28:6 the three means by which God might be expected to speak to a reigning king are brought together: "When Saul inquired of Yahweh, Yahweh did not answer him, either by dreams or by Urim or by prophets."

If the Pentateuch lays the foundation for the coming of Christ, the historical books relate the preparation for his coming. Since the revelation at Mt. Sinai Yahweh had chosen to identify with one nation. To that people he gave his revelation (Rom 3:2). Through his special ambassadors, the prophets, he shaped and molded that people. He carved out of national Israel a spiritual remnant which longed for the Messiah. This remnant kept faith alive even in the most trying circumstances. From the vantage point of the New Testament, Old Testament history consists of a myriad of arrows pointing to the fullness of times (Gal 4:4-5). Even so, Old Testament history is not merely a period of aimless waiting. Throughout these millennia God was moving decisively toward the goal of redemption for all people in Christ Jesus.[10]

Israel was called of God to be a light to the nations of the world, a testament to the power and grace of God. The ultimate plan was to bless all nations through Christ, the seed of Abraham, Isaac and Jacob. To that end the Lord endured a thousand years of indifference and outright apostasy broken up only occasionally by periods of renewal and revival. The history of Israel is in many ways a tragic history with a predictable conclusion. As horrendous as it was, the destruction of Jerusalem in 586 BC marked a turning point, at least as far as overt idolatry was concerned. When the Jews returned from exile in Babylon the old Canaanite idolatry which had polluted the nation since the days of Joshua was a thing of the past.

The message of the historical books revolves around four axes: kingship, prophets, the sanctuary and worship. Regarding kingship, the message is that God was faithful to the promises he made to David. Man-made kings were a disaster. Regarding prophets the message is that God sought at every opportunity to evoke repentance in his people. Through interpretation of past disasters and warnings of worse things to come mingled with assurances of blessing to reward fidelity, the prophets sought to impress upon Israel the need for a daily walk with the Lord.

As regards the sanctuary, the historical books make the point that the physical sanctuary—tabernacle or temple—was the earthly dwelling place of God. The one God required and permitted but one sanctuary and that could be located only at the place of his choosing. Worship was the standard by which the biblical historians measured the characters who appeared on this millennial stage. No matter what a person's accomplishments might be, if he did not worship the Lord in spirit and truth that man is judged by these historians to be a failure. The sanctuary was the nerve center of the nation.

IMPORTANCE OF OLD TESTAMENT HISTORY

Many Christians have never made a serious study of the Old Testament historical books because they perceive them to be boring and impractical. What possible relevance can anything have which happened "way over there" on a sliver of real estate called Canaan over 2500 years ago? The main characters in this history have now been dead for thirty centuries or so. Even when alive they lived in a world totally different from anything experienced by the contemporary Christian. Some of their beliefs and practices offend modern sensitivities and seem, on the surface at least, to oppose the spirit of Christ. So why bother with the twelve historical books?

Many good reasons can be advanced for studying these books. First, Israel's historians produced great literature, though that was not their purpose. They tell thrilling stories with consummate skill. Indeed the books of Samuel and Kings "contain some of the noblest and most moving stories in all literature." Like all great literature these books have the power to uplift, delight, console, encourage and warn the human heart.[11]

The historical books have a certain ethical power. Both by example and warning they inspire noble conduct. The challenging stories found here challenge the readers to make a decision to emulate what is worthy and to shun what is base.[12]

Even more important, the twelve historical books were part of the Bible of the Lord Jesus. He knew and loved these books. If no other reason could be offered for a study of Old Testament history this alone should cause the disciple of Christ to want to master the content of these books.

The Apostle Paul suggested that Old Testament history offered many valuable lessons for Christians (Rom 15:4; 1 Cor 10:11). The Scriptures of the Old Testament were capable of making one wise unto salvation (2 Tim 3:15). In these books are prophecies and pointers toward Christ (John 5:39; Luke 24:44f.).

Still other good reasons for the study of the historical books can be advanced. First, these documents are completely true (John 10:35; 2 Tim 3:16; 2 Pet 1:21). Virtually every issue of archaeological journals contains verification of details of the history contained in these books.

Second, the historical books of the Old Testament have had a major influence on the fine arts.[13] Third, these books contain the record of God's dealings with a unique and wonderful people. Fourth, these books are valuable for homiletical purposes. Fifth, these books throw invaluable light upon ancient practices and beliefs. Sixth, they furnish a framework in which the message of Israel's prophets can be understood.

Perhaps the best statement ever written about the value of studying Old Testament history was penned by F.K. Sanders in 1914.

The study of history ought to inspire students with generous ideals of active and responsible citizenship, with sincere ambitions for sane, strong leadership, with convictions regarding national policies and the power to distinguish between that which is clever and that which is fine and noble. No history surpasses that of the Hebrew people in its power to transmit and impress such results as these.[14]

INTERPRETING BIBLICAL HISTORY[15]

About forty percent of the Old Testament is in narrative form. Most of that material is contained in the twelve books which are the subject of this study. Those who read these narratives tend to make several mistakes in interpretation. They tend, for example, to regard these narratives as simply being stories about those who lived in Old Testament times. The biblical authors were not entertainers who could spin a good yarn. It is the work of God through people which should be emphasized. In the final analysis God is the hero of Old Testament narrative.

Others treat the stories as allegories which teach mysterious truths. Some even go so far as to read into the narratives such outlandish things as space ships and extra-terrestrials.

Another mistake which is commonly made is the attempt to identify some direct lesson or moral in each story. Every individual account is like the piece of a puzzle, which when joined to other pieces, presents the big picture. Biblical narrative illustrates what is explicitly taught elsewhere. One should not attempt to formulate doctrinal propositions based solely on a narrative.

Interpreters of Old Testament history should remember that narratives record what actually happened, not necessarily what should have happened. Therefore, the conduct of individuals in these accounts is often less than praiseworthy, and sometimes just plain despicable.

By its very nature narrative is selective and incomplete. Not all questions about an episode that one might wish to be answered are in fact answered. For this reason the Old Testament deuterographs—substantially the same narrative appearing in two separate books—may seem on the surface to be contradictory. One writer chose to emphasize certain details of what took place, while another adds additional details. A student would do well to purchase a harmony of Samuel, Kings and Chronicles before undertaking a serious study of these books. In the bibliography for the monarchy books two of these tools will be cited.

ENDNOTES

1. The twofold arrangement is reflected in such passages as Matt 5:17 and Luke 16:16-17; the threefold in Luke 24:44.

2. R. Laird Harris, *Inspiration and Canonicity of the Bible* (Grand Rapids: Zondervan, 1969), pp. 140-48.

3. F.F. Bruce, *The Canon of Scripture* (Downers Grove, IL: InterVarsity, 1988), pp. 68-97.

4. J. Sidlow Baxter, *Explore the Book* (Grand Rapids: Zondervan, 1960), 1:15-20.

5. Meredith G. Kline, *The Structure of Biblical Authority* (Grand Rapids: Eerdmans, 1972).

6. Kline did not address the issue of the Song of Solomon in relation to his covenant theory. The core document, however, has much to say about sexuality. The Song may be a positive expansion of those stipulations dealing with sex.

7. These sources are conveniently itemized by Willis J. Beecher, "Chronicles, Book of" in *International Standard Bible Encyclopaedia* (Grand Rapids: Eerdmans, 1956), 1:630.

8. Peter Craigie, *The Old Testament, its Background, Growth and Content* (Nashville: Abingdon, 1986), p. 144.

9. R. Laird Harris, "What Books Belong in the Canon of Scripture?" in *Can I Trust the Bible?* (Chicago: Moody, 1968), pp. 71ff.

10. Walter Roehrs, *Survey of Covenant History* (St. Louis: Concordia, 1989), p. 11.

11. Gordon Robinson, *Historians of Israel (1)* in "Bible Guides" (Nashville: Abingdon, 1962), p. 81.
12. *Ibid.,* p. 83.
13. Cynthia P. Maus devotes over six hundred pages to a discussion of the art, music and literature generated by the events in Israel's history. *The Old Testament and the Fine Arts* (New York: Harper, 1954).
14. F.K. Sanders, *The History of the Hebrews* (New York: Scribners, 1914), pp. 6-7.
15. The material in this section is a summarization of the excellent chapter on the proper use of Old Testament narrative in *How to Read the Bible for All its Worth* by Gordon Fee and Douglas Stuart (Grand Rapids: Zondervan, 1982), esp., pp. 74-78.

BIBLIOGRAPHY: GENERAL

Included are works (1) which cover the entire sweep of the history of Israel from the conquest through the restoration; and (2) which survey the twelve historical books of the Old Testament library.

A. Introductions.

Archer, Gleason. *A Survey of Old Testament Introduction.* Revised pb ed. Chicago: Moody, 1985.

Baxter, J. Sidlow. *Explore the Book.* Six vols. in one. Grand Rapids: Zondervan, 1960.

Harrison, R.K. *Introduction to the Old Testament.* Grand Rapids: Eerdmans, 1969.

Jensen, Irving L. *Jensen's Survey of the Old Testament.* Chicago: Moody, 1978.

LaSor, William Sanford, David Hubbard, Frederic Bush. *Old Testament Survey.* Grand Rapids: Eerdmans, 1982.

Slemming, C.W. *The Bible Digest.* One vol. ed. Grand Rapids: Kregel, 1968.

B. Histories.

Bright, John. *A History of Israel.* Philadelphia: Westminster, 1959.

Castel, Francois. *The History of Israel and Judah in Old Testament Times.* Trans. Matthew J. O'Connell. New York: Paulist, 1985.

Davis, John and John Whitcomb. *A History of Israel*. Grand Rapids: Baker, 1980.

Edersheim, Alfred. *Old Testament Bible History*. Grand Rapids: Eerdmans, 1977 reprint in one volume.

Harrison, R.K. *Old Testament Times*. Grand Rapids:Eerdmans, 1970.

Hayes, John H. and J. Maxwell Miller. *Israelite and Judaean History* in "The Old Testament Library." Philadelphia: Westminster, 1977.

Herrmann, Siegfried. *A History of Israel in Old Testament Times*. Philadelphia: Fortress, 1981.

Lemche, Niels Peter. *Ancient Israel; a New History of Israelite Society*. Sheffield: JSOT, 1988.

Merrill, Eugene H. *Kingdom of Priests*. Grand Rapids: Baker, 1987.

Orlinsky, Harry M. *Ancient Israel*. 2nd ed. Ithaca, NY: Cornell, 1960.

Peritz, Ismar. *Old Testament History*. New York: Abingdon, 1915.

Pfeiffer, Charles. *Old Testament History*. Grand Rapids: Baker, 1973.

Schultz, Samuel. *The Old Testament Speaks*. 2nd ed. New York: Harper & Row, 1970.

Shanks, Hershel ed. *Ancient Israel; a Short History from Abraham to the Roman Destruction of the Temple*. Washington: Biblical Archaeology Society, 1988.

Smith, William. *Old Testament History*. Revised and amended by Wilbur Fields. Joplin, MO: College Press, 1967.

Soggin, J. Alberto. *A History of Ancient Israel*. Philadelphia: Westminster, 1984.

Stanley, A.P. *Lectures on the History of the Jewish Church*. 3 vols. New York: Scribners, 1892.

Wade, G.W. *Old Testament History*. 3rd. ed. London: Methuen, 1904.

Wood, Leon. *A Survey of Israel's History*. Revised by David O'Brien. Grand Rapids: Academia Books, 1986.

PART ONE

THE SETTLEMENT

PERIOD

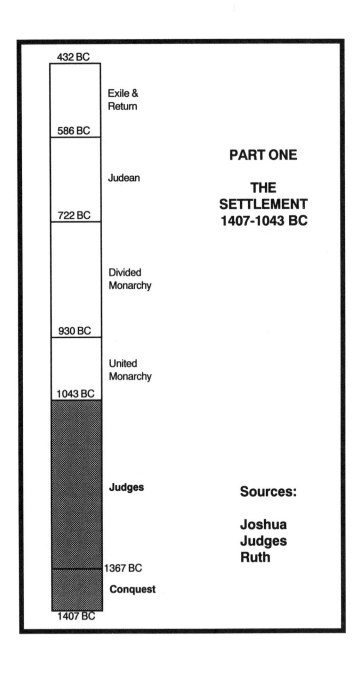

432 BC

Exile & Return

586 BC

Judean

722 BC

Divided Monarchy

930 BC

United Monarchy

1043 BC

Judges

1367 BC

Conquest

1407 BC

PART ONE

THE SETTLEMENT 1407-1043 BC

Sources:

**Joshua
Judges
Ruth**

CHAPTER TWO

The Pre-monarchy Books
An Introduction

Joshua, Judges and Ruth describe Israel's history between 1407 and 1043 BC. This is sometimes called the Settlement Period of Old Testament history. These four centuries may be subdivided into the Conquest Period (1407-1367 BC) and the Judges Period (1367-1043).

THE BOOK OF JOSHUA

The Book of Joshua occurs at a strategic place in the Old Testament canon. The book forms a bridge between the Pentateuch and that which follows. The Pentateuch concludes with the account of the death of Moses, the great Lawgiver. The Book of Joshua begins with the words *"After the death of Moses the servant of the Lord, it came to pass that the Lord spoke to Joshua the son of Nun, Moses' minister . . . ."* Thus the Historical Books take up the account of God's dealings with Israel where the Pentateuch left off.

The Mosaic books depict Israel moving toward Canaan. Joshua describes Israel entering into Canaan.

Besides this continuity of event, the book indicates continuity of authority. Joshua succeeded Moses. In many respects Joshua functioned like a second Moses. He enjoyed many of the privileges accorded the great Lawgiver. Scripture, however, takes care to point out frequently that the entire conquest of Canaan corresponded to the arrangements Moses had set forth as God's command.[1] Thus Moses is honored as the architect of the Conquest. Joshua is presented as the faithful executor of Moses' will (cf. Deut 31:3-8).

Continuity, however, is not the whole story. The Book of Joshua is a kind of climax of all which had gone before. The land promise made to Abram almost seven centuries earlier (c. 2092 BC) was now fulfilled. Israel's earlier failure to enter the land (Num 14:39-35) was now reversed. The glorious *vision* of faith set forth by Moses in his closing speeches (Deut 26-33) now became the *venture* of faith. The prospect of a land flowing with milk and honey now became possession of Canaan. Israel was on the pinnacle. The predominant note (with an occasional sour note) in Joshua is one of joy, confidence and exuberance.

With the possession of the land a new phase of Israel's history began. Joshua is the threshold of a thousand years of sacred history. Here and there the book anticipates the future. The last speeches of Joshua contain admonitions for continued faithfulness and warnings that all will be lost if Israel proves unfaithful (23:15-16; 24:19-20).

Thus the Book of Joshua honors past revelation, celebrates present success and anticipates future problems. It is a connecting link between the promise made to the Fathers and the perils which tested the people of God once that promise had been realized. In the words of Baxter, Joshua is "complementary to the five books of Moses, and introductory to the new historical group of twelve books."[2]

A. Background.

After emerging from the wilderness, Israel fought major battles in Transjordan with the Amorite kings Sihon and Og. While camped at Shittim on the edge of Canaan, the men of Israel yielded to the seduction of the Midianite women and their fertility dances. Moses launched

a holy war of retribution against the Midianites because of this incident. Following his final discourses to the nation, Moses climbed Mt.
Nebo to view the Promised Land and depart to meet his Maker. After
an appropriate period of mourning for the death of Moses, the
Israelites were ready to march into the land of promise under the
leadership of Joshua the son of Nun.

B. Circumstances of Writing.

The sixth book of the Old Testament is named after the leading
character of the narrative. The name Joshua means "Yahweh is salvation." In the Greek language the name *Joshua* becomes *Jesus*.
Hebrews 4:8 in the King James Version has confused some students
because it uses the Greek spelling *Jesus* to refer to the Old Testament
leader.

Jewish tradition ascribes the authorship of the sixth book in the
Old Testament to Joshua himself. No solid reasons have been put
forth for categorically rejecting this view. Certainly Joshua knew how
to write (8:32). In fact, Joshua 24:26 states that he wrote covenant
stipulations in *"the book of the law of God."* This indicates that
Joshua was regarded even during his lifetime as a prophet inspired of
God. Only one who spoke inspired words would have been permitted
to add anything to the writing of the great prophet Moses.

The author of the book participated in the events which he narrates (5:1,6). Rahab, the harlot who was spared when Jericho fell to
the Israelites was still living when the book was written. Thus the
author must have been part of the Conquest. No better candidate
than Joshua has been proposed as the author of this book.

The concluding verses of the book which narrate the death of
Joshua were no doubt appended by a later prophet. This prophet
may have been Samuel. Two accounts in the book may have been
inserted into the book by this same prophetic figure. The first episode
is Othniel's capture of Kiriath-sepher (15:13-17; cf. Judg 1:9-13).
The second episode which might be post-Joshuanic is the Danite
migration of Joshua 19:47 (cf. Judg 18:27-29). The chronological
placement of these events is problematic.

C. Chronology of the Book.

Chart No. 2

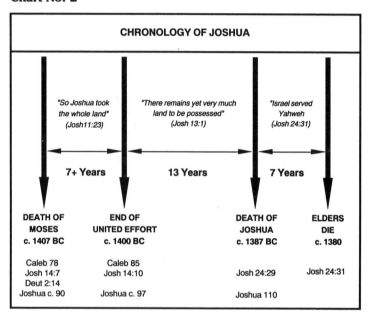

CHRONOLOGY OF JOSHUA

"So Joshua took the whole land" (Josh11:23)	"There remains yet very much land to be possessed" (Josh 13:1)	"Israel served Yahweh (Josh 24:31)
7+ Years	13 Years	7 Years
DEATH OF MOSES c. 1407 BC	END OF UNITED EFFORT c. 1400 BC	DEATH OF JOSHUA c. 1387 BC	ELDERS DIE c. 1380
Caleb 78 Josh 14:7 Deut 2:14 Joshua c. 90	Caleb 85 Josh 14:10 Joshua c. 97	Josh 24:29 Joshua 110	Josh 24:31

The crossing of the Jordan by the children of Israel (ch. 3) can be dated about 1407 BC. The last event recorded in the book is the assembly at Shechem in which Joshua delivered his farewell address to the nation (ch. 24). A comment by Caleb (Josh 14:7-10) enables the modern student to compute the length of time which the united effort against the Canaanites took. Caleb was forty when he had been sent forth from Kadesh-barnea with eleven others to spy out Canaan. He was eighty-five at the time he was given his personal inheritance within the tribal territory of Judah. Presumably this took place after the united tribal conquest led by Joshua. Of the forty-five years which elapsed between Kadesh-barnea and the designation of Caleb's inheritance in Joshua 14, thirty-eight years were consumed in the wilderness wandering (Deut 2:14). Thus seven years must have been consumed in the united conquest of Canaan. The final allotment of the newly conquered land must have been made about 1400 BC.

How much time is covered in the Book of Joshua after the final allotment of the land cannot be computed precisely. The only clue is found in the concluding verses of the book. Israel served Yahweh during the lifetime of Joshua and the elders who outlived Joshua (Josh 24:31). Twenty years would be a conservative estimate of the time which elapsed from the time of Caleb's inheritance to the passing of Joshua and the elders. The Book of Joshua, then, covers a period of roughly twenty-seven years.

D. Contents of the Book.

The Book of Joshua contains a variety of types of literature, some inspirational and exciting, others, quite frankly, boring to the average reader. The historical narrative of the book pulsates with excitement. The divine revelation, farewell speeches, and prayers are full of spiritual challenge. On the other hand, nothing in the Bible is less interesting than the seemingly endless lists of villages assigned to this or that tribe (chs. 12-21).

Chart No. 3

THE STRUCTURE OF JOSHUA				
PREPARING FOR VICTORY	ENGAGING THE FOE	CONQUERING THE LAND	POSSESSING THE INHERITANCE	ENCOURAGING THE COMMITMENT
chs.1-5	chs. 6-9	chs. 10-12	chs 13-22	chs. 23-24
The Lord Reveals the Plan	The Lord Gives the Victory	The Lord Empowers Israel	The Lord Fulfills the Promise	The Lord Demands Fidelity
THEME:THE VICTORY OF FAITH				

The theme of the Book of Joshua is *the victory of faith.* Joshua 1:3 is probably the key to the entire book *"Every place upon which the sole of your foot shall tread, to you I have given it, just as I spoke unto Moses."*[3] The key thought in the book is *God's faithfulness.* The God who brought them out of Egypt also brought them

35

into the Land of Promise (Deut 4:37f.), and that in spite of the unworthiness of two generations of Israelites.

The Book of Joshua opens with a word of the Lord for Joshua. That opening speech virtually outlines the entire book. *"Arise, go over Jordan"* (1:2) points to the preparation for conquest (chs. 1-5). *"No man shall be able to stand before you"* (1:5) announces in advance the result of the Israelite-Canaanite clash (chs. 6-12). *"You shall cause this people to possess this land which I swore to give to their fathers"* (1:6) is prophetic of what is described in chapters 13-22. The exhortation *"Be strong . . . to guard to do* [i.e., to carefully do] *according to all the law which Moses my servant commanded you" (1:7)* anticipates the concluding hortatory section of the book (chs. 23-24) in which Joshua pleads with the people to be faithful to the Lord. Chart 3 diagrams the structure of the book.

E. Teaching of Joshua.

Christians who find significance only in Old Testament books which prophetically portray the coming of Christ will be disappointed with the Book of Joshua. The book contains no personal messianic prophecy. Some see in the Captain of Yahweh's host (5:13-15) a Christophany or a pre-incarnate manifestation of Christ (cf. Rev 19:11-14). While this view is probably correct, the passage is not predictive. Consequently it adds little to the great stream of messianic revelation in the Old Testament.

According to Hebrews 3-4, Old Testament Canaan is a type of the believer's present position and possessions in Christ. Thus the Christian teacher does not err by suggesting comparisons between the present spiritual warfare and the ancient efforts of Israel to conquer Canaan.

The Book of Joshua illustrates two great principles of Scripture. The first is, *"Yahweh is a man of war"* (Exod 15:3). Yahweh ordered Israel into battle against the Canaanites. The God of holiness is in perpetual conflict with the forces of evil. To be sure, this move to exterminate the Canaanites came only after lengthy probation (Gen 15:16) and only after dramatic illustrations of Yahweh's wrath against immorality right there in the land of Canaan (Gen 18-19). In the course of time the cup of Canaanite iniquity was full. The holiness of

God could no longer overlook the corruption of those peoples (Lev 18:24-27). He therefore commissioned Joshua to unleash his wrath upon these hardened sinners. Total surrender to Yahweh was the only escape from destruction. Every Canaanite who surrendered to Yahweh was spared. Thus even in the midst of judgment the Lord showed mercy to those who sought it.

The second grand principle which is illustrated in the Book of Joshua is found in 1 John 5:4. *"This is the victory which has overcome the world, even our faith."* In battle after battle the Israelites fought against superior numbers and superior weaponry. Yet they prevailed. God gave the victory! When they marched, walls came tumbling down!

THE BOOK OF JUDGES

The seventh book of the Old Testament takes its name from a series of twelve individuals who arose in Israel as military leaders in emergency situations. Even the chapters which do not speak directly of the Judges (chs. 1,9,17-21) contribute to explaining the underlying causes of the national predicaments which caused God to raise up these military reformers. This book, then, is appropriately named. One should not conclude, however, that this book contains the accounts of *all* of Israel's Judges. Both Eli and Samuel (1 Sam 1-7) are said to have judged Israel, but they differed in important respects from those who are introduced in the Book of Judges.

In general the following observations can be made about Israel's Judges. They were God's vice-regents in the land. They seem to have experienced some "call" from God and thereafter served lifelong. No regular succession of Judges is in evidence. God raised them up as needed. They served without pomp and equipage. They had no power to make laws, for the law had already been given at Sinai. They had no power to interpret laws, for that was the responsibility of the priests. Their prime responsibility was to enforce God's law or justice and thereby bring "rest" to the land.

A. Background of the Book.

The united tribal effort to conquer Canaan lasted seven plus years.

Once Joshua had broken the back of Canaanite resistance, he assigned the tribes to their territories within the land. The individual tribes were required to eliminate any remaining enclaves of Canaanites within their borders. This process actually began before the death of Joshua in about 1387 BC. For a brief time after the death of Joshua the tribes attempted to continue clearing the Canaanites from the land. Gradually, however, conquest gave way to toleration, accommodation and assimilation. Israel departed from the Lord. God then sent against them a series of foreign invaders. This process began with the invasion of Cushan-rishathaim from Mesopotamia. With this invasion at about 1367 BC the period of the Judges began.

B. Circumstances of Writing.

Although the Book of Judges is anonymous, several clues point to the time of its origin. Judges was composed after the death of Joshua (2:7) and after *"the captivity of the land"* (18:30). This "captivity" is sometimes taken to be a reference to the Assyrian captivity of the northern kingdom which occurred in stages toward the end of the eighth century BC. This interpretation, however, is not necessary. The reference is probably to the Philistine captivity of Israel which occurred in the Judgeship of Eli (1 Sam 4-6). The book was probably written before the seventh year of David's reign (1004 BC) since the Jebusites still were holding Jerusalem (Judg 1:21; cf. 2 Sam 5:6). The book was written from a prophetic point of view (cf. 3:7; 4:1). A date of about 1035 BC during the reign of Saul would be close to the time of the composition of this book. Jewish tradition assigns the authorship to Samuel, and nothing in the contents precludes his authorship.

The immediate purpose of the author of Judges was to record the major events from the death of Joshua to the founding of the monarchy. By so doing the author was attempting to explain the establishment of the monarchy as necessitated by the social and political chaos which resulted from disobedience to God's word.

C. Chronology of the Book.

One of the most difficult problems facing the student of the Old Testament is the chronology of the Book of Judges. Part of the problem is created by the structure of the book itself. The opening verse announces the death of Joshua and gives the impression that what follows occurred after the old warrior had departed this world scene.[4] Some of the episodes narrated in that first chapter, however, have already been recounted in the Book of Joshua. To complicate matters further, the death of Joshua is narrated a second time (2:8). Apparently the author began this book with a series of episodes, some of which happened before the death of Joshua and some of which followed his death.[5]

A still more formidable chronological problem faces the interpreter in the last five chapters of Judges. Two episodes are recorded in these chapters: (1) the Danite migration; and (2) the civil war against the tribe of Benjamin. A careful study of the details in these episodes indicates that they most likely transpired even before the invasion of Cushan in 1367 BC. Since the Danite migration is recorded in the Book of Joshua (Jos 19:47), Judges 17-18 may be narrating an event which transpired even before the death of Joshua!

Aside from these internal chronological problems, reconciling the data in Judges with external chronological data is extremely difficult. The stated periods of oppression and rest in the book total 370 years. Scholars opting for the late date for the Exodus are forced to reduce this figure by almost fifty percent in order to make the period of the Judges fit between an Exodus in 1275 BC and the crowning of Saul at about 1043 BC. However, even scholars opting for the early date for the Exodus (1447 BC) cannot comfortably fit in a period of Judges lasting 370 years. Therefore, some compression seems necessary. Some of the Judges must have been regional heroes whose Judgeship was concurrent with similar leaders in other parts of the land. Determining how much compression must be applied to the figures in Judges, and where that compression should be applied are difficult problems. Chart 4 (next page) indicates the scheme adopted in this survey.

D. Contents of the Book.

The transition from the Book of Joshua to the Book of Judges is abrupt. If Joshua rings with shouts of victory, Judges echoes with sobs of defeat. Possession of the land becomes oppression within the land. Freedom and progress give way to bondage and regression. The

Chart No. 4

CHRONOLOGY OF THE BOOK OF JUDGES 306 Years			
AGENTS	PERIOD	YEARS	DATE BC
TRIBES	TRANSITION	20	1387-1367
CUSHAN	OPPRESSION	8	1367-1359
OTHNIEL	DELIVERANCE	40	1359-1319
EGLON	OPPRESSION	18	1319-1301
EHUD	DELIVERANCE	80	1301-1221
SISERA	OPPRESSION	20	1281-1261*
DEBORAH	DELIVERANCE	40	1261-1221*
MIDIAN	OPPRESSION	7	1221-1214
GIDEON	DELIVERANCE	40	1214-1174
ABIMELECH	OPPRESSION	3	1174-1171
TOLA	JUDGESHIP	23	1171-1148
JAIR	JUDGESHIP	22	1148-1126
AMMON	OPPRESSION	18	1126-1108
JEPHTHAH	DELIVERANCE	6	1108-1102
IBZAN	JUDGESHIP	7	1105-1098*
ELON	JUDGESHIP	10	1097-1087
ABDON	JUDGESHIP	8	1089-1081*
*Overlaps previous period.			

faithfulness of God's people in Joshua is countered by their faithlessness in Judges. If the Israelites are walking by faith in Joshua, they are living in the flesh in Judges. Jensen calls Judges "one of the saddest parts of the Bible . . . a book of failure.[6] Baxter calls Judges "a pathetic anticlimax" to the Book of Joshua.[7]

Judges does not offer a wide variety of literary genres. The book is mostly historical narrative with a few speeches and one song (ch. 5) mixed in. Two verses vie for the designation of key verse in the book. The first is 2:19 (*"And it came to pass when the Judge died they again acted more corruptly than their fathers to follow after other gods and bow down to them; they did not cease from their practices nor their stubborn ways"*). The second is 17:6 (*"In those days there was no king in Israel; every man did what was right in his own eyes"*). The key word in the book is *deliver* and its cognates (some 49 times). The key phrase is *"did evil."*

Those who characterize the Book of Judges as consisting of cycles

40

of rebellion, retribution, repentance and rest have not given careful attention to the text. The history of this period did not go in cycles like a carousel. Rather it moved like the plunge of a roller coaster with peaks and valleys, yet ever winding its way toward rock bottom. To change the metaphor, the author traces the deterioration of Israel from good health in the days of Joshua through the stages of ill, seriously ill, to critically ill.

The Book of Judges consists of a central core of narratives which focus on Israel's sin, servitude, supplication and salvation over the course of some three centuries. Each episode in the central core is introduced by a literary framework which when complete contains five elements.[8]

Chart No. 5

THE STRUCTURE OF JUDGES "THE DARKNESS OF DISOBEDIENCE"				
EXPLANATORY PROLOGUE		THE NARRATIVE CORE	ILLUSTRATIVE EPILOGUE	
		God's Awesome Wrath		
National Sin	**National Servitude**		**A Migration**	**A Mustering**
1:1-2:5	2:6-3:6	**SIN SERVITUDE SUPPLICATION SALVATION** 3:7-16:31	chs. 17-18	chs. 19-21
Review	**Preview**	*God's Amazing Grace*	Idolatry in Dan	Immorality in Benjamin

The core material in Judges is framed by a prologue (1:1-3:6) and epilogue (chs. 17-21) which depict the disunity of Israel. The prologue contains two distinct parts. In the first the conquest efforts of the various tribes before and after the death of Joshua are reviewed (1:1-2:5). The prologue then goes on to preview the theological rhythm of the period of the Judges. Ever increasing sin was followed by ever more severe oppressions, and these in turn by ever less spectacular deliver-

41

ances (2:6-3:6). The epilogue contains two narratives illustrating the extent to which idolatry and immorality had permeated Israel in this period. If the prologue stresses the need for political unity, the epilogue emphasizes the need for moral unity. Chart 5 diagrams the structure of the Book of Judges.

E. Teaching of the Book.

The Book of Judges demonstrates the terrible consequences of disobedience to God. The path to destruction is clearly marked in the book. Disregard for God's command to drive out the Canaanites led to toleration, compromise, intermarriage and outright apostasy. This path led to political disunity, foreign oppression, social chaos, and individual immorality. A basic lesson in Judges can be discovered by placing in juxtaposition two emphases. Twice the book declares that *"every man did what was right in his own eyes"* (17:6; 21:25). Seven times Judges states that *"the children of Israel did evil in the sight of Yahweh"* (e.g., 2:11). These two emphases stress that the natural man is inclined to do evil. Without revelation and the motivation to obey it man will inevitably choose the path of destruction.

Judges illustrates the methods God employs in dealing with his people. Here the anger of God burns against sin (2:14,20). He *"sold"* his people (2:14; 3:8; 4:2; 10:7) or *"gave"* them (2:14; 6:1; 13:1) into the hand of some enemy. Once God is said to have *"strengthened the hand"* of an enemy against Israel (3:12). Thus the God of holiness cannot and does not ignore sin but on the contrary, he punishes it.

The Book of Judges also illustrates the principle that where sin abounds, grace abounds much more (Rom 5:20). Five times Israel *"cried"* (za'aq) unto Yahweh (3:9,15; 4:3; 6:6; 10:10). Three times God spoke to his people, presumably through prophet-like individuals (2:1-3; 6:8-10; 10:11-14). Only once is national repentance clearly indicated in the text (10:10-16).[9] Nonetheless, the Lord was moved to pity by the the groaning of his people in the midst of their various oppressions (2:18). Therefore, he raised up a deliverer for them (3:9,15) through whom the current enemy was subdued (3:30; 4:23; 8:28; 11:33). Then the land would enjoy *"rest"* for a time (3:11,30; 5:31; 8:28). The lack of emphasis on the repentance of Israel in the text serves to underscore the amazing grace of God in this book.

On a more devotional level, Judges illustrates the principle that God chooses weak and foolish things to confound the wise and powerful things of this world (1 Cor 1:27). To gain the victory in Judges God used an ox goad (3:31), a nail (4:21), some trumpets, pitchers and lamps (7:20), a millstone (9:53) and the jawbone of a donkey (15:15). Some of the deliverers God raised up were most unlikely candidates: a bastard son, a ladies' man, a left-handed butcher, a mother, and a cowardly idol worshiper.

THE BOOK OF RUTH

Two books in the Bible bear the names of women: Ruth and Esther. Both of these heroines were great and good women. Here, however, the similarity ends. Ruth was a young Moabite girl who came to live with the Israelites. Esther was a Jewess who lived in faraway Persia. A marriage figures prominently in both books. Ruth married a wealthy Israelite farmer and became part of the royal line of David. Esther married a foreign king and became a queen. Ruth knew the discipline of field work. Esther was pampered with beauty treatments in the royal harem. The books named for these women are a contrast as well. They differ in size (four chapters vs. ten) and the degree to which the heroine is involved in the story. The Book of Ruth is the only instance in the Bible in which an entire book is devoted to a woman.

A. Background.

The setting of the Book of Ruth is *"in the days when the Judges ruled"* (1:1). Yet the contrast between this small book and the Book of Judges is stark. After navigating through the turbulent rapids of Joshua and Judges the reader comes at last to the placid waters of the Book of Ruth. Here there are no more sordid stories of crime and bloodshed, of lawlessness and savage revenge. The atmosphere of simple devotion pervades the story. One senses throughout the overruling providence of God quietly moving forward with his program in those dark days of the Judges.

43

B. Circumstances of Writing.

The Book of Ruth has been dubbed a "masterpiece . . . one of the world's greatest short stories."[10] Such language suggests that the book is an independent composition which may have had as its original purpose merely the entertainment of the reader. Actually the "book" of Ruth was originally the concluding portion of the Book of Judges. Ruth derives its ultimate significance from its original context as part of the larger book.

When was the story of Ruth excised from the Book of Judges? Sometime after the time of Josephus (c. AD 90). Why was this done? Apparently to facilitate the ease with which this material could be read at the feast of Pentecost. The newly created book was placed along with four other short Old Testament books in a collection called in Jewish tradition *Megilloth* ("Scrolls"). Rabbinic tradition required that each of these small books be read at major religious observances.[11]

Since Ruth was originally part of Judges, this book must have been penned by the author of that book. As noted above, Samuel is the traditional author of Judges.

C. Chronology of the Book.

Chart No. 6

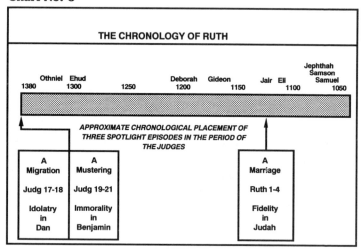

THE CHRONOLOGY OF RUTH

Othniel	Ehud		Deborah	Gideon		Jair	Eli	Jephthah Samson Samuel
1380	1300	1250	1200	1150		1100		1050

APPROXIMATE CHRONOLOGICAL PLACEMENT OF THREE SPOTLIGHT EPISODES IN THE PERIOD OF THE JUDGES

A Migration	A Mustering		A Marriage
Judg 17-18	Judg 19-21		Ruth 1-4
Idolatry in Dan	Immorality in Benjamin		Fidelity in Judah

The Book of Ruth is a sidestep book. Like the two appendices which follow the Samson saga in the Book of Judges (chs. 17-21), Ruth does not advance the history of God's people. The last five chapters of Judges and the four chapters of Ruth—three distinct episodes—are like three spotlights on social life during the period of the Judges. Though the events in Ruth clearly took place during the period of the Judges (1:1), exactly at what point in those three plus centuries is not easy to determine. Since Boaz was the great grandfather of David (Ruth 4:21), a date of about 1130 BC for these events would not be far off. For this reason several scholars date events in the book to the judgeship of Jair (1148-1126 BC).

D. Contents of the Book.

The purpose of Ruth must have been the same as the two episodes with which the present Book of Judges concludes, viz., to shed light on the everyday life in Israel during the period of the Judges. In the first two episodes the author depicted the idolatry in the tribe of Dan and the immorality in the tribe of Benjamin. Ruth stresses fidelity in the tribe of Judah. All was not completely black in Israel's dark ages. Boaz, *"a man of wealth"* (NASB) or *"standing"* (NIV), is portrayed as a devout and obedient follower of Yahweh. Boaz stands out in this period as one stalwart oak in a forest of fallen timber. Ruth's devotion to the Lord is even more amazing. In spite of her pagan Moabite upbringing, in spite of seeing God's people in circumstances of suffering and deprivation, in spite of Israelite prejudice against her race, she still chose to worship Yahweh and identify with his people.

E. Teaching of Ruth.

No personal messianic prophecy is found in Judges-Ruth. In Ruth, however, rich typology is present. The kinsman redeemer (*go'el*) in Ruth is taken to be a type of Christ. Archer goes so far as to say that Ruth is one of the most instructive books in the Old Testament concerning the mediatorial work of Christ.[12] Ruth demonstrates that the *go'el* must (1) be a blood relative; (2) have the wherewithal to purchase the forfeited inheritance; (3) be willing to buy back that inheritance; and (4) be willing to marry the wife of a deceased kinsman.

The genealogy at the end of Ruth deserves special attention. Such genealogies in Scripture remind the reader of "the continuity of God's purpose through the ages."[13] Behind the romantic short story is the genealogy of Messiah. Thus the author relates to his readers the long-range consequence of Ruth's devotion to Naomi and her God. Her faith and love put her into the direct line of the Messiah.[14]

For the second time in the historical books the principle is established that those who were far off from the covenant promises could become part of the family of God through obedient faith. Rahab the Canaanite and Ruth the Moabite demonstrate that those who cried out to Yahweh for refuge found a loving welcome.

In a more devotional vein the book teaches that it is possible to live for God in the darkest circumstances. Boaz was loyal to God while surrounded by immorality and idolatry. Materially and socially speaking, Ruth had everything to lose and nothing to gain by casting her lot with the people of God. Yet she chose Yahweh. Although God's grace is free and open to all, it can save only those who make it theirs by an act of deliberate choice.

ENDNOTES

1. C. J. Goslinga, *Joshua, Judges, Ruth* in "Bible Student's Commentary" (Grand Rapids: Zondervan, 1986), pp. 5f. Passages indicating compliance with Mosaic instruction: 8:31; 11:15,20,23; 13:8,15,32,33; 20:2.

2. J. Sidlow Baxter, *Explore the Book* (Grand Rapids: Zondervan, 1960), I, 237.

3. These other passages have been nominated as the key texts in the Book of Joshua: 1:5-9; 23:3b-11; 24:14-15.

4. A. E. Cundall considers Judg 1:1a to be the title for the whole book. He assigns the events of 1:1b-2:6 to the lifetime of Joshua. *Judges, An Introduction and Commentary* in "Tyndale Old Testament Commentary" (Downers Grove, IL: InterVarsity, 1968), p. 51.

5. K. A. Kitchen cited by M. Woudstra, *The Book of Joshua* in "The New International Commentary on the Old Testament" (Grand Rapids: Eerdmans, 1981), p. 10.

6. Irving Jensen, *Jensen's Survey of the Old Testament* (Chicago: Moody, 1978), p. 152.

7. Baxter, *op. cit.*, II, 9.

8. The five parts of the literary framework of the Book of Judges are: (1) the assessment of evil (*"Israel did evil"*); (2) the assertion of judgment (Yah-

weh "sold" or "delivered" them into the hand of an enemy, or "strengthened" an enemy against them); (3) the appeal for intervention ("Israel cried
unto Yahweh"); (4) the announcement of action ("Yahweh raised up a
deliverer" or "subdued" the enemy); (5) the analysis of results ("the land
had rest").

9. Dale Ralph Davis questions whether Israel's cry implies repentance.
His study of the uses of the Hebrew za'aq led him to conclude that the word
by itself does not connote repentance. See Such a Great Salvation (Grand
Rapids: Baker, 1990), pp. 49f.

10. J. Lawrence Eason, The New Bible Survey (Grand Rapids: Zondervan, 1963), p. 128.

11. The other four books of the Megilloth and their place in the annual
cycle of religious observances were Song of Solomon (Passover), Lamentations (Ninth of Ab), Ecclesiastes (Tabernacles) and Esther (Purim).

12. Gleason Archer, A Survey of Old Testament Introduction (Rev. ed.;
Chicago: Moody, 1985), p. 287.

13. Leon Morris, Ruth, An Introduction and Commentary in "The Tyndale Old Testament Commentaries" (Downers Grove, IL: InterVarsity, 1968),
p. 318.

14. Ruth is one of four women listed in Matthew's genealogy of Christ
(Matt 1:1-16). The other three—Tamar, Rahab and Bathsheba—are associated with unworthy conduct. Ruth's life is without blemish, unless it be that she
was a Gentile by birth and once gave allegiance to pagan gods.

BIBLIOGRAPHY: SETTLEMENT

Atkinson, David. *The Message of Ruth* in "The Bible Speaks Today." Downers Grove, IL: InterVarsity, 1984.

Blaikie, William G. *The Book of Joshua*. 1908. Minneapolis: Klock & Klock, 1978.

Boling, Robert G. *Judges*. Vol. 6A in "The Anchor Bible." Garden City, NY: 1975.

Boling, Robert G. and G. Ernest Wright. *Joshua*. Vol. 6 in "The Anchor Bible." Garden City, NY, Doubleday, 1982.

Bush, George. *Notes on Joshua-Judges*. 1852. 2 vols. Minneapolis: James & Klock, 1976.

Butler, Trent C. *Joshua*. Vol. 7 in "Word Biblical Commentary." Waco: Word, 1983.

Coffman, James B. *Commentary on Joshua*. Abilene, TX: ACU Press, 1988.

Campbell, Jr. Edward E. *Ruth*. Vol. 7 in "The Anchor Bible." Garden City, NY: Doubleday, 1975.

Cooke, G.A. *The Book of Joshua* in "The Cambridge Bible for Schools and Colleges." Cambridge: University Press, 1918.

_____. *The Book of Judges* in "The Cambridge Bible for Schools and Colleges." Cambridge: University Press, 1918.

Cox, Samuel and Thomas Fuller. *The Book of Ruth*. Two separate vols. reprinted as one. Minneapolis: Klock & Klock, 1982.

Cundall, Arthur E. and Leon Morris. *Judges: An Introduction and Commentary* and *Ruth: An Introduction and Commentary* in "The Tyndall Old Testament Commentaries." Downers Grove, IL: InterVarsity, 1968.

Davis, Dale Ralph. *Such a Great Salvation; Exposition of the Book of Judges*. Grand Rapids: Baker, 1990.

Dods, Marcus. *Israel's Iron Age*. London: Hodder and Stoughton, n.d.

Fausset, A. R. *Commentary on the Book of Judges*. Reprint of 1885 ed. Minneapolis: James and Klock, 1977.

Freedman, H. and Judah Slotki. *Joshua* and *Judges* in "The Soncino Books of the Bible." London: Soncino, 1950.

Garstang, John. *Joshua-Judges*. Reprint of 1931 ed. Grand Rapids:

Kregel, 1978.

Goslinga, C.J. *Joshua, Judges, Ruth* in "Bible Student's Commentary." Trans. Ray Togtman. Grand Rapids: Regency Reference Library, 1986.

Gray, John. *Joshua, Judges and Ruth* in "The Century Bible; New Edition." Greenwood, SC: Attic Press, 1967.

Hals, Ronald M. *The Theology of the Book of Ruth.* Philadelphia: Fortress, 1969.

Hamlin, E. John. *Judges: At Risk in the Promised Land* in "International Theological Commentary." Grand Rapids: Eerdmans, 1990.

Hubbard, Robert L. *The Book of Ruth* in "The New International Commentary on the Old Testament." Grand Rapids: Eerdmans, 1988.

Klein, Lillian R. *The Triumph of Irony in the Book of Judges.* Sheffield: Almond, 1988.

Mayes, A.D.H. *Judges* in "Old Testament Guides." Sheffield: JSOT, 1985.

_____. *Israel in the Period of the Judges.* Naperville, IL: Allenson, 1974.

Mazar, Benjamin, ed. *Judges.* Vol. II in "The World History of the Jewish People." Tel-Aviv: Massada, 1971.

Morris, Leon. *Ruth: An Introduction and Commentary* in "The Tyndall Old Testament Commentaries." Downers Grove, IL: InterVarsity, 1968.

Moore, George F. *A Critical and Exegetical Commentary on Judges.* Second ed. Edinburgh: T. & T. Clark, 1903.

Redpath, Alan. *Victorious Christian Living* (Joshua). Westwood, NJ: Revell, 1955.

Sasson, Jack M. *Ruth.* Sheffield: JSOT, 1989.

Schaeffer, Francis A. *Joshua and the Flow of Biblical History.* Downers Grove, IL: InterVarsity, 1975.

Soggin, J. Alberto. *Joshua, a Commentary* in "The Old Testament Library." Philadelphia: Westminster, 1972.

_____. *Judges, a Commentary* in "The Old Testament Library." Philadelphia: Westminster, 1981.

Webb, Barry G. *The Book of Judges.* Sheffield: JSOT, 1987.

Winter, Willard W. *Studies in Joshua, Judges and Ruth* in "Bible Study Textbook Series." Joplin: College Press, 1969.

Woudstra, M.H. *The Book of Joshua* in "The New International Commentary on the Old Testament." Grand Rapids: Eerdmans, 1981.

Chart No. 7

CHAPTER THREE

Preparing for Victory
Joshua 1:1-5:12

As the Book of Joshua opens, the people of Israel are poised to push into Cis-jordan, the heart of the land promised to Abraham, Isaac, and Jacob. The plan of God revealed by Moses required the armies of Israel to cross the Jordan and dislodge those who were occupying the territory which was Israel's by divine decree. That would not be an easy task. Canaanite cities were well fortified; their armies were well equipped. In theory at least Canaan at this period was under Egyptian hegemony. The Pharaoh's assistance to his vassal clients was always a possibility. Even with his limited military experience Joshua must have realized that, humanly speaking, his forces faced incredible odds against success beyond the Jordan.

The opening chapters of Joshua focus on the preparations which were ordered before the commencement of the campaign. Four types of preparation are in evidence here: (1) hortatory, (2) military, (3) logistical, and (4) spiritual.

51

HORTATORY PREPARATION
Joshua 1:1-18

The Book of Joshua opens and closes with exhortation. The first chapter consists of three hortatory utterances: (1) Yahweh to Joshua, (2) Joshua to the tribes, and (3) the people to Joshua.

A. Yahweh to Joshua (Josh 1:1-9).

At about the age of ninety Joshua must have been filled with apprehension about succeeding Moses. The very fact that God would speak directly to him (1:1) was of itself a significant encouragement to this aging man of God. Previously the Lord had spoken only to Moses, *"the servant of Yahweh."*[1] Joshua had been only Moses' servant, a position of honor and apprenticeship (cf. Num 27:15-23; Deut 1:38; 3:21f.), but nonetheless a secondary position. Now Joshua would be the intermediary for divine revelation to Israel. That God broke the silence was the first of several steps taken by the Lord to bolster the confidence of Joshua and to magnify him in the eyes of the people. In his message the Lord first brought encouragement and then he offered exhortation to Joshua.

Chart No. 8

LIFE OF JOSHUA					
IN EGYPT	IN THE DESERT	IN CANAAN	A WARRIOR	AN ADMINISTRATOR	AN ORATOR
			3 Great Campaigns	Land Division	2 Great Speeches
A SLAVE	A SERVANT	A SPY	chs. 1-12	chs. 13-22	chs. 23-24

PREPARATION	Death of Moses 1407 BC	LEADERSHIP
c. 90 Years		c. 20 Years

1. The encouragement (1:2-5). The encouragement took several forms. First, Yahweh assured Joshua that the plan to conquer Canaan had not been altered by the death of Moses. Joshua and the people were to arise and pass over Jordan (1:2a). Earlier the Lord had told Joshua that he would lead Israel into the Promised Land (Deut 31:7,23). Now he was being encouraged to assume that leadership role. Second, Yahweh reassured Joshua that he was about to give them (a participle implying imminent action) the land (1:2a).[2]

In the third and fourth words of encouragement God is addressing the entire nation through Joshua. This is indicated by the switch from the singular to the plural second person pronoun in the Hebrew. The Lord declared that he had already given (perfect form of the verb) every place within that territory where they would have the faith to tread (1:3). The gift would be in proportion to the faith which they exercised in marching through the land. God always rewards courageous faith!

To magnify the promise just made, the Lord gave a verbal sketch of the broad contours of the territory he intended to give Israel (1:4).[3] Their territory would stretch from the wilderness[4] to the Lebanon mountains and Euphrates river in the north, and from the territory they already occupied in the east to the Great (Mediterranean) Sea in the west. The Lord specifically indicates that *"all the land of the Hittites"* would be theirs. The Hittites had in recent years been an international power which controlled territory in Syria and northern Palestine.[5]

Fifth, God assured Joshua—the pronoun now reverts to singular—that, though Israel would face resistance, anyone who would try to defend the land would not be able to stand before him (1:5).[6] Sixth, the Lord repeated what Moses had already told Joshua (cf. Deut 31:8), that he could count on the same divine assistance which Moses had received during his tenure as leader. With his own eyes Joshua had seen the supernatural intervention with which the Lord had come to the aid of Moses in crisis after crisis.

2. The exhortation (1:6-9). The promises just made to Joshua were conditional. Joshua was commanded three times to *"be strong and courageous."*[7] He must manifest a fearless confidence in God's ability to fulfill what he had sworn to do for his people.[8] Joshua must

53

believe that he would lead his people to *"inherit"*[9] their land (1:6). If he would enjoy success in his work he must manifest that same fearless confidence in executing exactly what Moses had commanded in the Law regarding the Conquest. Joshua's *"way"*—his life and leadership—would be prosperous if he was careful to obey the stipulations of God's word (1:7-8). Finally, God commanded fearless confidence because that is the only appropriate disposition for one who has God as a traveling companion (1:9). Fear and anxiety are tantamount to unbelief.

B. Joshua to the Tribes (Josh 1:10-15).

Bolstered by the encouraging revelation from the Lord, Joshua immediately began to exercise his authority over the people. He spoke first to the officers, and then to the eastern tribes.

1. *Commandment to the officers (1:10-11).* A chain of command within Israel was recognized. The tribal officers[10] were to pass on to the people a command, an explanation and a promise. The command was to "prepare provisions" (NASB), i.e., to gather up all supplies they might need to sustain them until they were established in Canaan.[11] The explanation for the command was that within three days they would be crossing over Jordan to possess their inheritance. The promise was that God would give them that land as their own possession.

2. *Conversation with the eastern tribes (1:12-15).* Joshua immediately sought out the leaders of the two and a half tribes which were intending to settle in Transjordan. He reminded them that Moses had already given them their rest—their inheritance (cf. Num 32:16-32). That gift, however, had been made conditionally. The Reubenites, Gadites and half tribe of Manasseh were to leave their families in Transjordan and lead the way across the Jordan "in battle array" (NASB) or "fully armed" (NIV).[12] They were to help their brothers until they had been given rest, i.e., the cessation of hostilities, and had possessed their inheritance. Joshua understood that in the wars of the Lord God's people must be united. The issue which Joshua explored with these tribes was that of leadership. Would they honor their word to Moses? Would they recognize Joshua as Moses' legitimate successor?

C. The People to Joshua (Josh 1:16-18).

The leaders of the eastern tribes immediately recognized the authority of Joshua. *"All that you have commanded us we will do."* They would leave their families behind and march together with their brothers until the victory was achieved. They were willing to go wherever Joshua might wish to send them. The eastern tribes would render to Joshua the same cheerful obedience which they had given to his predecessor. Furthermore, they would regard as treason any rebellion against the authority of Joshua. The death penalty would be executed against any who refused to obey the voice of the new leader (cf. Deut 17:12).

The speech of the Transjordan leaders contains provisos which are certainly wishes and may be prayers. Both are introduced by the word *"only."* First, they expressed the hope (condition?) that God would be with Joshua as he had been with Moses. These men realized that divine intervention would be necessary if the campaign in Canaan was to be successful. Second, the easterners prayed that Joshua might *"be strong and courageous."*[13] They knew that without courageous leadership the mission would fail.

MILITARY PREPARATION
Joshua 2:1-24

Jericho was the first objective beyond the river. Joshua needed to know what he was up against there. Perhaps he anticipated receiving information which would bolster troop morale on the eve of the river crossing. In any case, the dispatching of the two spies is evidence of Joshua's foresight as a general.

A. The Mission of the Spies (Josh 2:1-7).

Joshua secretly dispatched two men from Shittim[14] to spy out Canaan, especially Jericho. Why secretly? Did he not wish his own people to know what he had done? Did he think that such a move might imply that his faith was not strong? Or was the stealth necessary to avoid Canaanite patrols on the western bank of the Jordan? The text offers no clue. Nor does the account describe what must have been a harrowing adventure for these two men in crossing that rampaging, flood-swollen river (2:1).

The spies proceeded immediately to Jericho. They found lodging in the house of a harlot[15] named Rahab. Perhaps they chose this house of ill repute because they thought that fewer questions might be asked of them there. Even so, the men were quickly spotted, recognized as Israelites, and reported to the king of the city. Messengers were sent to Rahab ordering her to bring out the men who had entered her house. If Rahab was a sacred prostitute connected with one of the temples of the city that might explain why the authorities did not simply barge into the house and seize the strangers (2:2-3).

Rahab was not too sure that the sanctuary of her house would be respected by the king's men. She took the precaution of hiding her guests among stalks of flax on the flat roof of her house. As it turned out, this was unnecessary. Rahab was able to convince the soldiers that the strangers had indeed come, but they had left about sundown when the city gate was closed. She feigned concern that the soldiers pursue immediately after these men so that they might overtake them (2:4-6).

The soldiers followed the woman's advice. They searched every road leading to the Jordan. Though a sizable search party must have been sent out of the city, precautions were taken to shut the gate after their departure. Fear gripped the city that the Israelites might launch a surprise attack even during the night (2:7).

B. The Covenant of the Spies (Josh 2:8-21).

After the soldiers left, Rahab went immediately to the roof to converse with her two guests. At the door of her home she had taken a stand. She had renounced her country and its gods. Now she enthusiastically embraced Yahweh as *"God in heaven above and earth beneath."* She confessed her faith in the program of God: *"I know that Yahweh has given you the land."* Her conviction grew out of personal observation and prior testimony. Rahab had personally observed that the Canaanites already had lost their land because they were too terrified to offer effective resistance.[16] This fear grew because of reports of what Yahweh had done for Israel over the past forty years. Through traveling merchants the Canaanites knew of the crossing of the Red Sea on dry land. Within the past few months fugitives from the Amorite kingdoms of Sihon and Og had reported how

56

Israel had put their nations under the curse (cherem) of total destruction. These reports led to two results: fear and faith. For most Canaanites it was only fear; for Rahab, both fear and faith (2:8-10).

Rahab not only believed in the power of Yahweh, she must have also believed in his mercy. For this reason she pled with the spies to enter into a covenant with her that she and her household might be spared in the day of attack. On condition that she tell no one about their mission the two spies pledged on their lives that Israel would deal *"in covenant loyalty and faithfulness,"* i.e., they would honor the covenant with Rahab (2:12-14).

In the overcrowded city of Jericho Rahab's house had been built upon the wall. When the men descended by rope from the window of her house they would be outside the walls. Rahab urged the men to head west toward the nearby mountains which are honeycombed with caves. If they waited there for three days it would be safe for them to return to their camp east of Jordan (2:15-16).

Before leaving the scene the spies underscored again the conditions of the oath which they had just made to spare Rahab and her house. The oath would not be binding if these conditions were not met. First, she would need to tie *"this cord"*—apparently the rope upon which they had descended—in her window. This rope was made of bright scarlet thread woven together; it would be easily recognizable in the day of battle. (At this point the men assumed Jericho would fall by battle). Second, she would be responsible for gathering her family into the designated house. The spies would not guarantee the safety of anyone outside the house. Third, they underscored again the necessity of absolute secrecy. Rahab agreed to those conditions. She put the scarlet cord in her window apparently that very night (2:17-21).

C. The Report of the Spies (Josh 2:22-24).

The spies disappeared into the night. They followed the advice of Rahab and headed for the hills, exactly the opposite direction of that which the pursuers assumed they had taken. There they hid for three days. Then they returned to camp by the route they had come. They reported to Joshua that the Canaanites had melted away in fear before Israel. Their conclusion was *"Surely Yahweh has given all the land into our hands."* This is now the fifth utterance of this glorious truth. The Lord said it to Joshua (1:2,3), Joshua said it to the officers and the Transjordan tribes (1:11,15), Rahab said it to the spies (2:9) and now the spies say these words to Joshua.

LOGISTICAL PREPARATION
Joshua 3:1-4:18

Before undertaking the Conquest one formidable challenge had to be met. The Jordan river, never easy to cross, was in flood (3:5). Though two robust spies had navigated that river, now an army of thousands, not to mention women, children and livestock, would have to cross.

A. Approaching Jordan (Josh 3:1).
After three days of breaking camp (1:11), Joshua led the Israelites to a position closer to the Jordan. No hint had yet been given as to how they would be able to negotiate that raging river. In miles the distance from Shittim east of Jordan to Gilgal on the western bank was not more than six miles. Those miles, however, were potentially the most difficult and terrifying traveled thus far by Israel. Yet if there was to be a Conquest at all, Joshua had to reposition his forces in a staging area west of the river. For three days they awaited further instructions.

B. Further Instructions (Josh 3:2-13).
After three days the plan for crossing Jordan began to take shape. Instructions were passed from the Lord to Joshua, and from Joshua and the officers to the people.
1. Instructions of the officers (3:2-4). The plan was for the people to follow the ark of the covenant as it was carried by the Levitical priests.[17] Because of the vast number of people, the ark would be 2000 cubits (3000 feet or over half a mile) in front of the group. That way every Israelite would know that Yahweh was leading them forward. The rationale for letting the Lord lead is as valid for the believer today as for the Israelites then: *"You have not passed this way before."* The officers mentioned nothing of a miraculous crossing on

58

dry land. That, apparently, had not yet been revealed. They simply were trusting God to provide a way through an impassable barrier.

2. Initial instructions of Joshua (3:5-6). Joshua addressed first the people and then the priests. He urged the people to *"consecrate"* themselves. He challenged them to believe that on the morrow they would see Yahweh *"do wonders"*[18] among them. He did not state, however, what those wonders would be. Perhaps his words would bring to their mind what had happened at the Red Sea some forty years earlier.

Joshua then spoke to the priests, directing them to take up the ark and move forward ahead of the people. They immediately obeyed. What great faith was being demonstrated by these men of God! God's people can only do the impossible when the leaders of the faith are willing to be out in front.

3. Instructions of the Lord (3:7-8). Yahweh revealed a bit more of the plan to Joshua. He was first assured that the events of that day would exalt him in the eyes of his people. They would realize that Joshua enjoyed the divine blessing upon his work as much as Moses had before. What God had promised in his commission (1:5,9) would now be fulfilled. The great miracle would be initiated by the courage of the priests. Joshua was to command those men to wade out into the the river and stand there. The Lord needed to say no more. Joshua got the picture. He hastened to pass his vision on to the people.

4. Final instructions by Joshua (3:9-13). Joshua introduced his final pre-crossing directive to the people as *"the words of Yahweh."* This suggests that Joshua received more direct information from the Lord than has been recorded in the text in 3:7-8. The miracle of the crossing would lead to experiential knowledge of two key propositions of faith. First, what happened at the river would prove that the "living God" was among his people. Second, the river crossing would be a pledge that all the "ites"—the seven ethnic groups which occupied Canaan—would be dispossessed by the invading Israelites (3:9-10).

Joshua pointed out that the ark was already moving forward. He ordered that one man from each of the twelve tribes be designated. Presumably they were to follow the priests into the river. Joshua then indicated that at the moment those priestly feet entered the river, the

Jordan would stop flowing south (3:11-13). That Joshua was able to *predict* the miracle adds to to the wonder of the event. God may have used natural means to produce the path across the river, but the timing of that action requires that the event be regarded as thoroughly supernatural.

C. Crossing Jordan (Josh 3:14-17).

The remaining verses in typical Hebrew style relate in detail how the predictions of Joshua came to pass. When the priests carrying the ark dipped their feet into the river, the flow of water was cut off *"a great distance away at Adam."* The priests stood on dry ground in the middle of the river bed while all the people passed over on dry ground.

D. Commemorating the Crossing (Josh 4:1-9).

After the crossing, Yahweh spoke directly to Joshua for the third time. The function of the twelve men previously designated (3:12) was now indicated. These men were to pick up twelve stones from the place where the priests had stood in the midst of the riverbed. They were to carry these stones to the lodging place on the western bank and erect them as a monument. Those stones would be a *"sign"* or monument to provoke inquiries from future generations. Adults would be able to rehearse in the ears of the children the wondrous act of covenant faithfulness which God had performed for them through his ark (4:1-8).

Joshua himself erected a twelve-stone monument in the riverbed where the feet of the priests had stood. Those stones still protruded above the waters of the river at the time the Book of Joshua was written, about twenty years later (4:9).

E. Conclusion of the Crossing (Josh 4:10-18).

The conclusion of the crossing account stresses the obedience of all those who participated. Joshua had faithfully carried out all that the Lord had spoken to him in the past through Moses and more recently in direct communication. The priests had also done exactly as Joshua had commanded them. The people cooperated by hurrying across the dry riverbed (4:10).

When the crossing ended the ark of God again moved to the lead position in the march formation.[19] The Transjordan contingent—forty thousand strong[20]—followed the ark. Again the emphasis is on the obedience of these warriors to the instruction which Moses had given them (4:11-13).

Yahweh honored his own word that day. He had promised to exalt Joshua in the eyes of the people. That is exactly what he did. The people came to revere Joshua all the days of his life just as they had revered his predecessor (4:14).

The description of the ark's departure out of the Jordan is every bit as dramatic as that of the ark's approach to the river. The priests left the riverbed at Joshua's command which was issued in obedience to the directive of the Lord.[21] As soon as their feet touched the western bank a raging wall of water came down the riverbed. The water again overflowed its banks as before. The timing of the return of the waters was just as much a miracle as the crossing had been a few hours before (4:15-18).

SPIRITUAL PREPARATION
Joshua 4:19-5:12

After crossing the river the people camped at Gilgal (location uncertain). The event is so important that the date was long remembered. Israel camped in Canaan for the first time on the tenth day of the first month in the forty-first year after leaving Egypt (4:19). While encamped there the children of Israel made spiritual preparation for the long struggle to follow.

A. Covenant Faithfulness Recalled (Josh 4:19-5:1).

Under Joshua's direction the twelve stones taken from the midst of the Jordan were set up in Gilgal. The establishment of this memorial was accompanied by a brief speech by Joshua. As he had previously indicated (4:6f.), those stones were to have a pedagogical purpose. Children over the years would be inclined to ask what those twelve huge boulders, obviously stacked by human hands, meant. Adults would then be able to recount the glorious story of the crossing. The crossing of the Jordan is linked by Joshua to the crossing of the Red Sea. Both

61

miracles were designed to teach all peoples that Yahweh is indeed mighty. At the same time, both miracles were designed to underscore God's special relationship with Israel. Such mighty acts should have made Israel reverence Yahweh their God forever[22] (4:19-24).

Rahab had alluded to the Red Sea crossing and the effect of that miracle on the peoples in Canaan who had heard about it. The author now indicates the effect of the Jordan crossing upon those same people. Not just the common people, but even the kings of the region melted in fear at the news that Israel had transversed the Jordan on dry ground. The kings knew that they would now be compelled to face the armies of the Living God, the God of heaven and earth (5:1).

B. Covenant Sign Renewed (Josh 5:2-9).

In the fourth direct divine communication with Joshua, the Lord ordered a renewal of the rite of circumcision. This very basic covenant rite (Gen 17:11) had been suspended during the years of desert punishment, but for what reason is a matter of conjecture. In any case, Joshua was ordered to make flint knives[23] and circumcise that second generation of Israelites who had never received the sign of the Abrahamic covenant in their flesh. The place where the surgery was performed was called Gibeath-haaraloth, the hill of the foreskins. The men were forced to remain in camp until all were healed (5:2-8).

A declaration of the Lord to Joshua—the sixth divine communication to him—provided the name for that first camping spot. Now that Israel had been brought into the land flowing with milk and honey, and through circumcision had recommitted themselves to the covenant of the fathers, *"the reproach of Egypt"* had been rolled away. The Egyptians had heaped ridicule on the people of God with their dreams of a homeland. This was especially the case when the Israelites had been forced to wander so many years in the desert. Merchants and desert nomads kept the Egyptians informed of the whereabouts of this nation of former slaves. While Israel wandered in circles in the desert they must have been the butt of many a joke in Egypt. But no more. The God who had brought them out of Egypt had now brought them into Canaan. So they called that first camping spot Gilgal, *"rolling,"* to commemorate the fact that God had rolled away their reproach (5:9).

C. Covenant Meal Revived (Josh 5:10-12). The first Passover was observed in the Egypt the night of the death plague against the firstborn of the land. The second Passover was observed while Israel was camped at Mt. Sinai. So far as the record goes, the third observance of this great festival took place at Gilgal. Henceforth the Passover celebration would not only commemorate the "going out" (Exodus), it would also commemorate the "entering in."

Like circumcision, Passover seems to have been suspended during the period of wilderness wandering. In fact, no uncircumcised person was permitted to participate in the Passover ritual (Exod 12:48). Therefore, as the years of wandering progressed, an ever increasing percentage of Israelites would have been disqualified from observing the feast. Now that barrier had been removed. On the fourteenth day of Nisan, four days after the circumcision (cf. 4:19), the nation observed the first of thousands of Passovers in the Promised Land. Most of the males were still quite sore from the surgery which had been performed upon them. Nonetheless, the celebration must have been joyous indeed (5:10).

A special feature of this Passover was the eating for the first time of the *"produce of the land."* They ate *"parched grain"* along with the unleavened bread which was normally eaten at Passover. Once they were able to feed upon the fruits of Canaan, God no longer miraculously provided for them the manna which he had supplied over the past forty years (5:11-12).

In preparing for victory God's people had to overcome four great obstacles: (1) the death of Moses (ch. 1); (2) the morale of the troops (ch. 2); (3) the raging waters of Jordan (chs. 3-4); and (4) the spiritual condition of the people (ch. 5). The first obstacle was surmounted by words of encouragement and exhortation; the second, by information derived from reconnaissance; the third, by dramatic manifestation of the power of God; and the fourth, by renewal of basic ceremonies which marked Israel as the special people of God.

ENDNOTES

1. Moses is called *"the servant of the Lord"* in Deut 34:5 and frequently in the Book of Joshua. At the conclusion of his life Joshua was given this title (Josh 24:29). Others who were called *"the servant of the Lord"* were Abraham (Gen 26:24), David (1 Kgs 8:66) and even Nebuchadnezzar (Jer 25:9).

2. The theme of the "giving" of the land can be traced back to the Patriarchal narratives. See Gen 12:7; 13:15; 15:18; 26:3-4. That which had been promised was about to be fulfilled (cf. 13:1).

3. In different language, but with the same geographical vista, the boundaries of the Promised Land are given in Gen 15:18; Deut 1:7; 11:24. Only during the days of David and Solomon did Israel control all the territory encompassed here.

4. "The wilderness" in Josh 1:4 is the desert of Zin or perhaps the desert of Paran lying south of Canaan (Num 13:3,21).

5. "Hittites" may be used in Josh 1:4 in a representative sense to embrace all those who lived within the territory broadly sketched out here. For centuries after the time of Joshua the region of Syria-Canaan was known as the "Hatti (Hittite) land" in the Near East.

6. The promise given to the entire nation in Deut 11:25 is now given to Joshua personally as the leader of that people.

7. In the Hebrew the terms *"be strong"* and *"be courageous"* are virtually synonymous.

8. God's oath to the fathers concerning the land can be found in Gen 15:18; 24:7; Exod 32:13.

9. The verb inherit (*nachalah*) and the derived noun are important words in Joshua. They appear in 11:23; 14:13; 16:4; 17:6. Cf. also Deut 1:38; 12:10. The word argues for Israel's legitimate claim to the land. The concept has been carried over into the New Testament to speak of kingdom blessings which are inherited by the believer (e.g., 1 Pet 1:4).

10. The Hebrew term translated *"officers"* (NASB; NIV) literally means "literate men" or "scribes." The same term is used in Josh 3:2; 8:33; 23:2. These men were probably civil servants rather than military men.

11. The *"provisions"* would not include the manna, which could not be stored from day to day. Deut 2:6 suggests that Israel was able to secure other provisions now that they were out of the desert.

12. The Hebrew term *hamushim* literally means "a fivefold arrangement of army troops."

13. Joshua was hearing the exhortation *"be strong and courageous"* for the fifth time. Previously he had heard these words from Moses (Deut 31:6) and three times from the Lord (Josh 1:6,7,9).

14. Shittim is probably the same as Abel-shittim (Num 33:49). Here Israel sinned with Baal of Peor (Num 25:1-3). "Shittim" means "acacia trees." The site is uncertain.

15. Rahab is called a *zonah*. Heb 11:31 and Jas 2:25 confirm that she was a harlot or prostitute. Josephus and the Jewish Targums call her an "innkeeper."

16. Rahab's words confirm the fulfillment of one of the Exodus promises, viz., that God would put his terror in the hearts of those who inhabited the Promised Land. See Exod 15:14ff.; 23:27.

17. Literally, *"the priests, the Levites."* Normally the Levites of the clan of Kohath carried the ark. On special occasions, however, the priests carried the ark. See e.g., Deut 31:9; 1 Kgs 8:3,6. They are called Levitical priests, not to distinguish them from other priests (Woudstra) but to underscore the signal honor bestowed upon their tribe through its priestly members in leading the procession into the Promised Land.

18. Hebrew *niphla'oth*. Literally, "things to be astounded at."

19. Another understanding of the expression *liphne ha 'am* is *"before the eyes of the people,"* i.e., while they were watching from the western bank.

20. The forty thousand from the Transjordan tribes constitutes less than forty percent of the men of war of these tribes counted in the census taken a few weeks before by Moses (Num 26).

21. Josh 4:15f. is the fourth direct revelation to Joshua. The ark is here called *"the ark of the testimony"* because the ark contained the testimony (Exod 31:18), i.e., the tablets containing the ten commandments.

22. *"Fearing Yahweh"* includes all that is in involved in Old Testament religion. The expression conveys the recognition of God's glory and loving obedience to his commandments.

23. *Flint* knives may have been used to convey the thought of the antiquity of the ceremony as dating to a time before the use of metal was common.

CHAPTER FOUR

Engaging the Foe
Joshua 5:13-9:27

In the initial engagements of the Canaan campaign the Israelites encountered three very different types of enemies. At Jericho the enemy was holed up within their fortifications. At Ai the enemy was more bold, venturing beyond their walls to attack the Israelites. The Hivites who dwelled in Gibeon resorted to trickery to avoid a military confrontation with Israel.

FAITH INSTRUCTED
Joshua 5:13-6:5

A parenthetical note (6:1) makes clear the condition of the first enemy which Israel faced. The city gates were tightly shut. No one was entering and leaving the city. Israel was unskilled in siege warfare. The situation was hopeless from a military standpoint.

Thus far the author has indicated six occasions when Yahweh spoke directly to Joshua. The seventh divine communication came in

67

a theophany—a visible manifestation of God. The captain of Yahweh's host revealed to Joshua the battle plan for the first campaign in Canaan.

A. The Encounter (Josh 5:13-15).

Joshua had assumed even before the river crossing that Jericho would be the first objective in Canaan. From a distance he reconnoitered the city and contemplated what strategies might give Israel access to those walls with the least amount of causalities. Joshua thought he was alone with his thoughts. As he lifted up his eyes, however, he was shocked to see *"a man"* standing before him with a drawn sword, i.e., ready for combat. The scene was full of ambiguity. Joshua drew near with a question: *"Are you for us or for our adversaries?"* (5:13).

The stranger responded that he was not a mere soldier fighting on either side. Rather he was the commander of the host of Yahweh.[1] Joshua immediately bowed to the ground in respect to this one who was his military superior. He indicated that he was prepared to receive any orders which the captain might have for him. The captain let Joshua know that mere respect such as one officer might have for a superior was not sufficient. He, like Moses at the burning bush, was standing on holy ground. He needed to remove his sandals. This was a symbol of the removal of impurity and a token of respect for the holy presence of God. Joshua immediately complied (5:14-15).

Clearly a superhuman presence is depicted here. This person was undoubtedly the same as the angel of the Lord who appeared at various points in Patriarchal history,[2] a visible manifestation of God's presence. The drawn sword conveyed the thought that God himself would fight for Israel.

B. The Plan (Josh 6:1-5).

In the person of the captain of Yahweh's host the Lord assured Joshua that *"I have given Jericho into your hands."* The king of the city and all his valiant warriors would fall into Joshua's hands. Chapter 6 of the Book of Joshua celebrates the most outstanding instance of God's "giving" of the land to Israel.[3] God always has a better plan. The fall of Jericho would be an act of faith (Heb 11:30) as well as an act of God. What a relief those words must have been to Joshua (6:2).

The plan was simple. The Israelite army was to march around the walls of Jericho every day for six days. Seven priests carrying ram's horn trumpets were to escort the ark in that procession. On the seventh day the Israelite troops were to march seven times around the walls. The number seven is obviously symbolical, recalling God's works of creation.[4] Then the priests were to blow their trumpets, and the people were to shout with a great shout. At that moment, God promised, the walls would *"fall down flat."* At whatever point in the procession an Israelite soldier might find himself, he would be able to move straight ahead into the city. The protective walls of Jericho would virtually melt away (6:3-5).

FAITH TRIUMPHANT
Joshua 6:6-7:1

The Hebrew narrative skillfully employs repetition to underscore what the author considered important in the account. His style emphasizes the exact compliance with the directives of the captain of Yahweh's host.

A. The Plan Presented (Josh 6:6-10).
Joshua immediately passed on the instructions of the Lord. He first explained the role of the priests (6:6). He then told the people (6:7) about the march around the city. A unit dressed in full battle array would precede the ark. This may be a reference to the forty thousand Transjordan contingent of 4:13. The advanced guard was followed by the priests who marched *"before Yahweh"* i.e., the ark which symbolized Yahweh's presence. Another military contingent—the rear guard—would follow the ark. Apparently the strange plan for the conquest of Jericho was accepted without question. Both the people and the priests fulfilled their respective roles in the strategy (6:8-9). A final detail of the plan was that the procession was to march in silence. Not one word was to be spoken until Joshua gave the signal (6:10).

B. The Plan Executed (Josh 6:11-15).
Apparently on the same day the captain of Yahweh's host

appeared to Joshua, the Israelites began their march around the walls. Given the known size of ancient Jericho—about thirteen acres—a trip around the walls would have only taken about an hour. The text gives the impression that the first day's march took place late in the day. When the ark—the emphasis on the ark should be noted—had made its trip around the walls the first day the soldiers returned to the camp at Gilgal where they spent the night (6:11).

The march was repeated on each of the next five days. On the seventh day the procession marched around the wall seven times as God had ordained (6:12-15).

Chart No. 9

VICTORIOUS FAITH: A COMPARISON		
Hebrews 11:30		Galatians 3:26,27
The Walls of Jericho Fell Down	WHAT	You are all the Children of God
by Faith	HOW	by Faith
after they had been Compassed about Seven Days	WHEN	for as many of you as have been baptized into Christ have put on Christ.
TO SAY THAT WE ARE SAVED BY FAITH WITHOUT OBEDIENCE IN BAPTISM IS TO SAY THE WALLS OF JERICHO WOULD HAVE FALLEN WITHOUT MARCHING		

C. The Ban Applied (Josh 6:16-25).

On the seventh circuit of the seventh day the priests gave a special blast on the trumpets. Joshua signaled for the shout of victory. Standing before those towering walls which as yet had shown no signs of weakening Joshua made a great proclamation of faith: *"Yahweh has given you the city!"* (6:16).

At this point the text records Joshua's orders regarding the ban (*cherem*) which was to be placed on the city. He probably had given these orders to tribal officers earlier in the camp, but they are placed here in the account because they were about to be executed. The concept of the ban was simple: everything within the city belonged to God either to be used in his worship or destroyed. In this case all metallic objects were to be considered holy, i.e., set apart for God, and therefore placed in the treasury of the Lord. No captives were to be taken. All human inhabitants and animals were to be slain.[5] To confiscate for private use anything within the city would bring a curse on the camp. The only exception to the these general rules was Rahab. Since she had hidden the Israelites spies, Rahab and her family were to be spared (6:16-19).

When the trumpets blew and the people shouted with a great shout, the walls of Jericho *"fell down flat,"* i.e., crumbled before them. The Israelite soldiers surged forward and took the city, apparently with some resistance on the part of the inhabitants (cf. 24:11). Every living thing in the city was utterly destroyed with the edge of the sword. The exception was Rahab and her family (6:20-21).

Joshua assigned the task of protecting Rahab's family to the two spies who had stayed in her home. Apparently one portion of the wall had been left standing, viz., the portion where Rahab's house was located. The converted harlot and her relatives were brought out safely. Since they were Gentiles and inhabitants of a city under God's curse they were ceremonially unclean (Lev 13:46; Deut 23:3). They were therefore compelled to live for a time outside the camp of Israel. After certain days, Rahab lived in the midst of Israel. Eventually she even married an Israelite man. She was still living in the midst of Israel at the time the Book of Joshua was written (6:22-25). Israel was a community of faith. Purely racial components never have defined "Israel."[6]

D. Concluding Notes (Josh 6:26-7:1).

Joshua made the children of Israel take an oath that Jericho would never be refortified.[7] Anyone who violated that oath would be cursed before Yahweh. In the process of trying to rebuild the walls and gates of the place the violator would lose his own sons in death (6:27).[8]

What happened at Jericho is a magnificent example of the divine assistance promised at the outset of the campaign. Because Yahweh was with him, the fame of Joshua spread throughout the region (6:27).

71

The account of the glorious triumph at Jericho is marked by one sour note. The terms of the ban were not strictly observed by everyone. Achan of the tribe of Judah took for his personal use some objects which were under the ban, and which therefore belonged to God. Although only one man was the offender, the entire people were viewed as having "*acted unfaithfully.*"[9] God considered Israel an organic unity. A sin by one brought guilt upon all. Achan's sin caused the anger of the Lord to burn against the sons of Israel. Corporate guilt and individual responsibility go hand in hand in Joshua 7.[10] Thus the author prepares the reader for the account of the first setback experienced by Israel in their inheritance campaign (7:1).

FAITH FALTERING
Joshua 7:2-26

Following the great victory at Jericho, Joshua was determined to press his advantage. His strategy was to knife up into the mountains and dissect the land separating the powerful Canaanite forces in the northern part of the land from those in the south. Joshua soon learned that not all the enemy would cower within walled cities. He learned too that on the road to ultimate victory Israel would have to cope with setbacks.

A. Defeat at Ai (Josh 7:2-5).

Joshua determined that Ai would be the next objective of the campaign. Ai was a military outpost in the mountains which guarded the approach to the larger city of Bethel. Ai is said to have been near to Beth-aven (location uncertain).[11] Following the same strategy he had used at Jericho, Joshua dispatched some men to reconnoiter Ai. These men returned with the report that Ai was not heavily defended. Two or three thousand men should be sufficient to capture the place. The entire armed forces need not make the toilsome trip up into the mountains (7:2-3).

Joshua dispatched three thousand troops to attack Ai. The defenders launched a counterattack which caught the overconfident Israelites off guard. Joshua's troops "*fled from before the men of Ai.*" Thirty-six Israelites died on the mountain slopes, the first to taste death in the inheritance campaign. This setback rekindled fear in the hearts of the people of Israel. In their first attempt to take a city of Canaan by military means they had failed. God was not going to hand them Canaan on a silver platter. They would have to fight for their inheritance, and in the process of that fighting many would die (7:4-5).

B. Distress in the Camp (Josh 7:6-9).

Joshua was distraught by this experience of defeat. He tore his clothes and fell to the earth on his face before the ark of the covenant. Both he and the elders put dust on their heads as a symbol of mourning. The leaders remained prone before the ark until that evening (7:6).

Out of his despondency Joshua voiced a pathetic prayer. He began with the word *"Alas!"* by which he expressed deep pain and perplexity." Second, Joshua requested light in the present darkness. *"Why did you, Lord, bring this people over the Jordan only to deliver us into the hands of the Amorites?"* How prone are believers in times of discouragement to blame God for life's setbacks (7:7).

Third, Joshua actually expressed the wish that the entire nation had remained on the eastern side of Jordan. Fourth, he used narrative prayer to describe to God the tragedy which so concerned him: *"Israel has turned their backs before their enemies."* The anticipated result of this would be that the inhabitants of Canaan would be emboldened by this news. They would surround and exterminate Israel at Gilgal. Finally, Joshua made an oblique request in the form of a question: *"Then what will you do for your great name?"* Yahweh's reputation was linked with the people who worshiped him. If Israel disappeared, so would any reputation that Yahweh might have among the Gentiles. Thus Joshua was appealing for help. He was suggesting that helping Israel would be in God's own self-interest (7:8-9).

C. Directions for Joshua (7:10-15).

The Lord rebuked Joshua for lingering in this prayer of discouragement. He should have known when God did not aid his people at Ai that there must be sin in the camp. After all, Joshua had just warned Israel that if they violated the ban at Jericho they would bring trouble to the camp (6:18). That was exactly what had happened. Israel had sinned in regard to the things which were put under the ban at Jericho. The contraband objects were still in the camp. Thus a curse rested upon the camp. Until those objects were destroyed God would no longer be with his people. The sons of Israel would continue to flee before their enemies (7:10-12).

So what must be done? First, God told Joshua to "rise up." Prayer must never be a substitute for action! Second, he was to order the people to "consecrate" themselves. Third, he was to announce to the people what most would be horrified to hear: "Things under the ban are in your midst." Fourth, he was to indicate the results of the presence of this forbidden material within the camp: "You cannot stand before your enemies." Fifth, he was to outline a process by which the guilty party could be identified. Tribes, clans, families, households and finally individuals would "come near" presumably to the ark of the covenant. There by lot God would indicate where the guilt lay.[12] Sixth, he was to stipulate the punishment which would be heaped upon the guilty party. The violator and all which belonged to him would be burned (following execution by stoning) because of the magnitude of the sin committed. The guilty party had "transgressed" and and committed a "shameful thing" in Israel (7:13-15).

D. Discovery of the Culprit (Josh 7:16-21).

Early the next morning Joshua did exactly what God told him to do. In the lengthy process of finding the culprit first the tribe of Judah was taken, then the clan of the Zerahites, and finally the family of Zabdi. When Zabdi brought his family near the ark the lot fell on Achan (7:16-18). Why did not the Lord simply reveal the name of the trespasser to Joshua? Why this time-consuming identification process? Probably the intention was to give the guilty party opportunity to repent. By refusing to come forth earlier in the process Achan revealed his hardened and defiant heart.

Joshua pled with Achan to acknowledge his guilt. Though it was too late for forgiveness, his admission would at least bear witness to the omniscience of God in pointing him out. Now that the finger of accusation pointed straight at him, Achan admitted what he had done. He confessed to stealing from the contraband (1) a beautiful garment from Shinar (Babylon), (2) two hundred shekels of silver (about 6.5 lbs.), and (3) a wedge of gold weighing fifty shekels (about 1.1 lbs.). The irony of his sin is that he never received any benefit at all from that which he had stolen. In his own words, he *saw, coveted, took* and *concealed* that which he had taken in the soil beneath his tent (7:19-21).

E. Death to the Guilty (7:22-26).

Messengers were dispatched immediately to the tent of Achan. There they found the contraband just where Achan had said. These items were brought to Joshua and the congregation. They were then *"poured out before Yahweh"* in acknowledgment that the Lord was the true owner. None of these items, however, could be placed in the treasury. The taint of Achan's sin required their destruction (7:22-23).

Joshua and all Israel took Achan, the items he had stolen, and all his possessions and brought them to a valley which after this event was named Achor ("Trouble"). Before the execution Joshua pointed out the appropriateness of what was taking place. Achan had troubled Israel; now he was to be troubled. All Israel then stoned Achan and his children. The fact that the children (Achan seems to have been a widower) were also stoned suggests that they were accessories after the fact (if not actual accomplices) to the transgression. The bodies of the guilty were then burned along with all the possessions of the man (7:24-25).

A great heap of stones—the third thus far—was raised up over the charred carcass of Achan to bear witness through the years to the necessity of rendering unto God his due. Thus was the fierce anger of the Lord, which had come against Israel because of Achan's transgression (7:1), now turned away (7:26).

FAITH REBOUNDING
Joshua 8:1-29

Once the camp had been purged, the time had come to get back on the victory trail. After the Ai debacle Joshua needed special encouragement if he was to continue in his mission. He would not dare have renewed the Conquest without an express word from the

Lord. In his ninth direct revelation to Joshua the Lord commanded his captain to take all the army and proceed to Ai. This directive contains an oblique rebuke to Joshua for having misjudged the enemy strength earlier. At the same time it was a reminder that the Conquest was to be a united effort of all the people. God promised that he would now give Ai into the hands of the Israelites (8:1).

The rules of engagement were a bit different. First, like Jericho, Ai was to be completely destroyed. All the inhabitants of the place were to be executed. Second, permission was granted for the spoils and livestock to be taken as plunder by the Israelites.[13] This was the standard procedure both before (Deut 2:34f.; 3:6f.) and after Jericho. Third, the Lord briefly revealed how Joshua was to organize the attack against Ai. The method of victory this time would be a military stratagem (8:2).

Joshua sent forth 30,000 valiant warriors by night to become part of an elaborate ambush at Ai. The plan was for the main body of troops to lure the soldiers out of Ai by feigning a rout. The ambushment would then seize the city and burn it.[14] Joshua assured the men that the strategy came from the Lord. If they followed that strategy they would be victorious over Ai. With these words of reassurance the thirty thousand immediately departed and assumed their position "between Bethel and Ai" on the west of Ai (8:3-9).

Joshua and the elders led the main body of troops to Ai early the next morning. He pitched camp on the north side of Ai in a valley. Joshua dispatched another five thousand men to serve as a rear guard still further to the west of where the ambushment had been deployed the previous night. These men were probably guarding against any attempted intervention from Bethel (8:10-13).

The strategy at Ai worked to perfection. The king of Ai saw Joshua and some of his men deployed in the valley. A sortie was sent forth to test the attackers. Then Joshua feigned a rout. The king of Ai ordered a total mobilization to pursue the Israelites. No one was left behind to guard Ai or Bethel.[15] At this point the Lord took direct control of the operation. He ordered Joshua to give the signal to begin the full attack on Ai. This tenth direct divine communication with Joshua concluded with the encouraging words "I have given it into your hands" (8:14-18).

When they saw Joshua raise his javelin, the ambushment arose, entered Ai, and set the town ablaze. This fire was probably intended as the signal for the retreating Israelite forces to turn and press the attack toward the city. When the men of Ai looked behind them they knew they were trapped *"in the midst of Israel."* Every soldier of Ai was cut down. Only the king was spared and brought to Joshua. Once the field army was destroyed the troops returned to the burning city and put the rest of the inhabitants to the sword (8:19-24).

Twelve thousand inhabitants of Ai died that day, the entire population. The Israelites took the spoils of Ai as their own. Ai was left *"a heap,"* i.e., a total ruin. The king of Ai was killed (cf. 10:26) and then his corpse was impaled on a tree until evening. This disgrace demonstrated the curse of God upon those who resisted the movement of God's people. The body of the king was then buried beneath a heap of stones in front of the gate of Ai (8:25-29). This is now the fourth heap of stones erected by Joshua during the Conquest.

FAITH RENEWED
Joshua 8:30-35

Now that resistance in central Canaan had been neutralized, Joshua was able to carry out a directive of Moses (Deut 11:29; 27:2-8). He led the tribes to the area of Shechem, right in the center of Canaan. At Mount Ebal he built an altar of uncut stones in order to avoid even the slightest hint of the *"graven images"* forbidden in the Ten Commandments. There they offered burnt offerings (symbolic of complete commitment) and peace offerings (symbolic of unbroken fellowship with God) before the Lord. On plaster covered stones (cf. Deut 27:1-8) Joshua wrote the law of Moses in the presence of the sons of Israel. How much of the law was written on the stones is not indicated (8:30-32).[16] This mound of stones—the fifth to be erected by the Israelites—proclaimed the sovereignty of Yahweh over the entire land.

Something else took place at the twin mounts. The new generation of Israelites formally accepted Yahweh as their king by accepting the terms of his law. Joshua positioned the tribes, half on Mount Ebal and half on Mount Gerizim just as Moses had commanded. The Levit-

ical priests who carried the ark of the covenant were positioned in the
valley between the two mountains. Joshua read aloud the blessings
and the curses of the law. The people responded by saying *"Amen"*
(cf. Deut 27:11-26). All Israel, including women and children, recommitted themselves to observe the law of Moses (8:33-35).

The importance of the covenant renewal ceremony at the twin
mounts cannot be overstated. The passage is a key for understanding
the Book of Joshua. The main point is that possession of the land
was granted those who voluntarily chose to place themselves under
the authority of God as revealed in the Sinai covenant. The ceremony
also served to formally recognize Joshua as Moses' successor.[17]

FAITH ENDANGERED
Joshua 9:1-27

Among the inhabitants west of Jordan two reactions to Joshua's
initial successes manifested themselves. Most of the city states determined to band together to withstand the advance of the Israelites. The
inhabitants of Gibeon,[18] however, *"acted craftily."* They determined
that they would try to trick the Israelites into a solemn nonaggression
treaty (9:1-3).

The Gibeonite plan was simple. They sent envoys to Joshua who
pretended to be from a distant land. These men were dressed in tattered clothing, they carried worn-out sacks and mended wineskins.
Even their bread was dry and crumbled. From their home in the
mountains these envoys traveled the nineteen miles to Gilgal to which
Israel had returned after the covenant renewal ceremony at Mount
Ebal (9:4-6).[19]

Though the Israelites suspected a ruse, the envoys nonetheless
convinced them that they had come from a distant land. They claimed
that the fame of Yahweh had caused them to seek out Joshua. They
had heard of what the Lord had done for his people in Egypt and in
Transjordan. They were too cunning to mention the more recent
news of the fall of Jericho and Ai since news of these victories would
not yet have reached a distant land. The elders[20] of Gibeon had dispatched these envoys with instructions to seek a peace treaty with
Israel (9:7-13).[21]

Because they were suspicious, the men of Israel checked the provisions in the knapsacks of the travelers. Everything seemed to be as the envoys claimed. Therefore, the men of Israel *"took some of their provisions"* (NASB).[22] Here, however, the leaders of Israel were making a tragic mistake. They were trusting their senses. *"They did not ask counsel of Yahweh."* Joshua made *"peace"* and a *"covenant"* with the Gibeonites. The leaders of Israel bound themselves to the covenant with a solemn oath (9:14-15).

Three days after the covenant had been negotiated, the Israelites discovered that these envoys were Hivites who came from a city within the territorial limits which Yahweh had assigned to Israel. The Israelites immediately marched toward Gibeon to demand an account. No doubt the Gibeonites met them at the border to remind them of the covenant and to point out that the terms of that covenant also applied to three neighboring villages under Gibeon's jurisdiction. The advance troops refused to attack because of the oath which the leaders had taken. Though they honored the oath, the whole congregation grumbled against the leaders (9:16-18).[23]

The leaders explained to the people that an oath taken in the name of God could not be broken even if that oath had been negotiated under false pretenses. Israel would incur the wrath of God should they slay any of these Hivites. The terms of the covenant, however, did not prohibit other kinds of action against the Hivites. The plan was to subject the Hivites to rigorous and humiliating servitude (9:19-21).

Joshua summoned the Hivite leaders to report the decision to them. He first reproached the Hivites for their deception. He then announced that these people would be under a perpetual curse as slaves to Israel. The Hivites attempted to explain their actions. They had heard that Yahweh had commanded Moses to give the land of Canaan to Israel and to destroy all the inhabitants of the land. *"We feared greatly,"* the Hivites admitted. They seemed to be very grateful to accept whatever fate short of death that the Israelites might assign them (9:22-25).

So Joshua prevented the Hivites from being killed. He made them, however, lowly servants from that day forth. Their twofold task was to serve as hewers of wood and drawers of water for the congregation in non-religious activities, and for the worship center as well. Since the Lord had not yet indicated where his sanctuary would be, the text does not name the place where the Gibeonites would serve (9:26-27).

ENDNOTES

1. Yahweh's army is composed angels (1 Kgs 22:19; Ps 103:20f.; 148:2). In other passages the term includes to the armies of Israel.

2. The Angel of the Lord appeared in Gen 16:7-14; 21:14-21. Later he appeared in Judg 2:1 and 6:12,22.

3. M. H. Woudstra, *The Book of Joshua* in "The New International Commentary on the Old Testament" (Grand Rapids: Eerdmans, 1981), p. 108.

4. *Ibid.*, p. 111.

5. Transjordan also had been placed under the *cherem* (Josh 2:10; Num 21:21-35; Deut 2:34; 3:4). The temporal *cherem* foreshadows the final judgment upon rebellious sinners at the end of days.

6. Woudstra, *op. cit.*, p. 116.

7. The curse does not apply to those who merely used the site of Jericho for habitation. See Josh 18:21; Judg 3:13; 2 Sam 10:5.

8. Exactly how the builder of the fortifications would lose the lives of his sons is not clear, whether by sacrificial rite on his own part or by divine action. In any case, 1 Kgs 16:34 reports the fulfillment of the curse.

9. The Hebrew *ma'al* literally means "to act under cover; to deal treacherously." It indicates a breach of trust (Lev 5:15), usually against the Lord.

10. Woudstra, *op. cit.*, pp. 120f.

11. Hosea and Amos use Beth-aven ("House of Nothingness") as a mocking name for Bethel (e.g., Hos 4:15). Here, however, Beth-aven is clearly distinguished from Bethel.

12. Just how the lot was cast in such situations is unknown. The suggestion has been made that white and black stones were used. A black stone drawn from the pouch would indicate guilt. Whatever the mechanics of the process, the lot was under the direction of God. This was but another means by which God revealed information to his people.

13. The ban was enforced more strictly because (1) this was the first Canaanite city to fall to Israel in the Promised Land; and (2) because the army of Israel played such a small role in the victory there.

14. The Hebrew uses two different verbs to distinguish this initial burning by the ambushment and the final burning of the city in 8:28. The first limited blaze was designed to signal the soldiers of Ai that their cause was now hopeless.

15. Either the defenders of Bethel had reinforced the garrison at Ai before the arrival of Joshua, or some communication system existed between the two sister towns. The Book of Joshua, which gives only an outline of the Conquest struggles, does not mention the capture of Bethel. The king of Bethel, however, is named among those slain by Joshua (12:16).

16. The stones may have contained only the Ten Commandments. Others have suggested that they contained the blessings and curses from Deut 28.

17. This conclusion is based on what is known of ceremonies of covenant renewal in countries surrounding Israel. The best treatment of the present passage in the light of ancient Near Eastern custom is found in M. G. Kline, *Treaty of the Great King* (Grands Rapids: Eerdmans, 1963), pp. 36, 121ff.

18. While some still dispute the location of Gibeon, most scholars have settled on a site called el-Jib eight miles north and slightly west of Jerusalem. An imposing ancient water works has been found at this site. See *New Bible Dictionary* (2nd ed.; Wheaton: Tyndale House, 1982) s.v. "Gibeon."

19. Some scholars think a different Gilgal, one in the region of Shechem, or Shiloh is intended. For a listing of the various Gilgals of the Book of Joshua, see *New Bible Dictionary, op. cit.*, s.v., "Gilgal."

20. Elders are mentioned at Gibeon, but no king. Perhaps Gibeon was under the jurisdiction of the king of Jerusalem. The other alternative would be that Gibeon's government differed from the other cities of the region.

21. The words *"we are your servants"* (9:8) were a formal expression of courtesy in the Near East, not an offer of subordination. C. J. Goslinga, *Joshua, Judges, Ruth* in "Bible Student's Commentary" (Grand Rapids, Zondervan, 1986), p. 92.

22. The men of Israel took the provisions in order to inspect them. Another possibility is that they shared the provisions of the Gibeonites in a meal intended to seal the treaty which had just been made.

23. The verb used here (*lun*) is the same one used to describe the murmuring of Israel during the wilderness wandering. See e.g., Num 16:41 (Heb. 3:17).

81

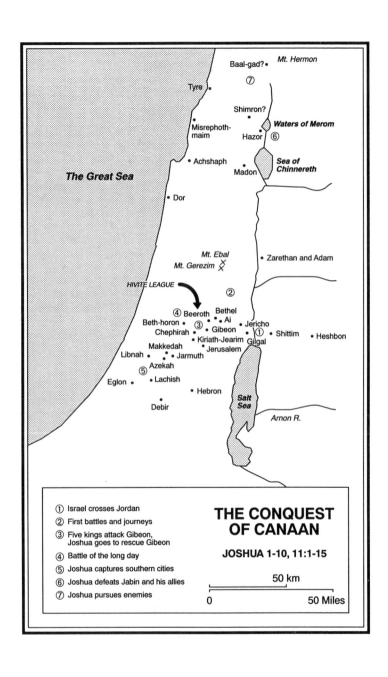

THE CONQUEST
OF CANAAN

JOSHUA 1-10, 11:1-15

① Israel crosses Jordan
② First battles and journeys
③ Five kings attack Gibeon,
Joshua goes to rescue Gibeon
④ Battle of the long day
⑤ Joshua captures southern cities
⑥ Joshua defeats Jabin and his allies
⑦ Joshua pursues enemies

50 km

0   50 Miles

CHAPTER FIVE

Conquering the Land
Joshua 10-12

With the conquest of Jericho and Ai and the capitulation of Gibeon Joshua was the master of central Canaan. The remaining city states of the area were resolved to band together to resist the Israelite invaders. Unfortunately, from their point of view, Joshua had driven a wedge through the midst of their territories. Nonetheless, two major coalitions did emerge, one in southern Canaan, the other in the north.

THE SOUTHERN CAMPAIGN
Joshua 10:1-43

Adoni-zedek king of Jerusalem was concerned about the destruction of Ai and the capitulation of Gibeon. Ai was a relatively small village. Gibeon, however, was "a great city." Historians theorize that Gibeon was within the jurisdiction of the king of Jerusalem. Therefore Gibeon's treaty with Israel would be a renunciation of its allegiance to Jerusalem.

A. Attack Against Gibeon (Josh 10:1-8).

Adoni-zedek invited four other kings of the region to join him in an attack against Gibeon. By military pressure the coalition would punish Gibeon for having taken the part of the Israelites. So the five kings went up, camped against Gibeon and initiated the hostilities. This assault was the first serious effort on the part of the Canaanite kings to resist the invasion of the Israelites (10:1-5).

Chart No. 10

THE SOUTHERN COALITION Joshua 10			
KING	CITY	AMARNA LETTERS	LOCATION
Adoni-zedek	Jerusalem	yes	
Hoham	Hebron	no	19 Miles SSE of Jerusalem.
Piram	Jarmuth	yes	16 Miles W of Jerusalem.
Japhia	Lachish	yes	25 Miles SW of Jerusalem.
Debir	Eglon	yes	Near Lachish (?).

The Gibeonites reported what had happened to Joshua. They requested immediate help against the hill country coalition. Probably the covenant which the Israelites had signed with the Gibeonites provided for such military support (10:6).

Joshua immediately mobilized his troops. He took not only the elite troops (*"valiant warriors"*) but all the rest of the army as well. In his eleventh direct communication to Joshua, Yahweh urged his general not to be afraid. He promised to deliver the enemy into the hand of Joshua. Not one of the enemy would be able to stand before the army of Israel (10:8).

B. Victory by Israel (Josh 10:9-11).

Joshua 10 clearly reveals again the principle which has appeared again and again in this book, viz., that God *gives*, and Israel *takes*.[1] The narrative alternates between the actions of Joshua's army and the supernatural acts of God.

By means of a night march up steep terrain Joshua was able to position his troops for an attack upon the southern coalition. The forced march caught the enemy by surprise. The summary of the

great battle is first stated, and then the details are added. Four statements are made about the outcome. First, *"Yahweh confounded"*
the enemy before Israel.² Whether the enemy was confounded by the
surprise attack or by the hailstorm which followed is not clear. Second, Yahweh *"slew them"* with a great slaughter at Gibeon. Third,
when the enemy fled via the road leading to Beth-horon,³ Yahweh
pursued them. The Canaanites fled in a westerly direction toward the
coastal plain. The slopes above the road gave the Israelites excellent
opportunity to continue to bombard the fleeing remnants of the
enemy army. Finally, Yahweh continued to strike down the enemy as
far south as Azekah and Makkedah (10:10).

Yahweh used a hailstorm to smite down the enemy troops as they
tried to escape from the Gibeon area. The *"great stones"*⁴ continued
to fall upon them from the *"ascent of Beth-horon"* as far as Azekah.
More died in the hailstorm than died by the sword of the Israelites
(10:11).

C. Miracle in the Heavens (Josh 10:12-15).

The narrator has established that the Lord fought for Israel in the
battle of Beth-horon after the initial rout of the enemy at Gibeon.
Next he explains how the divine intervention came about. *"Then
Joshua spoke unto Yahweh,"* i.e., he prayed. When? After the hailstorm? Not necessarily. *"Then"* (*'az*) in Hebrew does not necessarily
imply sequence. It is an indefinite indication of time. The prayer *may*
have come before the great hailstorm. In any case, the prayer was *"in
the sight of Israel."* Perhaps Joshua assumed some posture which
the Israelites immediately associated with prayer. He must have
uttered his words audibly with Israel as eyewitness (10:12a).

Joshua's prayer was that the sun might *"stand still"* at Gibeon
and the moon over the valley of Aijalon (10:12b). The verb used here
(*damam*) literally means "to be still, dumb or silent." Why did Joshua
utter such a prayer? Three basic positions have been taken by the
commentators. First, the oldest interpretation is that Joshua wished to
prolong the sunlight so that the enemy might be completely destroyed
before darkness provided an opportunity to escape. Second, some
have suggested that Joshua was praying for relief from the heat of the
day so that his troops could press the attack more effectively. Third,

others have proposed that Joshua wished to maintain the advantage of darkness as he attacked the enemy in the earliest part of the day. In the first and third views Joshua's objective was virtually to make time stand still. The inspired writer next describes how Joshua's prayer was answered. The sun *"stood still"* (another form of the verb *damam*) and the moon *"stopped"* (*'amad*). The verbs could be understood to indicate that the heavenly bodies ceased in their motion or that they ceased in their function. Joshua 10:13 could be understood to declare that either the daylight or the darkness was prolonged. If the sun stopped, or appeared to stop, in its *motion*, then daylight would be prolonged. If the sun stopped in its *function*, then the darkness would be prolonged. In any case, this unusual day continued until *"the nation avenged themselves of their enemies"* (10:13).

In what he has reported thus far about the battle of Beth-horon the author of the Book of Joshua has been citing the Book of Jashar (lit., upright, just). Holy Spirit inspiration does not mandate originality, only accuracy and truthfulness. The Holy Spirit often guided Biblical writers to cite resource material. The Book of Jashar is mentioned one other time in the Old Testament (2 Sam 1:18). It appears to have been a poetic composition describing the wars of Yahweh. The original Book of Jashar is not extant. It is not properly speaking "a lost book of the Bible." Had God intended for it to be part of the sacred collection the book providentially would have been preserved. A spurious edition of the Book of Jashar is available, but it is worthless for any serious historical investigation (10:13).

Some commentators attempt to explain away the miracle of Joshua 10 as poetic exaggeration. The Israelites supposedly accomplished as much in one day as they would normally accomplish in two. This approach to the text is entirely unacceptable. Though it is true that Joshua's prayer is cited in poetic form, the sacred historian himself verifies that a miracle actually happened in the heavens in response to that prayer. *"The sun stopped* [or ceased] *in the midst of the sky."* The sun *"did not hasten to go down* [or come] *for about a whole day."* The report of what happened, like the prayer which called it forth, is ambiguous. The Hebrew verbs could just as easily be taken to refer to a prolonged night as to a prolonged day (10:13).

Whatever happened that day in the sky over Gibeon was a miracle wrought in answer to Joshua's prayer. Never before nor since had the Lord listened to the voice of a man to alter the normal routine of the heavenly bodies. By answering Joshua's prayer Yahweh *"fought for Israel"* (10:14). This phrase used in verse 14 in connection with the sun *"standing still"* recalls the language of verses 10-11 where the Lord caused great hailstones to fall on the enemy. When the Lord caused the sun to *"stand still"* he created the weather conditions which produced the hailstones of verses 10-11. A rapid cooling of moisture laden air is the natural cause of hail. Joshua's prayer was answered when God caused the sun to cease producing light. This may have been done by means of a cloud. The sudden change in temperature produced the hailstorm. Fleeing down the ascent of Beth-horon the Canaanites were pelted by the huge hailstones.

At the conclusion of the great victory over the armies of the southern coalition Joshua and his troops returned to the camp at Gilgal (10:15). To the western reader 10:15 seems out of place. It signals the end of the story whereas it is clear from what follows that another dramatic incident occurred on that same day. The verse serves to mark the conclusion of phase one of the conquest in the south, viz., the defeat of the enemy host. Now having related the striking defeat of the armies of the southern coalition, the author relates another incident which occurred later that same day—the capture and execution of the five kings.

D. Execution of the Kings (Josh 10:16-21).

During the flight from the battle of Beth-horon, the five kings had hidden themselves in *"the cave at Makkedah."* After an unspecified period of time, the Israelites found the kings. Their whereabouts was reported to Joshua. The general issued an order that the cave be sealed and guarded. The troops were to continue to press the remnants of the southern coalition. Every effort was to be made to prevent these Canaanites from returning to their cities (10:16-19).

How long the great campaign in the south lasted is not stated in the text. After the southern coalition was completely crushed and the few survivors had entered their cities, the Israelites returned to the camp which Joshua had established at Makkedah. No one dared challenge Israel or even utter a negative word against them in view of the smashing success which they had experienced (10:20-21).

Joshua then ordered the cave of Makkedah opened and the five kings brought out. He ordered that the military officers who were with him on this campaign come near and put their feet upon the necks of the captive kings. This act symbolized what God would do to all the enemies of Israel. Therefore, Joshua urged his subordinates to *"be strong and courageous"* (10:22-25). These words had previously been spoken to Joshua by Moses, the Lord and the people (e.g., 1:6,18). Now he for the first time uses these words to encourage his subordinates.

The kings were then executed, and impaled on five *"trees"* until evening. One who hung on a tree was considered cursed of God (Deut 21:23; Gal 3:13). In compliance with the law of Moses (Deut 21:23), before sunset Joshua ordered the corpses taken down. They were thrown in the cave in which earlier they had taken refuge. Huge stones were then placed over the entrance of the cave to serve as another stone monument, the sixth in the book (10:26-27).

E. Capture of Cities (Josh 10:28-39).

At this point the author lists a number of cities in southern Canaan—the future territory of Judah—which were captured by Joshua. The passage is characterized by a certain monotony of repetition. It emphasizes the role of Yahweh in *"giving"* these cities into the hands of Israel. In each case the ban was applied. All the inhabitants were executed including the king. Six southern cities are listed: (1) Makkedah (10:28); (2) Libnah (10:29-30); (3) Lachish (10:31-32); (4) Eglon (10:34-35); (5) Hebron (10:36-37); and (6) Debir (10:38-39). Three of these cities were mentioned earlier in the chapter as part of the southern coalition. While the author presents a stereotypical description of the capture of each of these cities, certain individual variations in the reports are present.

1. In four of the six reports the execution of the king is mentioned. No mention is made of the fate of the kings of Lachish and Eglon.

2. The language used to describe the movements of Joshua's army is different depending on the geographical circumstances of each particular city. So Joshua *"passed on"* or *"went up"* or simply *"returned"* (NASB).

3. The city of Lachish received aid from the king of Gezer delaying the capture of that city by one day. The army from Gezer was crushed (10:33).

4. Both Debir and Hebron had to be recaptured at a later period.[5]

5. The mention of the execution of the king of Hebron in 10:37 is interesting in the light of 10:23 in which he was executed on the day of the smashing victory. The conquests reported in 10:28-39 must have stretched over considerable time. The citizens of Hebron had replaced their fallen king.

F. Southern Region Summary (Josh 10:40-43).

The author of the Book of Joshua next gives a description of the territory controlled by Israel at this point in the Conquest. First, he describes the four natural regions which had fallen into Israelite hands: (1) the hill country; (2) the Negev; (3) the lowland; and (4) the slopes. The hill country and the lowland (Shephelah) were mentioned in 9:1-2 as areas in which the kings were alarmed over the success of Joshua. The Negev ("dry area") is the region roughly south of the Gaza-Beersheba road. The southern border of the Negev merges into the highlands of the Sinai Peninsula. This region of about 4,500 square miles is nearly half the area of the modern state of Israel. The "slopes" mentioned here lie between the Judean mountains and the Shephelah (10:40a).

Second, the author indicates that Joshua applied the ban to all inhabitants within the area conquered. This was done, the reader is again reminded, at the command of Yahweh. In the light of verses to follow (15:14f.,63) it is clear that some inhabitants of these cities did escape. The text therefore means that no one was deliberately spared by Joshua's forces (10:40b).

Third, the author gives the dimensions of the territory thus far conquered in terms of terminal points in four directions. Kadesh-barnea marked the southernmost point of Conquest. This is the oasis in the wilderness of Zin where the Israelites had faltered in their faith some forty years before (Num 13). On the west the Israelites had taken Gaza. They controlled all the land of Goshen. This was a border region between the Judean mountains and the Negev. It is not to be confused with the famous land of Goshen in Egypt. The northern extremity of the Conquest at this point was Gibeon (10:41).

Fourth, the southern region had all been captured *"at one time,"* i.e., in one campaign. The author does not indicate how long the campaign lasted. It probably extended over several months (10:42a).

Fifth, the author again inserts a reminder that all the victories in the south had been made possible *"because Yahweh, the God of Israel, fought for Israel"* (10:42b).

Finally, when all the united effort in the south concluded, Joshua and the army returned to the camp at Gilgal (10:43).

THE NORTHERN CAMPAIGN
Joshua 11:1-23

The text does not indicate how much time elapsed between the southern and northern campaigns. The entire united effort of the tribes lasted over seven years. Thus it is clear that only the highlights of the Conquest are recorded in the Book of Joshua.

A. Northern Coalition (Josh 11:1-5).

Hazor was the leading city in northern Canaan.[6] Jabin, the king of Hazor, heard of the successes of Joshua in southern Canaan. He realized that the only chance his region stood of remaining free of Israelite domination was for city states to band together.

So Jabin formed an alliance with several neighboring kings. Only one is named, viz., Jobab king of Madon. Two other cities are specifically mentioned—Shimron and Achshaph. Also included in the coalition were the kings of four geographical areas: (1) the hill country to the north of Hazor; (2) the Arabah (Plain) south of Chinneroth (Sea of Galilee); (3) the lowland; and (4) the heights of Dor to the west. The alliance included six ethnic groups, normally at odds with one another, united in order to thwart the advance of the people of God (11:1-3).

The northern coalition was powerful. Using Near Eastern hyperbole to underscore this point, the author indicates that the armies of the northern kings were as numerous as *"the sand that is on the seashore."* They also had superior weaponry. Because of the terrain in northern Canaan chariots could be employed for the first time against Israel. This powerful force assembled at the waters of Merom to the north of the Sea of Galilee to make their stand against Israel (11:4-5).

B. Battle at Merom (Josh 11:6-9).

Once again prior to the battle the Lord spoke words of encouragement to Joshua. This was now the twelfth recorded time when Yahweh spoke directly to Joshua. First, the Lord urged Joshua not to be afraid. Without doubt the general already knew through reconnaissance the strength of the enemy forces. Second, there was the gift promise: *"I will give all of them as slain before Israel."* Third, Yahweh gave new instructions. Joshua was to hamstring their horses and burn their chariots. To hamstring a horse—cutting the tendons at the hoof or knee—renders the animal unsuitable for further military usage (11:6).[7]

The next day the Israelite army swooped down *"suddenly"* upon the northern kings near the waters of Merom. True to his word, the Lord gave the northern army into the hand of Israel. The coalition broke apart. Every contingent fled for its own territory. The Israelite forces chased them in three different directions. No survivor was left to the Canaanite forces. Following the battle Joshua carried out exactly the orders he had been given by the Lord. He hamstrung their horses and burned their chariots (11:7-9).

C. Capture of Cities (Josh 11:10-15).

Once the main force of the enemy had been routed, Joshua turned his attention to capturing the various cities in the north. Hazor, *"the head of all those kingdoms"* is mentioned first. The king—presumably Jabin had escaped to the safety of his walls—was put to the edge of the sword. All the inhabitants of the city were destroyed. For the first time since Jericho and Ai Joshua ordered the city burned. Because Hazor had held the leading position among the northern cities it received a special exemplary punishment (11:10-11).

All the other cities of the northern coalition were captured. Their kings and populations were executed, utterly destroyed, just as Moses the servant of the Lord had commanded. However, no city in the north was burned except Hazor. Apparently the Israelites took possession of these cities, thus fulfilling the promise of Deut 6:10. The plunder of the cities belonged to Israel, but the inhabitants were executed. That standing order had originated with the Lord. It was passed down to Moses, and from Moses to Joshua. The author is anxious to emphasize that Joshua carried out exactly what he had been instructed to do (11:12-15).

THE ENTIRE CAMPAIGN
Joshua 11:16-12:24

Following the account of the southern and northern campaigns the author presents an overview of the entire campaign.

A. Geography of the Conquest (Josh 11:16-18).

The author loved to paint verbal pictures of the extent to which the Israelites had been successful in the conquest. He first states a generalization: *"Joshua took all that land."* The author emphasized that point by enumerating the various regions which comprised *"that land:"* (1) the hill country; (2) the Negev; (3) *"all that land of Goshen";* (4) the lowland; (5) the Arabah or plain; (6) the hill country of Israel; and (7) the lowland of Israel. To be more precise, the area conquered by the united effort of the tribes extended from Mount Halak[8] in the south to the Mount Hermon in the north. Baal-gad at the foot of Mount Hermon is the northernmost site mentioned. In this entire region the kings were all executed. The duration of this phase of the conquest is said to have been *"a long time."* From data presented later in the text that *"long time"* can be computed to be just over seven years.

B. Theology of the Conquest (Josh 11:19-20).

Not one city attempted to make peace with Israel with the exception of the Gibeonites who used deception to secure a peace treaty (cf. ch. 9). All of the territory acquired by Israel was won on the battlefield. But why did none of the city states sue for peace? *"It was of Yahweh to harden their hearts, to meet Israel in battle."* The destruction of the Canaanites was a judicial act of God. His will was that the Canaanites should be completely destroyed.[9] They should receive no mercy. That will was first revealed to Moses, and Moses laid the burden of execution on Joshua.

Yet it is a fact that one Canaanite begged for mercy and received it (cf. ch. 2). All the Canaanites knew of the mighty acts of God on behalf of his people. Only one was willing to renounce idolatry and embrace the Living God. God is said to harden a heart when an individual has rejected all prior efforts to effect moral change. The hardening of the heart is a withdrawal of further efforts to soften the heart; it is an introduction of circumstances which tend to make the wicked become ever more belligerent. In the case of the Conquest, the more territory Israel captured the more determined the Canaanites were to withstand their advance.

C. Climax of the Conquest (Josh 11:21-22).

No mention has been made heretofore in the book about those dreaded Anakim which had so terrified the ten spies in the initial reconnaissance of the land (Num 13:33). This was a giant race of people which made the Israelites feel like grasshoppers. Anakim were encountered at various locations in the hill country of Judah and in the hill country of Israel. Joshua utterly destroyed them with their cities. No Anakim were left in the land of Israel. Only in three locations in the Philistine plain did any of this race survive. The author surely withheld any information to this point about the Anakim to suggest that in defeating these giants a climax in the Conquest had been reached.

D. Concluding Statement (Josh 11:23).

To his account of the united Conquest the author adds a concluding summary. In it he states first that Joshua took the whole land. In so doing he fulfilled the promises regarding the Promised Land which God had made to Moses. The conquered territory was then divided up as an inheritance to the tribes of Israel. The details of how that was done will be recounted in the following chapters. *"Thus the land had rest from war."* This note must be understood in a limited sense. The author refers to the massive confrontations of armies and bloody sieges of cities. Certainly he does not mean that once the territory was divided there was no more conflict, for that would contradict what he relates in subsequent chapters. He means that the enemy's chief resistance was now broken. The united effort of *"all Israel"* was now over. From this point on it would remain for each tribe to remove remaining pockets of Canaanites from their inheritance.

E. An Appendix (Josh 12:1-24).

To the narrative account of the Conquest the author has appended a systematic listing of thirty-three kings defeated by the Israelites. This boring list is in reality a song of praise for the triumph of the King of Kings over the kings of this world. The author speaks first of the conquests under Moses east of Jordan, and then of the more recent conquests under Joshua west of Jordan.

1. Kings conquered east of Jordan (12:1-6). The geographical extent of the territory conquered by Israel east of Jordan is first given. This may have been done for three reasons: (1) to draw another parallel between Moses and Joshua; (2) to stress the unity of Israel; and (3) to underscore that the Transjordan area was now considered part of the Promised Land. The Arnon river valley marked the southern boundary, the foothills of Mount Hermon, the northern boundary. This territory included all the Arabah or plain of the Jordan east of the river (12:1).

King Sihon was the first to be conquered when Israel emerged from the desert (Num 21:21-35). His capital was Heshbon. This Amorite kingdom stretched from the Arnon river to the Jabbok river. It included all the valuable Arabah (Plain) between the Sea of Chinneroth (Galilee) and the Salt (Dead) Sea (12:2-3).

The second territory conquered east of Jordan was that of Og who ruled the region north of the Jabbok known as Bashan. Og was a remnant of the Rephaim, a giant race of people. He had two capitals, one at Ashtaroth, the other at Edrei (12:4-5).

Both Sihon and Og were defeated by Israel under the leadership of Moses. This territory was then given to the tribes of Reuben, Gad and half of the tribe of Manasseh (12:6). Twice in this verse Moses is called "the servant of Yahweh," perhaps to underscore the legitimacy of Israel's claim to the Transjordan territory.

2. Kings conquered west of Jordan (12:7-24). The author next lists the kings conquered by Joshua west of the Jordan. These kings had ruled collectively a large territory extending from Baal-gad at the foot of Mount Hermon to Mount Halak in the south. This territory embraced several distinct geographical regions: (1) hill country, (2) lowlands, (3) Arabah, (4) slopes, (5) wilderness and (6) Negev. Several different ethnic groups lived in this region: (1) Hittite, (2) Amorite, (3) Canaanite, (4) Perizzite, (5) Hivite and (6) Jebusite. Within this territory Joshua conquered thirty-one kings whose cities are now enumerated without comment. Perhaps this list was intended to be recited from time to time to remind the Israelites of the glorious victories that had been theirs when they experienced tribal unity under Joshua's leadership. Four observations regarding this list are in order.

Chart No. 11

CONQUERED KINGS Joshua 12			
Kings East of Jordan Defeated by Moses Sihon Og			
Kings West of Jordan Defeated by Joshua			
1. Jericho	8. Gezer	16. Bethel	24. Achshaph
2. Ai	9. Debir	17. Tappuah	25. Taanach
3. Jerusalem	10. Geder	18. Hepher	26. Megiddo
4. Hebron	11. Hormah	19. Aphek	27. Kedesh
5. Jarmuth	12. Arad	20. Lasharon	28. Jokneam
6. Lachish	13. Libnah	21. Madon	29. Dor
7. Eglon	14. Adullam	22. Hazor	30. Gilgal
	15. Makkedah	23. Shimron-meron	31. Tirzah

First, the list of defeated kings follows roughly the order in which events have been narrated in the preceding chapters. Second, half of the names on the list have not been mentioned in the Conquest narratives. Most of the new names are of cities in central and northern Canaan, where the narratives were extremely sketchy. Third, from subsequent narratives it becomes clear that the Canaanites were not permanently driven out of all of these towns. Some even had to be re-conquered.

Fourth, the most puzzling name on the list is the thirtieth—the king of Goiim in Gilgal. Goiim could be translated *"nations."* Here,

95

however, it is probably the name of a small tribe. Obviously the *"Gilgal"* here is not the camping spot near Jericho. This seems to have been a Gilgal in the region of Galilee. In fact, the Septuagint here reads *"Galilee"* which may well be the most ancient reading.[10]

ENDNOTES

1. The observation of K. Gutbrod, cited by M. H. Woudstra, *The Book of Joshua* in "The New International Commentary on the Old Testament" (Grand Rapids: Eerdmans, 1981), p. 171, n. 12.

2. The Hebrew term *hamam* is used of various meteorological phenomena which God employs against the enemies of Israel on the battlefield. See Exod 14:24; Judg 4:15; 5:20f.; 1 Sam 7:10; 2 Sam 22:15.

3. In Joshua 10 the road to Beth-horon is called both an ascent (v. 10) and a descent (v. 11). The road from Gibeon to Upper Beth-horon first goes up, and then descends to the village. From Upper Beth-horon the road descends sharply to Lower Beth-horon.

4. Some scholars (e.g., Velikovsky) think the "great stones" came from a rain of meteorites.

5. On the recapture of Hebron and Debir see Josh 14:6-15; 15:15-17; Judg 1:10-13.

6. Hazor is mentioned in the Mari tablets dating to the eighteenth century BC as well as the Amarna tablets from the fourteenth century. The city at its height could have accommodated forty thousand people. See *The New Bible Dictionary* (2nd ed. Wheaton: Tyndale House, 1882) s.v. "Hazor" p. 456.

7. H. Freedman, *Joshua* in Soncino Books of the Bible (London: Soncino, 1950), p. 64.

8. In 10:41 the southernmost point conquered was Kadesh-barnea which lay further west than Mount Halak ("Bald Mount"). Mount Halak is said to rise toward "Seir" or Edom.

9. God also hardened Pharaoh's heart. For a discussion of the concept see James E. Smith, *The Pentateuch, A Survey*, 2nd ed. (Joplin, MO: College Press, 1992), pp. 275f.

10. C. J. Goslinga, *Joshua, Judges, Ruth* in "Bible Student's Commentary" (Grand Rapids: Zondervan, 1986), p. 112.

CHAPTER SIX

Possessing the Inheritance
Joshua 13-24

The united effort of the tribes in the conquest of Canaan took just over seven years. Under the brilliant generalship of Joshua and the providential intervention of the Lord, the backbone of Canaanite resistance had been broken. The second half of the Book of Joshua deals with issues surrounding the occupation of the land. In these chapters the author discusses (1) the distribution of the land, (2) the dispute among the tribes, and (2) the final discourses of Joshua.

DISTRIBUTION OF THE LAND
Command and Precedent
Joshua 13:1-33

Joshua was now approaching a hundred years of age. He is described as *"old and advanced in years"* (13:1). Joshua still had one major part of his commission to carry out. The land which had previously been conquered needed to be parceled out to the various tribes. This long unit begins by citing the revelation which Joshua received mandating the distribution of the land. The author then describes the allotment east and west of Jordan. The unit concludes with a discussion of the cities of refuge and the Levitical cities.

A. The Divine Command (Josh 13:1-7).

The thirteenth divine communication to Joshua began with a recitation of the lands which were yet to be controlled by Israel. At this point *"very much of the land"* remained to be possessed. This statement, however, seems to be at variance with what the previous chapter declared: *"Joshua took the whole land. . . . Thus the land had rest from war"* (11:23). The victories which Joshua had won gave Israel the possession of the land in principle. No Canaanite forces were left which were capable of presenting any effective resistance to Israel. Occupation in principle, however, is not the same as possession of the land. Pockets of Canaanite resistance remained here and there. These areas are now identified by the author (13:1).

1. The territory of the Philistines and allied Geshurites[1] along the southwest coast of Canaan. Though the Philistines were not themselves Canaanites, this territory was reckoned as *"Canaanite"* probably since the Canaanites occupied the territory before the Philistines arrived on the scene in force about 1200 BC. Since this was Canaanite territory it was part of that Promised Land which God had deeded to the Israelites.

2. The *"whole land of the Canaanite"* along the Phoenician coast as far as Aphek some twenty-three miles north of modern Beirut (13:4).

3. The land of the Gebalite and *"all of Lebanon"* eastward (13:5).

4. The mountain regions from Lebanon to Mesrephoth-maim which was located just south of the so-called Ladder of Tyre on the Mediterranean coast. This area is said to be occupied by the Sidonians (13:6a).

God promised that he would drive out all the remaining inhabitants of the area. In this statement the principle is again operative, God gives, but Israel must take. Even though some of the land was not yet fully possessed, it was to be divided among the nine and a half tribes as an *"inheritance."* Thus, not all of the land assigned to the various tribes actually was under effective Israelite control at this time. The very act of assigning that territory was an act of faith (13:6b-7).

B. Allotments East of Jordan (Josh 13:8-33).
As has been his custom thus far, the author first deals with Transjordan, then with Cis-jordan. The tribes of Reuben, Gad and half of Manasseh had received their inheritance east of Jordan. The boundaries which had been worked out for each tribe by Moses "the servant of the Lord" are now set forth.

The description of the Transjordan territory given here follows what was presented earlier (12:2-6; cf. Deut 3:8-17). To this general geographical description of Transjordan the author appends two notes. First, he notes that the children of Israel did not dispossess the Geshurites or Maacathites who lived in the vicinity of the Sea of Galilee (13:13). Second, he notes that no inheritance was given to the Levites in Transjordan. The offerings made by fire to the Lord were their inheritance (13:14).The reference is to the portions of various sacrifices which were designated for the Levitical priests.

Having introduced the Transjordan allotments the author verbally maps out the areas assigned to the two and a half tribes. The territory was assigned essentially in the order it was conquered. From the Arnon river north to Sihon's old capital at Heshbon was given to Reuben (13:15-23). The territory between Heshbon and Ramoth-gilead—virtually the entire Jordan valley east of the river—belonged to Gad (13:24-28). Manasseh occupied Bashan, the territory formerly ruled by King Og (13:29-31).

The description of the Transjordan allotments concludes with a note that (1) stresses the authority by which these tribal assignments were made; and (2) underscores again that no land inheritance was given to Levi because of the greater spiritual inheritance which that tribe enjoyed (13:32-33).

THE GILGAL DISTRIBUTION
Joshua 14:1-17:18

While the territory east of Jordan was apportioned by Moses, that west of Jordan was done by committee. Joshua, Eleazar the high priest, and the tribal leaders shared in the decision (14:1). Nine and a half tribes were given territories west of Jordan. All together then, counting the two and a half territories east of Jordan, twelve tribal areas were assigned. The descendants of Joseph received two portions, for Joseph's two sons had become full-fledged tribes in Israel. The Levites, the author continues to emphasize, did not receive a tribal allotment. They did, however, receive cities scattered throughout the tribes. All of these arrangements were exactly what Moses had stipulated (14:3-5).

A. The Tribe of Judah (Josh 14:6-15:63).

The discussion of the allotment to Judah emphasizes the role of Caleb in the settlement of the tribal area. Caleb's faith and courage are held up as a model for what God expected from all of the tribal units. The request of Caleb for an inheritance is followed by a verbal description of the geography of Judah, a note about the early successful efforts of Caleb and Othniel, and a list of the cities which were in this tribal area.

1. The request of Caleb (14:6-15). The first of two apportionments in Canaan occurred at Gilgal. Caleb led a delegation to Joshua and reminded him of the commitments which had been made to him in the wilderness (cf. Num 14:24,30). In making his claim Caleb rehearses the history of how he had been sent from Kadesh-barnea to spy out Canaan. Because Caleb had been fully committed to the Lord, Moses swore that he would have his own personal inheritance in the Promised Land. Now some forty-five years later Caleb at age eighty-five claimed his inheritance. In the wilderness Caleb had risked his life to bring to his countrymen a positive report regarding Canaan. Now Caleb's land inheritance is placed at the head of all the allotments in Cis-jordan (14:6-10).

In spite of his age, Caleb was not inclined to seek retirement. He felt he was as strong as ever. Therefore he requested as his inheritance the hill country where the Anakim—the giants—were located. Apparently some of the Anakim who had escaped Joshua's initial conquest of the area (11:21f.) had returned to the area. Caleb believed that the Lord would honor his word (cf. 13:6) and drive those Anakim from the land. Thus Caleb was modeling the faith which God desired all his people to have at this stage of the Conquest. This is how Caleb received Hebron and environs as his inheritance. The city, once named Kiriath-arba after Arba the greatest of the Anakim, was now renamed Hebron. Following the conquest of Hebron *"the land had rest from war"* at least for a time. The cessation of hostilities made possible the further distribution of the land (14:11-15).

2. *The borders of Judah (15:1-12).* The author meticulously traces the tribal borders of Judah. Each tribe's territory was designated by lot by which divine guidance was assured. The phrase *"according to their families"* suggests that tribal areas where broken down into smaller portions. Mercifully the Holy Spirit has spared modern readers the details of the family assignments. For the Israelites such lists had a legal purpose. Perhaps these boundary lists were also recited in worship liturgy in celebration of the faithfulness of God in keeping his covenant promises. Since many of the places listed in tribal areas were still in Canaanite hands, the boundary lists also served the purpose of establishing a program of expansion for each of the tribes. The overriding spiritual truth in all this is that God has a place in his kingdom for every one of his children.

3. *Caleb's settlement model (15:13-19).* The author relates how Caleb was successful in driving out from Kiriath-arba (Hebron) the three giant sons of Anak. Caleb then proceeded to attack Kiriath-sepher (Debir), another city previously conquered (10:36-39) but reoccupied by Canaanites. He offered his daughter Achsah in marriage to the man who could conquer this town. Othniel, his brother or half-brother,[2] captured Hebron and thereby won the hand of Achsah. This young lady was very insightful and determined. She knew that land without water was worthless. So she persuaded her husband to allow her to ask Caleb for some nearby springs of water as a wedding present. Pleased with the pluck of his daughter, Caleb gave her *"the upper and the lower springs"* (15:13-19).

4. *Cities of Judah (15:21-62).* The text next lists 114 cities along with some villages which were not reckoned as "cities." The cities are listed in four major regions: the Negev (15:20-32), lowlands (15:33-47), hill country (15:48-60) and desert (15:61-62). Some of these cities would later be taken from Judah and given to the tribe of Dan. A most significant note comes at the conclusion of the long city

catalog. This tribe was unable to drive the Jebusites out of Jerusalem (15:63). Not until the time of David did the city finally and permanently come under Israelite control.

B. The Joseph Tribes (Josh 16:1-17:18).

The descendants of the two sons of Joseph, Ephraim and Manasseh, were reckoned as two separate tribes in Israel. The author first presents a general picture of the lot that fell to the Joseph tribes (16:1-4). He then discusses individually these two tribes.

1. *The inheritance of Ephraim (16:5-10).* To the outline of Ephraim's boundaries (16:5-9) the author adds an important note. The tribe of Ephraim did not drive out the Canaanites who lived in Gezer (16:10). They could have, but they did not. Instead the Ephraimites chose to make forced laborers out of these Canaanites.

2. *The inheritance of Manasseh (17:1-13).* Part of the tribe of Manasseh had already been given an allotment east of Jordan (17:1). The rest of the tribe received ten portions of land in an area west of the Jordan. Five of those tracts were given to the daughters of Zelophehad. Zelophehad had died in the wilderness. He had no sons. In the plains of Moab his five daughters had come to Moses requesting that they be recognized as the rightful descendants of their father. The young ladies won their case. As long as they did not marry outside their tribe they would each be entitled to a portion in the Promised Land (Num 27:1-11; 36:5-9). Joshua honored the word of the Lord as spoken through Moses regarding these women (17:2-6).

The author next gives a verbal description of the borders of Manasseh (17:7-10). Because the area contained few cities, Manasseh was assigned six cities in neighboring tribal areas (17:11). Unfortunately Manasseh was not able to take control of all these cities. When Israel became strong, however, they put the Canaanites to forced labor (17:12-13).

3. *The complaint of the Joseph tribes (17:14-18).* The Joseph tribes complained to Joshua about the size of their portion. In point of fact at least three other tribes were more numerous. Joshua, however, did not argue with them. He challenged them to carve out a settlement in *"the forest"* which covered a considerable portion on the northwest of their allotment. Of course there they would have to

tangle with the Perizzites and Rephaim (17:14-15).

Joshua's answer did not satisfy the Joseph tribes. They felt the hill country was not large enough. The Canaanites who lived in the valley of Jezreel possessed *"chariots of iron."* Perhaps the Josephites expected some kind of favoritism from Joshua since he was of the tribe of Ephraim. Joshua, however, would not budge. He repeated their own boasts to them. They were a numerous people. They needed more land. So take the hill country, he charged, and drive the Canaanites out. If they would only assert themselves they would have all the land they needed in spite of the iron chariots of their enemies (17:14-18).

THE SHILOH DISTRIBUTION
Joshua 18:1-19:51

Shiloh was the site at which the final allotment was made. The tent of meeting was set up there once the main Canaanite resistance had been removed. By some revelation God had designated that spot as the site of his earthly palace (cf. Deut 12:11; Jer 7:12). The site was ideal for a sanctuary because of its central location among the tribes (18:1). The complaint of the Josephites had indicated that tribal self-interest threatened national unity. The relocation of the tabernacle at this point in the tribal area of Ephraim was intended to counter this trend.

After describing how the Shiloh distribution was organized, the author proceeds to describe the territories of the tribes which had not yet received their inheritance. The tribal distribution chapters conclude with a note concerning a special portion given to Joshua.

A. Organization of the Distribution (Josh 18:1-10).

At this point seven tribes had not yet received their inheritance. Joshua chided these tribes for not entering their respective areas to take possession of them. Three men from each of these tribes were organized into a survey team. They were to go through the land, write a description of the prospective areas, and divide the remaining territory into seven areas. Then Joshua would cast lots *"before Yahweh our God"* to determine how the seven allotments would be assigned.

Joshua used this public speech to do what he did at every opportunity, viz., underscore the national unity of the twelve tribes. He did this by alluding to the Transjordan tribes, the two and a half tribes already assigned territory in Cis-jordan, and the Levites who had the priesthood as their portion (18:2-7).

The twenty-one man survey team completed their work. Probably a good portion of what is recorded in Joshua 13-19 is the result of their work. They described the land *"by cities in seven divisions in a book."* Joshua cast lots for them before the Lord in Shiloh (18:8-10).

Chart No. 12

COMPARATIVE SIZE OF TRIBAL TERRITORIES *In Square Miles*		
MANASSEH (EAST)		2,500
JUDAH	1,400	306,000 Population
GAD	1,300	162,000 Population
SIMEON	1,000	88,800 Population
MANASSEH (WEST)	800	210,800 Population*
NAPHTALI	800	181,600 Population
REUBEN	700	174,920 Population
EPHRAIM	600	130,000 Population
DAN	500	257,600 Population
ISSACHAR	400	257,200 Population
ZEBULUN	300	242,000 Population
ASHER	200	213,600 Population
BENJAMIN	200	182,400 Population

Population estimates based on the military census of Num 26 x 4 for an average family. Manasseh east and west are combined.

B. Final Tribal Allotments (Josh 18:11-19:48).

The lot fell in the following order: Benjamin (18:11-28), Simeon (19:1-9), Zebulun (19:10-16), Issachar (19:17-23), Asher (19:24-31), Naphtali (19:32-39), and Dan (19:40-48). Discussion of the multitude of geographical problems in this unit is beyond the scope of this survey. Concerning these allotments, however, the following observations are in order:

1. The lot of Benjamin is the most carefully described. It consists of both border stations and a city list of twenty-six entries.

2. The lot of Simeon was taken from within the tribal area of Judah because the portion of Judah was *"too large for them."*

3. A portion of the tribe of Dan migrated to the north beyond the

territory assigned to any tribe. There they captured the town of Leshem situated near the headwaters of the Jordan. They subsequently renamed the town Dan. The details of this tribal migration are reported in Judges 18. This event probably took place after the time of Joshua. If that is the case, an editor of the Book of Joshua has placed this brief note here in order to round out his account of the allotment of Dan.

C. Joshua's Inheritance (Josh 19:49-51).

The discussion of the tribal allotments west of Jordan began with the reference to the area assigned to Caleb. The same unit ends with a reference to the personal allotment of Joshua. Caleb and Joshua had risked their lives by bringing a good report regarding the land when Israel was camped at Kadesh-barnea (Num 14:6-10). How appropriate then that the author has used the inheritance of these two men as a frame around the allotment chapters.

In compliance with the commandment of the Lord, "the sons of Israel" gave Joshua an inheritance in their midst. The exact command regarding Joshua's inheritance is not recorded, but the idea may be implied in Numbers 14:30. He asked for and received the city of Timnath-serah in the hill country of Ephraim about sixteen miles southwest of Shechem. Joshua is said to have "built" (i.e., rebuilt) this city and settled it.

With the allocation of Timnath-serah to Joshua the western tribal allotment came to an end. Eleazar, Joshua and the tribal leaders had fulfilled their responsibility. The final phase of the allotment was performed at Shiloh "before Yahweh" at the door of the tent of meeting (19:51).

DESIGNATION OF SPECIAL CITIES
Joshua 20:1-21:45

Appended to the descriptions of the various tribal areas are two lists of important towns, viz., the cities of refuge and the Levitical cities. Actually all six cities of refuge were also Levitical cities which served a special function in the judicial system.

A. Cities of Refuge (Josh 20:1-9).

In the fourteenth direct address to Joshua[3] Yahweh directed that cities of refuge be appointed. In this communication the Lord repeated the principles by which this system of asylum would operate (cf. Deut 19:1-13). Cities of refuge were sanctuaries for those who had committed manslaughter. The *"avenger of blood"* could not execute the manslayer as long as he resided within the walls of one of these cities. Some commentators think the avenger of blood was a kinsman of the person who had been killed. Another view is that the avenger was a title for a government functionary whose job it was to execute those who had committed murder.

The elders of the city of refuge would decide who was eligible for the sanctuary within their walls. The sanctuary could be temporary, i.e., until a formal trial could be conducted, or indefinite where unintentional manslaughter had been determined. In the latter case the manslayer had to remain in the city until the death of the high priest.[4] Then he was free to return to his own city (20:1-6).

Three cities of refuge had already been appointed by Moses east of Jordan: Bezer in Reuben, Ramoth in Gad and Golan in Manasseh. Now Joshua and his advisers appointed three additional cities west of Jordan: Kedesh in Naphtali, Shechem in Ephraim and Hebron in Judah (20:7-9).

B. Levitical Cities (Josh 21:1-45).

Under Moses' leadership the decision had been made that Levites would be given cities throughout the tribal areas of Israel (Num 35:1-8). Chapter 21 relates how each of the three major branches of Levites received by lot its own cities. Thus the Levites occupied their towns by divine appointment.

The Levites approached Eleazer and Joshua at Shiloh to request that they might be given cities in which to settle. Forty-eight cities were assigned to them. Apparently these teachers of the law and religious leaders were to be readily available to all of the people of God. The descendants of Aaron were situated in the tribal areas of Judah, Simeon, and Benjamin. Thus the priests were located relatively close to Jerusalem which God later would designate as the site for his temple.

Chart No. 13

THE LEVITICAL CITIES		
LEVITICAL CLANS	**LOCATION OF CITIES**	**NUMBER**
Family of Aaron	Judah-Simeon (9) Benjamin (4)	13
Other Kohathites	Ephraim (4) Dan (4) Manasseh West (2)	10
Gershonites	Issachar (4) Asher (4) Naphtali (3) Manasseh East (2)	13
Merarites	Zebulun (4) Reuben (4) Gad (4)	12
TOTAL LEVITICAL CITIES ────────▶		48

DISPUTE AMONG THE TRIBES
Joshua 22:1-34

Chapter 22 indicates how the national unity which Joshua had cultivated during his years of leadership was nearly broken by foolish actions of the tribal leaders.

A. Tribal Unity Praised (Josh 22:1-8).

After the years of united tribal warfare, Joshua summoned to Shiloh the military contingent from the two and a half Transjordan tribes. This group which crossed the Jordan seven years earlier forty thousand strong had served faithfully. They had honored the word which they had given to Moses about fighting with their brethren. They had obeyed every command which Joshua had issued during the campaign. Now that the Cis-jordan tribes had achieved their "rest" it was time for these valiant soldiers to return to the possession which Moses had appointed them on the other side of the Jordan. Joshua, however, did have a parting admonition for these men. He urged them carefully to observe the law of Moses. This involved loving the Lord, walking in all his ways, keeping his commandments, holding fast to him and serving him with *"with all your heart and with all your soul."* Only then would they be able to enjoy their rest in Transjordan (22:1-5).

With these words of commendation and admonition Joshua *"blessed"* the troops and sent them away. The *"blessing"* took the form of an imperative. He encouraged them to share with their tribal brothers all the spoils which they had captured in battle. These spoils are called *"great riches."* They consisted of livestock, silver, gold, bronze, iron and *"very many clothes"* (22:6-8).

B. Tribal Unity Threatened (Josh 22:9-20).

The Reubenites, Gadites and half-tribe of Manasseh departed for the land of Gilead across the Jordan. In the vicinity of the Jordan they decided to build a large altar. When the other tribes heard of this, they gathered together at Shiloh to go into Gilead and make war against their brethren. From a distance it appeared that the eastern tribes were attempting to introduce an altar to rival the one authorized altar at the Tabernacle. A second place of worship would be a serious violation the law of Moses (22:9-12).

Fortunately cooler heads prevailed. A committee consisting of ten tribal leaders led by Phinehas, the son of the high priest, was dispatched to Transjordan to challenge the construction of the altar. Phinehas' zeal for Yahweh had already been demonstrated in the incident which had taken place at Baal-Peor (Num 25:7).

The committee was harshly accusatory with the eastern tribes. They accused their brethren of an *"unfaithful act"*[5] or *"turning away from following Yahweh."* By building the altar the eastern tribes had committed a trespass of the magnitude of what had transpired at Peor in the last days of Moses. The committee seemed most afraid that the altar transgression would bring God's wrath on the entire nation. The committee reminded the eastern tribes that they were welcome to cross the river and take up residence among the nine and a half tribes. By building the altar, however, they were rebelling both against Yahweh and their brothers. The committee closed its presentation with the ominous reminder of what happened when Achan had acted unfaithfully. The entire congregation had been punished for the sin of one man. Thus the other tribes had a legitimate concern about the purpose of this altar near the Jordan (22:13-20).

C. Tribal Unity Preserved (Josh 22:21-34).

The eastern tribes responded to the broadside of the committee of tribal leaders with shock and humility. They had not intended their altar to be an act of rebellion. Their altar was not intended for sacrificial purposes. Rather it was a monument to the unity of the nation. A future generation west of Jordan might wish to disown the eastern tribes and cut them off from participation in Tabernacle worship. In such an event the altar near the Jordan would be a reminder of the fact that the eastern tribes had fought alongside their brothers in the conquest of Canaan. Thus the newly constructed "altar" was really a monument celebrating the spiritual unity which bound the tribes on both sides of the Jordan into one nation. The large altar had even been modeled after the altar of the Tabernacle and thus was another expression of their loyalty to Yahweh. The eastern tribes were horrified at the thought that their actions were misconstrued as rebellion against the Lord (22:21-29).

The response from the Transjordan tribes pleased the investigative committee. A serious threat had been averted. No illegal act had been committed. Therefore there was no reason to think that Israel would experience the hand of divine wrath. God was still in their midst. Phinehas and his ten committee members returned from the land of Gilead in Transjordan and reported their findings. The report pleased the congregation. All talk of war against the eastern tribes ceased (22:34).

Misunderstanding between brethren arises when one group launches into some activity without seeking approval from the congregational leadership and without explaining intentions. Often brothers jump to conclusions about motives without first carefully investigating the situation. Joshua 22 contains several lessons which can be helpful in maintaining the unity of the spirit in the bond of peace.

This account concludes with a note that the eastern tribes named the Jordan altar "Witness." The altar was intended to bear witness that Yahweh is God (22:34).

JOSHUA'S FAREWELL ADDRESS
Joshua 23:1-16

Joshua 23-24 contain Joshua's last words to the people he had served throughout his lifetime. The tone of these chapters is hortatory. Thus the Book of Joshua ends as it began with words of exhortation. Though the two chapters have a great deal in common, certain differences are clear. Chapter 23 is oriented toward what God would do in the future, whereas chapter 24 focuses on what God had done in the past. The location of the two meetings probably was different. Also the scope of the assembly in chapter 24 seems to to larger ("*all the tribes of Israel*") than that in chapter 23.

Joshua's farewell address was delivered when he was "*old and advanced in years.*" Since this same language is used in 13:1 at the time of the land apportionment, it is impossible to determine how much time, if any, had elapsed since that event. Joshua summoned all Israel, but to what place is not indicated. The likely possibilities include Shiloh, Shechem and Timnath-serah. "*All Israel*" was represented in the person of its elders, heads, judges and officers. The address consists of three calls to covenant obedience each of which is preceded by a recitation of past favors bestowed by the Lord (23:1-2).

A. A Call to Covenant Faithfulness (Josh 23:3-5).

Joshua began his speech by calling attention to his great age. He was approaching 110. He apparently intended his words to be regarded as a kind of last will and testament. He spends very little time rehearsing the victories of the Conquest period. He first gives credit to the Lord for what was accomplished on the battlefields of Canaan. He then explained that he had given Israel as an inheritance two kinds of land: the land of nations which had been "*cut off;*" and the land of nations which yet remain. Joshua could make these allocations because he was fully confident that Yahweh would fulfill his promises and drive the remaining nations out of the inheritance he had given to Israel (23:1-5).

Joshua urged these leaders of Israel to "*be very firm*" (lit., be strong) to observe the commandments of Moses. Specifically, Joshua was referring to the Mosaic commands regarding absolute separation between the people of God and the peoples remaining in the land. Israel was not to *"associate"* with them. To do so would result in gradually making mention of the names of their gods. This certainly would include prayer to those gods.[6] That in turn would lead to taking oaths in the names of their gods, and even worse, the worship of those non-existing deities. To be successful in their inheritance Israel needed to continue to *"cling"*[7] to Yahweh (23:6-8).

B. Second Call for Covenant Faithfulness (Josh 23:9-13).

Based on their recent experience there was every reason to remain faithful to Yahweh. The Lord had driven out mighty nations before Israel. No man had been able to stand before their armies. Because the Lord fought for Israel, one Israelite soldier had been able to put to flight a thousand of the enemy. The Lord had kept his word in a marvelous way (23:8-10).

Israel must not assume that such divine aid as they had recently experienced would automatically continue. The Lord's help was conditional. Israel must continue to love Yahweh, and love for him was an exclusive thing. In Canaan they would be constantly tempted to *"go back"* (i.e., commit apostasy) and *"cling"* to surrounding nations. They would be tempted to give the same kind of loyalty to these pagans that they should have been giving to the Lord. Intermarriage is one example of what Joshua meant by clinging to the nations. In the event of such apostasy, God would abandon Israel. No longer would he drive out those nations before Israel. Those heathen nations would become a snare and a trap. They would torment Israel producing pain like that of a whip upon the back or thorns poking into an eye. Ultimately the heathen influence would cause Israel to *"perish from off this good land"* which they had just received from the Lord (23:11-13).

C. Third Call for Covenant Faithfulness (Josh 23:14-16).

Joshua reminded his audience of his impending death: *"I am going the way of all the earth."* Both Joshua and these leaders had observed that every promise which God had made had been fulfilled. Not one word of promise had failed. The same God who kept his positive promises to Israel would also keep his threats. He would in fact destroy them from off that land if they did not continue to cling to him. Faithfulness to the covenant was the key. If Israel began to take up with other gods, the Lord would *"burn"* against them. Israel would then *"quickly perish"* off the good land which their God had just given them (23:14-16).

COVENANT RENEWAL
Joshua 24:1-28

Because of its ancient Patriarchal connections, Joshua chose Shechem[8] as the site for the final covenant renewal ceremony of his life. *"All the tribes"* were present, at least in the person of their representatives. The elders, heads, officers and judges presented themselves *"before God."*[9] Joshua then addressed the assembly (24:1).

A. The Basis of the Appeal (Josh 24:2-13).

Joshua began his covenant renewal speech by reviewing the history of God's dealings with Israel, beginning with Abraham.[10] He mentions Abraham's journey to Canaan, the birth of Isaac, the descent of Jacob and his sons into Egypt. He speaks of the plagues against Egypt, the crossing of the sea, the destruction of the Egyptian army and the preservation of Israel in the wilderness *"for a long time."* Most of this would be ancient history for the audience of Joshua (24:2-7)

Joshua then began to speak of events with which his audience would have been personally acquainted. He mentioned the defeat of the Transjordan Amorites, and the reversal of the curses of Balaam (Num 22-24). He reminded them of the battle at Jericho and the long campaign against all the ethnic groups which inhabited the land of Canaan. God sent *"the hornet"*[11] before Israel which drove out *"the two kings of the Amorites."* At this very moment, because of God's unspeakable blessing, Israel was living in cities which they had not built, and eating from vineyards and groves which they had not planted (24:8-13).

B. Exhortation and Response (Josh 24:14-24).

All that he had been saying was building up to a challenge. *"Now*

112

therefore, fear Yahweh and serve him in sincerity and truth." This would entail two specific actions, one negative and the other positive. (1) They must put away the gods which their fathers served beyond the Euphrates river and in Egypt;[12] and (2) they must serve Yahweh. Service (i.e., worship) to Yahweh must be exclusive. If they did not wish to serve Yahweh, then they should choose which gods they would serve, either the old gods of Mesopotamia or the newer gods which they had encountered in Canaan. In any case, Joshua let the assembly know what his choice would be: *"As for me and my house, we will serve Yahweh"* (24:14-15).

The assembly responded in a forceful way. To forsake Yahweh and serve other gods would be a horrifying thought. After all, it was Yahweh who brought up *"us"* and *"our fathers"* out of the *"house of bondage,"* i.e., Egypt. Yahweh is the God who performed great signs in *"our sight."* Yahweh had preserved this people in whatever hostile circumstances they had found themselves over the years. He had driven out the Amorites, i.e., inhabitants of Canaan before Israel. Since Yahweh had demonstrated himself to be their God, the Israelites formally committed themselves anew to serving him (24:16-18).

Joshua then raised the bar of commitment to a higher level. He reminded his audience that Yahweh was a holy God. Yahweh was *"a jealous"*[13] God who would not merely ignore their dalliance with *"strange"* deities. If they turned from serving Yahweh to serve the foreign gods, Yahweh would turn against them and consume them as a nation. Disobedience turns covenant blessings into covenant curses (24:19-20).

Once again, and doubtless even more vociferously, the people declared their intention to serve Yahweh. Then Joshua coaxed yet another statement of commitment from them. They declared that they were witnesses against themselves that they had chosen to serve Yahweh in full knowledge of what the consequences would be if they lapsed into pagan religion. The people affirmed: *"We are witnesses"* (24:21-22). By setting forth the voluntary acceptance of covenant obligation on the part of Israel, the author is making clear that any later calamities which befell Israel for covenant unfaithfulness cannot be blamed upon God.

After these several verbal declarations of devotion to Yahweh, Joshua put the people to the true test of sincerity. *"Put away the foreign gods which are in your midst."*[14] Such an act would demonstrate that their hearts were inclined to Yahweh. For the fourth time the people declared their intention to serve Yahweh. They add, *"And we will obey his voice."* Presumably they were referring to the commandments regarding recognizing other gods or making graven images (24:24-25).

C. Covenant Documentation (Josh 24:25-28).

All which had just transpired is described as *"a covenant."* That covenant became the law of the land. Joshua wrote down these words in the Book of the law of God. Presumably the reference is to the writings of Moses. What Joshua wrote was the nucleus of the present Book of Joshua. The fact that Joshua was permitted to add words of any kind to the book already deemed sacred indicates that the people regarded him as a prophet inspired of God. That which Joshua wrote was immediately regarded as Scripture (24:25-26a).

To mark the spot of this covenant renewal, Joshua erected a large stone and set it under the oak that was *"near the holy place of Yahweh"* (NIV). The sanctity of that spot near Shechem went back to the time of Abraham (Gen 12:6). The stone had been a silent witness to the words of the Lord which Joshua had just spoken. The gracious acts of the Lord which Joshua had rehearsed before Israel at Shechem would testify against them should they ever be unfaithful to the covenant. Having made provision for the stone of witness, Joshua dismissed the tribes, each to its own inheritance (24:26b-28).

EPILOGUE
Joshua 24:29-33

The Book of Joshua concludes with four notes of historical interest. First, it reports that Joshua died at the age of 110 (c. 1387 BC). His age at death was the same as that of Joseph whose final burial is mentioned in the following verses. In this concluding note about him Joshua is given for the first time the title Moses had worn: *"servant of Yahweh."* Joshua was buried in his own inheritance of Timnath-serah in the hill country of Ephraim (24:29-30).

Second, the sacred historian reports that Israel served Yahweh all the days of Joshua and all the days of the elders who outlived Joshua. This probably represents a period of seven years or so. By that time most if not all of the elders who had seen the mighty acts of God in the wilderness and in Canaan would have passed from the scene (24:31).

Third, the Israelites buried the bones of Joseph which they had brought up from the land of Egypt. The burial plot was a piece of ground which Jacob had purchased from the local inhabitants some five centuries earlier (Gen 33:19). That piece of ground had now at long last become part of the inheritance of the sons of Joseph. This had probably been done on the first visit to the vicinity of Shechem early in the Conquest (Josh 8:30-35). The report is delayed until this point in order to serve as a kind of climax to the book. Before Joseph died he had expressed his faith in the fulfillment of God's land promise (Gen 50:25). Now Joseph's faith in God's promise had been vindicated (24:32).

The book concludes with a note on the passing of Eleazar the son of Aaron who was Joshua's lieutenant during the Conquest. The author may be suggesting that Eleazar's death (c. 1380 BC) marked the end of the period of the elders who outlived Joshua (24:33).

ENDNOTES

1. These Geshurites are not to be confused with a people by the same name which occupied an area in the vicinity of the Sea of Galilee (Josh 13:11,13; Deut 3:14).

2. The relationship between Othniel and Caleb is disputed. Othniel was the son of Kenaz. If Kenaz was the brother of Caleb, then Othniel would be his nephew. Jewish tradition takes Kenaz to be the father of both Caleb and Othniel.

3. In 20:1 the Hebrew uses the verb *dibber* ("spoke") rather than *'amar* ("said") which was used in the previous instances of direct divine communication to Joshua. For this reason Jewish tradition regards this as merely passing on to Israel what the Lord had previously said to Moses. See H. Freedman, *Joshua, Judges and Ruth* in "Soncino Books of the Bible" (London: Soncino, 1950), p. 120.

4. Scriptures do not state why the death of the high priest would mean release for the manslayer. These theories have been offered: (1) the death of the high priest had a kind of atoning effect since he had been anointed with oil. (2) Since the high priest was the head of the tribe of Levi, his death released the hold of the Levitical city (city of refuge) over the manslayer. (3) The death of the high priest signaled the end of an era and thus a general amnesty was declared.

5. The same Hebrew word (*ma'al*) is used of the offense committed by Achan (Josh 7:1; 22:20).The word basically refers to a breach of trust or unfaithfulness.

6. *"Making mention of their names"* might also refer to using the names of pagan gods as part of their personal names. Later in the family of Saul two sons had names which included the name of the god Baal. See 1 Chr 8:33; 9:39.

7. *"Cling"* (*dabhaq*) is the same verb used of the husband-wife relationship in Gen 2:24.

8. Shechem is specifically mentioned in the book only in 24:1. The city had special meaning to the Israelites. Here Abraham built his first altar in Canaan (Gen 12:6f.) and Jacob purchased a parcel of ground from the local inhabitants (Gen 33:18-20)

9. The expression *"before God"* suggests, but does not require, that the ark had been brought from Shiloh for this solemn service.

10. Here Joshua reveals that Israel's forefathers *"beyond the river"* in Mesopotamia had served other gods. The language is not clear as to whether Abraham himself was involved in this idolatry before God called him. Most likely he was.

11. The hornet (*tsir'ah*) is difficult to identify. Is a plague of insects intended? Others have taken the *"hornet"* to be a symbol for the stinging, paralyzing fear which seized the Canaanites before the arrival of Israel (cf. 2:9; 5:1). Garstang thought that the reference is to Palestinian campaigns of certain Pharaohs one of whose symbol was a bee or hornet.

12. The fact that Israel was serving idols in Egypt at the time of the Exodus is also emphasized by Ezekiel (20:7; 23:3,8).

13. God's jealousy is his zeal for the maintenance of his honor. This zeal can be shown in acts of punishment against those who have violated his holiness or in acts of vindication on behalf of his people who have been wronged by unbelievers (cf. Exod 20:5; 34:14; Deut 5:9).

14. The text does not record how this command was actually carried out. Some believe that Joshua is speaking of idolatry of the heart. Others think he is referring to the idols of the pagan nations living in the land.

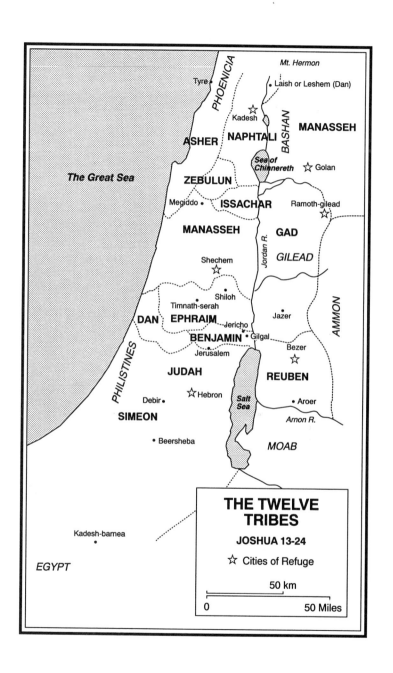

Mt. Hermon

Tyre

PHOENICIA

• Laish or Leshem (Dan)

☆ Kadesh

BASHAN

MANASSEH

ASHER NAPHTALI

Sea of Chinnereth

☆ Golan

The Great Sea

ZEBULUN

Megiddo •

ISSACHAR

Ramoth-gilead ☆

MANASSEH

Jordan R.

GAD

GILEAD

Shechem
☆

Shiloh
Timnath-serah •

Jazer •

DAN EPHRAIM

Jericho •

AMMON

BENJAMIN • Gilgal

Bezer
☆

Jerusalem •

JUDAH

REUBEN

Debir •

☆ Hebron

Salt
Sea

• Aroer

SIMEON

Arnon R.

• Beersheba

MOAB

THE TWELVE
TRIBES

JOSHUA 13-24

☆ Cities of Refuge

Kadesh-barnea

•

50 km

EGYPT

0

50 Miles

CHAPTER SEVEN

The Roots and Fruits of Apostasy
Judges 1:1-3:4

Judges is a book about apostasy. The opening paragraphs of the book trace the roots of that apostasy to the failures of the tribes to carry out the orders of God in their dealings with the Canaanites. At the same time these paragraphs sketch in broad outline some of the bitter fruits which apostasy produced for Israel.

Actually the introductory paragraphs of the Book of Judges constitute two separate, but partially parallel, introductions to the book. The first (1:1-2:6) is an historical epilogue to the Conquest period. The second (2:7-3:4) is a prophetic prologue to the period of the Judges. The first is more reportorial, the second, analytical.

A REQUEST FOR GUIDANCE
Judges 1:1-2

The Book of Judges begins on a positive note. The death of Joshua about 1387 BC triggered a renewed interest in driving the

Canaanites from the land. The Israelites, however, were hesitant to begin the program without some direction from the Lord. So the *"sons of Israel"* in the person of their leaders assembled to *"inquire of the Lord."* They wished to know which tribe should initiate the hostilities with the Canaanites. Doubtless they approached Eleazer the high priest. Through the priestly oracle—the Urim and Thummim[1]— Eleazar would have been able to answer their question. So far as the record goes this is the first time the Israelites asked advice from the Lord in this way.

Why the tribes felt they needed to have one tribe lead out in the tribal conquest is not stated. Perhaps there was a doubt whether the Lord would continue to drive out the Canaanites now that Joshua was gone from the scene. One tribe would "test the waters" for the others. The success of that tribe would signal all the others to launch their own campaigns. In spite of the uncertainties in the opening verses of Judges, two positive developments were triggered by Joshua's death: (1) interest in tribal conquest was rekindled; and (2) the tribal leaders were concerned to seek God's direction about the campaign.

The response of the Lord indicated that the tribes were right to renew the conquest and right to seek his will. The Lord indicated that Judah should go up first against the Canaanites. The Lord assured this tribe that he would give the land into their hand (1:1-2).

SUBSTANTIAL PROGRESS IN THE SOUTH
Judges 1:3-21

Judah invited the tribe of Simeon to *"come up"* to the Judean hill country to fight the Canaanites. Judah pledged to return the favor and subsequently aid the Simeonites in their territory. This was all together appropriate since the territory of Simeon was entirely within the territory of Judah (1:3). The allied tribes first attacked Bezek, then Jerusalem and other cities in the hill country, and finally the Negev and the coastal areas.

A. At Bezek (Judg 1:4-7).

First objective in the Judah-Simeon campaign was Bezek, the location of which is uncertain. The Canaanite king Adoni-bezek ("Lord of Bezek") was able to field an army of ten thousand, a considerable force for this small city state. Nonetheless, Yahweh gave his combined force of Canaanites and Perizzites into the the hands of the two Israelite tribes. The king fled the scene; but he was pursued and apprehended. In just vengeance for his cruel reign of terror in the area the Israelites cut off his thumbs and big toes (1:4-6). Adoni-bezek recognized the justice of what had befallen him. He himself had maimed seventy other kings over the years by cutting off their thumbs and toes. He had further humiliated his victims by making them gather scraps under his table like a pack of wild dogs. This cruel and proud king finally got a dose of his own medicine. Adoni-bezek was taken to Jerusalem where he subsequently died (1:7).

B. At Jerusalem and Hebron (Judg 1:8-10).
Technically Jerusalem was not part of the tribal inheritance of Judah. The city, however, was right on the border with Benjamin. Therefore, the Judahites, perhaps in concert with the Benjaminites, captured Jerusalem, put its inhabitants to the sword, and then burned the city (1:8).

Judah next undertook a campaign against Hebron, formerly known as Kiriath-arba (1:10). The author of the Book of Joshua was concerned to emphasize the individual role of Caleb in this campaign (15:13f.). The writer here sees it as an illustration of tribal success. Both accounts are true. Caleb certainly did not defeat the Anakim there single-handedly. In 1:20 Judges gives Caleb due credit for what was accomplished at Hebron (1:9-10).

C. At Debir (Judg 1:11-15).
Likewise Judges considers the conquest of Kiriath-sepher ("Booktown"), later called Debir, as a tribal victory. Yet Othniel was the hero of the battle. He had been challenged to undertake the campaign out of romantic considerations. Caleb had promised to give his daughter to the man who could capture the city. Othniel, Caleb's younger brother, won the prize, presumably not without the acquiescence of Achsah. Uncle-niece marriages were not one of the forbidden categories of marriage under the law of Moses (1:11-12). This account

121

serves to set the stage for the judgeship of Othniel in chapter 3. The man was already a military hero in Israel before he was called to be Israel's first Judge.

The author of Judges appreciated the pluck of the women of Israel. Achsah is the first woman to appear in the book. She was not merely chattel, a possession gained by bloody fighting. She was a shrewd, determined, and far-sighted woman. When Achsah *"came to him"* in marriage she persuaded her husband to request a field in addition to the city of Debir itself. She is the one who immediately pressed the request, with or without the permission of her husband. She pointed out to her father that a town in the Negev needed a water supply. So Caleb gave his daughter a *"blessing"* or wedding gift of two springs near Debir (1:14-15).

Aside from the author's interest in portraying women in a positive light, what might have been the purpose for the inclusion of this rather private and inconsequential event in Holy Scripture? This is a question which may not be conclusively answered. Certainly at the least it illustrates the principle, "Ask and you shall receive."

D. Other Campaigns (Judg 1:16-18).

The success of Judah in the Negev is indicated by the fact that the Kenites left the region of Jericho (*"city of palms"*) and went to live among the Judahites in the wilderness area south of Arad (1:16). The Kenites were a Midianite tribe skilled in working with metals. Moses' in-laws were Kenites. Hobab, Moses' brother-in-law, had apparently accepted Moses' offer to accompany the Israelites to the Promised Land (cf. Num 10:29).

The Judah-Simeon coalition next undertook the conquest of Zephath, a city allotted to Simeon. The city was *"utterly destroyed"* and thus was given the name Hormah ("Destruction").[2] Some twenty years earlier the Israelites had done the same thing to the cities of this region (cf. Num 21:1-3).[3]

In the Mediterranean coastal area the Judahites were able to take the Philistine cities of Gaza, Ashkelon, and Ekron and surrounding territories. Unfortunately these cities did not remain under Israelite possession for very long.

E. Status Report on the South (Judg 1:19-21).

Whatever success Judah had in clearing the hill country of Canaanites was due to the presence of Yahweh. The Judahites, however, did not fare well against the inhabitants of the lowlands to the west because they had *"iron chariots"* (1:19). Why was Yahweh unable to help them in the lowlands? The problem was that (1) Judah did not press the initial advantage in the lowlands; and (2) failed to settle the areas which had been conquered.

Benjamin did even worse. They did not follow up on the initial Judahite victory over Jerusalem. The Jebusites returned, and the Benjaminites made no effort to drive them out. At the time the Book of Judges was written the Jebusites were still living *"with the sons of Benjamin"* in Jerusalem (1:21).

UNEVEN PROGRESS IN THE NORTH
Judges 1:22-36

The author now paints a picture of the progressive failure of the northern tribes to dispossess the Canaanites. The campaigns start well enough, but then tribal efforts slack off. Finally the Canaanites got the upper hand in one area and forced the relocation of the tribe of Dan.

A. Initial Success (Judg 1:22-26).

The house of Joseph (the tribes of Ephraim and Manasseh) followed the example of Judah and launched a campaign to clean the Canaanites out of their territory. Bethel, which was initially conquered by Joshua (Josh 12:16), was their first target. *"The Lord was with them"* in this effort. Spies spotted a man coming out of the city. They requested that he show them *"the entrance"* of the place.

City entrances in this period had various configurations ranging from very simple to extremely complex zigzag affairs. To storm the entrance without having some advance knowledge of its construction would mean needless death to many soldiers. Like Rahab the Bethelite apparently was sympathetic to the Israelite cause. Upon a promise of kind treatment from the attackers, the man diagramed the entrance to the city.[4] Bethel was subsequently smitten with the sword, i.e., put

123

to the ban. The informer, however, was released. Unlike Rahab, this unnamed man chose not to join the people of God. He moved north outside of Canaan to the land of the Hittites. There he built a city which he named Luz after the original name of Bethel.

B. Failures of the Joseph Tribes (Judg 1:27-29).

Manasseh had been assigned certain cities from the tribes of Issachar and Asher (Josh 17:11). Four of these towns were in the Esdraelon valley, and one was on the coast. Manasseh *"did not"* take possession of these cities. They could have, but they did not. If fear was the initial reason for inaction, it did not continue to be a factor. The problem was not tribal strength, for at some point *" Israel became strong."* Still the Canaanites were not driven from the land. They were only put to forced labor. One can only speculate as to the possible reasons for Manasseh's failure (1:27-28).

The Ephraimites made the same mistake as their brethren the Manassehites by not driving out the inhabitants of Gezer. Again, the text does not say that Ephraim *could not* drive out the enemy. They simply left this strategic city in Canaanites hands (1:29).

C. Failures of the Other Tribes (Judg 1:30-36).

Zebulun left two cities in the hands of the Canaanites. Zebulun was strong enough, however, to subject the Canaanites to forced labor (1:30). Asher and Naphtali *"lived among the Canaanites."* This language suggests that at some point these tribes were actually at the mercy of the natives who lived in their territories. In the case of Dan, the Amorites forced a retreat back into the hill country of Ephraim. The Danites never were able to gain the upper hand (1:31-36).

And so the litany of failure concludes. Seven times in these verses the sad words appear: *"did not drive out."* Certainly there were good reasons to have carried out God's initial orders to drive the Canaanites from this land. Some of the sites left in Canaanite hands were geographically strategic. The danger from Canaanite enclaves, however, was fundamentally spiritual, not military or economic. Toleration would lead to association and that to accommodation. Yahweh would come to be regarded as just another deity, one among many, that needed appeasement from time to time. Here in Judges 1 are the roots of the apostasy so prevalent later in the book: failure to obey the primary command of God to expel the Canaanites.

From the standpoint of the author of Judges—a true preacher—the record of tribal activity in the north was one of dismal failure. The text, however, acknowledges that the Israelites did come eventually to dominate their Canaanite neighbors militarily and economically. Four times (vv. 28,30,33,35) he stresses that the Canaanites were put to forced labor. Thus the accusation here is not that Israel could not because of lack of faith drive out the Canaanites. Rather the charge is that Israel *deliberately disobeyed* the commandment of God. Israel *chose* to live side by side with Canaanites. Thus the text suggests that success may be measured by many yardsticks. Judged physically, Israel's occupation of Canaan was a success. Judged spiritually, Israel had miserably failed.

A DIVINE REBUKE AND WARNING
Judges 2:1-6

When the tribal efforts to expel the Canaanites ceased, the angel of Yahweh, whose directives launched the Conquest at Jericho (cf. Josh 5:13-15), appeared again. His message now was one of rebuke and warning.

A. The Appearance (Judg 2:1a).

The terminology *"angel of Yahweh"* is never used of a human messenger or prophet in the historical books.[5] The angel of Yahweh is a theophany, a visible manifestation of Yahweh.This appearance should be dated sometime between the death of the faithful elders who outlived Joshua c. 1380 BC and the rise of the first foreign oppressor c. 1367 BC.

The angel of Yahweh *"went up"* from Gilgal in the Jordan valley to Bochim. The location of Bochim is unknown, but apparently some prominent place in the hill country is meant. Since the passage indicates that the place received the name Bochim ("Weepers") from what transpired in this passage, the site must have been known by another name before this event. Since the text indicates that the "angel" spoke to *"all Israel"* some place of national assembly must be intended. Two places appear possibilities: Shechem where Joshua led Israel in covenant renewal, and Shiloh where the tabernacle was located.[6]

Why does the text speak of going up from "Gilgal"? The "angel" did not physically follow a road from the one site to the other. The text only means to say that the same divine personage who issued the initial battle plan at Gilgal now appeared at Bochim. At Gilgal the reproach of God's people had been rolled away. There the covenant feast and covenant sign had been renewed after thirty-eight years of suspension. At Gilgal Israel learned the power of obedient faith; at Bochim the dismay of disobedience. Thus the phrase "from Gilgal to Bochim" expresses the decline of Israel from spiritually lofty heights to the pit of spiritual despair.[7]

B. The Message (Judg 2:1b-3).

The "angel" did not introduce his speech with a messenger formula (*"thus says Yahweh"*) because the "angel" is Yahweh. What he said is something that only Yahweh could say. The message began with a reminder of three things. First, the "angel" reminded Israel of his gracious acts, how he had brought them out of Egypt; how he had brought them into the land which he had sworn to give to their fathers. Thus he is the God of dramatic power and faithful promise. Second, he reminded Israel of his gracious commitment. Yahweh had promised never to break the covenant with Israel. Third, he reminded Israel of covenant obligations. Israel was not to make a covenant with the inhabitants of Canaan. This reminder suggests that formal covenants had been made with the native population promising to spare their lives (cf. Josh 9). Furthermore, Israel was to destroy all Canaanite altars and symbols of worship (2:1b-2a).[8]

Following the reminder, the "angel" brought an accusation against Israel in the form of a direct statement and a question. *"You have not obeyed me."* Nothing could be more plain and forceful than this terse statement (three words in the Hebrew). The question (*"What is this you have done?"*) is designed to underscore the shocking nature of such flagrant and deliberate disobedience to the Lord (2:2b).

Finally, the "angel" uttered a threat against Israel. It is couched in language previously used by the Lord in the days of Moses (Num

33:55) and in the days of Joshua (Josh 23:13). First, Yahweh threatens not to drive the Canaanites out before Israel. Second, these nations would be like thorns in the side of Israel, i.e., they would oppress them. Third, the Canaanite gods would be snares to entrap and finally destroy Israel. They would be infected by the cancer of Canaanite idolatry. Thus would Israel be ensnared in its own folly (2:3).

Chart No. 14

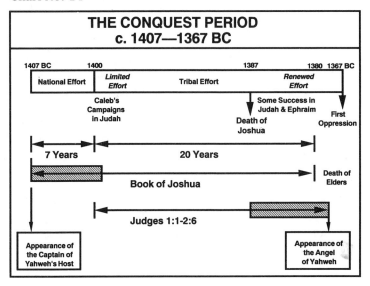

THE CONQUEST PERIOD
c. 1407—1367 BC

C. The Reaction (Judg 2:4-5).

In reaction to the appearance and message of the angel of Yahweh the people did three things. First, they lifted up their voice and wept. They were not yet so hardened as to be unmoved by the reminder of their spiritual failings. Second, they named the place Bochim ("Weepers"). Third, they sacrificed to the Lord.[9] Yet the text does not indicate that there followed any concerted effort to drive the Canaanites from the land. The tears of Bochim were those of remorse, but not real repentance.

A PROPHETIC PROLOGUE
Judges 2:6-3:4

In his first introduction to the Book of Judges (1:1-2:5) the author has concluded the record of the Conquest period. That period which began with such promise had a painful conclusion. Now the author presents a second introduction to the book, one which focuses on what will be emphasized in the chapters to follow. This section is a prophetic explanation—for the author was indeed a prophet—of all the tumult and turmoil of the period of the Judges. In these verses the text speaks of the peril of Israel, the person of God and the power of sin.

The second preface is not a continuation of 1:1-2:5 but rather parallels it. Both units begin with the death of Joshua; both conclude with the divine decision not to drive the Canaanites from the land. Here certain phrases from Joshua 24:28-31 are repeated almost verbatim. The conclusion of the former book has become one of the means by which this author opens his accounts of the various Judges. These verses interpret the stories of the Judges which follow in the book. In particular they reveal what God was doing during the period of the Judges.

A. God's Assessment (Judg 2:6-13).

The author hints at a number of perils which Israel faced toward the end of the Conquest period. Basically these verses describe how Israel got into the mess she was in during the days of the Judges.

1. Loss of godly leadership (2:6-9). The people served the Lord all the days of Joshua and the elders who survived Joshua (cf. Josh 24:31) or for about twenty years after Joshua dismissed them to their individual tribal areas. This does not mean that they obeyed all that the Lord had commanded. It only means that they had not yet taken up with any of the Canaanite gods.

2. Lack of experiential knowledge of the Lord (2:10). Joshua's generation knew by experience the miraculous works of the Lord on behalf of Israel. After the death of Joshua and the elders, however, a new generation arose which had no experiential knowledge of Yahweh or of the mighty work which he had done for Israel. Knowing *about* the Lord is totally different than knowing the Lord.

3. Lure of Baalism (2:11). Israel's spiritual decline came slowly,

128

almost imperceptibly. Disregard for the command to dislodge the Canaanites led to toleration of their practices and worse. The new generation *"did evil in the sight of Yahweh"* by serving the various types of Baal gods and their female counterparts, the Ashtaroth. Baal was the fertility god worshiped throughout Canaan. Each community had its own version of Baal. This fertility religion with its sacred prostitutes appealed to all the baser instincts of man.

4. *Lapse of historical memory (2:12-13).* They forsook Yahweh, the God of their fathers *"who had brought them out of the land of Egypt."* Forsaking Yahweh is depicted as a gross act of ingratitude. Taking up with such gods constituted a rejection of the exclusive claims of Yahweh. Forsaking Yahweh meant regarding him as only one deity among many.

B. God's Actions (Judg 2:14-18).

Davis suggests that the thrust of the second paragraph of this preface is on "the astonishing character" of God. Basically these verses present an overview of three centuries with a view to explaining how God dealt with the apostasy of his people.[10]

1. *Amazing in his anger (2:14-15).* Already the author has mentioned the fact that the unfaithfulness of Israel *"provoked Yahweh to anger"* (2:12). That thought is now further developed. God's anger burned against Israel. He *"gave them"* into the hands of *"plunderers"* who robbed them of their material goods. He *"sold them"* into the hands of enemies so that Israel could no longer stand up to them. No matter what direction they turned, the hand of Yahweh was against them just as he had warned them by solemn covenant oath.[11] Israel was severely distressed.

2. *Amazing in his salvation (2:16).* God did not immediately "write off" Israel at the first sign of apostasy. The distress of Israel called forth further demonstrations of divine grace. He sent "Judges" to deliver them. He *"raised up"* these deliverers, i.e., he called and commissioned them, and then equipped them to successfully carry out their mission.

3. *Amazing in his patience (2:17).* Israel did not respond to grace any more than to judgment. They did not listen to their Judges. Thus their guilt became all the more pronounced. They *"played the*

harlot" with other gods by bowing down to them. The Sinai covenant was like a marriage bond. Therefore, dalliance with other deities constituted spiritual adultery. Israel quickly turned aside from the path of obedience which their fathers had trod apparently even within the lifetime of the various Judges.

4. *Amazing in his pity (2:18).* In spite of Israel's disobedience Yahweh would raise up Judges to deliver them. The enemy could not prevail during the days of the Judge. God would give his people blessing and rest. Why did the Lord continue to show this kindness to his fickle people? Because he *"was moved to pity by their groaning"* in the face of their oppression. Even though his people were undeserving and unworthy the Lord had compassion on them during days of hardship.

Nothing God did during those centuries brought anything but temporary correction. Once a godly Judge died the people of Israel would revert to their idolatrous ways. They would act ever more *"corruptly."* Each generation seemed to get worse. Sin became ingrained. The people refused to abandon their practices or their stubborn (lit., stiffnecked) ways. Thus it would appear that whereas the Judge might hold in check the outward manifestations of idolatry he could not erase the tendency toward this evil from the lives of his people (2:19).

C. God's Anger (Judg 2:20-3:6).

The structure of Judges 2 needs to be studied carefully. The angel of Yahweh appeared to announce that God would no longer drive out the Canaanites (2:1-5). The rest of the chapter explains in effect the reason for that announcement. The apostasy of Israel provoked the Lord to anger (2:12). His anger *"burned against Israel"* (2:14,20). In the concluding unit of this second introduction to Judges the anger of God is further explained.

In his anger Yahweh issued a sovereign decree. When was this decree issued? At some point after the death of Joshua and before the appearance of the angel of Yahweh. In fact the angel of Yahweh appeared to announce to Israel the decree which God had already determined against them. In other words, Judges 2:20 is a continuation of 2:12. The intervening verses are a prophetic preview of the entire period of the Judges.

God's policy regarding the Canaanite nations had changed. The reason is clearly stated. Israel had (1) transgressed the covenant and (2) disobeyed God. By serving pagan gods they transgressed the covenant (Exod 34:14-16). By tolerating Canaanites in their tribal areas they were disobeying the direct command of God. Israel's unfaithfulness released God from his commitment to destroy the Canaanites before Israel. He would no longer drive out from before them any of the nations which were left in the land when Joshua died. These nations would serve a further end in God's program. They would constitute a test for Israel as to whether or not Israel would walk in the way of Yahweh as their fathers had done (2:20-23).[12] Thus the inhabitants of Canaan were no longer under the ban. They would have a new standing before God as tools which he would use to test the loyalty of Israel.

In concluding his second introduction to the book, the author has appended two notes of clarification. First, he clarifies the particular group of Israelites which God had targeted for the "testing." Some Israelites were still on the scene (e.g., Othniel) who had participated in the great war against the Canaanites. The majority, however, had not really experienced the wars of Canaan. The testing applied to this new generation which had no firsthand experience of war. Instead of experiencing "rest" they would experience oppression, fear and bloodshed (3:1-2).

Second, the author clarifies the nations by whom the testing would be accomplished. The list of nations here is much like that which appeared in Joshua 13:2-6 at the conclusion of Joshua's military career. These nations included the inhabitants of the coastal plain (Philistines, Canaanites, Sidonians) and the Hivites who lived in the region of the Lebanon mountains. Thus the author listed only nations that lived beyond the reach of Joshua's conquests, not those that had largely been destroyed and survived only as scattered remnants within the conquered territory (3:3).[13]

Third, the author clarifies the intention of the testing. National trouble and war would test each new generation to see if it would choose to obey Yahweh's commandments which had been given through Moses (3:4).

131

ENDNOTES

1. On the Urim and Thummim see Exod 28:30 and Num 27:21. In Judg 20:28 the text is explicit about inquiry through the high priest.

2. The Book of Joshua already used the name "Hormah" for this city. See Josh 12:14; 15:30; 19:4. Either this episode in Judg 1:17 took place before Joshua was written, or some later editor of Joshua updated the name of the town in these three places after the event of Judg 1:17.

3. Another possibility is that Num 21:3 was added to the text of Numbers after the Israelite Conquest to document that the wilderness vow had been fulfilled. In that case, Num 21:3 would be describing the same campaign as is here related in Judges 1:17.

4. Another interpretation is that he showed the Israelites some secret entrance to the city.

5. The prophet Haggai is called "messenger (angel) of Yahweh" (Hag 1:13). Malachi calls a priest "the messenger (angel) of Yahweh" (Mal 2:7).

6. From Judg 20:26f. it appears that the ark of the covenant was kept at Bethel for a time. In the light of this passage the identification of Bochim with Bethel (as is actually done in the LXX) is possible.

7. C.J. Goslinga, *Joshua, Judges, Ruth* in "Bible Student's Commentary" (Grand Rapids: Zondervan, 1986), pp. 259-262.

8. Commands to destroy Canaanite altars and paraphernalia are found in Exod 19:5f.; 23:32f.; 34:12-15; Deut 7:2-6.

9. That they offered sacrifices there suggests, but does not require, that the site of Bochim was Shiloh. Under the law of Moses altars could be constructed at any spot sanctified by God's presence.

10. Dale Ralph Davis, *Such a Great Salvation* (Grand Rapids: Baker, 1990), p. 37.

11. By virtue of Yahweh's covenant with Israel the threats contained therein actually had the force of an oath. See Exod 24:1-8; Deut 29:12,21; Josh 24:19-24.

12. Judges 2:23 serves to answer the question why any Canaanites were left in the land at the end of Joshua's campaign. God's intention had been to destroy the Canaanites gradually (Exod 23:29f.). Joshua had fulfilled his role in the master plan, but the tribes had not.

13. Goslinga, *op. cit.*, p. 275.

CHAPTER EIGHT

A Strange Salvation
Judges 3:5-5:31

The focus of Judges 3-16 is on the glory of God's salvation.[1] The author has selected several stories of sin, supplication and salvation in order that his readers might appreciate God's salvation even more. Since God refused to drive out the native population any longer, the Israelites had no alternative except to live among the Canaanites. Thus at the outset of the period of the Judges Israel was living at peace with people who should have been their enemies. Toleration of pagan ways led to accommodation, integration and finally apostasy. Israel's distinct identity was thus compromised. Israelites married Canaanite women and served their gods (3:5-6). The warning from the Angel of Yahweh (2:1-5) obviously went unheeded.

The first four oppressions and deliverances of Israel in the Book of Judges fell roughly within the period 1367-1221 BC. The oppressors during this period were Cushan, Eglon, the Philistines and Jabin. The deliverers were Othniel, Ehud, Shamgar and Deborah. These deliverances arose from unexpected quarters. Thus a certain strangeness characterizes the salvation of God's people.

Chart No. 15

THE EARLY JUDGES
1367-1221 BC

SALVATION THROUGH AN OLD MAN
Judges 3:7-11

The account of the first oppression and deliverance sets a literary pattern for those which follow in the Book of Judges. Though Othniel was the tool used by the Lord in this situation, the spotlight is really on God throughout. The text speaks of the anger, grace, action and gift of God.

A. The Anger of God (Judg 3:7-8).

The author outlines in three steps the circumstances which led to the first oppression of Israel by an external power. These steps move from the general to the specific. First, Israel *"did what was evil in the sight of Yahweh."* Second, Israel forgot Yahweh their God, i.e., forgot his claims, his commands, his character, and his mighty acts on behalf of the nation. Third, Israel served the various Baal gods of the Canaanites along with their female counterparts, the Asheroth (3:7).

The apostasy of Israel triggered the anger of Yahweh. His anger is a jealous anger which refuses to let go of his people. He would not allow them to be comfortable in their sin. God *"sold them"* into the hands of Cushan-rishathaim king of Aram Naharaim (NIV)—"Aram of the two rivers."[2] *"Rishathaim"* was a nickname bestowed upon this oppressor by the Israelites. It means "double wicked." Thus the Israelites called their oppressor "Double trouble from twin rivers."

The name "Cushan" appears to be Hittite. Cushan may have been a king of the kingdom of Mitanni who was a vassal of the powerful Hittite empire. He was probably attempting to extend his kingdom southward into Canaan. Apparently the entire land of Canaan was subject to him. For eight years (c.1367-1359 BC) Israel *"served"* this king. Presumably this meant that the Israelites paid tribute to Cushan. Throughout Old Testament history God frequently gave expression to his anger against unfaithfulness by empowering a Gentile ruler against his people.

B. The Grace of God (Judg 3:9).

The Israelites *"cried unto Yahweh."*[3] God was moved by those tears to raise up for his people a *"deliverer."* To *"raise up"* means to call, commission and empower a person to do a certain job. In this case, the job was to deliver Israel from the oppression of Cushan. The author has previously introduced this deliverer. He was Othniel ("lion of God"), Caleb's younger brother. Many years had elapsed since Othniel had established his credentials as a warrior in the capture of Debir. If he were as much as twenty years younger than Caleb he would have been about eighty-six at this point. The "lion of God" was indeed a harmless old lion. Even so, he had the spirit of his more famous brother who at the same age looked for giants to conquer! Othniel was the most prominent representative of that older generation which had witnessed God's mighty deeds in the conquest of Canaan.

C. The Action of God (Judg 3:10).

God used Othniel for great things. *"The Spirit of Yahweh"* came upon him. By that Spirit he was enabled to *"judge"* Israel. The function of the Judge was to set right what was wrong in the land. In this case, the wrong was the heartless oppression of Cushan. So *judging* Israel eventually meant going to war with Cushan. No details of the crucial battle are recorded. The text simply states that the Lord *"gave"* Cushan the double wicked into the hands of Othniel. The result was that Othniel *"prevailed"* over Cushan.

D. The Gift of God (Judg 3:11).

The land of Israel had *"rest"* for forty years after the expulsion of Cushan. *"Rest"* does not merely mean the absence of war. The term has a more positive side to it. To have *"rest"* means to have peace, happiness and well-being.

The text mentions the death of Othniel after the forty years of rest. This is probably not to be taken to mean that Othniel lived through that entire forty years. If so he would have been amazingly old—about 125—at the time of his death. Whereas in early Old Testament history some lived to this age and beyond, in this period people were not living such long lives. Surely note would have been taken of the fact had Othniel lived so much beyond the century mark. Most likely, then, the *"rest"* achieved by Othniel on the battlefield continued long after his death. This rest is probably to be dated about 1359-1319 BC.

SALVATION THROUGH A LEFTY
Judges 3:12-30

Judges goes into more detail concerning the second oppression and deliverance. The text speaks of the oppressor, the deliverer, the assassination of the oppressor and the victory over his forces.

A. The Oppressor (Judg 3:12-14).

Israel again began to do evil immediately after the death of Othniel and probably during the forty years of *"rest."* Thus even while enjoying the blessing of Yahweh the people again did what was contrary to his will. A new generation had grown up after the oppression by Cushan. They ignored the lessons of their history and turned again to the paths of apostasy which their fathers had trod. At the conclusion of the forty years of *"rest"* God punished his people a second time by means of a foreign adversary. He *"strengthened"* Eglon, king of Moab, against Israel (3:12).

Eglon with his allies the Ammonites and Amalekites invaded and defeated Israel in some decisive battle. The forces of the king occupied *"the city of palm trees"* in the general vicinity of old Jericho. From that headquarters Eglon was able to wield authority over the Israelites for eighteen years (3:13-14).

B. The Deliverer (Judg 3:15-16).

Yahweh was moved again by the agonizing cries which his people directed unto him. The Lord therefore *"raised up"* Israel's second deliverer. Concerning Ehud the text relates the following. First, he was the son of Gera. What significance may be attached to the mention of his father is not indicated. Second, Ehud was a Benjamite. Chronologically, the civil war which almost wiped out the tribe of Benjamin (Judg 19-21) probably already had taken place. Ehud would be one generation removed from that time when his tribe had almost become extinct. Because of that bloody civil war "Benjamite" must have been in this period a designation of contempt.

What is more, Ehud was left-handed. Left-handedness in the ancient world was considered a stigma. The fact that Ehud was left-handed does not necessarily mean that his right arm was useless. In a right-handed world the left-handed enjoyed certain military advantages.[4] Some who trained to be warriors would have their right hand bound to their side throughout their youth so that they might become skilled in the use of their left hand. Within the tribe of Benjamin at the time of the civil war there were six hundred such warriors (Judg 20:16). Ehud may have been descended from one of them.

Ehud seems to have been designated as leader of the groups which annually carried the tribute to Eglon. Whether or not this was deemed an honor is questionable. Ehud had probably been in or led that delegation several times during the eighteen years of Moabite oppression. He saw clearly what action must be taken if Israel was to be liberated from these oppressors (3:15).

Apparently without telling anyone of his intentions, Ehud fashioned a two-edged sword a cubit (c. 18 inches) in length. This weapon he strapped on his right thigh under his garment. He had observed that the guards always checked the left side of those who sought an audience with the king. They (rightly) assumed that a right-handed man would draw his sword from his left side. Since he was left-handed Ehud thought he would be able to smuggle his weapon into the presence of Eglon. The weapon probably had no crosspiece on it and thus would have been easier to conceal under the long flowing robes (3:16).

C. The Assassination (Judg 3:17-22).

Ehud had the assassination of Eglon carefully planned. First, he presented the tribute to the obese king as he had doubtless done many times before. Then he made sure his companions got safely through the Moabite perimeter in the Jericho region. He went with them as far as the *"idols"* at Gilgal.[5] There he turned back toward Eglon's headquarters. He was readmitted to the king's presence by announcing that he had *"a secret message"* for the king. Eglon may have thought that Ehud was about to reveal some secret Israelite plan to rebel against him. In any case, it is clear that Eglon trusted Ehud. He ordered all attendants from the room (3:17-19).

In the cool roof chamber of the headquarters building, Ehud approached the king. He explained as he did so that his secret message was from God. Pagan people had no problem embracing many gods. Eglon probably believed that Israel's God Yahweh was to be respected in this land. So he rose, out of respect for the God from whom he believed he would receive a message. At this point Ehud reached for his sword. Before the king could take evasive action or even cry out for help, the sword was buried in his fat belly. Ehud struck the king with such force that even the handle of the razor-sharp blade entered the body of the king. Ehud did not attempt to withdraw the sword. The king's entrails came out around the gaping wound (3:20-22).

Some have voiced great concern over the ethics of Ehud's actions. These points need to be stressed: First, Ehud was raised up by God. His calling as a Judge required him to rid the land of those who were causing oppression. Second, Ehud did not act out of base motives of selfishness or personal vengeance. Third, the Bible does not explicitly nor implicitly condemn Ehud for the course he followed.

D. The Escape (Judg 3:23-26).

The details of Ehud's escape from the scene of the assassination are not clear. Somehow he was able to lock the doors to the upper room where the king had died. One view is that he used a key taken from the person of the dead king to lock the doors from without. Another view is that he bolted the doors from the inside and then fled through a back door or window, or possibly even through the toilet shaft.[6] It is not clear whether or not the king's servants actually noticed Ehud leave. When they attempted to return to their stations in the upper room, they found the door locked. The locked door plus the odor that must have been generated by the rupture of the king's anal sphincter led the courtiers to conclude that the king was defecating (lit., "covering his feet") in the upper chamber. No doubt Israelites told this story over the years with a chuckle over the stupidity of the Moabite soldiers (3:23-24).

The royal guards waited until they became anxious. They then secured the key and opened up the upper room. There they were shocked ("behold!") to find their master lying on the floor dead. Meanwhile Ehud had escaped to Seirah, an otherwise unknown location in the hill country (3:25-26).

E. The Victory (Judg 3:27-30).

Ehud blew the trumpet throughout the hill country of Ephraim. After explaining what he had done, the Israelites followed him back down toward the Jordan. He assured the hastily assembled troops that Yahweh had given their enemies into their hand. The Israelite hosts seized the Jordan fords leading to Moab. None of the enemy was allowed to escape. About ten thousand Moabites were killed in the struggle (3:27-29).

The defeat of the Moabite army at the Jordan eliminated the threat from that quarter for a number of years. "Moab was subdued that day under the hand of Israel." Consequently that part of the land was undisturbed for eighty years (3:30).[7]

SALVATION THROUGH A GENTILE
Judges 3:31

Only one verse describes the career of Shamgar. The name is not Hebrew. For that reason scholars think he probably was a Gentile. He is called "the son of Anath." Anath was the name of a female goddess of sex and war among the Canaanites. This may be the intended meaning here, but other possible explanations have been proposed.[8] A note in chapter 5 (5:6) suggests that Shamgar was a man of considerable influence for some time. Though little is recorded about him in the Bible he must have been a legend in his own time.

God used Shamgar to deliver Israel from a new threat from the west. Shamgar's exploits against the Philistines should be dated about 1300 BC or shortly thereafter. Shamgar was able to strike down six hundred Philistines using as his weapon an ox goad, a sharp-pointed stick used to prod oxen. The strangeness of God's salvation is indicated by the odd instruments which the deliverers used against the enemy. Ehud used a homemade dagger, Jael a hammer and peg. Now Shamgar is said to have used an ox goad. God can win great victories with whatever is in the hand of a willing servant.

SALVATION THROUGH A WOMAN
Judges 4:1-24

The author of Judges appreciated godly women. Already he has given a cameo of Achsah, Caleb's lovely and clever daughter (Judg 1:13-15). In the fourth deliverance account of Judges the author introduces two women totally different in personality and station, but equally committed to the kingdom of God.

A. The Need for Salvation (Judg 4:1-3).

The text does not actually relate when Ehud died. Most likely he did not live to the conclusion of the eighty years of *"rest"* which followed his victory over the Moabites. A suggested date would be 1281 BC. In any case, when he died *"the sons of Israel again did evil in the sight of Yahweh."* Commitment which depends on some external force (e.g., Ehud) is not real commitment. Sin is soberingly repetitious. This apostasy most likely began in the northern tribes where the influence of Ehud's work had been felt the least.

The Lord *"sold them"* into the hand of a Canaanite king named Jabin whose capital was in Hazor. This is not the same Jabin who ruled Hazor in the days of Joshua almost a century and a half earlier (Josh 11:10-13). *"Jabin"* may have been a dynastic title for all the rulers of this city. Perhaps while Israel had been occupied with the oppressions by Cushan and Eglon this Canaanite city had gradually risen to power.

The commander of Jabin's army was Sisera whose military headquarters was in Harosheth-hagoyim (location unknown). The main source of Sisera's power was a unit of nine hundred iron chariots. For twenty years (c. 1281-1261 BC) he was able to dominate northern Israel (4:1-3).

B. The Tools of Salvation (Judg 4:4-11).

Deborah differed from all the other Judges who appear in the book in four respects. First, she was a woman, *"the wife of Lappidoth."* Women in positions of political or spiritual leadership during Old Testament history were rare. Second, unlike the other Judges who began their careers in response to a foreign oppression, Deborah seems to have been active for some time prior to the deliverance from Sisera. She was *"judging Israel at that time."* Third, Deborah is described as *"a prophetess."* She received direct revelation from the Lord which enabled her to interpret the past, give direction in the present and announce the future. Fourth, Deborah had a regular spot from which she judged Israel. Under a palm tree between Ramah and Bethel in the hill country of Ephraim Deborah held court. The sons of Israel came there to her for *"judgment."* Life in the heart of Israelite territory could proceed as usual. Jabin's influence had not spread much further south than the valley of Esdraelon (4:4-5).

How long Deborah ministered prior to the great deliverance is not stated. At some point she summoned Barak from Kadesh in the tribal area of Naphtali. Kadesh was further north than Hazor. Undoubtedly Deborah was following divine direction when she summoned this man. Barak came from the tribe which had suffered the most under the Canaanite oppression. Deborah shared with him a prophetic revelation which directed him to assemble ten thousand men and march them to Mount Tabor overlooking the valley of Esdraelon. He was to secure his troops from the tribes of Naphtali and Zebulun. God promised to *"draw out"* (lit., pull or drag out) Sisera to the river Kishon which flowed through the valley. He promised to give Sisera into the hand of Barak (4:6-7).

Barak agreed to carry out this divinely ordained mission if Deborah would accompany him. Was Barak showing cowardice? Was his faith wavering in spite of the assurances which Deborah had given? Not necessarily. He may simply have wanted Deborah to be present for the value of her prophetic advice. In any case, Deborah was quite willing to go with Barak. She warned Barak, however, that the honor associated with a victorious campaign would not belong to him. She predicted that the Lord would *"deliver Sisera into the hands of a woman."* That prediction is fulfilled in an amazing manner later in the chapter (4:8-9).

Encouraged by Deborah's agreement to go to Kadesh with him, Barak raised his army of ten thousand men. These men came from the two tribes most affected by Jabin's oppression, Naphtali and Zebulun. Other tribes, however, contributed to the effort (cf. 5:14). Deborah kept her word and went up to Kadesh with Barak (4:10).

A parenthetical note introduces another aspect of the strangeness of God's salvation. Heber separated himself from the Kenites who had migrated to the southern part of Judah (cf. Judg 1:16). He moved north to the general region of Kadesh. Jael, Heber's wife, will be yet another tool used by God in the deliverance from Sisera. Thus the author of Judges would have his readers reflect on the providence of God which led a family to relocate and thus position itself to be the agent of God's salvation (4:11).

C. The Day of Salvation (Judg 4:12-16).

The movement of ten thousand men from Kadesh to Mount Tabor could not be kept secret, nor did the Israelites wish to keep it so. Sisera heard that this army had positioned itself on Tabor. He therefore massed his nine hundred chariots and supporting infantry. He slowly began to move his forces from his headquarters to the Kishon river in the valley of Esdraelon. Sisera probably thought this show of force would intimidate the Israelites as it had done many times before. The position of the Israelites atop Mount Tabor was a strong one, but they could not stay there forever. As soon as they dared to come into the valley of Esdraelon Sisera aimed to destroy them (4:12-13).

Deborah the prophetess was not intimidated. She urged Barak to launch the attack. She predicted that this day Yahweh would deliver Sisera into the hand of Barak. *"Behold,"* she said cryptically, *"Yahweh has gone out before you."* His faith strengthened by the words of the prophetess, Barak led the charge down the slopes of Mount Tabor (4:14).

The Lord *"routed"* (lit., threw into confusion)[9] Sisera and his army *"with the edge of the sword"* before Barak. That, however, was not the whole story. Apparently a driving rainstorm made the floor of the valley impossible terrain for the chariot forces (cf. 5:20f.). When Sisera saw that the battle was lost he fled on foot. Meanwhile Barak pursued the chariots and infantry back to their headquarters at

Harosheth-hagoyim. Not one of the enemy troops survived the onslaught by Barak's men (4:15-16).

D. The Completeness of Salvation (Judg 4:17-24).

While his army fled west, Sisera on foot fled north and east. At Zaanamim he came upon the tent of Heber. As he approached, Jael went out to meet him. She invited him to come into her tent. She urged him not to be afraid. Since there was peace between King Jabin and the Kenites, Sisera thought he might find sanctuary within Jael's tent. She then *"covered him with a rug."* The general requested a drink of water. Jael gave him goat's milk instead. Sisera requested that Jael stand in the doorway of the tent to divert possible pursuers (4:17-20).

When Sisera fell asleep, Jael seized the opportunity to strike a blow for freedom. She took a tent peg and hammer. These were items she knew well how to use, for among the desert peoples the pitching of the tent was the work of the women. She cautiously approached the sleeping general. Sisera, however, was so exhausted by his flight that he was fast asleep. Jael drove the tent peg through his temple. The tyrant of the past twenty years was dead. As Barak approached her tent, Jael came out to meet him. She invited him into the tent to see *"the man whom you are seeking."* There Barak saw Sisera lying in a pool of blood with a tent peg in his temple (4:21-22).

With his army totally annihilated it was only a matter of time before King Jabin himself fell before Israel. *"The hand of the sons of Israel pressed heavier and heavier upon Jabin."* Finally he was destroyed, just as Joshua had destroyed the earlier Jabin who had ruled Hazor.

SALVATION'S STRANGE SONG
Judges 5:1-31

Deliverance from a ruthless adversary demands celebration. Judges 5 is a song sung by Deborah and Barak on the day of the great victory over Sisera. This ancient piece of Hebrew poetry is difficult to translate. Popular English versions of the Bible reflect a wide range of possible renderings of this chapter. Nonetheless, this poem is regarded as one of the masterpieces of world literature.[10]

A. The Savior (Judg 5:1-11).

The poem begins with praise for Yahweh. First, the Lord is praised because the leaders led and the people volunteered to follow them. Without courageous leaders and loyal followers God's work cannot be accomplished (5:2). Second, the poem praises Yahweh for his awesome presence. Yahweh is depicted going out *"from Seir"* or Edom. As he marched forth the ground trembled, the heavens dripped water. At Sinai the mountains quaked at the presence of Yahweh. This same God who with such awesome power appeared at Sinai had now come to the aid of his people against Sisera (5:3-5).

The presence of God among his people was much needed. The situation in Israel had been desperate in the days of Shamgar and Jael.[11] Major highways controlled by the Canaanites in the north and the Philistines in the south were deserted. New gods were being worshiped. Though war threatened their cities Israel had no courage to take up shield or spear in defense of the land. Forty thousand could have been hurled against Sisera, but no one would fight in those desperate days before Deborah arose.[12] She inspired confidence in the troops. Deborah realized, however, that she would not have been able to gain the victory without the aid of valiant commanders. For them she praised the Lord (5:6-9).

All segments of society are called upon to join the song of joy now that some normalcy had been restored. The ruling class *("who ride on white donkeys")*, the merchants *("who travel on the road")* and the shepherds all have reason to celebrate *"the righteous deeds of Yahweh"* (5:10-11).

B. The Summons (Judg 5:12-18).

Next the poem recalls how the people of Israel responded to the appeal to rise up against their enemies. Barak responded first to the challenge to take captives of the enemy. Then those who had survived the twenty years of oppression responded. *"The people of Yahweh came down to me* [Deborah] *as warriors."* Leaders from the tribes of Ephraim, Benjamin, Machir (west Manasseh), Zebulun and Issachar joined Deborah for the rebellion. They followed Barak into the valley of Esdraelon (5:12-15a).

Not all the tribes were interested in fighting against Sisera for the freedom of God's people. The Reubenites had *"great resolves of heart,"* i.e., good intentions. They talked about joining the fray. They searched their heart. Finally, however, the Reubenites decided that they were just too busy with their sheep. The Gileadites (the tribes of east Manasseh and Gad) also remained safely on the other side of Jordan. West of Jordan no help was offered by Dan and Asher. These two coastal tribes were caught up in a profitable maritime trade. Those who rest secure while their brothers fight the battle nearby stand condemned by the Lord (5:15b-17).

The unit dealing with "the summons" closes on a positive note. If there were tribes which refused to fight for freedom, there were two in particular which merited special praise. Zebulun was *"a people who despised their lives even to death."* They courageously threw themselves into the struggle without considering the fact that they might lose their lives in the battle. The same was true of Naphtali (5:18).

C. The Struggle (Judg 5:19-23).

The kings of Canaan—those who were allies with Jabin—sent their armies to fight the insurgents. At Taanach near the waters of Megiddo in the valley of Esdraelon the two armies clashed. The Canaanites were not able this time to take plunder. *"The stars fought from heaven"* against Sisera. This is a poetic way of speaking of how the Lord intervened in the battle. A terrific rainstorm caused the normally placid Kishon river to become a raging torrent. The horses mightily struggled to pull their chariots through the morass, but to no avail (5:19-22).

The third unit of the poem closes with a reference to the failure of another group of Israelites to assist in the battle. Through Deborah the *"angel of Yahweh"* put a curse on Meroz *"because they did not come to the help of Yahweh"* in the struggle against the enemy warriors. This city was near to the scene of the battle. Even after the battle had been won these Israelites did not help in the pursuit (5:23).

D. The Slaying (Judg 5:24-27).

The fourth unit of the poem celebrates Jael's contribution to the struggle for freedom. Her blessing stands in sharp contrast to the curse on Meroz. She is called *"most blessed of women."* She was an ordinary woman of a tent-dwelling tribe. She normally attended to duties about *"the tent."* Jael, however, is celebrated for her cleverness, courage and strength. Sisera asked for water which might refresh him. She cleverly gave him milk instead. This hastened his sleep. She took her life in her hand as she approached the sleeping general. She used all of her strength to pound that tent peg through the temple of the sleeping tyrant.

E. The Sorrow (Judg 5:29-30).

While there is jubilation in Israel, Deborah paints a sad picture of the sorrow that filled at least one heart. As a mother Deborah could understand the pain which one woman must be feeling. Every Sisera has a mother, someone who loves him in spite of his cruelty. So Deborah imagines how it must have been that day for Sisera's mother.

In typical motherly concern Sisera's mother paced in the palace, looking out the window from time to time to see if she could see any evidence that the troops were returning from the battle. She could not understand the delay that day. Those about her—*"her wise princesses"*—attempted to console her by suggesting various explanations for the inordinate delay. Perhaps the division of the spoil captured from the Israelites was so great that it was taking longer than usual to divide it among the soldiers. Perhaps females had been captured as a result of the battle and the soldiers were having their way with them. In any case, Sisera would return shortly bringing wonderful garments for his mother and others in the palace. Sisera's mother heard these suggestions, and even convinced herself that they were correct. She repeated them to herself. She knew not that another mother had engineered the defeat of her son on the battlefield. She had no idea that even while she was anticipating sharing the spoils of the battle, her son lay dead at the feet of a humble tent woman (5:28-30).

F. The Supplication (Judg 5:31).

Deborah was not a hard woman. She could appreciate the pain that the death of a Sisera might have on another mother. At the same time Deborah was not guided by feminine sentimentality. She loved the Lord and the people of the Lord more than life itself (5:31a).

The poem concludes with a twofold prayer. First, she prayed "*Thus let all your enemies perish, O Yahweh.*" The prophetess thus regards Sisera as one of the enemies of the Lord. Wicked oppressors frequently respond to no inducement to moderate their ways. They respond only to force. In essence Deborah was praying that God's kingdom might be established on earth as it is in heaven. She longed for the day when God's people would enjoy permanent "*rest*" because the last of their oppressors had been destroyed. Second, Deborah prayed that those who love the Lord might be "*like the rising of the sun in its might.*" God's people are meant to be a light in this world which dispels the power of darkness (5:31b).

The account of Deborah concludes with a note that the land had rest for forty years (5:31c). The rest can be dated to about 1261-1221 BC.

ENDNOTES

1. Dale Ralph Davis reached a similar conclusion in *Such a Great Salvation* (Grand Rapids: Baker, 1990), p. 47.

2. The NASB rendering "Mesopotamia" is not accurate.

3. The dominant connotation of the Hebrew za'aq is desperation. When repentance is included another word is added for clarity. Therefore the cries for help in Judges do not necessarily imply real repentance. See Davis, *op. cit.*, p. 50.

4. Baruch Halpern, "The Assassination of Eglon," *Bible Review*, December 1988, p. 35.

5. The "*idols*" may refer to the twelve stones erected at Gilgal by Joshua when Israel crossed the Jordan. Goslinga, however, thinks the idols were Moabite, that the Gilgal is not the famous site by that name, but the place mentioned in Josh 15:7 which was southwest of Jericho on the road to Jerusalem. *Joshua, Judges, Ruth* in "Bible Student's Commentary" (Grand Rapids: Zondervan,1986), p. 282.

6. For a discussion of the various views and a fascinating presentation of the "toilet" view see Halpern, *op. cit.*, pp. 35-41.

7. The eighty years of rest following the Moabite oppression should be dated about 1301-1221 BC. Most likely this period of rest in the south was coterminous with the oppression of Jabin, and the deliverance and rest under Deborah in the north.

8. Some think "Anath" was an abbreviation for the name of a town such as Beth-anat in Galilee (Josh 19:38).

147

9. The same Hebrew word is used in reference to the Egyptians (Exod 14:24f.) and the Amorites (Josh 10:10).

10. Goslinga, *op. cit.*, p. 295.

11. The reference in Judg 5:6 has implications for the chronology of the book. A casual reading of the text suggests that Shamgar delivered Israel from the Philistines at least twenty years before Jael slew Sisera. Yet in this poem the two are viewed as contemporaries dealing with the same general set of circumstances.

12. Deborah arose *"a mother in Israel"* or *"as a mother in Israel."* In the first translation Deborah would be claiming that she was in fact a mother. In the second she would be saying that she adopted all Israel as her children and served them with motherly devotion.

CHAPTER NINE

Strength in Weakness
Judges 6-8

The first four instruments used by Yahweh in the period of the Judges illustrate the strangeness of God's salvation. The fifth— Gideon—illustrates how God demonstrates his strength through human weakness. God delights in using the weak things of this world to confound the wise.

THE NEED FOR SALVATION
Judges 6:1-6

At some point during the forty years of rest after the deliverance from Jabin, the Israelites again *"did evil in the sight of Yahweh."* About 1221 BC the Lord *"gave them"* into the hands of the Midianites for seven years. This desert people were descended from Abraham through his concubine Keturah (Gen 25:2). Because the Midianites were distant relatives of the Israelites this oppression was particularly onerous. Each year at harvest the Midianites, along with their allies, would sweep in from the desert, cross the Jordan, proceed up the Esdraelon valley, the bread basket of Canaan, and then south through the coastal plain. They confiscated all the grain which they could carry away with them. The Midianites would bring their camels with them in such numbers that an accurate count was impossible. Like a locust plague they would strip the land. The invaders would leave virtually no means of sustenance for the people of Israel or their animals. The Israelites salvaged what they could in mountain caves and dens.

A PROPHETIC EXPLANATION
Judges 6:7-10

These annual incursions brought the Israelites low. They cried to the Lord. The answer to their prayer came in a strange way. God sent a prophet to them. That Israel should understand the present predicament was more important than the immediate deliverance from their oppressors (6:6-8a). God gave them what they really needed, not what they wanted. Understanding a problem may be more important than eliminating the problem. The word of God is the key to such understanding.

The unnamed prophet began with a messenger formula: *"Thus says Yahweh."* This is a claim that what the prophet was saying was directly spoken by *"the God of Israel."* First, the Lord reminded his apostate people of his gracious acts in the past. He had brought them out of slavery in Egypt. He had delivered them from the hands of the Egyptians at the Red Sea. Those *"oppressors"* who stood in Israel's path en route to Canaan (e.g., Sihon and Og) were dispossessed before the people of God. The Lord gave to his people the land of all their enemies (6:8b-9).

Second, the prophet stressed the relationship which existed between God and Israel, a relationship which had been initiated by the Lord himself. Often God had declared Israel to be his people. He had bound himself to them by covenant.

Third, the prophet repeated the basic demand of Yahweh's covenant: Israel must not *"fear"* (i.e., worship or serve) the gods of the Amorites in whose land they were dwelling.

Finally, after these various reminders, the Lord through his prophet made this charge: "You have not obeyed me" (6:10). The word of the Lord exposes and rebukes human failings. How gracious God is to bring his word of judgment to bear upon the lives of his wayward people!

The text does not indicate directly what effect the preaching of the prophet throughout the land might have had. The purpose of his coming was to bring the nation to repentance and thereby prepare them for the deliverance from Midian. When the prophet had finished his work, the Angel of Yahweh himself appeared in the land.

THE CALL OF A DELIVERER
Judges 6:11-40

More is known about the call of Gideon than of any of the other Judges. His call involved three types of divine revelation. In the first the Lord appeared directly to Gideon. In the second, God spoke verbally to Gideon. The third revelation involved supernatural deeds of God. These three types of revelations were designed to equip Gideon spiritually and psychologically for the great work he was about to do.

A. A Theophanic Revelation (Judg 6:11-24).

In a theophany God appeared directly to individuals in the Old Testament period. When he assumed human-like form the theophany is called the Angel of Yahweh. That Angel who last appeared at Bochim at the conclusion of the Conquest period (Judg 2:1-5), now made his first appearance during the Judges period.[1]

1. The challenge presented (6:11-16). The Angel sat down under a well-known oak tree on the property of Joash who was of the Abiezrite clan of the tribe of Manasseh. Joash's son Gideon was nearby beating out wheat in a wine press. By threshing his wheat in this unlikely place Gideon hoped to preserve a portion of the harvest from the Midianites (6:11).

The Angel made himself known to Gideon through an abrupt greeting: "May Yahweh be with you." This was a common greeting in the days of the Judges (cf. Ruth 2:4). The Angel addressed Gideon as "valiant warrior." Gideon was in no mood for pleasantries. He challenged the assumption that Yahweh would be with any Israelite. If Yahweh were with us—the shift to plural is noteworthy—then *"why has all this happened to us?"* The unstated premise upon which this question rests is that God would not allow such unpleasant circumstances if he were really with his people. He surely could not look askance while his people suffered. He would surely perform some mighty act on their behalf. Where were all the miracles which Yahweh was said to have performed in former generations? Since he had seen no evidence of miraculous intervention, Gideon could only conclude that Yahweh had abandoned his people. He had given them over to the power of Midian (6:12-13).

God answered Gideon's objections by revealing more of himself to the man. The Angel of Yahweh (who now is identified simply as Yahweh) faced Gideon. Gideon could see that the stranger was not making light of him. He was in dead earnest. Then came the commission: *"Go in this your strength and deliver Israel from the hand of Midian."* The *"strength"* to which the Angel alluded was the power which God supplies to those he calls to do his bidding. The question *"Have I not sent you?"* calls attention to that divine source of power (6:14).

Gideon was beginning to realize that the one with whom he was speaking was no ordinary person. He questioned, not the power of God, but the wisdom of God's choice: *"How shall I deliver Israel?"* Gideon saw his family as being the least in the tribe of Manasseh. He was the youngest in his family. He was lacking two essential ingredients of leadership: influence and maturity (6:15).

Yahweh bolstered the self-confidence of Gideon by reiterating the words of the greeting with which the conversation had begun. What was first stated as a mild wish now became a solid promise. *"Surely I will be with you."* God's presence would enable Gideon to smite the entire Midianite army as though he were smiting only one man (6:16).

2. The credentials offered (6:17-24). Gideon wanted proof that it really was the Angel of Yahweh who was speaking to him. He requested a *"sign,"* (i.e., supernatural verification) of the identity of this stranger. Gideon wished to present an offering to the stranger, as Abraham had done so many years before (Gen 18:5-8). Gideon specified no particular miracle. He must have assumed that an "*offering*" would give the Lord opportunity to show his power in some manner. The Angel agreed to remain until the offering was presented (6:17-18).

Gideon prepared an elaborate meal to present as an offering to his guest—a young goat and a tremendous quantity of unleavened bread.[2] He put the meat in a basket and its broth in a pot and brought it to the Angel who was waiting patiently beneath the oak tree. The Angel directed him to place the goat and the unleavened bread on a rock which became a makeshift altar. The broth he was to pour out, perhaps on the offering. The Angel then put out the end of his staff and touched the offering. Fire sprang up from the rock and consumed the goat and the unleavened bread. At the same time the Angel vanished from his sight (6:19-21).

Gideon now was certain that he had been conversing with the Angel of Yahweh, a manifestation of God himself. He was immediately stuck with fear. "*Alas*" signifies the deepest agony. Gideon apparently felt that to look upon the Angel of Yahweh face to face would mean death. What irony! Gideon needed assurance of Yahweh's promise (v. 16), but when the assurance came he was intimidated, not emboldened (6:22).

God spoke to him, no doubt in an audible voice. He urged him not to be afraid. He would not die. Gideon immediately built an altar to Yahweh to mark the spot of this manifestation. He named that altar "*Yahweh is Peace*" to celebrate the fact that he had seen the Angel face to face without tasting death. At the time the Book of Judges was written that altar was still present in Ophrah (6:23-24).

B. A Verbal Revelation (Judg 6:25-32).

In the theophanic revelation Yahweh had indicated that he was committed to Gideon. That very night in a verbal revelation Yahweh demanded that Gideon demonstrate his commitment to his God.

1. Requirements of Gideon's God (6:25-27). Gideon was directed to destroy his father's Baal altar and the Asherah pole beside it. Those who would be leaders of God's people must first set in order the affairs of their own house. Gideon was then to build an altar to Yahweh "*on top of this stronghold.*" The two altars could not exist side by side. One cannot serve both Yahweh and Baal (6:25).

153

Gideon was to use the wood of the Asherah pole for kindling. Then he was to offer up to Yahweh the seven-year old bull. The deliberate mention of the bull's age may be an allusion to the fact that Midian had oppressed Israel for seven years. Offering up the bull would then symbolize national rededication after this length of time.[3] Be that as it may, Gideon took ten men of his servants and carried out the instructions of the Lord. Because he anticipated interference from his father's household and the men of the city, he destroyed the Baal altar by night (6:26-27).

2. *Reactions of Gideon's neighbors (6:28-30).* The men of the city discovered the next day that the Baal altar and Asherah had been destroyed. A new altar of the fashion used in Yahweh worship had been constructed. They could tell that the new altar had been used during the night for sacrificial purposes. Diligent inquiry revealed that Gideon was guilty. The town leaders demanded that Gideon be handed over by his father to be executed for the sacrilege.

3. *Response of Gideon's father (6:31-32).* Joash refused, however, to hand over Gideon. He argued in effect that Baal, if he really were a god, could take care of himself. Here Gideon's father seems to be taking a decisive stand against Baal and his worshipers. Growing out of this incident Gideon received the nickname Jerubbaal, "Let Baal Contend Against Him" (6:28-32). This passage makes crystal clear that the struggle against foreign oppression and the struggle against foreign gods were inextricably linked.

C. Action Revelations (Judg 6:33-40).

Gideon heard no further from the Lord until the Midianites swept into the land on their annual raid. Then he received a new revelation, not in words, but in actions. These new revelations equipped him for his mission and confirmed him in it.

1. *The equipping revelation (6:33-35).* At the time the Midianites and their allies came up into the valley of Jezreel, the Spirit of God *"came upon Gideon"* (lit., clothed himself with Gideon). He was empowered to assume leadership. He blew a trumpet in the area of his clan, and the Abiezrites came together to follow Gideon into battle. Messengers were sent throughout the tribe of Manasseh and neighboring tribes. Thousands responded and joined Gideon and his

nucleus of Abiezrites (6:33-35).

2. *The confirming revelation (6:36-40).* Gideon still need reassurance that God would deliver Israel. This is cautious faith, but it certainly is not unbelief. Gideon thus put out his fleece on a threshingfloor. He requested that the fleece be wet the next day, and the ground about it dry. That would prove that the Lord would use Gideon to deliver Israel. The next morning Gideon found the fleece soaking wet. Still he needed reassurance. He put the same fleece out and requested that it remain dry while the ground round about was wet. Since wool has a tendency to absorb moisture, the fleece could only remain dry by supernatural intervention. The next morning the fleece was dry. Gideon was now ready to lead his troops against the Midianites (6:36-40).

The Lord granted both signs to Gideon because his request was not a demand made in unbelief, nor was it an arbitrary test of God's faithfulness.[4] A double sign was appropriate because Gideon would shortly experience a double testing of his faith. God delights in strengthening fragile faith. Far better to admit weakness and ask for strengthening than to go into battle with a cocky faith.

THE METHODS OF FAITH
Judges 7:1-18

The account of the deliverance by Gideon reveals clearly the methods of faith. God delights in teaching his people absolute dependence on him. Hence in this unit the narrator discusses the reduction of Gideon's army, the concessions which God made to Gideon's weakness, and the preparations for the battle.

A. Reduction of the Force (Judg 7:1-8).

Gideon may have been ready for confrontation with the Midianites, but God was not. Gideon had positioned his troops at the spring of Harod. The Midianites were encamped beneath in the valley of Jezreel. The Lord spoke to Gideon there on the eve of battle. Gideon's army was too large to be an effective tool of God. If the battle were won using such a large force, the Israelites would attribute victory to their own power. God's people have a propensity for glorifying their own efforts, for stealing the praise that belongs to the Lord (7:1-2).

Gideon was instructed to use the provision of the law of Moses (cf. Deut 20:8) and dismiss all those who were afraid when they looked down upon the Midianite camp. Twenty-two thousand men left the army. Gideon now had but ten thousand men to face the hordes below (7:1-3).

Gideon must have been a bit apprehensive as he saw two-thirds of his troops walk away. Again the Lord declared *"The people are still too many."* Gideon was directed to bring his remaining forces down to the water so that God might test them there. Only those who passed the water test would be permitted to go with Gideon into battle. At the water Gideon was told to segregate those who lapped water as a dog from those who knelt down to drink. The "lappers" scooped up water in the hand and drank while standing. They refused to break ranks. These numbered three hundred. The 9,700 who knelt down to drink were dismissed. The three hundred men apparently took the provisions of those who left including their trumpets (7:4-8).

The major question regarding the river episode is whether the "lappers" were intrinsically better soldiers than those who knelt to drink. Those who preach on this passage usually affirm that the "lappers" were more vigilant, more disciplined than the others. Commentators are divided on the question. Many feel that God simply used the drinking exercise as a mechanism for further reducing the force to "faith size." Certainly the text is silent about any military superiority of the "lappers" over the "kneelers."

B. Concession to Weakness (Judg 7:9-14).

That night the Lord again spoke to Gideon. If he had the least bit of fear regarding his mission, he was to go to the enemy camp. If he was afraid to go alone, he was authorized to take with him his personal servant Purah. God wanted Gideon to eavesdrop on a conversation in the Midianite camp which would *"strengthen"* his hands, i.e., give him confidence. What a concession to human frailty! God knows how scared circumstances can make his servants.

Gideon did not feign courage. He was not the stereotypical hero with ice water in his veins. He had no concern to maintain his macho image, not with God at least. He was doubly afraid—afraid to take on the Midianites with three hundred men, and afraid to attempt to penetrate their camp alone. So Gideon took Purah and descended into the valley to one of the outposts of the vast Midianite camp (7:9-12).

When Gideon and his servant got within listening distance of the outpost they heard a strange thing. One Midianite soldier was relating a dream to a companion. A loaf of barley bread was tumbling into the camp of Midian smashing a tent before it. His companion interpreted that dream without a moment's hesitation. Since the Israelites were grain farmers, the barley loaf represented the sword of Gideon. God had given Midian and the camp into the hand of Gideon (7:13-14). From this it is clear that the Midianites had heard of the resistance movement headed by Gideon. They must have heard some rumors about a divine visitor who had dispatched Gideon on this mission. Finally, Gideon would have concluded from what he heard that the rank and file of the Midianite army were terrified at the prospects of having to face the Israelites in battle.

C. Preparation for Battle (Judg 7:15-18).

When he heard the dream in the Midianite camp, Gideon bowed and worshiped God on the spot. Having had his own morale lifted, Gideon returned to his camp and inspired his men with the assurance that Yahweh had given the Midianite camp into their hands.

In preparing his three hundred men for battle, Gideon took advantage of what he had heard in the camp. His plan was to provoke panic within the enemy camp by feigning an all out attack on three sides by three hundred *companies* of men. No thought was ever given to defeating the Midianite camp by force of arms (7:15).

Gideon divided his men into three companies. Each man was equipped with a trumpet, a pitcher and a torch, the light of which was shielded by the pitcher. All were to look to Gideon's company for the cue as to what to do. He would lead his company to the outskirts of the Midianite camp, perhaps to the very spot where he and Purah had been earlier that night. When those who were with Gideon blew their trumpets all the others were to do the same. Then they were to shout the battle cry: *"For Yahweh and for Gideon!"* (7:16-18).

THE DEFEAT OF MIDIAN
Judges 7:19-8:28

The account of the defeat of the Midianites is difficult because it is abbreviated and because it contains geographical references which are hard to identify. Therefore the movements of the two forces are not always easy to decipher. Four key developments are clear: (1) the initial rout of the enemy; (2) the involvement of the reserve forces; (3) the pursuit of the Midianites; and (4) the return from the battle.

A. The Initial Rout (Judg 7:19-22).

The plan worked to perfection. Gideon's company approached the outskirts of the camp at the beginning of the middle watch just after the new guards had been posted. At Gideon's signal the three companies blew their trumpets, smashed their pitchers, held their torches high above them, and shouted the battle cry. While the Israelites each stood in their places around the Midianite camp, the enemy began to panic. They thought they were being attacked from all directions by three hundred companies. The Midianites fled down the Jezreel valley toward the Jordan. Later prophets regarded this victory as one of the greatest in the history of Israel (cf. Isa 9:4).

B. The Involvement of Reserve Troops (Judg 7:23-8:3).

Once the Midianites were put to flight, Gideon summoned the stand-by army—those men who previously had been dismissed—to take up the pursuit. The Ephraimites, who had no part in the original mobilization, were encouraged to seize the Jordan river crossings, thus thwarting the Midianite escape. Since Ephraim bordered the Jordan this made good sense. The Ephraimites responded in a positive way. They were able to capture two Midianite princes, Oreb and Zeeb. The Ephraimites brought the heads of these two princes to Gideon *across the Jordan*. Gideon and his men had been the first to reach and cross the river in hot pursuit of the enemy (7:24-25).

The Ephraimites were very angry that they had not been included in the original battle against Midian. Perhaps they felt that they were going to miss out on the spoils of war. On the other hand, perhaps the exclusion had wounded the ego of the temperamental

Ephraimites. In any case, Gideon had to deal with this difficulty. He "smoothed their ruffled feathers" by lauding them for the capture and execution of Oreb and Zeeb. Whereas it was true that Gideon and his men had been permitted to reap the harvest, i.e., strike the initial blow, in this case the *gleanings* were more important. Capturing the Midianite princes was more important than anything which Gideon had achieved that night. Furthermore, since God had given the victory to Israel there was no room for boasting by any man. By these wise and disciplined words Gideon put to rest the Ephraimite anger (8:1-3). Sometimes keeping peace in the camp is more of a challenge than chasing the enemy!

C. The Pursuit of the Midianites (Judg 8:4-12).

Gideon and his three hundred continued the pursuit of the Midianites deep into Transjordan. At the Israelite city of Succoth, located where the Jabbok empties into the Jordan, he requested some provisions for the troops. The leaders of Succoth were still cautious. Zebah and Zalmunna, the Midianite kings, had still not been captured.[5] As a city close to the desert Succoth would suffer severely if the Midianites were to be able to successfully counterattack. Prudence—or was it cowardice—demanded that they reject Gideon's request. They even *"taunted"* (cf. v. 15) Gideon, i.e., mocked or insulted him. They sided with the enemy and acted like the enemy, so Gideon would treat them like the enemy. He warned the leaders of Succoth that when he returned from the pursuit of the Midianite kings he would *"thrash"* their naked flesh with *"thorns of the wilderness and with briers"* (8:4-7).

At Penuel (NIV Peniel), a bit further east on the Jabbok river, Gideon received a similar response to his request for aid. There he threatened to tear down the tower of the city when he returned (8:8-9).

Zebah and Zalmunna attempted to reassemble what was left of their forces at Karkor. The exact location of Karkor is unknown, but it is thought to have been near Rabbah, the modern Amman Jordan, far to the southeast of Penuel. Only 15,000 of an original force of 120,000 were still intact. Gideon tracked down these forces. The Midianites were no doubt demoralized. Both the size of their remaining force and the distance from the original battlefield perhaps contributed to lack of military discipline. In any case, Gideon was able to launch another surprise attack. The Midianite army again was routed. Zebah and Zalmunna fled. Gideon, however, was able to capture them (8:10-12).

The final defeat of the Midianites was achieved basically without the enthusiastic support of God's people. The Ephraimites were more concerned about their tribal status than about smashing the enemy. The Transjordan towns of Succoth and Penuel chose neutrality rather than jeopardize their security. Everyone wants to join the victory parade. Few are willing to hazard their lives in the heat of battle. A wise warrior will expect disappointment from God's people. He will, nonetheless, press on to victory.

D. The Return from the Battle (Judg 8:13-26).

The return from the battle of Karkor was eventful. Gideon had three punishments to mete out. He also had to deal with the exuberance of his victorious troops.

1. Punishment of two Israelite cities (8:13-17). Gideon returned to Succoth to make good on the threat he had made before the final battle with Midian. A captured youth revealed the names of the seventy-seven leading men of the city. Gideon showed them the two captured Midianite kings. Then he disciplined the elders of the city with the thorns and briers, i.e., he administered corporal punishment. From there he proceeded to Penuel where he tore down the tower, as he had threatened, and executed the men in the city. Why Penuel received the harsher punishment is not clear. Both towns, however, had been guilty of treason. Both paid the price for failing to come to the aid of their countrymen in a time of national peril.

2. Execution of the two kings (8:18-21). After returning to Ophrah[6] Gideon confronted Zebah and Zalmunna with one of their crimes against the Israelites. He reminded them of a massacre which they had ordered at Tabor. There, it turned out, those two kings had killed the blood brothers of Gideon. The implication is that Gideon's brothers had been treacherously murdered under the orders of these two kings rather than killed in fair combat. If only they had showed mercy to his brothers, Gideon would have spared their lives (8:18-19).

Gideon turned to his firstborn son Jether and ordered him to slay the kings. Perhaps the point here was to inflict humiliation upon the kings by having them slain by an inexperienced youth. On the other hand, maybe Gideon was giving Jether a chance to show his manhood. In any case, Jether refused to draw his sword *"because he was still a youth."* The two kings then requested that Gideon himself wield the sword of execution. He was strong enough to slay them with one blow. Gideon compiled with their request. As a trophy of his defeat of Zebah and Zalmunna Gideon took the crescent ornaments which were on the necks of their camels (8:20-21).

3. *Recognition of Gideon (8:22-26)*. The men of Israel were overwhelmed with gratitude for what Gideon had done for the nation. They were willing to make him their ruler on the spot. While they refrain from using the word *king,* they clearly have in mind a hereditary regime. Gideon declined their offer insisting *"Yahweh shall reign over you."* Gideon, however, did suggest that the troops could show their gratitude by each contributing one earring from his spoil. Since the enemy were *"Ishmaelites"* each had an earring.[7] The earrings had been taken from the corpses of the slain. The weight of the gold contributed to Gideon came to 1,700 shekels (about 43 lbs.). With this contribution plus the other valuable items which were taken from the two Midianite kings, Gideon became a wealthy man.

CLOSING NOTE ABOUT GIDEON
Judges 8:27-35

Following the victory over Midian the land had rest for forty years (8:28). This is the last time in the Book of Judges that such a declaration is made. The forty years ended about 1174 BC. Thereafter the land seems to have suffered constant war. The gift of *"rest"* would no longer be granted to a people who so many times before had abused it.

The last days of Gideon were disappointing. His gold shekels were *"fashioned into a ephod."* An ephod was the upper garment worn by the high priest at the Tabernacle. The ephod described in Exodus 28 and 39 was very ornate and costly. It was woven with gold thread and contained numerous jewels. To what extent Gideon's ephod

161

resembled that worn by the high priest cannot be ascertained. None-theless, it is clear that to make a proper ephod would require consid-erable gold.[8] Gideon placed his new ephod in his city of Ophrah (8:27-28).

Perhaps the narrator was pained to recount all the details regard-ing this ephod. In the Old Testament the ephod with its breastpiece is associated with divine revelation. Several times before the battle Gideon had received direct communication from the Lord. Perhaps the ephod was an attempt to continue to receive divine guidance. Did Gideon himself attempt to function as a priest? Was he attempting to establish an alternative channel of divine communication? Did he feel that the normal means of revelation were not adequate? These are questions which cannot be answered. This much the text does clearly state: *"All Israel played the harlot with it there."* That ephod became a snare to Gideon and his household (8:27-28). These words suggest that some kind of illegitimate worship centered around the ephod at Ophrah.

Gideon became a religious innovator rather than a reformer bent on bringing Israel back to the old paths. Believers must be careful about ephod-making—of attempting to solicit direction from God in ways which he has not authorized. In Scripture God has already pro-vided all that the believer needs for his growth and direction.

Chart No. 16

THE MIDDLE JUDGES
1221-1126 BC

Another disappointing fact about Gideon is that he took many wives. He had concubines in various cities. All together Gideon had seventy sons who were his direct descendants (8:29-30). God had warned that Israel's kings should not multiply wives (cf. Deut 17:17). How much more this would apply to those who were not kings.

A third disappointing fact is related about Gideon. He named the son of one of his concubines *"Abimelech"* which means "My father is king."**9** The narrator has introduced this fact to point out the contradiction between what Gideon said about kingship in 8:23 and the way he acted. Gideon, it seems, refused to be a king. Nonetheless, he wanted to live like a king. Like many believers he had a hard time bringing his walk into harmony with his talk. His theology was correct. God alone should be king. His psychology was imperfect. He regarded himself as a king (8:31).

The closing words regarding Gideon's life remind believers that even the greatest champions of the faith can be brought low by avarice, lust and pride. Gideon died *"at a ripe old age"* (NASB) and was buried in the tomb of his father in Ophrah (8:32).

ENDNOTES

1. For a discussion of the identity of the Angel of Yahweh see comments on Judg 2:1-5.
2. An ephah of flour would be just short of a bushel.
3. C.J. Goslinga, *Joshua, Judges, Ruth* in "Bible Students' Commentary" (Grand Rapids: Zondervan, 1986), p. 328. That God here authorized a sacrifice to be offered by a man who was not descended from Aaron "shows how abnormal things had become in Gideon's day." *Op. cit.*, p. 329.
4. *Ibid.*, p. 333.
5. The question of the men of Succoth, *"Are their hands in your hands?"* may be asking Gideon to show them the severed hands of the two Midianite chieftains.
6. The presence of Jether (8:20) at the time of the execution of the two Midianite kings suggests that Gideon and his men had returned to base. That a young boy like Jether would have been among the three hundred chosen men who accompanied Gideon into Transjordan is not likely.
7. In this context *"Ishmaelites"* has lost its ethnic significance. It has the more general meaning of "desert peoples" and thus includes the Midianites. The interplay between Ishmaelites and Midianites is found in Gen 37:25,36.
8. Perhaps some of the gold was used to pay the craftsmen who fashioned the ephod.
9. Literally the text states: *"he appointed his name Abimelech."* According to Robert Boling, the terminology refers to renaming. See *Judges* in "The Anchor Bible" (Garden City, NY: Doubleday, 1975), p. 162.

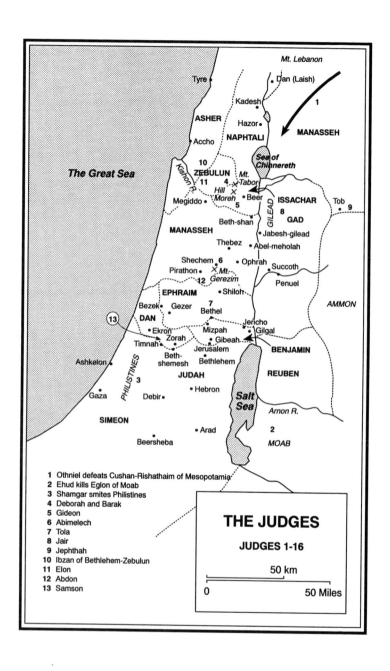

Mt. Lebanon

Tyre •

• Dan (Laish)

Kadesh •

ASHER   Hazor •

Accho •   NAPHTALI

The Great Sea

10
ZEBULUN   Mt.
11   4. Tabor
Hill X
Moreh • Beer
5

Megiddo •

Beth-shan

MANASSEH

Thebez •

Shechem • 6
Pirathon •   X Mt.
12 Gerezim
• Shiloh

EPHRAIM

Bezek • Gezer   7
Bethel

DAN

• Ekron   Mizpah
Zorah • Gibeah
Timnah •
Jerusalem
Beth-   Bethlehem
shemesh
JUDAH

Ashkelon •

• Hebron

Gaza   Debir •

SIMEON

• Arad

Beersheba •

Sea of
Chinnereth

MANASSEH

ISSACHAR   Tob
8   9
GAD

• Jabesh-gilead

• Abel-meholah

• Ophrah
Succoth

Penuel

AMMON

Jericho
Gilgal

BENJAMIN

REUBEN

Salt
Sea
Arnon R.

2
MOAB

1 Othniel defeats Cushan-Rishathaim of Mesopotamia
2 Ehud kills Eglon of Moab
3 Shamgar smites Philistines
4 Deborah and Barak
5 Gideon
6 Abimelech
7 Tola
8 Jair
9 Jephthah
10 Ibzan of Bethlehem-Zebulun
11 Elon
12 Abdon
13 Samson

THE JUDGES

JUDGES 1-16

50 km

0   50 Miles

CHAPTER TEN

Israel's Critical Condition
Judges 9-12

The author of the Book of Judges has presented the history of a nation whose spiritual health deteriorated from ill, to seriously ill, to critically ill. In the present unit Israel has reached the third stage in this ugly process. Here the oppressions were more ruthless, the deliverances less dramatic, and the deliverers less noble. Above all, in this unit Israel no longer enjoyed periodic seasons of God-given rest.

ABIMELECH: TRAGIC AMBITION
Judges 9:1-57

Gideon's son Abimelech, though of lowly birth (cf. 8:31), had grandiose ambitions. He wanted the kingship which his father had declined. Abimelech was not a Judge. If anything he was an oppressor of Israel. Israel's unfaithfulness was punished, not by some foreign foe, but by internal discord and bloody civil strife. Chapter 9 should not be viewed merely as an appendix to the story of Gideon. The

165

chapter serves to underscore the political implications of Baal worship. It portrays the terrible decline which set in after Gideon's death. It illustrates how God frequently brings about the demise of wicked men by turning them against one another. It represents another level in the social, moral and spiritual decline of the nation.

A. Sinful Ambition Unleashed (Judg 9:1-6).

Abimelech anticipated that the seventy sons of Gideon would share the rule over Israel after their father was dead. He therefore contacted relatives in his native town of Shechem. He urged them to press the city leaders to recognize him, their own flesh and bone, as their sole ruler. The text offers no evidence that the sons of Gideon had any plan to rule Israel as an oligarchy. Abimelech appears to have been using scare tactics to get what he wanted from the men of Shechem (9:1-2).

The leaders of Shechem were inclined to follow Abimelech because he was related to them through his mother. They even gave him silver from their temple—the house of Baal-berith—to aid him in his bid for power. Abimelech hired some thugs and took them to Ophrah. There he rounded up his brothers and killed them *"on one stone."* Only one, the youngest of the seventy sons of Gideon, escaped (9:3-5).

Having ruthlessly removed his potential rivals, Abimelech returned to Shechem. There the men of Shechem and all Beth-millo—an independent part of the city of Shechem—assembled for his coronation. The ceremony was held by the oak of the pillar which was in Shechem. This was the very spot where Joshua (cf. Josh 24:26-27) had many years earlier called upon Israel to be faithful to God's covenant (9:6).

B. Sinful Ambition Exposed (Judg 9:7-21).

Jotham, the surviving brother of Abimelech, went to Shechem. From a safe distance on an outcropping of Mount Gerizim he interrupted the coronation with a shout. He then delivered a fable[1] to the men of Shechem that they might realize the stupidity of what they were doing. In the fable the trees were looking for a king. Various noble trees—the olive, fig, the vine—all declined the invitation. Only the worthless bramble agreed to become king. The bramble even threatened to burn the rest of the forest if they did not anoint him as king (9:7-15). The basic point of the fable is that Abimelech, a man of ruthless temperament, is the least qualified to serve as king. How often God's people are attracted to the leadership of the men least qualified to lead!

Jotham then began to remind the Shechemites of all that Jerubbaal (Gideon) had done for the nation. He had risked his life to deliver the land from Midian. Now the Shechemites had joined a plot to wipe out all of his sons. Was this deed done *"in truth and integrity?"* If so, then a happy relationship should exist between Shechem and their new "king." But if not, then Jotham predicted that the "king" and his subjects would destroy one another. His point is that "a friendship based on ambition, ingratitude, disloyalty, and bloodshed could only have disastrous consequences for both sides" (9:16-20).[2]

Having finished his speech Jotham fled. He took refuge in Beer (location unknown) and remained there because of the danger from the ruthless Abimelech (9:21).

C. Sinful Ambition Thwarted (Judg 9:22-29).

Abimelech claimed to rule all Israel. In truth his "reign" was limited to the region around Shechem. After three years the prophecy of Jotham began to come to pass. God sent *"an evil spirit"* between Abimelech and the men of Shechem. Even the evil spirits are subject to the will of the Creator. What God permits, he is said in the Old Testament to have done. One of the ways God destroys evil men is by turning them against each other. That is exactly what happened in Judges 9. The men of Shechem began to deal *"treacherously,"* i.e., to be disloyal, to Abimelech (9:23-24).

The Shechemites set ambushes along the busy road which passed through their city. Merchants and travelers were robbed and abused. Such actions were designed to discredit the "reign" of Abimelech, to make it appear that the new king was totally incapable of maintaining civil order. The sin of murdering the seventy sons of Gideon was now about to be visited on Abimelech. At the same time, the Shechemites would be punished for their supportive role in those murders (9:25).

At this point another ambitious and vain man entered the picture.

167

Gaal the son of Ebed and his relatives moved into Shechem. He quickly gained the confidence of the men of Shechem who were looking for someone who could protect them from Abimelech. The Shechemites put their trust in Gaal. Now they could openly break with Abimelech (9:26).

When the grape harvest was complete, the town celebrated in a drunken feast in the temple of their god. Emboldened by their drink, the men cursed Abimelech. Gaal in drunken bluster challenged Abimelech to gather his army and come out for a showdown (9:27-29).

D. Sinful Ambition Punished (Judg 9:30-57).

God punished the sinful ambition of Abimelech and simultaneously the wickedness of the citizens of Shechem and their new leader Gaal. The events unfolded in four stages.

1. Judgment on Gaal (9:30-41). Abimelech still had at least one loyal friend in the city, Zebul the mayor. Perhaps he had been appointed to his position by Abimelech. Be that as it may, Zebul was enraged at the treasonous talk of Gaal. He sent word to Abimelech *"deceitfully,"* i.e., secretly, appraising him of the situation. Zebul urged Abimelech to bring his army that night and position it about the city. At sunrise he should rush upon Gaal and his supporters (9:30-33).

Abimelech moved that night. He positioned his soldiers in four companies about Shechem. Gaal and his men went out of the city in the morning. Perhaps they were going on a raid, or maybe they were intending to protect the workers in the fields. In any case, Abimelech launched the attack prematurely. Gaal thought he saw something moving down from the mountains. Zebul, stalling for time, convinced Gaal at first that he was seeing only shadows. A few minutes later, however, Gaal realized that he was coming under attack from several directions. Zebul now threw Gaal's boasts of the previous day back into his face and challenged him to go out and fight Abimelech (9:34-38).

So Gaal, the rebellious leader of Shechem, went out to face Abimelech. The skirmish was no contest. Gaal fled. Most of his supporters were slain. At the same time Zebul drove out all the relatives of Gaal so that they could no longer live in Shechem (9:39-41).

2. The judgment on Shechem (9:42-45). The next day the She-chemites assumed that all was back to normal. Gaal and his support-ers were gone. Abimelech appeared to have withdrawn from the area. The people, therefore, left the safety of their walls and went out into the fields to work. Abimelech, however, had not yet vented his anger on the city for tolerating rebellion against him. His troops were strate-gically placed in three places about the city. One company seized the city gate; the other two attacked the workers in the field. Abimelech waged war the whole day against Shechem. One by one he con-quered each quarter of the city. The inhabitants were all slain. The city was razed. Then as a symbolic gesture of eternal desolation, Abimelech sprinkled salt upon the ruins (9:42-45).

3. Destruction of the temple fortress (9:46-49). A number of the leaders of Shechem happened to be in the tower fortress part of the city when Abimelech's attack began. They hurriedly took refuge in the inner chamber of the temple of El-berith. This appears to have been a subterranean chamber. Abimelech took his men to the nearby woods and cut large branches. These were set afire over the entrance to the inner chamber. The thousand men and women who had taken refuge there were either burned alive inside or forced by the smoke to come out and face the swords of Abimelech's men (9:46-49).

4. The attack on Thebez (9:50-55). Abimelech then marched to nearby Thebez about six miles north of Shechem. This city also was in rebellion against him. He easily captured the city itself, but the fortress tower in the center of the city was a different matter. Abim-elech attempted to burn the entrance of the tower. A certain woman, however, threw an upper millstone on Abimelech's head mortally wounding him. He quickly called for his armorbearer to thrust him through lest it be said that he had been slain by a woman. The armor-bearer obliged his master. Thus ended the brief and turbulent career of Israel's first "king." When Abimelech's supporters saw that he was dead, each departed for his home (9:50-55).

E. A Prophetic Explanation (Judg 9:56-57).

The long account of Abimelech ends with a solemn appraisal of what has just been narrated. In the conflict between Abimelech and Shechem God was at work. Abimelech was being punished for the

murder of his brothers. The Shechemites were being punished for *"all
their wickedness"* which included blatant idolatry, violence, and support for the ruthless Abimelech. The curse of Jotham, the youngest
son of Gideon, came upon the lot of these gangsters (9:56-57).

TRAGEDY MITIGATED
Judges 10:1-5

Two minor Judges followed Abimelech. They are only minor in the
sense that the sacred historian has not seen fit to supply any more
than the barest of information about them. Here there is no catas-
trophic oppression, no desperate cry, no divine call of a deliverer. At
the same time, no "rest" is mentioned. These were not days of decisive battles but of constant turmoil. The brief notes about Tola and
Jair suggest that the glory days of Ehud, Deborah and Gideon were
part of Israel's past.

A. Judgeship of Tola (Judg 10:1-2).
Not much is known about Tola. His lineage (*"son of Puah, the
son of Dodo"*) is cited, perhaps indicating that he came from an outstanding family. He was of the tribe of Issachar, yet he lived in Shamir
in the hill country of Ephraim. This suggests that his leadership was
accepted by this fractious tribe. That he judged Israel for twenty years
(c. 1171-1148 BC) suggests that he provided a stable and helpful
leadership for the people. Though Abimelech comes between Gideon
and Tola, it is reasonable to assume that Tola must have been the
divinely ordained successor of Gideon.[3]
The most important thing said about Tola is that he *"arose to
save Israel"* after the death of Abimelech. The author seems to have
regarded Abimelech as equivalent to an oppressor. The influence of
this thug, and his cooperation with the idolaters at Shechem, created
an environment throughout the land from which Israel needed deliverance. Tola apparently did what he could to curtail the negative influence which Abimelech had exerted on the nation.

B. Judgeship of Jair (Judg 10:3-5).
The seventh Judge of Israel was a Gileadite, i.e., he hailed from

170

the region beyond the Jordan known as Gilead. Presumably that is where he also exercised his judgeship for twenty-two years (c. 1148-1126 BC). Jair had thirty sons which is good evidence that he had multiple wives. Gideon had apparently established a precedent. The sons rode on thirty donkeys which in that age was a mark of importance. Each son administered a city in Gilead. These towns were called Havvoth-jair ("Villages of Jair")[4] even to the day when the Book of Judges was written.

The polygamous marriages and the nepotism of Jair hint at a further degeneration in the concept of judgeship. When Jair died he was buried in Kamon (location unknown).

ISRAEL: TRAGIC APOSTASY
Judges 10:6-16

From what has been related about the town of Shechem, Abimelech and the Judges who followed him, one can conclude that the unfaithfulness of Israel had reached a new low. That conclusion is confirmed by the author himself who now paints the worst picture yet of the apostasy of the nation. The unit begins with words that have become by this time familiar to the reader of Judges: *"Then the sons of Israel again did evil in the sight of Yahweh."* The author then gives a rapid-fire presentation of the accusations against Israel. Not only were they worshiping the Baals and Ashtaroth of the native Canaanites, they were embracing the gods of other peoples as well. From north of Canaan they embraced the gods of Aram and Sidon. From east of Jordan they were attracted to the gods of Moab and Ammon. The gods of the Philistines to the west also attracted them. This plethora of gods caused Israel to *"forget Yahweh."* This does not mean that they forgot about him. They forgot him in the sense of failing to practice their faith, to walk by his law, to confess his exclusive claims to divinity. Failing to serve the Lord exclusively is forgetting him (10:6).

The degradation of Israel called forth for the first time a double-barreled oppression.[5] West of Jordan the Philistines were the oppressors while east of Jordan (mainly) the Ammonites were the enemy. Israel was *"crushed"* by these two enemies *"that year,"* probably c.

1126 BC. This suggests that the resistance of Israel crumbled in the same year the oppression started.

At some point during the eighteen years the Ammonites trampled Transjordan. They crossed the Jordan to harass the tribes of Judah, Benjamin and Ephraim. Caught as they were between two mighty enemies, it is no wonder that the author says that *"Israel was greatly distressed."*[6] The author proceeds to discuss first the Ammonite oppression (ch. 11) and then that of the Philistines (chs. 13-16).

Israel cried out unto Yahweh. This time the *"cry"* is accompanied by a confession of sin which appears here for the first time in the book. The confession admits to the twin sins of (1) having forsaken Yahweh (2) to serve the Baal gods (10:10).

In response to the cry and confession, Yahweh spoke to his people, most likely through a prophet (cf. 6:8-10). His words suggest that the Israelite confession of sin was not completely sincere. In order to make Israel realize the depth of their sin, Yahweh lists several of the times he had rescued them from their enemies, beginning as always with the deliverance from Egypt. Under Joshua he had kept his people from being crushed by massive Amorite armies. The current enemies—the Ammonites and Philistines—had been the oppressors of Israel once before, but Yahweh had delivered his people. The Lord mentioned the deliverances from the Sidonians, the Amalekites and the Maonites, none of which are specifically mentioned in the sketchy narrative of the Book of Judges (10:11-12).[7]

In each case of oppression the Israelites had cried unto Yahweh and he had effected their deliverance. In spite of these repeated acts of God's grace the Israelites continued to forsake Yahweh and serve other gods. No more would he deliver them. They should cry to the gods they had chosen to serve. Let those gods deliver Israel out of distress if they could (10:13-14).

Again the children of Israel confessed their sins. They placed themselves in the hands of God, resigned to face whatever fate he deemed appropriate. Yet they pled with him to deliver them from the oppressors. This prayer was accompanied by the removal of the foreign gods from among them. When they began to serve Yahweh, he could no longer endure their misery (10:15-16).

JEPHTHAH: A TRAGIC FIGURE
Judges 10:17-11:11

The Ammonites began to press their claims in Transjordan. They brought a host into Gilead and camped there. The Israelites gathered an army to Mizpah to block the Ammonite advance. Faced with a spirited resistance, the Ammonites delayed the attack. Meanwhile, the leaders of the Gileadites found themselves with no one qualified to lead the defense of the land. They were so desperate that they offered to make the general of the army the ruler of all Gilead. The deliverer in this crisis was not raised up by God. Rather he was selected by the leaders of Gilead (10:17-18).

The obvious choice for leadership of the army was Jephthah. He was a valiant warrior; but he had no social standing. He was the son of a harlot. His half-brothers had driven him out of the family so that he would have no part in the family inheritance. Jephthah had fled from his brothers to the land of Tob. There a gang of *"worthless fellows"* gathered about him. Jephthah was virtually an outlaw leader (11:1-3).

Faced with the Ammonite invasion, the elders of Gilead went to Tob to ask Jephthah to lead the army. These elders had sanctioned the expulsion of Jephthah from the land. He made them eat the proverbial humble pie when they came to him with this emergency request (11:4-7).

Jephthah let the elders squirm for a bit. He made them repeat the offer to make him ruler over Gilead if he should defeat the Ammonites. The leadership offer was confirmed by the elders with a solemn oath. Thus reassured, Jephthah returned with the elders. He was made leader of the Gileadites in a solemn ceremony ("before Yahweh") there at Mizpah (11:8-11).

KING OF AMMON: TRAGIC STUBBORNNESS
Judges 11:12-28

Jephthah was a peace loving man. He first attempted to settle the dispute with the king of Ammon through negotiation. His messengers inquired of the Ammonite what quarrel he had with Israel that he had brought an army into Israelite territory. The king in his response accused the Israelites of having taken his land when they came out of Egypt. He was therefore expecting all the territory between the Arnon and Jabbok rivers to be returned to him (11:12-13).

Jephthah then sent a second group of messengers to the king of Ammon. Through them he presened a marvelous defense of the Israelite claim to the territory in Transjordan. First, he offered an argument based on history. When the Israelites emerged from the wilderness back in the days of Moses they did not seek military confrontation with any kings of the area. They circumvented Edom and Moab when they were refused permission to pass through those territories. The Amorites were then controlling the Transjordan territory. Israel requested permission from their king Sihon to pass through that territory. Sihon, however, gathered his armies and fought against Israel. Yahweh gave Sihon and all his people into the hand of Israel. That was how Israel came to possess the land of the Amorites which now the king of Ammon was claiming (11:14-22).

Jephthah next raised a theological argument. Yahweh the God of Israel had driven the Amorites from the land before his people. He had in effect deeded the land to Israel. What right then did the king of Ammon have to claim that territory? The land ruled by the king of Ammon is what Chemosh[8] had given his people (11:23-24).

Jephthah's third argument was based on precedent. Balak the king of Moab never disputed Israel's claim to the Transjordan lands back in the days of Moses (Num 22:6). He never tried to drive them from that land.[9] Nor had any king of Ammon ever disputed the claim to this territory in the three hundred years Israel had lived there (11:25-26).

On the basis of these arguments Jephthah concluded that Israel had not *"sinned"* against Ammon, but rather vice versa. Yahweh, the ultimate Judge, would determine which people had just claim to the land. Jephthah correctly anticipated that the king of Ammon would reject any overtures towards a peaceful settlement of the dispute. The stage was thus set for a military showdown (11:27-28).

JEPHTHAH: A TRAGIC VOW
Judges 11:29-40

What amazing grace that God would use this man Jephthah to

deliver his people. He was the son of a harlot, rejected by his own family, and the leader of an outlaw band. The account of Jephthah revolves around a vow which he took on the eve of battle.

A. Circumstances of the Vow (Judg 11:29-33).

Though God did not raise up this Judge as he had done in previous deliverances, he did equip him for leadership. This was tantamount to having endorsed the selection of Jephthah by the Gileadites. Under the influence of God's Spirit Jephthah first marched through Gilead and Manasseh (the land north of the Jabbok river). Presumably he was organizing his forces. With his reinforcements he then returned to the camp at Mizpah. Jephthah then seized the initiative and went out to face the Ammonites (11:29).

Before leading his troops into battle Jephthah made a vow to Yahweh, a vow he lived to regret. He pledged that if the Lord would give him a victory over the Ammonites, he would give to Yahweh *"whatever comes out of the doors of my house to meet me when I return."* His exact words were *"it shall be Yahweh's, and I will offer it up as a burnt offering"* (11:30-31).

Only a modicum of information is presented about the battle with the Ammonites. Jephthah initiated the hostilities *"and Yahweh gave them into his hand."* He struck them with a very great slaughter all the way back to Ammon. A lengthy pursuit followed the battle. Twenty cities which had been occupied by Ammonites were retaken. The Ammonites were forced to retreat within their own borders (11:32-33).

B. Compliance with the Vow (Judg 11:34-40).

When Jephthah returned to his home at Mizpah his daughter came out to meet him with tambourines and with dancing in celebration of the victory. She was his only child, the apple of her daddy's eye. He obviously did not expect that she would be the first to come out to meet him. He screamed his agony, and tore his clothes while he explained his vow to her. Jephthah had a lot of faults, but lack of integrity was not one of them *"I have given my word to Yahweh, and I cannot take it back"* (11:34-35).

Jephthah's daughter heroically accepted her fate. She recognized that her father could not renege on a vow made in the name of Yahweh. She did request, however, that she be given two months to go to the mountains to mourn her virginity with her companions. Marriage and motherhood, the essence of life for an Israelite girl, would never be hers to experience. Her father was perfectly willing to comply with this last request of his daughter before she became the Lord's (11:36-38).

At the end of two months Jephthah's daughter returned to her father. He *"did with her according to the vow which he had made."* She was given to Yahweh. Then the note is added: *"And she had no relations with a man."* Obviously the writer wished to underscore that this young lady was given to the Lord in a state of virginity. Four days each year the daughters of Israel went (to the tabernacle?) to commemorate[10] the daughter of Jephthah. They recalled the willing sacrifice which she made in order that her father might fulfill his vow (11:39-40).

Jephthah certainly gave his daughter to the Lord. Did he also offer her up as a burnt offering? Scholars are divided. The text does not actually say that she was slain and then immolated. For this reason some scholars have proposed that Jephthah gave up his daughter to a celibate life of service at the tabernacle.[11] At least two passages speak of females who had ministry responsibilities at the tabernacle (Exod 38:8; 1 Sam 2:22).

Human sacrifice was illegal under the law of Moses. A person vowed to God could be redeemed by the payment of a stipulated amount (Lev 27); but obviously in this case no redemption money was paid. The question of human sacrifice here is mute. Good arguments can be made for and against that interpretation of the text. This much is certain: If Jephthah actually sacrificed his daughter he sinned in a grievous manner. No vow should be kept if the keeping of that vow involves a greater sin than the breaking of that vow.

EPHRAIM: A TRAGIC PRIDE
Judges 12:1-7

At some point the Ephraimites had been summoned to send troops to aid in the war against Ammon. They arrived just after the battle and rebuked Jephthah for having gone into battle without them. In their blustering the Ephraimites threatened to burn down Jephthah's house in retaliation for bruising their egos (12:1).

Jephthah explained that he had summoned the Ephraimites before the battle. He waited as long as he dared, but the Ephraimite contingent never showed up. He therefore was forced to undertake the battle with only the forces he had mustered in Transjordan. Yahweh graciously had given the Gileadites the victory over Ammon. There was no reason for the Ephraimites to be showing hostility toward Jephthah (12:2-3).

The Ephraimites accused the Gileadites of being "renegades of Ephraim" (NIV). Perhaps the suggestion is that Gilead, which is situated between the big tribes of Manasseh and Ephraim, was so insignificant that it had no right to go to war on its own. At the least this was an ethnic slur; but it may also have hinted of Ephraimite desires to annex the territory of Gilead. In any case, the Gileadites were threatened by these words. They were willing to go to war against the Ephraimites (12:4).

Jephthah regathered his troops and fought Ephraim. The Gileadites captured the fords of the Jordan opposite Ephraim. Any individual attempting to cross the Jordan at that point was challenged to pronounce the word "Shibboleth." Apparently the Ephraimites could not pronounce the "sh" sound. Chronologically this was the second civil war during the period of the Judges, the third if one counts the Abimelech strife with Shechem. Some 42,000 Ephraimites fell in this civil war (12:5-6).

Jephthah's judgeship was comparatively short. It lasted only six years. When he died he was buried in "one of the cities of Gilead." The great victory which he won over the Ammonites was overshadowed by the tragic vow which he made, the tragic stubbornness of the Ammonite king and the tragic civil war which erupted because of the pride of Ephraim (12:7).

TRAGEDY MITIGATED
Judges 12:8-15

Three minor Judges followed Jephthah. Not much is known about these men. Certain clues, however, do exist that they represent a further deterioration of the office of Judge. Things may have appeared to be normal on the surface. After Gideon, however, there is no reference to the God-given rest which is mentioned in connection with the earlier Judges. If the chronology adopted for this study is correct, Ibzan, Elon and Abdon were all Judges in their respective tribal areas while the Philistines were oppressing Israel in the south.

A. Judgeship of Ibzan (Judg 12:8-10).

Ibzan was from Bethlehem, but probably not the famous village of that name in Judah. More likely he was from the Bethlehem in Zebulun (cf. Josh 19:15). Ibzan had thirty sons and thirty daughters. Thus he must have been married to several wives. He gave his daughters in marriage to those "outside," and took thirty wives for his sons from those "outside." The reference is probably to intermarriage with non-Israelites. Ibzan may have had an ecumenical spirit, but he was violating one of the most fundamental of God's laws of separation (12:8-9).

Daughters are mentioned in connection with only Jephthah and Ibzan. Jephthah had but one, and was forced by his foolish vow to surrender her while she was still a virgin. Ibzan had thirty daughters, all married, and thirty married sons as well. The fullness of Ibzan serves to underscore the barrenness of his predecessor in consequence of his vow.[12]

Ibzan's judgeship was probably limited to Zebulun and tribal areas bordering on Zebulun. After serving seven years Ibzan died. He was buried at in his hometown. His judgeship can be dated to about 1105-1098 BC (12:10).

B. Judgeship of Elon (Judg 12:11-12).

Elon from the tribe of Zebulun judged Israel for ten years. That is all that is said about him. Like a lot of church leaders, Elon merely held a title. He did not accomplish anything worth noting during his years of leadership. He was buried at Aijalon (location unknown) in the land of Zebulun. His judgeship can be dated to about 1097-1087 BC. That judgeship was not hereditary is made clear here. Nothing is said about how the office passed to Elon.

C. Judgeship of Abdon (Judg 12:13-15).

Abdon is called the Pirathonite, i.e., he was from the town of Pirathon in the hill country of Ephraim.[13] During his judgeship no doubt Ephraim regained some of the tribal prestige which had been lost in the humiliating defeat by the Gileadites (12:6). Like Gideon, Ibzan and Jair, Abdon was a polygamist. He had forty sons and thirty grandsons who rode about on seventy donkeys. That would be a symbol of affluence and authority. One senses here a bit of pomp, arrogance and nepotism.

Abdon was buried at Pirathon in the land of Ephraim, *"in the hill country of the Amalekites."* This note suggests that an enclave of the Amalekites had become entrenched in territory belonging to Ephraim. Apparently Abdon had not been very successful in reclaiming this territory for Israel.[14] Perhaps he never even tried. The judgeship of Abdon can be dated to about 1089-1081 BC.

ENDNOTES

1. The only other example of a fable used in the Bible is found in 2 Kgs 14:9.

2. C.J. Goslinga, *Joshua, Judges, Ruth* in "Bible Student's Commentary" (Grand Rapids: Zondervan, 1986), p. 361.

3. *Ibid.*, p. 375.

4. The name Havvoth-jair had already been given to these towns in Gilead by an earlier Jair from the tribe of Manasseh (Num 32:41; Deut 3:12-14). Perhaps that name was renewed in honor of the judgeship of this Jair.

5. In 3:13 the sons of Ammon and Amalek were allies of Eglon of Moab and in 6:3 the Amalekites could come up against Israel with the Midianites; but only here in 10:7 is the Lord said to have sold Israel into the hands of two separate peoples simultaneously.

6. The language *"greatly distressed"* is used only here in the book. This indicates that the author intended the reader to see in each successive oppression something worse than had been experienced previously. Thus the worst oppression of Israel was at the time that the Ammonites crossed the Jordan and pressed the Israelites from the east while at the same time the Philistines were pressing from the west.

7. The reference could be to the times when the Amalekites had joined forces with Moab (3:13) and later Midian (6:3) in attacking Israel. More likely some more recent incursion of the Amalekites is intended. No references are to be found to oppressions by the Sidonians or the Maonites. Perhaps these

179

were deliverances effected through the instrumentality of the so-called minor judges Tola and Jair.

8. Chemosh was actually the god of Moab and Molech was the god of Ammon. Jephthah is subtly suggesting that the Ammonites were legitimately occupying the territory formerly occupied by Moab.

9. Balak was nervous about having such a large population on his border. He did attempt to have Israel cursed by Balaam (cf. Num 22).

10. The same verb appears in 5:11. It could be translated "celebrate in song, recite." Thus Jephthah's daughter was honored for her courageous act of self-surrender by which she allowed her father to fulfill his vow.

11. Barry G. Webb, *The Book of the Judges: An Integrated Reading,* JASOT Supplement Series 46 (Sheffield: JSOT, 1987), p. 161.

12. The view that Jephthah's daughter was offered in some kind of celibate service originated with the Jewish rabbi David Kimchi (c. AD 1232). The majority of ancient sources discussing the problem accept the view that Jephthah offered his daughter as a burnt offering.

13. Another great Pirathonite of the Bible was Benaiah, one of David's mighty men (2 Sam 23:30).

14. Another possibility is that an Amalekite settlement had existed in this area prior to the Israelite invasion.

CHAPTER ELEVEN

The Beginning of Deliverance
Judges 13-16

The double oppression by Ammonites and Philistines began about 1126 BC. After eighteen years of misery Jephthah had been able to deliver the Transjordan area from the Ammonites (c. 1108 BC). West of Jordan, however, the oppression continued. All together the Philistines dominated the Israelites for forty years, until about 1085 BC. Thus the last oppression in the Book of Judges is twice as long as the next longest. From this oppression Judges records no deliverance, only a bit of periodic relief through the instrumentality of Samson.

Samson judged Israel for twenty years *during* the Philistine oppression. He was not a military leader like Gideon or Jephthah. He used his own strength to inflict devastating blows upon the oppressors. Samson, however, was never able to free the land from the power of the Philistines. That remained for Samuel, the man of prayer, to accomplish.

Chart No. 17

THE LATER JUDGES
1126-1043 BC

Though Samson was extraordinary in many ways, he does not appear to have been a zealous servant of the Lord. Nor does the text supply evidence of any close bond between Samson and his countrymen. On the contrary, Samson was very friendly with the Philistines. He seemed particularly attracted to Philistine women. He was a man of impulse who was controlled by sensual desires. Revenge dominated his thinking, even in his prayers.[1]

GLORIOUS IN HIS BIRTH
Judges 13:1-25

Whereas other Judges were raised up in times of crisis to deliver God's people, Samson was dedicated to his task before his birth. Of the twenty-three references to the Angel of Yahweh in this book, thirteen are found in the account of Samson's birth. Samson is the only deliverer in the Book of Judges about whose birth anything is related. The birth announcement demonstrated (1) the painstaking steps that Yahweh took to provide his people with a Judge; and (2) that deliverance would only come through a special work of God. God's people were so powerless in themselves, they could only receive that deliverance as a gracious gift from Yahweh.

A. First Appearance of the Angel (Judg 13:2-7).
Something is missing in the account of Samson. The narrator begins by announcing another apostasy on the part of Israel and the judgment which followed it. He then tells the story of the birth of the man who would be Israel's deliverer. He does not, however, mention any cry to Yahweh, either out of repentance or sheer misery. Sin is

like that. Sin crushes and beats down until a people have no will to change their circumstances however miserable. Yet here the glorious truth stands out that God begins his great work of deliverance even though his people do not have the good sense to cry out to him. Thank God that he does not give help to his people only when they pray![2]

About a century had elapsed since the Angel of Yahweh appeared to Gideon at a winepress near Ophrah. About 1125 BC the Angel appeared again to the wife of a Danite named Manoah. This woman was barren—a shameful condition in those days. What is more, she is nameless in the text. Nonetheless, Manoah's wife is portrayed as a woman of great faith and calm assurance. She is another of the great feminine faces to appear in the book. This woman underscores the blessed truth that God delights in working through anonymity and powerlessness to accomplish his purpose.

The stranger began by revealing his knowledge of the circumstances in the life of this godly wife. She was barren. That, however, was about to change. She would conceive and give birth to a son. In preparation for the birth of this son the woman was to be careful not to drink any strong drink or eat any unclean thing. The son was to be a Nazirite to God from the womb.[3] God would use this consecrated man to *begin* to deliver Israel from the hands of the Philistines (13:2-5).

The woman reported the incident to her husband. She described her visitor as *"a man of God."* This was terminology commonly applied to prophets. Nonetheless, she gave a description of the visitor which made clear to her husband that this man was no ordinary prophet. His appearance was *"like the angel of God, very awesome"* (NASB). Intimidated as she was by this appearance, she had not asked the stranger where he was from. Nor had the stranger volunteered to tell her his name. Then she repeated the instructions and the prophecy which the Angel of Yahweh had given her (13:6-7).

B. Second Appearance of the Angel (Judg 13:8-23).

Manoah believed his wife, but he felt he needed more information regarding the birth of the son. So he prayed that the man of God might come again to teach Manoah and his wife what needed to be done in regard to the boy. God heard that prayer. Again the Angel appeared to the woman. She ran quickly to inform her husband (13:8-10).

After verifying that this man indeed had visited his wife earlier, Manoah asked the question that was uppermost in his mind. When the prophecy was fulfilled (note that Manoah had no doubt) what would be the rule for the boy's life and work? The Angel responded that the woman should obey all his previous instructions. Those instructions were then repeated in the presence of Manoah. Though God answers the prayers of believers, he also places limits upon their actions. If one is to be used to accomplish anything for God he must follow directions (13:11-14).

Manoah still thought at this point that he was dealing with a prophet of God. Wanting to be hospitable, he offered to prepare a meal for his guest. The Angel said that he would not eat of a meal, but he would wait if Manoah cared to offer a burnt offering to Yahweh. Manoah recognized the clue here. His guest was much more than a prophet. Since he was not a human being, he wanted an offering rather than a meal (13:15-16).

Manoah then inquired as to the name of the Angel. The Angel refused to answer except to say that his name was "wonderful," i.e., beyond comprehension. For this reason Manoah was not to inquire about the name of the guest. While a person may know God, he cannot know God perfectly. Man must learn to be content with those things which God has revealed about himself. The person of God is mysterious beyond human understanding. Those who deal with the things of God on a regular basis must never lose their sense of awe (13:17-18).

Manoah prepared the offering and laid it on the rock which served as an altar. Then Yahweh performed wonders while Manoah and his wife looked on. As the flame began to ascend from the sacrifice, the Angel of Yahweh ascended in the flame and disappeared. The two witnesses fell on their faces to the ground in reverence. Manoah was convinced then of what he probably suspected earlier, viz., that he had been conversing with the Angel of Yahweh. Manoah panicked in the stress of the moment. He believed that he and his wife would die because they had seen God. Mrs. Manoah is portrayed as much more calm, logical and confident. If God had intended to slay them he would not have (1) accepted the sacrifice, (2) performed wonders, nor (3) revealed good tidings. Here again, as frequently in Judges, the godly wisdom of a woman outshines that of the men surrounding her (13:19-23).

C. Birth and Growth of the Child (Judg 13:24-25).

As predicted, the woman gave girth to a son. She named him Samson which means "sunshine" or perhaps "sunny" for short. His birth meant the dawn of a new day in the house of Manoah and for Israel. The childhood of Samson is passed over in silence. The text simply says that *"the child grew up and Yahweh blessed him."* As he came into his adult years *"the Spirit of Yahweh"* began to *"stir"* him in *"Mahaneh-dan"* (lit., camp of Dan), a nearby place in Judah. This was the first of many times when Samson received overpowering impulses from the Spirit of God which drove him on and enabled him to perform amazing feats of strength.

WEAK IN HIS JUDGMENT
Judges 14:1-20

The key word in Judges 14 is the verb *yarad* ("to go down"). The chapter focuses on several trips—the exact number is unclear—which Samson made into Philistine territory. Each of these journeys centers around a secret stated or implied in the text.[4]

A. The Attraction Trip (Judg 14:1-4).

First, Samson *"went down"* to nearby Timnah. The reason for his trip is not stated. There Samson saw a Philistine woman who attracted him. He returned to his home and requested that his parents arrange a marriage with this woman. Samson's parents tried to dissuade him. Could he not find a suitable mate among the Israelite women? Physical attraction, however, prevailed over wisdom and parental objection. *"Get her for me,"* Samson said, *"for she looks good to me!"* The lust of the flesh is a foundation of sand upon which to build the temple of marriage (14:1-3).

The first secret in Judges 14 belonged to God. Neither Samson himself nor his parents realized that God's providence was at work. God was seeking an occasion to inflict upon the Philistines blows of judgment. Israel as a whole was too crushed to fight for liberty. Through the personal grievance of Samson God would bring devastation and death upon the oppressors. The marriage to the Philistine woman was the first step in stirring up Samson to anger against the enemies of God's people. While the readers of Judges 14 know God's secret, the main characters in the chapter do not (14:4).

B. The Arrangement Trip (Judg 14:5-7).

The second trip down to Timnah was for the purpose of making marriage arrangements. Samson's parents accompanied him, for they would be involved in the marriage negotiations customary in that time. On this trip Samson turned aside into some vineyards. There he was attacked by a young lion. For the first time *"the Spirit of Yahweh"* came mightily upon him. He tore the lion with his bare hands as one might tear a kid. Now Samson had a secret. He did not tell his parents what he had done perhaps because touching something dead would be a violation of his Nazirite vow. Here for the first time Samson had occasion to test his own strength (14:5-6).

The marriage negotiations and "courtship," such as it was, went well. After talking with the woman, Samson still found himself attracted to this Philistine (14:7).

C. The Celebration Trip (Judg 14:8-18).

When Samson returned to take his bride, he turned aside to see the carcass of the lion he had slain on the earlier trip. There he found a swarm of bees and honey. He scooped up the honey in his hands and ate it as he walked along. When he caught up to his parents he gave them some as well, but he did not tell them where he had secured the honey. Again Samson had a secret, and his parents were in the dark (14:8-9).

Following the custom of the time, Samson gave a marriage feast. Apparently his father helped in the arrangements. The family of his bride brought together thirty companions to be a part of the weeklong celebration, a *mishteh* or drinking feast. In eating honey from the carcass of the lion Samson had violated the Nazirite rule about touching something that was dead. Now he appears to have violated the rule against drinking the fruit of the vine. In sports metaphor, this was strike two against Samson.[5]

To impress the snobbish friends of his bride, Samson proposed a challenge to his Philistine guests. He would propound a riddle. If the guests could solve the riddle during the seven days of the feast Samson promised to give to them thirty changes of garments including underwear. If, however, they were unable to solve the riddle then each of them would provide for him a similar change of garments. The Philistines agreed to the challenge not believing that any Israelite hillbilly could outwit the sophisticated men from the plains. So Samson put forth a two line rhyming riddle: *"Out of the eater, something to eat; out of the strong, something sweet"* (14:10-14).

By the third day the Philistines still had not solved the riddle. On the fourth day they approached Samson's bride. If she did not coax the answer from him before the seventh day, they threatened to burn her and her father's house. They did not intend to be financially disadvantaged because they had agreed to attend a wedding feast honoring her husband (14:15).

Samson's wife turned on the tears at this point. She accused Samson of hating her, of not trusting her with his secret. Samson responded that he had not told his parents the riddle, so why would he tell her, a woman he hardly knew even though she was his wife. The woman, however, continued to plead for Samson to tell her the riddle. On the seventh day the pressure became so intense that Samson gave in. She went immediately and told the wedding guests (14:16-17).

Before sunset on the seventh day the Philistines explained the riddle. What is sweeter than honey? What is stronger than a lion? Samson knew immediately that they had secured this answer from his wife. He spoke another poetic couplet as he stormed out of the place: *"If you had not plowed with my heifer, you would not have found out my riddle"* (14:18).

D. The Vengeance Trip (Judg 14:19-20).

For the second time the Spirit of Yahweh came mightily upon Samson. Empowered by God's Spirit, Samson began to fulfill his destiny. Samson went down to Ashkelon and killed thirty Philistines. He took the garments from these men back to Timnah and threw them down in front of those who had solved his riddle. This was the beginning of deliverance from the Philistine oppression. Yahweh's secret (v. 4) was starting to be revealed. The Lord does not always sanitize his deliverances. They are often messy. Bloodshed is often the only means of breaking the yoke of tyrants.

With his anger still burning over the Philistine conniving, Samson *went up* to this father's house. Even as he was at home trying to regain his composure, actions were being taken in Timnah which would trigger round two in the pummeling of the Philistines. While he was away, Samson's wife was given in marriage to *"his friend,"* i.e., his best man, who also was a Philistine (14:19-20).

MIGHTY IN HIS VENGEANCE
Judges 15:1-20

Judges 15 contains three examples of the kind of blows which Samson was able to inflict against the Philistines during his twenty year career. Each Philistine provocation was met with swift and devastating vengeance. The chapter concludes with Samson at the point of death, crying out to God for deliverance.

A. First Provocation and Response (Judg 15:1-6a).

After a time Samson's anger cooled. During wheat harvest, a time of great celebration, he visited his wife in Timnah with a young goat. He was thereby proposing a reconciliation feast. The woman was still living in her father's house even though she had been given in marriage to a Philistine. Her father prevented Samson from entering his wife's room. He explained that he thought Samson had deserted his wife for good, and that he therefore had given the woman to Samson's best man. The desperate father tried to assuage the anger of Samson by offering to him his younger daughter. The father considered her even more beautiful than her older sister. Apparently Samson did not agree. As he again left that house in anger Samson shouted for all to hear that he now had a right to get even with the Philistines for what they had done to him (15:1-3).

Samson then rounded up three hundred foxes (or jackals). By twos he tied the tails of the foxes to a burning torch. The terrified animals drug the torches hither and yon through the grainfields and vineyards of Philistia. A good portion of the crop was totally destroyed (15:4-6a).

B. Second Provocation and Response (Judg 15:6b-8).

The Philistines soon ascertained the name of the culprit who burned their fields and the reason he had created this devastation. Unable immediately to get their hands on Samson, a group of angry Philistines went to Timnah and torched Samson's wife and her father (15:6b).

The death of his wife at Philistine hands caused Samson to launch another vendetta against the enemies of God's people. Details of the confrontation have been omitted. The text simply states that Samson struck them ruthlessly with a great slaughter. Then he went down to live in a cave at the rock of Etam. Perhaps he was still grieving over the death of his wife. Perhaps he had grown weary of the slaughter (15:7-8).

C. Third Provocation and Response (Judg 15:9-17).

At this point the Philistines launched a mass attack against Israel with the prime objective being the capture and death of Samson. The men of Judah wished no hostilities with the Philistines. They were perplexed by this incursion. When they learned that the objective of the invasion was the binding of Samson, the men of Judah, cowards that they were, agreed to hand him over to them (15:9-10).

Three thousand men of Judah went down to the cave where Samson was holed up. With two biting questions they challenged his wisdom and love for his countrymen. Was Samson so stupid that he did not know that the Philistines were rulers over Israel? Why would he provoke these enemies and thus trigger an invasion by them? Samson responded that he was living by the iron rule: As they have done to me, so I have done to them. Samson does not seem to have grasped the significance of his role as Israel's deliverer. He was motivated strictly by personal revenge. Samson made no effort to mobilize the Israelites for a decisive battle against the Philistines. That was not his style. Perhaps he knew that, given the attitude of his people, military resistance would be impossible to organize (15:11).

Samson agreed to surrender peacefully to his countrymen if they would swear not to kill him. The Judahites agreed only to bind him and hand him over to the Philistines. They must have known that a fate worse than death awaited Samson should the Philistines get their hands on him. Nonetheless, they bound him with two new ropes and brought him up from the rock at Etam (15:12-13).

The Philistines shouted triumphantly as they saw Samson being led into their camp at Lehi. Then, however, for the third time the Spirit of Yahweh came mightily upon Samson. He snapped the ropes that bound him as if they were charred flax. He grabbed a new donkey's jawbone from the ground. Using that as his weapon he was able to slay a thousand Philistines. Some think this feat was accomplished with the help of the Judahites who were emboldened by his actions. In any case the remainder of the Philistine force fled in panic back to their own territory. Samson celebrated his victory with a poetic verse. He then named the spot Ramath-lehi, i.e., the high place of the jawbone (15:14-17).

D. A Personal Crisis (Judg 15:18-20).

The heat of battle, which must have lasted the better part of the day, had taken a physical toll on Samson. He was very thirsty, yet there was no source of water immediately available. For the first time the narrator mentions that Samson sought the Lord. His prayer recognized the fact that God had given the victory over the Philistines through him. Yet now he was in danger of dying from thirst. If that should happen his body would fall into the hands of the uncircumcised Philistines for mutilation (15:18).

The Lord heard that prayer. God *"split the hollow place"* that was in Lehi so that water came forth. The fresh water revived Samson. He named the spot where God provided the water *"En-hakkore"* ("spring of the caller"). That spring was still producing water in the days that the Book of Judges was written.

PITIFUL IN HIS DOWNFALL
Judges 16:1-31

Judges 16 sketches the pitiful details of the downfall of Samson. Chapters 14-15 contain three references to the overpowering of

Samson by the Spirit of God. No such reference appears in chapter 16. The author seems to be placing in juxtaposition two contrasting portraits of Samson, the first with the Spirit (chs. 14-15), and the second without the Spirit. Here Samson is self-sufficient and out of control. The chapter begins with Samson's head on a harlot's pillow; it concludes with his hands on a god's pillars. The tragedy unfolds in four stages. Samson was (1) cornered at Gaza, (2) entrapped in Sorek, (3) bound in a prison, and (4) mocked in a temple.

A. Cornered at Gaza (Judg 16:1-3).

For some unexplained reason Samson journeyed to the Philistine city of Gaza. There he met a harlot and went into her. When the men of Gaza heard that Samson had come to their city they surrounded the harlot's house. They intended at first light of day to slay their Israelite nemesis (16:1-2).

Somehow Samson learned that his enemies were prepared to ambush him in the morning. At midnight he slipped out of the house and passed the sentries. He went down to the city gates which had been bolted shut for the night. He ripped the doors of the gate off their hinges. Along with the posts and bars of the gate, Samson carried the doors on his shoulders to the top of a hill near Hebron. Thus in the heartland of Judah Samson left tangible evidence of his latest humiliating blow against the Philistines (16:3).

B. Entrapped at Sorek (Judg 16:4-20).

Samson could not resist Philistine women. Even after his fiasco at Timnah, and his near escape from the house of the harlot in Gaza, Samson became involved with yet another Philistine woman, the infamous Delilah.[6] Tradition says that she was the younger sister who had been spurned by Samson a few years earlier. Samson "loved" Delilah. He never suspected for a moment that she would bring about his downfall (16:4).

The Philistine lords took note of the attraction which Samson had for Delilah. Each promised to pay the vixen eleven hundred pieces of silver if she could discover the secret of Samson's strength. Their intention was to overpower Samson, and then afflict him (16:5). Revenge is a motive devoid of scruples. These Philistines would stop at nothing.

To his credit Samson resisted the feminine wiles of Delilah for a time. He lied to her three times about the secret of his strength. Had he been as tough mentally as he was physically Samson would have refused to discuss the matter with her. He seemed to sense that she could not be trusted, but he could not resist her charms. He first told Delilah that if he should be bound with seven fresh cords he would be as weak as other men. Next Samson told Delilah that if he were bound with new ropes he would lose his supernatural strength. In both cases when the woman aroused Samson with the shout that the Philistines were upon him, he snapped the the restraints as if they were mere thread (16:6-12).

Even when it became obvious that Delilah was laying a trap for him, Samson still was unable to resist her seduction. He walked into her temptations with open eyes. Delilah increased the pressure, and Samson told a third lie. If one were to weave the seven locks of his hair into the web of the loom and fasten it with a pin he would become weak like other men. Delilah's cry brought Samson to his feet. He pulled out the pin which tied his hair to the loom. Still the secret of his strength was intact (16:13-14).

Delilah continued to press Samson on a daily basis to reveal to her the secret of his strength. The man's soul *"was annoyed to death"* (NASB). Finally he told her that he had been Nazirite to God from birth. The secret of his strength was in his unshorn hair which was the outward symbol of that Nazirite vow. Delilah could sense that her man had now revealed the truth. She summoned the Philistine lords and received her wages of betrayal. Then she put Samson to sleep on her lap. A servant came in and cut the seven locks of his hair. When she aroused him, Samson again jumped to his feet. He thought that he would *"shake himself free"* from any attackers as on previous occasions. *"But he did not know that Yahweh had departed from him"* (16:15-20).

C. Bound in a Prison (Judg 16:21-22).

The Philistines seized Samson with little resistance. They gouged out his eyes to render him permanently harmless. He was then taken to Gaza, bound with bronze chains. There he was made to serve as a grain grinder, a job normally performed by oxen. It involved pushing a

large round grinding stone in a circle over stalks of grain. How humiliating! Even as he performed this exhausting labor, however, his hair
was beginning to grow back. This the Philistines failed to notice. Of
course there was nothing magical about Samson's hair. His strength
came from the Spirit of God. Yet the hair was the symbol of his
strength. The sincere repentance which grew in the sightless darkness
of the mill chamber positioned Samson for one last heroic act in the
drama of redemption (16:21-22).

D. Mocked in a Temple (Judg 16:23-30).
The lords of the Philistines assembled to offer a great sacrifice to
Dagon[7] their god. Little did they realize that they were setting the
stage for the greatest feat of Samson. The assembly was filled with
joy. When they saw Samson the people praised Dagon for delivering
Samson into their hands. When they were in *"high spirits"* the crowd
demanded that Samson be brought forth into the temple to amuse
them. For a time they entertained themselves by playing a cruel game
of blind man's bluff with the helpless Israelite (16:23-25).

Three thousand jeering Philistine men and women joined their
leaders in heaping their abuse upon the once formidable enemy. They
were sitting on a balcony overlooking a courtyard where Samson was
being tormented. When Samson sensed that he was standing near the
main pillars of the structure, a plan formed within his mind. He asked
the lad who was leading him by the hand to let him lean against the
great pillars upon which the house rested (16:26-27).

In his desperation Samson cried out to the Lord. He asked for one
last infusion of divine strength that he might be avenged of the
Philistines for the loss of his two eyes. He then braced himself
between the two main pillars, with his right hand on the one and the
left hand on the other. After praying that he might die with the
Philistines, Samson pushed with all his might against the pillars. The
author seems to delight in the irony that he who was brought into that
building as an entertainer literally brought the house down upon the
revelers. In this final act of defiance, Samson slew more of the
Philistines than he had slain during his lifetime. At the same time, this
final blow wiped out the entire leadership of the Philistine people
(16:28-30).

At the conclusion of chs. 14-15 Samson was at the point of death after the slaughter of the thousand. He cried out to Yahweh, and the Lord intervened with a miraculous supply of water. The climax of chapter 16 is likewise the prayer of Samson. He asked God for vindication and for death. Both requests were granted. Surely the author is stressing the principle that man's extremity is God's opportunity. Prayer is the key that brings to bear on desperate circumstances the powerful resources of heaven. One cannot escape the conclusion that if the Lord hears the prayers of a backslidden philanderer like Samson, he will surely hear the fervent prayer of a righteous man.

E. Epilogue (Judg 16:31).

Samson's family came down to Gaza to retrieve the lifeless body of Israel's great hero. They buried him in the tomb of his father Manoah. Samson had judged Israel for twenty years, roughly 1105-1085 BC.

In retrospect one might ask how God could choose to use an unfaithful and immoral man like Samson. Here is a man who violated his vows and abused his gifts. Samson's physical prowess was not matched by his moral strength. Who can explain the sovereign choices of the Almighty? The tools which God employed during the entire period of the Judges are certainly not those who might be selected as leaders of God's people today. In Samson's defense only this can be said. He would fight when no one else would. He knew who the enemy was, and he inflicted countless blows against them.

ENDNOTES

1. C.J. Goslinga, *Joshua, Judges, Ruth* in "Bible Student's Commentary" (Grand Rapids: Zondervan, 1986), p. 404.
2. Dale Ralph Davis, *Such a Great Salvation* (Grand Rapids: Baker, 1990), p. 160.
3. The ordinary Nazirite vow was voluntary and temporary. In the case of Samson, God ordered a permanent Nazirite separation from birth.
4. On the structure of Judges 14 see Davis, *ibid.*, pp. 169-70. Davis is correct in emphasizing "secrets" as the motif of this chapter. It is all about what people do not know.
5. The text does not actually say that Samson imbibed at the feast, but it would be hard to imagine that he did not.
6. The text does not explicitly identify Delilah as a Philistine. She may

have been an Israelite woman who sold out to the enemy.

7. The Philistines had another temple for Dagon in Ashdod (1 Sam 5:2). Outside the Bible, worship of Dagon is attested at Ebla, Mari, and Ugarit. In some Ugaritic texts he is referred to as the father of Baal.

CHAPTER TWELVE

The Moral Mess
Judges 17-21

Chapters 17-21 constitute an appendix to the Book of Judges. The materials here are not in chronological order. As a matter of fact, certain indications in the text suggest that these episodes happened within a few years of the death of Joshua, even before the invasion of the land by Cushan (3:8). These chapters have been included in the book in order to illustrate the apostasy, lawlessness, immorality, disunity and legalism which characterized most of the 324 years of the period of the Judges.

APOSTASY ILLUSTRATED
Judges 17:1-13

In chapter 17 the author of Judges illustrates what chronologically must have been the first blatant indulgence in idolatry during the period of the Judges (cf. Judg 2:11-23). The account revolves around an Ephraimite named Micah and his relationship to his mother, his shrine and a certain Levite.

A. Micah and His Mother (Judg 17:1-3).

Micah, which means "Who is like Yahweh," had stolen eleven hundred pieces of silver[1] from his mother. Without realizing that her son was the thief, the mother pronounced a curse on the one who stole her money. When the renegade son returned the silver his mother sought to reverse the curse with a blessing. She then dedicated the money to Yahweh *"for her son."* By this action she was probably attempting to remove the dangers which were associated with the initial curse.

The mother apparently thought she would be performing an act of devotion by providing *"a graven image and a molten image"*[2] to assist in the worship of Yahweh. This is the technical language of Deuteronomy 27:15 where a curse is pronounced against anyone who would make such an object. Thus again the author is pressing home his consecrated sarcasm. Micah's mother was attempting to negate a human curse by bringing her son under a divine curse! (17:1-3).

B. Micah and His Shrine (Judg 17:4-6).

Two hundred shekels of the silver were given to a silversmith who fashioned the desired images. These images were kept in the house of Micah in the hill country of Ephraim. That a man with the orthodox name Micah would be cited as the first after the entry into Canaan to represent the invisible God by means of cultic objects is an irony the author surely intends his readers to note (17:4).

Little by little Micah's illegal worship expanded. He built a shrine for his gods. He made an ephod, an upper garment worn by those in priestly service. He constructed *"household idols"* (teraphim) in addition to the images constructed with his mother's silver. To preside over his shrine Micah consecrated one of his sons as priest. The author of Judges explains that this idolatrous cancer was tolerated because *"there was no king in Israel; every man did what was right in his own eyes."* The right kind of king would have been loyal to the covenant. He would have squelched this incipient idolatry (17:4-6).

C. Micah and His Levite (Judg 17:7-13).

An itinerant Levite provided Micah the opportunity to add to the prestige of his idolatrous shrine. This young man from Bethlehem

Judah[3] was traveling through Ephraim when he happened to spend the night at Micah's house. When Micah learned that this Levite was attached to no particular sanctuary, he offered him employment. Micah agreed to pay the young man ten silver pieces per year, furnish him with a new suit of clothes, and provide his maintenance if the Levite would be *"a father,"* i.e., spiritual advisor, *"and a priest"* at his shrine (17:7-10).

The Levite sinned when he accepted the offer to be Micah's priest. He lived in Micah's house. As time went on this sacerdotal employee was treated more like a son. Micah was overjoyed with his good fortune at having secured a man from the priestly tribe to serve at his idolatrous shrine. He actually thought Yahweh would smile upon him and bring him prosperity now that a Levite officiated at all the worship activities in his house (17:11-13).

For Micah worship was private business. He wanted to do his own thing. He bought into the philosophy that as long as one is sincere strict compliance to God's word was not necessary. Though he did not totally abandon Yahweh, he borrowed worship forms from his pagan neighbors to "enrich" his own approach to God. Though modern man may not make a graven image, he still displays much of the same attitude about worship which guided Micah down a dead end street. Biblical worship is God-centered, not man-centered. To please God must be the ultimate obsession of the worshiper. God cannot be pleased when his specific commands about worship are either violated or ignored.

LAWLESSNESS ILLUSTRATED
Judges 18:1-31

The account of the illicit worship in the hill country of Ephraim is continued in chapter 18 but with a new element. The chapter illustrates the lawlessness which was prevalent in Israel during the decades prior to the monarchy. The action centers about certain families in the tribe of Dan.

A. A Spy Mission (Judg 18:1-10).
To this point in time—shortly after the death of Joshua—the Dan-

ites had not been able to control their original allotment. So the tribal elders dispatched five men to search for a location which might be suitable for a tribal inheritance (18:1-2).

1. *The spies at Micah's house (18:1-6)*. Apparently the spies turned aside at the house of Micah because they recognized, even at a distance, the voice of the Levite. They seem to have been most surprised to encounter him there in the hill country of Ephraim. When the Levite explained that he was now serving as a Micah's priest, the Danites requested that he inquire of God[4] as to the success of their mission. The Levite assured them that Yahweh approved of the way they were going (18:3-6).

2. *The spies at Laish (18:7-10)*. The five Danites proceeded on northward to the town of Laish (Leshem in Josh 19:47) north of the Sea of Galilee. This was a Phoenician city loosely associated with Sidon. Because of the considerable distance from Sidon, Laish was basically independent. It had no strong army to protect it (18:7).

The five spies reported back to their brethren what they had found. The tribe made the decision immediately to move against Laish. This spacious region of abundance would easily fall into the hands of these fierce fighters (18:8-10).

B. A Tribal Migration (Judg 18:11-26).

Six hundred armed Danites set out with their families toward Laish. En route they passed through the hill country of Ephraim (18:11-13).

1. *The Danite theft (18:14-20)*. As the Danites approached the house of Micah, the five spies told their brethren about the religious paraphernalia which was there. The armed men determined that they would take these objects with them to Laish, and they would invite the Levite to go with them as well (18:14).

Backed by the small army, the five spies entered into the shrine. They gathered up the images and ephod. They offered the Levite the position of *"father and priest"* to the Danites. Much better, they argued, to be the priest of a tribe than the priest of one man. The Levite was overjoyed with this "call" to a larger pulpit. He himself supervised the theft of the religious objects. Then he joined the group for the march to Laish (18:15-20).

The religious decline of the nation is clearly illustrated in this passage. Contrary to the design of the law of Moses, Israelites had developed a strong desire for local shrines. They apparently believed that the mere possession of sacred objects guaranteed success in their ventures. Character counted for nothing in religious figures if they could demonstrate some measure of genealogical legitimacy. In these new attitudes the influence of Canaanite paganism is in evidence.

2. *Micah's confrontation with the Danites (18:21-26)*. The Danites anticipated some violent response when Micah learned of the theft of his religious objects and the pirating of his personal clergyman. They arranged their column so that the little ones and valuables were in front. The six hundred armed men acted as a rear guard. As expected, Micah assembled the men of the community, and they overtook the Danites. Micah, however, accused them of having taken his *gods* and his priest. In these verses the author underscores the folly of idolatry. A god that can be carried off is a non-god. The author has made Micah, the first idolater of the settlement period, to testify to the ultimate stupidity of idolatry (18:21-24).

The Danites, unable to refute the accusation, responded belligerently. Micah had best keep his complaints to himself or he and the men with him would be attacked by *"hot-tempered"* (NIV) or *"fierce"* (NASB) men. The Danites apparently held to the philosophy that "might makes right." Micah realized that he and his ill-equipped force were no match for the Danites, and so he turned back to his own house. Thus Micah who had stolen from his mother was now repaid by a theft of that which he revered. The author wishes his readers to note that the sanctuary at Dan had its origin in a double theft (18:24-26).

C. A Capture (Judg 18:27-29).

Following the confrontation with Micah, the Danites and their new priest continued their migration to Laish. They struck the quiet town with the edge of the sword, and burned down the place. The remoteness of the town made rescue by the city of Sidon impossible. Why the city was put to the torch is not clear. Perhaps they were motivated by some superstitious fear that they might be harassed by the guardian spirit of the dwellings.[5] In any case, after totally destroying the place, the Danites rebuilt Laish and named the place Dan after their tribal ancestor (18:27-29). This town became the northernmost settlement of the children of Israel in the land of Canaan.

Did the Danites have the right to attack Laish? The city was within the boundaries of the Promised Land. Certainly Israelites would have had the right to conquer the place. Laish, however, was within the tribal limits of Naphtali. The Danites were acting in a cowardly way by failure to press the attack within their own allotment. The peaceful inhabitants of Laish were no military challenge to the Danites. Furthermore, the Danites did not follow the general principle of Deuteronomy 20:10-15 by first offering peace to the inhabitants of the place.

The author depicts the Danites in the worst possible light. They stole what belonged to another man. They had as their spiritual head a priest who could be bought. They pounced on a defenseless city. They established a shrine which was the rival of the house of Yahweh at Shiloh.

D. A Cult (Judg 18:30-31).

The Danites established their own religious shrine in the newly built city. They installed therein the graven image which they had confiscated from Micah back in the hill country of Ephraim. The wandering Levite who was consecrated to be the priest of that shrine is at last identified. His name was Jonathan. He was a grandson or great grandson[6] of Moses.[7] This fact provides a chronological framework for the first appendix to Judges. The involvement of Moses' grandson (or great grandson) would date the Danite migration shortly after the death of Joshua (18:30a).

The prestigious Levitical family continued to serve at the illegal and idolatrous shrine until *"the captivity of the land."* The reference is probably not to the Assyrian captivity of Israel which did not begin until about 745 BC. Most likely the reference is to the Philistine captivity of the land, when the ark of God was captured and Shiloh was destroyed (1 Sam 4-5). A date of 1080 BC probably would not be far off.[8] This explanation of the *"captivity of the land"* fits well with the note with which the first appendix to Judges closes. Micah's graven image continued to be worshiped *"all the time that the house of God* (i.e., tabernacle) *was at Shiloh."* The point seems to be that the idolatrous shrine in Dan was a rival of the legitimate worship center in Shiloh until the latter was destroyed (18:30b-31).

IMMORALITY ILLUSTRATED
Judges 19:1-30

Judges 19 illustrates a third dimension of the moral mess which characterized the years immediately following the death of Joshua. Again a Levite is involved, and he is portrayed in a less than favorable light. The account opens with the reminder that *"in those days Israel had no king"* (19:1). This note seems intended to link chronologically the events of the two previous chapters to those about to be narrated. At the same time the author intends to warn his readers that he is about to relate shocking events, events which would never have transpired had there been a strong, god-fearing king in those days.

A. A Trip to Bethlehem (Judg 19:1-9).

The Levite, who lived in the remote part of Ephraim's hill country, had taken a concubine[9] from Bethlehem in Judah. She, however, had *"played the harlot"* (*zanah*) against him. She deserted her husband and returned to the house of her father.[10] After four months of painful separation the Levite set out for Bethlehem with a servant and a pair of donkeys. He went after his concubine to *"speak tenderly"* (lit., speak upon her heart) in order to persuade her to return with him to their home. He must have mended the relationship, for she brought him into her father's house. The Levite's father-in-law was glad to see his daughter's husband. For three days the men feasted. The overly gracious father-in-law persuaded the Levite to spend a fourth day and night in Bethlehem. Not until afternoon of the fifth day was the Levite able to depart for his home in Ephraim (19:3-9).

B. A Stopover in Gibeah (Judg 19:10-21).

By the time the travelers had gone six miles or so it was late in the afternoon. The Levite's servant proposed that his master turn aside for the night into the Jebusite city of Jebus (Jerusalem). The Levite, however, refused to lodge in a city occupied by *"foreigners."* He was determined to press on for Gibeah or Ramah (19:10-13).

By the time the threesome reached Gibeah the sun had already set. They entered the city and sat down in the public square. Normally citizens would provide lodging for weary travelers. Gibeah, however, was most inhospitable. Finally an old man, who was an Ephraimite living in Gibeah, came in from the field. When he learned that the Levite was an Ephraimite, he was most cordial. The Levite assured the old man that he would provide the food for himself, his concubine, servant and donkeys. He would not be a burden. The old man, however, insisted that the travelers come into his home and accept his provisions. The Levite quickly accepted the invitation (19:14-21).

C. An Attack by the Gibeahites (Judg 19:22-26).

The joyous evening meal was interrupted by a pounding on the door. The men of the city, certain *"sons of Belial"* (worthless fellows), had surrounded the house. They demanded that the old man surrender the Levite to them that they might *"know"* (i.e., have carnal relations with) him. This unnatural lust (cf. Rom 1:27) shows how corrupt the men of Gibeah had become. The old man pled with his neighbors not to contemplate such *"foolishness"* (nebhalah).[11] To dramatize the magnitude of the sin of homosexual rape, the old man offered to surrender to the mob his own virgin daughter and the concubine of his guest. The mob could ravish these women and do with them as they pleased if only they would cease attempting to rape the Levite (19:22-24).

The moral perversity of the Benjamites was only matched by the moral insensitivity of the old man. He regarded a heterosexual rape even of a virgin, as bad as that might be, as far less of a crime than a homosexual rape. Granted, under the code of the east, he had a responsibility to protect his guest from danger. The end, however, does not justify the means. That the men in this account have a very low estimation of the value of women is rather clear. One should remember, however, that the very purpose of this story is to illustrate the disgusting immorality which was sweeping the land in the days just after the death of Joshua. Certainly Biblical *teaching* does not support the notion that the rape of a woman is a lesser offense than the rape of a man, or that heterosexual immorality is less serious than homosexual immorality.

The Levite was as morally perverse and insensitive as the old man and the mob. When he saw that the mob would not listen to the old man, he seized his concubine and shoved her out the door. Accepting this sacrifice to their perverted lust, the men of Gibeah showed no further interest in the old man or his guest. They raped the woman and abused her all night long. At the approach of dawn they released her. She staggered to the door of the house, and fell. There she breathed her last breath (19:25-26).

D. Reaction to the Atrocity (Judg 19:27-30).

Early in the morning the Levite arose to continue his journey. He saw the crumpled body of his concubine at the doorway. When she did not respond to his cold command to arise, the Levite realized that she was dead. He placed her on his donkey and continued on toward the hill country of Ephraim. At his house the Levite took a knife and dismembered the corpse. The man had as little respect for his spouse in death as he had had for her in life. He sent the pieces of her body throughout the territory of Israel. The entire nation was shocked at the sordid tale of the sin of the Benjamites. Nothing like that had ever happened in Israel since the day that the children of Israel had come up from Egypt (19:27-30).

The crime at Gibeah illustrates the depths of the moral depravity into which many of the Israelites quickly had fallen after the death of Joshua and the elders of his generation. Hosea regarded this outrageous sin as the standard by which to measure all other depraved acts (9:9); he saw in this narrative the initial act of apostasy after Israel entered Canaan (10:9). This chapter, taken together with the one which follows, however, also illustrates the divine law of sowing and reaping. The woman who played the harlot died by being sexually abused. The Levite who sacrificed his spouse to save his honor lost her altogether. The men of Gibeah, along with thousands in their tribe who condoned their actions, died in a war of retribution.

DISUNITY ILLUSTRATED
Judges 20:1-48

The moral perversity of the men of Gibeah set in motion a chain of events which drove a wedge between the tribes. The internecine bloodshed which was narrowly averted in the days of Joshua (cf. Josh 22) became a bloody reality shortly after his death.

A. The Assembly (Judg 20:1-10).
From Dan to Beersheba and from Gilead as well the sons of Israel assembled *"as one man"* at Mizpah. The tribal chiefs took their stand in the assembly of the people. Some 400,000 swordsmen were present. The author is much impressed with the unity of the tribes, for three times he states that they gathered *"as one man."* Yet one tribe—Benjamin—was not represented. By failing to appear the Benjamites were signaling that they were siding with the men of Gibeah. So the unity of Israel here is directed against one of their own tribes. Three times the author seems to lament the tragedy of the whole situation by noting that the united tribes and the Benjamites were *"brothers"* (20:1-3a).[12]

The assembly requested from the Levite a firsthand report of what had happened that night in Gibeah. The Levite rehearsed the dreadful details of the event, being careful to place his own despicable conduct in the best possible light. He alleged that the men of Gibeah intended to kill him. Though the narrative of the previous chapter does not state this explicitly, the Levite is probably not exaggerating when he states that his life was in jeopardy. His gruesome butchery of the woman's corpse was justified by the magnitude of the sin committed against her by the Benjamites. They had committed *"a lewd and disgraceful act"* in Israel (20:3b-6). The word *"lewd"* (*zimmah*) denotes a sin so vile that the perpetrator must be *"cut off"* from the nation (cf. Lev 18:17,29). The word translated *"shameful act"* (*nebhalah*) is the same term used by the old man when he appealed to the men of Gibeah to abandon their sinful course (cf.19:23).

The shocking dismemberment of the corpse had accomplished exactly what it was intended to accomplish, viz., the massing of the national assembly. Now the Levite called upon those assembled to give advice and counsel regarding the incident (20:7).

Those assembled pledged not to return to their homes until a military campaign had been launched against Benjamin. Following the holy war traditions, they cast lots to set aside ten percent of their number to serve as a quartermaster corps to provide food for the army. The others marched against Gibeah of Benjamin (20:8-10).

B. The Positions (Judg 20:11-17).

Messengers were dispatched throughout the tribe of Benjamin to demand the surrender of the "sons of Belial" in Gibeah. Only the death of those rapists and murderers could remove the wicked blot from Israel. The Benjamites refused to join the national effort to punish the atrocity at Gibeah. On the contrary, an army of 26,000 swordsmen rushed to Gibeah to bolster the defense of the town. Among the Benjamite defenders were 700 left-handed slingers who could sling a stone at a hair and not miss (20:11-16). By taking the side of their tribesmen the Benjamites came to share the guilt of the murderers. They too came under the ban which had been imposed on Gibeah.

The united tribes numbered their swordsmen at 400,000. This constituted an advantage of almost fifteen to one. That this vast army did not immediately crush the Benjamites and in fact suffered heavy casualties at their hands suggests that Yahweh was punishing the united tribes as well as Benjamin in this account (20:17).

C. The Battles (Judg 20:18-35).

Over the next several days the united tribes clashed with the Benjamites three times. In the first two battles Benjamin was victorious. In the third clash the united tribes virtually wiped out the Benjamites.

1. The first attack against Gibeah (20:17-21). Representatives of the eleven tribes went to Bethel to seek by priestly oracle direction concerning the war with Benjamin. The text makes no mention of any request for divine wisdom or even divine help for that matter. Nor is there any record of offerings being brought in worship. Their only question was, Which tribe would lead the campaign against Benjamin? The same question was asked in reference to the warfare against the Canaanites in Judges 1:1. The response there and here is that Judah should lead the tribes into battle. The next day as the men of Israel approached Gibeah, the Benjamites came out to meet their attackers. Some 22,000 men of Israel became casualties in the first clash of the war (20:17-21).

2. The second attack against Gibeah (20:22-25). The united tribes were discouraged by their heavy losses, but they were not yet ready to relinquish the effort to punish the lawless Benjamites. Again they arrayed themselves for battle in the same position which they had held on the previous day. Representatives of the eleven tribes again *"went up before Yahweh"* (at Bethel?). Until evening time they wept and inquired of the Lord. Should they renew hostilities with Benjamin? Their tears were not those of real repentance. They were attempting to coerce Yahweh to be sympathetic to their cause. The priestly oracle directed them to resume the attack. The oracle, however, offered no assurance of victory (20:22-23).

The results of the second battle were similar to those of the first clash. The Benjamites again came out against the united tribes and cut down 18,000 swordsmen. Thus far Israel had received the favor of divine guidance but not divine aid in the battle itself. Yet the significance of this should not be overlooked. In spite of all that was wrong in Israel, that people still had access to divine guidance through the high priest.[13] This Benjamin did not have (20:24-25).

3. The third attack against Gibeah (20:26-35). In the two disastrous defeats the Israelites had learned that victory would not come through their military might, but only through empowerment by the Spirit of God. They dared not go forward with their campaign against Benjamin until they were assured that the Lord would give them victory. So all of the people went up to Bethel to inquire of the Lord. Phinehas, the grandson of Aaron, stood before the ark and ministered there. The Israelites fasted and wept, and offered various sacrifices before the Lord. They again asked if they should go up against Benjamin. This time, however, they add the words *"or not."* They were now willing to break off the attack if that be the will of Yahweh. No longer were they presuming that their plan to punish Benjamin was within the will of God. Again the priestly oracle directed the united tribes to attack Gibeah a third time. This time victory was assured (20:26-28).

A new strategy was employed by the united tribes in the third attack against Gibeah. They set men in ambush around the city with the obvious intention of catching the Benjamites in a pincher movement. The main body began the attack, then feigned retreat. The

Benjamites, overconfident because of their previous victories, began to pursue the retreating men of Israel. The maneuver worked. The Benjamites where lured out into the open where they were attacked from three directions. The battle was fierce. The Benjamites did not suspect that their army was about to be decimated (20:29-35).

D. The Victory (Judg 20:36-46).

Having given a thumbnail sketch of the third clash, the author now explains how that victory was possible. One contingent of the ambushment rushed the city itself. When they saw the smoke rising from Gibeah, the Benjamites lost their will to fight. They attempted to flee toward the wilderness. The battle, however, overtook them. The Lord struck the Benjamites before Israel (20:36-43).

The Benjamite casualties in that third day of battle were staggering. The total is said to be 25,100 swordsmen (v. 35).[14] (20:44-46). A band of 600 Benjamites made it to the rock of Rimmon where they remained for four months. Having crushed the army of Benjamin, the united tribes turned back against the territory of Benjamin. The non-combatants were struck with the edge of the sword, the cattle were destroyed and the cities burned. The entire tribe was under the ban of total destruction since it had taken the side of the men of Gibeah (20:47-48).

LEGALISM ILLUSTRATED
Judges 21:1-25

In their shock over the behavior of the Benjamites, the men of Israel had taken a rash vow before the war. They had sworn in solemn oath that they would not give their daughters in marriage to Benjamites. Now they realized that an entire tribe was about to be lost. The leaders of Israel consequently devised a scheme whereby they could technically keep the terms of their sacred oath, and at the same time provide wives for the surviving Benjamites. In this kind of hypocritical legal fiction the Israelites became skilled with the passing of years. The scribes of Jesus' day were experts in knowing how to keep the letter of the law while at the same time breaking the spirit of that law.

209

A. Virgins of Jabesh (Judg 21:1-14).

The prospect of losing one of the tribes entirely was a matter of great concern. Again the people went to Bethel where they expressed their grief all day before the Lord. In their zeal to punish the atrocity of Gibeah they had entered into a rash vow. Now they bemoaned the consequences of their own stupidity. Sacrifices were offered in an attempt to move the Lord to heal the breach in their nation (21:1-4).

After a day of lamentation and worship, a potential solution occurred to some of the leaders. When the national assembly had been called to Mizpah (20:1-11), another oath had been taken. This oath obligated them to put to death soldiers who failed to assemble before the Lord. A roll call of the army indicated that no contingent from Jabesh-gilead had aided in the war against Benjamin (21:5-9).

The assembly determined to put Jabesh-gilead under the ban. A contingent of twelve thousand men was dispatched with orders to put to death the inhabitants of the place. Thus human logic determined to resort to massacre of their countrymen in order to undo the results of the massacre of other countrymen. Only the young virgins were to be spared. Since virgins wore distinctive clothing in ancient cultures, they easily would be identified by the attacking forces. The original oath, however, must either have applied only to the men of military age, or to the entire population of towns which sent no support to the war effort. The sparing of the virgins was completely arbitrary. The desperate effort here was to undo the effects of one rash vow by the selective implementation of another (21:10-11).

Four hundred virgins were found among the inhabitants of Jabesh-gilead. These girls were brought back to Shiloh, the site of the tabernacle. Then a peace offering was sent to the six hundred Benjamites at the rock of Rimmon. They left their stronghold in the wilderness, came to Shiloh, and claimed as brides the four hundred virgins from Jabesh. Still, however, two hundred of the Benjamites did not have wives (21:12-14).

B. Daughters of Shiloh (Judg 21:15-25).

More wives were needed. Another solution occurred to some of the rulers. Though not as violent, it was equally bizarre. During the annual feast at Shiloh the Benjamites who still needed wives were to conceal themselves in the vineyards. When the daughters of Shiloh came out to join in the dancing, the Benjamites were to rush forth from the vineyards and seize wives for themselves. Should fathers or brothers complain to the leaders, they would be assured that they were innocent of any violation of the oath. They had not actually *given* their daughters or sisters to the Benjamites. No one seems to have cared that a festival of the Lord was being used for this chicanery (21:15-22).

The Benjamites did as they were told. Each single man captured one of the dancing daughters of Shiloh and carried her off, cave-man style, to be his wife. A more despicable desecration of marriage can hardly be imagined. The Benjamites then returned to their tribal inheritance with their new brides to rebuild and occupy their towns. The national assembly of the eleven tribes, having served its purpose, also dissolved. The men of Israel returned to the territories of their respective tribes and clans. The narrative concludes with a final reminder of how such unpleasant episodes could have taken place. There was no central government during the days of the Judges. Everybody simply did what he thought was right (21:23-25).

Judges 21 is ambiguous. It contains a record of consistency and inconsistency. The punishment of Jabesh-gilead was justified, but was needlessly severe. That Israel was concerned to honor an oath to God is commendable, but to do so by trampling on the rights of the Shiloh girls and their families was perverse. God's grace even shines through the clouds of this chapter. Old Sodom was completely destroyed in Genesis 19. In New Sodom—Benjamin—a remnant of six hundred was spared.[15]

ENDNOTES

1. NIV margin states that 1100 silver shekels would weigh 28 lbs. Goslinga, however, gives the weight as 40 lbs.

2. The term *pesel* usually denotes an image that is carved from wood or stone. The term *massekhah* always denotes a cast idol. Did the woman have two idols made? The Hebrew verb in verse 4 is singular and this argues against the notion of two separate idols. Probably the combination *pesel-massekhah* denotes a single idol with two distinct parts. Cf. Goslinga, *op. cit.*, p. 457, n.8.

3. Bethlehem was not a Levitical city. The text says literally that the Levite *"lived as a sojourner"* there. This may have been because his assigned city was not yet in Israelite hands.

4. That the Danites used the general name *'Elohim* rather than the covenant name *Yahweh* suggests that they did not regard Micah's shrine as a legitimate sanctuary of Israel's God.

5. Goslinga, *op. cit.*, p. 469.

6. According to 1 Chr 23:16 Gershom's son was Shebuel. Jonathan may have been the son of Shebuel, hence a great grandson of Moses. Skipping a generation is not uncommon in Old Testament genealogy.

7. Apparently the Hebrew text originally read *"Moses"* in Judges 18:30. Later scribes could not accept the fact that a grandson of Moses would have agreed to serve as priest at an idolatrous shrine. They assumed that the original reading was *Manasseh* rather than *Moses*. The difference between the two names in the Hebrew text is a single consonant. In some Hebrew manuscripts the scribes have "restored" the missing letter by inserting above the line of writing a small letter *nun* at the appropriate place.

8. A divine judgment on Shiloh is alluded to in Ps 78:60; and Jer 7:12,14; 26:6,9. Presumably these references refer to what happened to Shiloh just after the death of Eli. Limited habitation of the site, however, must have continued after 1080 BC (1 Kgs 11:29; Jer 41:5).

9. A concubine was a wife of secondary rank who did not enjoy the economic protection provided by the *mohar*. A *mohar* was a substantial sum of money left on deposit with the father of a bride which provided for the woman in the event of premature death or desertion by her husband.

10. It is not clear whether the author meant to say that leaving the Levite constituted committing harlotry, or whether the concubine played the harlot and then left her husband.

11. *Nebalah* is rendered *"disgraceful thing"* (NIV) and *"act of folly"* (NASB). The word is used of shameful acts of sexual immorality such as rape (Gen 34:7) and incest (2 Sam 13:12).

12. The united tribes and the Benjamites are called *"brothers"* in 20:13,23,28. On the tragic disunity of Israel in this account, see Dale Ralph Davis, *Such a Great Salvation* (Grand Rapids: Zondervan), p. 218f.

13. Davis, *op. cit.*, p. 222.

14. The exact count of casualties on the third day of battle is said to be 25,100 (v. 35). This is rounded off to 25,000 in v. 46. The number of Benjamite casualties added to the 600 survivors falls 1,000 short of the figure given for the Benjamite forces at the beginning of the war. The text is silent about any Benjamite casualties in the first two clashes. The 1,000 unaccounted for in the casualty figures from the third clash may have been lost in the first two clashes.

15. Davis, *op. cit.*, p. 226.

CHAPTER THIRTEEN

A Point of Light in a Dark Night
Ruth 1-4

The setting for the Book of Ruth is the period when the Judges ruled Israel.[1] No specific Judge, however, is named. Jewish tradition suggested the Judge was Ibzan (1105-1098 BC). Modern scholars are more likely to suggest Jair (1148-1126 BC). The book was originally a kind of third appendix to the Book of Judges. The author apparently wished to illustrate that even though the days of the Judges were morally and religiously dark, yet some within Israel were faithful to God and to his law.

A SAD HOMECOMING
Faith Encompassed by Tragedy
Ruth 1:1-22

The focus in chapter 1 is on the family of Elimelech ("My God is King") an "Ephrathite"[2] from Bethlehem Judah. Elimelech's wife Naomi ("Pleasant") is one of two leading characters in the book. Her sons Mahlon ("Sickness") and Chilion ("Vanishing") may have been given their names because of the sad plight of the nation during the dark days of the Judges.

A. Leaving Bethlehem (Ruth 1:1-5).

The land of Judah experienced a famine. Although famines were common in the days of the Patriarchs some eight hundred years earlier (cf. Gen 12:10; 26:1; 43:1), this is the first recorded famine encountered by Israel since entering the land of Canaan.

Elimelech decided to move his family to the land of Moab east of the Dead Sea to wait out the famine. Because of this decision Elimelech is vilified in rabbinical exegesis as an arrogant and evil man. His death in Moab is viewed by the rabbis as just punishment for having left the Promised Land. Naomi *"was left"* (lit., she remained) with her two sons in the land of Moab (1:1-3). Again rabbinical exegesis sees Naomi here as defying the divine warning of the death of her husband by choosing to remain on foreign soil. Nothing in the text, however, suggests that Elimelech sinned by moving his family to Moab. Nothing suggests that his death was anything more than coincidental with his abiding in that foreign land. The passage does suggest, however, that godly people do experience unexpected tragedies, and sometimes in rapid succession.

After the death of Elimelech, the two sons took Moabite wives. They thus, in the eyes of Jewish commentators, sinned more grievously than their father. If this passage is intended to be a protest against religious intermarriage it certainly is a mild one. That the women converted to the worship of the Living God before the marriages is not inconceivable. Technically, the marriage to Moabite women was not illegal. The law only forbade Moabite *males* from joining the assembly of the Lord (cf. Deut 23:3).

For about ten years the Israelite men and their wives Orpah and Ruth lived in Moab. They had apparently given up all thought of returning to Bethlehem. The widow Naomi remained with her sons. In those days a widow was almost totally dependent upon her sons for support. As fate would have it, however, Naomi was shortly left destitute. Her two sons both died (1:4-5).

B. Contemplating Return (Ruth 1:6-18).

Through travelers Naomi learned that conditions in Judah had improved. Yahweh had *"visited his people,"* i.e., had intervened on their behalf, to provide food. Naomi considered her chances of surviving without a male provider to be greater in her native land than in Moab. Following eastern customs, her two daughters-in-law accompanied her for some distance on the road to Judah (1:6-7).

One of the unusual features of the Book of Ruth is that fifty-five of the eighty-five verses in the book are dialogue. At some point along the road Naomi urged her two daughters-in-law each to return to her mother's house.[3] She then pronounced a blessing upon them in the name of Yahweh. She prayed that the Lord would be as kind to these two Moabite women as they had been kind to their dead husbands and to Naomi. She further prayed that Yahweh would help each to find *"a resting place"* each in the house of her husband. The term *"resting place" (menuchah)* carries the meaning of both peace and happiness.[4] The term summarizes all the qualities of an ideal marriage in which a godly woman can find strength, security, material wellbeing and love. Naomi then kissed Orpah and Ruth. At this point the three could restrain their emotions no longer. They lifted up their voices and wept (1:8-9).

The young women expressed determination to accompany Naomi all the way to Bethlehem. Naomi, however, insisted that they go back to their country. She could not provide husbands for them in any reasonable length of time. Knowing that she must be deprived of the companionship of the two fine daughters-in-law made Naomi's burden even harder to bear. She had lost both her husband and sons to death. Now she was about to lose the last dear ones she had on earth through separation. All of this misfortune Naomi attributed to the actions of Yahweh. This frank and logical analysis of the situation caused the women again to burst into tears. Orpah yielded to Naomi's logic and submitted to her directions. She kissed her mother-in-law and departed for her home. Ruth, however, *"clung"* to Naomi and refused to leave (1:10-14).

After some time passed Naomi began to urge Ruth to follow the example of her sister-in-law. Orpah had returned to her people and *"to her gods."* If the women had embraced Yahweh when they mar-

215

ried the Israelite men, Naomi knew that it would be impossible for Orpah to remain faithful to the Lord while surrounded by Moabite idolatry. Orpah's gods would doubtless include the god Chemosh who demanded child sacrifice from his devotees. Perhaps Naomi's words to Ruth should not so much be interpreted as a directive but as an invitation to declare her complete allegiance to Yahweh (1:15).

Ruth could not bear the thought of returning to the heathen environment in which she had grown up. If she had not fully repudiated the gods of Moab before, Ruth does so at this point. She would hear no more of Naomi's urging to return to Moab. On the contrary, Ruth committed herself for better or worse to Naomi, Naomi's people, and Naomi's God. She did not even desire to return to her native Moab for burial. Nothing but death would separate her from Naomi. This commitment she sealed by a self-malediction or curse in which she used the name of Yahweh: *"Thus may Yahweh do to me, and worse, if anything but death parts you and me."*[5] The use of Yahweh's name exclusively in this oath again suggests a complete conversion on Ruth's part (1:16-17).

When Naomi saw that Ruth was determined to go on to Bethlehem with her, she ceased urging her to return to Moab (1:18).

C. Returning to Bethlehem (Ruth 1:19-22).

The entire village of Bethlehem was astir when Naomi and Ruth arrived. The sight of two women traveling alone toward the city was unusual. As they drew near the women of Bethlehem thought they recognized Naomi, and inquired if the traveler was she. Naomi responded: *"Do not call me Naomi* (i.e., "Pleasant") *but call me Mara* (i.e.,"Bitter")." By this Naomi signaled that the decade in Moab had taken its toll in more ways than one (1:19).

Naomi blamed her misfortune on the Lord. Shaddai, the Almighty,[6] had afflicted her, or so she thought. When she had left Bethlehem she had been living a full life. She had a fine husband and two fine sons. Yahweh, however, had brought her back empty. By bringing this misfortune upon her Yahweh had witnessed against Naomi, i.e., had shown her to be a terrible sinner undeserving of his blessing. Instead of using his power to protect this woman, Shaddai had turned his power against her (1:20-21).

If Naomi referred to the permissive will of the Lord, her theology was impeccable. Her words, however, seem to blame all her misfortune directly on the Lord. God may have permitted her misfortune. To deny this would be to deny the omnipotence of God. That God initiated or directly caused Naomi all the pain she had experienced is never suggested in the text. Here is an example of that theology which so often rears its ugly head, viz., that calamity in one's life means that one is being punished for some sin. This theology is decisively laid to rest in the Book of Job.

The dialogue between Naomi and the women of Bethlehem underscores dramatically the theme of the first chapter of the book, viz., the terrible ordeal of Naomi. The narrative of the homecoming concludes by emphasizing (1) the loneliness of the return—only the two women without their loved ones; (2) the sacrifice of the return—Ruth was a Moabitess who was forsaking all for her commitment to Yahweh's people; (3) the wisdom of the return—they came from Moab, a land where Chemosh was honored, to Bethlehem Judah in the Promised Land; and (4) the time of the return—at the beginning of the barley harvest. In April the barley crop ripened and was ready for harvest (1:22).

A PROVIDENTIAL MEETING
Faith in Everyday Circumstances
Ruth 2:1-23

Chapter 2 begins with the introduction of the third leading character of the book. Boaz is described as (1) an acquaintance (NASB margin) of Elimelech; (2) a man of great wealth; and (3) a member of the family of Elimelech. The exact relationship between Elimelech and Boaz is left unclear. The rabbinical thesis that Boaz was a cousin of the dead man is without foundation. Another tradition would make Boaz Naomi's nephew by marriage.

A. Polite Requests (Ruth 2:2-7).

Ruth was an industrious woman. She was not afraid to work. She politely requested permission from her mother-in-law to go out into the fields where the barley was being harvested. Perhaps there she could find a friendly land owner who would allow her to follow behind the harvesters picking up the stalks which they might leave lying on the ground. Mosaic law stipulated that the gleanings of the field were to be left for the poor, for strangers and for widows and orphans.[7] Either this custom prevailed also in Moab, or Ruth had learned of it from local women, perhaps as she drew water at the public well. In any case, Naomi granted permission for Ruth to proceed with her plan (2:2).

At some point in her forays into the harvest fields Ruth happened upon the field of a wealthy farmer named Boaz. Providence must have brought her to that place because Boaz was from the same tribe as Elimelech (2:3).

That Boaz was a godly man is stressed from the moment he is introduced in the account. When he came out from Bethlehem to inspect the harvest he greeted his reapers in the name of Yahweh. They responded in kind. Where both labor and management share the same faith in the Lord, peace and satisfaction will reign supreme (2:4).

Noticing Ruth walking behind the reapers, Boaz inquired of the foreman who this might be. The foreman introduced Ruth as *"the Moabite woman who returned with Naomi from the land of Moab"* (NASB). She had requested permission to glean after the reapers in the field, and the foreman had granted that request. Ruth had been hard at work in the field since early morning, except for a brief respite in the hut which was used by the reapers for rest and refreshment (2:5-7).

B. Gracious Offer (Ruth 2:8-13).

Boaz addressed Ruth in a most courteous manner. Since he was considerably older than the Moabitess, he calls her *"my daughter."* He invited her to join the women who were working for him. Ruth could follow them from field to field during the harvest. Boaz had given strict orders to his male servants not to touch or in any way hinder the efforts of Ruth. He further invited Ruth to help herself from the water jars which the servants might draw from some nearby well (2:8-9).

Ruth was overwhelmed by this display of kindness by the Israelite.

In typical Oriental exaggerated respect, she bowed her face to the ground. She could not help but ask why she, a foreigner, should have found favor in his sight. Boaz explained that he had heard of all that Ruth had done for her mother-in-law after the death of her husband. Boaz had been particularly impressed by Ruth's willingness to leave her mother and father and the land of her birth to stay with Naomi in a strange land (2:10-11).

Boaz then pronounced a blessing on Ruth in the name of Yahweh. He prayed that the Lord might continue to bless the work of Ruth, that he might provide for her *"a full reward"* (BV) for all she had done. The Gentile had sought refuge under the *"wings"* of Yahweh, and therefore was entitled to his blessing. The language here is obviously metaphorical. Perhaps the reference is to the wings of the cherubim which were spread out over the ark of the covenant in the Tabernacle. In any case, the language here definitely confirms what was suggested in the previous chapter, viz., that Ruth had given her heart to the Lord (2:12).

Ruth responded to this spiritual blessing with gratitude and humility. She did not consider herself equal to any one of Boaz's maidservants. Nonetheless, the farmer had bestowed favor upon her. This *"comforted"* or touched the heart of Ruth (2:13).

C. Generous Provision (Ruth 2:14-17).

At mealtime Boaz again was gracious to Ruth. He invited her to come and eat with the reapers. The meal of bread, with a special dip, and roasted grain was typical of that region. Ruth had more than enough to eat. As she arose to resume her labor, Boaz issued three orders to his servants. First, Ruth was now to be allow to glean among the tied sheaves which the harvesters placed upright on the ground. Here the grains were more numerous. In addition, the servants were told to *"drop some heads for her on purpose"* (BV).[8] Finally, no servant was to rebuke Ruth as she gleaned.

Ruth continued to glean in Boaz's field until evening. Then she beat out what she had gleaned. The kernels of grain were knocked loose from the stalk with a stick. The Moabitess was able to carry home that day an ephah[9] of barley, enough to last the two widows for a number of weeks.

D. Grateful Acknowledgment (Ruth 2:18-23).

Ruth returned to the city with the fruit of her labor. She shared with Naomi what remained of the bountiful lunch which Boaz had provided for her in the field. Naomi was amazed at the good fortune of her daughter-in-law. She pronounced a blessing on the benefactor, and then inquired as to his name. When she learned that it was Boaz, she again pronounced a blessing. Boaz, as it turned out, was a close relative, a kinsman-redeemer *(go'el),* in the family of Elimelech (2:18-20). In the Old Testament social structure the kinsman-redeemer had three responsibilities: (1) He had the right to recover forfeited property of a kinsman (Lev 25:25). (2) If one had fallen into slavery, the kinsman-redeemer was to purchase his freedom (Lev 25:47-49). (3) Should a brother die leaving no male heir, the kinsman-redeemer was to marry the widow to raise up seed in the name of the dead relative (Deut 25:5-10; Gen 38:8-10). Some think the kinsman-redeemer also had the responsibility to avenge the murder of a family member (Num 35:19).

With great excitement Ruth informed Naomi that Boaz had invited her to stay with his servants until the harvest was finished. Naomi was very pleased with this news. She knew that righteous Boaz would not allow any harm to come to the young widow while she work in his fields (2:21-22).

For the next several weeks Ruth stayed close by the maids of Boaz in order to glean. When the barley harvest was complete she continued in this relationship into the wheat harvest as well. All the while she continued to live with her mother-in-law (2:23).

A DRAMATIC PROPOSAL
Faith Taking Initiative
Ruth 3:1-18

Ruth 3 begins and ends with dialogue between Ruth and Naomi. These dialogue scenes introduce and evaluate the major scene of the chapter which depicts a late night meeting between Ruth and Boaz at the threshingfloor.

A. Introductory Dialogue (Ruth 3:1-5).

The introductory dialogue between Ruth and Naomi is essential to a correct perspective of the principal scene which follows. While Ruth took the initiative in chapter 2, here it is Naomi who proposes a bold move. Ruth only acts in this chapter on orders from Naomi. On her part, Naomi appears to be compelled by what she considers her moral obligation to seek for her daughter-in-law *"a resting place,"* i.e., marriage (3:1). Ruth did not belong in the fields with the hired hands. A woman of her worth deserved to be the queen of a home. Naomi recognized that when a godly woman marries a godly man, and both are committed to building their home upon divine principles, matrimony is a *"rest"* as much as anything on earth can be so called. Only in such a situation could Ruth *"prosper"* (BV), i.e., fulfill the deepest longings of her soul.

Naomi knew that Boaz would be winnowing barley on the threshing floor that night. He would then sleep there to protect his crop from thieves. Naomi directed Ruth to bathe, anoint herself with fragrant oils, and put on her best clothes. Ruth should go down to the threshingfloor. She should conceal herself until after Boaz had finished his evening meal. After the man had gone to sleep, Ruth should uncover his feet and lie down there. Boaz then would tell her what she was to do (3:2-4).

Naomi's directions and Ruth's willingness to comply (3:5) therewith must be judged by the standards of the times in which those women lived. On her part, Naomi had confidence in the good behavior and resolute chastity of her daughter-in-law. She knew that Boaz was a deeply religious man who would recognize immediately that he was being nudged ever so gently to perform his duty to his dead kinsman by marrying Ruth. On her part, Ruth trusted her mother-in-law's judgment and knowledge of local customs. She believed she was fulfilling a duty of love to her dead husband by approaching Boaz to remind him of his kinsman obligations.

B. A Marriage Proposal (Ruth 3:6-15).

Ruth did exactly as Naomi had directed. After his meal Boaz's *"heart was merry."* From the shadows Ruth watched him lie down at the end of the heap of grain. Then she quietly approached him, uncovered his feet, and lay down (3:6-7).

A midnight Boaz was startled to feel something soft and warm at his feet. He instinctively bent forward and discovered Ruth. In the dark he did not recognize her. Ruth identified herself. She then asked that he *"spread"* his *"wing"* over her since he was a kinsman-redeemer. The reference here is to the placing of the corner of the garment over a maiden as a token of marriage (3:8-9).

Boaz responded to the marriage proposal with a blessing on Ruth. Her desire to marry a kinsman of her dead husband was commendable, especially since Boaz was considerably older than Ruth.[10] Boaz urged Ruth not to fear. The Moabitess had the reputation of being a virtuous woman. He would be glad to do as she suggested. A problem, however, did exist. Whereas Boaz was a kinsman-redeemer, there was another who was closer than he. This anonymous relative first would have to relinquish his legal rights to *"redeem"* Ruth. If this nearer kinsman was unwilling to perform the function of the kinsman-redeemer, than Boaz assured Ruth by oath that he would do it (3:10-13).

Boaz invited Ruth to remain with him on the threshing floor that night. Concern for Ruth's reputation caused both to arise before sunrise. Boaz urged Ruth not to let it generally be known that she had been to the threshingfloor. As an added precaution, Boaz measured out to Ruth six measures of barley[11] and laid it on her, i.e., put it on her head. If someone should spot her that morning it would appear that she had merely gotten an early start on the day's work by transporting this sizable allotment of grain from the threshingfloor to her quarters. Ruth then departed for the city (3:14-15).[12]

C. Concluding Dialogue (Ruth 3:16-18).

When Ruth approached the house, Naomi inquired, *"Who are you, my daughter?"* The early morning darkness may have obscured the identity of Ruth. More likely, however, Naomi's question meant: Are you one dishonored by rejection or one protected as a wife? She wanted to know if the plan had worked! Ruth then told her mother-in-law all that had taken place. The generous gift of the barley signaled Boaz's favorable disposition toward the two women. Naomi counseled Ruth to be patient. She was confident that Boaz would not rest until he had settled the matter with the nearer kinsman (3:16-18).

A SIGNIFICANT MARRIAGE
Faith Finding Rest
Ruth 4:1-22

In the early morning Boaz went to the city gate. In ancient cities the gate complex was the center of social life. Legal judgments were rendered there. Before Boaz was able to function as the kinsman-redeemer of Naomi and Ruth, a legal proceeding was required.

A. A Legal Proceeding (Ruth 4:1-12).

When the nearer kinsman passed by, Boaz called him to turn aside and sit down. At the same time Boaz asked ten of the elders of the city to sit down to witness the proceedings (4:1-2). The nearer kinsman is called *"friend" (peloni almoni)*. Probably the author of Judges deliberately has suppressed his name to spare him embarrassment for refusing to perform his family duty.[13] Apparently the right of the *go'el* was exercised according to an order of kinship priority which is found in Leviticus 25:49. The order is: the paternal uncle, his son, then other relatives.

Boaz formerly notified the closest kinsman that Naomi had to put her husband's property up for sale. The closest kinsman had the right of purchase. Boaz hints that he might be willing to purchase the property, but he has no legal right to do so. The closest kinsman was quite willing to make the purchase. Apparently he thought that the property belonged solely to Naomi, and that his duty would end with the purchase of the field from her. When he learned, however, that the transaction would include marriage with Ruth, he withdrew. He felt that marriage to Ruth would in some way jeopardize his own inheritance (4:3-6).

Transfer of the legal rights of the *go'el* was symbolized by the removal of a sandal. Presumably it was the closest relative who gave the sandal to Boaz in the presence of the witnesses.[14] Boaz then acknowledged before the witnesses and *"all the people"* that he had acquired *(qanah)* from Naomi all which once had belonged to her husband and sons. In addition, Boaz proudly claimed that he had also acquired *(qanah)* Ruth as his wife. The legal terminology is the same with regard to the acquisition of the property and the wife. There, however, the similarity ended. Boaz clearly distinguishes between the acquisition of the property and the marriage to Ruth. In Biblical teaching a wife is never regarded as property, but as a full partner in the sacred task of building a home. Apparently the ceremony had attracted many of the townspeople of Bethlehem. They would be most happy to see the plight of the two impoverished women alleviated by the legal intervention of the wealthy Boaz (4:7-10a).

Unlike the closer kinsman, Boaz announced before the witnesses that he would be most happy to perform the responsibility of the Levirate marriage to raise up a descendant for Mahlon. All the people in the gate responded to Boaz's announcement with the proper legal formula: *"We are witnesses."* Then they spontaneously pronounced a blessing first on Ruth, then on Boaz. They prayed that Yahweh would make her as fruitful as Rachel and Leah from whom the whole house of Israel sprang. Regarding Boaz the people prayed for wealth and fame. They prayed that his household might be like that of Perez the son of Judah (Gen 38). Why Perez? Probably because he was the offspring of Levirate marriage similar to that of Ruth and Boaz (4:10b-12). Perez was the progenitor of one of the clans of the tribe of Judah (Num 26:21).

B. A Joyous Blessing (Ruth 4:13-17).

True to his public commitment, Boaz *"took,"* i.e., married, Ruth. He *"went in unto her,"* i.e., had sexual relations with her, that he might fulfill the responsibilities of a Levirate husband. Not long after the marriage the Lord *"gave her conception."* She who had not been able to conceive by her young husband Mahlon, was enabled by God to conceive by the much older Boaz (4:13).

One of the themes of the Book of Ruth is the bitterness of Naomi. She left Bethlehem *"full,"* i.e., finding fulfillment in her family. She returned to Bethlehem *"empty,"* i.e., having lost both her husband and sons (1:21). With the birth of a grandson, however, she experiences anew the satisfaction and security afforded by male offspring. The women of Bethlehem blessed the Lord in joyous praise. The newborn son would assume the responsibilities of the nearest kinsman toward both his mother and grandmother. The women pray that he may become a famous man in Israel. They pray that he may be to

Naomi a *"restorer of life,"* i.e., one who gave new meaning to living. The women also pray that the child would one day sustain Naomi in her old age (4:14-15a). The fear of every woman in Israel was to grow old without a male provider. The women of Bethlehem considered Naomi blessed, not only because of the newborn child, but because she had a daughter-in-law who loved her *"more than seven sons."* A mother of many sons in the Old Testament world was a happy mother. As long as she had no descendant, Naomi was so bitter that she could not really appreciate the blessing which Ruth represented in her life. Now that the stigma of childlessness had been removed, Naomi could come to appreciate how blessed she really was. Her life was indeed *"full"* of God's blessing (4:15b).

Naomi took the child and laid him in her lap. She became his *"nurse"* (*'omeneth*), i.e., she raised the child. The action here appears to be some kind of formal ceremony in which guardianship of the child was assumed. The child hereafter would be recognized as the son of Naomi as well as the son of Ruth. Certainly the neighbor women recognized this to be the case. They even were given the honor of naming the lad. They chose the name Obed, one who serves. Obed became the father of Jesse, and the grandfather of David (4:16-17).

C. A Concluding Genealogy (Ruth 4:18-22).

The concluding genealogy indicates the purpose and meaning of the entire Book of Ruth. The author aims to demonstrate that David came from solid Israelite stock even though he had Moabite blood in his veins.

ENDNOTES

1. Literally the Hebrew reads: *"in the days of the judging of the Judges."* Here the verb has the generic sense of exercising power. Hence the rendering of the NASB is *"in the days when the judges governed."*
2. Ephrath was the ancient name for Bethlehem Judah.
3. Since Ruth's father was still living (2:11), the reference to *"mother's house"* is puzzling. Jewish commentators suggest it is because "a proselyte has no legal father." Others have suggested that females lived in the mother's tent. Still others have pointed out that among the ancient Arabs a trace of

matriarchal organization can be documented in which the tent was actually the property of the wife.

4. The term *"resting place"* is used in the OT of (1) a camping place for the ark and people of God (Num 10:33); the Promised Land (Deut 12:9; 1 Kgs 8:56; Ps 95:11) and of Zion as the residence of Yahweh (Ps 132:8,14). Any place God dwells is a resting place for his people. The term also has a military significance meaning a place free of strife (e.g., Judg 20:43).

5. The idea behind this curse or oath formula is this: May the Lord do to me such and such unmentionable deed, and may he repeat it an unspecified number of times if I go back on this commitment. In English this is equivalent to saying, I swear I will never go back on this commitment.

6. Shaddai, as a divine title, is used forty-eight times in the OT. Seven times it is preceded by 'el (God). The exact meaning of the term is disputed. The LXX thought the word meant "all powerful" and most English versions have followed this lead. Recent scholarship suggests that Shaddai means "mountain." Hence El Shaddai would mean "God of the Mountain." This name for God seems to emphasize the power of God as it is channeled into the lives of individuals. The name is frequently linked with God's promise of progeny to the Patriarchs Abraham, Isaac and Jacob.

7. See Lev 19:9,10; 23:22; and Deut 24:19-22.

8. Literally, *"pull out for her from the bundles"* (tsebhathim). The Hebrew word appears only here and is to be distinguished from the tied sheaves of the preceding verse. These *"bundles"* were the quantity of grain the harvester could hold in his left hand when he was cutting with the sickle.

9. The exact size of the ephah is unknown. Some commentators give 40 liters as the capacity of an ephah. That would make it a bit larger than a bushel. Others, however, think the ephah had a capacity of only 22 liters, a bit over half a bushel.

10. In Jewish tradition Boaz was only a nephew of Elimelech whereas the nearer kinsman was a brother. Furthermore, the tradition is that Boaz was an octogenarian.

11. The measure is not stated in the text. Certainly the ephah is not intended. The Jewish Targum suggests the measure was the se'ah (one-third of an ephah), but even this measured by six likely would be too heavy for a woman to carry any great distance. Most likely the measure was the omer (one-tenth of an ephah).

12. The standard Hebrew text reads "he went to the city." Most English versions, however, read the verb as a feminine. Jewish Midrash explains the masculine by suggesting that Boaz accompanied Ruth to the city.

13. In the other two places (1 Sam 21:3; 2 Kgs 6:8) where the term peloni almoni appears in the Old Testament a name has been omitted deliberately.

14. The Targum (ancient Aramaic paraphrase of Ruth) favors the view that the purchaser—Boaz—was the one who removed his sandal.

226

PART TWO

THE

MONARCHY PERIOD

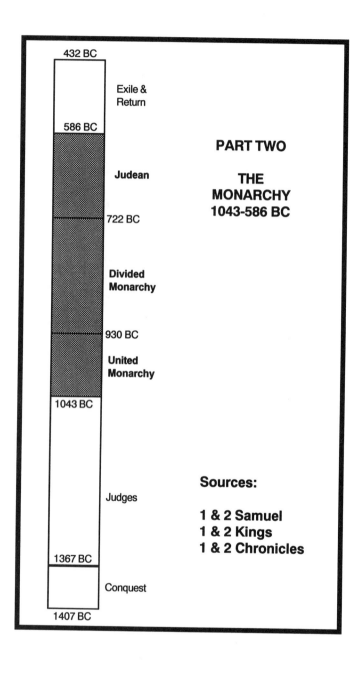

432 BC

Exile &
Return

586 BC

Judean

722 BC

PART TWO

**THE
MONARCHY
1043-586 BC**

Divided
Monarchy

930 BC

United
Monarchy

1043 BC

Judges

Sources:

**1 & 2 Samuel
1 & 2 Kings
1 & 2 Chronicles**

1367 BC

Conquest

1407 BC

CHAPTER FOURTEEN

The Monarchy Books
An Introduction

Originally the six monarchy historical books—the two Samuels, the two Kings, and the two Chronicles—were but three books. The division of the original works came when these books were translated into the Septuagint (Greek) version late in the third century BC. The Hebrew language of the Biblical period did not write symbols for vowel sounds in words. When the Hebrew was translated into the Greek language the vowel letters virtually doubled the size of the scroll. Hence to make the use of the scroll more manageable, the material in each case was somewhat arbitrarily divided into two separate scrolls.

THE BOOKS OF SAMUEL
Birth and Expansion of the Kingdom

With regard to the names of the ninth and tenth books of the Old Testament, two ancient traditions can be documented among the Jews. The Talmud (AD 500), representing a much older tradition, regarded this historical material as one book called "Samuel." Hebrew manuscripts continued to treat Samuel as one book until printed editions of the Hebrew Bible began to appear. The division into two books was first introduced into the Hebrew Bible edited by Daniel Bomberg in AD 1517.

In the Greek and Latin the original book of Samuel appears as two separate books as noted above. Christian Greek manuscripts of the Old Testament (c. AD 350) designate these two books as 1 & 2 Kingdoms. This tradition was followed in Jerome's Latin Vulgate. In later Vulgate tradition "Kingdoms" was shortened to "Kings." Older English versions combined both traditions in the headings of these books, e.g. in the King James version, "The First Book of Samuel otherwise called the First Book of Kings." Most English versions of the twentieth century have opted to follow exclusively the Samuel tradition for these books.

A. Background.

The "sea peoples," as they are called in non-biblical sources, settled en masse in the coastal region of Palestine about 1200 BC. About 1126 BC they began to extend their influence into the lowlands and mountains where they clashed with the Israelites. The chariots and weaponry of this powerful people intimidated the Israelites for forty years (Judg 13:1). Samson vented his personal vengeance against the Philistines for the twenty years of his judgeship (1105-1085 BC).

Eli's ineffective judgeship of forty years (1 Sam 4:18) paralleled the forty years of Philistine oppression. During those years of Samson's exploits and Eli's decline, a young lad was growing to manhood at the tabernacle in Shiloh. His name was Samuel. The opening chapters of 1 Samuel give the details of his birth and boyhood, his call to prophetic office, and his moral and spiritual influence on Israel.

The name of Samuel came to be attached to the ninth and tenth books of the Old Testament primarily because of the prominent role this prophet played in this period. He was the last of the Judges and the first of a new line of prophets. Samuel was the instrument through whom God founded the monarchy in Israel. He anointed Saul and David, the first two kings. In the career of David the influence of

Samuel lived on long after his death in 1 Samuel 25:1.

B. Circumstances of Writing.

The Book of Samuel is anonymous. The Jewish tradition that Samuel was the author seems untenable in view of the fact that the history is continued far beyond his death in 1 Samuel 25:1. Jewish tradition is most likely correct, however, in regarding the author of the book as a prophet.

The fact that the death of David is not recorded in Samuel suggests that the book was written before he died. Because of the length of time covered in Samuel no one person could have been a contemporary of all the events. Hence the author guided by the Holy Spirit must have used some sources. According to 1 Chronicles 29:29 the acts of King David, from first to last, were written "in the chronicles of Samuel the seer, in the chronicles of Nathan the prophet, and in the chronicles of Gad the seer." The "chronicles" written by these three prophets probably constituted the sources from which the author drew his material.[1]

The immediate purpose of the Book of Samuel was to narrate the circumstances surrounding the founding of the monarchy in Israel. 1 Samuel relates the birth of the monarchy. 2 Samuel narrates the expansion of the kingdom of Israel into an important world power. An appropriate caption for the two books of Samuel would be "The Birth and Expansion of the Kingdom." The ultimate purpose of the books was to reveal the divine origin of the messianic house of David, i.e., the family through whom the Messiah would one day come (2 Sam 7:12f.).

C. Chronology of the Books.

Combined, the books of 1 & 2 Samuel cover about 140 years. The opening event, the birth of Samuel, can be assigned to the year 1110 BC. The closing event, the death of David, probably occurred in 971 BC. Breaking this down according to the two books, 1 Samuel covers about a century, and 2 Samuel about forty years. Chart 13 depicts the chronological relationship between the major leaders and events in the books.

Chart No. 18

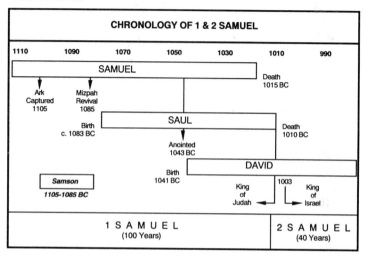

CHRONOLOGY OF 1 & 2 SAMUEL

D. Contents of the Books.

For the most part the books of Samuel consist of historical narrative. Other literary forms which appear in the books are prayers,
songs (e.g., 1 Sam 2; 2 Sam 22,23), and lists (e.g., 2 Sam 21:15-22;
23:8-39).

Childs has done commendable work in analyzing the structure of
the books of Samuel.[2] Clearly the introductory formula in 1 Samuel
13:1 marks a major division in this material. The same is true of
2 Samuel 1:1. The division of the original book into two separate
books recognized the structural significance of 2 Samuel 1:1. The language of 2 Samuel 21:1 is similar to that which was used in Ruth 1:1
to set off an historical appendix which is dischronological. Based on
these indicators, the text of the Samuel books falls into four main divisions.

The first main division (1 Sam 1-12) is focused on the transition to
monarchy. The unit begins with the birth of Samuel and ends with his
valedictory address. The text clearly indicates two major subdivisions.
The first seven chapters focus on the last days of judgeship government. The high priestly Judge Eli is depicted as a failure both in
respect to his governance of the worship center, and in respect to his

inability to cope with the Philistine menace. These failures led to the rise of a new type of Judge. In Samuel the roles of prophet and Judge were combined. The climax of this subsection is the victory over the Philistines which Yahweh granted in response to the prayer of Samuel (1 Sam 7).

Chart No. 19

<table>
<tr><td colspan="8" align="center">THE BOOKS OF SAMUEL</td></tr>
<tr><td colspan="4" align="center">1 SAMUEL</td><td colspan="4" align="center">2 SAMUEL</td></tr>
<tr><td colspan="4" align="center">The Birth of the Kingdom</td><td colspan="4" align="center">The Expansion of the Kingdom</td></tr>
<tr><td>Judgeship of Samuel</td><td colspan="3" align="center">Kingship of Saul</td><td colspan="4" align="center">Kingship of David</td></tr>
<tr>
<td>Transition

to

Monarchy</td>
<td>The Appointment
(8-12)

&

The Dis-
appointment
(13-14)</td>
<td>S

I

N</td>
<td>Saul's
Kingship
Rejected

&

David's
Kingship
Anticipated</td>
<td>David

under

the

Blessing
(5:12)</td>
<td>S

I

N</td>
<td>David

under

the

Curse
(12:11ff.)</td>
<td>APPENDIX

David in

Retrospect

&

Prospect</td>
</tr>
<tr>
<td>Locus:
Shiloh

1-7</td>
<td>Locus:
Gibeah

8-14</td>
<td>15</td>
<td>Locus:
Wilderness

16-31</td>
<td>Locus:
Hebron/
Jerusalem
1-10</td>
<td>11</td>
<td colspan="2" align="center">Locus:
Jerusalem

12-20   21-24</td>
</tr>
<tr>
<td>↓
Hannah's
Hymn
(2:10)</td>
<td colspan="3" align="center">Predictions with messianic
implications</td>
<td>↓
Nathan's
Oracle
(7:12-16)</td>
<td></td>
<td colspan="2" align="center">↓
David's
Last Words
(23:5)</td>
</tr>
</table>

The phrase *"and it came to pass when Samuel was old"* in 1 Samuel 8:1 clearly marks the beginning of the second subsection of the first main division. Here the focus is on the interaction between Samuel and Saul. Saul was selected by God, anointed privately and publicly by Samuel, and finally, after vindication through military leadership, embraced by the people. Once the people accepted their king, Samuel resigned from his role as Judge. He indicated such by a marvelous farewell address (1 Samuel 12).

The second main division of the material begins in 1 Samuel 13:1. The kingship was now in place. This division, which terminates with the death of Saul in 1 Samuel 31, also has two subdivisions. The account of Saul's disobedience in 1 Samuel 15 brings to an end a period in which he received public support and private guidance from Samuel. From Samuel's point of view Saul's reign was a disaster from the outset. God had punished his people for their premature and worldly-motivated request for a king by giving them exactly the kind of king they had requested. After the great sin of 1 Samuel 15, Samuel anointed a king after God's own heart. In the last sixteen chapters of 1 Samuel Saul did everything he could to consolidate his own power and thwart the elevation of David to the throne.

The third main division of material (2 Sam 1-20) focuses on the forty-year reign of David. David's reign, like that of Saul before him, is divided by the author into a "before and after" pattern, with David's great sin with Bathsheba being the watershed event (2 Sam 11). Before the sin David enjoyed God's blessing (cf. 2 Sam 5:12). After the sin David was under a divine curse (cf. 2 Sam 12:11ff.).

The last four chapters of 2 Samuel serve as an appendix to the David narratives. These chapters are carefully crafted to present "a highly reflective, theological interpretation of David's whole career."[3]

E. Teaching of the Books.

Three texts in the Samuel material indicate the main point which the author was attempting to get across. These texts are (1) the song of Hannah (1 Sam 2), (2) the oracle of Nathan (2 Sam 7), and (3) the last words of David (2 Sam 22-23).[4]

In Hannah's song God is central. Hannah praised the character, the strength of God and the ultimate day when God would judge the ends of the earth through his anointed king. The history which unfolds in the Samuel material illustrates the truth of which Hannah sang. Virtually every line of her song finds its counterpart in the pages which follow. The author has placed this poem near the beginning of his work in order to set forth the perspective from which he writes the history of Israel.

The Nathan oracle is the pinnacle of the blessings which God showered on David in 2 Samuel 1-10. Here the general expectations of Hannah are made more specific. The blessings bestowed on David are projected into the distant future. God would bless the *"house"* of David *"forever."* Thus David is regarded as the fulfillment of Yahweh's ancient promise to give his people a king. At the same time, he regarded David as a type of the ultimate Ruler who would sit on God's throne forever. The treatment of Saul's reign and that of David stand in stark contrast. In the same chapter where Saul's reign began, Samuel announced that his kingdom would not endure forever. God was seeking a man *"after his own heart"* to replace Saul. After Saul's great sin (1 Sam 15) the prophet announced that the kingdom would be given *"to your neighbor who is better than you"* (v. 28). Thus the author of the books of Samuel regarded Saul's kingship as a false start. Saul was a king like those who ruled all the surrounding nations. David was God's choice.

The final passage with crucial significance for the message of these books is 2 Samuel 22:1-23:7. This passage contains two separate poetic compositions, the first (2 Sam 22:1-51) coming from the time when Yahweh had delivered David from all his enemies, including Saul (2 Sam 22:1). The second composition comes from the last days of David (2 Sam 23:1). This material has been placed at the conclusion of the books of Samuel for strategic purposes. The thanksgiving hymn in chapter 22 echoes many of the themes articulated in Hannah's praise hymn (1 Sam 2). The poem looks back over the career of David and underscores the grand proposition which is the overriding message of this material, viz., that God rewards the righteous, and brings judgment upon the unrighteous.

The thanksgiving poem concludes with an allusion (2 Sam 22:51) to the Nathan oracle which announced Yahweh's eternal involvement with the house of David. This theme of the eternal duration of the Davidic dynasty is stated even more forcefully in the following poem (2 Sam 23:5). Thus in spite of the terrible sin with Bathsheba and the other shortcomings of David's career, the promise of an enduring house was still valid.

Appearing as they do at the beginning of the material, (roughly) the middle, and at the conclusion, the four poetic compositions cast a messianic shadow over the books of Samuel. One cannot read these passages without concluding that God had great things in store for the house of David: an everlasting covenant, an eternal throne, and a righteous king who ultimately would judge the very ends of the earth. The testimony of the New Testament is that such promises find their fulfillment in Jesus of Nazareth.

THE BOOKS OF KINGS
Glory and Decline of the Kingdom

The sixth and seventh books of the Old Testament have been designated by several different titles. Jews sometimes refer to these books by the initial Hebrew words *vehammelech David ("now King David")*. This designation is attested by Origen, the great church father of the third Christian century. The ancient Syriac version contained this cumbersome but very accurate title: *"The Book of the Kings who Flourished Among the Hebrews, Containing also the History of the Prophets who Flourished in their Times."* The Septuagint (Greek) translators dubbed this book *Kingdoms*. In the early Hebrew Bible the book was called *Kings*. English versions have generally adopted title 1 & 2 Kings, occasionally using as a subtitle 3 & 4 Kingdoms when the books of Samuel were designated 1 & 2 Kingdoms.

A. Background.

After twenty years or so of glory, David committed a trespass which altered the course of his reign. Because of the Bathsheba incident and the consequent murder of her husband David finished his reign under the cloud of God's chastisement. His son Absalom led a rebellion which forced David to flee temporarily into Transjordan. No sooner was that rebellion crushed, then another broke out led by a radical Benjamite named Sheba.

As 1 Kings opens, David was *"old and advanced in age"* and suffering from some malady which threatened his life. Unknown to him, his eldest son Adonijah was attempting to launch a coup which would depose David and sweep himself into power.

B. Circumstances of Writing.

In their present form the books of Kings could not have been written before 560 BC, for that is the date of the last historical incident narrated (2 Kgs 25:27-30). These last four verses may be an appendix to the original book, added perhaps by Ezra. If that is the case, the bulk of the Kings material was probably written shortly after the fall of Jerusalem in 586 BC.

The author of Kings is not known for sure. Jewish tradition
assigned the book to Jeremiah the prophet.[5] A remarkable affinity
exists between the language of Kings and that of the Book of Jeremiah. Even those who deny Jeremianic authorship would concede that
the author must have been a pupil of the great prophet.

C. Chronology of the Books.

The Book of Kings covers about four centuries of Israel's history,
from just before 971 BC to just after 562 BC. Excluding that material
which appears as an appendix at the end of the concluding chapter,
Kings covers the story of God's people from the accession of
Solomon to the destruction of Jerusalem. Stating the matter another
way, Kings begins (roughly) with the building of the temple and concludes with the burning of that same edifice.

The four centuries reviewed in Kings are clearly divided by the
author into three periods: (1) Solomonic kingdom (40 years); (2) sister
kingdoms (210 years); and (3) surviving kingdom (136 years). Chart
20 indicates the way in which the author has allocated his material to
these three periods.

Chart No. 20

THE CHRONOLOGY OF KINGS		
SOLOMON'S KINGDOM	SISTER KINGDOMS	SURVIVING KINGDOM
40 Yrs.	210 Years	136 Yrs.
David to Solomon	In Judah Rehoboam to Ahaz In Israel Jeroboam to Hoshea	Hezekiah to Zedekiah
11 Chs.	28 Chapters	8 Chs.
1 Kgs 1-11 ▼	1 Kings 12 — 2 Kings 17	▼ 2 Kgs 18-25
971 BC 930		722 586
David's Death Kingdom Divided		Samaria Fell Jerusalem Destroyed

Kings contains abundant chronological data. Two kinds of figures
are given in respect to the various kings. For most kings an absolute

figure of the total number of years of reign is given. The author usually has dated the beginnings of the reigns of the kings of one kingdom
in terms of the contemporary ruler in the sister kingdom. From the
earliest times devout scholars have been aware of a number of apparent discrepancies within these data.

Basically, the problems in the chronological notations are three in
number. First, sometimes the synchronous data disagrees with the
absolute regnal years of a monarch which are stated elsewhere.[6] Second, the sum of the regnal years for the kings of Israel for a given
period sometimes fails to tally with the years of the kings of Judah of
the same period.[7] Third, sometimes the chronological data in Kings
appears to be variance with the established chronology of the
Mesopotamian powers.[8]

Thanks to the extensive research of Edwin Thiele[9] most of the
chronological difficulties in Kings have been resolved satisfactorily. His
work is firmly grounded in the computational methods known to have
been used by ancient scribes. Coregencies, differences in the way the
accession "year" was computed,[10] and different calendars[11] are some
of the factors which must be taken into account when dealing with the
chronology of Kings.

D. Contents of the Books.

Kings does not manifest the variety of literary forms which other
Old Testament books display. The book is almost entirely written in
prose.[12] The two dominant forms are narrative and speech. To a lesser extent one finds lists, chronological notices, obituaries, building
specifications and even one bona fide fable (2 Kgs 14:9).

The plan of the books is primarily chronological, although occasionally the material is arranged topically. The topical arrangement is
readily apparent in 2 Kings 2:1-8:15 which treats the ministry of
Elisha.

One distinctive feature of Kings is not pleasant to the modern
reader. The reigns of many of the kings are introduced and concluded
with a somewhat stereotyped formula.

Chart No. 21

THE CONTENTS OF KINGS *"The Glory and Decline of the Kingdom"*				
FIRST KINGS		**SECOND KINGS**		
Solomonic Kingdom	Sister Kingdoms	Focus on N. Kingdom	Dual Focus	Focus on S. Kingdom
1 King 11	4 Kings South 7 Kings North 22	3 Kings 10	9 Kings N. 8 Kings S. 17	8 Kings 25
STRENGTH	STRUGGLE			STORM
United Kingdom	Divided Kingdom			Surviving Kingdom

E. Teaching of the Books.

The historians of Israel were prophets. History in their hands had "purpose," i.e., religious aim. Aided by the Holy Spirit, the author of Kings could see the hand of God at work in the period of the monarchy. The lessons which he wished to teach were spiritual, not political. For this reason he focuses on two crisis periods, viz., the reigns of Ahab in the north and Hezekiah in the south. He judges individual kings, not by their political achievements, but by their religious policies.

The building of the temple was of great significance to the author of Kings. This is immediately evident in the amount of space devoted to the construction of this holy edifice and the furnishings thereof. After that sanctuary was dedicated the author viewed all other worship centers *("high places")* as illegitimate. For this reason the author condemns the state-controlled Yahweh worship of the northern kingdom. From the day Jeroboam set up his golden calves in Bethel and Dan, the northern dynasties came under divine condemnation.

The author also attacked the infiltration of Baal worship in both kingdoms. Nearly one third of the material in Kings is devoted to the ministries of Elijah and Elisha, who labored mightily against Jezebelian Baalism in the northern kingdom. In miracle after miracle Yahweh demonstrated his superiority to Baal. In this large section of the book chronological and political narration is suppressed. The emphasis is on building up the remnant of the faithful.

Another concern of Kings is the Davidic monarchy. To the author, David was the standard by which all other kings were measured. The glorious promise of 2 Samuel 7—in the words of Keil—is the red thread which runs through the history of the kings from Solomon to the exile. Twenty descendants of David followed him on the throne in Jerusalem. Kings documents how God chastised the rulers of the Davidic dynasty. Yet *"for the sake of David my servant"* God continued to back the royal claims of this dynasty.

The author of Kings viewed the roles of the prophets as crucial in the history of the monarchy. Because of their teaching the people were without excuse in respect to their apostasy. By dwelling on the prophets the author magnifies the guilt of the people. He demonstrates that the destruction of Jerusalem and captivity of God's people were justified in spite of God's promise to David.

THE BOOKS OF CHRONICLES
Focus on David and his Dynasty

Jewish rabbis refer to Chronicles as *dibhre hayyamim,* "the affairs of the days." In the Septuagint (Greek) translation the book was called *Paraleipomenon* ("the things left out"). That name came over into the Latin Vulgate and the Douay, the first Catholic English version which was based on the Vulgate. Jerome (c. AD 400) suggested that Chronicles be called "A Chronicle of the Entire Sacred History." Modern English versions, whether Catholic or Protestant, employ the name *Chronicles.*

In the modern Hebrew Bible Chronicles is separated from the books of Samuel and Kings and placed in the *Kethubhim* or Writings. As a matter of fact, this book is the final book in the Hebrew Bible. In the Septuagint, however, Chronicles came after Kings, and that is the arrangement which has been followed in the English versions.

A. Background.

Like the Book of Ruth in the first triad of historical books, Chronicles is a "side-step" or focus book. It does not advance the history, but reiterates the history of the monarchy from a different perspective. In Chronicles the focus is on the Davidic dynasty. Information regarding the Northern Kingdom is incidental.

B. Circumstances of Writing.

After the captivity was over the remnant in Judah needed to be reminded of their heritage, the covenant, the temple, the dangers of apostasy, and the messianic hope through the Davidic line. The Jews of the post-captivity period needed every encouragement to rebuild their nation. Chronicles is a clear warning to the Jews never again to forsake the temple and the worship of the Living God.

The book then was written in the postexilic period. Chronicles was written from a priestly point of view. A continuity in substance, viewpoint and style with the Book of Ezra, suggests that the two books were written by the same person. Therefore, the Jewish tradition which assigns Chronicles to Ezra the priest and scribe is probably correct.

C. Chronology of the Books.

The genealogies of 1 Chronicles 1-9 stretch back to Adam and creation. Thus it can be said that Chronicles covers the longest period of any of the books of the Bible. Excluding these genealogies the first event narrated in Chronicles is the death of Saul in 1010 BC. The last event in the book is the edict of liberation issued by Cyrus in 538 BC. Thus Chronicles narrates 472 years of the history of God's people.[13]

Chart No. 22

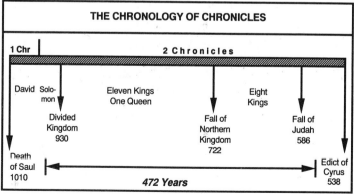

THE CHRONOLOGY OF CHRONICLES

1 Chr	2 Chronicles

David Solomon

Eleven Kings
One Queen

Eight Kings

Divided Kingdom 930

Fall of Northern Kingdom 722

Fall of Judah 586

Death of Saul 1010

Edict of Cyrus 538

472 Years

D. Contents of the Books.

Following a lengthy genealogical preface, Chronicles relates the history of Judah during the monarchy. Twenty chapters are devoted to David's reign, nine chapters to his son Solomon. During the Divided Monarchy period the author only gives notice to the northern kingdoms in situations where that kingdom interacted with Judah.

Chart No. 23

A casual reading of Chronicles suggests it is nothing more than a repetition of the contents of Samuel and Kings. This is familiar terrain. The stories of David, Solomon and their successors fill these pages. About one half of the material in Chronicles is repeated virtually verbatim from the earlier books. This book, however, is not Samuel and Kings warmed over. A closer examination indicates a number of differences which mark Chronicles as a distinctive work. This book has "a freshness and flavor" about it. When its purposes are understood, it furnishes "rich nourishment for theological thought."[14] The following chart tabulates those differences.

Chart No. 24

PERSPECTIVES ON ISRAEL'S HISTORY	
Samuel-Kings	**Chronicles**
1. More Biographical	1. More Statistical
2. More Personal	2. More Official
3. Prophetic Standpoint	3. Priestly Standpoint
4. Focus on Two Kingdoms	4. Focus on Judah Alone
5. Emphasis on the Throne	5. Emphasis on the Temple
6. Indictment of the Nation	6. Incitement of the Nation
7. Exposing Guilt	7. Encouraging Loyalty
8. Chronological Progression	8. Review Previous History
9. Political History	9. Religious History

The accuracy of Chronicles has frequently been called into question. The author is accused of exaggerating numbers, especially in regards to opposing armies. In 1 Chronicles 21:5, for example, Israel's army of 1,100,000 faced Judah's army of 470,000. The census of Joab a few years earlier gave the numbers of those two armies as 800,000 and 500,000 respectively. While the figures in Chronicles do occasionally seem extraordinarily high, they are not consistently higher than those which appear in Samuel and Kings. In five of seventeen cases of apparent discrepancy the numbers in Chronicles are lower. The differences in these numbers in parallel accounts is due to scribal errors or different methods of reckoning. These matters will be addressed further in the discussion of the individual passages.

Chronicles used as its main source the books of Samuel and Kings.

In addition the author names some twenty-five other sources which he consulted (e.g., 1 Chr 9:1; 2 Chr 27:7). In respect to the accuracy of the Chronicles version of Israel's history, the opinions of critics is mellowing to some degree. Though the author's method of presentation is somewhat homiletical, his story has been found to be accurate wherever it can be checked.[15]

E. The Teachings of the Books.

The purpose of Chronicles is to preserve the record of priestly worship from Saul to Cyrus. The book underscores the essential and central role of worship in the life of God's people. For the author the temple was (1) a symbol of the unity of the nation; (2) a reminder of the nation's high calling as a priestly people; (3) a sign that Yahweh was in the midst of his people; and (4) a standard by which national faithfulness could be measured.[16] Good kings loom large in these books, and good are those who led revivals and restored the temple.

The author of Chronicles lived in the post-monarchy period. The throne was gone, but God still had a purpose for his people. The fall of Babylon and the liberation edict of Cyrus fulfilled the predictions of Isaiah and Jeremiah. In spite of the exile Israel survived as a people. Furthermore, the prophetic promise for the future still remained. Even after the fall of Jerusalem the Davidic line was still intact, and the Messiah was to come from this line. The author was confident that the most glorious days of the Davidic dynasty were still in the future.

ENDNOTES

1. Probably Samuel was the source for most of what appears in 1 Sam 1-24; Gad for 1 Sam 24-2 Sam 5:3; and Nathan for 2 Sam 5:4-1 Kgs 3:28.

2. Brevard S. Childs, *Introduction to the Old Testament as Scripture* (Philadelphia: Fortress, 1979), pp. 271-77.

3. *Ibid.*, p. 275.

4. Analysis of the teaching of Samuel is based on Childs, *ibid.*, pp. 272-275.

5. Talmud, *Baba Bathra* 14b.

6. For example, Omri is said to begin to reign in the thirty-first year of Asa (1 Kgs 16:23). But the twelve year reign of Omri is said to end in the thirty-eighth year of Asa (1 Kgs 16:29).

7. Jehu of Israel and Athaliah of Judah both began to reign in 841 BC.

The city of Samaria fell to the Assyrians in the sixth year of Hezekiah of Judah (2 Kgs 18:10). The regnal years of the kings of Israel from Jehu to the fall of Samaria tallies 143 years. Yet the regnal years of the kings of Judah from Athaliah to the sixth year of Hezekiah tally 165 years, a discrepancy of 22 years.

8. The period from the accession of Jehu to the fall of Samaria in Assyrian chronology is 120 years. This figure is as much as 45 years out of kilter with the figures given in the previous note.

9. Edwin Thiele, *The Mysterious Numbers of the Hebrew Kings*, revised (Grand Rapids: Eerdmans 1965); *A Chronology of Hebrew Kings* (Grand Rapids: Zondervan, 1977).

10. The ancients had two different systems for counting the remaining months of the calendar year in which a king came to the throne. Sometimes they would call these months an accession year and not compute them as part of the regnal years of the king. At other times those few months were counted as a full year. The practice in Israel and Judah was not consistent over the course of the history of the two kingdoms.

11. The northern kingdom of Israel began its civil year in Nisan (in the spring), while the southern kingdom regarded Tishri (in the fall) to be the first month of the year.

12. The RSV prints only three passages in poetic verse.

13. W.F. Albright argues in favor of the Jewish tradition which sees Ezra as author of the books of Chronicles, Ezra and Nehemiah. "The Date and Personality of the Chronicler," JBL 40 (1921): 104-124.

14. William S. LaSor, David Hubbard, Frederic Bush, *Old Testament Survey* (Grand Rapids: Eerdmans, 1982), p. 630.

15. J.M. Myers, *1 Chronicles* in vol. 12 of "Anchor Bible" (Garden City, NY: Doubleday, 1965), p. LXIII.

16. J. Sidlow Baxter, *Explore the Book* (Grand Rapids: Zondervan, 1960) II, p. 172.

CHAPTER FIFTEEN

Transition to Monarchy
1 Samuel 1-7

Even before Samson began waging his personal warfare against the Philistines, another kind of Judge was ruling in Shiloh. Eli was the high priest of the nation as well as a Judge. He judged Israel for forty years (1145-1105 BC). He was followed in the judgeship by the prophet Samuel. His long judgeship of over forty years paved the way for the establishment of the monarchy.

In terms of national history, the first seven chapters of 1 Samuel revolve around two major events. The people of God reached their all-time low point when the ark of God was captured in battle. A dying mother made the most telling comment on this disaster when she whispered with her dying breath the name for her new son: "Ichabod," (the glory has departed)! (1 Sam 4:20). Twenty years later a grateful prophet shouted the name "Ebenezer" (stone of help) as he erected a monument to God's grace after Israel smashed the Philistines in battle. Thus Willmington is correct when he captions this unit of the book "From Ichabod to Ebenezer."[1] Samuel assumed leadership when Israel was in the pits of degradation. By bringing the people back to God he restored their national pride, power and purpose.

DEDICATION OF A CHILD
1 Samuel 1:1-2:11

While the conditions in the period of the Judges continued to deteriorate, God was preparing to write the next chapter in the thrilling story of redemption. In the sinful darkness of those days God found a godly woman through whom he would bring a great reformer into the world.

A. Hannah's Plight (1 Sam 1:1-8).

Elkanah was a Levite who lived in Ramathaim-zophim (Ramah) in the hill country of Ephraim. While basically a godly man, he had taken two wives. The notation that Hannah had no children suggests that her infertility had driven Elkanah to marry a woman (Peninnah) who could produce an heir (1:1-2).

Elkanah would take his family each year to the annual feast at the Shiloh tabernacle some eighteen miles north of Jerusalem. The trips were most painful for Hannah. Her husband showed his greater love for her by giving her an extra portion at the sacrificial meal. Peninnah, however, made life miserable for Hannah, using her fertility to lord it over her rival (cf. Gen 16:4; 30:1-24). Year after year the scene replayed itself. Peninnah would provoke her rival; Hannah would become so emotionally upset that she could not eat. Elkanah attempted to comfort his beloved wife. *"Am I not better than ten sons?"* he would say. While intending to cheer his wife, these words only made this desperate woman feel all the more her emptiness (1:3-8).

B. Hannah's Petition (1 Sam 1:9-19a).

While at Shiloh on one occasion Hannah finished the ritual meal. Near the entrance to the temple[2] she wept and poured out her heart to *"Yahweh of hosts."*[3] She approached him reverently as can be seen in her threefold reference to herself as *"handmaid"* of the Lord.

248

She vowed that if the Lord would give her a son, she would dedicate him all the days of his life as a Nazirite.[4] As she continued praying before the Lord, Eli the high priest, who was sitting by the doorpost of the temple, took note of her. Because Hannah was praying silently and only her lips were moving, Eli thought she was drunk. Tragic it is when a leader of God's people cannot recognize true piety when he sees it (1:9-13).

Since it was his high priestly duty to guard the courts of the sanctuary from desecration, Eli rebuked Hannah. He ordered her to *"put away"* her wine. Hannah replied firmly but politely. She had not been drinking wine. She was not *"a worthless woman,"* i.e., a woman without respect for sacred things. Rather she was oppressed in spirit; she was pouring out her heart to the Lord. Eli then dismissed Hannah with a blessing: *"May the God of Israel grant your petition."*[5] Hannah then returned to her meal. Because she was now confident that God would hear her petition, her face was sad no longer (1:14-18).

The eventful trip to Shiloh ended with a final time of worship. Then Elkanah took his family and returned to Ramah (1:19a).

C. Hannah's Presentation (1 Sam 1:19b-28).

Elkanah *"knew"* his wife, i.e., had marital relations with her. The Lord *"remembered"* Hannah, i.e., granted her petition. She conceived and bore a son. Hannah named the child Samuel, *"name of God."* She knew that this baby was truly an answer to prayer (1:19b-20).

At the next annual sacrifice Elkanah was prepared to offer *"his vow."* Unless repudiated by the husband, the vow of a wife became an obligation upon her husband. Hannah elected not to go to the sanctuary until she had weaned the child and could present him to the Lord. Under the Mosaic law a woman was not obligated to attend the annual festivals. Elkanah agreed that this would be the wisest course. He expressed aloud his prayer that the Lord would *"confirm his word,"* i.e., Yahweh would bring Hannah's vow to fruition (1:21-23).

Eastern women nursed their babies up to three years. When the child was weaned, Hannah took him and a generous offering to the sanctuary. The family first offered their sacrifice. Then Hannah presented the young boy to Eli. She reminded the priest of the incident some three years earlier when he had mistaken her earnest petition as drunken gibberish. Since God had answered her prayer, Hannah dedicated the lad to the Lord for as long as he lived. In gratitude Eli bowed in worship (1:24-28).

D. Hannah's Prayer (1 Sam 2:1-11).

When Hannah presented her son to Eli, she burst forth in a magnificent hymn-prayer inspired by the Holy Spirit. Yahweh is the central figure in this beautiful poem. She began on a most positive note. Hannah identified four sources of joy. First, she rejoiced in the personal deliverance from a life of misery which she had recently experienced (2:1). Second, Hannah rejoiced in the person of God—his holiness, his strength, and his knowledge (2:2-3). He is the Judge who weighs actions. Third, she rejoiced in the government of God (2:4-8). Hannah pointed out that often those who are rich, powerful and blessed are humbled. At the same time those who are poor, weak and dishonorable are suddenly exalted. The Lord *"brings low and exalts."* Over the long haul life has a way of evening out. Hannah's own experience is a prime example of this principle.

Fourth, Hannah rejoiced in her hope (2:9-10). The righteous are under the watch care of God; the wicked, however, are swallowed up in darkness when God withdraws the light of his grace. At this point Hannah's poem becomes predictive. She announces that ultimately God would (1) judge the whole world, (2) give strength to his king, and (3) exalt the horn or power of his anointed.[6] The context here of universal judgment suggests that the prophecy points to the Coming One, the Messiah.[7]

Following the presentation of Samuel at the tabernacle, Elkanah and his family returned to their home in Ramah. The lad Samuel, however, remained at Shiloh ministering to the Lord under the supervision of Eli the high priest (2:11).

DOOM OF ELI'S HOUSE
1 Samuel 2:12-4:1a

The narrator draws a stark contrast between the degeneracy of Eli's sons, and the spiritual growth of the young lad Samuel.

A. The Sins of the Priests (1 Sam 2:12-26).

The sons of Eli were *"sons of Belial,"* i.e., worthless men. Though they were priests of God, *"they did not know Yahweh"* in the experiential sense. Their brazen disregard for sacred ritual manifested itself in several ways. For example, they sent their servant to fish out of boiling cauldrons the priest's portion before the Lord had received his portion. Those who insisted that the Lord's portion should first be burned on the altar were threatened with violence. Thus these priests were treating the offerings of the Lord with contempt (2:12-17).

The boy Samuel was quite a contrast to the sons of Eli. He wore a linen ephod and ministered before the Lord. Each year his mother would make him a little robe and take it to Shiloh. Eli would pronounce a blessing on Hannah for having given Samuel to the Lord. Hannah's fertility continued. She bore three more sons and two daughters (2:18-21).

When Eli learned that his sons were having sexual relations with the women who served at the tabernacle, he tried to deal with them. He warned them that a sin against God was far more serious than a sin against man. The young men would not listen to the voice of their father. The sacred historian explains their intransigence as due to the fact that Yahweh desired to put them to death. Meanwhile Samuel was maturing and gaining favor with both the Lord and with men (2:22-26).

B. The Sentence Against the Priests (1 Sam 2:27-36).

An unnamed *"man of God"* or prophet came to Eli with an unpleasant message. He first reminded Eli of the tremendous privilege which was his to be a priest of God. The Lord had revealed himself to Aaron even before the Exodus. He had chosen the family of Aaron for the priestly honor. Eli, however, was responsible for the disrespect which was being shown for God's sacrifice at Shiloh. The priests at Shiloh were getting fat with the choicest pieces of the sacrificial offerings. Eli had honored his sons more than the Lord. As chief religious officer, he was ultimately responsible for all the evil which was being tolerated at Shiloh (2:27-29).

God indeed had promised the priesthood (*"walk before me"*) to the house of Eli and to Eli's father's house (the Aaronides). God, however, will only honor those who honor him. Thus fidelity is the implied condition attached to every promise God makes. So in the case of Eli, God announced punishment. First, God would *"cut off the strength"* of the priestly house, i.e. the sons of that family would die before honorable old age. Three times in the prophecy this point is stressed. Second, Eli would live to see the distress of God's dwelling, the tabernacle, i.e., the destruction of the place. Third, the priestly family would lose altar rights. Fourth, as a *"sign"* that the long range aspects of this prophecy would be fulfilled, Eli's two sons would both die on the same day (2:30-34).

To replace the Aaronide priesthood once it was cut off Yahweh would raise up a faithful priest. This future priest would carry out the will of God perfectly. To acknowledge his faithfulness, Yahweh would build him *"an enduring house"* or family, i.e., an eternal priesthood. Commentators generally conclude that the faithful priest was Samuel or Zadok. Samuel, however, if he was a priest in any sense, certainly did not have an enduring house. The slaughter of the priests at Nob (1 Sam 22:11-23) and Solomon's banishment of Abiathar, the last representative of the house of Eli, certainly fulfilled a portion of the prophecy made to Eli (cf. 1 Kgs 2:27). The anonymous prophet, however, predicted that the house of Eli's father (contextually, Aaron) would also be removed from office. Since Zadok was of the family of Aaron (cf. 1 Chr 6:1ff., 50ff.), he certainly did not fulfill that portion of the prophecy. The Aaronide priesthood was not totally removed from priestly office until the destruction of Jerusalem in AD 70. The faithful priest, then, was neither Samuel nor Zadok.

Who is the faithful priest of 1 Samuel 2:35? The prophecy is best interpreted messianically. The faithful priest is Jesus, God's anointed. For him God built a enduring house, the royal priesthood of 1 Peter 2:9. Before the Faithful Priest, a *"house"* or priestly family would *"walk"* or minister.[8] Members of the old Aaronic priesthood would have to bow before God's anointed, Messiah, if they would occupy a place of priestly service (2:35-36). When many of the Aaronide priests became obedient to the faith (Acts 6:7) this passage found ultimate fulfillment.

C. The Call of Samuel (1 Sam 3:1-18).

During the days when the sanctuary of Yahweh was at Shiloh

prophetic revelations, whether auditory or visionary, were rare. For this reason the narrative goes into some detail about the first revelatory experience of Samuel (3:1). Aged, blind Eli and the lad Samuel had retired for the night. Only the fading light of the lamp of God from within the Holy Place gave any illumination to the area where Samuel abode. Three times in the darkness Samuel heard the voice of God but mistook it for the voice of Eli. The narrator excuses this mistake by saying that Samuel did not yet know Yahweh experientially, nor had he received any revelation. Three times he rushed to the side of the old man. Finally Eli recognized that God was calling the boy. He instructed his protege to respond to any further call of his name by saying: *"Speak, O Yahweh, for your servant is listening"* (3:1-9).

Yahweh came to Samuel a fourth time *"and stood and called"* as at other times. The lad was experiencing what theologians call a theophany, a visual and auditory manifestation of the deity. Samuel responded on this occasion as Eli had instructed him (3:10).

What Samuel heard from the Lord was basically what the man of God had told Eli some time earlier. What God was about to do would make the ears of all who heard of it *"tingle."* The family of the old priest would fall under divine judgment because his sons had made themselves contemptible and Eli had failed to rebuke them.[9] The Lord had assured the house of Eli by oath that no sacrifice could atone for the sins they had committed (3:9-14).

Samuel lay down until the morning. He performed his usual chores, all the time trying to avoid a confrontation with Eli. He was afraid of hurting his beloved mentor should he be forced to divulge what he had learned during the night. Finally Eli sent for the lad and put him under a solemn curse if he withheld any part of the revelation. So Samuel told him everything. Eli accepted the disconcerting news with godly resignation. He knew Yahweh had revealed his will to Samuel. He believed that Yahweh would only do what was right. Therefore, he resigned himself to accept the verdict of God (3:15-18).

D. The Fame of Samuel (1 Sam 3:19-4:1a).

As Samuel grew to physical maturity, Yahweh was with him. The Lord let none of his words *"fall to the ground,"* i.e., go unfulfilled.

His fame spread throughout the land, from Dan in the far north, to Beersheba on the edge of the Negev in the south. Because his prophecies were constantly being fulfilled, the people recognized that he was confirmed as a prophet.[10] Yahweh continued to *"appear"* at Shiloh to Samuel. He revealed himself again and again *"by the word of Yahweh."* What a sharp contrast there is here between the fully accredited Samuel on the one hand, and the very old Eli and his wicked sons on the other.

DEFEAT OF ISRAEL
1 Samuel 4:1b-11

In the days of Eli the Israelites attempted to put an end to Philistine incursions into the land. When these enemies camped at Aphek, the Israelites formed their ranks nearby at Ebenezer about two miles east of Aphek. In the ensuing battle some four thousand[11] Israelites were slain *"in the field."* These last words suggest that the Israelites had held their ground in spite of the losses (4:1-2).

In the camp that night the Israelites concluded that the Lord had delivered them into the hands of the Philistines because the sacred ark had been left at Shiloh. So they sent to Shiloh for the ark. Hophni and Phinehas accompanied the ark back to the Israelite encampment (4:3-4).

The Israelite army greeted the arrival of the ark with thunderous jubilation. The Philistines soon learned the reason for the shouting, and they became fearful. They recognized the sacred box as guaranteeing the presence of God. These pagans knew the traditions of how the "gods" of the Israelites—the Philistines assumed the Israelites were polytheists—had smitten the mighty Egyptians with plagues. They feared lest now the lowly *"Hebrews"*[12] would gain the advantage over them and make them slaves. Therefore, with desperate determination they urged one another to fight all the harder (4:5-9).

Again the Philistines defeated Israel, this time inflicting over seven times the number of casualties (30,000) experienced in the first engagement. What was worse, the ark was captured, and the two sons of Eli were slain (4:10-11).

DEATH OF ELI
1 Samuel 4:12-22

A disheveled messenger brought the grim message to Shiloh from the battlefield some eighteen miles distant. The aged Eli, now ninety-eight, was sitting on a stool beside the road awaiting the results of the battle. He feared for the safety of the ark. When Eli heard the tumultuous outcry of the city, he inquired as to its cause. The messenger ran to the blind old man and blurted out the news with four hammer-like blows: (1) the Israelites had deserted the field; (2) the army had experienced heavy losses; (3) Eli's two sons had been killed; and (4) the ark had been captured. When he heard that the ark had been captured, Eli fainted or experienced a stroke. He fell backward off the stool, falling in such a way that his neck was broken. In this inglorious way the forty year judgeship of Eli came to an end (4:10-18).

The trauma of that day hastened the labor of Phinehas' wife. Through great difficulty she gave birth to a son. The neighbor women tried to calm the terrified woman with the news that she had given birth to a son. She, however, could only think of the great loss which both she and the nation had experienced that day. The high priest was dead. Her husband was dead. Israel had been humiliated by enemies. Worse still, the ark of God had fallen into pagan hands. With her last breath she whispered the name of the baby: *Ichabod* (lit., "glory has gone into captivity"). Ever after the name of this child would recall the day when the ark of God had departed from Israel (4:19-22).

DEFEAT OF DAGON
1 Samuel 5:1-12

Though the Philistines had defeated Israel twice on the field of battle, a confrontation on a different level was about to take place. Israel's God would now show himself superior to the chief god of the Philistines.

The ark of God was deposited in the temple of Dagon in Ashdod (cf. Judg 16:23). In the morning the priests of Dagon discovered that the statue of their god had fallen on its face to the ground before the ark of God. So the priests set Dagon in his place again. The second morning the priests rose *early*—they must have been concerned for the welfare of their god—to find the statue of their god in the same position, except this time the head and hands of the image had broken off at the threshold of the shrine.[13] Dagon was reduced to a stump without a head for thinking or hands for acting. For that reason no one thereafter would step on the threshold of that temple lest they defile the place where pieces of the statue of Dagon had lain. The main point here is that Yahweh defeated Dagon in his own temple. The memory of that humiliation was perpetuated in this religious superstition for generations (5:1-5).

The hand of Yahweh (i.e., his power) was heavy against any Philistine city where the ark lodged. The Lord *"ravaged"* (NASB) or *"brought devastation on them"* (NIV). The same verb is used for the destruction of vines and fig trees in Hosea 2:12.[14] The Lord smote the men of Ashdod with tumors. Because of the connection of the tumors with rodents (cf. 6:4-5, 17-18), many scholars think that some form of bubonic plague spread throughout the land (5:6-7).[15]

When the Ashdodites complained to the lords of the Philistines, they were directed to take the ark to Gath. Again Yahweh smote the men of the city, both the young and the old, with the tumors. When the ark approached Ekron, the citizens of that place feared for their lives. The deadly plague broke out there just as in Ashdod and Gath earlier. Many died. Those who did not suffered with tumors. The Ekronites were panic stricken. They petitioned the lords of the land to return the ark to Israel. At the same time the agonizing cry of the city *"went up to heaven."* This narrative underscores the point that Yahweh was master even in Philistine territory (5:8-12).

DISASTER AT BETH-SHEMESH
1 Samuel 6:1-7:2

After seven months of tumult, the Philistines had had enough of the ark. They consulted their diviners as to the proper method of returning the ark to its rightful place in Israel. If the plague was to be removed, the Philistines needed to send a guilt offering along with the ark as reparation to appease the God whose anger had been unleashed against them. Five golden *"tumors"* would magically grant relief from the terrible disease which plagued the land.[16] They should be accompanied by five golden mice, in the likeness of the mice which ravished the land. By so doing the Philistines would be giving glory to God and thereby making it possible for him to withdraw his hand from them. The diviners urged the lords of the Philistines not to be more hardened of heart than Pharaoh who eventually allowed Israel to depart from his land. Ancient peoples often feared the gods of other peoples, even those of their enemies (6:1-6).

The pagan diviners suggested a method by which the lords of the Philistines could determine whether their national misfortune was simply a natural disaster, or whether it was due to the judgment of God. Two cows were separated from their calves and hitched to a cart, a *new* cart which had not been defiled by secular labor. The ark was placed on the cart. Alongside the ark was a box containing the guilt offering of golden tumors and mice. They then put the cart on the road to the nearest Israelite town of Beth-shemesh. Rather than turn back to their calves, the cows went straight down the road lowing as they went under divine compulsion away from their calves. They turned neither to the right nor to the left. The lords of the Philistines followed the cart to the borders of Beth-shemesh, some ten miles east of Ekron. This guaranteed that no one would tamper in any way with the experiment. The unnatural behavior of the cows convinced them that the disaster which had befallen their land was not mere chance. The hand of Yahweh had smitten the Philistines. Ironically the test proposed by the Philistine diviners only gave Yahweh another opportunity to demonstrate his power (6:7-12).

The farmers of the Levitical village of Beth-shemesh rejoiced when they saw the ark. The cows stopped near a large stone in the field of one named Joshua. The Levites removed the ark and placed it on the large stone. A fire was built with the wood of the cart. The cows were slaughtered and offered to Yahweh as burnt offerings. Other sacrifices apparently were also offered. From a distance the lords of the Philistines looked on as the box containing their guilt offering was opened. There the Israelites found five golden mice and five golden tumors representing the Philistine Pentapolis: Ashdod, Gaza, Ashkelon, Gath and Ekron. The large stone where the ark had been

257

placed became a kind of national monument, a witness to the day the when the ark came home (6:13-18).

At this point the narrative takes a surprising turn. In their exuberance over the return of the ark, the men of Beth-shemesh made a serious mistake. They looked into the ark. Their motives may have been innocent enough. They probably wished to see if the Philistines had removed any of the memorial objects which were contained in the ark. Nonetheless, looking into the ark with profane curiosity was strictly forbidden (cf. Num 4:20). So Yahweh smote the people of the area with a great slaughter. The leaders of Beth-shemesh quickly sent to Kiriath-jearim to ask them to come and take away the ark (6:19-21).

The number of people affected by the plague at Beth-shemesh is in dispute. Actually the Hebrew text contains two numbers side by side, seventy and fifty thousand. NIV chooses the smaller figure, apparently regarding the fifty thousand as a gloss. NASB follows the Septuagint in combining these numbers into one figure, 50,070.[17]

Kiriath-jearim was ten miles northeast of Beth-shemesh and nine miles west of Jerusalem. The men of this village showed great faith and reverence by coming and removing the ark. The sacred chest was housed on the property of Abinadab. Eleazar, the son of Abinadab, was consecrated to care for the ark. For twenty years the Israelites lamented after Yahweh (7:1-2).

Chart No. 25

The ark remained in Kiriath-jearim for several decades. Probably it was not returned to Shiloh because that place had been defiled if not destroyed by the Philistines.[18] As far as the record is concerned the ark disappeared from national life. Even when the tabernacle was reconstructed and located at Nob, the ark remained at Kiriath-jearim. The extent to which the ark played any role in the religious life of Israel cannot be determined. Only after David had established Jerusalem as his capital did the ark surface again as an important object in Israelite worship.

REVIVAL AND VICTORY
1 Samuel 7:3-17

After twenty years of spiritual malaise,[19] Samuel sensed that the time was right for revival. He called upon his people to return to Yahweh with all of their heart. If they would remove the foreign gods including the popular female idols of Ashtaroth, and if they would serve Yahweh alone, the Lord would deliver them from the hand of the Philistines. Samuel's message struck a responsive chord. The Israelites removed the Baals and their female counterparts. They devoted themselves exclusively to Yahweh. Samuel then called for all Israel to assemble at Mizpah where he promised to pray for them (7:3-5).

The Mizpah meeting, some eight miles north of Jerusalem, was one of the great revivals in Biblical history. The people fasted that day. To symbolize the surrender of their entire beings, they drew water and poured it out before the Lord.[20] They confessed their sins. They recognized the authority of Samuel by allowing him to *"judge"* them (7:6).

The lords of the Philistines regarded this show of national unity in Israel as a threat to their hegemony. They came out against Israel in full force. The news of the Philistine approach struck terror in the hearts of the Israelites. They begged Samuel to keep on crying to Yahweh on their behalf that he might save them. Samuel immediately offered up a lamb as a whole burnt offering to Yahweh. The sacrifice was accompanied by earnest petition which Yahweh immediately answered (7:7-9).[21]

As Samuel was offering his sacrifice, the Philistines were forming their battle lines. Yahweh thundered against the attackers with a great thunder. The Philistines were thrown into confusion. They fled before the men of Israel. The Israelites pursued and struck the enemy all the way to Beth-car (7:10-11).

Chart No. 26

THE LIFE OF SAMUEL *Proposed Chronology*			
EVENT	DATE BC	YEARS	AGE
Birth	1118		
Shiloh Destroyed	1105		13
Ark at Kiriath-jearim		➤ 20 Yrs.	
Mizpah Revival	1085		33
Samuel Judges		➤ 42 Yrs.	
Saul Anointed	1043		75
Advisor to Saul		➤ 11 Yrs.	
David Anointed	1033		86
Retirement		➤ 19 Yrs.	
Death	1014		105

To commemorate the victory over the Philistines Samuel erected a monument between Mizpah and Shen. The stone was named Ebenezer, "stone of help." That victory marked the beginning of Israelite resurgence. All the days of Samuel the Philistines never again were successful in invading the territory of Israel *"for the hand of Yahweh"* was against them. Cities which had been lost to the Philistines were recovered. The ascendancy of Israel also caused the Amorites who lived within the borders of Israel to cease their hostilities (7:12-14).

Thus, Samuel the man of prayer was able to accomplish what Samson the man of strength could not accomplish. The prophet judged all Israel all the days of his life. His judicial circuit, however, was limited to a relatively small area of central Palestine. He moved about in a circuit from Bethel to Gilgal to Mizpah and back to his home at Ramah. In these places he *"judged"* Israel. At Ramah Samuel built an altar to Yahweh. The text thus hints that Ramah became the center of national worship.

ENDNOTES

1. Harold Willmington, *Willmington's Survey of the Old Testament* (Wheaton, IL: Victor Books, 1987), p. 214.

2. The term *doorpost of the temple* (1 Sam 1:9) suggests that some kind of permanent structure had been constructed perhaps to protect the ancient tent of meeting from the elements.

3. The title *Yahweh of hosts* appears here for the first time in the Bible. The title is used ten times in the books of Samuel, and one additional time as *Yahweh God of hosts* (2 Sam 5:10). The name Yahweh contains the Hebrew root which means "to be." Some understand the name to mean "He who exists" or "the Eternal;" others take it to mean "He who causes to exist" or "the Creator." The *"hosts"* may be the armies of Israel, armies of angels, the stars of the heavens, or all of the above. The combination *"Yahweh of hosts"* stresses the supreme authority of Yahweh as well as his omnipotence.

4. Nazirites were bound by three rules. They could not consume any product of the fruit of the vine, touch a corpse, or cut their hair (Num 6).

5. The blessing of Eli could be interpreted as a firm promise if the verb is parsed as an imperfect: *"The God of Israel will grant your request which you have asked of him."*

6. This is the first use of the term *mashiach* (Messiah) in the Old Testament.

7. For a discussion of the messianic implications of Hannah's prediction see James E. Smith, *What the Bible Says about the Promised Messiah* (Joplin: College Press, 1984), pp. 76-78.

8. That which walks before God's anointed in 1 Sam 2:35 is not the faithful priest, but his *"house."* The latter is the nearest antecedent to the third person masculine pronoun. To *"walk before"* means to serve or minister as in 2:30. Hence, the *"house"* of the Faithful Priest ministers or serves under his scrutiny or supervision. For a detailed discussion of the messianic interpretation of the passage, see James E. Smith, *What the Bible Says about the Promised Messiah* (Joplin: College Press, 1984), pp. 78-82.

9. Obviously God did not regard what Eli said to his sons in 2:22-25 as a rebuke, or at least as an effective rebuke. The only rebuke that would have been acceptable would have been to remove the two brothers from the priestly office.

10. No unanimity exists among scholars as to the etymological significance of the term *nabhi'* ("prophet"). In context here, however, the meaning is clear. A prophet is one who received revelation from God and who, on the basis of that revelation, was able accurately to predict the future.

11. P.K. McCarter understands the word *'eleph*, usually translated "thousand," to be a technical name for a military unit of undetermined size. *I Samuel* in "The Anchor Bible" (Garden City, NY: Doubleday, 1980), p. 107. If an *'eleph* consisted of thirty troops, for example, the losses here would be four times thirty or 120 men. While this approach to the battle figures in the Old Testament is possible in some passages, the methodology is not capable of consistent application.

12. The significance of the term "Hebrew" is unclear. Most occurrences are in discourse spoken by or addressed to non-Israelites. Many see in the term a derogatory nuance. The term is consistently ethnic and thus does not refer to foreign mercenaries or outlaws as some have suggested. See M.G. Kline, s.v., "Hebrews" in *New Bible Dictionary,* second ed. (Wheaton, IL: Tyndale House, 1982), pp. 466-67.

13. Decapitation was the ultimate humiliation inflicted in ancient warfare (1 Sam 17:51; 31:9). Ralph Klein thinks that the hands on the threshold symbolized that Dagon was seeking refuge in his own temple. Thus the loss of head and hands indicates Dagon's utter capitulation to Yahweh. *1 Samuel* in "Word Biblical Commentary" (Waco, TX: Word, 1983), p. 50.

14. Howard Vos, *1,2 Samuel* in "Bible Study Commentary" (Grand Rapids: Zondervan, 1983), pp. 28f.

15. The bubonic plague is characterized by swellings in the lymph glands especially in the groin and armpit. Other interpretations: boils or abscesses at the anus; sores resulting from dysentery (Josephus); hemorrhoids (Masoretes).

16. A general principle among the ancients was that like cured like. At the ancient site of Corinth visitors may view an entire museum gallery full of statuary of diseased body parts sent to the temple of Asclepius, the god of medicine and healing, as offerings.

17. In his *Encyclopedia of Biblical Difficulties,* Gleason Archer argued for the smaller number as the original reading of the passage. He points out that (1) the customary Hebrew word order is not used in expressing the figure 50,070; (2) Josephus (*Ant.* VI.i.4) refers to the loss of life at Beth-shemesh as only seventy, with no mention whatever of the fifty thousand; (3) a few Hebrew manuscripts entirely omit the fifty thousand; and (4) given the size of the village of Beth-shemesh the lower figure is probably the original. No one, however, has given a credible explanation of how the fifty thousand figure crept into the text.

18. The Psalmist (Ps 78:60) and Jeremiah allude to the destruction of the sanctuary at Shiloh (Jer 26:6,9). Excavations at Shiloh indicate that the place was destroyed about the middle of the eleventh century BC, during the time of Philistine hegemony over Israel.

19. Vos, *op. cit.,* p. 32.

20. Pouring out the heart like water is an expression of sorrow in Lam 2:19. The woman of Tekoa regarded water poured on the ground to indicate utter defeat (2 Sam 14:14).

21. The role of Samuel as intercessor is emphasized by the notation that *he* cried unto Yahweh rather than that the people cried as is usual in the Book of Judges.

CHAPTER SIXTEEN

A King Like All the Nations
1 Samuel 8-12

The Mizpah revival and subsequent victory over the Philistines
(1 Sam 7) were the highlights of Samuel's long judgeship. These
events occurred about 1085 BC. The anointing of Saul took place
about 1043 BC. Some four decades are passed over in silence in the
text. In 1 Samuel 8 the great prophet appears advanced in years.

ISRAEL'S DEMAND PRESENTED
1 Samuel 8:1-22

In his old age Samuel made a tragic mistake. He appointed his two
sons, Joel and Abijah, to judgeships in Beersheba some fifty miles
southwest of Jerusalem.[1] Apparently he was trying to make the office
of Judge hereditary. Samuel's sons, however, did not walk in the righteous path of their father. Out from under his watchful eye they
turned aside after dishonest gain, and took bribes to pervert judgments (8:1-3).

263

The elders of Israel used Samuel's sons as a pretext for demanding a king. They came to Ramah to request that Samuel appoint for them a king *"like all the nations."* God had promised to give his people kings (Gen 17:16; 35:11). The law of Moses anticipated the day when Israel would have a king (Deut 17:14-20). Nevertheless, the request offended the prophet. He interpreted it as a rejection of his life and ministry. So Samuel did what all wounded souls should do. He went to the Lord in prayer (8:4-6).

Yahweh instructed Samuel to listen to the voice of the people. They had not rejected the judgeship of Samuel, but the kingship of God (cf. Judg 8:22-23). This was but another example of the spiritual rebellion manifested by Israel ever since God had brought them out of Egypt. While Samuel was to yield to the request for a king, he was first to go on record with a warning of what kingship would mean in Israel (8:7-9).

Samuel spoke all the words of Yahweh to the people. He warned them of five actions which they could expect from their king: (1) conscription for military service (vv. 11-12); (2) seizure of private property (v. 14); (3) the corvée, a kind of labor tax (vv. 12,16); (4) impressment of persons into royal service (vv. 13,16); and (5) heavy (ten percent!) taxation (vv. 15,17). Ultimately all Israelites would be servants of the crown. Then, Samuel warned, the people would cry to Yahweh for relief because of the king which they were now demanding. The Lord, however, would not respond to their prayer in that day (8:10-18).

In spite of the very negative portrayal of kingship, the people insisted that a king should rule over them as in surrounding nations. Their king would be a Judge and a leader in battle as well. Samuel repeated all the words of the people to the Lord. Yahweh authorized Samuel to appoint a king for Israel. After assuring the people that they would get their king, Samuel dismissed the assembly to their respective cities (8:19-22).

ISRAEL'S REQUEST GRANTED
1 Samuel 9:1-10:27

Though the people indicated the kind of king they desired, they left the appointment of the candidate up to God's prophet.

A. Saul Selected (1 Sam 9:1-25).

The narrator next introduces the man whom God had selected as Israel's first king. First, Saul was from Benjamin, smallest of the tribes. Leaders of the larger tribes would view this selection as a happy compromise designed to eliminate tribal jealousies. Second, he was from a prominent family. This is indicated by the inclusion of a brief genealogical record in the text. Third, Saul's father Kish was *"a mighty man of valor."* The reference is not so much to his physical strength as to the power which comes through wealth or influence. Fourth, Saul had outstanding physical attributes. He was handsome and he was tall, in fact taller than any of the people (9:1-2). The elders desired a king like all the nations. In ancient pictures of royalty the king is usually depicted as taller than any of his subjects.

A curious set of circumstances resulted in the initial contact between Samuel and Saul. Kish had dispatched his son from Gibeah, three miles north of Jerusalem, to search for some lost donkeys.[2] A wide-ranging search through several districts in central Palestine did not locate the lost animals. Saul was ready to give up the search lest his father become anxious over his whereabouts. His servant, however, suggested that Saul consult the local *"man of God"* about the donkeys. This man of God had a reputation for accurate prediction. Saul thought the servant's suggestion was a good one. He pointed out, however, a problem. The provisions were exhausted. There was nothing suitable to serve as the customary offering—an interview fee— to the man of God for his services. Fortunately, the servant had a fourth of a shekel of silver. Since coins were not used until much later in Israel's history, this quarter shekel was a weight. For that amount the man of God[3] would be willing to give prophetic advice. Saul and his servant then set out for nearby Ramah, the city of Samuel (9:3-10).

As they approached the city the two travelers met some young women going out to draw water. They learned that Samuel was scheduled to officiate at a sacrificial meal that very day. The people were waiting on him to arrive, for they would not begin the festivities without his blessing. The women advised the two men to intercept the prophet on his way to the *"high place"* where only invited guests would be permitted to assemble. As Saul and his servant proceeded toward the city, they met Samuel on his way up to the *"high place"* (9:11-14).

Yahweh prepared Samuel for his meeting with Saul. The previous day the Lord had revealed (lit., uncovered his ear) that within twenty-four hours he would send to Samuel *"a man from the land of Benjamin."* This man was to be anointed *"prince"* and be given the commission to save the people from the Philistines. When the prophet saw Saul, Yahweh made the identification even more specific. This was the man who would rule over (lit., keep within bounds) God's people (9:15-17).

Saul approached Samuel to inquire where the seer lived. Obviously he had never met the prophet before. Samuel identified himself. He then invited Saul to the *"high place"* as his personal guest. Before Saul had an opportunity to mention the problem of the lost donkeys, the prophet assured him that they had been found. Samuel thus demonstrated to Saul his supernatural knowledge. Then he asked two cryptic questions to pique the curiosity of Saul. *"To whom is all the desire of Israel? Is is not to you and to all the house of your father?"* The meaning is simple. Saul would be the one who would fulfill the desire of Israel for a king. He was the chosen one. Saul sensed that some great honor was being announced. However, he could not understand why Samuel would speak to him in this manner. He was from Benjamin, the smallest tribe, and even within that tribe his father's family had little standing (9:18-21).

The communal meal over which Samuel presided that day functioned as an anticipation of a coronation banquet. Saul was treated royally. He was seated in the most honored place at the head of the thirty invited guests. Then a choice portion of meat was set before him. Samuel told him that this portion had been reserved for him since the day this special feast had been announced. Samuel hinted that the whole purpose of the meal was to honor Saul! That night Saul was a guest at Samuel's home (9:22-25). All of this was designed to prepare Saul for the great announcement to be made the following day.

B. Saul Anointed (1 Sam 9:26-10:16).

Early in the morning, Samuel aroused Saul from his sleep on the

266

flat roof of the prophet's home. He walked with Saul and his servant to the edge of the city. There the servant was dismissed, so that Samuel might declare the word of God to Saul privately. The prophet then took a flask of oil and poured in on Saul's head, kissed him on the cheek, and explained these actions with a rhetorical question: *"Is it not so that Yahweh has anointed you as a prince over his inheritance?"* The term *"prince"* (*naghid*) in this context probably means something like "crown prince" or "king designate" (9:26-10:1).

Three supernatural signs would confirm that Saul's anointing indeed had been ordained by Yahweh. First, Saul would encounter two men near Rachel's tomb who would report that the donkeys had been found and that Saul's father was worried about his whereabouts. Second, he would meet three men at the oak of Tabor who were on their way to worship at Bethel carrying various items to be offered as sacrifice. One of these strangers would greet Saul, and give him two of the three loaves of bread he was carrying. Third, at the hill of God where a Philistine garrison was stationed Saul would meet a group of prophets coming down from a *"high place,"* playing their musical instruments and *"prophesying."*[4] In their presence Saul would be overwhelmed by the Spirit of Yahweh. His whole personality would be changed and he too would join in the vigorous prophetic praise of God. These three signs would assure Saul that God was with him in a special way (10:3-7).

Guided by God, Saul was to do for himself what the occasion required. The reference most likely is to the Philistine menace, for this seems to form the background for the demand for a king (cf. 9:16). One restriction was placed on Saul as he exercised his God-guided military leadership. Before he initiated hostilities against the Philistines, he was to go down to Gilgal in the Jordan valley and wait seven days for Samuel. The prophet intended to do two things: (1) to offer sacrifices; and (2) show Saul what he should do. The campaign to deal with the Philistines must be launched with divine blessing and prophetic guidance (10:8).

As Saul turned to leave Samuel, *"God changed his heart."* The three signs announced by Samuel came about that very day. The Spirit of God rushed upon him thus indicating that Saul was a deliverer like the Judges before him (cf. Judg 11:29; 14:6 etc.). The quiet

country boy became a vigorous public proclaimer of praise to Yahweh, and that right in the shadow of a Philistine garrison (cf. v. 5).
People who previously knew Saul were astonished that one so shy
would now be drawn to a band of religious enthusiasts. A bystander
rebuked the shocked observers by means of the question, *"Who is
their father?"* The question suggests that one is not born a prophet.
God's Spirit is what compelled men to join the prophetic band (10:9-
13).[5]

When Saul reached home, his uncle questioned him about his long
absence. In the light of the context of 1 Samuel this uncle was most
likely Abner who later became the general of Israel's army. Saul
briefly rehearsed the events of the past few days, but he did not vol-
unteer information about the matter of the kingdom (10:14-16).

C. Saul Presented (1 Sam 10:17-27).

One may assume that Samuel called for the people to *"gather to
Yahweh at Mizpah"* very soon after the private anointing at Ramah.
The old prophet opened the assembly with a brief speech in which he
reminded the audience of all that God had done for them in the deliverance from Egyptian bondage and oppressions by neighboring
nations. By taking the initiative in demanding a king, the people had
rejected the God who had delivered them from all their past calamities. Nevertheless, Samuel ordered the people to present themselves
before Yahweh by their tribes and clans (10:17-19).

Though the mechanics of the sacred lot in Old Testament times
are not known, certainly the process was controlled by Yahweh. In
the person of their representatives, all the tribes of Israel one by one
drew near to Samuel. Presumably the tribe of Benjamin, descended
from the youngest of Jacob's twelve sons, was last. The lot indicated
that Yahweh had chosen this tribe. Then the representatives of the
clans of Benjamin drew near to Samuel and the Matrite clan was chosen. At this point the names of all the heads of families within the
Matrite clan where perhaps placed on potsherds. By lot Saul the son
of Kish was selected. When they looked for Saul, however, he could
not be found. Further inquiry of Yahweh through the prophet Samuel
revealed that Saul was hiding by the baggage (10:20-22).

Leaders hastened to bring Saul from his hiding place. When Saul stood among the people he was head and shoulders taller than any of his countrymen. Physically Saul qualified to be the kind of king Israel wanted. Samuel made sure that the audience understood that the unusual proceedings of that day were Yahweh's means of making known his selection for Israel's king.[6] The people ratified the appointment by shouting the traditional *"Long live the king"* (10:23-24).

Samuel then set forth *"the judgment of the kingdom,"* i.e., the constitutional, historical and spiritual basis for the monarchy in Israel. This material was written by the prophet in *"the scroll."* The reference may be to the scroll of Scripture which Samuel was now expanding.[7] The scroll was then placed *"before Yahweh,"* i.e., in a sacred shrine, perhaps even before the ark of God. This act recognized that the written words of Samuel possessed divine authority like Moses and Joshua before him (10:25).

When Samuel dismissed the people from Mizpah, Saul returned to Gibeah. Some valiant men *"whose hearts God had touched"* went with him. Certain *"sons of Belial,"* i.e., worthless men, mocked the appointment of the timid farmer from Gibeah. They despised him and brought him no gift in token of submission to his authority. Saul wisely refused to take action against his critics. He knew that he would have the opportunity soon enough to prove his mettle (10:26-27).

Chart No. 27

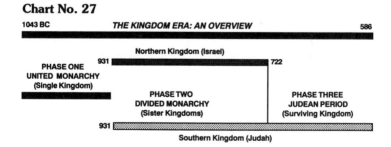

1043 BC   *THE KINGDOM ERA: AN OVERVIEW*   586

Northern Kingdom (Israel)

PHASE ONE | 931 ... 722
UNITED MONARCHY
(Single Kingdom)

PHASE TWO   PHASE THREE
DIVIDED MONARCHY   JUDEAN PERIOD
(Sister Kingdoms)   (Surviving Kingdom)

931
Southern Kingdom (Judah)

GOD'S CHOICE VINDICATED
1 Samuel 11:1-15

The test for Saul's leadership unexpectedly came, not from the

Philistines to the west, but from the Ammonites across the Jordan. Nahash besieged the Israelite outpost of Jabesh in the region of Gilead.[8] Realizing that they had no chance of successfully resisting the siege, the men of Jabesh expressed willingness to become vassals of the Ammonite. Nahash, however, was not willing to settle for this type of submission. He wanted to inflict a humiliating defeat upon this Israelite town. Only if the men of Jabesh would allow Nahash to gouge out their right eyes would he be willing to enter into a covenant with them.[9] He wanted to make Jabesh *"a reproach"* in all Israel (11:1-2).[10]

When they realized that Nahash was in no mood to negotiate, the elders of Jabesh requested a seven-day reprieve so that they might seek deliverance from other tribes. Nahash was so confident of the political disarray of Israel that he actually granted the request of the elders. Even if other tribes should respond to the plea of Jabesh, Nahash was confident that he would be able to defeat the Israelites (11:3).

The messengers headed straight for Saul's town of Gibeah. Apparently few, if any, of the trappings of royalty marked the earliest days of the monarchy in Israel. Saul was out working with his oxen in the fields when the messengers arrived. The people of Gibeah lamented loudly when they heard the news from Jabesh.

When Saul learned of the brutal demands of Nahash, *"the Spirit of God"* rushed upon him.[11] As a result he was filled with righteous anger. Whereas in other contexts the blowing of a horn mustered the tribes for a holy war, Saul determined that more dramatic action was necessary. He dismembered a yoke of oxen and sent the pieces throughout the territory of Israel by messengers, perhaps the same messengers who had come from Jabesh. The chunks of meat were to be visual aids to reinforce the the first royal edict. If any man failed to report for military duty to follow Saul and Samuel, his oxen would be slaughtered (cf. Judg 19:29-30) Mentioning Samuel's name in this call to arms indicates the insecurity which Saul felt in his royal rank at this period (11:4-7).

This dramatic action put the fear of Yahweh in the men of Israel. They assembled as one man to Bezek, the town near the Jordan which had been designated as the staging area for the Jabesh operation. There Saul numbered and organized his men. From Judah 30,000 men had responded, and from the other tribes 300,000 (11:8).

The messengers from Jabesh were sent back with the glad news that deliverance was at hand. By the time the sun got hot the next day, the army of Israel would be there to rescue them. The men of Jabesh immediately sent word to Nahash that they would surrender themselves to him the following day and he could then do with them whatever he had determined to do. This report no doubt lulled Nahash into a false sense of security. He most likely took no ordinary military precautions to prevent a surprise attack (11:9-10).

During the night the Israelite forces drew near. Saul organized his troops into three units, probably to facilitate a pinchers movement against the enemy.[12] Sometime during the morning watch (2 AM to 6 AM) the attack was launched. The battle turned out to be a slaughter of Ammonites. Only a few stragglers survived (11:11).

The brilliant and decisive defeat of the Ammonites convinced everyone that Saul indeed was the right choice for king. The people came to Samuel—he apparently had accompanied the troops to Jabesh—to urge that those who had vocally opposed Saul's anointing now be executed. Saul, however, would have none of that. Yahweh had granted deliverance in Israel. This was no day for recrimination, but for celebration. Samuel agreed. Capitalizing on the current enthusiasm, Samuel urged the people to assemble in the ancient shrine of Gilgal to "renew the kingdom," i.e., to give everyone an opportunity to express their support for Saul. So the people went to Gilgal and "made Saul king" before Yahweh. Burnt offerings and peace offerings were presented to the Lord. Unlike the Mizpah meeting which ended in mixed opinion about Saul a few months (?) earlier, at the Gilgal assembly Saul and all the men of Israel rejoiced together greatly (11:12-15).

THE EXPLANATION OF ISRAEL'S GUILT
1 Samuel 12:1-25

At the Gilgal assembly Samuel delivered his valedictory. In so doing he resigned, in effect, from the office of Judge. The speech is interspersed with responses from the people and the description of a manifestation of God, a theophany.

A. A Testimony for Samuel (1 Sam 12:1-5).
In the prologue to his speech, Samuel elicited from the people an acknowledgement that the integrity of his leadership had not been compromised. First, he mentioned the fact that he had done what they had asked him to do, *viz.*, he had appointed a king for them. Their king was now *"walking before"* them, i.e., installed in office. Second, he refers to himself as *"old and gray,"* perhaps suggesting that it was time for him to step down from his role of political leader. Third, he made reference to his sons who are *"with you."* Perhaps this was a father's way of admitting the painful truth that his sons were not in fact worthy of succeeding their father in the office of Judge (cf. 1 Sam 8:3,5). Fourth, he reminds them of his lengthy service to the nation *"from my youth even to this day."* Samuel had *"walked before"* them, i.e., he had been a public figure his entire life (12:1-2).

Samuel then challenged the audience to bear witness against him if they knew of any situation in which he had abused his power as Judge by taking bribes or defrauding citizens. The assembly unanimously agreed that Samuel had never abused his office in any way. Then Samuel in effect made the people swear before Yahweh and his anointed Saul that they could find no ill-gotten gain in his hand (12:3-5).

B. A Testimony for the Lord (1 Sam 12:6-12).
Samuel devoted a major part of his address to demonstrating the many *"righteous acts"* which Yahweh had performed for his people. When the Israelites cried out in the midst of Egyptian bondage, Yahweh raised up Moses and Aaron to bring them out of the land of oppression. The Lord settled his people in Canaan. When, however, they proved time and again to be unfaithful to him, Yahweh would deliver them into the hands of oppressing nations. In each of those oppressions the people would cry out to Yahweh, confessing their sins and begging for deliverance. The Lord responded by sending Jerubbaal (Gideon), Bedan (Barak?), Jephthah and Samuel to deliver

Israel from the hand of their foreign oppressors.

The request for a king had been triggered by the oppression of Nahash the Ammonite.[13] Instead of trusting God to supply deliverance, the people had resolved to find their own solution. They insisted on having a king like all the nations even though the Lord had never failed them in so far as they were faithful to him. Thus history bore testimony that God faithfully had performed the royal office. The request for a king had been premature, unnecessary, and insulting to the Lord (12:6-12).

C. A Testimony Against Israel (1 Sam 12:13-18).

Samuel next addressed the present realities. Israel had now formally chosen as king the man God had ordained. Hence *"Yahweh has set a king over you."* As always, the requirement of Israel was to fear Yahweh, i.e., to serve and obey him. Following the Lord would lead to national blessing. On the other hand, the path of disobedience would bring the hand of Yahweh against them just as it had been against their fathers in times of their spiritual rebellion (12:13-15).

A miraculous sign would be needed to underscore in the minds of the people the gravity of their sin in requesting a king. Samuel called attention to the time of the year. Wheat harvest was in progress. This was the dry season when rain scarcely ever falls in Palestine. Yet Samuel announced that he would call upon Yahweh to sent thunder and rain. One wonders if this announcement was greeted with skepticism by the assembly. Be that as it may, when the old prophet prayed, the thunder and rain came that day. Then the people greatly feared Yahweh and his servant Samuel (12:16-18).

D. A Final Testimony (1 Sam 12:19-25).

The ferocious thunderstorm got the message across. The people feared for their lives. They sensed the enormity of their sin against Yahweh. They immediately pled for Samuel to make intercession for them that they might not die. Samuel calmed their fears. Yet he used the occasion to press for future strict and heartfelt obedience to Yahweh. If they ceased to serve Yahweh, they would inevitably follow after *"futile things,"* i.e., idols. Such *"gods"* were of no benefit to any nation since they could not deliver from danger. Yahweh, on the other hand, had chosen Israel as his own people. His divine name (honor, reputation) was bound up in the fate of this nation. Therefore he would not abandon Israel even though the nation may have committed a grievous sin against him (12:19-22).

Even though he was stepping down as Judge, Samuel did not relinquish his office of prophet. His prophetic responsibilities under the monarchy would be twofold: (1) prayer and (2) instruction. Under no circumstances would Samuel sin against Yahweh by ceasing to pray for Israel. Intercessory prayer was a fundamental attribute of a prophet (cf. Gen 20:7,17). In addition to his prayers for Israel, Samuel would continue to instruct them *"in the good and right way"* (12:23).

Samuel's valedictory concluded with an admonition for Israel to *"fear Yahweh and serve him in truth."* Heartfelt and cheerful obedience were the only proper responses to all the great things which Yahweh had done for his people. On the other hand, if Israel arrogantly insist upon its own way, both the people and their king would be swept away (12:24-25).

ENDNOTES

1. The reason for the appointment of Samuel's sons is not clear. Nor is it clear why two sons were appointed in one city. Were they a replacement for Samuel? Were they appointed to relieve Samuel of judicial responsibilities at a distant site?

2. Asses or donkeys were the riding animals of prominent people in early Old Testament times. See Judg 5:10; 10:4;12:14. The loss of these animals would (1) strip the family of one of the insignia of leadership and authority; and (2) be an economic blow.

3. The author of Samuel supplies very crucial information when he notes that those who formerly were called *"seers"* in Israel later were known as *"prophets."* The former term emphasized the visionary aspect of prophetism, the latter the proclamation function.

4. This *"prophesying"* surely was neither prediction nor preaching, but rhythmic chanting to the accompaniment of instrumental music. The connection between *"prophesying"* and instrumental music is again made in 1 Chr 25:1 and 2 Kgs 3:15.

5. The question *"Who is their father?"* has been interpreted in a variety of ways. Some think the sense is that the prophets have no father and hence are a disreputable band with whom Saul should have nothing to do. Others think the term *"father"* refers to the leader and interpreter of the group, *viz.*, Samuel. Hence the thought would be, Why criticize Saul for joining the prophetic band when their *"father"* is none other than Samuel?

6. In the books of Samuel and Kings only Saul and David are designated as God's *chosen* or *elect.*

7. Joshua wrote the record of the covenant which he had made with Israel *"in the book of the law of God."* So now Samuel is writing his record for that same book. The material which Samuel wrote on this occasion may have been the nucleus of what today is known as Judges and 1 Sam 1-10.

8. According to the LXX, the Nahash incident occurred one month after the first anointing of Saul.

9. Josephus (*Ant.* 6.5.1) suggests that the gouging of the right eyes would effectively disarm the Gileadites since in battle the buckler would cover the left eye.

10. On the basis of one of the Dead Sea scrolls (4Q Sam[a]) NRSV "restores" material which may have fallen out of the standard text of Samuel in the process of copying. This "missing" text relates how Nahash had been oppressing the Transjordan tribes for some time, gouging out the right eyes of all who fell into his hands. Seven thousand who had escaped from his hand had entered into Jabesh-gilead. About a month after they took refuge there, Nahash came against the city. P. Kyle McCarter, Jr. defends this material as part of the original text. *I Samuel* in Vol. 8 of The Anchor Bible (Garden City, NY: Doubleday, 1980), pp. 199f. The argument for regarding this material as part of the original text of Samuel is far from convincing. See also James C. VanderKam, *The Dead Sea Scrolls Today,* (Grand Rapids: Eerdmans, 1994), pp. 130-132.

11. The same language was used of Samson (Judg 14:6,19; 15:14. In 10:6,10 the Spirit turned the timid Saul into a vigorous leader in public worship. In chapter 11 the same Spirit equipped Saul for leadership in a holy war.

12. Gideon (Judg 7:16,20) and Abimelech (Judg 9:43) and even the Philistines (1 Sam 13:17-18) also employed the three-prong military strategy.

13. Apparently the attack on Jabesh was only the latest in a series of menacing attacks by Nahash.

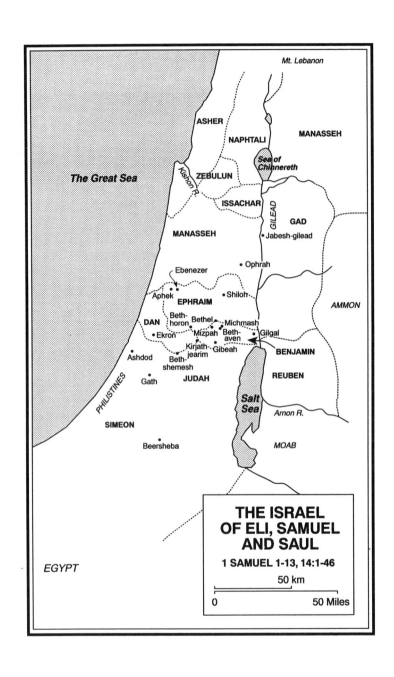

EGYPT

**THE ISRAEL
OF ELI, SAMUEL
AND SAUL**

1 SAMUEL 1-13, 14:1-46

50 km

0   50 Miles

CHAPTER SEVENTEEN

The King Rejected
1 Samuel 13-17

Two important pieces of chronological data are missing in 13:1: the age of Saul when he began to reign; and the length of Saul's reign.[1] The English translators have supplied in italics figures which represent an intelligent guess. Saul was probably between thirty and forty at the time he was anointed king. The length of his reign was something like thirty-two years. For some reason in the ancient transcription of the text of Samuel these figures dropped out.

The purpose of 1 Samuel 13-17 seems to be to document the deterioration of the reign of Saul. The author speaks of Saul's sinful impatience, foolish zeal, blatant rebellion, and faltering leadership. In three steps the rejection of Saul is made clear. First, Samuel announced that Saul would have no lasting dynasty. Second, Samuel declared that Saul personally had been rejected by the Lord. Third, Samuel went to Bethlehem to anoint that one who would be Saul's replacement in kingship.

SAUL'S SINFUL IMPATIENCE
1 Samuel 13:1-23

Once the reins of government had been turned over to him, Saul devoted himself to the priority of his reign, viz., rescuing his people from the Philistines (cf. 1 Sam 9:16).

A. Beginning of Hostilities (1 Sam 13:2-4).

How much time elapsed between the defeat of Nahash and the events of 1 Samuel 13 is not stated. Probably Saul would want to capitalize on the zeal which the people manifested for his reign at the reaffirmation ceremony in chapter 12. Be that as it may, at some point Saul began to organize a standing army. As a nucleus he chose for himself 3,000 men. Of these, a thousand stayed with Saul at Michmash, while another thousand under the direct authority of the king were stationed near Bethel. The third thousand was with Saul's son Jonathan at Gibeah of Benjamin. The rest of the people were sent home (13:2).

Hostilities with the Philistines were triggered by the actions of Jonathan. He and his men attacked the Philistine garrison[2] at Geba. Whether Jonathan acted on orders from his father or on his own initiative cannot be determined. In any case, this action made the Israelites odious to the Philistines. Anticipating a retaliatory invasion by the Philistines, Saul had the trumpet blown throughout the land. He alerted the *"Hebrews,"* those Israelites and kindred souls who had been mercenaries of the Philistines. Then he summoned the people of Israel to Gilgal (13:3-4).

B. Philistine Invasion (1 Sam 13:5-7).

The Philistines assembled a massive army to invade Israel: 30,000 chariots, 6,000 horsemen,[3] and infantry without number. This force camped at Michmash, Saul's former headquarters. The men of Israel had no will to resist such a vast host. They began to desert, taking refuge in terrain which they thought was inaccessible to the Philistines. Some of the Hebrews even fled across the Jordan. Though Saul and his troops remained in Gilgal, they were trembling at the prospects of having to do battle with the Philistines.

C. The Assembly at Gilgal (1 Sam 13:8-14).

Saul waited seven days for Samuel to appear in Gilgal. Each day more of his troops were deserting. Finally Saul ordered burnt offerings and peace offerings to be prepared. He himself seems to have officiated at the sacrifice. Just as Saul finished offering the burnt offering, Samuel appeared. Saul went out to greet him as though nothing were amiss (13:8-10).

Samuel demanded an explanation for Saul's action. The king defended himself with three arguments. First, he blamed his actions on the people. They were scattering, and he needed to do something to boost morale. Second, he blamed Samuel: You (the pronoun is emphatic in the Hebrew) did not appear within the appointed days. Third, he blamed the Philistines. They were assembling at Michmash for an all-out attack on Israel. Saul was convinced that the Philistines would attack him at Gilgal. Offering sacrifices before a holy war was customary. Therefore, the king said: *"I forced myself"* to offer the burnt offering (13:11-12).

Samuel did not bother to answer any of Saul's excuses. He simply stated a twofold assessment of the king's actions. First, Saul had acted foolishly; and second, he had disobeyed the commandment of Yahweh. Had he been obedient Saul would have been the founder of a long-lived dynasty. Now, however, the divine sentence is that Saul's dynasty would not endure. Yahweh had already sought out for himself *"a man after his own heart."* This unnamed man would become the ruler of God's people because Saul had not done what the Lord had commanded him (13:13-14).

D. Saul's Predicament (1 Sam 13:15-23).

Saul was now in quite a predicament. Samuel deserted him. He had left Gilgal bound for Gibeah of Benjamin. Saul would not have the benefit of prophetic guidance. Then Saul numbered *"the people"* and found only six hundred still with him.[4] With this little band Saul took up defensive positions near Geba of Benjamin. He was helpless to deal with the raiding parties dispatched to the north, to the south and to the west from the Philistine base camp at Michmash. Yet he was determined to defend his own tribal area of Benjamin (13:15-18).

Lack of proper weaponry exacerbated Saul's predicament. The

Philistines had removed all the blacksmiths from Israel, thus thwarting the manufacture of swords and spears. Israelites were forced to travel down to the Philistine plain to get their agricultural implements sharpened. Since the Philistines had a monopoly on the smelting and working of iron, they charged exorbitant prices—two thirds of a shekel—just to sharpen or repair their tools. Such prices made weapons unaffordable to the average Israelite. All of this the author relates so that his readers may understand why it was that only Saul and Jonathan had proper spears and swords on the eve of battle. The rank and file were armed with clubs, slings and perhaps other weapons made of bronze (13:19-22).

The showdown with the Philistine invaders began when the enemy base camp moved south toward the pass of Michmash. The courage of Saul in facing this force with only six hundred underarmed soldiers is to be commended (13:23).

<h2 style="text-align:center">SAUL'S FOOLISH ZEAL
1 Samuel 14:1-52</h2>

Early in his reign Saul decided to challenge the Philistine domination of Israel. The initial effort against this formidable foe was successful almost in spite of Saul. The king here is depicted as pious, though his piety seemed to paralyze rather than energize the effort. Yet through the courageous faith of Jonathan and the awesome power of Yahweh the Philistines were put to flight. In the previous chapter Saul lost the hope of dynastic succession. Here the author portrays the sterling qualities of Jonathan, the man who might have been king.

A. Yahweh's Initial Victory (1 Sam 14:1-15).

For a time Saul failed to take any action against the Philistines. Once again (cf. 13:3) Jonathan decided to initiate the battle by attacking an outpost guarding the pass between Michmash and Geba. His courageous faith stands out in bold relief against the background of Saul's paralysis. The king had only six hundred men in his encampment on the outskirts of Gibeah. Saul's force was small, yet the high priest was there wearing the ephod and the ark of God was also there (v. 18). Perhaps the author intends to say that Saul's situation was

280

desperate, but not hopeless (14:1-3).

Jonathan attempted to bolster the confidence of his young armor-bearer by reminding him of two things. First, the enemy was "*uncircumcised.*" This was a kind of ethnic slur used to mock the enemy and thus express confidence in victory (cf. 1 Sam 17:26,36). Second, Jonathan stressed that Yahweh is capable of giving victories to the few as well as to the many. Yet Jonathan did not presume that his action automatically would fall within the will of God. "*Perhaps,*" he said to his armorbearer, "*Yahweh will work for us.*" The armorbearer indicated that he would stand with Jonathan no matter what decision he made (14:4-7).

The plan was to cross the valley and reveal themselves to the Philistines who controlled the heights above. If the enemy ordered them to halt they would not ascend the height where the enemy was camped. If the Philistines challenged them to climb up, Jonathan would regard that as a sign that Yahweh would give a victory. Such a challenge would indicate overconfidence, even carelessness on the part of the defenders. Since this fight with the Philistines was a holy war ordered by a prophet (10:8) and consecrated by sacrifices, Jonathan believed that God would make his will clear (14:8-10).

When the Philistines spotted Jonathan and his armorbearer, they assumed that they were "*Hebrews*" coming out of hiding. They therefore challenged the two to climb up to their camp. Jonathan then began to make the precipitous climb confident that the victory was his. When they reached the top Jonathan and his armorbearer slew twenty of the enemy in a very small area.[5] Before the main force of the Philistines could come to the aid of their outpost, a tremendous earthquake began to shake the ground. The enemy was thrown into panic and began to flee back to their homeland (14:11-15).

B. Yahweh's Complete Deliverance (1 Sam 14:16-23).

Israelite lookouts observed great confusion in the Philistine camp. Saul suspected that some of his men had attacked the enemy. A quick numbering of his troops revealed the absence of Jonathan and his armorbearer. Saul ordered the high priest to bring the ark of God forward. Saul was making inquiry through the priestly oracle about his next move. Before the priest could complete the ritual inquiry, however, it became obvious that the Philistine camp was engaged in battle. Saul rallied his troops to join the fray (14:16-20a).

As they approached the battlefield Saul witnessed the total confusion of the enemy. The Hebrew mercenaries within the Philistine army had rebelled. The Philistines were in full retreat. News of the rout of the Philistines spread like wildfire. Israelites who had hidden away in the mountains came forth to join the pursuit. The battle spread beyond Beth-aven. So Yahweh delivered Israel that day (14:20b-23).

C. Saul's Rash Curse (1 Sam 14:24-46).

After reporting the glorious victory, the author focuses on a rash curse which nearly turned victory into calamity. Anxious that his men not lose the advantage over the Philistines, Saul placed a curse on anyone who stopped during the day to eat. The well-being of his men was of no concern to Saul *"until I take vengeance on my enemies."* These words suggest selfishness on Saul's part, even fanatical zeal. He had lost the sense that the Philistines were Yahweh's enemies, and he was fighting Yahweh's battle.[6] Not only did Saul's foolish oath work a hardship on his soldiers; other terrible consequences followed as well.

1. The violation by Jonathan (14:25-30). Pursuing the enemy through a forest, the Israelite soldiers spotted an abandoned honeycomb which was oozing wild honey. None of the soldiers dared to touch that tempting treat because they feared the curse of their king. Jonathan, however, knew nothing of the oath. Therefore as he continued the pursuit, he dipped the end of his staff in the honeycomb and put it to his mouth. Immediately *"his eyes brightened,"* i.e., he experienced a sudden surge of energy. When informed about his father's oath Jonathan was discouraged. He called attention to the difference in his energy level and that of the men. An even greater victory over the Philistines would have been possible had Saul not *"troubled the land"* with his foolish oath. Perhaps Jonathan should not have spoken so critically of his father in front of the troops.

2. The defiled troops (14:31-35). Another direct result of Saul's curse occurred at the end of the day. The Israelites had chased the Philistines as far as Aijalon some twenty miles west of where the battle was first joined. The troops now were faint from lack of food. As soon as the sun set, they pounced on the spoil of livestock. The animals were slaughtered on the ground. No provision was made for the proper drainage of blood (cf. Lev 19:26; Deut 12:16). The meat was eaten *"with the blood,"*[7] which was a violation of Mosaic law (14:31-32).

Saul was soon told that his troops were sinning against Yahweh by eating *"with the blood."* Saul referred to what his men had done as *"treachery."* He ordered a stone rolled to the spot. Officers circulated among the troops ordering them to bring their livestock to the central stone for slaughter. The stone was considered an altar, the first altar which Saul erected (14:33-35).

3. The silent oracle (14:36-39). After the men had eaten, Saul determined that perhaps it would be a good idea to press the attack against the Philistines into the night. The officers agreed, but the priest (Ahijah) suggested that it might be wise to *"draw near to God,"* i.e., seek an oracle regarding the proposed pursuit. So Saul inquired of God about the matter, but he did not answer him on that day through the Urim and Thummim of the high priest.[8] By this silence Yahweh rebuked the rash piety of Saul in taking the oath in the first place (14:36-37).

Saul realized that there must be sin in the camp. He called upon his officers to investigate and report how the sin occurred. Then Saul took another oath. Even if the guilty party were prince Jonathan, he would still die for having violated the solemn curse of the king. Though it was generally known through the ranks that Jonathan had violated his father's curse, no one ventured to point the finger of accusation at him (14:37-39).

4. The jeopardy of Jonathan (14:40-45). Since no one would report any violation of the royal curse, Saul would find the guilty party in another manner. He determined to cast lots. The first lot would be between the royal family (Saul and Jonathan) and the troops. The king prayed that the Lord would give a perfect lot. Saul must have been shocked when the lot indicated that the guilt was in the royal family. A second lot was cast between Saul and his son. The lot indicated Jonathan (14:40-42).

Saul then interrogated Jonathan, and the prince confessed to tasting a little honey during the midst of the battle. Now that Saul had bound himself by an oath to execute the guilty party, Jonathan was fully prepared to accept his fate.[9] Then Saul took a third oath which reinforced the second, that Jonathan would surely die (14:43-44).

At this point the troops intervened. These soldiers gave the credit for the victory over the Philistines to Jonathan. He could only have accomplished what he had accomplished if he had *"worked with God."* Therefore Jonathan should not die. The troops took an oath that not one hair of Jonathan's head would fall to the ground.[10] Thus it would appear that the oath of the many took precedence over the oath of the one, even if the one was the king. In this case Saul must have been very relieved that his troops overruled him (14:45).

5. *The end of the battle (14:46).* Since his troops in effect had mutinied against him, any hopes of further pursuit of the Philistines became impossible. Saul and his men returned home. The Philistines withdrew from Israelite territory. They would return to fight another day.

D. Summary of Saul's Reign (1 Sam 14:47-52).

The author now interjects a brief summary of other accomplishments of Saul's reign. Saul was successful in campaigns against Moab and Ammon to the east, Edom to the south, Zobah to the north, and the Philistines to the west. Saul was credited with defeating the Amalekites and other marauding desert tribes who *"plundered"* Israel from time to time (14:47-48). Thus Saul was doing what Israel's judges had done before him (cf. Judg 2:16).

By his wife Ahinoam[11] Saul had three sons and two daughters.[12] The sons were Jonathan, Ishvi and Malchishua. The daughters were Merab and Michal. The captain of Saul's army was his uncle[13] Abner (14:49-51).

Chapter 14 closes with one other negative note about the king. Saul's recruiting policy marked a major shift from the emergency tribal levy which had served Israel to this point. Any men capable of military leadership were pressed into service on the royal staff. Such a policy became necessary because of the uninterrupted nature of the conflict with the Philistines (14:52).

SAUL'S BLATANT REBELLION
1 Samuel 15:1-35

Chapter 15 is devoted completely to events surrounding Saul's war with the Amalekites. Saul's dynasty was rejected in chapter 13. Here the king personally is rejected for disobedience to a direct command of Yahweh. The text supplies no information which would allow one to compute the time interval between chapters 14 and 15.

A. Commission of Saul (1 Sam 15:1-3).

Yahweh had directed Samuel to anoint Saul as king of Israel. As Yahweh's anointed, Saul had an obligation to listen to what Yahweh said through his prophet Samuel. The Lord had determined to punish Amalek for the obstruction which they had been to Israel at the time of the Exodus (Ex 17:8-16; Deut 25:17-19). Though some four centuries had elapsed, Yahweh had not forgotten the threat which he had made concerning the Amalekites. Since in the intervening centuries Amalek had shown no signs of national repentance,[14] that nation should now be put under the ban, i.e., totally destroyed (Deut 7:2; 20:17). Nothing was to be spared.

B. Disobedience to the Word (1 Sam 15:4-9).

Saul promptly summoned the people for a holy war against Amalek. Saul numbered his troops at the staging area of Telaim in the Negev of Judah some thirty miles south of Hebron. His large force—200,000 from Israel, and 10,000 from Judah[15]—would be necessary in chasing the Amalekites across the sprawling desert. The point is that Saul had enough forces to carry out his mandate (15:4).

Before going to war against the Amalekites, Saul warned the Kenites to leave the area lest they be caught up in the fighting. The Kenites were old allies of Israel dating back to the days of the Exodus (15:5-6).

While Saul concentrated on *"the city of Amalek,"* contingents of his army chased down the Amalekites from Havilah (northwest Arabia) to the borders of Egypt. He executed every Amalekite he could get hands on with one exception. He spared their king Agag.[16] He and his troops were also unwilling to destroy the best of the livestock.

Hence Saul had failed to put Amalek under the ban as ordered. He had, in effect, committed the same sin as Achan had committed during the conquest (15:7-9).

C. Confrontation with Samuel (1 Sam 15:10-21).

By revelation Samuel learned the sad truth about Saul. The king's actions had caused Yahweh to be sorry that he had ever made Saul king. At the outset Saul had been warned that only if he honored God through obedience would he be blessed, and if he did not he would be rejected. Thus Yahweh's change of attitude toward Saul was not a change of purpose. For God to be unchanging in his purpose, he had to now change his attitude toward Saul. Samuel felt great distress over the matter. He cried out all that night in prayer to the Lord (15:10-11).

Early in the morning Samuel set out to find Saul. He learned from travelers that Saul had returned to Carmel, a town seven miles south of Hebron. There Saul had erected a monument to celebrate his victory over Amalek. So much for the modesty of this man before his coronation. From there Saul was proceeding to Gilgal. As Samuel approached Saul gave him a warm greeting in which he enthusiastically declared that he had carried out the commandment of Yahweh. Either Saul is bluffing, or he is part of that group in every age who think that partial obedience is acceptable to the Lord (15:12-13).

Samuel cut short the blustering of the king. He called attention to the noise being made by the numerous livestock spared by Saul. The king then blamed *"the people,"* i.e., his troops, for sparing the best of the animals so that they might offer sacrifices to Yahweh. Saul was making two grave leadership mistakes here. First, he was attempting to shift the blame to others. Even if true these excuses would be tantamount to an admission that Saul had no control over his troops. Second, he attempted to use a religious pretext as an excuse for disobedience. He seems to be arguing that religious sincerity is a valid substitute for obedience to God. Besides this, in the peace offering most of the sacrificial animal was eaten by the worshipers. Had Saul really wished to give those animals to God he would have slain them as ordered in the first place (15:14-15).

"Stop" (NIV) Samuel said. Enough of your excuses! Hear what

Yahweh revealed to me last night. Saul agreed to listen. A rhetorical question reminded Saul that Yahweh had elevated him to kingship even when he in his own eyes was unworthy of such honor. He also reminded Saul of the precise words of the recent commission. The Amalekites were sinners. He had been commissioned to fight against them until they were exterminated. Why then, Samuel asked, did Saul commit evil by disobeying the voice of Yahweh? Samuel rejected any distinction between what Saul had done and what the troops had done. He placed total responsibility on the king (15:16-19).

Saul strongly rejected Samuel's accusation that he had disobeyed the Lord. He had spared only Agag. The people had spared the choicest livestock to sacrifice to Yahweh "*your*" God at Gilgal (15:20-21). Saul ignored the fact that the Amalekite livestock had already been devoted to God by being placed under the ban. They therefore could not legitimately be presented to God as sacrifice (Lev 27:29; Deut 13:16).

D. Rejection by the Lord (1 Sam 15:22-31).

Samuel forcefully rejected Saul's contention that religious intention justifies selective obedience. *"To obey is better than sacrifice."* No amount of religious ritual can substitute for doing what God commands. To be valid, external religious observance must reflect internal faith and piety. Rebellion and insubordination are sins equivalent in seriousness to divination[17] and idolatry. Conscious disobedience is like idolatry in that one makes an idol out of the human will. The punishment would suit the crime. Saul had rejected the word of Yahweh, therefore *"Yahweh has rejected you from being king!"* (15:22-23).

Samuel's announcement knocked the bluster out of Saul. He now realized the seriousness of what he had done. In humble contrition Saul confessed his transgression in listening to the voice of the people rather than to the words of Yahweh and his prophet. He begged that he might be pardoned, that Samuel might join him in public worship (15:24-25).

Samuel at this point refused to join Saul in worship. The king might interpret his presence as tantamount to forgiveness of the transgression. Saul had been rejected as king and therefore Samuel could not any longer give him public support. With that parting word

Samuel turned to leave. In desperation Saul seized Samuel's robe. This constituted a final act of supplication on his part. The robe tore. The prophet used the torn robe to illustrate his announcement. Yahweh had torn the kingdom out of the hands of Saul and had given that kingdom to someone more worthy of it. Furthermore, Samuel added, *"the Glory of Israel,"* i.e., Yahweh, would not lie, nor would he change his mind about the kingdom (15:26-29).

For the second time Saul acknowledged his sin and accepted his fate. He made one last request of the prophet. He asked Samuel to honor him before the elders and people by accompanying him back to Gilgal. This time Saul's request was not accompanied by request for pardon. Since the king would not misunderstand his presence, Samuel followed him back to Gilgal. There Saul worshiped Yahweh, i.e., offered sacrifices to him. Samuel's presence acknowledged that the sinful king retained his office for the time being (15:30-31).

E. Execution of Agag (1 Sam 15:32-33).

After the worship ceremony had concluded, Samuel demanded that Agag be brought to him. Agag came to him *"cheerfully"* (NASB) or *"confidently"* (NIV). The joyous worship celebration had convinced him that his life was no more in danger. Samuel, however, was of a different mind. He first pronounced sentence on the Amalekite. Agag's sword had made many women childless, so now his own mother would be childless. With those words of judgment Samuel hewed Agag to pieces *"before Yahweh,"* i.e., before Yahweh's altar, at Gilgal. By slaying Agag, Samuel was executing the death sentence which the Lord had already pronounced against this king and his people.

F. Separation from Saul (1 Sam 15:34-35).

After the episode at Gilgal both Samuel and Saul returned to their respective homes at Ramah and Gibeah. Samuel did not see Saul again in his advisory capacity until the day he died. During Samuel's last days he grieved over Saul. Yahweh also *"regretted that he had made Saul king,"* i.e., Yahweh grieved over the tragic fall of Saul as well.

SAUL'S ANOINTED RIVAL
1 Samuel 16:1-23

The text does not indicate how many people knew that Saul had been rejected as king. Perhaps the matter was private, just between Samuel and Saul. When Samuel no longer appeared at the royal court, the people became uneasy. They must have suspected that all was not well between the prophet and the king.

A. Samuel's Trip to Bethlehem (1 Sam 16:1-5).

Samuel's continued mourning over the downfall of Saul was deemed inappropriate because *Yahweh* had rejected him. The prophet was commanded to take his horn of oil to the house of Jesse in Bethlehem. Yahweh had selected a new *king* (not *prince* as in 9:16) from among the sons of Jesse. Samuel feared for his life, and for the life of anyone he might anoint. Furthermore, anointing a new king might trigger a civil war. These considerations explain Samuel's reticence to carry out his instructions (16:1-2a).

Yahweh directed Samuel to take with him a heifer to use as a sacrificial animal in Bethlehem. The animal was not a subterfuge, but a means of verifying his sacrificial intentions should he be challenged by Saul's agents. Jesse's family was to be invited to the sacrifice. At that time God would show Samuel what he should do. To anyone who inquired about his trip, Samuel should tell the truth, but not the whole truth. He should tell them he had come to sacrifice. Withholding the whole truth from those who have no right to know it is not unethical (16:2b-3).

So Samuel went to Bethlehem. The distance he traveled according to commentators ranges from 10 to 25 miles depending on which of four locations is identified as the home of Samuel. Since it was unusual for the prophet to be in their area, the elders feared the worst. They undoubtedly knew of the rift between the prophet and the king, and they did not wish to get involved. Samuel indicated that he had come in peace to offer a sacrifice.[18] He told the elders to consecrate themselves for the service. He specifically invited Jesse and his sons (16:4-5).

B. David's Anointing (1 Sam 16:6-13).

Apparently after the public sacrifice, Samuel retired to the house of Jesse to partake of the sacrificial meal. As each of Jesse's sons entered the room for the sacrificial meal, Samuel sized them up. When he saw Jesse's firstborn Eliab he thought surely this was *"Yahweh's anointed."*[19] Yahweh, however, told the prophet not to look on the outward appearance. Yahweh looks on the heart (16:6-7).

All seven of Jesse's sons passed before Samuel but in each case Yahweh rejected the candidate. Through inquiry Samuel learned of an eighth son who had been left to tend the sheep. Samuel directed Jesse to send for his youngest son. The family would not sit down to eat of the fellowship meal until David had been brought in (16:8-9).

David finally arrived. He made a pleasing appearance. He was *"ruddy,"*[20] i.e., with reddish tint of hair and even skin. He had beautiful eyes and handsome features. He had an even more beautiful heart. Samuel was told to anoint this son. This he did *"in the midst of his brothers."* From that day forward the Spirit of Yahweh rushed upon David. After the anointing Samuel departed for Ramah. The next time he would see David the young man would be in flight from Saul (16:12-13).

C. Saul's Deterioration (1 Sam 16:14-23).

The same equipping Spirit which came upon David, left Saul. He no longer had the resources to administer the kingdom. His own mental health deteriorated. An evil spirit from Yahweh, i.e., permitted by Yahweh, terrorized the man. This may have been a demonic spirit which Yahweh permitted to invade the mind of the king. On the other hand, the evil spirit may have been a psychological state sent on Saul as a divine judgment (16:14).[21]

Saul's servants suggested that soothing music might help alleviate the panic caused by the evil spirit. So Saul authorized his servants to seek out a skilled harp player. Someone immediately thought of David who had a reputation as a skilled musician. David also possessed all the other attributes which Saul prized in his courtiers. He was prudent in speech, handsome, a warrior and *"a mighty man of valor,"* i.e., he was from a family of standing (cf. 1 Sam 9:1). By slaying ferocious wild animals (cf.17:34-35) David probably got the reputation of being a warrior (16:15-18).

So Saul sent a draft notice to Jesse demanding that David be sent to the royal court. Jesse complied with the king's demand. Along with David Jesse sent a donkey loaded down with gifts for the king (16:19-20). David began to attend Saul, and the king developed a special affection for him. Eventually David was given the high honor of being named armorbearer to the king. Saul sent a message to Jesse indicating that David would become part of his permanent staff (16:21-22).

David's main function during this period was to play his harp whenever Saul was troubled by the evil spirit. This procedure worked well, for Saul would be refreshed, and the evil spirit would temporarily depart from him (16:23).

SAUL'S FALTERING LEADERSHIP
1 Samuel 17:1-58

An invasion by the Philistines demonstrated that Saul was faltering in his leadership. The Philistines brought with them a giant who single-handedly intimidated the entire army of Israel including King Saul. On the other hand, the Philistine-Israelite standoff in the valley of Elah was David's first opportunity to publicly demonstrate his courage and commitment to Yahweh.

A. The Challenge (1 Sam 17:1-11).

Periodically the Philistines invaded the territory of Israel. Chapter 17 reports one occasion when they penetrated as far as Socoh, about fourteen miles west of Bethlehem. They camped at Ephes-dammim in the vicinity of Socoh. Saul countered by calling up the army. The Israelites camped on a height overlooking a ravine (the valley of Elah) to block any further advance by the enemy. On the elevation across the valley the Philistines pitched their camp (17:1-3).

Each day a *"champion"* named Goliath would come forth from the Philistine camp to taunt the Israelites. His size was intimidating: six cubits and a span (over nine feet tall).[22] Goliath was a descendant of the tall Anakim race, the remnants of which had settled in the Philistine plain after the Israelite invasion under Joshua (Josh 11:22).

He wore a helmet and shin guards of bronze. His body armor weighed five thousand shekels (125 lbs.). He was armed both with a bronze javelin thrown over his shoulder and a spear. The shaft of that spear was as thick as a weaver's beam (part of a large loom), its head weighed six hundred shekels of iron (15 lbs.). As if that were not enough, the warrior had a shield bearer who walked before him (17:4-7).

When the Israelites drew up in battle formation, Goliath would propose that single combat replace fighting between armies. If some Israelite warrior could kill Goliath, the Philistines agreed to become servants of the Israelites. The opposite would be true if the Philistine should prevail. This daily winner-take-all challenge dismayed and intimidated Saul and all Israel. For forty days the daily challenge continued. Neither army moved during that period (17:8-11).

B. The Mission (17:12-19).

The three older sons of Jesse were part of Saul's army. Evidently David was no longer serving in Saul's court. As the youngest member of the family, David's job was to carry supplies to his brothers in the field. Apparently families were expected to supply provisions to their men in the field. During the standoff at the valley of Elah, Jesse dispatched David with food for his brothers and their commander. He was to check on the welfare of his brothers and bring back *"their pledge,"* i.e., some token that would confirm the delivery of the food and the well-being of the brothers (17:12-19).

C. The Discussion (1 Sam 17:20-30).

As David approached the perimeter of the Israelite camp the troops were moving into battle positions shouting the battle cry as they did. The Philistine army across the valley was going through the same exercise. David left his supplies with the quartermaster corps and hastened to the battle line to greet his brothers. While he was there Goliath made his daily appearance. Again the men of Israel *"fled"* from him, i.e., they refused to move forward. David heard the troops talking among themselves of the tremendous rewards which Saul would give to any man who would kill Goliath. The king would enrich that man, give his daughter to him in marriage, and exempt his father's house from taxation (17:20-25).

David could not believe that no one would take up the challenge of this *"uncircumcised Philistine."* He grew increasing interested in the promised reward which he overheard the troops discussing. By questioning several men, David verified the truth of the reward rumor. When Eliab, David's oldest brother, heard these discussions, his anger burned against David. He wrongly rebuked David for abandoning his responsibilities of tending a small flock of sheep. He falsely accused David of having a perverse interest in watching the battle which was about to take place. David's response is typical of younger brothers throughout the centuries: *"Was it not just a question?"* David turned away from Eliab and began to question other men at the front (17:26-30).

D. The Preparation (1 Sam 17:31-40).

Saul soon heard about the brash young man who showed no fear of the Philistine. David lost none of his confidence in the presence of the king. He even volunteered to fight Goliath. Saul scoffed at this suggestion. Goliath had been trained as a warrior; David was but a youth. David, however, defended his fighting credentials. He had slain a lion and a bear in defense of his sheep. Goliath had taunted the armies of the living God. David therefore was confident that Yahweh would deliver him from the hand of Philistine just as he had delivered him earlier from the paw of the lion and bear. Saul was convinced. He prayed Yahweh's blessing upon his efforts (17:31-37).

Saul tried to clothe David in his personal armor.[23] David tried on the armor, but felt so uncomfortable that he removed it. Since he had never *"proved"* or *"tested"* this armor in battle, he felt it would be more of a hindrance than a help. Rather he took his shepherd's stick (to help him negotiate his way down the steep ravine) and his sling.[24] As he moved toward Goliath he paused at a wadi (dry stream bed) in the valley and picked up five smooth stones (17:38-40).

E. The Victory (1 Sam 17:41-53).

Goliath came out to meet his challenger. When he saw that he was a youth and that he had no armor or sword, Goliath cursed David in the names of his gods. He considered it a personal insult that the

Israelites would send an unworthy opponent to fight him. Goliath mocked David's boyish appearance. He tried to verbally intimidate David by threatening to give his flesh to the birds and beasts (17:41-44).

David continued to advance toward Goliath. The giant had never faced such bravado before. David employed his own version of psychological warfare. *"You come at me with a sword, spear and javelin; but I come to you in the name of Yahweh of hosts, the God of the armies of Israel, whom you have taunted. This day Yahweh will deliver you into my hands."* David went on to boast that he would decapitate Goliath and give the bodies of the Philistines to the birds and beasts. Through this victory all the earth would know that there was a God in Israel. Those present on the battlefield would come to know that Yahweh does not deliver by sword or spear. *"The battle is Yahweh's, and he will give you into our hands"* (17:45-47).

As Goliath rose and moved ponderously toward him, David began to run right at him. As he did so he loaded his sling and let fly a missile. The stone struck the one place where the giant had no armor. Goliath fell stunned to the ground. David ran forward, took the giant's own sword,[25] slew him, and cut off his head (17:48-51a).

When the Philistines saw that their champion had fallen, they broke ranks and fled. Saul's army pursued them to the very gates of their cities, about seven miles from the valley of Elah. As they returned to their own borders, the Israelites plundered the Philistine camps (17:51b-53).

F. The Epilogue (1 Sam 17:54-58).

Commentators are perplexed about the conversation between Saul and Abner which took place as David was going out to face the Philistine. In the light of the fact that David had served for a time in Saul's court, that Saul loved him, and had even made him the royal armorbearer, how could it be that neither he nor Abner recognized David? Various solutions have been offered. First, David may have matured considerably during his absence from the court. Second, in his disturbed state Saul may have paid little attention to the features of David as he played his harp. Third, the account of David serving in

Saul's court may be chronologically later than the Goliath episode. Actually the text does not say that Abner and Saul did not recognize David. The identity of David's father is the point at issue. This information would be necessary if Saul were to fulfill his pledge to make the father's house free of tax obligations. When David returned from killing Goliath, Abner brought him before Saul. David still had the Philistine's head in his hand. The king asked David about his father, and David proudly identified Jesse the Bethlehemite as his father (17:55-58).

David took Goliath's head and showed it to the Jebusites and Israelites who jointly occupied Jerusalem[26] as a testimony to the greatness of Israel's God. David put Goliath's weapons in his own tent. Later, however, the sword was deposited in the tabernacle (17:54; cf. 1 Sam 21:9).

ENDNOTES

1. Josephus (*Ant.* 6:14,9) states that Saul reigned eighteen years before Samuel's death, and twenty-two years afterward, a total of forty years. Paul assigned forty years to the reign of Saul (Acts 13:21), but he may have been including the reign of Ish-bosheth, Saul's son, in this figure.

2. The word commonly translated *"garrison"* (13:3) may also mean resident administrator, or even monument. Whatever it was that Jonathan attacked at Geba the Philistines interpreted his action as rebellion against Philistine hegemony.

3. Some manuscripts give the number of chariots here as 3,000. This would correlate better with the 6,000 *"horsemen,"* i.e., charioteers. Two-man chariots are well known in Egypt.

4. The six hundred who remained were of *"the people"* who had assembled to Gilgal at Saul's direction (cf. v. 4). Presumably the three thousand men of Israel whom Saul had chosen (v. 2) were still intact.

5. The slaughter took place in a space equal to about half the distance across an acre field, or 15-20 yards. See Ralph Klein, *1 Samuel* in "Word Biblical Commentary" (Waco, TX: Word, 1983), p. 137.

6. In a holy war Israel takes vengeance on their (and Yahweh's) enemies. See Josh 10:13.

7. Others understand the text to say that the troops ate *upon* the blood, i.e., upon bloody ground.

8. The Urim and Thummim were placed in or on the breastpiece of the high priest (Exod 28:30; Lev 8:8). Apparently the one stone(?) represented a positive answer, the other a negative. In a context of judgment, Urim may have indicted "guilty" while Thummim indicated "not guilty."

9. Some point to the parallel of Jephthah's daughter (Judg 11:36) who also seemed willing to accept the death sentence resulting from a foolish vow made by her father.

10. The text says that the troops "redeemed" (*padah*) Jonathan. This may mean they rescued him by insisting on his release. On the other hand, if the word "redeem" is used in its legal sense some price may have been paid for Jonathan's redemption, either money (Exod 21:30; Num 3:46-51), or an animal substitute (Exod 13:13,15; 34:20). Some modern writers have even proposed that another man died in the place of Jonathan.

11. Saul had at least one other wife or concubine, Rizpah (2 Sam 3:7; 21:1-14).

12. Elsewhere Ishvi is known as Ish-bosheth (Eshbaal). See 1 Chr 9:49; 2 Sam 2-4. Saul also had a son named Abinadab who probably was born to another wife (1 Sam 31:2; 1 Chr 9:49).

13. The *"uncle"* in 14:50 could have been either Ner or Abner as its antecedent. Whether Abner was Saul's uncle or cousin is unclear. Supporting the first interpretation are 1 Chr 8:33 and 9:39. According to this interpretation Ner has been omitted between Kish and Abiel in 1 Sam 9:1. The second view sees Ner and Kish as brothers, sons of Abiel (1 Chr 9:36). This interpretation requires that one emend the word "son" to "sons" in 1 Sam 14:51.

14. The Amalekites had opposed Israel's entrance into Canaan (Num 14:25). They had been been implacable enemies during the period of the Judges (Judg 3:13; 6:3). More recently they had been guilty of numerous atrocities (1 Sam 15:33).

15. Here again skepticism regarding these large numbers has caused some scholars to propose that the word *"thousand"* should be understood as a military unit of undetermined size. In this case, Israel would have furnished 200 such units, and Judah ten.

16. Why Saul spared Agag is not clear. He may have wished to use him as a trophy of war, or negotiate some kind of deal with him. On the other hand he may have avoided slaying a fellow king out of superstition that a similar fate would befall him.

17. Divination is the use of some external object in an attempt to probe the future. It is a practice consistently condemned in Scripture. E.g., Deut 18:10; 2 Kgs 17:17; Jer 14:14; Ezek 13:6 etc.

18. Since no central sanctuary existed in these days, public sacrificial services appear to have been conducted in various places.

19. Klein (*op. cit.*, p. 160) has called attention to the fact that of thirty-four times in which the term *"anointed"* is used of a royal person, it always appears with the name Yahweh, or a possessive pronoun referring to him.

20. The same adjective is used of Esau in Gen 25:25.

21. God sent an evil spirit between Abimelech and the men of Shechem (Judg 9:23). He put a lying spirit into the mouth of the false prophets in the days of Ahab (1 Kgs 22:19-22).

22. The LXX read "four cubits and a span" which would make Goliath 6'9" tall.

23. Whether the armor and sword David received were Saul's is not clear. The text may simply be saying that Saul supplied David with his garments (uniform?) and armor.

24. A slingstone was held in a pouch with cords attached at opposite ends. The sling was whirled over the head until one end was suddenly released. In the hands of one who was proficient, the sling was a deadly weapon (cf. Judg 20:14-16). Ancient armies had units which specialized in use of the sling.

25. The text is not clear whether David used his own sword or the sword of the giant to decapitate him. The result was the same in either case.

26. Israelites took up residence in Jerusalem during the days of the conquest under Joshua (Josh 15:63). The tribe of Judah was also able to conquer at least a part of Jerusalem (Judg 1:8). The fortress on Mt. Zion, however, remained in the hands of the Jebusites until it was conquered by David (2 Sam 5:6). It is possible that the text is simply saying that the trophy of Goliath's head eventually came to reside in Jerusalem just as the remains of Saul were moved from Jabesh to the tomb of Kish in Benjamin (2 Sam 21:12-14).

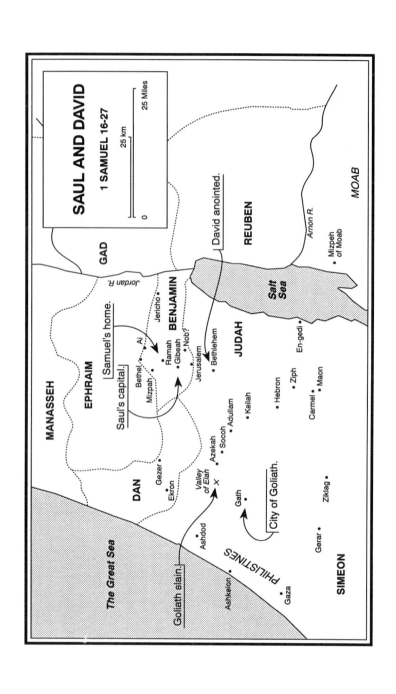

SAUL AND DAVID

1 SAMUEL 16-27

25 km

25 Miles

0

MANASSEH

EPHRAIM

DAN

GAD

Jordan R.

Samuel's home.

Bethel Ai
Mizpah
Ramah
Gibeah
Nob?

Saul's capital.

Gezer

Ekron

Jerusalem

BENJAMIN

Jericho

David anointed.

REUBEN

Arnon R.

Mizpeh
of Moab

MOAB

Salt
Sea

JUDAH

Bethlehem

En-gedi

Ziph

Hebron

Carmel
Maon

Keilah

Adullam

Socoh

Azekah

Valley
of Elah
X

Gath

City of Goliath.

Ashdod

Goliath slain.

Ashkelon

PHILISTINES

Gaza

Gerar

Ziklag

SIMEON

The Great Sea

CHAPTER EIGHTEEN

The King and His Rival
1 Samuel 18-27

In the victory over Goliath David proved himself to be a worthy leader of men. From that point on his fortunes were on the rise, while King Saul continued to decline both in popularity with the people and in his capacity to rule. In chapters 18-27 David's relationship to Saul passes through four stages. Here the author describes David as (1) a courtier, (2) a fugitive, (3) an outlaw, and (4) a mercenary.

DAVID THE COURTIER
1 Samuel 18:1-19:17

The events of chapter 18 follow immediately on those of chapter 17. Saul did not allow David to return to his home. From this point on David would be a national figure.

A. The Friendship of Jonathan (1 Sam 18:1-9).

Jonathan, the son of Saul, became the closest of friends with

David following the Goliath episode. His soul *"was knit"* (lit., chained itself) to the soul of David. He came to love David as he loved himself. Jonathan entered into a covenant of brotherhood with David and symbolized the same by bestowing on David his robe and armor. Many in recent years have viewed this "male bonding" between David and Jonathan as some kind of homosexual covenant. Nothing could be farther from the truth. Both men were married and had children. David was later lured in an adulterous act by the sight of a naked woman. This is hardly conduct typical of homosexuals (18:1-4).

During those early days in the court David continued to impress the king. He carried out whatever orders he was given. Eventually Saul made David a commander in the army. This move met with the approval of the people in general and Saul's advisors in particular (18:5).

B. The Adoration of Israel (1 Sam 18:6-16).

Saul's jealousy was triggered by the adoration bestowed on David by the women when the troops returned from battles with the Philistines. To the accompaniment of musical instruments the women would chant: *"Saul has slain thousands, but David his tens of thousands."* Saul believed that this popular adulation would catapult David to the throne itself. Therefore, from that day forward he viewed David with suspicion (18:6-9).

The *"evil spirit from God"* continued to trouble Saul from time to time. David would play the harp in an attempt to bring peace to the king. On two occasions when Saul was raving under the influence of the evil spirit, he tried to slay David with his spear (18:10-11).

Saul was afraid of David. He saw that Yahweh was with the Bethlehemite. Saul himself no longer sensed the direction of God's Spirit. Therefore Saul made David a captain of a thousand to get him out of the court. Yet with Yahweh's blessing, David continued to prosper. This only fueled Saul's resentment. Yet the people of both Israel and Judah loved David (18:12-16).

C. The Love of Michal (1 Sam 18:17-30).

Saul schemed to bring about the death of David. He offered him the hand of Merab, his oldest daughter, if he would engage the

Philistines in battle. David felt unworthy to be son-in-law to the king. On the day Merab was to become David's bride, Saul found some pretext to give her to another. This, no doubt, was intended to humiliate David (18:17-19). Saul's second daughter loved David. When the king discovered this he again began to plot against his rival. David had no wealth to pay a dowry suitable for a king's daughter. Saul, however, sent word that he desired as a dowry a hundred foreskins of slain Philistines. In this vulgar stipulation Saul was following the custom of other peoples of the ancient Near East who cut off the genitals of enemy soldiers as a trophy of victory.[1] Again Saul was hoping that David would fall by the hands of Israel's enemies (18:20-25).

David was happy to become the king's son-in-law on the terms stipulated. He and his men slew the requisite number of Philistines and brought their foreskins to Saul. The king this time honored his word and gave Michal to David. When he saw that his daughter really loved his rival, Saul was even more afraid of David. As son-in-law to the king David now had established a possible claim to the throne. Saul became David's implacable enemy (18:26-29).

Chapter 18 closes with a note that even the Philistine commanders began to take note of David. He behaved himself more wisely than any of Saul's officers, i.e., his tactical skills were superior to any other commander (18:30).

D. The Jealousy of Saul (1 Sam 19:1-17).

Finally Saul made public in his court what he had been thinking in his heart for some time. He wanted David dead! Jonathan warned David. He promised to signal his friend if he could not persuade his father to cancel the death warrant (19:1-3).

Jonathan gave an impassioned plea on behalf of David. He reminded his father that David had never committed any sin against him. On the contrary, David's activities had only benefited Saul, and that at great risk to his own life. On this occasion Saul listened to reason. He vowed that David should not be put to death. Jonathan immediately went and brought David back to the court (19:4-7).

New military accomplishments by David triggered the jealous spirit within Saul. Again while David was playing for the king, Saul tried to

301

pin David to the wall with his spear. David escaped unharmed. Saul then dispatched assassins to wait outside David's house to slay him in the morning. Michal warned her husband that he must flee that night if he would save his life. Michal helped David escape out a back window. Then she fixed up a decoy which was designed to buy some time for her husband. She took a teraphim (household god) and put it in bed. She fixed the life-size statue to resemble a human figure. When Saul's agents came looking for David, Michal told them he was sick. No doubt she allowed them to peek into the bedroom from a distance. In the dim light the teraphim looked the part of a sick man (19:8-14).

Saul ordered his agents to bring David to him on his sick bed so he could kill him. Only then did the agents discover that they had been tricked. They took Michal with them instead. Saul rebuked his daughter for aiding his enemy. To get back in the good graces of her father Michal lied. She only had aided David because he had threatened her life. This lie, of course, only fueled Saul's hatred of David (19:15-17).

DAVID THE FUGITIVE
1 Samuel 19:18-22:5

At this point David was forced to become a fugitive. He was aided during the next several weeks by a number of individuals.

A. David and Samuel (1 Sam 19:18-24).

David went first to Ramah to meet with Samuel. For a short time he resided in Naioth, the little community of prophetic students which was located near Ramah. When Saul heard where he was residing, he dispatched agents to arrest David. As they entered the area where the prophets were prophesying under the direction of Samuel, the Spirit of God came upon Saul's agents and they also prophesied. The same thing happened to a second and a third group of agents. Thus divine intervention prevented the capture of David at this point (19:18-21).

Finally Saul decided to go to Ramah himself. While en route to his destination the Spirit of God came upon Saul and he also prophesied. When he arrived at Naioth Saul continued to prophesy before Samuel. He stripped off his outer garments and lay down *"naked,"* i.e., without his outer robes, all that day and even through the night.

302

People were stunned once again by the religious devotion of Saul (19:22-24).

By the great manifestation of the Spirit of God at Naioth, Yahweh was demonstrating how he could disarm the most determined foe. God rebuked Saul's anger and gave David opportunity to escape again.

B. David and Jonathan (1 Sam 20:1-42).

David next sought out his friend Jonathan. The prince knew nothing of any new death warrant on David, and Saul always discussed his intentions with his son. David explained that Saul was now withholding such information from Jonathan because he knew of their friendship. In reality, David said, *"there is but a step between me and death"* (20:1-3).

David asked Jonathan to ascertain whether Saul was still determined to kill him. At the New Moon[2] celebration if Saul should ask about his absence, Jonathan should tell his father that he had gone to Bethlehem for the annual family sacrifice.[3] If Saul became angry about this excuse that would signal that Saul still harbored murderous thoughts toward David. The problem, however, was how the information could be communicated to David if the disposition of the king was still hostile (20:4-11).

Jonathan agreed to convey the information to David whether the news was good or bad. The prince asked his friend to enter into a covenant that he would not cut off his house in the day that Yahweh gave him victory over his enemies. Thus Jonathan recognized that David would be the next king of Israel. David gladly entered that covenant with Jonathan (20:12-17).

The plan for conveying the disposition of Saul to David was now worked out. David was to hide himself in the spot where he previously had hidden. Jonathan would shoot three arrows. As the servant went to retrieve the arrows, Jonathan would say *"the arrows are beyond you"* or *"the arrows are on this side of you."* The first would indicate danger, the second, that everything was all right with Saul (20:18-23).

On the second day of the New Moon celebration Saul inquired about the absence of David. Jonathan gave the prearranged excuse. Saul exploded with anger, hurling a vicious epithet at his son, one in which he made disparaging comments about Jonathan's mother. Because of his friendship Jonathan had brought shame to *"his mother's nakedness."* He asserted that the kingdom would never be Jonathan's as long as David lived. He ordered his son to bring David to him so that he might die (20:24-31).

Jonathan tried to reason with his father as he had done a few weeks before. Saul, however, hurled his spear, narrowly missing his son. Jonathan knew now that David would never again be safe in Saul's presence. He left the room in anger because of the way his mother and his best friend had been treated by Saul. Jonathan fasted in grief over the treatment of David (20:32-34).

The next morning under the pretext of practicing archery Jonathan went out into the field to keep his appointment with David. A little lad accompanied him. Jonathan carried out the prearranged signal with David because he feared that he might be watched. After the danger signal had been given, however, Jonathan threw caution to the wind. He gave his bow and quiver to the lad and sent him back to the city. David then came out of hiding. Both friends thought that this would be the last time they would ever see one another. David expressed gratitude to Jonathan by bowing three times to the ground. In eastern style the friends kissed one another and wept. Jonathan reminded his friend of the covenant which had been made between them earlier. Then David and Jonathan went their separate ways (20:35-42).

C. David and Ahimelech (1 Sam 21:1-9).

David proceeded immediately to Nob, a couple of miles away on the northern outskirts of Jerusalem. The tabernacle was now located there. Ahimelech[4] the high priest came trembling to meet David. He must have known of Saul's hatred of David. That David was traveling alone was a clue that he was no longer employed in government service. David told the priest he was on a secret royal mission. His entourage would meet him at a designated spot.[5] David requested five loaves or any food which Ahimelech might have there at the sanctuary (21:1-3).

Ahimelech told David that the only bread in the place was holy. This bread was eaten by priests each sabbath day (Lev 24:9). The priest determined[6] that he could release that bread if David and his men were consecrated as soldiers normally were when they fought in a holy war. Abstinence from sexual relations was apparently a minimal requirement of consecration.[7] If David's men had kept themselves from women, Ahimelech could share the consecrated bread with them. David assured the priest that (1) both he and his men had indeed abstained from sexual relations; and (2) their *"vessels"* (NASB), i.e., their clothing and/or bodies were *"holy,"* i.e., ritually clean (21:4-5).[8]

Having been thus reassured, Ahimelech gave David the consecrated bread of the Presence which had just recently been replaced with freshly baked bread. Unfortunately, one of Saul's loyal servants was at the tabernacle that day. Doeg the Edomite, the overseer of Saul's herdsmen, *"was detained before Yahweh,"* probably on some ceremonial impurity (21:6-7).

David then asked the priest if he had available a weapon of some kind. He explained that the urgency of the king's business had prevented him from securing his own weapon. Ahimelech reminded David that the sword of Goliath was now housed in the tabernacle. He was welcome to that sword should he want it. *"Give it to me,"* David said, *"for there is none like it"* (21:8-9).

D. David and Achish (1 Sam 21:10-15).

David determined that the only way to escape Saul was to leave his kingdom. For this reason he went over to the Philistine King Achish of Gath. The king apparently welcomed the defection of David. His servants, however, were suspicious. They reminded their king that David was virtually *"king of the land,"* and that he had the reputation of having slain even more Philistines than Saul (21:10-11).

Sensing that he was in danger, David began to feign madness. He *"scribbled"* (NASB), i.e., *"made marks"* (NIV) on the doors of the gate. He allowed his spittle to run down into his beard. A normal person would never have permitted such an indignity to himself. Achish was convinced. He wanted nothing to do with such a madman. The Philistines observed the code of the east which regarded the insane as possessed of the gods, and therefore sacrosanct. The fugitive was safe for the moment (21:12-15).

305

E. David and the Four Hundred (1 Sam 22:1-2).

David departed from Achish in peace. He returned to Judah, to the cave of Adullam about ten miles from Gath and about twelve miles west of Bethlehem. There his relatives joined him. All those who were not prospering in Saul's kingdom joined David at Adullam. David became the captain of some four hundred men.

F. David and the King of Moab (1 Sam 22:3-5).

How long David remained at Adullam is not stated. From there he traveled south around the Dead Sea to Mizpah of Moab.[9] He requested that the king of Moab allow his mother and father to stay in his land *"until I know what God will do for me."* As long as David was in the *"stronghold"*[10] his parents remained in Moab (22:3-4).

The prophet Gad was among those who followed David. He advised David to depart from the *"stronghold"* and return to the land of Judah. Gad was probably thinking that David's claim to the throne might be jeopardized by remaining out of the country. David followed Gad's advice and entered the forest of Hereth in the Judean wilderness (22:5).

DAVID THE OUTLAW
1 Samuel 22:6-26:25

Now that David was back in his kingdom, his capture became the priority of Saul's reign. Five times David narrowly escaped from his determined father-in-law.

A. An Ominous Massacre (1 Sam 22:6-23).

Saul finally got word about David's whereabouts. He summoned his servants to a war council. Saul's court was simple. He sat under a tamarisk tree on a hill in Gibeah. Saul's spear served as his scepter. All his Benjamite courtiers stood in front of him. Saul appealed for the loyalty of his servants (22:6).

By means of two rhetorical questions Saul affirmed that he, not *"the son of Jesse,"* had given them property and appointed them to military commands. Yet none of these servants had kept Saul informed about the covenant between Jonathan and *"the son of*

Jesse." None of the servants felt sorry that Saul's son had stirred up *"my servant"* (David) against the king. No one seemed concerned that the son of Jesse was lying in ambush against Saul at that very moment. Of course Saul had it wrong. Jonathan had nothing to do with stirring up David against his father. In fact there was no evidence that David was hostile in any way to Saul, much less that he was setting an ambush for the king (22:7-8).

Doeg the Edomite was standing by the servants of Saul. He now stepped forward to report what he had seen at Nob a few weeks before. Saul immediately summoned all the priests from Nob. He began to harangue against Ahimelech. He accused the priest of conspiring with *"the son of Jesse"* against the crown by inquiring of God for him and giving him bread and a weapon. Thus Ahimelech was responsible for the ambush which David had set for Saul in the wilderness (22:9-13).

Ahimelech eloquently defended himself. First, he argued that David was as faithful a servant as Saul had. Second, it was not unusual for the priest to inquire of God on behalf of David. Third, he pled ignorance of *"this whole affair,"* i.e., any conspiracy against the king (22:14-15).

Saul refused to listen. In his mind there was a conspiracy against him, and the priests were part of that conspiracy. Saul, therefore, ordered his servants to slay the priests. His servants, however, refused to put forth their hands against the holy men. The king then ordered Doeg to do the deed. He slew eighty-five members of the priestly family that day. He also smote the city of Nob, utterly destroying the place and all who lived there. Thus Saul enforced against the innocent populace of Nob the ban which he refused to execute against the Amalekite sinners (22:16-19).

Only one priest, Abiathar, escaped the slaughter. He fled to David and reported to him what had happened. David had suspected that Doeg would tell Saul what had transpired at Nob. He felt personally responsible for the death of the priests. He invited Abiathar to join him and promised to give the priest protection from Saul (22:20-23).

B. David's First Escape (1 Sam 23:1-14).

In the Forest of Hereth David heard how the Philistines were plundering the threshing floors of Keilah. Through the prophet Gad he inquired of Yahweh as to whether or not he should go to the rescue of this city. The oracle was positive. Since his men objected to doing battle with the Philistines, David made a second inquiry with similar results. So David's small band went to Keilah and engaged the Philistines. Not only did he deliver the town of Keilah from being plundered, he was able to capture the Philistine livestock which his men desperately needed (23:1-5).

David's location at Keilah soon became known throughout the land. Abiathar (cf. 22:20-23) found him there. Saul also heard the reports. The king was confident that David could now be captured since he apparently had made the strategic mistake of occupying a walled city. Saul interpreted David's mistake as an indication that God had now rejected David. He still failed to grasp that he was the one who had been rejected. Nevertheless, Saul mobilized his army and marched toward Keilah (23:6-8).

Sympathizers soon sent the report of Saul's plans to David. He immediately inquired of the priestly oracle whether or not the reports about Saul were true, and whether or not the men of Keilah, if threatened with annihilation, would surrender David to his enemy. On both counts the priestly oracle was positive. David and his men—now numbering some six hundred—quickly returned to their wilderness haunts. When he heard that David had escaped Keilah, Saul canceled his campaign against that city and chased David into the Wilderness of Ziph (23:9-14).

C. David's Second Escape (1 Sam 23:15-29).

While David was at Horesh ("thicket") in the wilderness of Ziph Jonathan came to *"encourage him in God."* The Saulites knew that some day David would be king, and Jonathan would be his lieutenant. The two made another covenant to this effect. Then Jonathan departed for his home (23:15-18).

The Ziphites reported David's general location to Saul. They promised to deliver him into the hands of the king. Saul sent the Ziphites back as scouts before his army to get an exact fix on David. They found that David had moved to the Wilderness of Maon to the south of Jeshimon, a wasteland along the western shore of the Dead

Sea. When he heard that Saul was again in hot pursuit, David retreated to *"the rock"* in the wilderness of Maon (23:19-25).

With the aid of intelligence supplied by the Ziphites, Saul marched straight toward that mountain. Saul was in the process of positioning his men to surround David when a messenger arrived who reported that the Philistines had invaded the land. Saul withdrew his troops to deal with the new threat. Because of David's narrow escape the rock in the wilderness of Maon became known as the Rock of Escape. David then relocated to the strongholds of Engedi, a mountain oasis midway along the western side of the Dead Sea (23:26-29).

D. David's Third Escape (1 Sam 24).

Once the Philistine threat was over, Saul again turned his attention to tracking down his rival. In response to reports that David was hiding in the area of Engedi, Saul took three thousand men and marched in that direction. En route Saul entered one of the caves that was part of a sheepfold to *"cover his feet"* (KJV), i.e., relieve himself. David and some of his men were hiding in the inner recesses of that very cave. One of his men reminded David that Yahweh had promised one day to deliver his enemies into his hand.[11] David crept forward in the dark and cut off the edge of Saul's robe.[12] He returned to his men guilt stricken because he even had dared to cut the robe of God's anointed. David's attitude persuaded his men not to touch Saul (24:1-7).

After Saul had gone a safe distance, David went out of the cave and called after him. He bowed to the ground and addressed Saul respectfully as *"my lord the king."* With great emotion he tried to make his father-in-law see that he was being manipulated by certain men who stood to profit by removing David from the scene. He pointed out that he could have slain Saul in the cave had he been so minded. The missing edge of Saul's robe was proof of that. Perhaps Yahweh would avenge the wrong which Saul had done to him, but David would not. Saul was wasting his time seeking him, for David was no more a threat than a single flea on a dead dog. David concluded his speech by appealing to Yahweh to deliver him from the hand of Saul (24:8-15).

Saul was moved to tears by the words of David. He acknowledged that David had been more righteous than he. He recognized for the

moment that David must not have considered him as an enemy, else
he would have slain him in the cave. Saul prayed Yahweh's blessing
on David because he had refrained from slaying the king. Saul
acknowledged that David one day would be king. He concluded by
requesting an oath from David that he would not wipe out the family
of Saul, an action frequently taken when a new dynasty came to
power (24:16-21).

This request for an oath must have been a face-saving action by
Saul. If David would not kill the king, he would have no reason to kill
the descendants of the king. Nonetheless, David quickly gave Saul the
oath he wanted. Saul then returned home. David went up to *"the
stronghold,"* in this case, the most rugged part of the Wilderness of
Judea (24:22).

E. David's Fourth Escape (1 Sam 25).

During the days of wilderness hiding, Samuel died. All Israel
mourned for the prophet. They buried him at his house in Ramah.
Meanwhile, David kept on the move. He relocated temporarily about
a hundred miles to south in the Wilderness of Paran[13] on the border
between Canaan and the Sinai peninsula (25:1).

In the vicinity where David was hiding, a wealthy businessman was
shearing his sheep. Nabal was a descendant of Caleb, but he certainly
did not possess the disposition of his ancestor. He was harsh and evil
in his dealings. His wife Abigail, however, was both beautiful and
intelligent (25:2-3).

When he heard that Naboth was shearing sheep in Carmel (8 miles
SE of Hebron), David sent ten of his men to request a donation of
provisions. Sheep shearing was a festival time in which the spirit of
generosity prevailed. All the time he had been in that area David's
men had never taken any of Nabal's livestock. In fact the presence of
the small army of men probably keep thieves and raiding parties at
bay. In any case, David felt he had a solid basis upon which to make
his request (25:4-8).

The ten messengers were rudely rebuffed by Nabal. He regarded
David as nothing more than an ordinary rebel. He had no intentions
of sharing what belonged to him with the likes of a David (25:9-11).

When the ten messengers reported back to camp, David was furious. He ordered his four hundred men to strap on their swords. He prepared to lead the attack personally. He felt that Nabal had returned to him evil for good. In a fit of rage David swore that by morning no male associated with Nabal would be alive (25:12f.; 21f.).

One of the servants told Abigail what had happened. He confirmed what the messengers of David had asserted, *viz.,* that David's men had provided protection for those who tended sheep for Nabal in the field. The servant rightly judged that David would not ignore the insults of Nabal. The entire household was facing danger. Yet no one could approach the know-it-all Nabal because he was such a *"worthless man"* (25:14-17).

Abigail gathered a sizable amount of provisions from all the good things which had been prepared for the festival. She loaded this food on donkeys and secretly departed for David's camp, led by one of her servants. As it happened, David and his men where coming down from their mountain stronghold even as Abigail approached (25:18-22).

When she saw David, Abigail dismounted, and bowed herself to the ground. She accepted the total blame for the lack of hospitality shown the ten messengers. She urged David to pay no attention to *"this worthless man"* Nabal, for he lived up to the meaning of his name. The name Nabal means "fool" and this man acted the part (25:23-25).

Abigail used sweet but persuasive logic to urge David to accept the gift which she had brought on the donkeys and to forgive *"your maidservant."* She argued that (1) through her actions God had kept David from the guilt associated with shedding blood and avenging himself; (2) God was the true avenger of folly like that of Nabal; and (3) David should accept her gift for the sake of his men (25:26-27).

Abigail then made a direct plea for forgiveness. Since David was one who would be greatly blessed, he could afford to be gracious. David's blessing included (1) an enduring house, i.e., a long-lasting dynasty; (2) divine protection of his life;[14] and (3) the casting out of his enemies as a stone is hurled from a sling. Should David proceed to take vengeance on Nabal his conscience would bother him for having avenged himself rather than allowing the Lord to take vengeance for him (25:28-31).

311

In David's reply he (1) praised God for having sent Abigail; (2) thanked Abigail for keeping him from bloodshed; (3) graciously thanked the woman for the gifts; and (4) dismissed her in peace (25:32-35).

Abigail returned to find Nabal already feasting. Since he was very drunk, she did not attempt to tell him at that time what she had done. The next morning when he was sober Nabal learned of his wife's mission. When he heard, *"his heart died within him so that he became like a stone."* The text appears to be describing a paralyzing stroke triggered by rage. Nabal lingered ten days. Then Yahweh struck him, i.e., he had another seizure, and he died (25:36-38).

The news of Nabal's death caused David to bless Yahweh. The Lord had restrained David from the evil of personal vengeance, but at the same time Nabal had been repaid for the reproach which he had heaped upon God's anointed. David then sent servants to invite Abigail to become his wife. She greeted the offer with humility. Nonetheless, she arose quickly, and with her five maidservants, followed the emissaries to David's camp (25:39-42).

Abigail was the third wife of David. During his absence from court, Michal, his first wife, had been given to a certain Palti. At some point prior to marrying Abigail, David had taken Ahinoam of Jezreel as a wife (25:43-44). Polygamy stands condemned in Scripture both by the original marriage pattern of the garden and by the law of Moses (cf. Lev 18:18).

F. David's Fifth Escape (1 Sam 26).

The Ziphites again reported to Saul that David was hiding in the hill of Hachilah which was before the Jeshimon. Saul led his three thousand troops to the vicinity of that hill. David took evasive action when he ascertained that Saul was on his trail again. From a distance David noted that Saul was spending the night ringed by his troops (26:1-5).

David determined to enter the camp of Saul that night. Abishai, brother of Joab,[15] volunteered to go with David on this dangerous mission. The two invaders found the entire camp of Saul asleep. No one was guarding the king. Abishai sought permission to take the spear which was stuck in the ground near the king and run his enemy through. David, however, had qualms about striking Yahweh's anointed. Saul would die a natural death, or be smitten by Yahweh, or die in battle. David would not touch him. Instead, David told Abishai to take the king's spear and jug of water (26:6-11). David and Abishai were able to escape from Saul's camp undetected. Yahweh had caused all the troops of Saul to sleep with a sound sleep. The two men crossed the road and climbed the mountain on the other side. From that distance David shouted to awaken Saul's camp. He first addressed Abner. He accused Abner and his troops of being guilty of dereliction of duty worthy of death for failing to guard the life of the king. He then displayed the spear and jug which proved that security in Saul's camp had been breached (26:12-16).

David then addressed Saul. He asked why his father-in-law was pursuing him. Was it Yahweh who had stirred Saul up against David? Perhaps a sacrifice by the two of them would suffice to placate him. Was it his advisers who had stirred up Saul against David? Let them be cursed before Yahweh. These advisers were attempting to drive David from "the inheritance of Yahweh," i.e., from Israel. They could care less if David rendered devotion to the gods of one of the surrounding nations. David did not wish to die on foreign soil, and he pled with Saul not to hound him into foreign exile (26:17-20).

Once again David's words struck a responsive chord in Saul. He confessed his sin. Saul summarized his life with serious self-condemnation: "I have played the fool and have committed a serious error." He invited David to return. He promised not to harm him because David had spared his life that day (26:21).

David then invited one of Saul's servants to come and fetch the royal spear. He further expressed his confidence that Yahweh would reward his righteousness and faithfulness in not taking the life of the king that day. Yahweh would regard David's life as precious just as he had regarded Saul's life. David concluded his speech by expressing his desire for Yahweh to deliver him from distress. Saul responded by pronouncing a blessing on David. In it he expressed confidence that David would both accomplish much and surely prevail one day in receiving the crown. After these words, the two men went their separate ways never to see one another again (26:22-25).

DAVID THE MERCENARY
1 Samuel 27:1-12

David became very discouraged about his plight. If he remained in the land of Israel some day Saul would succeed in taking his life. He therefore determined to escape Saul's wrath by fleeing to the land of the Philistines (27:1).

A. David at Gath (1 Sam 27:2-6).

David took his six hundred men along with their families to Gath. He placed himself under the authority of Achish. When Saul heard that David had fled to Gath he gave up the search (27:2-4).

Achish on this occasion readily received David for two reasons. First, David brought with him a sizable force which he offered to place at the disposal of the Philistine king. Second, at this point David was the archenemy of Saul, who in turn was the archenemy of the Philistines.

After David had proved his worth to Achish, he requested of that king his own city. From David's standpoint it was important to remove his followers from the corrupting influence of a pagan culture. Achish saw the request as an opportunity to put a trusted ally in a strategic post on the outskirts of his territory. So the Philistine gave the city of Ziklag[16] to David. That city remained a possession of the kings of Judah at the time the Book of Samuel was written (27:5-6).

B. David at Ziklag (1 Sam 27:7-12).

David spent sixteen months in the land of the Philistines. Out of his headquarters at Ziklag, he attacked various of the old pagan inhabitants of the land: Geshurites, Girzites and Amalekites. The first two peoples are otherwise unknown in the Bible. Saul virtually had wiped out the Amalekites (1 Sam 15:8-9), but a new wave of these desert marauders was attempting to press into Canaan out of the desert (27:7-8).

David apparently would launch a retaliatory attack against the desert peoples whenever they attempted to invade the south of Judah. He would exterminate these enemies of Israel and take all their plunder. These raids accomplished two things. First, David was able to supply the needs of his followers. Second, his victories over the enemies of his people helped him build a base of support in Judah (27:9).

When Achish inquired about the raids, David would give deliberately misleading reports. They were worded in such a way that Achish assumed the raids were against Israelite territory. He became confident of David's loyalty. Achish was prepared to integrate David's six hundred soldiers into the Philistine army (27:10-12).

The conduct of David during the sixteen months in Ziklag cannot be condoned. These were dark days in the life of the future king. He was spiritually depressed. During this period there is no record of any communication with the Lord.

Chart No. 28

DAVID IN THE WILDERNESS					
	1ST ESCAPE 23:1-14	**2ND ESCAPE** 23:15-29	**3RD ESCAPE** Ch. 24	**4TH ESCAPE** Ch. 25	**5TH ESCAPE** Ch. 26
General Location		Wilderness of Maon	Wilderness of Engedi	Wilderness of Maon	Wilderness of Ziph
Specific Location	Keilah	"Rock of Escape"	"Rocks of the Wild Goats"	Carmel	Hill of Hachilah
Betrayal	Anonymous	Ziphites	Anonymous	Nabal	Ziphites
Dangers	Attack on Keilah; David could be surrendered to Saul	Saul's men were surrounding David	Saul & David in a cave together	David about to take vengeance on Nabal	David's 600 just opposite Saul's 3000; Saul's life in David's hands
Advisor	Abiathar: Warning	Jonathan: Encouragement	David's Men: Incitement	Abigail: Pacification	Abishai: Incitement
Relief Action	David departed from Keilah	Philistine Invasion	David cuts off a portion of Saul's robe	Abigail gives provisions to David	David takes spear and jug from Saul
Outcome	Saul gave up pursuit	Saul goes to engage Philistines	Temporary reconciliation	David relents; God smites Nabal	Temporary reconciliation

ENDNOTES

1. Howard Vos, *1,2 Samuel* in "Bible Study Commentary" (Grand Rapids: Zondervan, 1983), p. 69.

2. Scholars debate whether the New Moon was celebrated every month or four times each year.

3. Most commentators take the position that the story of the family sacrifice in Bethlehem was pure fabrication. That David may have actually made a quick trip to Bethlehem on the first day of the New Moon is not impossible. The distance from Gibeah to Bethlehem was only about 8.5 miles.

4. Jesus stated that this episode occurred *"in the days of Abiathar the high priest"* (Mark 2:26). Did Abiathar share the high priesthood with Ahimelech? Or is the epithet *"high priest"* used proleptically?

5. Most commentators bluntly accuse David of lying to Ahimelech about his mission and his men. That Saul had assigned to David some mission prior to his departure from the court is not inherently impossible. That he had men with him is confirmed by the statement of Jesus in Mark 2:26.

6. If the testimony of Doeg the Edomite can be trusted, Ahimelech *"inquired of Yahweh"* before he gave provisions and the sword to David (1 Sam 22:10). This testimony seems authentic, because it would not seem likely that Ahimelech would give priests' food to David without divine approval.

7. Even an involuntary nocturnal emission forced a soldier to move outside the military encampment. He had to bathe before reentering the camp at sundown (Deut 23:9-11).

8. Vos, *op. cit.,* p. 76.

9. David may have chosen Moab because of his Moabite ancestry (Ruth 4:17,22). On the other hand, David may have felt he would be safe in the territory of one of Saul's adversaries.

10. Some think the *"stronghold"* is Masada. The text, however, suggests that the location was in Moab.

11. No record exists of any promise made to David that one day God would deliver Saul into his hands. To what promise David's men had reference in 1 Sam 24:4 is not clear.

12. Coming into the dark cave from the bright sunlight meant that Saul's eyes were not as accustomed to the darkness as were the eyes of David. Evidently the king left his outer garment near the entrance of the cave while he went into a side chamber to relieve himself. The noise of men and animals outside the cave would have drowned out any noise David might have made in getting to the robe.

13. The Septuagint reads in 1 Sam 25:1 *"wilderness of Maon"* instead of *"wilderness of Paran."* The NIV and JB follow this Greek reading, thus avoiding a somewhat lengthy journey by David. Though difficult, the Hebrew reading is to be preferred.

14. The idea of David's life being *"bound in the bundle of the living"* (NASB) is an allusion to the bundle in which a man might tie together silver or other precious objects.

15. Abishai and Joab were sons of David's sister Zeruiah (1 Chr 2:16) and hence were nephews of David.

16. Ziklag was located some fifteen miles northwest of Beersheba, and some twenty-five miles south of Gath. During the conquest Ziklag had been assigned to the tribe of Simeon. The gift of Ziklag suggests (1) that the city was under Philistine jurisdiction; and (2) that the site was virtually uninhabited at this time.

The Great Sea

Mt. Hermon

Tyre

PHOENICIA

Sea of Chinnereth

Saul consults witch before battle.

Endor

Shunem
Jezreel
× Mt. Gilboa
Beth-shan

Saul's body fastened to a wall by Philistines.

Jabesh-gilead

Saul and Jonathan slain in battle.

Jordan R.

Aphek

PHILISTINE MARCH

SAUL'S MARCH

Saul's body rescued by men of Jabesh-gilead.

PHILISTINES

Ramah
Gibeah

Gath

David accompanies Philistines part way.

Salt Sea

Arnon R.

Brook Besor

Ziklag

Amalekites smitten.

David pursues raiders of Ziklag.

THE SOUTH (NEGEV)

EGYPT

SAUL'S THIRD PHILISTINE WAR

1 SAMUEL 28-31

50 km

0   50 Miles

CHAPTER NINETEEN

David Becomes King
1 Samuel 28-2 Samuel 4

During his reign Saul had been fairly successful in preventing the Philistines from making significant inroads into Israel. From the viewpoint of these enemies, however, the time was now ripe for a major thrust into Israel. Samuel, the spiritual leader of the nation, was dead. The most capable soldier in Israel's army had defected to the Philistines. Saul was losing his political grip and perhaps even his sanity. These factors convinced the lords of the Philistines to band together under the leadership of Achish to attempt an invasion of Israel.

THE PHILISTINE INVASION OF 1010 BC
1 Samuel 28:1-25

The Philistine invasion came about 1010 BC. The plan was to march north along the coastal plain to the valley of Jezreel, then knife eastward across that valley. In this region Saul's defenses were thin,

319

and the flat terrain gave the Philistines military superiority because of their chariotry.

A. David's Awkward Position (1 Sam 28:1-2).

The Philistine attack put David, who was now a trusted ally of King Achish, in an awkward position. The king insisted that David go to war with him against Israel. David was in no position to refuse since he had placed himself at the disposal of the Philistine king.[1] Achish trusted David so much that he appointed his men to be the royal bodyguard during the battle.

B. Saul's Desperate Plight (1 Sam 28:3-14).

The plight of Saul is indicated in three statements in the text. First, the author reminds the reader that Samuel was dead. In this national crisis Saul could count on no counsel from the great prophet. Second, Saul had removed from the land those who were mediums and spiritists. This statement indicates that Saul had attempted to fulfill his responsibilities as king to remove from the land all practitioners of the occult. This action meant, however, that in this crisis he could not easily consult with these prognosticators. Third, the Philistines camped in Shunem seven miles east of Megiddo in the Valley of Jezreel. The Israelites were camped just across a narrow valley on the slopes of Mt. Gilboa. When he saw their camp, Saul trembled with fear. Finally, when he tried to inquire of the Lord, the king received no answer by any of the unusual means of revelation: dreams, Urim (the priestly oracle), or prophets (28:3-6).

In his desperation Saul decided to resort to necromancy (consulting the dead). He ordered his servants to seek out a woman who was a medium. Though outlawed,[2] witches still secretly practiced their Satanic religion. The servants knew of a woman in Endor who was a medium. In Jewish tradition this woman is identified as the mother of Abner, Saul's general (28:7).

Saul disguised himself by changing his clothes in order to conceal his identity from Philistine patrols and from the medium herself. He and two men made the perilous journey through the night around the Philistine lines to Endor.[3] The witch was cautious when the unidentified visitor requested to contact a dead spirit. She suspected the request might be an effort at entrapment. Saul swore an oath in Yahweh's name that no punishment would come to the woman. The woman inquired about who she should call up (28:8-11).

As soon as Saul mentioned the name Samuel, the prophet appeared. The witch, who had performed none of her usual seance antics, *"saw"* him. She cried out in fear. If she had any suspicions as to the identity of her tall visitor they now were confirmed. She chided Saul for having deceived her. The king calmed her fears and begged her to describe what she saw. The witch said she saw a *"divine being"* (NASB), i.e., supernatural being, coming out of the earth. Saul then inquired as to the form of what she saw. The witch described the form as (1) an old man who was (2) wrapped in a robe. At this point it seems that Saul himself saw the spirit. He *"knew"* that this was the spirit of Samuel. In respect to the old prophet, Saul bowed himself to the ground (28:12-14).

C. Samuel's Ominous Prophecy (1 Sam 28:15-25).

A conversation took place between Samuel and Saul apparently without the mediation of the witch. First, Samuel asked Saul why he had disturbed him by bringing him up, i.e., causing him to return from Sheol, the abode of the dead, to the land of the living. The language suggests that Sheol for the saint was peaceful. Second, Saul responded by describing his plight. In the face of the Philistine invasion he needed divine counsel, but Yahweh had departed from him. Third, Samuel raised a second question. If Yahweh had become his enemy, why then did he now seek the counsel of Yahweh's prophet? (28:15-16).

Samuel then spoke ominous prophetic words to the king. He announced (1) political judgment. By the violence of the coming battle the kingdom would be torn from Saul's hand and given to David. The disobedience regarding Amalek (ch.15) would be avenged even as Samuel had predicted years before. Then Samuel spoke of (2) military judgment. On the morrow Yahweh would deliver the army of Israel into the hands of the Philistines. In this battle Saul would experience (3) personal judgment. He and his sons would join Samuel in Sheol on the morrow, i.e., they would die in battle (28:17-19).

Faint with hunger and overwhelmed with fear, Saul fell prostrate on the ground.[4] Seeing the terror in the eyes of her king, the woman tried to be a source of comfort to him. Since she had done as Saul had asked, she now requested him to listen to her. He should eat some food before attempting to return to the camp. With the assistance of his servants, the woman finally persuaded Saul to eat. The king arose from the ground and sat on the bed while the kindly witch quickly prepared meat and bread for him. After they had eaten that fare the royal entourage departed (28:20-25).

DAVID'S PROBLEMS
1 Samuel 29:1-30:31

The Philistine invasion of 1010 BC created problems for David as well as Saul. He faced problems with Achish, at Ziklag and with his own troops.

A. Problems with Achish (1 Sam 29).

The Philistines gathered their forces to Aphek. There they organized their army for the thrust into Israel. As royal bodyguard, David's unit was to the rear of the attacking forces. The Philistine commanders were very uncomfortable with a sizable "Hebrew" unit to their rear. Achish, however, defended David. In all the time he had been in the land of the Philistines, never had Achish ever had occasion to find fault with him. Yet the commanders angrily insisted that David be sent back to Ziklag. They were afraid that in the heat of battle he would attack the Philistines and thus try to win his way back into the good graces of Saul (29:1-5).

Achish summoned David and dismissed him, but not without first praising him for his fidelity during his years of service. The text seems to suggest that the king could not overrule the collective will of the Philistine lords. David protested his dismissal, but it is hard to believe that in his heart he did not breathe a silent sigh of relief. Achish reiterated his own satisfaction with David who had been as pleasing as *"an angel of God."* Nevertheless, because the commanders had insisted, he ordered David to leave at first light. In the morning David and his men went south toward the land of the Philistines while the armies of Achish marched east toward Jezreel to confront Saul (29:6-11).

322

B. Problems at Ziklag (1 Sam 30:1-6).

The trip from Aphek to Ziklag—about seventy-five miles—took three days. The troops arrived only to find the city in ruins. In the absence of the fighting men, those pesky Amalekites had made a raid on the city. They had taken captive all those who remained in the city. Then they had burned the place. David and his men burst forth in agonizing lamentation at the realization that their wives, sons and daughters were in the hands of Amalekites. Ahinoam and Abigail, David's wives, were among those who had been kidnapped. The agony over this loss was compounded by the murmuring of the troops. Blaming him for leaving the city without adequate defenses, they spoke of stoning David. *"But David strengthened himself in Yahweh, his God,"* i.e., his faith in God enabled him to deal with this crisis effectively (30:1-6).

C. Problems with his Troops (1 Sam 30:7-25).

David sought the counsel of God through the priestly oracle administered by Abiathar. By this means he ascertained that a pursuit of the Amalekites into the desert would be successful. Forgetting their fatigue, the six hundred desperate men set out in pursuit of the enemy. Exhausted by their three-day trip from Aphek, two hundred of David's men collapsed at the Brook Besor, about ten miles from Ziklag. David left them there to guard the baggage while he and four hundred stalwarts proceeded with the chase (30:7-10).

The search for the Amalekites discovered an Egyptian lying in the sand. Because he had had neither food nor water, the man was all but dead. He was taken to David where he received food and drink. When questioned, the Egyptian reported that he had been a servant of the Amalekites. When he had fallen sick three days earlier, the Amalekites had left him to die in the desert. He agreed to lead David to their camp if David would swear not to kill him nor hand him over to the Amalekites (30:11-15).

At what they considered a safe distance from the scene of their attack, the Amalekites were celebrating when David came upon them. They were eating, drinking and dancing because of the great spoil which they taken both from the Philistines and from the people of Judah. David launched a night attack against the sprawling camp.

Until evening the next day his men chased and cut down fleeing Amalekites. Only four hundred young men who rode camels were able to escape (30:16-17).

So David was able to rescue his two wives. He recovered all which the Amalekites had taken. The other livestock which was in the Amalekite camp was regarded as David's personal spoils of victory (30:18-20).

On the return trip to Ziklag, David had to settle a dispute among his men. Some of the worthless men among David's four hundred thought that the spoils of war should go only to those who actually went into battle. Those who had guarded the baggage should receive only their family members *"that they may lead them away and depart."* Apparently they wanted these baggage handlers excommunicated from the community. David, however, would have none of that. Credit for the victory belonged to Yahweh, not the four hundred. Therefore, David issued a ruling which became part of Israelite military law: Those who guarded the baggage in war would receive equal share of the spoils with those who actually fought (30:21-25).

D. Epilogue: Gifts to Judah (1 Sam 30:26-31).

Upon his return to Ziklag, David sent part of the spoils from the victory to the elders of various towns throughout Judah. By this diplomatic move David was positioning himself to be elevated to kingship by his native tribe immediately after the death of Saul.

THE BATTLE OF MT. GILBOA
1 Samuel 31:1-13

While David was defeating the Amalekites in the desert, Saul was facing the judgment of God at Mount Gilboa.

A. The Death of Saul (1 Sam 31:1-6 // 1 Chr 10:1-6).

The Philistines initiated the attack against Israel. Saul's troops fled. The slopes of Mt. Gilboa were covered with the corpses of his fallen men. Three of Saul's sons fell that day. Then the battle pressed in on the king himself. He was wounded by Philistine archers. Fearing that he might fall into enemy hands to be abused and finally slain, Saul ordered his armorbearer to thrust him through. The armorbearer, however, feared to take the life of the king. So Saul took his sword and fell on it. His loyal armorbearer followed the example of the king. Thus was the prophecy made by Samuel in his post-mortem appearance fulfilled (31:1-6).

After describing how the Philistines had forced Saul to suicide, the Chronicler affirms that Yahweh slew him. He cites two reasons for the downfall of Saul: (1) his trespass which he committed against Yahweh *"because of the word of Yahweh which he did not keep;"* and (2) he did not inquire of Yahweh,[5] but rather sought counsel of a witch. For these reasons Yahweh turned the kingdom over to David (1 Chr 10:13-14).

B. Valor of the Gileadites (1 Sam 31:7-13 // 1 Chr 10:7-12).

In the aftermath of the Philistine victory at Gilboa, the Israelites withdrew from the Valley of Jezreel and even certain vulnerable areas east of Jordan. For a time the Philistines occupied those cities. When the Philistines returned to Gilboa to strip the slain of valuables, they discovered the bodies of Saul and his sons. They decapitated the corpse and stripped his weapons. These trophies of victory triggered joyous celebration throughout the land of the Philistines. Saul's weapons were eventually deposited in the temple of Ashtaroth, the goddess of sex and war.[6] The Philistines nailed Saul's body and those of his sons to the wall of the town of Beth-shan[7] near the Jordan river (31:7-10).

Across the Jordan in Jabesh-gilead courageous men decided to end the desecration of Saul's body. They marched all night to Bethshan. They took the bodies of the royal family from the wall and returned to Jabesh. There they cremated the remains in order to prevent any further desecration of them. Then they buried the remains beneath a tree near their city. To show respect for the dead the Gileadites fasted for seven days (31:11-13).

DAVID'S REIGN ESTABLISHED
2 Samuel 1:1-2:7

Three days after returning to the burned out site of Ziklag, David received news from the battle at Mount Gilboa.

A. A Battle Report (2 Sam 1:1-10).

An Amalekite who had been in the camp of Saul made his way to Ziklag to report to David the outcome of the battle. The man was tattered and torn. He had dust on his head to symbolize lamentation. This man related the sad news that Israel had been put to flight before the Philistines, and that Saul and Jonathan were dead. To this point the report was accurate. The remainder of the report was fabricated by the Amalekite for self-serving purposes (1:1-4).

David wished more verification that the king and prince were dead. The Amalekite then reported coming upon Saul leaning on his spear on Mt. Gilboa. With Philistine chariots pressing in on him Saul supposedly asked this Amalekite to end the agony of his wound by slaying him. The Amalekite reported that he did as Saul had asked. He produced Saul's crown and bracelet as evidence of the truth of his account. The Amalekite apparently thought that he could curry favor with David by claiming that he had been the one to kill the king. The truth is that he must have been lurking nearby when Saul committed suicide as reported in the previous chapter (1:5-10).

B. A Just Execution (2 Sam 1:11-16).

The reaction in Ziklag to the news of Saul's death must have shocked the Amalekite. David's men followed their beloved leader in the ritual mourning until evening. Then David summoned the Amalekite and rebuked him for having stretched out his hand against Yahweh's anointed. He then ordered one of his men to slay this man who claimed to have slain the king. The Amalekite had condemned himself to death by his own testimony.

C. A Bitter Lamentation (2 Sam 1:17-27).

David then composed a poetic lament over the deaths of Saul and Jonathan. The composition was called *"the song of the bow."* It appeared in the extrabiblical Book of Jashar[8] as well as here in 2 Samuel (1:17-18).

The poem began with a reference to the royal figures as *"the beauty"* and *"mighty"* of Israel. David could not bear the thought that the *"uncircumcised"* Philistines might be rejoicing over the death of the royal family. He called for Mt. Gilboa to remain barren to mark the tragedy. There the royal shields were defiled in spite of the fact that both Saul and Jonathan had been valiant in battle (1:19-22).

David's lament continued by describing the loving relationship between Saul and Jonathan in life. They were not separated in their death. David described their physical prowess as *"swifter than eagles"* and *"stronger than lions."* He called on the daughters of Israel to weep over Saul who had brought them prosperity (1:23-24).

The lament concluded with a special word about Jonathan. David was especially distressed over the death of this man that he considered a *"brother."* His relationship with Jonathan brought David more satisfaction and joy than his relationship with any woman in his life (1:25-27).

D. A Royal Elevation (2 Sam 2:1-4a).

Following the period of lamentation over Saul and Jonathan, David inquired of Yahweh regarding his next step. By this means he ascertained that he should move immediately from Ziklag to Hebron, the political and geographical center of the region. All of his men and their families relocated in the villages around Hebron. The tribal leaders then came to Hebron and anointed David king over the house of Judah.

E. A Proper Recognition (2 Sam 2:4b-7).

When he learned of the heroic actions of the men of Jabesh, David immediately sent a congratulatory message to that city. He wished Yahweh's lovingkindness upon them. He promised to show *"goodness"* to them because they had shown kindness to Saul. David's message closed with mention of the fact that the house of Judah had anointed him king. The congratulatory message was an oblique appeal to the elders of this distant city of Israel to recognize him as king.

DAVID'S REIGN CHALLENGED
2 Samuel 2:8-3:5

Saul had many loyal followers throughout the land who were determined to prevent David from becoming king of Israel. Their problem was that the most qualified successor of Saul had died with his father at Gilboa. Abner, Saul's uncle and general, sought to rally support for Ish-bosheth[9] the sole surviving son of the late king.

A. The Plot of Abner (2 Sam 2:8-11).

Mahanaim in Transjordan was Abner's base of operations. The presence of the Philistines west of Jordan made it impossible to maintain a capital in that region. Gradually Abner was able to secure for Ish-bosheth the support of various regions of the country. After about five years it could be said that Ish-bosheth ruled over "all Israel," i.e., all of the tribes besides Judah. He ruled all Israel for two years. Meanwhile, David ruled in Hebron over Judah for seven and a half years (2:8-11).

B. The Clash at Gibeon (2 Sam 2:12-32).

When he had gathered sufficient support, Abner decided to challenge David's rule of Judah. To thwart this offensive David's men advanced to Gibeon in the territory of Benjamin. At the pool there the two forces met. Joab the nephew of David was commanding the forces of Judah. Abner proposed that before the battle, champions from the opposing sides "make sport," i.e., fight a mini battle for the entertainment of the soldiers in both armies. Joab agreed. Twelve men from each side competed. The twenty-four soldiers were so skilled in hand to hand combat that all of them eventually fell wounded. The place thereafter was named Helkath-hazzurim, "the field of sword-edges." If this contest was meant to settle the dispute between the two armies, it did not. A general battle of severe intensity followed. Abner and his men were thoroughly defeated (2:12-17).

An incident occurred in the battle at Gibeon which was to have serious repercussions. Asahel was killed. He was the third son of Zeruiah and younger brother of Joab and Abishai. This youth was "swift of foot." During the course of the battle he set his sights on Abner. He determined to chase down the old general and kill him. As he scampered up and down the rough hills of Benjamin, Abner spotted the young soldier bearing down on him. Twice Abner warned Asahel to turn aside lest he be killed. Abner knew that if he killed this young warrior Joab would never forgive him. Asahel, however, refused to be deterred. As he closed in on Abner, the wily old general abruptly stopped and thrust backward with the butt of his spear. Asahel was struck with such force that the butt of the spear ripped through his belly and exited his back. Asahel died on the spot. Those who came on that spot the rest of the day paused in silent tribute to the valor of this dashing young officer (2:18-23).

Joab and Abishai continued to press the attack on Abner out into the wilderness. Abner was eventually able to rally his fleeing soldiers in a strategic position on the top of a certain hill. Abner called to Joab and suggested that it was time to end hostilities. After all, both the pursuers and those being pursued were *"brothers."* Observing that an all-out assault on the position of Abner would be extremely costly, Joab signaled his men to halt the attack. Under cover of darkness, Abner and his men marched through the Arabah (Jordan valley), crossed the river and returned to the safety of Mahanaim (2:24-29).

In the battle at Gibeon twenty of David's men had been lost while Abner's losses were 360. Asahel was buried with honors in the family tomb at Bethlehem. Then by an all-night march Joab and his troops returned to Hebron (2:30-32).

C. A Summary Statement (2 Sam 3:1-5).

Apparently the clash at Gibeon was the first of many encounters between those who supported the son of Saul, and those who followed David. Gradually the house of Saul grew weaker (3:1).

Chart No. 29

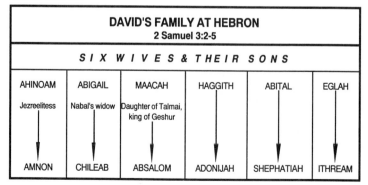

DAVID'S FAMILY AT HEBRON 2 Samuel 3:2-5					
S I X W I V E S & T H E I R S O N S					
AHINOAM	ABIGAIL	MAACAH	HAGGITH	ABITAL	EGLAH
Jezreelitess	Nabal's widow	Daughter of Talmai, king of Geshur			
↓	↓	↓	↓	↓	↓
AMNON	CHILEAB	ABSALOM	ADONIJAH	SHEPHATIAH	ITHREAM

During the seven plus years at Hebron David continued to prosper. He took three additional wives, one of whom was the daughter of the king of Geshur. Each of his wives bore him one son during this period.

DAVID'S REIGN SOLIDIFIED
2 Samuel 3:6-4:12

David's bid to succeed Saul as king of a united Israel was strengthened considerably by a strange turn of events among the supporters of the opposition.

A. Accusation against Abner (2 Sam 3:6-11).

Early on Abner was intensely loyal to the house of Saul. At the same time he viewed David as a threat to the nation. In Abner's view, David's associations with King Achish of Gath disqualified him from any consideration of kingship.

The text hints that at some point Abner began to have some personal ambition. With the weak Ish-bosheth totally dependent on him, Abner *"was making himself strong in the house of Saul"* (NASB). Ish-bosheth accused Abner of a sexual relationship with Rizpah, one of Saul's concubines. To take the wives of a king was a method of positioning oneself for a bid for the crown. Whether or not Abner was guilty as charged is difficult to ascertain from the text (3:6-7).

Abner exploded with anger at the accusation of Ish-bosheth. He could not believe that after all the kindness he had shown to the house of Saul that anyone could think him guilty of such treachery. At any time Abner could have delivered Ish-bosheth over to David. Now because he had been (falsely?) accused, Abner swore that he would use his influence to see David acknowledged as ruler of Israel from Dan to Beersheba. Ish-bosheth was so intimidated by this outburst that he could not say a word to his general (3:8-11).

B. Negotiations with Abner (2 Sam 3:12-21).

Abner immediately sent messengers to Hebron. He wanted David to enter into a covenant with him. If that came about, Abner promised to bring all Israel over to him. Before David would consider a covenant, however, he insisted that his first wife Michal, daughter of Saul, be returned to him. To re-establish his marriage with the daughter of the former king would strengthen David's claim to the throne in the eyes of many supporters of Saul (3:12-14).

With his chief military officer negotiating with his rival, Ish-bosheth was in no position to deny David's request. He took Michal from her current husband Paltiel (Palti) and had her escorted to Hebron. Her husband sorrowfully followed, helpless to reclaim his wife. When Paltiel reached Bahurim, Abner ordered him to return. The text gives no indication about Michal's attitude about being returned to her rightful husband (3:15-16).

True to his word, Abner began to consult with the elders of Israel about supporting David. He pointed out to them that in time past they had preferred David to Saul. Now Abner urged them to recognize him. He told them that Yahweh had designated David as the savior from the Philistines. After he had secured the support of the other tribes, Abner approached the tribe of Benjamin. This tribe was the base of Saul's support. Abner agreed to carry the concerns of the northern elders to David (3:17-19).

Abner with a twenty-man honor guard came to David at Hebron. They were welcomed with open arms. Details of the negotiations are not related. At the end of the feasts, however, Abner was prepared to gather all Israel that they might make a covenant with David. Abner was dismissed with David's blessing (3:20-21).

C. Murder of Abner (2 Sam 3:22-39).

At this point Joab returned with the troops from a raid. When he was informed that Abner had just left with the king's blessing, Joab rebuked David. He was suspicious that Abner was feigning support in order to spy out the strength of Judah. Without notifying David, Joab sent messengers to bring Abner back to Hebron. When he returned, Joab took him aside into the middle of the gate on the pretext of speaking to him privately. There he slew Abner *"on account of the blood of Asahel his brother"* (3:22-27).

David was shocked when he heard what his general had done. He publicly proclaimed his innocence in the matter. He pronounced a malediction on Joab and his descendants. He wished sickness,

331

poverty, weakness and hunger on Joab's family perpetually (3:28-30).

The king ordered his supporters, including Joab, to publicly lament the death of Abner. David himself followed the bier to the grave. There he and all his followers wept. The king chanted a lamentation which he had composed in honor of Abner. The man had experienced a death unworthy of him. He had not died in battle, nor had he been executed as a common criminal. Abner had been treacherously murdered (3:31-34).

After the burial, the people tried to get David to eat. He vowed he would not taste food until sundown. The people were pleased with this demonstration of grief over the murder of his former enemy. They rightly concluded that David had nothing to do with the cold-blooded murder of Abner. The king regarded Abner as *a prince and a great man* in Israel. His sense of justice called for punishment against Joab. Yet, even though he was king, he regarded the two sons of Zeruiah as *too difficult* to handle. All he could do was to call upon Yahweh to punish the evil which Joab had done (3:35-39).

D. The Death of Ish-bosheth (2 Sam 4:1-12).

The death of Abner sent shock waves throughout Israel. Ish-bosheth lost his courage (lit., "his hands went limp") and all his subjects were *"disturbed."* Two Benjamite brothers, who were commanders in Ish-bosheth's army, decided to take advantage of the situation. They decided to assassinate the king so as to gain some recognition from David. The author then notes parenthetically that no other viable candidate for the throne could be found within the royal family. The son of Jonathan was now only twelve. He had been crippled from childhood. He was unwilling or unable to press any claims to the throne (4:1-4).

On a hot day when Ish-bosheth was taking a siesta in his house, Baanah and Rechab made their move. Under the pretext of entering the house to get some wheat (probably rations for their troops), they entered the royal chamber and assassinated their king. They then decapitated Ish-bosheth. After making good their escape from Mahanaim, the two traveled all night through the Arabah (Jordan Valley) to make their way to Hebron (4:5-7).

The assassins presented the head of Ish-bosheth to David. They thought they would be rewarded for having eliminated David's enemy. They suggested that through their action Yahweh had taken vengeance on the house of Saul. David, however, was of a different mind. If he had ordered the execution of a man who thought he had brought good news of Saul's death, how much more would he execute those guilty of murdering an innocent man in his own bed. At that sentence, David's men fell on Rechab and Baanah and slew them. The hands and feet were removed from the corpses, and their bodies were hung up beside the pool in Hebron. The mutilation of the dead bodies was a sign that these men had raised their hands against royalty. Then David took the head of Ish-bosheth and buried it in the grave of Abner in Hebron.

Chart No. 30

THE LIFE OF DAVID *Proposed Chronology*		
EVENT	**DATE BC**	**AGE**
Birth	1040	
Anointed by Samuel	1029	11
In Saul's Court	1028	12
Fought Goliath	1021	19
In Saul's Army	1020	20
Flight from Saul	1016	24
In Achish's Army	1012	28
Anointed by Judah	1010	30
Anointed by Israel	1003	37
Sin with Bathsheba	982	58
Rebellion by Absalom	976	64
Death	970	70

ENDNOTES

1. David's response to Achish was actually ambiguous: *"You shall know what your servant can do."* Achish interpreted the words to mean that

David would fight heroically on behalf of the Philistine forces.

2. Lev 19:31; Deut 18:10-11. Anyone who dabbled in necromancy was to be stoned (Lev 20:6, 27).

3. Endor stood on the north side of the hill of Moreh, north of the Philistine lines. The town was some ten miles north of Saul's camp.

4. The pressure of the invasion had kept Saul from eating all that day and night. He had made a difficult journey to Endor. Now he had been given the sentence of death by a voice from beyond the grave. His physical and mental reaction to what has just taken place is understandable.

5. 1 Sam 28:6 states that Saul did inquire of Yahweh, but did not receive an answer. He must not have inquired with the right spirit or with persistence. Hence Chronicles insists that he did not inquire of the Lord at all.

6. The location of the temple of Ashtaroth where Saul's weapons were deposited is uncertain. Most commentators assume that the temple was located in the Philistine city of Ashkelon. A temple of this goddess has been located in Beth-shan. It would have been more convenient to put the battle trophies in this temple.

7. Beth-shan was located just east of the battlefield and about four miles west of the Jordan River. The city was built on a prominent hill. Its wall could be seen from a great distance.

8. The Book of Jashar is mentioned in Joshua 10:13 and in the Septuagint of 1 Kgs 8:53. It was apparently a book of war ballads. A modern "reconstruction" of the book which is available is a fake.

9. Ish-bosheth ruled Israel for two years while David ruled Judah from Hebron for seven and a half years (2 Sam 2:10). From this fact some have concluded that Abner waited five and one-half years before attempting to enthrone Ish-bosheth.

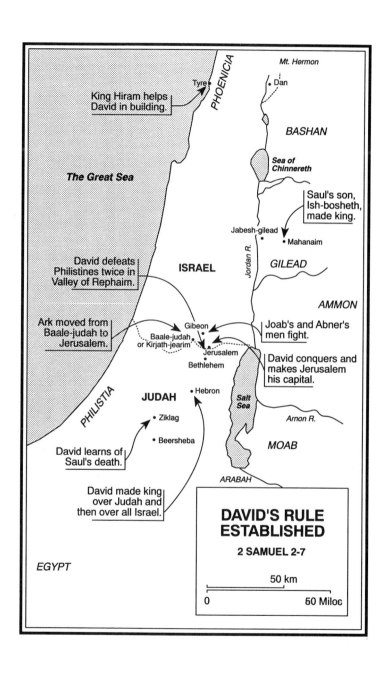

King Hiram helps
David in building.

Mt. Hermon

• Dan

Tyre

PHOENICIA

BASHAN

The Great Sea

Sea of
Chinnereth

Saul's son,
Ish-bosheth,
made king.

Jabesh-gilead

• Mahanaim

David defeats
Philistines twice in
Valley of Rephaim.

ISRAEL

Jordan R.

GILEAD

AMMON

Ark moved from
Baale-judah to
Jerusalem.

Gibeon

Joab's and Abner's
men fight.

Baale-judah
or Kirjath-jearim

Jerusalem

Bethlehem

David conquers and
makes Jerusalem
his capital.

JUDAH

• Hebron

Salt
Sea

PHILISTIA

• Ziklag

Arnon R.

• Beersheba

David learns of
Saul's death.

MOAB

David made king
over Judah and
then over all Israel.

ARABAH

**DAVID'S RULE
ESTABLISHED**

2 SAMUEL 2-7

EGYPT

50 km

0   50 Miloc

CHAPTER TWENTY

The Triumphs of David
2 Samuel 5-9

With both Abner and Ish-bosheth dead, the northern tribes quickly endorsed David as king. The early years in David's rule over united Israel were glorious in many ways. In chapters 5-10 the sacred historian recounts his triumphs.

POLITICAL ESTABLISHMENT
2 Samuel 5:1-25

During the long years after his anointing at Bethlehem, David made no effort to seize the throne by force. He patiently waited for the prophecy of Samuel to be fulfilled. He trusted God to work his will. In 2 Samuel 5 the text chronicles the steps by which David finally was established on the throne of united Israel.

A. Coronation at Hebron (2 Sam 5:1-5 //1 Chr 11:1-3; 12:23-40).

In response to the efforts of Abner the elders of the tribes came to

Hebron after the death of Ish-bosheth. They acknowledged that (1) they were David's *"bone and flesh."* (2) Even when Saul was king it was David who had been their military leader. (3) Yahweh had promised David that he would be *"shepherd,"* i.e., ruler,[1] of Israel. David then made a covenant with these elders. What concessions he may have made to secure the recognition of these elders is not stated. The elders responded by anointing David to be king of Israel (5:1-3).

The Chronicler relates more details about the glorious three-day celebration in Hebron at the anointing of David. Each tribe sent a sizable contingent of armed men as indicated in Chart 31. These all came *"with perfect heart"* to make David king. The celebration lasted three days. The locals provided most of the provisions; but tribes as far as Issachar, Zebulun and Naphtali brought great quantities of food on all means of conveyance. *"There was joy indeed in Israel"* (1 Chr 12:23-40).

Chart No. 31

DAVID'S THIRD ANOINTING 1 Chronicles 12:23-40		
TRIBE	**TROOPS**	**COMMENTS**
Judah	6,800	Bore shield and spear.
Simeon	7,100	Mighty men of valor.
Levi	4,600	Plus Jehoiada and 3,700 of the house of Aaron and Zadok with 22 captains.
Benjamin	3,000	
Ephraim	20,800	Mighty men of valor; famous men in their father's households.
W. Manasseh	18,000	Designated by name to come and make David king.
Issachar	200	Men who understood the times, with knowledge of what Israel should do.
Zebulun	50,000	Could draw up in battle formation with all kinds of weapons; helped David with an undivided heart.
Naphtali	37,000	With shield and spear; plus 1000 captains.
Dan	28,600	
Asher	40,000	
Reuben		
Gad	120,000	With all kinds of weapons of war for battle.
E. Manasseh		

David was thirty when he became king (of all Israel?). In round figures, he reigned forty years. Seven and a half years he ruled over Judah from Hebron. His rule over all Israel was 33 years (5:4-5).

B. Capture of Jerusalem (2 Sam 5:6-10 // 1 Chr 11:4-9).

Perhaps as a result of the covenant with the elders of the northern tribes, David's first order of business was to establish a new capital for the united nation. Jebus (Jerusalem), which was strategically situated on the border of Judah and Benjamin, was selected. The fortress of this city was still occupied by Jebusites. They were so confident of the impregnability of their city that they boasted that even blind and lame men could defend the place against David (5:6-7).

By three statements David challenged his men to capture Zion. (1) He indicated that those Jebusites who had sarcastically referred to themselves as *"blind and lame"* were *"hated"* by David, i.e., they were his enemies. (2) The way into the fortress was through the water tunnel.[2] (3) Whoever struck down a Jebusite first would be commander of the entire army (5:8;1 Chr 11:6).

Joab was the first to scale the vertical water tunnel and enter Jebus. He therefore became commander of the army. Once the city was secure David took up residence in that stronghold. Since the place had been conquered by David's men and since David resided there, the place was called *"the city of David."*[3] Jerusalem's fortifications were repaired and extended.[4] Once established in his new capital David became greater and greater because Yahweh of hosts was with him (5:9-10; 1 Chr 11:6-9).

C. Recognition by Hiram (2 Sam 5:11-12 // 1 Chr 14:1-2).

The mention of King Hiram's recognition of David at this point in the narrative gives the impression that he was among the first to enter into a covenant with David. Actually, archaeologists provide information which make it clear that Hiram did not begin to reign until 979 BC. At that time David was in his last years of life. Thus it is clear that the author of 2 Samuel was not narrating events in a strictly chronological sequence.

Certainly the author regarded the covenant between Hiram and David as a most significant development. The Tyrian king sent cedar wood and skilled craftsmen to Jerusalem to build a palace for David. This gesture of recognition caused David to realize that (1) Yahweh truly had established him as king of Israel; and (2) Yahweh had exalted his kingdom for the sake of his people Israel.

D. Growth in the Family (2 Sam 5:13-16 //1 Chr 3:5-9; 14:3-7).

Unfortunately David followed the example of foreign kings in building up a large harem.[5] He had six sons by six wives while living in Hebron (cf. 2 Sam 3:2-5). Thirteen sons are named as having been fathered by David in Jerusalem.[6] David also fathered several unnamed sons by concubines. Tamar, one of his many daughters, is named because of the prominence which she will have in later narrative (1 Chr 3:9).

E. Victories over the Philistines (2 Sam 5:17-25 // 1 Chr 14:8-17).

During the seven years in which David ruled in Hebron the Philistines appear to have been dormant. Perhaps they looked on David as a friend. The text says nothing about what became of the Philistines who occupied the villages of the Valley of Jezreel in 1010 BC (1 Sam 31:7). Presumably Abner had driven them out of the land at some point. Now that the tribes were united, however, the Philistines became concerned. They were determined to cut David off from his northern subjects by driving a military wedge through the center of the Israel.

1. The first invasion (5:17-21). The first Philistine invasion was intended to capture David. Most likely it should be dated prior to David's move from Hebron to Jerusalem. When David heard these old enemies were marching eastward in search of him, he went down to the *"stronghold,"* probably the old cave of Adullam. The Philistines spread out their forces in the Valley of Rephaim, the western approach to Jerusalem. His actions sanctioned by the priestly oracle, David attacked the Philistines and broke through their ranks. He named that spot Baal-perazim ("the master of breaking through"). In their flight the Philistines abandoned their idols. David and his men carried them away and burned them (cf. 1 Chr 14:12).

2. The second invasion (5:22-25). Some time later the Philistines returned to the valley of Rephaim. Again David inquired of Yahweh about a possible attack. He was told to circle behind the enemy. When he heard *"the sound of marching"* i.e., rustling, in the tops of the balsam trees, then he should attack. God would go before him into battle. David followed these instructions and secured the victory. His men struck down the army of the Philistines from Gibeon (six miles northwest of Jerusalem) and Geba even as far as Gezer, some fifteen miles further to the northwest. As a result of this victory the fame and fear of David spread to surrounding lands (cf. 1 Chr 14:13-17).

Chart No. 32

PARALLELS IN THE MONARCHY BOOKS					
1 Samuel		*2 Samuel*	*1 Kings*	*2 Kings*	
Preface: Judgeship of Samuel	Reign of Saul	Reign of David	Reign of Solomon	Reigns of Kings of Israel and Judah	Appendix
Chs. 1-7	Chs. 8-30	Chs. 1-24	Chs. 1-11 / Chs. 12-22	Chs. 1-25	25:27-30

1 Chronicles			*2 Chronicles*		
Preface: Genealogies		Reign of David	Reign of Solomon	Reigns of the Kings of Judah	Appendix
Chs. 1-9		Chs. 10-29	Chs. 1-9	Chs. 10-36	36:20-23

RELIGIOUS DEVELOPMENT
2 Samuel 6:1-23

Establishing Jerusalem as a center of worship for the entire nation was the priority of the early years of David's reign. The obvious first step in bringing this about was to transport the ark, the ancient symbol of the covenant, to Jerusalem. This was accomplished in two stages.

341

A. Learning Reverence (2 Sam 6:1-10 // 1 Chr 13:1-14).

After consulting with his military commanders, David proposed to the assembly of Israel that the ark be transported to Jerusalem, the new capital. The assembly concurred. The king then assembled an honor guard of thirty thousand men from all of Israel to escort the ark of God to Jerusalem. This representative force traveled the ten miles from Jerusalem to Baale-judah (Baalah; Kiriath-jearim) where the ark had resided for some seven decades.

Unfortunately David did not take time to research the proper manner of transporting the ark. He placed the sacred chest on an ox cart. Two brothers, Uzzah and Ahio, who been custodians of the ark, were accompanying the cart. Ahio was out in front; Uzzah was walking beside the cart. David and all his men were celebrating with religious fervor using musical instruments of various kinds (6:1-5).

When the procession had reached the threshingfloor of Nacon a tragedy took place. The oxen stumbled. The ark nearly toppled to the ground. Uzzah reached out his hand to steady the ark. Uzzah's good intentions notwithstanding, Yahweh's anger burned against him. Because of his irreverence, Uzzah died there beside the ark. As a Levite and one who had watched over the ark during its stay at Kiriath-jearim, Uzzah should have known the proper manner in which the ark was to be transported. (See Num 4:5,15,19-20). Touching the ark was the proverbial straw that broke the camel's back. It was but the culmination of a cavalier attitude which gave little consideration to sacredness of the ark (6:6-7).

David was angry over the incident. He probably blamed himself for not being more careful in his plans for moving the ark. Because he now feared the Lord, he wondered if the movement of the ark to Jerusalem would ever be possible. The king ordered the ark to be taken aside off the road to the nearby house of the Levite Obed-edom the Gittite, i.e., a man from Gath Rimmon (6:8-10).[7]

B. Celebrating Success (2 Sam 6:11-19 // 1 Chr 15:1-29).

The ark remained at the house of Obed-edom for three months. During that period Yahweh blessed this man with a blessing that must have been noticeable to others. David decided to try again to move the ark to Jerusalem for two reasons. (1) Yahweh was blessing Obed-edom; and (2) David had learned the reason for the initial failure (1 Chr 15:13).

Again David assembled *"all Israel,"* i.e., representative of all Israel, at Jerusalem. The assembly included the elders and the captains over thousands (cf. 1 Chr 15:25). The second movement of the ark, however, was attended primarily by 862 priests and Levites rather than military units. By royal order these religious leaders first consecrated themselves. After this had been done, the Levites reverently attached poles to the ark and hoisted the sacred chest to their shoulders *"as Moses had commanded according to the the word of Yahweh"* (1 Chr 15:3-15).

After they cautiously had moved the ark but six paces, the procession stopped and David offered an ox and a fatling to God. Apparently at various intervals along the way the procession paused to offered similar sacrifices *"because God was helping the Levites who were carrying the ark"* (cf. 1 Chr 15:26).

David was jubilant that all was going well. He enthusiastically led the procession with vigorous dancing. For this he had removed his royal robes and was wearing only an ephod, a short, sleeveless, garment. The people were shouting praise. Stringed instruments, horns and cymbals accompanied the loud praise. Chenaniah, chief of the Levites, directed the singing *"because he was skillful"* (2 Sam 6:13-15).

The ark was placed inside a special tent which David had erected for it. Again the king offered sacrifice before the Lord. This was followed by a fellowship meal for which David provided the food. The king then blessed the people in the name of Yahweh (2 Sam 6:17-19).

C. Defending Zeal (2 Sam 6:20-23).

As the procession enter Jerusalem Michal observed the religious zeal of her husband from a window in the royal residence. In her heart she despised David (6:16). Why Michal found David's actions so disgusting is not stated. Returning to his home in a joyous mood, David was greeted by a sullen, sarcastic wife. She verbally chastised her husband for acting like a fool by uncovering himself in the eyes of the maids of Israel. Though the actions of the king may been undignified, they were not immodest. David defended himself by saying that he had been celebrating before Yahweh. He was happy to abase himself before God and honor the Lord before the people. He reminded Saul's daughter that Yahweh had selected him over her father. He assured her that although he might in the future be even more lightly esteemed by people with the mindset of Michal, he would in fact be distinguished in the eyes of those maids to which his wife had referred (2 Sam 6:20-22).

Michal had no child to the day of her death. The placement of the verse at this point suggests that Michal's barrenness may have been a punishment for the attitude which she had toward the religious zeal of her husband. Others think the verse points to the permanent estrangement between David and Michal (2 Sam 6:23).

D. Ordering Worship (1 Chr 16:4-42).

When the ark was installed in Jerusalem, David appointed priests and Levites to ministerial posts. Asaph was the chief of those appointed to lead the praise before the ark. A lengthy psalm, apparently composed for the occasion, is recorded in Chronicles. It is not clear who authored this beautiful composition (16:1-36).

In addition to the Levites and priests who led the musical celebration at the tent in Jerusalem, David appointed Obed-edom and sixty-eight of his relatives as gatekeepers. Zadok was the priest in charge at the tabernacle which was now located at Gibeon. The prescribed morning and evening sacrifices were reinstituted. Levitical musicians were also assigned to the tabernacle. Heman and Jeduthun led the praise service there with trumpets and cymbals (16:37-42).

PROPHETIC ANTICIPATION
2 Samuel 7:1-29

The placement of chapter 7 in 2 Samuel may again mislead one regarding the chronology of the event. Most likely the chapter relates an event which occurred fairly late in David's reign. Once David was firmly established on the throne, he became obsessed with the desire to build a house for the ark of God. His conscience bothered him that he dwelled in house of cedar, i.e., a luxurious palace, while the ark of

God resided in a tent. The prophet Nathan, David's counselor, thought this was a splendid idea. He encouraged the king to proceed with all that was in his heart (7:1-3).

A. God's Promise (2 Sam 7:5-17 // 1 Chr 17:1-15).

Nathan's encouragement for David's building plans was premature. The prophet learned that very night that it was not God's will for David to build a temple to house the ark. Nathan was dispatched to bear that news to David (7:4-5).

The prophetic oracle began with two reminders. First, God had never requested a house. Since the days of the Exodus Yahweh had been content to dwell in a tent. Second, God had selected David to be ruler over his people. He had given him victory over all his enemies (7:6-9a).

Next, several specific promises were made to David. (1) God would make David's name great. (2) David and God people's would enjoy a rest from their enemies such as they had not experienced since the days of the Judges. (3) God would build a house, i.e., a dynasty for David (7:9b-11).

Finally, Nathan's oracle outlined promises for David's posterity. (1) God would establish the kingdom for one of David's direct descendants. (2) This future ruler would build a house for God's name. (3) The throne of his kingdom would endure forever. (4) This ruler would occupy the position of a son in relationship to God. (5) As such he would be corrected with the disciplinary rod of divine judgment. (6) Yet the covenant faithfulness of God would not depart from him. (7) The house, kingdom and throne of David would endure forever (7:12-17).

The "foreverness" of these promises points beyond David's son Solomon. Jesus the Messiah is a son of David. He is God's son par excellence. He is currently building a spiritual temple. On the cross he experienced the disciplinary rod of God, not for his own sins, but the sins of others. He sits even now upon the throne of God in the heavenly places.

B. David's Prayer (2 Sam 7:18-29 // 1 Chr 17:16-27).

Moved by the breadth and depth of these promises, David *"went in and sat before Yahweh,"* i.e., he entered the tent where the ark was housed. He opened his prayer by expressing amazement that God had brought him this far. Yet now through Nathan's oracle the Lord was making commitments to David concerning the distant future. The king then began to praise God (1) for this most recent revelation of his plans for David. (2) Such revelation set Yahweh apart from all other so-called deities. (3) With mighty acts God had redeemed Israel from nations and their gods. In so doing he had made a name for himself. (4) Yahweh had established a relationship with Israel as his people forever (7:18-24).

David then called upon God to confirm forever the word which he had just spoken through his servant. The fulfillment of these promises would cause the name of Yahweh to be magnified forever. The prayer concluded with a petition that God would indeed do what he had just promised to do (7:25-29).

GEOGRAPHICAL EXPANSION
2 Samuel 8:1-14

David expanded the territory controlled by Israel significantly in all directions. His conquests resulted in foreign tribute flowing into the coffers of his kingdom. Distant kings swore vassal allegiance to David.

A. Against Old Enemies (2 Sam 8:1-2 // 1 Chr 18:1-2).

Early in his reign David decisively had turned back two major Philistine invasions of Israel. When he was sufficiently strong he went on the attack against these old enemies. He subdued them and took control of their chief city, probably Gath (8:1; cf. 1 Chr 18:1).

After defeating the Moabites, David was especially harsh with the captives. They were forced to lay on the ground and then were measured with a line. Two lines were executed, and one was spared. These men had committed such notorious atrocities that David deemed the death penalty appropriate. The sparing of one third of the captives would have been viewed in the ancient world as a benevolent act. These remaining Moabites became servants of David, sending him annual tribute (8:2).

B. Against the Arameans (2 Sam 8:3-12 // 1 Chr 18:3-11).

David won a major victory when he defeated Hadadezer of the kingdom of Zobah near the Euphrates river. The captives numbered 7,000 cavalrymen, 1,000 chariots, and 20,000 foot soldiers.[8] Since the Israelite army at this time had neither cavalry nor chariotry, David ordered all but a hundred of the chariot horses hamstrung (lamed). This action rendered the horses useless for military purposes (8:3-4).

When the Arameans of Damascus attempted to come to the aid of Hadadezer, David won a second impressive victory in the north. Some 22,000 of the enemy were killed. Israelite occupation forces were stationed among the Arameans of Damascus. The Aramean people sent tribute to David throughout his reign (8:5-6).

From his campaigns in the north David returned to Jerusalem with valuable spoils. For example, from the servants of Hadadezer he had captured a number of golden shields. These eventually were housed in the treasury of the temple. Some of the cities in Hadadezer's kingdom yielded to David a large amount of bronze. Solomon later made use of this bronze to construct the brazen "sea," the huge pillars, and bronze utensils of the temple (8:7-8).

Toi (or Tou), king of Hamath, was grateful to David for defeating Hadadezer. He expressed his appreciation by dispatching his son with valuable gifts of gold, silver and bronze. Toi apparently was seeking either an alliance, or protection from David. These items, as well as all similar tribute, were dedicated to Yahweh (8:9-12).

C. Against the Edomites (2 Sam 8:13-14 // 1 Chr 18:12-13).

David's reputation as a military genius was enhanced when he won a decisive battle over the Edomites[9] in the Valley of Salt. Some 18,000 Edomites fell. The field commander in this operation was Abishai (1 Chr 18:12). David was able to put garrisons throughout Edom. The Edomites became his vassals.

BUREAUCRATIC GROWTH
2 Samuel 8:15-9:13

The growth of the kingdom necessitated the creation of new administrative positions.

A. Organization (2 Sam 8:15-18 // 1 Chr 18:14-17).

The greatness of David's kingdom is indicated by the growth in the royal court. Joab had won appointment as military commander by his heroics in the capture of the stronghold of Zion. Jehoshaphat was the recorder, charged with the responsibility of keeping the royal records. Zadok, the priest under Saul, shared the priesthood with Ahimelech the son of Abiathar, David's priest. Seraiah was secretary who penned the royal proclamations. Benaiah commanded a unit made up of mercenary Cherethites and Pelethites—peoples closely related to the Philistines—which served as the royal bodyguard. David's sons served as *"chief ministers,"* (lit., priests).[10] Thus Saul's simple court had now evolved into a complex royal bureaucracy.

B. Benevolence (2 Sam 9:1-13).

The benevolence of David toward the son of Jonathan indicates the soft side of his personality. Normally oriental kings would make the total elimination of the former royal house the first order of business in a new regime. David, however, was of a different spirit. From Ziba, a former servant in Saul's house, David learned that a crippled son of Jonathan was still living. David sent to Lo-debar in Transjordan for this son (9:1-5).

Mephibosheth[11] must have feared the worst as he prostrated himself before the king. David assured him, however, that he had nothing to fear. For the sake of Jonathan he promised to restore all the lands of Saul to this young man. In addition, David decreed that Mephibosheth should eat at the royal table regularly, i.e., he would be part of David's court. At this good news, Mephibosheth again prostrated himself and confessed his unworthiness to receive such honor (9:6-8).

David then summoned Ziba and appointed him to manage the lands of Mephibosheth. With fifteen sons and twenty servants of his own, Ziba was certainly in a position to assume such responsibility. This he agreed to do (9:9-11).

So Mephibosheth lived in Jerusalem. He ate at the king's table where he was treated like one of David's sons. In trying to ascertain the chronology of this incident, these facts need to be considered: (1) Mephibosheth was five when he was dropped by a nurse and became a cripple (2 Sam 4:4). David ruled seven and a half years at Hebron before becoming king of Israel (2 Sam 5:5). That would make Mephibosheth almost thirteen at the time David was recognized as king by all the tribes. Since Mephibosheth had *"a young son"* at the time he received his court position, one must place the recognition of Mephibosheth at least five years (and possibly more) into David's reign over all the tribes.

Why has the author of Samuel included the account of David's kindness to Mephibosheth here? At least three reasons have been suggested. (1) God had kept his word to David; so David now kept his word to Jonathan. (2) The account introduces two characters (Ziba and Mephibosheth) who figure prominently in the struggles of David later. (3) The account demonstrates that David was secure in the throne. He could afford to be magnanimous to a representative of the former royal family.

ENDNOTES

1. The term *"shepherd"* became a technical term for a ruler in Israel. See Jer 3:15; Ezek 34:2-3. The term is also found in reference to rulers in nonbiblical literature of the ancient Near East.

2. In 1867 Charles Warren discovered the fifty-two foot shaft by which it appears Joab entered the city. The shaft connected with a stairway that led within the walled fortress.

3. The *Zion* of this passage is not to be confused with the modern hill of that name in Jerusalem. Geographical Zion was the southeastern hill of Jerusalem.

4. The report that David built all around *"from the Millo and inward"* (NASB) is difficult. The term *"Millo"* means *"filling."* It was probably some tower which David incorporated into the already formidable walls of the fortress.

5. Deuteronomy 17:17 specifically commanded a king of God's people not to multiply wives unto himself.

6. 2 Samuel 5:14-16 lists only eleven sons of David born in Jerusalem. The two additional sons in the Chronicles passages were Elpelet and Nogah. These sons may have died very young. The list in 1 Chr 14:3-7 contains variant spellings of five of the names of the sons as listed in 1 Chr 3:5-8.

7. Obed-edom ("servant of Edom") was from the Korahite clan of the Levites (1 Chr 26:1-4). In the wilderness period the Korahite clan was charged with the responsibility of transporting the sacred furniture of the tabernacle, including the ark. Obed-edom probably received his name after being in servitude to the Edomites sometime during his life.

8. On the numbers here the text of 1 Chr 18:4 is probably more accurate than that of 2 Sam 8:4 which reads 1,700 cavalrymen and 20,000 infantry. No mention is made in Samuel of the captured chariots. In the process of copying the manuscripts the figures 1,000 and 7,000 got conflated into 1,700.

9. The Masoretic Text reads *"Arameans."* That this is a likely scribal error for *"Edomites"* is indicated by the following considerations: (1) It is improbable that the Arameans would have such a large force in the Valley of Salt near the southern end of the Dead Sea. (2) In Hebrew the words "Arameans" and "Edomites" look almost alike. (3) The parallel passage in 1 Chr 18:12, the Septuagint, and 2 Sam 8:14 all indicate that the war was against Edom.

10. In the parallel passage in 1 Chr 18:17 David's sons are called *"chiefs at the king's side"* (NASB). They must have functioned as royal advisers.

11. In 1 Chr 8:34 Mephibosheth is called Merib-baal.

CHAPTER TWENTY-ONE

David's Personal Troubles
2 Samuel 10-14

After discussing the triumphs of David, the author next narrates the troubles which David experienced as a result of his great sin with Bathsheba. The king's problems started during a protracted campaign against the Ammonites.

CAMPAIGN AGAINST AMMON
2 Samuel 10:1-19; 12:26-31

The results of the war against Ammon were summarized in 2 Samuel 8:3-8. That campaign here receives expanded treatment because (1) it was an extremely fierce struggle, one in which Israel met with near disaster; (2) it explains how distant Aramean city states became involved in hostilities with the kingdom of David; and (3) during this campaign David committed his greatest sin.

A. Diplomacy Rejected (2 Sam 10:1-5 // 1 Chr 19:1-5).

The Ammonite King Nahash,[1] who once had attacked Jabesh-gilead, had shown kindness to David. When he died his son Hanun ascended the throne. David sent high-ranking diplomats to convey his condolences over the father's death. Hanun's advisors, however, poisoned his mind against David. They suggested that these diplomats had come to spy out Rabbah—modern Amman, about twenty miles east of the Jordan—the Ammonite capital. The new king decided to humiliate David's representatives. He (1) shaved off half of their beards; and (2) cut off their robes at the hips thus shamefully exposing them. He then sent them away. The humiliated ambassadors were directed by David to tarry in Jericho until their beards had grown back before returning to Jerusalem.

B. The First Campaign (2 Sam 10:6-14 // 1 Chr 19:6-15).

The Ammonites realized that their disrespect for the Israelite ambassadors would lead to war. Consequently Hanun hired 33,000 mercenaries from the Aramean states to the north. When he received news of this large troop movement, David dispatched Joab and the army to attack Rabbah (10:6-7).

The Ammonites formed their battle ranks at the entrance of their capital. The Aramean mercenaries were strategically positioned nearby in the open field, probably out of sight. Their assignment was to attack Joab from the rear once the Israelite army launched a frontal attack on the Ammonites (10:8).

The Israelites apparently marched into a trap at Rabbah. Joab was forced to divided his army. He quickly selected some of the better units to lead personally against the Arameans. The remainder of the army was placed under the command of his brother Abishai to fight the Ammonites. Joab urged all the troops to fight courageously (10:9-12).

While Abishai held the Ammonites in check, Joab took the battle to the Arameans. After a fierce struggle the enemy broke ranks and fled. When the Ammonites saw that their allies had fled, they retreated behind the walls of their capital. At that point Joab terminated the campaign either because the casualties had been too heavy, or because he did not have the resources to lay siege to the city (10:13-14).

C. The Second Campaign (2 Sam 10:15-19 // 1 Chr 19:16-19).

The Arameans were determined to avenge the earlier defeat at the hands of Israel. Hadadezer assembled troops from several Aramean city states. A strong force assembled at Helam on the northeast border of Israel. The unified command was given to Shobach, the commander of Hadadezer's army (10:15-16).

In response, David mobilized his army and crossed the Jordan. He may have surprised the enemy with this rapid mobilization and deployment of troops. In the battle of Helam again the Arameans fled before Israel. David's forces killed 700 charioteers and 40,000 horsemen.[2] General Shobach also lost his life in the battle. All of Hadadezer's vassals then made peace with David. No more did they come to the aid of the Ammonites (10:17-19).

D. The Third Campaign (2 Sam 11:1; 12:26-31; 1 Chr 20:1-3).

The following year David dispatched Joab and the army to attack the Ammonites. The Israelites overwhelmed all resistance in the field. The Ammonites retreated behind the walls of Rabbah where they hoped they could outlast the siege efforts of Joab. Meanwhile David was back in Jerusalem (11:1). It was during this time that he committed his great sin with Bathsheba.

Although he sustained heavy losses, Joab was eventually able to overcome the lower city, *"the city of waters."* i.e., the area where the water supply was located. With the end in sight he sent for David to bring the remaining forces in order to administer the final blow. The loyal general wanted his king to receive the credit for capturing this important capital (12:26-28).

David did as Joab suggested. He led the final assault against the citadel and thus was credited with having conquered the place. The massive crown—it weighed 75 lbs.—displayed on the statue of the Ammonite god Milcam (*"their king"*) was captured. A jewel from this crown was put in David's crown. An enormous quantity of spoil was brought out of the city. Those who survived the siege were put to forced labor (12:29-31).

353

DAVID'S SIN AND REPENTANCE
2 Samuel 11:2-12:25

While the army was fighting successfully on foreign soil, David was losing the battle of temptation at home. His adultery marks the spiritual low point of the king's life, and a turning point in his reign.

A. The Sin of Adultery (2 Sam 11:2-13).

After an afternoon nap, David was walking on the flat roof of his palace. From that height he spied a beautiful woman bathing, probably in the courtyard of a house at lower elevation. David inquired about the woman and learned that she was the wife of one of his finest officers, Uriah the Hittite. Undeterred by her marital status, David sent messengers to fetch this woman. When she came to him— apparently voluntarily—he lay with her. Bathsheba *"purified herself of her uncleanness"* and then returned to her house. Apparently the two only spent the one night together. That night of sinful sex was to have repercussions which nearly destroyed the reign of David. A short time later the woman discovered she was pregnant. Of this fact she promptly notified David so that he might protect both himself and her (11:3-5).

In an attempt to cover the infidelity of Bathsheba, David ordered Uriah, a naturalized foreigner (Hittite), home from the battlefield. The king interviewed this officer concerning the conduct of the war. Then he urged the man to go to his house and refresh himself. As Uriah departed from the palace, David ordered a present (a guilt offering?) to be sent after him. Uriah, however, spent that night with the royal bodyguard at the door to the king's house. Whether Uriah suspected anything was amiss is difficult to determine. He may have heard reports from guards at the palace that Bathsheba had spent a night with the king. He also may have become suspicious because of the king's insistence that he visit his house (11:6-9).

When David was told that Uriah had not gone down to his house, he questioned the man. Uriah explained that as a professional military man he could not in good conscience enjoy the comforts of home as long as his troops were experiencing the deprivations of a long military campaign. For two more days Uriah remained in Jerusalem. At a royal banquet, David got Uriah drunk thinking that under the influence of the wine his inhibitions would erode. Still Uriah spent his nights with the king's servants outside the palace door (11:10-13).

B. The Sin of Murder (2 Sam 11:14-25).
David was driven by Uriah's obstinate refusal to visit his wife to a desperate scheme. He drafted orders to be carried to the battle front by Uriah. Joab was to assign Uriah to the front line where the battle was most fierce. Then he was to order the supporting troops to withdraw leaving Uriah to be struck down and killed by the Ammonites. General Joab faithfully executed the orders of his king. In one of the Ammonite sallies against the Israelite forces Uriah was killed (11:14-17).

Joab anticipated that David would be angry when he heard the report of heavy losses at Rabbah. He directed the messenger to respond to any royal outburst by reporting as a postscript the death of Uriah (11:18-21).

The messenger reported to David the details of the battle. The Ammonites had pushed the Israelites back from the city. Joab, however, had been able to rally his forces and push the Ammonites back to the gates of their capital. There the Ammonite archers were able to pick off many Israelites including Uriah. Hearing the news of Uriah's death, David realized that his royal orders led to the irresponsible conduct of Joab in ordering the men so close to the walls. He sent word back to his general urging that he not be distraught over the losses or of his complicity in the death of Uriah. In a rather calloused comment the king said *"the sword devours one as well as another."* He ordered Joab to continue the attack against Rabbah (11:22-25).

C. The Marriage to Bathsheba (2 Sam 11:26-27).
Bathsheba went through the motions of mourning for her dead husband. Whether this mourning was sincere or just part of the cover-up plot is not clear. In any case, following this time of mourning (usually seven days), David married Bathsheba. Soon after she brought forth the child which had been conceived in adulterous union. How many, if any, suspected what had taken place is not indicated. David's actions, however, were evil in the sight of Yahweh.

D. The Prophetic Rebuke (2 Sam 12:1-14).

Yahweh left David in his guilty state for almost a year. He then dispatched the prophet Nathan to administer a rebuke to the sinful king. He chose to use a parable in order to elicit from David a pronouncement of self-condemnation. The parable was simple. A poor man and rich man lived beside one another. While the rich man had many flocks and herds, the poor man had only a little lamb which was a family pet. When a traveler came to the rich man he was unwilling to feed him from his own flock or herd. Rather he took the poor man's pet lamb and made a meal of it for his guest (12:1-4).

David's anger boiled as he heard the story which he took to be a real occurrence. David swore an oath in the name of Yahweh that the rich thief deserved to die. He ordered that this man make a fourfold restitution for the stolen lamb (12:5-6).

Nathan then made the devastating application. *"You, David, are the man!"* You have pronounced judgment upon yourself. God had anointed David as king and had delivered him from the hand of Saul. He had given Saul's house including his wives into the care of David along with both Judah and Israel. The Lord would have given him many similar blessings. David, however, had despised the word of Yahweh by committing a horrendous evil. David was as guilty of murder as if he had struck Uriah with his own sword. He then had taken to himself the wife of the man whose death he had orchestrated. David had despised the Lord by taking Bathsheba for he denied by his conduct the omniscience of his God (12:7-10).

The penalty for David's sin is twofold. First, the sword would never depart from the house of David (v. 10). Second, God would raise up evil against David from within his own house. Third, one of David's associates would take his wives from him and lie with them in full public view (12:11-12).

David was moved deeply by the words of the prophet. He made no excuses for his conduct. He acknowledged forthrightly his sin. Nathan accepted the confession. He announced that God would not take David's life on account of the sin. However, because his conduct had given occasion to the enemies of Yahweh to blaspheme, God would punish him by taking the child which had recently been born (12:13-14).

E. The Punishment of David (2 Sam 12:15-23).

Yahweh struck the child of Bathsheba with serious illness. David inquired of God for the child, i.e., he prayed for him. He humbled himself by fasting and laying all night prostrate on the ground. His advisers encouraged him to eat with them, but he refused. After seven days of illness, the child died. The courtiers were afraid to tell their king of the infant's death. Observing how the child's illness had affected David, they feared that he might take his own life when he learned of the death (12:15-18).

From the whispering of the courtiers David sensed that the fortunes of the child had changed for the worse. When he ascertained that the child had died, David arose from the ground, washed, anointed himself, changed his clothes and went to the house of God to worship. Then he returned to his own house and requested food (12:19-20).

The royal servants were completely dumbfounded by the king's behavior. David explained that he had fasted and wept while the child was alive, hoping that Yahweh would be gracious and spare the life of his son. After the death, however, fasting was of no avail. No amount of mourning could bring back the dead. Then David's faith soared when he stated: *"I shall go to him, but he will not return to me."* The statement suggests a belief in infant salvation and immortality (12:21-23).

F. The Birth of Solomon (2 Sam 12:24-25).

David comforted Bathsheba over the loss of their son. Eventually she become pregnant a second time by David. The son who was born was named Solomon. Now Yahweh loved this child. He sent the prophet Nathan to bestow on the infant a special name: *Jedidiah*, "beloved of Yahweh."

AMNON'S INCEST AND DEATH
2 Samuel 13:1-33

The prophesied trouble within David's household was not long in making its appearance. By their lawless conduct, two of David's sons brought incalculable pain to the heart of their father.

A. Amnon's Plot (2 Sam 13:1-10).

Amnon, the eldest son of David, lusted after his stepsister. From a distance he watched in the courtyard where the unmarried women were kept in seclusion. The frustration of not being able to devise a way by which he might be alone with Tamar made Amnon ill (13:1-2).

Unfortunately Amnon had a *"friend"* and cousin named Jonadab. He is described as *"a very shrewd man"* (NASB). Jonadab had the solution to Amnon's problem. He suggested that Amnon feign illness. When David came to see him he should request that Tamar come and prepare some fancy cakes for him. David suspected nothing. He sent word for Tamar to go to her brother's house and prepare food for him (13:3-7).

If David was naive about Amnon's request, Tamar was even more so. When she entered his house Amnon was lying on his bed. Tamar took dough, kneaded it, made cakes in the sight of Amnon and baked them. She then set the cakes on a table in view of her half brother, but he refused to eat. Amnon then ordered everyone out from his presence. Then he asked Tamar to bring the cakes into the bedroom and feed him. Suspecting nothing improper, Tamar took the food to the bedroom (13:8-10).

B. Tamar's Rape (2 Sam 13:11-19).

Amnon seized his half sister and demanded that she lie with him. Tamar resisted as best she could. First, she pled with Amnon not to do such a horrible deed. Second, she argued that such disgraceful things were simply not done in Israel! Third, she pointed out that both of them would be ruined by such an act. Amnon would be considered a fool, i.e., a godless man, for having raped his own half sister. Finally, Tamar urged Amnon to ask the king for her in marriage if he could not control his lust. The king—so Tamar affirmed in the desperation of the moment—would not refuse such a request. At least marriage to his half sister, though forbidden in the law (Lev 18:9,11; 20:17), would be more honorable than rape. Amnon was in no mood to reason. He overpowered his sister and violated her (13:11-14).

Perhaps because Tamar refused to cooperate, the sexual experience was not what Amnon had fantasized. Immediately thereafter

Amnon went to the opposite extreme. He hated Tamar more than he ever had "*loved*" her. Because of his guilt and fear of exposure he ordered Tamar out of his presence. Tamar again tried to reason with Amnon. Sending her away after violating her was even worse than the violation itself. This would make it appear that Tamar had initiated the seduction. Amnon again would not listen. He ordered his attendant to throw Tamar out of the house and lock the door (13:15-17).

Humiliated by her experience, Tamar went into public mourning. She put ashes on her head. She tore the long-sleeved garment which virgin daughters of the king wore as distinctive garb. She placed her hand on her head to replace the veil which had been ripped off in Amnon's chamber. She cried aloud as she ran toward her brother's house (13:18-19).

C. Absalom's Revenge (2 Sam 13:20-29).

Absalom comforted his sister by inviting her to come and live in his house. There Tamar remained "*desolate*," i.e., childless and despondent. David heard about the incident, and he was very angry. The Scripture, however, does not indicate that he took any disciplinary action against his lawless son.[3] Perhaps he found it difficult to punish in his son the same sin which had marred his own life. On his part, Absalom refused to speak to Amnon. He hated his half brother for what he had done to Tamar (13:20-22).

After two years of seething anger, Absalom was ready to take his revenge on Amnon. He requested that the king and his sons attend a sheepshearing celebration at Baal-hazor about ten miles from the capital. David declined because he did not wish to burden Absalom with the expense of providing for the entourage which accompanied the king on all his outings. Absalom then requested that Amnon, the eldest son, be permitted to attend the festivities as a stand-in for the king. If David had any suspicions they are not indicated here. Permission was granted. Amnon and all the king's sons went with Absalom to Baal-hazor near Ephraim (13:23-27).

When Amnon became drunk, Absalom ordered his servants to slay him. When this happened all the other sons of David mounted their mules and fled (13:28-29).

D. David's Agony (2 Sam 13:30-36).

The initial report which reached David was that all the sons had been massacred by Absalom. David immediately went into mourning. Jonadab, however, came in to assure the king that only Amnon had died, the victim of a plot that had been in motion since the day Tamar had been raped. Shortly thereafter the king's sons were spotted returning on the Jerusalem road. They entered the palace to join David and his servants in mourning over the death of Amnon (13:30-36).

ABSALOM'S FLIGHT AND RETURN
2 Samuel 13:37-14:33

Absalom fled to the land of Geshur northeast of the Sea of Galilee where his maternal grandfather was the ruler. He remained there for three years. Meanwhile, David mourned for *"his son,"* probably the absentee Absalom. He longed to send for him to invite him to return. The king probably thought that to do so would be equivalent to endorsing the murder of his oldest son (13:37-39).

A. Joab's Plan (2 Sam 14:1-20).

Joab sensed that David was agonizing over the exile of Absalom. He also may have assumed that Absalom as the eldest son of David would succeed to the throne. Therefore Joab contacted a wise woman from Tekoa six miles south of Bethlehem. Joab urged the woman to feign mourning. He told her exactly what she was to say to the king. She was to tell a story similar to that of the king's situation (14:1-3).

The woman in the guise of a mourner fell prostrate before David beseeching his help. She told David that she was a widow with two sons. The two young men, however, had gotten into a fight while working in the field. One of her sons had been killed in the struggle. Now other family members were demanding that the murderer be handed over for execution. If this should happen, however, her husband would have no one to perpetuate his name (14:4-7).

David responded to the woman's problem in three stages as the woman continued to press for decisive action. First, the king attempted to brush aside the woman by saying that he would issue orders concerning the situation. Apparently he felt that if he defended the son, he would become involved in his guilt. The woman then offered to take any associated guilt upon herself. Second, David promised that if she would bring her tormentors to him he would order them not to harass her about the matter any longer. Finally, David swore an oath that not one hair of the surviving son would fall to the ground, i.e., he would not be harmed in any way (14:8-11).

The wise woman then made an application of her drama. While the king was willing to guarantee the safety of this "widow's son," yet the king would not guarantee the safe return of Absalom, favorite prince of the people. Life is like water spilled on the ground. It cannot be gathered up again. Therefore David should waste no time restoring his son. In so doing David would be acting in a God-like way, for the Lord is constantly looking for ways to restore the wayward. The woman completed her appeal by complimenting David on his keen sense of right and wrong. In this respect the king was like *"the angel of God"* (14:12-14).

To continue to throw off David, the woman then returned to her fictitious story. She wanted the king to think that was her only reason for coming to him. David, however, now saw through the deception. He suspected that Joab was behind the ruse of the woman from Tekoa. Perhaps Joab had attempted on various occasions to get David to take action regarding Absalom. Under questioning, the woman admitted that Joab had told her exactly what she should say (14:15-19).

B. Absalom's Return (2 Sam 14:20-27).

The king then summoned Joab and ordered him to bring Absalom back home. The general prostrated himself before David and thanked him for granting this request (14:18-22).

Joab went to Geshur immediately and brought Absalom back to Jerusalem. David, however, did not forgive Absalom completely. The crown prince would not be restored to the royal court. Absalom was forced to take up residence in his own house (14:23-24).

Absalom was a favorite of the people. No one was as handsome as the crown prince. There was no defect in his physical appearance.

Once each year he had his hair cut. The shorn hair weighed two hundred shekels (about 5 lbs.). Absalom had three sons and one daughter. His beautiful daughter was named Tamar after his disgraced sister (14:25-27).

C. Absalom's Restoration (2 Sam 14:28-33).

Two years passed and still there was no reconciliation between David and his eldest son. Twice Absalom attempted to get Joab to come and discuss his status. The general would not come. Finally Absalom ordered his servants to burn Joab's barley field which was right next door. That got Joab's attention immediately. Absalom demanded that he be restored to the court or executed as a murderer (14:28-32).

Joab made the king realize that by allowing Absalom to return he had recognized that the murder of Amnon was justifiable homicide. There was, therefore, no legal grounds to deny the prince his rightful place in the royal court. David then sent for Absalom. The prince did obeisance before his father. David kissed his son. Reconciliation had been effected, or so it seemed (14:33).

Chart No. 33

ENDNOTES

1. Others think the Nahash who died in 2 Sam 10 was the son or even the grandson of the Nahash who attacked Jabesh-gilead in 1 Sam 11. Approximately fifty years elapsed between the attack on Jabesh and the events of 2 Sam 10.

2. The casualty figures respecting charioteers in 1 Chr 19:18 is 7000 compared to the 700 reported in 2 Sam 10:18. Yet the Samuel text reports

7000 horsemen who fell. The more complete text of Samuel is the original. The text of Chronicles must be the result of a scribal miscopying.

3. In the Greek version an explanation for David's inaction is added to 2 Sam 13:21: *"he loved his firstborn son."*

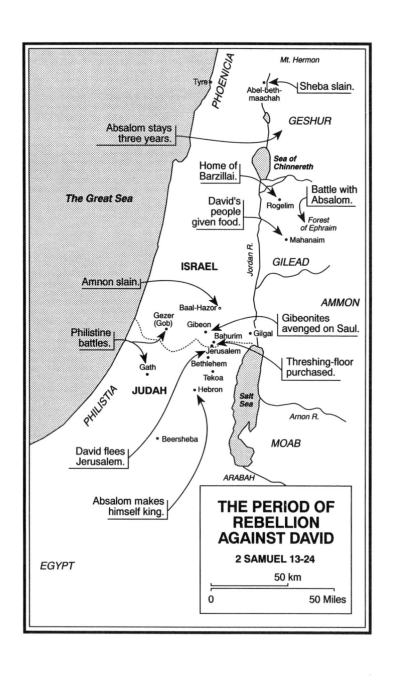

Mt. Hermon

Tyre •

PHOENICIA

Abel-beth-
maachah

Sheba slain.

GESHUR

Absalom stays
three years.

*Sea of
Chinnereth*

Home of
Barzillai.

Battle with
Absalom.

David's
people
given food.

Rogelim

*Forest
of Ephraim*

The Great Sea

Jordan R.

• Mahanaim

ISRAEL

GILEAD

Amnon slain.

Baal-Hazor ○

AMMON

Gezer
(Gob)

Gibeon

Gibeonites
avenged on Saul.

Bahurim • Gilgal

Philistine
battles.

Jerusalem

Threshing-floor
purchased.

Gath •

Bethlehem •

• Tekoa

• Hebron

*Salt
Sea*

PHILISTIA

JUDAH

Arnon R.

• Beersheba

MOAB

David flees
Jerusalem.

ARABAH

Absalom makes
himself king.

THE PERIOD OF REBELLION AGAINST DAVID

2 SAMUEL 13-24

EGYPT

50 km

0   50 Miles

CHAPTER TWENTY-TWO

David's Political Troubles
2 Samuel 15-20

Nathan predicted that the sword would never depart from the house of David as a result of his adultery with Bathsheba (2 Sam 12:10). The rape of Tamar and the subsequent murder of Amnon were but the first installments of this judgment. In his last years David faced two political rebellions led by his sons as well as one revolt led by a Benjamite.

ABSALOM'S REVOLT
2 Samuel 15:1-18

From the moment Absalom set foot on Israelite soil he plotted the overthrow of his father. The handsome devil, as some have called him, used several tactics not unfamiliar to the Christian. Satan often uses the same tactics in an effort to get people to join his rebellion against heaven's king.

First, Absalom put on a big show to impress his countrymen. He secured a chariot and horses. This is the first recorded use of horses by a member of the royal family. Compared to the mule which David used for transportation, these horses must indeed have been impressive. Furthermore, fifty runners preceded Absalom as he rode into the city. These advance PR men stirred up the crowds to give the crown prince a royal welcome (15:1).

Second, Absalom worked hard. He rose early and stood beside the way of the gate to greet the people much as a modern politician might "pump the flesh" at a factory entrance at the start of the morning shift. No palace hours for this prince!

Third, he showed a personal interest in all who came to the gate with court cases. He would inquire about the litigant's city and the nature of his case. Fourth, Absalom used flattery to good advantage. He would always agree that the legal claim of each petitioner was right. Fifth, he treated the litigants as more or less equals. If any came near to do obeisance Absalom would take hold of the man and greet him with a kiss upon the cheek. This crown prince developed the reputation of being down to earth, just one of the common folks.

Sixth, Absalom sought to discredit the king in the eyes of his subjects. He pointed out to each petitioner that no one was present to hear cases on behalf of the king. The implication was that King David was derelict in duty. Absalom would openly express the desire that he might be appointed judge so that he might render justice to all who sought it (15:2-5).

By these six stratagems Absalom was able to steal away the hearts of the men of Israel. After four[1] years of preparation Absalom was ready to launch his rebellion (15:6).

Absalom went to his father and requested permission to go to Hebron to honor a vow which he had made while still living in Geshur. While in exile, he had sworn that if he was restored to Jerusalem he would *"serve Yahweh."* Since David was a man of piety, he was anxious to encourage any spiritual inclination on the part of a son, especially this son. Suspecting nothing, David put his blessing on Absalom's trip. Absalom chose Hebron as the site to launch his rebellion because (1) it was in the heart of Judah, his base of support; (2) it was a royal city antedating Jerusalem; (3) it was the town where Absalom had been born (2 Sam 3:3); and (4) it was a safe distance from Jerusalem where David's soldiers might crush the revolt before it gained momentum (15:7-9).

Absalom dispatched secret agents throughout the tribes of Israel to alert his supporters that the moment was near. A trumpet signal relayed across the land would indicate that Absalom had been declared king (15:10).

Two hundred of the leading citizens of Jerusalem were invited to accompany the crown prince to Hebron. They had no idea that they were being used by a rebel. Absalom wanted it to appear in Jerusalem that his rebellion had massive support among the national leaders. He sent for the influential Ahithophel, David's counselor, who previously had assured Absalom of his support. Why Ahithophel was willing to back a revolt against David is not stated in the text.[2] His support, however, gave the entire effort credibility. The sacred historian indicates that the conspiracy was strong. Absalom's following kept on increasing (15:11-12).

A messenger arrived at David's palace with the news that the hearts of the men of Israel were with Absalom. David seems to have panicked. He ordered an immediate evacuation of Jerusalem. He probably wished to spare the capital the agony of a protracted siege. The king stressed the urgency of quickly departing from the city lest the forces loyal to Absalom overtake and slaughter them. The servants pledged themselves to do whatever the king ordered. Their support for David's plan to flee indicates that militarily evacuation was the best option (15:13-15).

David probably anticipated that his absence from Jerusalem would be of short duration. He therefore left ten of his concubines to tend the palace. He never anticipated that these women would become pawns in Absalom's bid for power (15:16).

The royal entourage stopped at the last house within the city limits. David sadly watched his servants and his six hundred foreign personal bodyguards march out before him (15:17-18).

DAVID'S FLIGHT
2 Samuel 15:19-16:14

David's humiliating flight from Jerusalem provoked two very different responses. Some heroically pledged themselves to serve David unto the death. Others took advantage of the situation to further their own interests or vent their anger toward the king.

A. The Committed (2 Sam 15:19-37).

At various points along the exit route David was met by friends who in different ways expressed their support for their humiliated king.

1. Ittai the Gittite (15:19-23). David questioned Ittai the Gittite,[3] the commander of the king's guards, as to why he was leaving. The royal bodyguard should remain with the new king. Ittai had only recently cast his lot with David. He did not need to feel obligated to follow David into an uncertain future. Ittai, however, replied that he would serve David wherever he may go and even to death. After hearing this resolute commitment, David permitted Ittai and his men and their families to leave Jerusalem with him. The sad procession marched down Mt. Zion, across the Kidron, up the ascent of Olivet in the direction of the wilderness. All the country was weeping with a loud voice (15:19-23).

2. Zadok and Abiathar (15:24-29). The chief priests Zadok and Abiathar and the Levites who where in Jerusalem stood beside the ark of God as David and his supporters exited the city. David ordered the ark returned to the city. He reasoned that if God showed him favor he would eventually return to Jerusalem to the ark and Yahweh's habitation. Yet if the Lord no longer took delight in David, this man of faith was prepared to accept whatever future God might have planned for him. Zadok and his sons could do David a great service by keeping him informed of developments in Jerusalem. David would wait at the fords of the Jordan until he received directions from Zadok. Since this priest was also a seer (prophet), David trusted his insight into the what actions he should take in response to Absalom's threat (15:24-29).

3. Hushai the Archite (15:30-37). The royal fugitives slowly made their way up the ascent of the Mt. of Olives. David was barefoot, his head was covered, and he was weeping. His agony was even greater when he learned that his close adviser Ahithophel was among the conspirators. David prayed that the counsel of Ahithophel might be turned to foolishness. As if in answer to his prayer, Hushai, another royal counselor, met David near the summit of Olivet. His clothing was torn and he had dust on his head in mourning over the turn of events. David suggested that Hushai would be of more help to return to Jerusalem and offer his services to Absalom. David wanted Hushai to (1) frustrate the counsel of Ahithophel; and (2) report Absalom's plans to Zadok and Abiathar. Zadok's two sons in turn would relay that information to David (15:30-37).

B. The Opportunist (2 Sam 16:1-4).

Ziba, the servant of Mephibosheth (son of Jonathan), met David a little beyond the summit. This opportunist was confident that Absalom's rebellion would fail. He was trying to position himself for a greater influence and power in the post-rebellion kingdom.

Ziba brought with him two donkeys loaded with food stuffs for the royal family and the king's servants. With these timely gifts Ziba won over the heart of the king. When David inquired about the whereabouts of Mephibosheth, Ziba slandered his master. He said that Mephibosheth had remained in Jerusalem anticipating that in all the political confusion the kingdom of his father Saul would be returned to him. This accusation was certainly plausible. Without making any further inquiry into the truth of this serious accusation, David on the spot decreed that all of Mephibosheth's possessions would now belong to Ziba (16:1-4).

C. The Antagonist (2 Sam 16:5-14).

At Bahurim, a village east of the Mount of Olives, David was met by Shimei, a man who was related to King Saul. The deep animosity of the Saulites towards David is indicated in this episode. Shimei walked along a ridge above the road David was traveling. He continuously cursed David, called him foul names and pelted his entourage with stones. He called David a man of blood and a son of Belial (worthless man). In his opinion David's misfortune had befallen him because of what he had done to the household of Saul (16:5-8).

Abishai wanted to chase down Shimei (*"this dead dog"*) and decapitate him. The sons of Zeruiah (Joab and Abishai) were addicted to the use of the sword to solve all problems. David, however, imme-

369

diately disassociated himself from such a vengeful spirit. He accepted this treatment by Shimei as part of God's judgment against him. If his own son Absalom was trying to kill him, how can this Benjamite be condemned for what he was doing? David had determined to place himself at the mercy of God. Perhaps the Lord would turn this cursing to good. So the procession continued on its way even as Shimei continued his harassment (16:9-14).

ABSALOM'S COUNSELORS
2 Samuel 16:15-17:23

Absalom entered Jerusalem unopposed. His chief counselor Ahithophel was at his side. Hushai, David's friend, approached and rendered homage to the new king. Absalom questioned Hushai about why he had not departed with *"his friend."* Hushai declared that his allegiance was to whatever king Yahweh, the people and the army selected. He was prepared to serve Absalom just as he had served David (16:15-19).

Absalom turned to Ahithophel to ask what his next step should be. This Old Testament Judas advised the young man to publicly go into the concubines of his father. Such an act would (1) be a public claim to the throne; (2) signal that the rebellion was irreversible; and (3) therefore strengthen the will of all who had committed themselves to his cause. Absalom immediately followed Ahithophel's advice. In those days this counselor's advice was regarded as equivalent to an oracle of God. A tent was pitched on the roof of the palace. There Absalom sexually humbled the concubines of his father (16:20-23).

Ahithophel next urged Absalom to let him take 12,000 men and immediately pursue David. The wise man reasoned that David was weary and exhausted from his flight. A swift attack would discourage his supporters. They would flee, and Absalom could then smite the king himself. Ahithophel felt he was the one who could secure for Absalom the support of all of those who had supported David. This plan would result in peace in the land rather than a protracted conflict. Ahithophel's plan pleased both Absalom and the elders of Israel (17:1-4).

Absalom submitted Ahithophel's plan to Hushai to see what he might think of it. David's friend, stalling for time, proclaimed the plan to be bad advice. David was a mighty warrior. His men were skilled soldiers. No doubt he was already hiding out in a cave in the wilderness ready to pounce on any force which might try to pursue him. Should David score a quick victory over Absalom's forces, those committed to the rebellion would lose heart and desert the cause (17:5-10).

Hushai then advanced his own plan to Absalom, one which would be advantageous to his friend David. He recommended that Absalom muster a huge army and then personally lead that army against his father. This army would search out David and totally crush him leaving not one of his supporters alive. If David attempted to take refuge in a city, that city would be totally dismantled. Hushai painted a picture which stirred the macho mentality of Absalom and his soldiers. They declared the counsel of Hushai to be superior to that of Ahithophel. The narrator explains that Yahweh had appointed that the wise advice of Ahithophel should be frustrated so that calamity might befall Absalom (17:11-14).

Hushai immediately went to the temple to convey the news to Zadok and Abiathar about what Absalom was contemplating. David must be advised to cross over the Jordan. He would be in grave danger at the fords of the Jordan should Absalom revert to the plan of Ahithophel (17:15-16).

The sons of Zadok, Jonathan and Ahimaaz, were hiding at En-rogel in the Kidron Valley southeast of Jerusalem. The plan was for a maidservant to relay information to them. They in turn were to carry the news to David. This plan was nearly upset when a lad spotted the two loyal supporters of David and reported their whereabouts to Absalom. The two young soldiers fled to Bahurim to the house of a man who had a well in his courtyard. They climbed down into the well, and a woman spread a covering over the opening of the well. On the covering she spread grain. Just at that moment the agents of Absalom arrived. They questioned the woman about Jonathan and Ahimaaz. She misdirected them across the brook of water. Not finding David's two friends in the area, Absalom's men returned to Jerusalem (17:17-20).

Jonathan and Ahimaaz conveyed their warning to David at the

371

fords of the Jordan. David ordered a nighttime crossing of the river. Thus by frustrating the counsel of Ahithophel, Hushai saved David's life. When Ahithophel saw that his advice was not followed, he was so depressed that he went to his home and committed suicide (17:21-23).

ABSALOM'S DEATH
2 Samuel 17:24-19:7

David made Mahanaim, the old capital of Ish-bosheth, his Transjordan headquarters. The people of this region were solid supporters of David. Three of the local leaders brought supplies for David and his men. Shobi was an Ammonite, the son of Nahash.[4] Machir from Lodebar had been a friend of Mephibosheth (cf. 2 Sam 9:4). Barzillai was a very aged and loyal supporter of David. These friends brought food, bedding and utensils of various kinds to David's troops (17:24,27-29).

Absalom soon led his army across Jordan into Gilead for the inevitable confrontation. His army was led by Amasa, Joab's illegitimate cousin (17:25-26).[5]

At Mahanaim David numbered and organized his forces. He appointed three commanders, each in charge of one third of the force: Joab, his brother Abishai, and Ittai. David intended to lead the army, but his troops vetoed this idea. His presence on the battlefield would become the focal point of the enemy attack. It would be better if David remain in the safety of the city with whatever reserve forces there may have been. The king reluctantly agreed. So David stood by the gate and reviewed his troops before the battle. In the hearing of the entire army David charged his three commanders for his sake to deal gently with his son Absalom. In spite of all that had happened, David still loved that rebellious son (18:1-5).

The two armies met in the forest of Ephraim.[6] David's troops gained the advantage almost immediately. In the wide-ranging battle the forest proved a formidable obstacle for Absalom's less skilled partisans. In all, Absalom lost twenty thousand troops that day, a good portion to the pits and perils of the forest (18:6-8).

As Absalom tried to escape the battle, his head[7] became lodged in a low hanging tree. He was jerked from the back of his mule and left dangling in mid air. His predicament was reported to Joab. The old general rebuked his troops for not slaying the rebel. They could have earned ten pieces of silver for their effort. The troops, however, respected the wishes of their king so much that a hundred times that amount would not have induced them to slay Absalom. The soldiers knew their general. Had they disobeyed the orders of the king Joab would not have stood up for them. Joab then took matters in his own hands. He took three spears and thrust them into the heart of Absalom while he was yet alive in the midst of the oak. Taking their cue from their commander, ten of the general's armorbearers gathered around Absalom and completed the execution (18:9-15).

Once Absalom was dead there was no need to continue the carnage. Joab blew the trumpet signaling an end to hostilities. His men unceremoniously threw the body of Absalom in a deep pit in the forest and piled stones over it. Absalom's supporters fled *"each to his tent,"* i.e., home. The prince himself had no male heir. Once earlier he had erected a monument and placed it in the King's Valley[8] to perpetuate his name. The point of mentioning that monument here is to underscore what a tragic end came to this talented and charismatic young prince (18:16-18).

David's close friend Ahimaaz wished to carry the news of the battle to David. For some reason unexplained in the text Joab denied the request of Ahimaaz.[9] He dispatched instead a Cushite (Ethiopian black man) runner. Still Ahimaaz pressed Joab for permission to carry the news to David. Perhaps he felt that the Cushite would not present the news of Absalom's death in a sympathetic manner. Joab finally consented to dispatch Ahimaaz. Taking a longer but quicker route, Ahimaaz outran the Cushite (18:19-23).

David waited anxiously *"between the two gates"* of Mahanaim for news from the battle. At last a watchman caught sight of a man running alone. David reasoned that the news must be good else the watchman would have seen many men fleeing in all directions from the battlefront back to the safety of the city. Then the watchman spotted the second runner. Again David consoled himself with the assessment that the news must be good. As the runners drew nearer, the watchman thought he recognized the unique running style of Ahimaaz. David was convinced now. Ahimaaz was a good man. He would surely be brining good news (18:24-27).

Ahimaaz approached his king and breathlessly blurted out the message *"All is well."* He then prostrated himself and praised Yahweh who had delivered up all those who had lifted their hands against the king. David anxiously inquired about the well being of Absalom. Ahimaaz avoided giving a direct answer. *"I saw great tumult,"* he said. The king ordered Ahimaaz to stand aside. At that moment the Cushite arrived with a similar message of good news. Again David asked about Absalom. The Cushite gave a forthright but discreet indication of his death. He wished that all the enemies of David might be as that young man. He needed to say no more. The king went to the chamber over the gate and sobbed uncontrollably. He sincerely wished that he had died that day in place of his son Absalom! (18:28-33).

As the troops returned from the battle their joyous spirit was quickly turned to gloom by the news that David was grieving over his dead son. His troops sulked back into the city as though they had lost the battle. The king continued to agonize over his son with such a loud voice that the men in the city could hear his wailing (19:1-4).

Sensing a major morale problem, Joab came and spoke bluntly to David. The king's agony had caused the men who had saved the lives of the royal family to feel as though they had done something wrong. David appeared to love those who hated him, and to hate those who loved him. Had the result of the battle been reversed, said the general, David would have been more pleased. If David did not immediately go out and express appreciation to his troops all of them would desert him that very night. Joab may have been threatening to lead the troops away from David. In any case, David was jarred into action. He went out and sat in the city gate. All his supporters gathered around him (19:5-8).

DAVID'S RESTORATION
2 Samuel 19:9-43

Following the victory over Absalom David waited in Mahanaim until a ground swell for his return developed on the other side of the

Jordan. Several different reactions to the restoration of the king are indicated in chapter 19.

A. The Bickering (2 Sam 19:9-10).

The people of Israel were in a dilemma. The king they had chosen for themselves was now dead. David was in exile in Transjordan. In the past David had delivered them from the hands of their enemies, especially the Philistines. The implication here is that without a strong king they again would be at the mercy of these enemies. Some action needed to be taken to formally reinstate David on his throne. David wisely waited until popular support for his return to power developed (19:9-10).

B. The Reluctant (2 Sam 19:11-15).

Though the northern tribes were debating about how best to reinstate David, Judah had made no moves in that direction. David contacted his avid supporters Zadok and Abiathar in Jerusalem. They were to speak to the elders of Judah regarding their lack of initiative in this matter. After all, David was their flesh and bone. David's agents were to inform Amasa, who had been Absalom's commander, that he would replace Joab as general of the army. This popular and diplomatic move united the men of Judah behind David. They sent word for David and his servants to return to Jerusalem. David made his way to the Jordan. The men of Judah assembled at Gilgal in order to assist the king in crossing the river (19:11-15).

C. The Desperate (2 Sam 19:16-23).

Two of the first men to greet David at the Jordan were Shimei and Ziba, both of the tribe of Benjamin. The former brought with him a thousand men; the latter brought his fifteen sons and twenty servants. Both men feared that David, once he was restored to power, would direct his wrath toward them, Shimei for cursing the king, Ziba for twisting the truth for personal advantage. These Benjamites kept crossing the river to assist the king's household in transit (19:16-18a).

As the king was about to cross the Jordan, Shimei fell down before him. He begged David to forget what he had done as he was climbing the ascent of Olivet. He confessed his curses on the king to be sin.

He asked David to take into account that he was among the first to greet him on his return to Jerusalem (19:18b-20).

Abishai raised the legal question of whether Shimei had committed a capital crime by cursing Yahweh's anointed. Technically Abishai was right. David, however, disassociated himself from this attitude of vindictiveness. This was a day for celebration, not revenge. Furthermore, as chief judicial officer in the land it was David's prerogative to decide if clemency would be extended. David swore an oath to Shimei that he would not die for the crime he had committed (19:21-23).

D. The Aggrieved (2 Sam 19:24-30).

Mephibosheth the grandson of Saul met David when he crossed Jordan. His appearance indicated that he had been in mourning for a long time. He had given himself no personal care since the day that David had departed from Jerusalem. David questioned him, however, about why he had not gone with him into exile. Mephibosheth explained that he had been deceived by Ziba. He had intended to saddle a donkey and depart with David, but his lameness had prevented him from doing this. Moreover, he charged, Ziba had slandered him. Yet Mephibosheth regarded David as *"an angel of God"* in respect to discerning between truth and falsehood. Mephibosheth knew that the house of Saul was as good as dead until David befriended him and allowed him to eat at the royal table. Therefore, whatever David might decide, Mephibosheth would utter no word of complaint (19:24-28).

David was not sure whether Ziba or Mephibosheth had told him the truth. He therefore decided that they would split the land which once had belonged to Saul. Mephibosheth said he was willing for Ziba to have it all. The only thing that mattered to him was that David had returned safely. Whether or not these words were spoken sincerely is difficult to ascertain from the text (19:29-30).

E. The Benefactor (2 Sam 19:31-39).

Barzillai the Gileadite had come down to the Jordan to escort David across the river. This wealthy octogenarian had supplied the king with his necessities while he was in Mahanaim. David invited Barzillai to go to Jerusalem with him so that he might return the hospitality (19:31-33).

Barzillai politely declined. He had few years yet to live. At his age he would not appreciate the finery of court life. In his declining years he would only be a burden to the king. He begged leave to return that he might die in his own land near the grave of his parents. Yet Barzillai was not reluctant to request that David take his son Chimham with him. So David announced that he would take the son of his friend with him to Jerusalem. The king would do for the son whatever the father thought appropriate. The king than kissed the old man, blessed him, and sent him on his way. Then David followed his supporters across the Jordan (19:34-39).

F. The Childish (2 Sam 19:40-43).

David was escorted to Gilgal by Chimham, the people of Judah, and half of the people of Israel. At Gilgal a brouhaha developed. Some of the northern tribes complained to David that they had been left out of the privilege of bringing the royal family across the Jordan. The men of Judah defended their right to take the lead in escorting the king by pointing out that the king was a member of the tribe of Judah. They further pointed out that they had received no royal compensation for what they had done. The men of Israel responded that they were ten tribes and therefore had ten times more claim to David than did Judah. Furthermore, they were the first to propose bringing back the king. Why then should the men of Judah treat them with contempt? Yet the words of the tribe of Judah were harsher than the words of the men of Israel.

THE REBELLION OF SHEBA
2 Samuel 20:1-26

The tribal argument at Gilgal abruptly concluded when a Benjamite named Sheba blew a trumpet and announced that the northern tribes had disowned David as their king. The men of Israel then withdrew from following David and went after Sheba. The men of Judah, however, remained with their king from the Jordan to Jerusalem (20:1-2).

The first order of business upon returning to Jerusalem was to deal with the ten concubines who had been humiliated by Absalom. David decided that they should be treated as widows, since Absalom, who had claimed them as his wives, was now dead. The king provided for these unfortunate ladies security and sustenance. They were shut off from society until the day of their death (20:3).

The next order of royal business was to dispatch Amasa to deal with the rebellion among the northern tribes. He was to recruit an army from the men of Judah within three days. Apparently the men of Judah had no taste for more war at this time. At the end of the three days Amasa still had not been successful in recruiting his force (20:4-5).

Time was of the essence as far as David was concerned. The rebellion in the north needed to be crushed immediately lest it become worse than that of Absalom. Abishai was commissioned to take the royal guard and pursue Sheba before he could find some fortified city to hole up in. So Joab's men, now under the command of Joab's brother Abishai, along with the palace bodyguard of foreign mercenaries, pursued Sheba. David left himself completely unprotected in the palace. This indicates how urgent he felt the situation was in the north (20:6-7).

Amasa met the northward bound force at the large stone in Gibeon. Joab feigned friendship with Amasa. He rushed forward to greet him. Joab arranged for his sword to drop from its sheath as he rushed forward. He then picked it up with his left hand. He took Amasa's beard by the right hand as he pretended to want to give his rival a kiss of greeting. Amasa was completely off guard. Joab then smote him with such a blow that the viscera of the man began to ooze out the wound (20:8-10).

Joab and Abishai left to pursue Sheba. One of Joab's soldiers then challenged those loyal to David to follow Joab. The troops, however, were paralyzed by the dastardly deed they had just witnessed. They did not wish to walk past the writhing body of Amasa lying in the middle of the road. Joab's servant removed the body to a field beside the road and threw a robe over it. The soldiers then hastened after Joab who had now assumed command of the forces (20:11-13).

Joab pursued Sheba through the tribes of Israel to the city of Abel Beth-maacah, about four miles west of Dan. The men of Judah laid siege to the city. They built a siege ramp up to the level of the walls. From the height of that ramp they were wreaking destruction on the walls of the city. When it appeared that the city was about to fall, a wise woman from within the city summoned Joab to a conference (20:14-17).

The woman pled for a cessation of hostilities. She argued that (1) the city of Abel was a part of Israel's heritage with a reputation as a place of wisdom; (2) the city was among the most peaceful and loyal in Israel; (3) the city was "a mother in Israel," i.e., a city which had produced much offspring for the nation; and (4) the city was part of the inheritance which Yahweh had given his people (20:18-19).

Joab assured the unnamed woman that he had no desire to destroy the place. Yet a rebel had taken refuge in that city. If the city would surrender this rebel, Joab would withdraw from the area. The woman promised that the head of Sheba would be thrown to Joab over the wall. The woman then returned to her people to persuade them to execute Sheba. When the head of the rebel came over the wall, Joab signaled an end to the conflict. His troops returned to their homes (20:20-22).

In view of all the turmoil he has narrated, the author of Samuel felt it was necessary to record the officers of David's government once again (cf. 8:16-18). For the most part the two lists are the same. Joab was reinstated as commander of the army. Benaiah commanded the mercenary royal bodyguard. Adoram (NASB) or Adoniram (NIV) was over the forced labor battalion. Jehoshaphat was the recorder. Sheva replaced Seriah as scribe. Zadok and Abiathar continued as priests. Ira the Jairite replaced the sons of the king in the office of "priest," i.e., personal adviser (20:23-26).

ENDNOTES

1. Following the Septuagint and the Syriac versions. Josephus (Ant. 7.9.1) also read here four years. The Masoretic Text reads forty years. Some think that this revolt came when Absalom was forty years old, or in the fortieth year of David's reign. Most likely, however, the forty years of the Masoretic Text is a scribal error.

2. Ahithophel was the grandfather of Bathsheba (2 Sam 11:3; 23:34). Perhaps David's adultery with Bathsheba and murder of Uriah so angered this wise man that he was willing to risk his life in backing the insurrection.

3. Jewish tradition makes Ittai the son of David's friend King Achish of Gath.

4. Shobi may, therefore, have been the brother of the Hanun against whom David had fought. Another interpretation makes Shobi the son of an Israelite Nahash. Shobi would then have been the Israelite governor of Ammon.

5. Amasa was the son of Jithra (contracted to Jether in 1 Chr 2:17). This Ishmaelite *"went in to"* (i.e., seduced) Abigail, the sister of of Zeruiah, mother of Joab (2 Sam 17:25). When Joab later murdered Amasa, he may have been motivated as much by family animosity as by political differences.

6. The Forest of Ephraim is a tangle of brush in Gilead where Jephthah had defeated the Ephraimites who crossed the Jordan many years earlier (Judg 12:4-6).

7. Josephus states that Absalom was caught by his long hair in the branches of the tree. Others think his head would have been covered with a helmet so that his hair could not have gotten caught in the branches.

8. The so-called Absalom monument in the Kidron Valley east of Jerusalem today dates only to the Hellenistic period. It consequently cannot be the monument mentioned here.

9. Commentators have reached exactly opposite conclusions as to why Joab did not at first dispatch Ahimaaz: (1) because he did not wish to have the news of Absalom's death softened; or (2) because he wished to soften the blow by sending a more detached messenger. Another possibility is that Joab wished to spare Ahimaaz the unpleasantness or even animosity of David.

CHAPTER TWENTY-THREE

The Testimonies of David
2 Samuel 21-24

The last four chapters of 2 Samuel contain a sixfold appendix to the book. The material here comes from different periods of David's life. Dating the individual units is virtually impossible. These materials, however, have been arranged by the author in a very artistic chiastic manner as illustrated below.

A. David's Discipline (21:1-14).
B. A List (21:15-22).
C. A Song (22:1-51).
C'. A Song (23:1-7).
B'. A List (23:8-39).
A'. David's Discipline (24:1-25).

DAVID'S DISCIPLINE: A FAMINE
2 Samuel 21:1-14

At some point in the reign of David Israel experienced three years of famine. When the famine persisted, David concluded that this was no ordinary quirk of nature. The king *"sought the presence of Yahweh,"* i.e., he consulted the priestly oracle, in order to verify his hunch (21:1a).

A. The Offended Appeased (2 Sam 21:2b-6).

The oracle indicated that Israel was being punished for Saul's criminal acts against the Gibeonites. Their lives were protected by an ancient covenant which Joshua had made with these people (Josh 9). In his zeal for Israel, Saul had been attempting to rid the land of these Amorites. Perhaps he wished to confiscate their property to reward the Benjamites who were loyal to him (cf. 1 Sam 22:7). In any case, Saul's actions were a national crime since a national covenant was broken. The people were guilty in that they permitted their king to act in this lawless manner. Murder left unpunished polluted the land (Num 35:33). The famine was the punishment for that pollution (21:2).

David asked the Gibeonite leaders what he should do to make atonement for Israel's transgression of a solemn covenant. He desired for the aggrieved people to turn their curses into blessings for *"the inheritance of Yahweh,"* i.e., the land which Yahweh had given to his people for their inheritance. The Gibeonites indicated that no amount of monetary payment would make things right. They further stated that it was not their place to execute any Israelite. To do so would only bring on them the wrath of the more powerful Israelites around them. The hint here was that execution—the shedding of blood—was the only way in which atonement could be made for the many Gibeonites who had died at the hands of Saul. David then committed himself to do for these Gibeonites whatever they stipulated as being just (21:3-4).

Saul had tried to exterminate the Gibeonites. Only the execution of seven of his sons (descendants) would atone for the violation of the covenant with Gibeon. The Gibeonites wished to *"hang them before Yahweh in Gibeah,"* i.e., impale them on sharp stakes in their native village. Perhaps some stipulation to this effect was actually written in the treaty which Israel had with Gibeon. In any case, David agreed to hand over the seven Saulites (21:5-6).

B. The Guilty Punished (2 Sam 21:7-9).

David took two sons of Saul by the concubine Rizpah, Armoni and Mephibosheth (not to be confused with the son of Jonathan who was spared). Merab's five sons—grandsons of Saul—were also taken. These men all *"fell together,"* i.e., they were executed at the same time in the first days of the barley harvest. They were then handed over to the Gibeonites for impalement (21:7-9).

If these seven men were innocent of any involvement in the crimes of Saul, then David violated God's law. No innocent family member was to be executed for the crimes of another member of the family. Since David is not here condemned for any violation of the law, one must assume that these seven had been personally involved in the ethnic cleansing attributed to Saul.

Does the chronology, however, allow for personal involvement of the seven men? Certainly Saul's two sons could have been involved. But what about his grandsons? Would they have been old enough? That depends on when this episode is dated.

Most likely, the famine occurred early in David's reign over all Israel. That would have been the earliest that he would have controlled the tribal territory of Benjamin and consequently be responsible for the actions of those living there. Merab had been married even before David was forced to leave Saul's court. The chronological clues sprinkled through the account of David indicate that at least fourteen years elapsed between David's departure from Saul's court and his coronation as king of all the tribes. Thus Merab's sons would have been teenagers at the time David became ruler of all Israel. They certainly would have been old enough to have joined other Saulites in the ethnic crimes against the Gibeonites.

C. The Devoted Rewarded (2 Sam 21:10-14).

Rizpah, the mother of two of the executed men, could not give the corpses of her sons proper burial without violating the royal edict. She did the next best thing. She spread out sackcloth on a rock and sat down near the decaying bodies of the seven men. She made sure neither the birds by day nor the beasts by night had access to the bodies. This dedicated, living scarecrow kept her faithful watch until the famine ended and the rains fell. By that time only the skeletons remained (21:10).

383

David was deeply moved by the dedication of Rizpah. Therefore he issued two commands. First, he ordered the bones of Saul and Jonathan brought from Jabesh-gilead and reburied in the tomb of Kish, the father of Saul. This action demonstrates that he had no personal animosity toward the house of Saul. Second, he ordered the bones of the seven recently executed descendants of Saul buried in the same tomb. Only after these men had been given a proper burial was God moved by the entreaty for the land (21:11-14).

A LIST: DAVID'S HEROES
2 Samuel 21:15-22

The second segment of the appendix is a list of the heroes who had distinguished themselves in various campaigns against the Philistines early in David's reign. One reason the list may have been placed here is to provide an historical context for the song of deliverance which follows. The episodes have in common that in each case one of the sons of *"the giant"* was defeated. These giants employed by the Philistines were the last surviving members of the Rephaim, a tall race which once inhabited that region in large numbers. With each new giant they could put forward, the Philistines took new courage in their ongoing battles with the Israelites. In each engagement, however, the giant was slain and the Philistines were trounced.

In one battle David became weary. A Philistine giant named Ishbi-benob pressed down upon him. This powerful man wielded a spear which had a point weighing three hundred shekels of bronze (8 lbs).[1] Had not Abishai aided the king he surely would have been killed. This near escape caused the troops to insist that David no longer go into battle with them lest *"the lamp of Israel,"* i.e., the king himself, be extinguished (21:16-17).

Two battles with the Philistines were fought at Gob near Gezer (cf. 1 Chr 20:4), about twenty miles southeast of modern Tel Aviv. In the first Sibbecai smote Saph, another of the Philistine giants. Sibbecai was a member of the Thirty, a military order attained through gallantry in battle (1 Chr 11:29). At some point he was made commander of the eighth division of David's army (1 Chr 27:11). In the second battle at Gob, Elhanan killed Lahmi the brother of Goliath the

384

Gittite (21:18-19; cf. 1 Chr 20:5).

A fourth Philistine giant had six fingers on each hand and six toes on each foot. He defied Israel before the battle much like Goliath had done (cf. 1 Sam 17:8-10). David's nephew Jonathan struck down this formidable adversary (21:20-22).

A SONG OF DELIVERANCE
2 Samuel 22:1-51

David composed a song to celebrate his deliverance from the hand of Saul and other enemies. Presumably this was written very early in his reign.[2] The text is essentially the same as Psalm 18, but dozens of variations between the two versions are in evidence. Which of these two versions represents the original song is not clear.[3]

A. Opening Praise (2 Sam 22:2-4).

The opening verses summarize the entire song. Various figures are employed to stress David's dependence on God. From time to time David had sought refuge from Saul in the rocky wasteland of the Judean wilderness. The Lord, however, was his true Rock. The figure conveys unchangeable faithfulness, permanence, and impregnable safety. Like the shield of a warrior God protected David. As with the horn of a wild beast he routed all who attacked the faithful. David continued to call upon the Lord and he continued to save him.[4]

B. Divine Deliverance (2 Sam 22:5-20).

The poet next describes his need for divine aid. He is a man drowning in the sea of death. He has been ensnared by death as in the net of a hunter. In his desperation David had called unto Yahweh his God. From his heavenly temple the Lord had heard that desperate cry (22:6-7).

God answered in a most dramatic way. His divine anger was unleashed against the enemies of David. The earth seemed to quake, the heavens seemed to sink down as Yahweh came riding in on a cherub (a winged lion), i.e., a black storm cloud. *"Coals of fire,"* i.e., lightning bolts, and claps of thunder witnessed to the anger of Yahweh. The enemies scattered before this mighty manifestation of divine power (22:8-15).

The waters of death which threatened to engulf David withdrew from the divine presence. The Lord drew David out of these danger-ous waters. These figures mean that God delivered David from his enemies. From the narrow straits of persecution God brought him forth into a broad place, i.e., rescued him. What a magnificent description of God's intervention on behalf of David (22:16-20).

C. Ground of Deliverance (2 Sam 22:21-28).

David felt he had been rewarded according to his righteousness. He had kept the statutes of God. He was blameless toward Yahweh, i.e., he sought to please God both in his public and private life. It is not absolute perfection which David claims. The context here is that of his persecution by Saul. David did not allow the frustration of that experience to cause him to reject the principles of the law. His hands were clean in that he had made no attempt to kill Saul (22:21-25).

From his own specific situation David derived a general principle. God reciprocates in like manner the *"kind,"* the *"blameless,"* and the *"pure."* He intervenes on behalf of the *"afflicted"* (NASB) or *"hum-ble"* (NIV).The corollary of this principle is also true. With the *"per-verted"* (NASB) or *"crooked"* (NIV) the Lord shows himself *"astute"* (NASB) or *"shrewd"* (NIV). He brings down the *"haughty,"* i.e., god-less (22:26-28).

D. Deliverance in Battle (2 Sam 22:29-46).

David next begins to reflect on what God had done for him in bat-tle. God had provided illumination in the *"darkness"* of weakness or depression. He provided strength and courage for David to charge a troop, or leap over the defenses of his enemies. The word of God's promise is put to the test in time of war. Yet he had proved to be a shield to all who take refuge in him. He alone is a "rock" or ground of hope. The Lord was David's fortress. God provided his servant with swift feet with which to escape his enemies and climb to inaccessible places (22:29-34).

The Lord provided David with the strength to use a *"bow of bronze,"* i.e., a powerful weapon, and *"the shield of salvation."* With God's help he had been able to walk with bold steps of confi-dence. He enabled David to pursue and destroy his enemies, to walk right over their fallen bodies. It was God who had girded David with battle strength. It was God who caused the enemies to flee from David. His enemies found no one to save them from the pursuit of David, not even Yahweh. David was able to pulverize them like dust of the streets (22:35-42).

God also delivered David from the *"contentions"* (NASB) or *"attacks"* (NIV) of his own people. Again the reference seems to be to the efforts of Saul to kill David. This deliverance from Saul laid the groundwork for David's success in conquering other nations. Foreign peoples merely hearing rumors of his approach were surrendering their fortresses and rendering homage to David (22:43-46).

E. Concluding Praise (2 Sam 22:47-51).

David concludes his song with praise for the God he loved so much. In contrast to the lifeless idols of the heathen, Yahweh lives! The poet exalts the *"rock"* of his salvation, i.e, the steadfast Savior. This is the God who executed vengeance on behalf of David and brought down his foes. This confidence enabled David to overcome temptations to raise his hand against Saul. This God had again and again rescued David by lifting him above the reach of his enemies (22:47-49).

David owed the Lord a debt of gratitude. He unashamedly would give his thanks to Yahweh among the nations. Yahweh had proved to be a *"tower of deliverance"* to his king. He had shown covenant faithfulness (*"lovingkindness"* NASB) to David. Yahweh would continue to be so disposed toward the descendants of David as well (22:50-51).

A SONG OF ANTICIPATION
2 Samuel 23:1-7

The second song in the appendix to 2 Samuel is designated as *"the last words of David."* These are certainly not the last words that David ever spoke (cf. 1 Kgs 2:1-9). This poem must be the last prophetic or inspired utterance of the king (23:1a).

The poem begins with a description of David himself. He was of lowly origin, *"the son of Jesse."* Yet God had exalted him. This shep-

herd became *"the anointed of the God of Jacob."* As such David
was a type of Christ, the anointed one par excellence. He was *"the
sweet psalmist of Israel."*[5] Some seventy-three psalms in the Book
of Psalms are attributed to him. Yet he was no ordinary song writer.
The Spirit of Yahweh spoke through David. Inspiration is not a quality attributed to writings centuries after they were written. The Biblical
writers were aware that they were being used as the instrument of the
Holy Spirit. David claims that what he was about to write in this particular song was an oracle of God. The Rock of Israel had given him
these words (23:1b-3a).

The language of this song is difficult. The words seem to have
messianic implications. David anticipates the rise of a king who would
rule over mankind in righteousness, i.e., justice. He would rule in the
fear of God, i.e., reverence for God. His appearance would signal a
new day for the world. Just as the warmth of the morning brings
refreshment and stimulates growth, so the reign of this king would
result in spiritual growth. This ruler would come from the house
(descendants) of David. That was the thrust of the everlasting
covenant which God had made with David. Because of that covenant
David was confident that God would provide salvation, i.e., deliverance from physical threat, for David personally. He would also make
his house grow in stature (23:3b-5).

In contrast to the glorious future of David's house, the ungodly are
compared to thorns which men dig up and burn in order to clear the
land. As they do so they must be well armed (protected) for the task.
So the future king—Messiah—would root out of his kingdom all
such *"thorns."* These will be cast into the furnace of God's judgment
fire (23:6-7).[6]

A LIST: DAVID'S HEROES
2 Samuel 23:8-39

The second list of military heroes in the appendix contains the
names of those who helped David win the throne and conquer Zion.
The names in 2 Samuel are arranged in three groups which are military orders of honor. Twelve from these groups were appointed commanders of divisions of David's army (1 Chr 27). Chronicles adds the

names of others that David deemed worthy of special honor for their commitment to him in the period before he received the crown.

A. Supreme Honor (2 Sam 23:8-12 // 1 Chr 11:10-14).
Three warriors received the supreme recognition from King David. The group was simply known as "the Three." The commander of this group was Josheb-basshebeth, also known as Adino the Ezrite. He had slain eight hundred men with his spear in one encounter (23:8).

The second member of the Three was Eleazar the Ahohite. In one battle against the Philistines he had refused to withdraw. He struck the enemy until his hand was weary and *"clung to the sword."* Because of his valor that battle was won. The other Israelites reappeared when the danger was past to strip the enemy corpses (23:9-10).

Supreme honor also was bestowed on Shammah the Hararite. In a battle with the Philistines he took his stand in a bean patch and refused to retreat though all of his unit fled from the field of battle (23:11-12).

B. Superior Honor (2 Sam 23:13-23 // 1 Chr 11:15-25).
Within a military order known as the Thirty were certain men who stood out. Though their exploits were not deemed as valiant as those of the Three, yet they enjoyed superior honor within the group known as the Thirty. These three may be called "the overshadowed," for while their deeds were valiant, they were made to appear less important by the courageous acts of others.[7]

Three officers qualified for this honor. They first distinguished themselves during a Philistine invasion. David had taken refuge temporarily in the cave of Adullam. He was overheard expressing a desire to taste again the water from a well in Bethlehem which he had known in childhood. For these loyal men David's wish was their command. They broke through the camp of the Philistine garrison which currently occupied Bethlehem to fetch the water for their king. David, when he learned of the circumstances, poured the water out on the ground. He would not drink of water which was secured at the risk of the lives of his men. Their well-being was more important to him then his personal comfort (23:13-17).

The individual deeds of valor of two of the three men who received superior honor are recorded. First, Abishai the brother of Joab was chief of the Thirty. He had slain three hundred with his spear in one battle. Second, Benaiah had distinguished himself with several deeds of valor. (1) He struck down *"two of Moab's best men"* (NIV). (2) He also had faced a lion in the middle of a pit on a snowy day. (3) Using only a club, he disarmed an impressive Egyptian warrior and slew him with his own spear. This valor earned Benaiah the position of captain of David's bodyguard (23:18-23).

Presumably the third unmentioned member of this second group of three was Joab. Perhaps the record of his deeds was erased when he lost command because of the Absalom incident.

C. Secondary Honor (2 Sam 23:24-39 // 1 Chr 11:26-47).

Nothing is known of the exploits of the rest of David's heroes. Their names are merely listed in honor roll fashion. Certain things, however, stand out about the list. First, the group known as the Thirty was not actually limited to thirty men. The group may have started out as literally thirty men. Others, however, were added to the roster when their deeds were equivalent to those of the original members. Perhaps other soldiers were elevated to the honor to fill vacancies created by death or retirement from military service. In any case the text explicitly states that there were thirty-seven members of the order at the time the list which appears in 2 Samuel 23 was composed.[8]

A study of the names here recorded indicates that these heroes came from throughout the land. Several were even foreigners who were fighting in David's army. The last name on the list in 2 Samuel is Uriah the Hittite. One wonders if the brave deed which earned him this honor was the battle in which he lost his life because David had ordered him to be abandoned on the battlefield. The Chronicles version of the list includes sixteen names following Uriah. These were men added to the order after the list in 2 Samuel was compiled.

D. Special Honor (1 Chr 12:1-22).

The Chronicler has named certain individuals and groups for special honor, not so much for specific acts of heroism, as for their general courage.

1. Benjamite marksmen (12:1-7). When Saul was still king and David was living in Ziklag (1 Sam 27), a unit of twenty-three expert marksmen from the tribe of Benjamin cast their lot with David. These men could sling stones or shoot arrows with either hand. They risked loss of property, and even their lives, by taking their stand with David at a time when the kingship issue had not yet been settled. Their marksman eye was equaled by their keen insight into David's future role in Israel.

  2. Skilled Gadites (12:8-15). During the earliest days of David's flight from Saul he was joined by a group of highly skilled soldiers from the tribe of Gad in Transjordan. They joined David when he was hiding out in the stronghold in the wilderness. These valiant men were particularly expert in the use of spear and shield. Because of their shaggy beards, they are said to have the faces of lions. Quickness of foot was also an attribute of this unit. These Gadites all became captains in David's army. In battle the least of these officers was equal to a hundred men, the greatest to a thousand. These men had made a reputation for themselves on one occasion by a surprise attack across the Jordan when it was in flood. They drove the enemy—probably the Philistines—from the valleys which opened onto the plain of Jordan.

  3. A Spirit-directed band (12:16-18). During those wilderness days David was joined by several from Benjamin and Judah. At first David was suspicious that this group might be intending to betray him to Saul. He committed judgment as to the intentions of this group to God. Then the Spirit came upon Amasai[9] and caused him to deliver to David a message of commitment and encouragement. What an unlikely mouthpiece for the message of God! These men were also made captains in David's army.

  4. The defectors from Manasseh (12:19-21). The last group to cast their lot with David before the days of his glory was from Manasseh. David had been dismissed by King Achish before the battle of Mt. Gilboa (cf. 1 Sam 29:4-5). As he was returning to Ziklag, seven high ranking officers from Saul's army defected to him. They aided David in dealing with the desert raiders who had destroyed Ziklag and kidnapped its population. David was not remiss in honoring these men who, though tardy in their commitment, nonetheless risked

391

everything by casting their lot with him while the issue of kingship was
still in doubt.

DAVID'S DISCIPLINE: THE CENSUS
2 Samuel 24:1-25

The sixth appendix to the Book of Samuel contains the account of
a census ordered by David. Almost immediately after the census was
over David realized that he had sinned.

A. The Pride of David (2 Sam 24:1-10).

After the Absalom rebellion the anger of Yahweh burned against
Israel. God permitted Satan (1 Chr 21:1) to incite David to take a
census in Israel. The king ordered Joab to register the people from
Dan to Beersheba *"so that I may know the number of the people."*
Joab, as worldly a man as he was, sensed that this census was very
wrong. His objections, however, were probably more on political and
social grounds rather than theological ones. In spite of Joab's remon-
stration, the king could not be dissuaded. So Joab and his commanders went out from the presence of the king to register the people
(24:1-4).

Joab began the census in the southern part of Transjordan. He
then proceeded in a wide arc through Gilead to Dan, then to Tyre
and Sidon, then south through Cis-jordan to Beersheba in southern
Judah. After almost ten months Joab returned to the capital and presented the king with the census figures. He had found 800,000
valiant swordsmen in Israel, and 500,000 in Judah (24:5-9).[10]

David's heart troubled him after the census. He confessed to the
Lord that he had sinned greatly and acted foolishly. He begged God's
forgiveness. Since merely taking a census was not sinful—Moses took
two of them—the sin here must have been connected with David's
attitude. This was a military census. David must have been anticipating a military campaign on some grand scale. The cities of the Hivites
and Canaanites were included. Perhaps David planned to draft these
peoples into his army (24:10).

B. The Punishment of Israel (2 Sam 24:11-17).

In the morning Yahweh dispatched Gad, David's seer, with a message for the king. The Lord in his grace would allow David to choose what punishment he should experience because of his sin. The alternatives were (1) seven years of famine,[11] (2) three months of flight from before his enemies, or (3) three days of pestilence. These alternatives brought David great distress. Nonetheless, he elected to *"fall into the hand of Yahweh"* in the pestilence. He concluded that since the mercies of the Lord are great, that punishment might be the less disruptive both for him personally and for his people (24:11-14).

Yahweh then sent a pestilence upon the land. It lasted from morning to *"the appointed time,"* i.e., the time of afternoon sacrifice. Seventy thousand men of the people from Dan to Beersheba died within a matter of hours. As the angel of death approached the major population center of Jerusalem, Yahweh stayed his hand. This cessation came in response to David's intercessory prayer. The king could *"see"* the angel who was striking down the people, i.e., the angel was visible. David was prepared to accept the wrath of God for what he had done, but why *"these sheep,"* i.e., innocent people? God heard that prayer, and the angel of pestilence stopped his deadly work by the threshing floor of Araunah the Jebusite (24:15-17).

C. The Place of Sacrifice (2 Sam 24:18-25).

The sentiment of David's prayer was right, but his facts were not accurate. Israel had in fact sinned. By supporting the rebellion of Absalom in such large numbers they had repudiated for a time God's anointed. Thus God accomplished a twofold judgment in this pestilence. Israel was punished for tolerating the Absalom and Sheba rebellions. David was punished by seeing his potential military force devastated.

The seer Gad returned to David, instructing him to build an altar on the threshingfloor of Araunah the Jebusite. First, however, the king had to purchase that ground. The Jebusite, suspecting that sacrifice at this spot might put an end to the pestilence, offered to give David the land and even the sacrificial animals. The king, however, insisted on purchase. His words on this occasion have challenged believers through the centuries: *"I will not offer burnt offerings to Yahweh my God which cost me nothing"* (24:18-24a).

So the purchase was made. David paid fifty shekels of silver for the threshingfloor and the oxen.[12] On that spot the king built an altar and offered sacrifices. By this action Yahweh was entreated for the land. The plague was restrained (24:24b-25).

TEMPLE PREPARATION
1 Chronicles 22:1-19

David's magnificent obsession was to build a temple for Yahweh. That he was forbidden to do. Nonetheless, he did everything he could to make that task easier for his son Solomon.

A. Site Selected (1 Chr 22:1).

The selection of the site for the temple was linked to the episode of the plague which was stayed at the threshingfloor of Araunah (Ornan). David had offered sacrifices at that spot in celebration of the cessation of the plague. Thereafter David feared to make the trip to the tabernacle in Gibeon *"for he was terrified by the sword of the angel of Yahweh"* (1 Chr 21:30). Apparently the visible evidence of the death angel's presence lingered in the sky for some time. During that time David was shown (2 Chr 3:1) that his personal altar on the threshingfloor of Araunah would become a national altar. On that site the house of God would be located.

B. Materials Gathered (1 Chr 22:2-5).

David knew that when he died a young and inexperienced Solomon would succeed him. The task of building a world famous temple would be a challenge for any ruler. David determined that he would gather as much material as he could for the project before his death. Resident aliens were organized to hew out stones. David prepared a large quantity of iron for making nails and clamps. More bronze was collected than could be weighed. David also secured a large quantity of timber from Tyre. Thus did David make *"ample preparation"* for the construction of the temple before his death.

C. Builder Charged (1 Chr 22:6-16).

Old King David charged his son Solomon to build a house to the

name of Yahweh. He explained first why he himself had not under-
taken the project. The word of Yahweh (through the prophet
Nathan?) had indicated that because he had shed so much blood in
his many wars, he would be forbidden to build the temple. The
prophetic word had indicated that the Lord would give the land rest in
the days of Solomon. This man of rest would be the one to build the
house of God. The Lord had also indicated that David's son would be
the son of God in a special sense. God had promised to establish the
throne of David's son forever (22:6-10).

David expressed his prayer that Yahweh might be with Solomon,
that he might be successful in building the house of Yahweh. He then
prayed that Yahweh would give Solomon discretion and understanding in his governance of Israel. If the young man would be careful to
observe the Mosaic law, he would prosper. There David urged his
sons, in the same words which Moses charged Joshua, "*Be strong
and courageous.*" If one knows that he is in step with God he has no
reason to fear whatever the future might hold (22:11-13).

David then enumerated all the materials which he had gathered for
his son to use in temple construction: 100,000 talents of gold (3,750
tons NIV), a million talents of silver (37,500 tons NIV), bronze and
iron beyond weight, timber and stone. Many skilled in masonry, car-
pentry and stone cutting had been identified and organized. All was
ready for Solomon to begin the task (22:14-16).

The amount of gold and silver gathered by David has been dismissed by most commentators as a gross exaggeration. The fact is
that it is impossible to estimate with any degree of certainty what the
"talent" was worth in the days of David. Slotki points out that both a
Babylonian and a Phoenician system of weights were current in
Canaan, and the value of the talent of the former was twice that of
the latter. Each of these systems also had a heavier and a lighter
scale, the former again being double the latter.[13] In view of the fact
that the system of weights employed by the author of Chronicles—
perhaps neither of the systems mentioned above—is unknown, it is
presumptuous to speak of the figures here being preposterous.[14]

D. Princes Charged (1 Chr 22:17-19).

David next addressed the leaders of the nation. He commanded them to assist Solomon in building the temple. He pointed out to them that Yahweh had subdued the land before David and his people. The land now enjoyed rest on every side. With these military challenges behind them, the leaders should now set their heart to seek Yahweh. They should build the temple for the Lord, then move to that sacred house the ark of the covenant and the *"holy vessels,"* i.e., other furnishings of the tabernacle.

ENDNOTES

1. Though extremely heavy, this giant's spear point weighed only half that of Goliath (1 Sam 17:7).

2. Vos, however, feels that this song was composed after the Absalom rebellion toward the end of David's reign. *1,2 Samuel* in "Bible Study Commentary" (Grand Rapids: Zondervan, 1983), p. 155.

3. David may have altered slightly the original song for liturgical purposes; or the author of Samuel may have altered the song slightly when he incorporated it into his book. In either case, 2 Sam 22 and Ps 18 convey the same message.

4. The two verbs in verse 4 are imperfect indicating continuing action.

5. David was skillful as a musician (1 Sam 16:14-23). He even invented musical instruments (Am 6:5). He composed lamentations (2 Sam 1:17-27; 3:33-34). He also organized the musical aspects of temple worship (1 Chr 6:31; 25:1; chs.15-16).

6. Cf. Matt 13:30; Rev 19:15.

7. Michael Wilcock, *The Message of Chronicles* in "The Bible Speaks Today" (Downers Grove, IL,1987), pp. 59f.

8. Three groups of heroes are listed in 2 Sam 23:8-39. The first contains three, the second two, and the third group thirty-one. The unnamed thirty-seventh probably was Joab.

9. Literally the text says that the Spirit *"clothed himself with Amasai."* This language is used earlier of Gideon the Judge (Judg 6:34) and Zechariah the prophet (2 Chr 24:20).

10. The census figures in 1 Chr 21:5 are 1,100,000 for Israel and 470,000 for Judah. Undoubtedly the original report to David had the numbers broken down into various categories, e.g., standing army, aliens, age categories, as well as tribal and village numbers. The authors of Samuel and Chronicles have simply added together those categories which they thought most important. Figures would be very different, for example, if Samuel omits the king's personal bodyguard from the count, or if Chronicles included but Samuel excluded the 288,000 men of the regular army in Israel (1 Chr 27:1-

15). Another suggestion is that Chronicles included the resident aliens in the count for Israel.

11. In 1 Chr 21:12 the first alternative is stated as *three* months of famine. Under the principle that the harder text is probably the correct one, the Samuel reading should be retained. A copyist of Chronicles inadvertently miscopied the original number as three under the influence of the other two numbers in the verse.

12. According to 1 Chr 21:25 David paid six hundred shekels of gold *"for the site,"* i.e., the larger area where the future temple would be built. Samuel records only the value of the ground where the altar was built.

13. I.W. Slotki, *Chronicles* in "The Soncino Books of the Bible" (London: Soncino, 1952), pp. 123f.

14. Barker calls attention to a passage in Pliny (*Nat. Hist.*, 32.15) which might give some standard by which to compare the figures given in 1 Chr 22:14. Pliny reports that Cyrus in a single campaign in Asia captured half as many talents of silver as are here mentioned, and 34,000 lbs. of gold. See "I Chronicles" in *Pulpit Commentary* (New York: Funk & Wagnalls, 1909), p. 356.

CHAPTER TWENTY-FOUR

The Last Days of David
1 Chronicles 23-29

The length of time between the census with which 2 Samuel concludes and the illness of David with which the Book of Kings opens cannot be determined. Equally difficult to determine is the precise relationship between the events recorded in 1 Kings 1 and the final days of David as depicted in 1 Chronicles 23-29. Various reconstructions are possible. The most reasonable scenario is that Solomon's initial formal nomination and elevation to the throne is recorded in 1 Kings 1. The national convention of 1 Chronicles 23-29 must have occurred shortly after the first anointing of Solomon. At that convention Solomon was made king *"a second time"* (1 Chr 29:22).

ADONIJAH'S REBELLION
1 Kings 1:1-53

David's final years were full of turmoil and tribulation. As he lay critically ill he was yet to experience one last heartbreak. His disgrun-

tled eldest son, Adonijah, tried to take advantage of his father's condition to usurp the throne.

A. David's Decrepitude (1 Kgs 1:1-4).

When David was advanced in age[1] he became for a time decrepit.
He could no longer maintain his body temperature. The royal counselors (physicians?) advised that he secure a young virgin to *"stand
before the king,"* i.e., become his servant. She was to become his
"nurse" (NASB) or companion. The text implies, but does not clearly
state, that this virgin would become a concubine of the king. With
David's consent the search was conducted. In the town of Shunem in
the tribal area of Issachar a suitable maiden was found. Abishag was
very beautiful (lit., fair to exceeding degree). She was apparently willing to become the intimate companion of the decrepit king. Yet
David *"did not know her."* This remark helps to underscore the
wane of David's physical faculties.[2]

B. Adonijah's Plot (1 Kgs 1:5-10).

Adonijah, the son of Haggith, was the fourth, and now apparently
the eldest surviving son of David (2 Sam 3:4).[3] He considered himself
to be entitled to the throne. Yet Yahweh had bestowed a name of
affection on Solomon at his birth (2 Sam 12:25). David discerned in
this that God had designated Solomon to be his successor. Long
before any public announcement was made, the palace personnel
knew that Solomon, not Adonijah, was David's choice to succeed him
on the throne.

While David's physical condition deteriorated, Adonijah was exalt-
ing himself. He boasted to his confederates that one day he would be
king. He made no effort to conceal his conspiracy. Borrowing a tactic
from Absalom, Adonijah prepared for himself a chariot, horses, and
fifty men to run before him to herald his coming (1:5).

Adonijah's calloused disregard for his father's wishes and physical
condition is explained in four ways. First, he was a spoiled brat who
had never been disciplined. Though David was a great man in many
respects, he was a failure in parenting. Second, because of his natural
gifts, especially physical attractiveness, Adonijah had an ego which
simply would not allow him to acquiesce in being bypassed in the suc-

cession. Third, he felt he was entitled to the throne because he was the eldest surviving son. Fourth, Adonijah was encouraged in his claim to the throne by two powerful national leaders: Joab, David's general, and Abiathar the priest. Both of these men had unwavering fidelity to David. Why they encouraged Adonijah in his plot can only be a matter of conjecture. In any case, other equally influential leaders—Zadok the priest, Benaiah the general, and Nathan the prophet[4]—supported Solomon. Solomon also had the backing of "the mighty men who belonged to David," i.e., the palace guard, who refused to be swayed by the charisma of Adonijah (1:6-8).

Adonijah planned to proclaim himself king at a great feast held at En-rogel in the valley southeast of Jerusalem. All the king's sons, except Solomon, were invited. The courtiers from the tribe of Judah, those who did not openly support Solomon, were in attendance. The fact that Solomon was excluded proves that Adonijah knew him to be David's choice as successor (1:9-10).

C. Nathan's Counter Measures (1 Kgs 1:11-27).

When Nathan heard of Adonijah's coronation festivities, he took prompt action to thwart the conspiracy. First, he enlisted Bathsheba, Solomon's mother, in his effort. The prophet stressed the urgency of the situation by suggesting that unless the plot could be countered, the life of both Bathsheba and her son would be in jeopardy (1:11-12).

The plan called for Bathsheba to approach the king first. She was to present the danger from her perspective as wife and mother of the designated successor. Lest David think that his wife had exaggerated the intentions of Adonijah, Nathan would come in on her heels to confirm what she had told the king (1:13-14).

Bathsheba went immediately to the king's private chamber, which was probably a breach of etiquette since the old king was there with his young companion Abishag. First, Bathsheba reminded David of a solemn oath regarding the succession which he had made to her privately. Then she informed David about Adonijah's feast with its suspicious guest list. Third, Bathsheba impressed upon the king that the entire nation was looking to him for a clear declaration regarding his successor. Finally, she warned her husband that should he die without installing Solomon on the throne, both Bathsheba and her son would be viewed by the new king as *"offenders,"* i.e., criminals (1:15-21).

As Bathsheba was finishing her emotional appeal to her husband, Nathan's presence was announced to the king. After paying proper respects, Nathan spoke his piece in a masterful manner. He innocently assumed that David must have authorized Adonijah's feast. He pointed out that David's closest friends—Nathan, Zadok and Benaiah—had not been invited to En-rogel. Neither had Solomon been invited. If David was responsible for what was happening at En-rogel he must have changed his plans regarding his successor without consulting with his closest advisers. Nathan's words were framed in such a way as to elicit from David a strong denial that he had authorized Adonijah's coronation (1:22-27).

D. David's Actions (1 Kgs 1:28-35).

The impassioned plea of Bathsheba and then timely confirmation of Nathan served to impress the ailing king with the urgency of royal action in favor of Solomon. First, he summoned Bathsheba again into the bed chamber. He assured her that he would honor his oath. That very day Solomon would be publicly enthroned (1:28-31).

Second, David ordered Zadok, Nathan, and Benaiah to take Solomon to the spring Gihon[5] and anoint him as king immediately. They were to blow the trumpet and render to Solomon the traditional coronation greeting. They were then to bring the young man back into the city and have him sit on David's throne (1:32-35a).

Third, David declared that he had appointed Solomon to be *"prince"* (*nagid*) over Israel and Judah (1:35b). Apparently David could nominate Solomon as *nagid,* but it remained for the tribal leaders to declare him king (*melech*).

E. Benaiah's Prayer (1 Kgs 1:36-37).

Benaiah as captain of the king's personal guard could constrain himself no longer. He responded to the king's order with an expression of hearty agreement ("Amen!") and a prayer for God's blessing upon the future reign of Solomon. With most of the military leaders supporting Adonijah, the support of the palace guard was essential if Solomon was to secure the throne. Benaiah prayed that the throne of Solomon might exceed in greatness the throne of David. History records that God answered that prayer in a marvelous way (1:36-37).

F. Solomon's Anointing (1 Kgs 1:38-40).

In short order Zadok, Nathan and Benaiah organized the coronation processional. The Cherethites and Pelethites[6]—the royal palace guard—provided armed escort for the brief march to and from the Gihon. Zadok anointed Solomon with a horn of holy oil (cf. Exod 30:23-25) taken from the the sacred tent on Mt. Zion (cf. 2 Sam 6:17). Then a trumpet sounded and the crowds roared, "Long live King Solomon." The procession then moved back to the palace on Mt. Zion. The ground seemed to tremble with the tumultuous sounds of the joyous crowds.

G. Adonijah's Flight (1 Kgs 1:41-53).

The sounds of the tumult at Gihon reached Adonijah's company at En-rogel just around the bend in the valley. The guests—even Joab—were filled with apprehension. The guests, however, did their host the courtesy of finishing their meal. Then a breathless messenger arrived with the news the conspirators dreaded most: David had made Solomon king! Jonathan the messenger then went on to report the details of what had happened that day at Gihon and at the palace (1:41-48).

Jonathan's report sent the conspirators scurrying in all directions. Adonijah fled immediately to an altar[7] where he thought he could find sanctuary by grasping the "horns."[8] He refused to leave that place of sanctuary until "king" Solomon swore that he would not execute him. Solomon responded to Adonijah with a simple promise—not an oath—that he would be safe as long as he proved to be a loyal subject. If, however, he committed any fresh crime against the crown, he would be executed. With that assurance, Adonijah "came down" from the elevated altar. He was then escorted into the presence of King Solomon where he rendered homage to his younger half-brother (1:49-53).

PERSONNEL ORGANIZATION
1 Chronicles 23:1-27:34

Chronicles begins the description of David's last days by stating that in his old age he "made his son Solomon king over Israel." The author of Chronicles makes no mention of the coup in which Adonijah almost succeeded. Energized by that episode, David regained sufficient strength to call for a national convention. At that time he organized the various groups of leaders for more effective service under Solomon (23:1-2).

A. The Levites (1 Chr 23:3-32).

The Levites over thirty years of age numbered 38,000. The majority of these Levites were charged with oversight of the house of God. Others served as officers and judges, gatekeepers, and musicians. The tribe of Levi consisted of three clans: the Gershonites, Kohathites, and Merarites. David organized these Levites into twenty-four "houses" (23:3-23; 24:20-31).

In the days of Moses the primary work of the Levites was the transportation of the tabernacle. David ordered the Levites over twenty counted. Since the duties of Levites would be increased when the temple was erected, a larger number of attendants was required. Hence David lowered the age of service from thirty to twenty (23:24).

Chart No. 34

THE LEVITES IN DAVID'S DAY 1 Chronicles 23	
WORK	COUNT
Oversee Temple Work	24,000
Officers and Judges	6,000
Gatekeepers	4,000
Musicians	4,000
TOTAL	38,000

The Levites were assigned to assist the sons of Aaron with the service of the house of God by (1) purifying all holy things; (2) offering praise morning and evening; and (3) offering all burnt offerings to the Lord on special occasions. The duties of Levites appear to have been expanded during the monarchy, possibly due to the inadequate number of those in priestly families (23:25-32).

B. The Priests (1 Chr 24:1-19).

Two sons of Aaron (Eleazar and Ithamar) survived long enough to establish households in Israel. The representatives of these two great priestly families in the days of David were Zadok and Ahimelech. These two priests assisted David in organizing the descendants of Aaron for priestly service. Sixteen of the courses of priests came from the descendants of Eleazar, the other eight from the descendants of Ithamar. In a formal service before the king, the princes and chief priests cast the lot to determine the order of the courses. The results were recorded by a Levitical scribe. The twenty-four courses of priests rotated in serving two week shifts of ministry in the temple.

C. The Singers (1 Chr 25:1-31).

David and his military commanders organized musicians for use in the praise service of the temple. These were all Levites, but with a specialized ministry. The musicians came from three main families: Asaph, Heman and Jeduthun. These men were all able *"to prophesy,"* (i.e., praise God) with various musical instruments. The singers were under the direction of David. The total of those trained in singing was 288. These, like the priests and Levites were organized by lot into twenty-four courses.

D. The Gatekeepers (1 Chr 26:1-19).

Another group of Levites had the duty of guarding the temple precincts. Several of these men are called *"mighty men of valor"* or *"valiant men."* They guarded the gates leading to the temple, the storerooms, and temple treasuries. One name in this list—Obed-edom—stands out. David deposited the ark at his house where it remained for three months (1 Chr 13:13f.). The list here contains ninety-three names (cf. vv. 8,9,11), all of whom were chiefs (v. 12). The total number of gatekeepers was 4,000 (cf. 1 Chr 23:5).

E. The Officers (1 Chr 26:20-27:34).

1. Treasury officers (26:20-28). Apparently often various national leaders would dedicate valuable objects to the Lord. These were stored in the temple.

2. *"Outward business" (26:29-32).* David had officers who had charge of the affairs of the kingdom in respect to the work of the Lord and the service of the king. The king had 1,700 *"capable"* men west of Jordan, and 2,700 east of the river. The exact duties of these officers is not known.

3. *Military officers (27:1-15).* David organized his army into divisions numbering 24,000, each with its own commander. These divisions served on active duty one month each year. Some of the commanders are familiar to the student of Israel's history, e.g., Benaiah and Asahel.

4. *Tribal officers (27:16-24).* Each of the tribes had its own *"prince."* In Judah David's brother Elihu held this position. Here the author includes a note about David's census. David did not count those under twenty years of age. To do so would have called in question the promise of Yahweh that he would multiply Israel as the stars of heaven. Joab had started to count them, but did not finish. Because he started, however, wrath came upon Israel. The incomplete census numbers were not included in the account of the chronicles of King David.

5. *Overseers of crown property (27:25-31).* Crown officers supervised storehouses, agricultural workers, vineyards, wine cellars, oil stores, vineyards, and livestock of various kinds.

6. *Counselors (27:32-34).* Jonathan, David's *"uncle"* (dod) or near relative was a counselor and scribe. The reference is probably to the Jonathan mentioned in 1 Chronicles 20:7 who was a nephew of David. Jehiel *"was with the king's sons,"* i.e., he was their tutor. The counselor Ahithophel was the Judas of the Old Testament. He deserted David during the Absalom rebellion. Hushai was *"the king's friend"* or close advisor. During the Absalom rebellion he remained loyal to David and frustrated the counsel of Ahithophel (cf. 2 Sam 15:32ff., 17:5ff.). Jehoiada the son of Benaiah replaced Ahithophel after the latter committed suicide. Abiathar was chief priest along with Zadok. He advised David in ritual matters. Joab was over the host. He advised David in military matters.

FINAL PUBLIC ACTS
1 Chronicles 28:1-29:22

The gathering of 1 Chr 23:2, which mainly consisted of religious leaders and senior officials, was expanded to include *"all the officials of Israel."* David addressed the group. Then he formally delivered over to Solomon the materials which he had gathered for temple construction. Finally, David publicly charged Solomon before the assembly.

A. The King's Address (1 Chr 28:2-8).

Because of the size of the group, David *"rose to his feet"* to speak. He explained to the assembly that he had intended to build a permanent home for the ark of God which was *"the footstool of our God."* To this end he had made preparation. The Lord, however, overruled his good intention. Because he was a man of war and had shed blood in battle, God had said that David must not be the builder of the temple (28:2-3).

David then shared with the assembly—perhaps for the first time publicly—the substance of the Nathan oracle (cf. 2 Sam 7). Although he would not be permitted to build a house for God, the Lord would build an enduring *"house,"* i.e., dynasty for David (28:4).

Through prophetic revelation—David was a prophet as well as a king—God had made known his choice of Solomon. Since Israel was the kingdom of Yahweh, God alone had the right to establish throne succession. The revelation had indicated also that Solomon would (1) be the temple builder, (2) be the *"son"* of God in a special sense, and (3) have a permanent kingdom if he faithfully followed the law of God as did David (28:5-7).

David concluded his address to the assembly by exhorting them to observe all the commandments of Yahweh. Only thus could they ensure that they would be able to bequeath the good land of Canaan to their sons (28:8).

B. First Charge to Solomon (1 Chr 28:9-10).

Before the entire assembly David charged Solomon to *"know,"* i.e., have a personal walk, with God. He urged him to serve Yahweh,

407

not just outwardly, but with his whole heart and mind. Mere outward observance of the law would not suffice because Yahweh *"searches all hearts, and understands every intent of the thoughts"* (NASB). If Solomon sought Yahweh, he would allow himself to be found. On the other hand, if Solomon should forsake the Lord, he in turn would be forever rejected. Solomon then should *"consider,"* i.e., take seriously, the fact that Yahweh had chosen him for a purpose. His duty would be to build the sanctuary of the Lord. The young prince needed to *"be courageous and act."*

C. Revelation of the Plans (1 Chr 28:11-19).

Next in the public ceremony David delivered to Solomon the divinely revealed plans regarding the temple. David had felt the hand of God upon him as he drew those plans. They included the design of the temple proper, its courtyards and accompanying structures, the organization of the priests and Levites and all the other temple personnel. Even the amount of gold or silver which would be required for each major piece of furniture and their accompanying utensils had been computed. Though this structure is frequently called "Solomon's temple," this text indicates that David had a great deal to do with the design. What is more important, the temple constructed by Solomon was built according to a pattern revealed by God himself.

D. Final Charge to Solomon (1 Chr 28:20-21).

David realized that the construction of the temple would be a formidable task in spite of all the preparations which he had made. He therefore encouraged his son to *"be strong and courageous and act."* Solomon should not be intimidated by the magnitude of the project because, his father assured him, *"my God is with you."* The Lord would stay with Solomon until the task was completed. At the same time the young king would have at his disposal the divisions of priests and Levites as well as the non-clerical officials. These men would faithfully carry out any commands the king might issue.

E. The King's Challenge (1 Chr 29:1-9).

David reminded the assembly of the tremendous task which the youthful Solomon faced in building the temple. He pointed out that he had already provided precious metals and stones in abundance for the work. Now he announced yet another 3,000 talents of the most precious gold (*"gold of Ophir"*) and 7,000 talents of silver. He then challenged the assembled rulers to be equally generous (29:1-5).

The princes, officials and commanders responded generously to the challenge of their beloved king: Gold (5,000 talents + 10,000 darics), silver (10,000 talents), brass (18,000 talents) and iron (100,000 talents). Whoever possessed precious stones gave them to the treasury of the house of Yahweh. All present rejoiced because their collective generosity *"because they had given willingly"* (29:6-9).

F. The King's Prayer (1 Chr 29:10-19).

The generous contribution to the work of the Lord prompted David to lead in a prayer of praise and thanksgiving. The opening words of this prayer remind one of the model prayer in the Sermon on the Mount. David addressed God as *"our father."* He spoke of the greatness, power, majesty, victory and dominion of the Lord. Then David acknowledged that riches and honor come from God. He alone deserves the praise for the "miracle" offering since he is the one who had provided the wealth which had now been contributed (29:10-15).

God knows the hearts of all men. He therefore knew that the gifts presented both by David and his officers had been given cheerfully. David prayed that God would preserve forever in the hearts of his people this focus on things divine. He asked that the Lord would give Solomon a *"perfect"* (NASB) heart to keep the divine commandments and to build the temple for which he had made such abundant provision (29:16-19).

G. Concluding Celebrations (1 Chr 29:20-22a).

Following his prayer, David called on the assembly to *"bless"* Yahweh. All present bowed low and did homage to the Lord and his earthly representative King David. The next day the group offered sacrifices to the Lord: a thousand each of bulls, rams and lambs. These peace offerings were accompanied by feasting *"before Yahweh"* with great gladness.

DAVID'S FINAL COUNSEL
1 Kings 2:1-9

Participation in the great national convention drained the last bit of strength from the old king. Feeling death's grip tightening upon him, David summoned Solomon to his side to impart to him his final private instruction.

A. General Instructions (1 Kgs 2:1-4).

First, David urged Solomon to *"be strong and be a man."* Second, he urged his son to *"keep the trust of Yahweh."* He could prosper only by faithful adherence to the law of Moses. Third, the young man should walk before Yahweh in truth with all his heart. Thereby Solomon would experience the fulfillment of God's promise of everlasting possession of the throne.

Chart No. 35

THE TWO CORONATIONS OF SOLOMON	
FIRST CORONATION	**SECOND CORONATION**
1 Kings 1:1-2:11	1 Chronicles 28:1-29:30
At Gihon	At the Palace
Necessitated by Adonijah's Actions	Planned by David's Authority
Made King by David	Made King by the Assembly
Anointed by Zadok	Anointed by the Assembly
"Then Solomon sat on the throne of Yahweh as king instead of David his father" (1 Chr 29:23).	

B. Special Instructions (1 Kgs 2:5-11).

Certain obligations which David had neglected to fulfill, or had promised to fulfill, now devolved upon his son and successor. First, Solomon must deal with Joab who literally had gotten by with murder during the reign of David. The fact that Joab had *"shed the blood of war in peace*" (cf. 2 Sam 3:22-27; 20:4-10) cried out for judicial revenge. Solomon should not allow Joab *"to go down to Sheol* (the abode of the dead) *in peace,"* i.e., he must not be allowed to die a natural death. Solomon must *"act in wisdom"* in this matter. He must find a plausible pretext for bringing Joab's just deserts upon him. Otherwise a rebellion in the ranks of the army might occur (2:5-6).

The situation is completely different with the sons of Barzillai. David owed this family a debt of gratitude dating back to the days when he fled into Transjordan to escape Absalom. Barzillai the Gileadite had brought David much needed supplies in those dark days (cf. 2 Sam 17:27-30). David encouraged Solomon to allow Barzillai's family to be included among those who ate at his table, i.e., provide them with a perpetual royal food allowance (2:7).

Chart No. 36

THE REIGN OF DAVID 1010-970 BC			
HEBRON YEARS	**WAR YEARS**	**REST YEARS**	**TROUBLE YEARS**
King of Judah	King of all Israel		
Civil War	Defensive Wars Offensive Wars	Ark Moved Nathan Oracle David's Sin	Family Problems Absalom Revolt Sheba Revolt Adonijah Plot
7 1/2 Years	8 Years (?)	19 Years	6 Years
Age 30-37	Age 37-45	Age 45-64	Age 65-70
2 Samuel 1-4	2 Samuel 5, 8, 10-12	2 Samuel 6-7, 9	2 Samuel 13-20 1 Kings 1-2
1010-1003 BC	1003-995 BC	995-976 BC	976-970 BC

Shimei the Benjamite had cursed David in the hour of his humiliation by Absalom (cf. 2 Sam 16:5-8). Cursing the king was a capital crime (cf. Exod 22:28). Yet when David was restored to his throne, he pledged that he would not execute Shimei. Solomon, however, was not bound by the oath of his father. He should be wise enough to

411

realize that a man like Shimei could not be trusted. Though Shimei was *"with Solomon,"* i.e., had supported his claim to the throne,[9] the new king must *"bring down his gray hair in blood to Sheol,"* i.e., execute the man (2:8-9).

The morality of David's instruction concerning Shimei and Joab has been called into question. These points, however, must be observed. First, no hint of malice or vindictiveness is evident in the passage. Second, verses 2-4 set the tone for these special instructions. What was uppermost in David's mind was strict observance of the law of God. That would include the execution of the murderer and the blasphemer. Third, David is tacitly admitting to failure on his own part in enforcing the law. To know that these errors would be corrected in the reign of his son would give David great comfort in his last hours.

DAVID'S DEATH
1 Kings 2:10-11

Shortly after David's final instructions to Solomon, the old man *"lay down with his fathers,"* i.e., he died. The language seems to suggest an awareness of reunion with his relatives in Sheol, the abode of the dead. David was buried in the City of David—that part of Jerusalem which his personal troops had conquered from the Jebusites. His sepulcher on Mt. Zion still existed in the time of Christ (Acts 2:29).[10] The total length of David's reign was forty years. He had reigned seven years in Hebron,[11] and thirty-three years in Jerusalem.

ENDNOTES

1. Depending on the interpretation of 2 Sam 5:4, David was either seventy or sixty-three when he died. Only three other kings of Judah (Solomon, Uzziah, and Manasseh) are known to have exceeded sixty years of age.
2. The fact that David had never had a sexual relationship with Abishag furnished the legal grounds upon which Adonijah later dared to request her hand in marriage after David's death.
3. David's firstborn, Amnon, had been slain in a plot instigated by his

younger brother (2 Sam 13:28ff.). Absalom, the third son of David, was slain in battle (2 Sam 18:15). Of the second son, Chileab (or Daniel as he is called in 1 Chr 3:1) little is known. That he died very young is most likely.

4. The other two prominent supporters of Solomon named in 1 Kgs 1:8 are not easily identified. Rei is completely unknown except from this passage. Shimei may have been David's brother whose name appears as Shammah in 1 Sam 16:9, and Shimeah in 2 Sam 13:3 and 21:21. Others think he is the son of Elah named in 1 Kgs 4:18. A third view is that he is the Shimei who once had cursed David (2 Sam 16:5), but who now was *"with Solomon."*

5. In Old Testament times the spring Gihon was on the slope of the City of David. Why David selected this spot is not clear. Perhaps it had something to do with the symbolism that as Gihon was vital to the life of Jerusalem, so also was the king. That the king in his frail condition would think of such symbolism, however, is difficult to imagine.

6. While the function of these soldiers is clear, the precise origin and meaning of the terms Cherethites and Pelethites is subject to dispute. These troops were of foreign extraction, probably Philistine.

7. To which altar Adonijah fled is uncertain. At this time there was an altar at Gibeon (1 Kgs 3:4), one on Mt. Zion (2 Sam 6:17), and one recently erected by David on the threshingfloor of Araunah (2 Sam 24:25).

8. The *"horns"* were small protrusions resembling animal horns on the four corners of the altar.

9. In 1 Kgs 1:8 a Shimei is listed among the supporters of Solomon.

10. Archaeologists believe that they have located David's tomb. See R. deVaux, *Ancient Israel, Its Life and Institutions.* Trans. John McHugh (New York: McGraw-Hill, 1961), p. 58.

11. The seven years of this passage is a round number. David actually ruled six months beyond seven years. See 2 Sam 5:5.

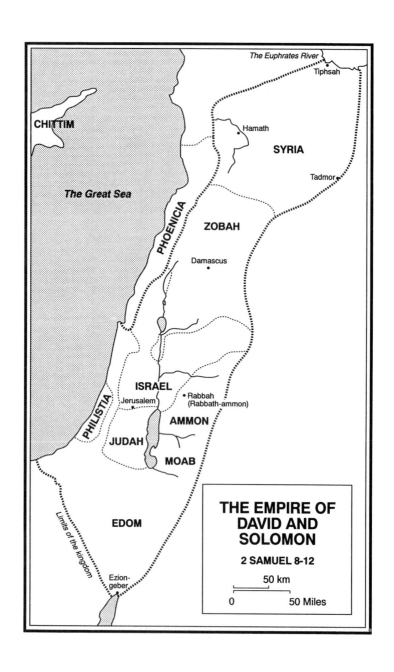

CHITTIM

The Euphrates River

Tiphsah

Hamath

SYRIA

Tadmor

The Great Sea

PHOENICIA

ZOBAH

Damascus

ISRAEL

Jerusalem • Rabbah
(Rabbath-ammon)

AMMON

JUDAH

MOAB

PHILISTIA

EDOM

Limits of the kingdom

Ezion-
geber

**THE EMPIRE OF
DAVID AND
SOLOMON**

2 SAMUEL 8-12

50 km

0   50 Miles

CHAPTER TWENTY-FIVE

Solomon's Great Wisdom
1 Kings 2:13-5:18

At the national convention in David's last days Solomon was made king *"a second time."* He was anointed again by Zadok the priest. The military leaders and all the other sons of David pledged their allegiance to the young king. God highly exalted Solomon in the sight of all Israel. He bestowed on Solomon royal majesty which neither Saul nor David had possessed (1 Chr 29:22b-25). The actions of the national convention firmly established Solomon on the throne (1 Kgs 2:12). Those who were his enemies, however, had not relinquished all hope of seizing the throne.

WISDOM IN POLITICAL MATTERS
1 Kings 2:13-3:1

After the collapse of his attempted coup, Adonijah had pledged his allegiance to Solomon (1 Kgs 1:53). Not long after the death of David, however, Adonijah attempted to lay the groundwork for another coup attempt.

415

A. A Subtle Plan (1 Kgs 2:13-18).

By means of Abishag, the former concubine of King David, Adonijah hoped to accomplish what his chariots, horsemen and banquets had not accomplished. He won the sympathies of the most powerful woman in the land, Bathsheba the queen mother. She was suspicious at first when Adonijah came calling. His tactics, however, disarmed her and turned her into an ally (2:13-14).

First, Adonijah resorted to self pity as a means of appealing to the sympathies of Bathsheba. The kingdom belonged to him, and *"all Israel"*—an obvious exaggeration—was prepared to make him king. Things turned around, however, and the kingdom became Solomon's. Second, he used hypocritical piety. He feigned resignation to the will of Yahweh in respect to the throne. Third, he pled with Bathsheba to help him: *"Do not deny me this one last request."* Fourth, he flattered Bathsheba by asserting that the king would never refuse a request from his mother. Fifth, he pretended to be in love. All he wanted as compensation for losing the throne to Solomon was the hand of Abishag the Shunammite (2:15-17).

Apparently Bathsheba did not question Adonijah about his motives for wanting to marry the the Shunammite. That love (or lust) partially may have motivated the request cannot be denied. Higher aspirations, however, were certainly involved as Solomon instantly recognized. Be that as it may, Bathsheba was taken in by Adonijah's tactics. She agreed to speak to the king on his behalf (2:18).

B. Bathsheba's Petition (1 Kgs 2:19-22).

Bathsheba went immediately to the throne room of Solomon. After the exchange of courtesies, she got right to the point. She referred to her petition as a *"small favor,"* and so it seemed to her. Solomon expressed his willingness to fulfill whatever request his mother might make, never dreaming that she would ask for anything which he could not grant. Thus reassured, Bathsheba stated her request on behalf of Adonijah.

Solomon exploded in rage when he heard his mother's request. He could not believe that his own mother did not realize the implications of her request. She might as well have asked the kingdom to be given to Adonijah, for that would be the upshot of a marriage to the

concubine[1] of the former king. Why so? Taking possession of a wife
or harem of a deceased king was equivalent to a claim to the throne
(cf. 2 Sam 12:8; 16:22). The mention of Joab and Abiathar in connection with Adonijah's request makes it appear that Solomon had
received from his intelligence officers some prior information indicating that another plot was brewing. Be that as it may, Solomon viewed
the petition of Adonijah as conclusive proof that Adonijah was
involved in another conspiracy (2:22).

C. Adonijah's Execution (1 Kgs 2:23-25).
Having been lenient with his elder brother once, Solomon was in
no mood to ignore further the threat that Adonijah posed to his rule.
In the presence of all those in the throne room he swore a solemn
oath that Adonijah would die that very day. He then dispatched Benaiah, captain of the palace guard, to execute his half brother. The
order was immediately carried out. This was the first in a bloody trilo-
gy of executions (2:23-25).
Those who might be tempted to look on the execution of Adonijah
as a ruthless misuse of royal power should ponder the following
points. (1) Had Adonijah's first rebellion succeeded both Solomon and
his mother would have been killed (cf. 1 Kgs 1:12). (2) By fleeing to
the altar following the collapse of his conspiracy, Adonijah was admitting that he deserved the death of a traitor. (3) Solomon displayed the
greatest magnanimity toward Adonijah when, instead of executing
him, he placed him on probation. (4) Adonijah had been warned that
if wickedness were found in him, he would be killed (1 Kgs 1:52).
(5) For Solomon to ignore this second offense might suggest that the
king was weak, and such weakness would be an encouragement to
sedition throughout the land.

D. Abiathar's Banishment (1 Kgs 2:26-27).
That Abiathar was again involved in the conspiracy to give the
throne to Adonijah is suggested by the actions which Solomon took
against him. This priest, who on the occasion of the earlier conspiracy escaped even censure, was summoned to the palace. The king
curtly ordered him to retire from the priestly office and return to his
hometown of Anathoth.[2] As far as Solomon was concerned, Abiathar

was worthy of death (lit., *a man of death*) for his treasonous conduct. On account of his past associations with David,[3] however, the king sentenced the old man to banishment rather than death (2:26).

Abiathar was the last descendant of the Ithamar branch of the priestly family. When he was banished, the high priesthood reverted to the descendants of Eleazar who was represented in Solomon's day by Zadok. Thus was fulfilled a prophecy made by an anonymous prophet (cf. 1 Sam 2:31-36) concerning the house of Eli (Ithamar branch) more than a century earlier.

E. Joab's Execution (1 Kgs 2:28-35).

When Joab heard of the execution of Adonijah and the expulsion of Abiathar, he knew that he would be next. Though Joab had not supported Absalom in his rebellion against David, he had lent his support to the ill-fated conspiracy of Adonijah. Realizing that his treason was a capital crime, Joab fled to the tent of Yahweh on Mt. Zion and clasped the horns of the altar. There he thought he would find sanctuary as Adonijah had found before him (cf. 1 Kgs 1:50). His flight to the altar indicates that he had been involved in the Abishag incident (2:28).

Solomon regarded Joab's flight to the altar as proof of his continuing treasonous intentions. He ordered Benaiah to go and slay the old general. When Joab refused his orders to come away from the altar, Benaiah was in a quandary. He finally returned to Solomon for further orders (2:29-30).

Good reasons existed for denying sanctuary to Joab. Solomon spelled out those reasons to Benaiah. The altar provided no sanctuary to murderers (Exod 21:14). Therefore the king ordered Benaiah to slay Joab at the altar. Only by the shedding of the blood of this guilty man could the innocent blood of Abner and Amasa be washed away from the house of David (cf. Num 35:33). As chief magistrate of the land, Solomon considered it his obligation to avenge the death of murder victims (2:31).

As if the execution of Joab needed any further justification, Solomon added that the victims of Joab's sword were better men than their assassin. Though many people, no doubt, suspected David of criminal complicity in these murders, the deeds were actually done without his knowledge. By avenging the death of the innocent, the stain of blood (obligation to punish) would be removed from the house of David. As a consequence, the descendants of David would prosper. On the other hand, the children of Joab would always have to live with the stigma that their father had been executed as a murderer (2:32-33). Having received royal authorization to slay Joab in the tabernacle, Benaiah hastened back to the altar to perform the deed. Joab was buried in the courtyard of his own house which was located near Bethlehem in the wilderness of Judah. To be so buried was considered an honor (cf. 1 Sam 25:1). This honor was accorded Joab in recognition of his years of faithful service to his country. Solomon filled the vacant posts of general of the army and high priest with his friends Benaiah and Zadok (2:34-35).

F. Shimei's Challenge (1 Kgs 2:36-46).

Even though Shimei had recently been *"with Solomon"* (cf. 1 Kgs 1:8), his earlier bitter outburst against David made Solomon suspicious of him. He was summoned to the palace and ordered to build a new home in Jerusalem. He was told never to leave the capital. Solomon wanted to keep Shimei under surveillance; he also wished to neutralize his considerable influence in his tribe of Benjamin (2:36).

Solomon warned Shimei that should he ever leave the city for any reason, he would be executed for his past crime against the crown. Specifically the king mentioned crossing the brook Kidron east of Jerusalem, for that would be the direction that Shimei might be expected to go in an effort to return to his home at Bahurim just over the Mount of Olives. Having been clearly warned, Shimei would be responsible for his own death should he venture out of the city. He swore an oath to comply with the terms of the probation. The sentence was better than Shimei deserved and probably better than he had expected especially in view of the fact that Solomon was not bound by the oath of David to refrain from slaying him (2:37-38).

After three years of probation in Jerusalem, two of Shimei's slaves ran away. They took refuge with Achish, king of Gath.[4] Learning of their whereabouts, Shimei immediately set out for Gath to retrieve them. Upon his return he was summoned to the palace. Solomon lodged a threefold charge against him. First, he had profaned the name of God by violating a solemn oath taken in the name of the deity. Second, he had violated the terms of his probation, thus disregarding the commands of the king. Third, Shimei had cursed and blasphemed the Lord's anointed, David. For these transgressions Shimei received divine recompense at the hands of Solomon. By executing Shimei, Solomon was acting in the service of God. He fully expected that God would be pleased with his action and bless him accordingly. Thus with no further hesitation, Solomon ordered Benaiah to execute Shimei (2:39-46a).

G. Pharaoh's Concession (1 Kgs 3:1).

By swiftly eliminating four potential antagonists—Adonijah, Abiathar, Joab and Shimei—Solomon firmly established himself as king (2:46b). He further strengthened his position by arranging a marriage to Pharaoh's daughter.[5] This marriage was strictly political. Treaties between nations were customarily sealed by intermarriage of the two royal houses. This alliance, however, must have been shocking to the average Israelite since Egypt was the ancestral foe of Israel.

Solomon brought his new wife to the city of David. There she lived in the palace formerly occupied by David (2 Chr 8:11) until Solomon was able to complete his building projects.[6] The text does not state that Pharaoh's daughter gave up her idols when she became Solomon's wife. Certain factors, however, lead to the conclusion that such was the case (3:1).[7]

WISDOM IN PETITION
1 Kgs 3:2-15//2 Chr 1:2-13

Because they had no temple, the children of Israel were sacrificing to Yahweh in the "high places." The only blemish on Solomon's commitment to the Lord in these early days was his participation in the high place worship. He loved Yahweh and walked in "the statutes of David," i.e., the laws of God which David had kept and which he commanded Solomon to keep (cf. 1 Kgs 2:4). The author of Kings does not say that worship in the high places was sinful at this time. He only is suggesting that it was less than ideal. God winked at this imperfection in the period before the temple was built (3:2-3).

The Bible explains Solomon's famous wisdom as a supernatural endowment which he received while worshiping at *"the great high place"* in Gibeon.[8] At this spot, six miles northwest of Jerusalem the tabernacle with its huge bronze altar was now located (2 Chr 1:3).[9] Upon that altar a thousand whole burnt offerings were offered (i.e., provided by) Solomon with the intention of seeking God's blessing upon his reign (3:4).

While he was at Gibeon, the Lord appeared to Solomon in a dream. The young king was instructed to name whatever it was he might desire from God (3:5).[10]

Solomon's reply was marked by both perception and piety. He began by acknowledging the great favor which Yahweh had bestowed on David to permit his son to follow him on the throne. He then humbly confessed his inability to handle the task that had been thrust upon his shoulders. He referred to himself as a *"little child."*[11] He did not know how *"to go out or come in,"* i.e., conduct himself in the office of king. Furthermore the nation had become so vast that the governance of it would be a major challenge even to the most mature man. In view of these circumstances, Solomon asked God to give him a discerning heart (lit., a hearing heart) that would qualify him to judge (i.e., rule) the people to God, to know the difference between what was true and false (3:6-9).

Solomon's response pleased Yahweh. Solomon might have asked for long life, or wealth, or victory over enemies. Since, however, he had asked for a gift that would enable him to better meet the needs of his people, God granted his petition. Solomon's wisdom would surpass all who had gone before him, and all who would follow. In addition God gave the young king what he had not requested, viz., riches and honor. The blessing of long life, however, had a condition attached. Only if Solomon continued to walk in the way of Yahweh would his days be lengthened (3:10-14).

Solomon awoke to discover that he had been dreaming. This, however, was no ordinary dream; it was a dream in which a divine revelation had been given to him. Solomon proceeded immediately to the other major sanctuary of that period, the tent which housed the ark of the covenant. There he offered new sacrifices to Yahweh. In addition to the burnt offerings made at Gibeon, he added peace offerings in gratitude for the endowment he had just received.[12]

421

WISDOM IN JUDGMENT
1 Kings 3:16-28

The classic case of two harlots, both claiming to be the mother of a baby, demonstrated the judicial wisdom which had been given to Solomon. The women had given birth to children out of wedlock within three days of one another. No third party was present at the births, hence independent collaboration was impossible. The plaintiff charged that her friend had smothered her child one night. She then allegedly switched her dead baby for the living one which was sleeping at the side of his mother. In the morning light the plaintiff discovered that the dead baby was not her own. The defendant naturally disputed all these contentions. She tenaciously maintained that the living child was really hers. Back and forth the women made their claims and counter claims (3:16-22).

Finally Solomon was ready to make a decision. He first summarized the problem as it had been presented to him. Then he ordered a sword to be brought. The child would be divided and half given to each woman. The real mother, the plaintiff as it turned out, was emotionally stirred by the decision which in effect would leave her son dead. In desperation she cried out to the king to spare the child and give it to her rival. She preferred to lose her case and see her rival rewarded than to have the child killed. The defendant, on the other hand, was perfectly content to allow the execution to take place. She did not really love the child. Her only objective had been to deprive her rival of the fruit of her womb (3:23-26).

Through this stratagem Solomon had learned the identity of the real mother. He ordered the plaintiff to be given custody of the disputed child. The people of Israel were impressed and even awed by this demonstration of royal sagacity. They rightly concluded that the wisdom of God was in this young king (3:27-28).

WISDOM IN ADMINISTRATION
1 Kings 4:1-6

Solomon's wisdom was also demonstrated in the area of kingdom administration.[13] To select faithful servants is one of the most difficult tasks of rulers. The welfare of the whole state depends on the choices. That the list of appointees reflects Solomon's wisdom is indicated by the following considerations: (1) Priority in this list is given of officers of peace. (2) In several positions Solomon retained the experienced servants of his father. (3) Positions of trust were filled by persons of piety—sons of priests or prophets.

Azariah was prime minister.[14] The scribes, Elihoreph and Ahijah, wrote letters and proclamations, drew up edicts and apparently had certain fiscal duties (2 Kgs 12:10). Jehoshaphat, a carryover from David's court (cf. 2 Sam 8:16), was the recorder. He scheduled palace activities and introduced people to royal audiences. Benaiah commanded the host. Zadok and Abiathar were the high priests.[15] Azariah son of Nathan (the prophet?) was over the the twelve district governors. Zabud, another son of Nathan, was chief minister (lit., *priest*) and *"friend of the king"* or confidential adviser. Ahishar was the steward and manager of the palace. Another carryover from David's administration was Adoniram (Adoram). He was in charge of the forced labor force (4:1-6).

WISDOM IN ECONOMICS
1 Kings 4:7-28

Solomon is credited with originating the first scientific system of taxation. He divided his entire realm into twelve tax districts, nine west of Jordan and three east of the river. The boundaries of the districts corresponded roughly to the old tribal boundaries. Over each district he set a governor who was responsible one month of the year to supply the produce and meat necessary to sustain the king's household. Judah is not included in the list of districts, probably because that area had been organized on a different basis by David.

The governors are listed in the order in which they were responsible for the royal provisions during the year. Two of them were married to daughters of Solomon (vv. 11,15). Five are known only by their patronymic (names of their fathers). No satisfactory explanation of this curious circumstance has yet been proposed (4:7-19).

The wisdom of the tax district system is indicated in 1 Kings 4:20. The population was so numerous that it was easier for the governors to collect the royal tribute. Solomon's subjects were *"eating, drinking and rejoicing."* Apparently the king's exactions did not deprive the people of necessary food; they had plenty to eat and drink.

Solomon's empire was vast, stretching from *"the river,"* i.e., the Euphrates in the north, to the land of the Philistines in the west and Egypt in the south. The northernmost point in his empire was Tiphsah, a town on the west bank of Euphrates river at its most important crossing place. The southernmost point was Azzah (Gaza), the last town in Palestine on the frontier of Egypt. All the kings in this region rendered tribute to Solomon. In spite of the large extent of his kingdom, peace prevailed (4:21,24).

The court provisions were commensurate with the size of his kingdom. Each day the royal household consumed approximately 340 bushels of fine flour and 155 bushels of meal.[16] Thirty head of beef, a hundred sheep, as well as wild game, were required for the palace table. Such a quantity of bread and meat would feed at least fourteen thousand people (4:21-23).[17]

Judah and Israel prospered under Solomon. From Dan, at the headwaters of the Jordan, to Beersheba, on the edge of the southern wilderness every person sat *"under his vine and under his fig tree."* This proverbial expression denotes rest and the undisturbed enjoyment of the fruits of the earth (4:25).

The peace was maintained by means of a huge cavalry and chariot force. The addition of these two units revolutionized the Israelite army which heretofore had been entirely infantry. Solomon had four thousand stalls[18] for his chariot horses. In addition the king kept twelve thousand cavalry horses. This great number of horses threw an extra burden on each of the twelve district governors (cf. 4:7-19). Yet these officers faithfully brought barley and straw to the various depots throughout the land where the animals were kept (4:26-28). Multiplication of horses by the king was a violation of God's law (cf. Deut 17:16).

WISDOM IN WORDS
1 Kings 4:29-34

God gave to Solomon practical wisdom, understanding (ability to solve difficult problems), and *"largeness of heart,"* i.e., comprehensive knowledge. The magnitude of his wisdom is indicated by four comparisons. His wisdom was like (1) *"the sand of the seashore."* (2) It exceeded that of the *"children of the east,"* i.e., the various Arab tribes dwelling east of Canaan including the Edomites who were famous for their wisdom. (3) It exceeded that of Egypt which was famous for the knowledge of geometry, arithmetic, astronomy and medicine. (4) it exceeded that of the wisest men of his own nation: Ethan, Heman, Calcol and Darda.[19] Solomon's reputation as a polymath spread throughout all the surrounding nations (4:29-31).

Only a small portion of the literary fruits of Solomon's wisdom has been incorporated into the Bible. During his reign this king spoke three thousand proverbs of which less than one third are preserved in the Book of Proverbs. Of his 1,005 songs, only three have survived: the beautiful Song of Songs, and two of the psalms (72 and 127). In addition, Solomon made observations based on his botanical and zoological studies. Solomon's great wisdom attracted the attention of the kings throughout the Near East (4:32-34).

WISDOM IN NEGOTIATIONS
1 Kgs 5:1-12//2 Chr 2:3-16

When Hiram (Huram) king of Tyre heard that Solomon had succeeded his father, he dispatched ambassadors to congratulate the youthful king. In a letter of response Solomon indicated that he now intended to pursue the dream of his father to build a house for the name of Yahweh. He made two requests of Hiram. First, he asked that Hiram continue to make available to him the valuable timber from the Lebanon mountains. Second, he requested that a skilled craftsman be sent to Jerusalem (2 Chr 2:7). In exchange for these provisions, Solomon agreed to supply manpower to assist in the logging operation and to pay the wages of the Sidonian laborers.[20] In a closing complimentary remark, Solomon alluded to the skill of the Sidonians in woodmanship (5:1-6).

Hiram rejoiced at the prospect of continued friendly relations with Israel. He praised Yahweh the God of Israel for having given David so wise a son as his successor. The wisdom of the youthful king was evident to Hiram because (1) he had chosen the path of peaceful coexis-

425

tence; (2) he earnestly desired to fulfill the purposes of his father; and (3) he had made the worship of God the foremost concern of his reign (5:7).

In his letter of reply, Hiram agreed to furnish the timber which Solomon had requested. The plan called for Hiram's servants to bring the logs down the rugged mountain road from Lebanon to the sea. There the timber would be lashed into rafts and floated down the Mediterranean seacoast to Joppa (2 Chr 2:16). At that point the logs would be separated and delivered to the Israelites. Solomon's men would be responsible for moving those logs the forty steep miles to Jerusalem. In exchange for these services Hiram asked that "bread," i.e., grain, might be supplied to his palace in Tyre (5:8-9).

The formal treaty negotiated with Hiram is regarded by the author of Kings as another manifestation of the wisdom of Solomon. Hiram sent the timber southward toward Jerusalem. Solomon paid Hiram annually, in addition to the wages Solomon had volunteered to pay the laborers, 20,000 kors of wheat (103,200 bushels), twenty kors (1,100 gallons) of *"beaten"* oil, i.e., oil that was obtained by pounding the olives before they ripened (5:10-12).

WISDOM IN ORGANIZATION
1 Kgs 5:13-18//2 Chr 2:1-2

Solomon made further preparation for the construction work by drafting out of Israel a labor force numbering some thirty thousand. These men were divided into three shifts of ten thousand. Each shift was compelled to labor in Lebanon four months of the year. Apparently these Israelites worked alongside of Hiram's servants and under their direction (5:13-14).

In addition to the thirty thousand Israelite draftees, Solomon compelled the remnants of the Canaanites to become tribute slaves (cf. 1 Kgs 9:20,21). The census by the king found 153,600 Canaanite men remaining within the Israel (2 Chr 2:17). Of these 70,000 became burden bearers, 80,000 became hewers of stone *"in the mountains,"* i.e., in the hill country of Canaan. The remaining 3,600 were Canaanite supervisors (2 Chr 2:18). Over these supervisors were 550 superior officers (cf. 1 Kgs 9:23).[21]

Having secured and organized the laborers, Solomon issued the order for the foundation stones to be cut out and brought to the temple site. Although the foundation stones would not be seen, equal care was given to their preparation. Ordinarily plain stones were used in foundations. The king, however, ordered for the temple great, costly, hewn stones. Some of these very stones can be viewed at the excavations on Mt. Moriah today. Solomon's laborers worked alongside the Phoenician construction crews preparing both the stone and the wood. Among the latter were the Gabalites. Gebal (Byblos) was a Phoenician city about twenty miles north of modern Beirut. The men of this town had a reputation (cf. Ezek 27:9) as skilled builders (5:17-18).

ENDNOTES

1. Abishag is never actually called David's concubine or wife in the text. Some think that had she actually been married to David, Adonijah would have been committing incest by marrying her under the laws of Lev 18:8 and 20:11. It may have been on the legal technicality that David had never been able to consummate the marriage with Abishag (assuming that he had married her) that Adonijah thought he stood a chance to gain her hand. What is clear is that in the eyes of the people Abishag would have been considered the wife of David regardless of her legal status.

2. Anathoth has been identified with the modern Anata, a village just north and east of Jerusalem about three miles. About three centuries later Jeremiah would be born here.

3. Abiathar had been with David during his wilderness flight from Saul (1 Sam 22:20f.). He was responsible for carrying the precious ark to Jerusalem (1 Chr 15:11). He had stood by David during the Absalom rebellion (2 Sam 15:24-29).

4. This Achish is probably the grandson of the Achish with whom David had taken refuge more than forty years earlier.

5. No other example has yet been found of a Pharaoh's daughter being given in marriage to a foreign royal house. A Babylonian king asked for the hand of the daughter of Amenhotep III. He was rebuffed in the following terms: "From of old, a daughter of the king of Egypt has not been given to anyone." See Abraham Malamat, "The Kingdom of David and Solomon in its Contact with Egypt and Aram Naharaim," *Biblical Archaeologist Reader III* (Garden City, NY: Doubleday, 1964), pp. 91-92.

6. Solomon began building the temple in the fourth year of his reign (1 Kgs 6:1), and his own house in his eleventh year (1 Kgs 7:1).

7. That Pharaoh's daughter may have surrendered her idols is suggested by three factors: (1) Solomon at this period of his life was an enthusiastic observer of the law of Yahweh; (2) the king is never condemned for this particular marriage; and (3) no trace of Egyptian idolatry or religious rites can be found in Israel at this time. See Joseph Hammond, *I Kings* in "The Pulpit Commentary" (New York: Funk and Wagnalls, 1909), p. 50.

8. Gibeon is probably called a *"high place"* because the ark of the covenant, with which Yahweh had bound up his presence, was in David's tent in Jerusalem.

9. The tabernacle was last mentioned as being at Nob (1 Sam 21:6). The Scriptures do not indicate how or when the sacred tent was transported to Gibeon.

10. The question *"What shall I give you?"* (3:5) seems to suggest that the objective of the sacrifices was to seek the help of God for his reign.

11. Rabbinic tradition has Solomon ascending the throne at age twelve. Josephus (*Ant.* 8.7.8) says he was fourteen. Modern scholars estimate that he was seventeen or eighteen. Solomon already had one child at the time of his accession as is indicated by the fact that he reigned forty years and his son Rehoboam was forty-one at the time of his father's death (1 Kgs 14:21).

12. In the peace offering, a token portion of the animal was offered on the altar. The remainder was eaten at a sacrificial meal by the worshiper and his guests.

13. The list of officials in 1 Kgs 4 does not necessarily represent the appointments of Solomon's early years. The mention of the king's two married daughters (vv. 11,15) seems to require that this list be assigned to a later point in his reign.

14. Azariah is designated in Hebrew as *ha-kohen, the priest.* The term *kohen* must have had a secular as well as a sacred meaning. In 2 Sam 8:18 David's sons are called *priests* whereas the parallel passage in 1 Chr 18:17 calls them *"first men."* Just as the sacred *kohen* represented the people before God, so the secular *kohen* represented the people before the king and vice versa.

15. Abiathar is listed here because he served for a time as high priest before being deposed by Solomon (1 Kgs 2:26f.).

16. Authorities differ as to how many bushels were in the *kor* measure. Estimates range from a high of eleven bushels to a low of 5.16 bushels. The lower equivalency has been used in the computation here.

17. J.A. Montgomery and H.S. Gehman, *The Books of Kings* in "The International Critical Commentary" (New York: Scribners, 1951) p. 137; John Gray, *I & II Kings* in "The Old Testament Library," (Philadelphia: Westminster, 1970), p. 137.

18. That the figure 40,000 in 1 Kgs 4:26 is a scribal error is indicated by two facts: (1) The parallel passage in 2 Chr 9:25 reads 4,000; and (2) the lower figure is more in line with the number of chariots (1400) possessed by

Solomon (10:26). Normally two horses were yoked to each chariot. A third horse was usually provided for each chariot in case of an accident.

19. Ethan, Heman, Calcol and Darda were the sons of Zerah (1 Chr 2:6). Heman and Ethan authored Pss 88-89, two of the wisdom psalms. The term *"Ezrahite"* which is applied to Ethan in 1 Kgs 4:31 and to both Ethan and Heman in the psalm titles is probably a variation of the family name Zerah. The Levites Ethan and Heman of 1 Chr 6:33,44 who were singers appointed by David may be the same men mentioned here. If this is the case, then these Levites, by virtue of their residence, would have been incorporated into the Judahite family of Zerah.

20. According to 2 Chr 2:10 Solomon paid the laborers 20,000 kors (103,200 bushels) each of wheat and barley and 20,000 baths (110,000 gallons) each of wine and oil.

21. Of the 550 superior officers, 250 were Israelites (2 Chr 8:10), while the balance were Canaanites. See James E. Smith, *I & II Kings* in "Bible Study Textbook Series" (Joplin: College Press, 1975), pp. 151f.

CHAPTER TWENTY-SIX

Solomon's Great Work
1 Kings 6:1-9:9

Without question the greatest achievement of Solomon's glorious reign was the construction of the Jerusalem temple. Using plans designed by David, and the expertise of Phoenician craftsmen, Solomon brought into being what surely must have been one of the wonders of ancient architecture.

CONSTRUCTION OF THE TEMPLE
1 Kgs 6:1-7:51//2 Chr 3:1-4:22

The material presented in Scripture is sufficient to allow one to get a general idea of what the temple may have been like. The omission of crucial architectural details, however, renders impossible absolute certainty about many points. The careful and detailed dimensions are proofs of the tender veneration with which the people of God regarded the temple. They are also indications of the belief that this house was for the Lord and not for man.

A. A Chronological Note (1 Kgs 6:1).

1 Kings 6:1 furnishes the key to Biblical chronology prior to the monarchy period. Temple construction began in Ziv, the second month (April), in the fourth year of Solomon's reign (967 BC). This was 480 years after the Israelites had come out of Egypt. This text seems to necessitate a date for the Exodus of about 1447 BC.

B. The Exterior of the House (1 Kgs 6:2-10).

The temple proper was a rather small building. Exclusive of the porch and side chambers, the building measured about 90 feet long, 30 feet wide, and 45 feet high.[1] The temple was never meant for the congregation of worshipers, but only for the presence of God and the priests who ministered before that presence. The congregation never met *within* this building; rather they offered their worship *towards* it. Worshipers congregated in the great courtyard which surrounded the temple (6:2).

Before the main building was a porch or vestibule fifteen feet deep which extended across the entire front (east end) of the temple. An unspecified number of immovable lattices were the windows of the house.[2] Around the outside wall of the entire building (exclusive of the porch) were three stories of staggered width which were divided by partitions into distinct compartments. Keil estimates that there were thirty of these chambers. The upper chambers were reached by means of a door through the external wall of the side chambers which led to a spiral stairway. The chambers were fastened to the house by means of cedar beams resting on rebatements in the walls of the house. The chambers served (1) as storage areas for temple treasures and gifts, (2) lodging for priests who were serving in the temple, and (3) possibly as a buttress to support the walls of the house (6:3-6,8).

The stones used in the temple were *"perfect,"* i.e., they were so hewn and prepared at the quarry[3] that no sound of any iron tool was heard at the temple site when the stones were brought together. The roof of the house, which was most likely flat, was made of beams and boards of cedar wood.

C. The Promise to Solomon (1 Kgs 6:11-14).

During the course of the building of the temple, Yahweh came to

Solomon with a gracious promise. The divine word came to the king probably through a prophetic intermediary (Nathan?). That God spoke directly is ruled out by 9:2 which alludes to the *second* direct revelation to Solomon. In effect the divine word contained an implied commendation of Solomon for having begun such a noble work. If Solomon continued to follow the direction of Yahweh (1) God would confirm the promise spoken to David in 2 Samuel 7:12ff.; and (2) God would dwell in the midst of his people. Thus encouraged by the gracious promise of Yahweh, Solomon proceeded with the construction of the interior of the temple.

Diagram No. 37

SOLOMON'S
TEMPLE

Drawn by Horace Knowles
British & Foreign Bible Society

D. The Interior of the House (1 Kgs 6:15-35).

The sacred historian next describes some of the outstanding features of the interior of the temple.

1. The holy place (6:15-18; 29-30). The interior stone walls of the house were lined with wood which was engraved with gourds and flower blossoms. The wood was in turn overlaid with small gold plates which were attached to the wood with nails. The walls were also ornamented with precious stones (2 Chr 3:6,9). The floor was covered with cypress wood. Thirty feet from the west end of the house a floor to ceiling partition separated the most holy place (the *debir*) from the rest of the house (6:15-18).

2. *The debir (6:19-22).* The holy of holies (the *debir*) at the rear of the structure housed the ark of the covenant. This part of the building was a cube (symbolizing perfection) of thirty feet. The *debir* was overlaid with pure gold (2 Chr 3:8) which weighed 600 talents (23 tons). Immediately in front of the *debir* was a stone altar covered with cedar which was overlaid with gold. Gold chains hung in front of the *debir*. The purpose of these chains is not stated. Above the *debir* were the *"upper chambers"* (2 Chr 3:9) which were also overlaid with gold. The relics of the old tabernacle may have been stored here.

3. *The cherubim (6:23-28).* Two huge cherubim (15' high) made of precious olive wood overlaid with gold dominated the interior of the *debir*. They faced east (2 Chr 3:13). Their outstretched wings reached across the entire width of the *debir* (30'). Between their bodies was a space of several feet where the ark of the covenant rested. Cherubim were angelic creatures which are usually depicted guarding something sacred. Their appearance is a matter of speculation.[4]

4. *The doors (6:31-35).* The doors leading to the *debir* were made of olive wood. They contained relief carvings similar to those on the walls. They were overlaid with gold. A curtain hung inside the *debir* which prevented any priest from gazing within when the doors were opened once each year on the day of atonement (2 Chr 3:14). The outer doors of the house were made of fir decorated with figures of cherubim, palm trees and flowers overlaid with gold. These doors were made of two panels, but it is impossible to determine whether they were divided lengthwise into two narrow leaves (Hammond) or width-wise about halfway up (Keil).

5. *Other construction details (6:36-38).* The inner court of the temple was enclosed by a low wall formed by three rows of hewn stones and a row of cedar beams. The size of this court is not stated. If it was twice the size of that of the tabernacle, the court would have

measured 300' by 150'.

The temple project was completed in the eleventh year of
Solomon's reign, in the month of Bul (October). This means that the
temple was 7.5 years in the building, rounded off by the sacred historian to seven years.

E. The Great Court (1 Kgs 7:1-12).

The palace complex dominated the outer court which surrounded
the temple mount. This complex was thirteen years in construction.
This longer period spent on the palace does not argue for selfishness
on the part of Solomon. On the contrary, his piety caused him to
build the temple first. The temple construction was much faster
because (1) David had gathered enormous quantities of materials in
advance; (2) Solomon employed a special force of laborers on the
temple; and (3) the temple was small in comparison to the palace
complex. The palace complex consisted of five major buildings.

1. *The house of the forest of Lebanon (7:2-5).* This building
received its name because it contained a virtual forest of cedar pillars.
This huge building (150' by 75') seems to have served as a treasury
and armory. Possibly it also served as the residence of the royal bodyguard (cf. 1 Kgs 10:17; Isa 22:8).

2. *The porch of pillars (7:6).* The porch of pillars was no doubt a
covered colonnade, i.e., it had a roof but no sides. It connected the
house of the forest of Lebanon and the hall of justice. Litigants probably waited here until called to present their case before the king.

3. *The hall of justice (7:7).* This building was open in the front,
and shut in by solid walls on the other three sides. It was covered with
cedar. Here the king held court and granted audiences.

4. *The palace (7:8a).* The hall of justice served as the principal
entrance into the king's personal residence. Little is known of this
structure except that it was within a courtyard, and it was built on the
same order as the hall of justice.

5. *House of Pharaoh's daughter (7:8b).* The queen's private residence seems to have been directly behind the palace.

All the stones used in the palace complex were of the finest quality, smoothed on all sides. The *"great court"* which enclosed both the
temple and the palace complex was formed by a wall consisting of

three rows of hewn stones and a coping of cedar. It thus resembled the wall surrounding the temple courtyard (7:9-11).

F. Hiram's Work (1 Kgs 7:13-51//2 Chr 4:1-22).

To construct the metallic furnishings of the temple, Hiram the king sent to Solomon, at his request (2 Chr 2:6), a workman who also bore the name Hiram.[5] His mother was a Danite by birth (2 Chr 2:14) who had married into the tribe of Naphtali. His father was a man of Tyre. Like his father before him, Hiram was a skilled worker in bronze as well as wood, cloth and other metals (2 Chr 2:14).

1. The bronze pillars (7:15-22). Perhaps the greatest achievement of Hiram was the casting of two enormous, hollow bronze pillars. The circumference of the pillars was 12 cubits (18'). The pillars stood 18 cubits (27.5').[6] A bronze, ornate capital roughly resembling a full-blown lily-cup added an additional 5 cubits (7.5') to each pillar. The pillars appear to have stood within the porch, not in front of it as some have suggested. These two pillars before the sanctuary symbolized the power and eternity of God. They were named *Jachin* ("he shall establish") and *Boaz* ("in him is strength").

2. The bronze sea (7:23-26). Hiram made for the temple courtyard a great bronze water basin which was called *"the sea"* on account of its unprecedented capacity. The sea was circular and measured 10 cubits (15') in diameter, 30 cubits (45') in circumference.[7] The sea rested on twelve bronze oxen, three of which faced each direction. The capacity when filled to ordinary height was 2,000 baths (11,500 gallons).[8] The weight of this giant laver must have been about thirty tons. Rabbinic tradition indicates that the sea was provided with taps or faucets. The text gives no indication how the sea was filled.

3. The stands and basins (7:27-39). Hiram constructed ten identical movable lavers for the temple court. These were made of bronze. They were decorated with cherubim, lions, palms and wreaths. Each laver could contain forty baths (230 gallons). Five of these lavers were positioned along the north side and five along the south side of the court. At these lavers the flesh and fat which were used in sacrifice were first washed. They were also used for the purification of worshipers (2 Chr 4:6), and for cleansing of the altar and court after bloody sacrifices. When filled with water these lavers would have weighed well over a ton.

Diagram No. 38, The Mobile Laver

In addition Hiram was also responsible for a number of the smaller implements used in the temple.The text explains that Hiram did the casting in Gilead between Succoth and Zarethan. No doubt this spot was chosen because of the abundance of water and good clay with which to form the molds (7:40-47). No attempt was made to discover the exact weight of the metal used on account of the vast quantities of bronze required. No mention is made here of the huge bronze altar. Someone other than Hiram must have constructed it.

4. *The interior temple vessels (7:48-51).* All the vessels used inside the temple were made of gold. Apparently Hiram had nothing to do with the making of these objects. The furniture within the holy place included (1) the altar of incense, (2) the golden table—actually ten of them (2 Chr 4:8)—upon which the twelve loaves of unleavened

bread were displayed; and (3) the ten lampstands, each with seven oil lamps, which were arranged five on each side of the *debir*.[9] The instruments used with the furnishings of the holy place included (1) tongs, (2) cups, (3) snuffers, (4) bowls, (5) spoons, and (6) firepans. Even the door hinges of the temple were of gold!

Even after the construction of all the temple vessels and furniture there was a surplus of precious metal and bronze. This excess was stored in the temple treasuries (7:51).

DEDICATION OF THE TEMPLE
1 Kgs 8:1-66//2 Chr 5:1-7:22

Because of its importance in the history of redemption, the sacred historian devotes considerable space to the dedication of Solomon's temple. Thousands of people flocked to Jerusalem to share in the paramount event. Without question the dedication of Solomon's temple was the grandest ceremony ever performed under the Mosaic dispensation. The solemn dedicatory transaction consisted of six acts.

A. The Procession (1 Kgs 8:1-13).

Solomon summoned all the leaders of the nation to Jerusalem to share in the dedication ceremonies. After years of waiting, a national sanctuary was to be dedicated which would supersede the tabernacle of Moses at which their forefathers had worshiped for five centuries.

The first order of business was the transfer of the ark of the covenant from Mt. Zion, the city of David, to its permanent resting place in the *debir* of the temple on Mt. Moriah.[10] Because it housed the sacred ark, the newly-built temple enjoyed the sanctity and national prestige of the sanctuary in Shiloh which had been destroyed by the Philistines about 145 years earlier (8:1).

In addition to the princes summoned by Solomon, *"all the men of Israel"* also came to Jerusalem to participate in the feast. Since the gathering took place in the month of Ethanim, the seventh month, the particular feast must have been the feast of tabernacles. No doubt the dedication was scheduled for this time of year because this feast was the greatest and most joyous gathering of the year (8:2).[11]

As on former occasions of extraordinary solemnity, the priests rather than Levites carried the ark of the covenant (cf. Josh 3:6ff.; 6:6). The Levites transported the tabernacle and its holy furniture. Innumerable sacrifices were offered before the ark to express the grateful joy of the populace (8:3-5).

The priests deposited the ark in its assigned place in the *debir*—the holy of holies—between the two giant cherubim. The wings of the cherubim completely covered the ark so that it was enveloped in darkness. The priests drew the staves forward toward the front end of the ark. These staves could be seen by one who might be standing in the holy place immediately in front of the *debir* (8:6-8).[12]

At the time the ark was placed in the temple it contained only the two tables of stone which had been put there by Moses at Horeb (8:9). The golden pot of manna and Aaron's rod (Heb 9:4) probably had been removed by the Philistines when they had temporary possession of the ark (cf. 1 Sam 6:19).

As the priests withdrew from the *debir,* the singers and trumpeters standing at the east end of the altar began their service of praise (2 Chr 5:13). At that exact moment the cloud which was indicative of the divine presence filled the house of the Lord (cf. Exod 40:34f.). Because of the cloud the priests for a time could not continue their ministrations (8:10-11).

As Solomon witnessed this divine manifestation, he was stirred to the depths of his being. That glorious cloud proved that his work of piety had been accepted. The almighty God had entered that earthly shrine to dwell in the darkness of the *debir.*[13] Solomon could only turn his eyes heavenward and utter a prayer of declaration in which he reaffirmed his purpose in building the temple. The structure was intended to be *"a house"* for God in contrast to the portable shrine of the tabernacle (8:12-13).

B. The Declaration (1 Kgs 8:14-21).

Turning his gaze from the house where the cloud appeared, Solomon faced the congregation assembled there and perhaps gestured to them that they might stand up. The king then *"blessed,"* i.e., greeted the people, and addressed them. First, Solomon praised God for bringing to pass what he had spoken through Nathan the prophet. Then the king enumerated the circumstances which led to the building of the temple. (1) God had selected David to rule Israel. (2) David desired to build a temple, and God approved of that desire. (3) Nevertheless, God had decreed that David's son would have the honor of being the temple builder. (4) The Lord had raised up Solomon and had aided him in building the temple which was a resting place for the ark.

C. The Adoration (1 Kgs 8:22-24).

The dedicatory prayer of Solomon is one of the most beautiful passages in the Bible. In it the temple is depicted as a house of prayer rather than a place of sacrifice.

Solomon began his prayer standing upon a bronze platform in the courtyard of the temple (2 Chr 6:13). His hands were spread toward heaven in a gesture of supplication. Solomon declared that no god in heaven or earth compared to Yahweh. This expression does not suggest that other gods really exist, but in effect means that Yahweh is the only God. That which distinguished Yahweh from the non-entities worshiped by other peoples is that he kept his covenantal word and extended mercy to those who sincerely tried to live by the terms of that covenant. As a particular example of God's faithfulness, Solomon cited the promises made to David. In the light of his succession and the completion of the temple, Solomon regarded those promises as fulfilled (8:22-24).

D. The Supplication (1 Kings 8:25-50).

In the second part of the prayer, Solomon presented his supplications before the Lord.

1. *General petitions (8:25-30).* God had also promised that David's descendants would continue to reign over God's people as long as these rulers were faithful to Yahweh. Solomon first asked that the Lord would keep that promise. The Israelites knew that God could not be contained in man-made buildings. Yet the king prayed that the Lord would take notice of the earnest prayer offered to him at the temple. This petition was not presumptuous because God had designated the temple as the place where his name, i.e., his revelation of himself, would dwell. Solomon prayed that the Lord would respond to penitent prayers by forgiving whatever trespass had been committed.

2. *Specific petitions (8:31-50).* Solomon next details seven specif-

ic situations which could be expected to arise in the future. Each situation is cast in the "if . . . then" framework. Frequently Solomon alludes to *"God in heaven."* Four times he mentions praying toward the temple.

The seven petitions may be briefly summarized as follows: (1) May God hear every oath taken before the temple altar and then intervene to punish the guilty and justify the innocent. (2) After military defeat may God restore to Israel those who might have been carried away captive. (3) May God hear the penitent prayers of his people when they had been chastised by drought. (4) In the midst of plagues may God listen to the cry of his people. (5) May God hear the prayers of any foreigners who might come to the temple to pray. (6) May God hear those who were fighting wars far removed from Jerusalem who might address their petitions toward the temple. (7) In his last petition Solomon contemplated the captivity of Israel. He prayed that God might intervene on behalf of his people when they came to their senses and repented (8:31-50).

3. Final appeal (8:51-53). Solomon brought his prayer to a conclusion by citing several reasons why God should hearken to the present prayer and all future prayers which might be offered before him. First, Israel was God's people. Second, God had brought this people out of the furnace of Egyptian bondage. Third, Yahweh had separated Israel from all peoples of the earth for his very own inheritance. The prayer closed with an appeal to the Lord to cause salvation and grace to go forth from the temple over his people (2 Chr 6:40-42).

E. The Benediction (1 Kgs 8:54-61).

At the conclusion of his prayer, Solomon rose up from his knees—he must have fallen to his knees at some point during the prayer—and, with hands spread toward heaven, blessed the congregation. The benediction began with praise to the Lord for the fulfillment of his promises, especially the promise of *rest* given through Moses (8:54-56).

The king then summed up his wishes for the good of his kingdom. First, he prayed that God might choose to teach Israel his commandments by positive guidance rather than through divine discipline. Second, he prayed that God might incline their hearts toward the Lord so that they might obey his commandments. Third, he prayed that the

441

words of his dedicatory prayer might ever be before the Lord that he might execute justice on behalf of both the king and the people. Finally, he prayed that Israel would be so blessed of God that all people of the earth would recognize that he alone was God (8:57-60).

Solomon concluded his prayer with a brief exhortation that the people continue to demonstrate the piety and loyalty to Yahweh which they had demonstrated in building the temple. According to 2 Chronicles 7:1 at that moment fire came down from heaven and consumed the sacrifices; and the glory of the Lord filled the house.

F. The Celebration (1 Kgs 8:62-66).

The king and his people celebrated the dedication of the temple with an enormous sacrifice. Some 22,000 oxen and some 100,000 sheep were slaughtered. In the peace offering only the fat was burned on the altar. The rest of the animal was eaten by the worshipers. The enormous number of animals would have been required to feed the vast multitudes which gathered for the dedication (8:62-63).

Even though the bronze altar in the temple courtyard had a top surface of 900 square feet,[14] it was not large enough to accommodate the offerings at the dedication. In addition to the enormous number of peace offerings just mentioned, burnt offerings and meal offerings appropriate to such an occasion were also offered. Therefore Solomon *"sanctified the middle court,"* i.e., the entire area of the court of priests which was before the house (8:64). This probably was done with holy anointing oil (cf. Exod 40:1-15). The whole space may have been regarded as one huge altar (Rawlinson), or temporary altars may have been erected all over the courtyard (Keil).

A great congregation had assembled from as far as the entrance of Hamath on the Orontes river in the north to the Wadi of Egypt in the south, i.e., from one end of the land to the other. These worshipers joined Solomon in a seven-day feast of dedication which was in turn followed by the seven-day feast of tabernacles (cf. 2 Chr 7:9f.). On the eighth day of the second feast—the twenty-second day of the seventh month—Solomon dismissed the multitude. The crowd reciprocated by blessing, i.e., saluting, their king. The next morning they departed for their tents, i.e., dwellings, full of joy because of what the Lord had done for his servant David and his people Israel (cf. 2 Chr 7:10).

REVELATION TO SOLOMON
1 Kgs 9:1-9//2 Chr 7:12-22

After Solomon had completed his building projects, Yahweh appeared to him a second time as he had appeared in the dream at Gibeon.[15] This communication is clearly God's response to the dedicatory prayer of Solomon. At least thirteen years had elapsed since that great prayer. Solomon was now at the height of his prosperity. With his building projects completed the king's heart was puffed up with pride. His love for the Lord was waning. He had begun that spiritual decline which eventually led to idolatry. This divine word served to remind Solomon of that wonderful prayer and youthful devotion which he was in danger of losing (9:1-2).

The Lord made the following points in this revelation: First, the Lord pledged himself to answer the prayers of his penitent people. *"I will hear from heaven, will forgive their sin, and will heal their land."* Second, Yahweh assured Solomon that he had chosen and consecrated the temple *"that my name may be there forever."* Third, he reminded Solomon of the conditional promise made to David. If his descendants were obedient to the Lord, then David's sons would continue to occupy the throne in Jerusalem (2 Chr 7:12-18).

The warnings against unfaithfulness are stern and uncompromising. If Solomon or any of his children turned from following Yahweh, God would deprive the nation of the land he had given them. Furthermore, the Lord would utterly reject the temple which he had so recently acknowledged. The condition of the nation would become so deplorable that people would allude to Israel when they wished to use an apt illustration of folly and unfaithfulness (9:6-7).

In case of unfaithfulness, the house of God would be a conspicuous example of the fate which befalls an unfaithful people. Those who observed the ruins on the temple mount would hiss or whistle in astonishment. They would ask one another why Yahweh would have treated the land of the temple in this manner. The answer would come back from those close at hand that Israel had forsaken the God who had brought them out of Egypt (9:8-9).

ENDNOTES

1. The figures given here assume the eighteen inch cubit.

2. C.F. Keil conjectures that there were no more than six on each side and probably none in the back. *The Books of Kings* in "Biblical Commentary on the Old Testament" (Grand Rapids: Eerdmans, 1950 reprint), p. 74.

3. Dr. J.T. Barclay, the first missionary dispatched by the churches of Christ, discovered in 1858 the entrance to a vast quarry beneath the temple mount. *The City of the Great King* (Philadelphia: James Challen, 1858), p. 118.

4. Modern scholars think of cherubim as resembling the Egyptian sphinx, i.e., lions with wings and human heads. Older commentators (e.g., Keil) thought of them as having human form and standing upright.

5. The name is also spelled Huram (2 Chr 2:13; 4:11,16). Because of his skills, in Chronicles he receives the title *'abhi* (" my father") which probably is equivalent to the English word "master." John Gray thinks Huram-abhi was the full name of the craftsman, thus regarding *'abhi* as part of his name, rather than a title. *I & II Kings* in "The Old Testament Library" (Philadelphia: Westminster, 1970), p. 171.

6. 2 Chr 3:15 gives the length (*'orech*) as 35 cubits (52.5'). Chronicles may be giving the total length of both pillars minus the pedestals to which they were anchored; Kings may be giving the height of each pillar individually, including the height of the pedestal. Another possibility is that the actual height of each pillar was 17.5 cubits which Kings has rounded off to 18. The 17.5 cubits of each pillar combined would yield the 35 cubits of 2 Chr 3:15.

7. The sacred historian here uses round figures, hence the small mathematical discrepancy in the ratio of the diameter to the circumference.

8. 2 Chr 4:5 gives the maximum capacity as 3,000 baths (17,500 gallons).

9. Some hold that the lampstands were arranged in a single row, in front of and parallel to the *debir*. Others picture the lampstands being arranged in two rows perpendicular to the partition of the *debir*. In the latter arrangement the lamps would furnish the light throughout the Holy Place. In the former arrangement the lamps would serve as a barrier before the *debir*. The idea that the ten lampstands rested on the ten tables mentioned in Chronicles is not supported in the text.

10. Originally the term *Zion* was restricted to the Jebusite fortress (city of David) on the southern and lower part of the hill on which the temple was built. In later times the name Zion denoted the temple hill (Amos 1:2; Isa 8:18; etc.) and the entire city of Jerusalem (Amos 6:1; Isa 10:24; etc.).

11. The temple construction was completed in the eighth month of Solomon's eleventh year (1 Kgs 6:38). The temple dedication was held in the seventh month (2 Chr 7:10), but of what year is not stated. It would seem, then, that the dedication was held prior to the completion of the work, or that the dedication was delayed for almost a year after the construction.

12. The meaning may be that the staves could be occasionally seen when the curtain was pulled aside to allow the high priest to enter the *debir* on the day of atonement. The traditional Jewish view is that the staves pressed against the veil which was hung before the *debir*.

13. Several passages speak of God appearing in thick darkness or in a cloud: Exod 19:9; 20:21; Deut 4:11; 5:22. The thick darkness may be an allusion to the fact that the *debir* was windowless.

14. According to 2 Chr 4:1 the bronze altar was twenty cubits by twenty cubits (30' x 30').

15. Solomon had received a message from Yahweh during the course of the temple building, but that message had probably come through the lips of a prophet (1 Kgs 6:11).

CHAPTER TWENTY-SEVEN

From Glory to Shame
1 Kings 9:10-11:43

Jesus once referred to *"Solomon in all of his glory"* (Matt 6:29). The author of Kings underscores the wisdom of Solomon's rule and the material blessing which resulted from it. Solomon's kingdom was surely the most glorious the world had yet seen, not because it was the largest or even the most prosperous, but because of the wisdom of its king and the perfection of its government.

THE GLORY OF MATERIAL POSSESSION
1 Kings 9:10-28

Whereas it was David who established the kingdom in its extent and power, it was Solomon who added the glamour. Some of the factors which enabled Solomon to erect so many magnificent buildings and gain such notoriety are set forth in 1 Kings 9:10-28.

A. Hiram's Cooperation (1 Kgs 9:10-14//2 Chr 8:1-2).

Solomon spent twenty years on his major building projects—seven years on the temple and thirteen years on the palace complex. That Solomon was able to build such magnificent buildings was due largely to his alliance with Hiram king of Tyre, from whom he had received enormous amounts of timber. At some point during the twenty years of construction, Solomon ran short of gold. He again turned to Hiram to supply his need. Probably the 120 talents (4.5 tons) of gold[1] were a loan rather than a gift advanced on the strength of anticipated profits from Solomon's share in the joint naval expedition to Ophir described in 1 Kings 9:26-28.

At the end of the twenty years of construction, Solomon ceded to Hiram the sovereignty over twenty cities in the land of Galilee, i.e., the northern part of the tribal territory of Naphtali.[2] Elsewhere this region is called *"Galilee of the Gentiles"* (Isa 9:1) because of the large number of Phoenicians who lived there. The villages given to Hiram were undoubtedly Canaanite communities which had not been taken over and developed into Israelite cities (9:10-11). Exactly why Solomon gave the twenty cities to Hiram is unclear.[3]

When Hiram went out to inspect his newly acquired territory, he was greatly disappointed. He had hoped to be awarded a rich grain-producing area, but had received instead a barren mountainous tract. Immediately he fired off a letter to Jerusalem to express his disappointment. Hiram addressed Solomon as *"my brother,"* the diplomatic language employed by friendly nations of that day. The letter referred to the recently acquired territory as *"Cabul."* Though the exact meaning of this word is not known,[4] it is almost certainly an expression of disparagement intended to mock Solomon's stinginess. The Chronicler intimates that Solomon regained possession of the cities (2 Chr 8:1-2). Perhaps Hiram simply refused to take jurisdiction of the area (9:12-13).

B. Compulsory Labor (1 Kgs 9:15-23//2 Chr 8:7-10).

The second means by which Solomon was able to construct so many buildings was the compulsory labor force (Heb. *hammas*). The object of the forced labor was the building of public works, the temple, palace, fortifications and strategic points in the provinces.

1. The Jerusalem projects (9:15a). In addition to the temple and palace complex, two projects constructed by compulsory labor are identified. The first, the Millo, is mentioned six times in Scripture, each time with the definite article. The Millo seems to have been a bastion which filled some weak point in the walls of the city. Second, Solomon's labor force extended the wall of Jerusalem, probably to enclose the temple mount.

2. *The fortress cities (9:15b-18).* Outside of Jerusalem Solomon constructed six fortresses located at points strategic for controlling the movement of caravans. (1) Hazor, situated in northern Galilee, controlled the routes from the north. (2) Megiddo was the great fortress which commanded one of the major passes through the mountains which intersected the coastal plains. The main highway from Egypt to Damascus passed through Megiddo. (3) Gezer was Solomon's fortress guarding the southern frontier of Israel.[5] (4) Lower Beth-horon guarded a main route leading from the coastal plains up to the highlands were Jerusalem was located. (5) Baalath was located in the tribal territory of Dan southwest of Beth-horon. (6) Tamar appears to have protected the route to the important Red Sea port of Ezion-geber. To the list of outer fortresses the Chronicler adds Upper Beth-horon and Tadmor which was 150 miles northwest of Damascus (2 Chr 8:4f.).

3. *Other cities (9:19).* In some cities public storage facilities were constructed. Such provisions were used for the troops and royal household, and possibly as insurance against seasons of scarcity. These may have been the cities where Solomon's twelve district administrators lived (cf. 1 Kgs 4:7). Other cities served as bases for Solomon's chariot forces and cavalry units.[6]

Solomon's levy of bond slaves was taken from among the foreign peoples which the Israelites had not destroyed. No Israelites were forced to become permanent bond slaves (cf. Lev 25:39), although some Israelites were compelled to render temporary government service (cf. 1 Kgs 5:13). For the most part Solomon used Israelites for the more exalted service in the army or in the royal court. At the top administrative level over Solomon's levy of bond men were 550 officers. As previously explained (cf. comments on 1 Kgs 5:16), 300 of these superior officers were Canaanites (9:20-23).

C. Pharaoh's Daughter (1 Kgs 9:24//2 Chr 8:11).

After completing the palace complex, Solomon had Pharaoh's

daughter brought up from the city of David to the loftier summit where her palace was situated. The Chronicler explains Solomon's motives for moving his Egyptian wife out of the city of David (cf. 1 Kgs 3:1). The ark of God had once been housed on that hill. The presence of this foreign princess in a place sanctified by the ark would not be appropriate (cf. 2 Chr 8:11).

D. Solomon's Worship (1 Kgs 9:25//2 Chr 8:12-16).

After the temple was built, Solomon ceased to sacrifice upon the altars of the high places (cf. 3:2). *"Solomon sacrificed burnt offerings and peace offerings to Yahweh"* on the bronze altar in the temple court. *"He also burned incense upon the altar which was before Yahweh"* (1 Kgs 9:25). The meaning is that Solomon as the builder of the temple provided the resources which were necessary to conduct the temple ritual properly (cf. 2 Chr 8:12f.).

After the completion of the temple, Solomon implemented the arrangements which David had made for the priests, Levites, and gatekeepers. Nothing which David had ordered was left undone (2 Chr 8:14-15).

E. Solomon's Navy (1 Kgs 9:26-28//2 Chr 8:17-18; 9:21).

Another source of Solomon's wealth was his commercial fleet. The king built ships at Ezion-geber in the land of Edom (cf. 2 Sam 8:14). Solomon himself made a trip to Ezion-geber (2 Chr 8:17), possibly to launch the fleet. In this maritime venture the Israelites and Phoenicians were partners. Phoenicians were renowned in the ancient world for their seamanship. The Chronicler adds that Hiram even provided the ships (2 Chr 8:18). This probably means that the ships were transported overland in sections, then reassembled at Ezion-geber. Hiram's interest in this venture was opening up the Red Sea trades routes to which he otherwise had no access.

The location of Ophir is uncertain. Modern scholarship has attempted to narrow the location to either India or East Africa. Wherever its location, Ophir supplied Solomon with enormous quantities of gold—420 talents (16 tons).[7] Whether all this gold was brought back on one voyage, or whether this figure represents the profits from several voyages to Ophir cannot be determined.

The "Hiram fleet" also brought large quantities of almug trees and precious stones. From this precious wood Solomon constructed "pillars," stairs (2 Chr 9:11) and various types of stringed musical instruments. The precise identification of the almug tree depends on the view one has of the location of Ophir. Only during Solomon's reign was this wood imported into Israel (1 Kgs10:11-12).

THE GLORY OF INTELLECTUAL PROWESS
1 Kgs 10:1-10//2 Chr 9:1-12

The wide-ranging voyages of the fleet spread the fame of Solomon to distant lands. An incredulous queen of Arabia came to inspect first hand the marvels of Solomon's city and court.

The precise identity of the queen of Sheba has not yet been ascertained. She was one of several prominent queens ruling trading colonies in southern Arabia during this period. The visit of the queen of Sheba was probably a trade mission rendered necessary by the Israelite control of the major land routes to the north and the economic threat to south Arabian trade with East Africa posed by Solomon's naval enterprise.

The queen was informed that Solomon's greatness was due to his relationship with the God of Israel. Part of her reason for going to Jerusalem was to test the king by means of enigmatic riddles in order to see for herself if he had supernatural wisdom. Such tests of practical sagacity were part of the diplomatic encounters of that time. A king's wit and poetic skill were evidence of the extent to which he was conversant with affairs and culture in the world of his day.[8]

The journey to Jerusalem from Sheba—a trip of some fifteen hundred miles—was no small undertaking in that day. The queen brought with her a very heavy force which included an armed escort and court attendants. She brought camels bearing spices, gold and precious stones to be bestowed upon her host.

When she reached Jerusalem, the queen spoke unto Solomon "all that was in her heart." The king was able to answer appropriately all the questions which were put to him. The queen was quite impressed with the wisdom of Solomon, and with the palace he had built as well. She was amazed as she watched Solomon's hundreds of servants gathered about the bountiful tables which the king spread for them. The rich and costly apparel of Solomon's personal attendants and his cupbearers (cf. 2 Chr 9:4) particularly caught her eye. The queen also took special note of the ascent[9] or private entrance by which the king entered the temple. The reaction of the queen to all the grandeur of Solomon's court is expressed in the words *"and there was no more spirit in her,"* i.e., she was beside herself with amazement (10:2-5).

The queen was not reluctant to express her feelings and reactions to Solomon. All that she had heard concerning his words and wisdom had proved to be true. While she had been incredulous prior to making her journey to Jerusalem, she now was of the opinion that the wisdom and prosperity of Solomon far exceeded any report which had come to her ears (10:6-8).

The queen rightly discerned that Solomon's prosperity and sagacity came from the God of Israel. For this reason, she directed her praise heavenward. Yahweh delighted in Solomon and set him upon the throne of Israel. The Lord loved Israel and desired a king to rule over his people who would execute justice and righteousness. Such sentiments were consistent with the polytheistic religion of this queen. Nothing in the text indicates that she became a worshiper of Yahweh after visiting Solomon's court (10:9).

The state visit concluded with an exchange of gifts. For her part, the queen gave Solomon 120 talents (4.5 tons) of gold, a vast amount of spices, and precious stones. Solomon made appropriate gifts to the queen in return for her generosity, and in addition gave her whatever she asked. This might well have included a satisfactory trade agreement (10:10).[10]

THE FAILURES OF SOLOMON
Wealth Multiplied
1 Kgs 10:14-22//2 Chr 9:13-27

In Deuteronomy 17:14-20 God stipulated three things that the future kings of Israel were not to do. They were not to multiply (1) horses unto themselves, or (2) wives, or (3) wealth. As the years went by Solomon violated all three of these stipulations.

A. Extent of his Wealth (1 Kgs 10:14-15//2 Chr 9:13-14).

In one year[11]—probably the year of the queen's visit—the gold revenues of Solomon weighed 666 talents (25 tons). According to the Berkeley Version, this gold would be worth $20,000,000. No doubt this amount includes the receipts from all sources—taxes, tribute, and voyages. This enormous income marked a turning point in the king's relationship to God. From this point on the story of Solomon is one of steady decline (10:14).

Solomon also received vast annual revenues from caravaneers who passed through his territory, the sheiks of the nomad tribes in Arabia, and *"the governors of the land,"* i.e., the twelve officers mentioned in 1 Kings 4. These contributions probably were in kind, i.e., produce or animals or goods. This explains why the author distinguished them from the gold revenues of the previous verse (10:15).

B. Use of his Wealth (1 Kgs 10:16-21//2 Chr 9:15-20).

From his enormous gold treasures Solomon made two hundred bucklers, i.e., body-length shields. Six hundred *bekas* (NIV) of gold (7.5 lbs.) went into each shield. In addition, Solomon made three hundred smaller shields, each containing three minas or 300 *bekas* (2 Chr 9:16), i.e., 3.75 lbs., of gold. These golden shields were carried by the royal bodyguard on special occasions. When not in use during royal ceremonies the shields were suspended from the walls of the house of the forest of Lebanon (10:16-17).

Solomon's throne, located in the porch of judgment, was another indication of the glory of his kingdom. It was made of ivory which was overlaid with pure gold.[12] Six steps led to the elevated throne. Perhaps the seven levels symbolized the perfection in the decisions rendered by the king when he was sitting in judgment. The top of the throne was rounded or arched in form. On either side of the arm rests were two wooden lions overlaid with gold. Twelve other lions were situated two on each step leading to the throne. The lion was a symbol of royalty in the ancient Near East. This animal also had special significance for the tribe of Judah (cf. Gen 49:9; Num 23:24). The twelve lions may represent the twelve tribes as the guardians of the throne of Israel. No throne in any kingdom of the time equaled that of Solomon (10:18-20).

All of Solomon's drinking vessels were of gold, as were also the vessels used in the house of the forest of Lebanon. None were made of silver, since silver had become so plentiful that it had lost all value (10:21).

C. Sources of his Wealth (1 Kgs 10:22-25//2 Chr 9:21-24).

The author of Kings already has referred to one major source of Solomon's wealth, viz., the Red Sea fleet (cf. 9:26ff.). Now he mentions two other sources of his wealth. First, Solomon also had a Tarshish fleet, i.e., a fleet which sailed to Tarshish on the southern coast of Spain. This fleet operated on a three-year schedule. It brought back exotic products from distant lands. The gold and silver were secured in Tarshish; the apes, baboons (NIV) and ivory were available through the trading colonies along the coast of Africa (10:22). The Tarshish fleet was probably based at some Mediterranean port.[13]

Second, dignitaries from distant lands came to Jerusalem to hear the wisdom of the man so richly endowed of God. These visitors bestowed upon Solomon luxurious presents including gold and silver vessels, garments, arms, spices and riding animals (10:23-25). The visit of the queen of Sheba is an example of what must have been occurring regularly.

THE FAILURES OF SOLOMON
Horses Multiplied
1 Kgs 10:26-29//2 Chr 9:25-28

In contravention of Deuteronomy 17:16 Solomon multiplied to himself horses. His force of 1,400 chariots would appear to have been maintained largely for the sake of pomp and display. The chariot is of little tactical value in the hilly terrain of Palestine and, furthermore, Solomon's reign was peaceful. Hence, he did not actually need such a large chariot force. The maintenance of 12,000 cavalry troops is further indication of Solomon's materialistic disposition. The various chariot and cavalry units were stationed throughout the land (cf. 9:19) a well as in Jerusalem, the royal residence (10:26).

In an obvious hyperbole the author declares that during the reign

SOURCES OF SOLOMON'S WEALTH

300 km 300 Miles

Persian Gulf

BETH-EDEN

Nineveh

Babylon

TRIBUTE, CORVEE

TRIBUTE, CORVEE

ARABIAN KINGS

From Sheba: perfumes, gold, precious stones, spices.

HORSES

KEVEH

Tadmor

KINGS OF ARAM

Hamath

Damascus

Jerusalem

COPPER

The Red Sea

Ezion-geber

Sidon

Tyre

TIMBER

Gaza

CHARIOTS

Tarshish fleet brings gold, silver, apes, baboons, ivory.

The Great Sea

On

Noph (Memphis)

From Ophir: gold, Almug wood, precious stones.

of Solomon, silver became as common as ordinary stones which cover the environs of Jerusalem. The highly valued cedar wood, imported from Phoenicia, became as common as the must less prestigious sycamore wood which heretofore, it would appear, had been used for building purposes (10:27).[14]

The source of Solomon's enormous silver reserves was his control of chariot and horse trading. He secured horses from Egypt and Kue, i.e., Cilicia in Asia Minor. During this period the Egyptians imported wood from Syria in order to manufacture chariots. Since Solomon controlled all the important trade routes from Cilicia and Egypt to Syria, he seems to have held a virtual monopoly on the horse and chariot trade in this region of the world. Thus, the neo-Hittite and Aramean kings to the north depended upon Solomon for Egyptian chariots, while the Egyptians depended on him for Cilician horses. As the middleman in this lucrative trade, Solomon no doubt made a handsome profit for himself. The established rate of exchange was 150 shekels (3.75 lbs.; $100 BV) for one Cilician horse, and for one Egyptian chariot 600 shekels (15 lbs.; $400 BV) (10:28-29).

THE FAILURES OF SOLOMON
Wives Multiplied
1 Kings 11:1-13

Solomon violated the law regarding kings by multiplying wives for himself. Besides his marriage to Pharaoh's daughter, the uniqueness of which has already been indicated, Solomon married many other *"strange"* or foreign women.[15] If chapters 9-10 describe the fame of Solomon, chapter 11 sets forth his shame.

A. Extent of the Marriages (1 Kgs 11:1-3).

Among his wives were women of Moab and Ammon. Ammonites and Moabites were not to be received into the congregation of the Lord until the tenth generation (cf. Deut 23:3). While marriage to a woman of these nations was not, strictly speaking, forbidden, such marriages must have been regarded as especially repugnant. The Edomites were viewed with more favor, being allowed to enter the congregation of the Lord in the third generation (cf. Deut 23:7).

The mention of Sidonians among the wives of Solomon gave rise to the tradition that Solomon married a daughter of Hiram.[16] The *"Hittite"* women were from those northern kingdoms which had once been subject to the Hittite empire prior to its collapse about 1200 BC. With the exception of Jehoram who married Athaliah, the semi-Phoenician daughter of Ahab, none of Solomon's successors on the throne of Judah married foreign princesses so far as the record goes.[17]

The law expressly forbade intermarriage with daughters of any of the seven nations of Canaan (Exod 34:11-16; Deut 7:1-4). Strictly speaking, only Solomon's Hittite, and possibly his Sidonian, wives violated this prohibition. The Sidonians were considered Canaanites. The rationale for the prohibition to the seven nations of Canaan, however, applied equally to all other idolaters, viz., *"they will turn away your sons from following after me"* (Deut 7:4). Thus by marrying any of these foreign women Solomon was certainly violating the spirit of the law.

Solomon clung unto these women in love. By placing the object of the preposition before the verb, the Hebrew suggests an emphasis which may be missed in the English: *"even them Solomon clung to."* Instead of clinging to God as commanded in the law (Deut 4:4; 10:20; 30:20), Solomon chose to cling to his women! (11:2).

B. Reason for the Marriages (1 Kgs 11:3).

Seven hundred of Solomon's wives were princesses, i.e., members of the royal houses of neighboring nations. His concubines—wives of secondary rank—numbered three hundred. These numbers, when compared with the practice of other monarchs of the near East, are not found at all to be incredible.[18]

The vast number of the harem suggests that Solomon was not motivated by sensuality in gathering these women. The mention that 700 of these women were *princesses* suggests that his object was to enhance his renown. As he exceeded other kings in glory, wisdom, chariots and horses, so he must also supersede them in the number of his wives. Pride rather than passion drove this king to violate God's command against the multiplication of wives (10:2).

C. Influence of the Marriages (1 Kgs 11:4-8).

Solomon paid the price for his pride. When he was old, i.e., toward the end of his reign, those women turned his heart away from God. This need not be taken to mean that Solomon himself took part in idolatrous practices, but only that he sanctioned such practices in the vicinity of Jerusalem.[19] In his early reign he had been uneasy at the mere presence of Pharaoh's daughter in the city of David; but now he crowned the hills overlooking the temple precincts with monuments to idolatry.

Three of the deities to whom Solomon showed favor are named in the text. First, Solomon *"went after"* Ashtoreth *"the goddess of the Sidonians."*[20] Ashtoreth is the Hebrew name of Astarte, one of the principal Phoenician goddesses. She was viewed by her adherents as a fertility goddess. As such she was worshiped by means of sexual intercourse in her temples. Small clay figurines of her with her breasts and pudenda accentuated have been found in Palestinian excavations in great abundance.[21]

Second, Solomon went after Milcom or Molech *"the abomination of the Ammonites."* The worship of this deity involved the sacrifice of little children. Whether or not Solomon permitted the child sacrifice rituals to be performed in Jerusalem cannot be determined.[22] Third, Solomon built a high place for Chemosh, *"the abomination of the Moabites."* Chemosh seems to be the Moabite name for the god called by the Ammonites Molech.[23]

The extent to which *"Solomon went after"* pagan gods is spelled out in the text. First, his heart was not wholly devoted to Yahweh as the heart of David had been. Second, Solomon did not follow Yahweh fully as David had done. Third, he did evil in the eyes of Yahweh by building shrines for the foreign gods. Two high places were located on the Mount of Olives east of Jerusalem, a site elsewhere called *"the mount of corruption"* (2 Kgs 23:13). The women made use of these sanctuaries by offering incense and animal sacrifices to their respective deities. The text never asserts that Solomon personally worshiped in the temples (11:7-8).

THE TROUBLES OF SOLOMON
1 Kings 11:9-40

At the close of the account of Solomon the author of Kings has gathered all the significant information concerning the adversaries of this king. These accounts have been placed here because (1) it is the habit of the author to collect into one passage material related to a particular facet of Solomon's reign; (2) it was only in his later life that these adversaries materially affected his position; and (3) because these troubles are regarded as a chastisement for Solomon's sin which has just been described. One should not conclude that these adversaries appeared only in the last days of the king.

A. The Lord's Anger (1 Kgs 11:9-13).

Yahweh was extremely angry with Solomon because his allegiance to him had grown cold. Exceptional favors had been granted to this king. Twice he had been permitted to receive direct revelations from God (cf. 1 Kgs 3:5; 9:2). Solomon had been solemnly warned about pursuing other gods, but he had disregarded this command of the Lord (11:9-10).

Chart No. 39

DIVINE COMMUNICATION TO SOLOMON			
TIME	REFERENCE	MEANS	SUMMARY
At the Beginning of his Reign	1 Kgs 3:5-14	In a Dream	Solomon Promised Riches and Honor as Well as Wisdom
During the Temple Construction	1 Kgs 6:11-13	By a Prophet	If he is faithful, God will Dwell in the Temple
At the Height of his Prosperity	1 Kgs 9:1-9	In a Dream	Warning that Apostasy would Lead to National Destruction
At the Time of his Apostasy	1 Kgs 11:11-13	By a Prophet	Announcement that the Kingdom would be taken from Solomon's Son

In his anger the Lord pronounced a solemn judgment upon Solomon. No doubt the pronouncement came through the mouth of one of God's prophets, for it hardly seems likely that God would condescend to grant this apostate prince yet another direct revelation. The message is dreadful. Because Solomon had failed to live up to his obligations before God, the Lord would rend the kingdom from him. A mere servant would be heir to all of Solomon's glory and treasure (11:11).

God tempered the judgment with two gracious and merciful limitations. (1) The blow would not fall until after the death of Solomon; and (2) the disruption would only be partial. One tribe, Judah, would remain under the Davidic dynasty.[24] Two reasons are given for these merciful limitations. Judgment would be mitigated (1) for David's sake, i.e., because of the promises made to David (cf. 2 Sam 7:13); and (2) for Jerusalem's sake. God had chosen Jerusalem as the site of his temple and as the appropriate capital of his earthly kingdom (11:12-13).

B. The Rebellion of Hadad (1 Kgs 11:14-22).

The first adversary raised up by Yahweh was Hadad, a member of the royal family of Edom. The Edomites had initiated hostilities with Israel by a fierce attack in the days of David. After general Joab had buried the dead Israelites, he led the armies of David into Edom in retaliation. The campaign there lasted six months. Every male who could be captured was executed (11:14-16).

To escape the slaughter, Hadad and some of the royal servants took refuge in the trackless desert of Midian south of Edom. Eventually he and his company pressed on toward Egypt, stopping in Paran to secure guides who would lead them across the Sinaitic peninsula to the kingdom of the Pharaohs (11:17-18a).

In Egypt Hadad and his party were graciously received. The Pharaoh gave to the young Edomite prince a house, land and provisions for his table. In due time Pharaoh gave Hadad the hand of his sister-in-law, the sister of Tahpenes[25] the queen consort. This action reflects the political hopes which the Egyptians pinned on the Edomite heir. Hadad's wife gave birth to a son, Genubath, who was reared in Pharaoh's palace with all the privileges of an Egyptian prince (11:18b-20).

When Hadad heard about the deaths of David and Joab, he

requested that Pharaoh might allow him to return to his own land. Pharaoh was reluctant to see Hadad, who now had lived in Egypt for at least twenty-five years, leave his court. Nonetheless, Hadad insisted that he be allowed to return to Edom. When he returned Hadad fomented rebellion against Solomon in Edom. Whether he succeeded in wresting any territory from Solomon's control or merely acted as a constant menace to the Israelite merchant caravans is unclear (11:21,22,25).

C. Rezon of Damascus (1 Kgs 11:23-25).

The second adversary raised up by God as an antagonist to Solomon was Rezon,[26] an Aramean who established himself in Damascus. Damascus, as part of the kingdom of Zobah, fell to David when Hadadezer of Zobah was defeated (cf. 2 Sam 8:3-12; 10:6-19). At that time Rezon deserted his master Hadadezer. He became the leader of an outlaw gang which preyed on Israelite interests in the north "all the days of Solomon." At some point—probably late in Solomon's reign—Rezon led a group of warriors against Damascus. He captured the city, settled in it, and finally established himself as the ruling power there. Eventually the entire region of Aram recognized Rezon as their king. Thus Solomon was faced with opposition simultaneously on the northern and southern frontiers of his empire.

D. Jeroboam the Ephraimite (1 Kgs 11:26-40).

The third adversary of Solomon was an Israelite, Jeroboam the son of Nebat. He was an Ephrathite, i.e., an Ephraimite (cf. Judg 12:5; 1 Sam 1:1) from the insignificant village of Zeredah. His mother's name, Zeruah, means *"leper."* She was a widow.[27] Perhaps these facts are recorded to emphasize Jeroboam's humble origins (11:26).

Because of his industry, Jeroboam had been appointed superintendent over the workers of the house of Joseph (Ephraimites) who had been drafted for service in the corvée. For the proud Ephraimites to be forced to labor on fortifications around Jerusalem must have been particularly galling. Jeroboam sensed the unrest among the workmen. He *"lifted up his hand against the king."* No account of this rebellion has survived. It apparently took place at the time Solomon was building the Millo (cf.1 Kgs 9:25), about the twenty-fifth year of his reign (11:27-28).

Ahijah the Shilonite (i.e., one from the town of Shiloh)[28] sought out Jeroboam and privately conferred with him in a field near Jerusalem. The prophet was clad in a new outer garment which he took in his hands and tore into twelve pieces. Israel is always reckoned as made up of twelve tribes. Since the tribe of Joseph had been divided into two, Ephraim and Manasseh, the total should have risen to thirteen. Levi, however, was omitted from the count because that tribe was scattered throughout all Israel. Ahijah instructed the young Ephraimite to take ten of the pieces of cloth, symbolizing the ten tribes which God would rend from the hand of Solomon (11:29-31).

One tribe, Benjamin, would be left to the rulers of Judah (cf. 1 Kgs 12:21; 2 Chr 11:3,23). God's graciousness to the house of David is based on two principles: (1) God's love for and promises to David himself; and (2) God's love for and choice of Jerusalem as his holy dwelling place. Judah and Benjamin shared possession of Jerusalem (11:32).

The disruption of the kingdom came about because of the idolatrous leanings of Solomon. The king certainly tolerated and perhaps subsidized the worship of Ashtoreth, Chemosh, Milcom and other deities. He had rejected the Davidic path of absolute commitment to God. Nevertheless, the divine judgment against the house of David was tempered in two ways. (1) The entire kingdom would not be taken from the Davidites; and (2) the judgment would be deferred until after the death of Solomon. God's graciousness to Solomon was based on his faithfulness to David. Solomon may have broken his covenant with God, but God would not break his covenant with David (11:33-36).

A major theme is reiterated here. David would always *"have a lamp"* before God. The lighted lamp is frequently used in the Old Testament as a symbol of life, happiness, and prosperity. The figure may have been derived from the custom of keeping a lamp burning in the tent or home. The extinction of the lamp symbolized the breaking up of the home.[29]

In Ahijah's closing words Jeroboam was assured that he would indeed become king. As such his every desire would be gratified. If he faithfully followed the Davidic path of steadfast obedience to God, Yahweh would (1) be with Jeroboam, and (2) give him a sure house, i.e., family or dynasty. Jeroboam was advised, however, that it was not God's intention to take away the kingdom from the house of David forever (11:37-38). Ahijah here intimates what later prophets specifically would predict, *viz.*, that in the future, the kingdom would be restored to the house of David.

As a consequence of Jeroboam's rebellion, Solomon sought to slay his Ephraimite overseer. Perhaps the rebellion was triggered by Ahijah's private prophecy. Still in no way would this justify any treasonous act on the part of Jeroboam. The fact that God had revealed his purposes to the young man was no reason for him to attempt to bring these things to pass. The rebellion was all the more inexcusable in view of the fact that Ahijah specifically had declared that Solomon was to retain the kingdom during his lifetime (11:40a).

Jeroboam fled for his life to Shishak in Egypt.[30] The fact that this pharaoh granted asylum to the fugitive proves that he was no friend of Solomon. The official attitude of Egypt towards Israel had drastically changed since the days when one of Shishak's predecessors had given Solomon the hand of his daughter in marriage (11:40b).

CONCLUSION OF SOLOMON'S REIGN
1 Kgs 11:42-43//2 Chr 9:29-31

Scripture writers list four sources which they used, guided by the Holy Spirit, in reconstructing the events of Solomon's reign: (1) the book of the acts of Solomon (1 Kgs 11:41); (2) the book of Nathan the prophet; (3) the prophecy of Ahijah the Shilonite; and (4) the visions of Iddo the seer concerning Jeroboam the son of Nebat. Neither the royal nor prophetic records of Solomon's reign are extant.

Like David, Solomon ruled for forty years. Scholars have computed that he could not have been more than sixty at the time of his death.[31] He was buried in the city of David—that portion of Jerusalem which David had conquered from the Jebusites. Solomon was succeeded by Rehoboam, his only son to be mentioned in Scripture.

ENDNOTES

1. The Berkeley Version computes the value of this gold loan to have been about $3,500,000.

2. Old Testament Galilee was not nearly so extensive as the territory called by that name in the New Testament. See Josh 20:7; 2 Kgs 15:29; Isa 9:1.

3. Three views can be found in the commentaries: (1) the cities were a gift in appreciation for the help Hiram had rendered throughout the twenty years of building (Slotki); (2) Solomon was forced to cede these towns to Hiram because he could not keep up with his annual financial obligations (Olmstead); and (3) the towns were put up as security for the loan of 120 talents of gold.

4. Keil, recently supported by Gray, holds that Cabul means "mortgaged." Others claim the name means "nothing" or "worthless."

5. Though Gezer was allotted to the tribe of Ephraim (Josh 16:3), and designated as a Levitical city (Josh 21:21), the Canaanite inhabitants had never been displaced. At some point Pharaoh captured the city. He subsequently gave Gezer to his daughter as a wedding present. The city was then rebuilt and fortified by Solomon.

6. Remains of stables dating to the time of Solomon have been found at Hazor and at Taanach four miles south of Megiddo.

7. According to 2 Chr 8:18 the fleet brought back 450 talents (17 tons). Probably Kings gives the amount of gold that actually entered the coffers of Solomon, while Chronicles includes thirty additional talents which went to Hiram for his services.

8. John Gray, *I & II Kings* in "The Old Testament Library" (Philadelphia: Westminster, 1970), p. 241. Josephus (*Ant.* 8.5.3) records a similar battle of wits between Solomon and Hiram.

9. Some think the *"ascent"* was an arched bridge or viaduct over the Tyropoeon Valley between Mt. Zion and the western wall of the temple area. Such a bridge would have been at least 350 feet high. Others, however, think the reference is not to some architectural achievement, but rather to the splendid retinue which accompanied Solomon on his visits to the temple.

10. Ethiopian Christians take these words as a basis for their belief that the queen bore a son by Solomon—Melimelek—from whom the recent monarchs of Ethiopia claimed to derive their descent.

11. The text does not necessarily imply that this income was annual. It may refer to the total income in Solomon's most prosperous year.

12. That the gold entirely covered and concealed the beautiful ivory is not likely. Some scholars think that the throne had ivory inlay rather than being made of solid ivory. See Leo L. Honor, *Book of Kings I* in "The Jewish Commentary for Bible Readers" (New York: Union of American Hebrew Congregations, 1955), p. 147.

13. Most commentators insist that the fleet mentioned in 10:22 is the same as the fleet mentioned in 9:26-28. The term *"Tarshish fleet"* is then taken to be a general name for all large, ocean-going ships or merchant vessels. That the term *can* have this meaning is clear from 1 Kgs 22:48, *"Jehoshaphat made ships of Tarshish to go to Ophir."* 2 Chr 9:21, however, proves that Tarshish in reference to Solomon's fleet is a geographical designation.

14. The sycamore fig is a large, well-rooted, spreading tree which grew profusely in the Shephelah or lowland region of Judah. The tree was considered important enough during the reign of David to have a royal overseer (1 Chr 27:28).

15. Solomon must have married Naamah the Ammonitess a couple of years before he became king, and thus before he married the Egyptian princess. Her son Rehoboam was forty-one when Solomon died at the end of a forty year reign (1 Kgs 14:21; 2 Chr 12:13).

16. Meander of Tyre states that Solomon married the daughter of Hiram. Quoted by Clement of Alexandria, *Strom.* 1.114.2.

17. Honor, *op. cit.*, p. 151.

18. Joseph Hammond, *I Kings* in "The Pulpit Commentary" (New York: Funk and Wagnalls, 1909), p. 221. Darius Codomanus took with him on his expedition against Alexander 360 female attendants.

19. A king who actually engaged in idolatry is said to have *"served"* other gods (cf. 1 Kgs 16:31; 22:53; 2 Kgs 16:3 etc.). The phrase *"went after other gods"* is sometimes used of actual idolatry (Deut 11:28; 13:2; 28:14); but in the majority of passages, even this phrase is joined to some more precise phrase (e.g., *"and served them"* or *"and worshiped them"*) when participatory idolatry is intended.

20. The singular form of the name is found only here and in 2 Kgs 23:13. More commonly the plural Ashtaroth is used in general statements about Canaanite paganism.

21. Millar Burrows, *What Mean These Stones* (New Haven: American Schools of Oriental Research, 1941), pp. 230f.

22. Human sacrifice among the Israelites is first explicitly attested under Ahaz in Judah (2 Kgs 16:3), and under Hoshea (2 Kgs 17:17) in Israel.

23. Gray, *op. cit.*, pp. 258f. Jephthah's reply to the Ammonites (Judg 11:24) seems to support this conclusion.

24. The tribes of Benjamin and Simeon were also a part of the kingdom left to the descendants of Solomon, but they were too small and insignificant to be specified at this point.

25. The name Tahpenes has not been identified in the few existing contemporary Egyptian sources. Some Egyptologists, however, are inclined to relate it to a name of a princess appearing on a statue dating to the twenty-first dynasty. See Abraham Malamat, "The Kingdom of David and Solomon in its contact with Egypt and Aram Naharaim" in *The Biblical Archaeologist*

Reader, 2 ; ed. Edward F. Campbell and David Noel Freedman (Garden City, NJ: Doubleday, 1964) pp. 90-91.

26. Some scholars think that Rezon is a variant of Hezion who appears to have founded the Damascus dynasty in 1 Kgs 15:18. Others think Hezion was the proper name of this king and Rezon was his title. Still others assume that after Rezon, Hezion founded a new dynasty in Damascus. See Benjamin Mazar, "The Aramean Empire and its Relations with Israel" in *The Biblical Archaeologist Reader, 2* (Garden City, NJ: Doubleday, 1964), pp. 133-134.

27. The Greek version says that Jeroboam's mother was a *harlot*. This would appear to be a deliberate effort to discredit Jeroboam.

28. The entire city of Shiloh had been destroyed by the Philistines in the days of Samuel (1 Sam 4:11; cf. Jer 7:12). A limited settlement, however, may have sprung up on the site of the former city.

29. Honor, *op. cit.,* 163. The allusion to David having a lamp in Jerusalem is repeated in 1 Kgs 15:4; 2 Kgs 8:19 and 2 Chr 21:7.

30. Shishak is the first Pharaoh in the Bible who can be identified with certainty. He is known in Egyptian history as Sheshonk I who began to reign between 988 and 980 BC.

31. I.W. Slotki, *Kings* in "Soncino Books of the Bible" (London: Soncino, 1950), p. 90.

CHAPTER TWENTY-EIGHT

The Division of the Kingdom
1 Kings 12-14

When Solomon died in 930 BC the kingdom appeared to be in good shape outwardly. Yet because of the idolatry introduced in his last days, the seeds of kingdom disintegration had already been sown. Even so, the speed with which that glorious kingdom shattered, and the devastating spiritual, political and economic consequences of that event are somewhat shocking and certainly sad.

THE ASSEMBLY AT SHECHEM
1 Kings 12:1-24

Rehoboam was forty-one at the time his father Solomon died (1 Kgs 14:21; 2 Chr 12:13). His succession to the throne does not seem to have been questioned in Judah. The northern tribes, however, insisted on their right to ratify the coronation of the new king. All Israel (the northern tribes) assembled at Shechem, the most important city in Ephraim, *"to make him king."* They had no concrete plans for rebellion at this time. Nonetheless, these tribes were disgruntled because of Solomon's high-handed tactics and rigorous taxation policies. Their insistence that Rehoboam meet with them on their own territory should have been a clear indication that they would brook no negative response to their demands (12:1).

A. Israel's Request (1 Kgs 12:1-5//2 Chr 10:1-19).

Jeroboam son of Nebat served as the spokesman for the dissident tribes at Shechem. Since the time of his abortive rebellion against Solomon, Jeroboam had resided in Egypt. When Solomon died, the elders of Israel immediately sent to Egypt to invite Jeroboam to speak on their behalf to Solomon's would-be successor. Putting forth Jeroboam as their spokesman was a second clear indication that the elders of the north did not mean to be ignored (12:2-3).

The dissidents complained that Solomon had placed a heavy yoke upon them. They requested that Rehoboam grant them a measure of relief. If this relief was forthcoming, the elders promised to serve Rehoboam. There is, of course, an implied threat in this conditional pledge of allegiance. The grievance of the northern tribes was real. While it is true that the reign of Solomon had brought prosperity to Israel, that national glory had been achieved only by means of a galling conscription and heavy taxation (12:4).

Rehoboam wisely postponed his decision regarding the northern ultimatum for three days. The new king did not suffer from impetuosity. He evidently sensed how much depended upon his reply. If he complied with the request, he was accepting the crown conditionally. On the other hand, if he denied their request, he faced the danger of revolt. Viewing Rehoboam's proposed three day delay as a reasonable interval, the dissidents peacefully departed (12:5).

B. Counselors' Recommendations (1 Kgs 12:6-11).

Rehoboam turned for advice first to the older men who were experienced in statecraft from their service in the court of Solomon. They advised him to "be a servant" unto the people for this day, i.e., accede to their demands. A little humility at this point would gain for the new king many servants forever (12:6-7).

Rehoboam was not in a mood to compromise. Spurning the

advice of his father's counselors, Rehoboam turned to young men who served as his personal courtiers and counselors. These were men who had grown up with Rehoboam in Solomon's harem. Of these friends Rehoboam asked the same question which he had asked the elders with three slight changes. (1) He emphasized the pronoun "*you*" in the Hebrew as though he anticipated a very different answer from that which he had heard from the elders. In the words "*that we may respond*" he identified these young men with himself. (3) He repeated the request of the dissidents, no doubt expressing his contempt for their audacity by the tone of his voice (12:8-9).

The young men viewed the request of the dissidents as presumptuous. They urged the king to follow a "get tough" policy. They suggested that he use what must have been a proverbial expression, "*My little finger is thicker than the loins of my father.*" The idea here is that Rehoboam's weakness would be stronger than his father's strength. The advice of the young counselors was based on the premise that appeasement would not work. Any attempt to placate the people by kindly words, they feared, would be interpreted as weakness (12:10-11).

C. Rehoboam's Reply (1 Kgs 12:12-15).

On the third day Jeroboam and the representatives of the northern tribes appeared again before Rehoboam. The new king spoke harshly to the petitioners, repeating verbatim the declaration of his young advisers. Whereas Solomon had chastised them with whips, Rehoboam promised to use "*scorpions.*" This term may be a reference to a particular kind of whip, one with barbed points like the point of a scorpion's sting. On the other hand, the term may be purely figurative for an even greater pain to be administered by Rehoboam (12:12-14).

Rehoboam's pride is inexcusable and reprehensible. Nevertheless, Yahweh used his incident to accomplish his purpose of bringing about a division within the kingdom. God may even use the sinful acts of men to accomplish his will. What happened at Shechem led to the fulfillment of the predictions made by the prophet Ahijah to Jeroboam some two decades earlier (12:15).

D. Israel's Rebellion (1 Kgs 12:16-20).

After briefly consulting among themselves, the representatives of the northern tribes defiantly replied to the king: *"What portion have we in David?"* i.e., we are receiving no consideration from David's seed, so why should we yield homage to him?[1] The dissidents further declared, *"Neither have we inheritance in the son of Jesse,"* i.e., his tribe is not ours; his interests are not ours. *"To your tents, O Israel,"* they shouted. As they angrily stomped out of the audience chamber they shouted one last warning, *"Now see to your own house, David,"* i.e., let the seed of David henceforth reign only over the tribe of Judah. With these ominous words the northern representatives departed for their tents, i.e., dwellings (12:16).

Those members of the ten tribes who happened to be settled within the territory of Judah (e.g. the Simeonites) rendered homage to Rehoboam. So also did the tribe of Benjamin (cf. v. 21). Probably the fact that Benjamin shared the magnificent city of Jerusalem with Judah induced that tribe to adhere to the house of David. In any case, from this point on, the term *"Israel"* is used by the author of Kings in its restricted sense as referring to the northern kingdom (12:17).

Rehoboam was determined to demonstrate to the rebels that he would not be intimidated. He therefore sought immediately to force the northern tribes to pay tribute and thereby recognize his sovereignty. The king ordered Adoram, the superintendent of forced labor, to collect the tribute.[2] The rebels stoned Adoram to death. Rehoboam realized the gravity of the situation. He therefore hastened south to the safety of Jerusalem (12:18).

The representatives of the northern tribes returned to their respective communities and reported what had transpired at Shechem. When the people heard that Jeroboam had returned from Egypt, they were anxious to crown him king. The text gives no indication where the ceremony took place. Most likely the event took place at Shechem. With the coronation of Jeroboam the secession of the northern tribes was complete (12:19-21).

E. Rehoboam's Reaction (1 Kgs 12:21-24//2 Chr 11:1-4).

Rehoboam was determined to crush the northern uprising with military force. He gathered a force of some 180,000 men from Judah and Benjamin.³ Crushing this rebellion by force, however, did not meet with the approval of God. Shemaiah the *"the man of God,"* i.e., prophet, ordered a halt to plans for an invasion of the north. Two reasons are given for the prohibition. First, the northern tribes were still *"brethren"* of those who lived in the south. Second, the national disruption was God-ordained. Thus a prophet of Judah (Shemaiah) confirmed what a prophet of Israel (Ahijah) had predicted. Because of the prophetic prohibition, the men of Judah called off the planned attack on the north and returned to their homes.

Chart No. 40

TWO KINGDOMS CONTRASTED	
ISRAEL	**JUDAH**
Northern Kingdom	Southern Kingdom
Ten Tribes	Two Tribes
First King: Jeroboam	First King: Rehoboam
Capitals: Shechem, Samaria	Capital: Jerusalem
Temples: Dan, Bethel, Samaria	Temple: Jerusalem
Dynasties: 9	Dynasty: 1
Kings: 19	Kings: 19 + a Queen
All Bad Kings	Good and Bad Kings
Duration: 209 Years	Duration: 344 Years
Destruction: 722 BC	Destruction: 586 BC
Land of Exile: Assyria	Land of Exile: Babylon
Longest Reign: Jeroboam II	Longest Reign: Manasseh
41 Years	55 Years
Shortest Reign: Zimri	Shortest Reign: Jehoahaz
7 Days	3 Months
Last King: Hoshea	Last King: Zedekiah

APOSTASY IN THE NORTH
1 Kings 12:25-14:20

Jeroboam's first concern as king of Israel was to find a suitable capital. First he *"built,"* i.e., fortified, Shechem, the most prominent city in the north. Then he was forced to temporarily move the seat of government across the Jordan to Penuel in the area of Gilead. This action may have been made necessary by the invasion of Pharaoh Shishak about which the text will speak later (12:25).

A. Worship Symbols (1 Kgs 12:26-30//2 Chr 11:1-4).

Another urgent concern of Jeroboam was the creation of a cult in the north which would rival the divinely revealed religion practiced in Jerusalem. He feared that if people continued to travel to the temple three times each year for the major festivals, the sentiment for the house of David would reassert itself in the north (12:26-27).

After taking counsel of his closest advisers, Jeroboam determined that the new religion should center about the images of two golden calves. He erected shrines for these calves at two convenient locations, Dan and Bethel. Propaganda poured forth from the palace in an attempt to persuade the people to change their religious affiliation. The king argued that it was inconvenient for his people to travel to Jerusalem for worship. Furthermore, he presented the golden calves as symbols of the divine personages who had led Israel out of Egypt. Jeroboam intended to link his calves to the calf erected by Aaron at Mt. Sinai (cf. Exod 32:4-8), i.e., he passed off his innovations as a restoration of something old. The people of the north zealously embraced their new religion (12:28-30).

Jeroboam's effort could hardly have succeeded if the calves erected at Bethel and Dan had been presented as images of the invisible Yahweh. The Semitic peoples never represented their gods zoomorphically. The calves must have represented the animal upon which Yahweh was understood to ride.[4] Eventually, however, theological distinctions faded. The calves became identified with Yahweh himself in popular religious understanding. For this reason Hosea regarded the calves as idols (Hos 13:2).

B. Worship System (1 Kgs 12:31-33).

Jeroboam built shrines on high places for his new faith. He made priests of *"all classes of the people"* thus rejecting the priestly prerogatives of the tribe of Levi. He ordered a great festival to be held on the fifteenth day of the eighth month, one month after the appointed time for the feast of tabernacles.[5] Jeroboam himself officiated as high priest, offering sacrifices and incense on special occasions before the calves which he had made.[6] Every aspect of the religion in the north was devised in Jeroboam's own heart (12:31-33).

Chart No. 41

THE DIVIDED MONARCHY
930-722 BC

Israel had Nineteen Kings

| 930 | HOSTILITY (Quarreling) | 885 | HARMONY (Embracing) | 841 | HUMILIATION (Bowing) | 790 | HEYDAY (Growing) | 750 | HOMAGE (Parting) | 722 |

Judah had Twelve Kings

Council at Shechem

Fall of Samaria

CALF WORSHIP CONDEMNED
1 Kings 13:1-34

Because Jeroboam had initiated his apostate religion in Israel, he lost the support of the prophetic order. He was denounced by a prophet from Judah as well as the prophet Ahijah within his own kingdom.

A. An Urgent Mission (1 Kgs 13:1-10).

God did not permit the inauguration of Jeroboam's first great feast at Bethel to proceed without prophetic protest. An unidentified prophet[7] from Judah was dispatched to deliver the divine word of warning to the king. With a precision rare, but not unique,[8] in Bible prophecy, Josiah,[9] a man who would not be born for some three hundred years, was named as the instrument who would bring God's wrath upon Bethel and its altar (13:1-2). For the fulfillment of this prediction see 2 Kings 23:20.

To give credibility to his long-range prediction, the prophet offered an immediate sign of confirmation. The altar would be rent and the ashes (lit., fatness, i.e., the fat of the sacrificial victim) poured out.

These words brought the proceedings to an immediate halt. In violent rage Jeroboam put forth his hand against the prophet, at the same time ordering him to be seized. The arm of the king, however, was stricken with paralysis so that he could no longer control it. At that very instant the altar was smitten by God as the prophet had announced. In one dramatic act God (1) demonstrated that the sacrifice being offered was unacceptable; (2) symbolized the ultimate overthrow of that altar; and (3) humbled a proud king (13:3-5).

Alarmed by the judgment he had experienced in his own person, Jeroboam begged the prophet to entreat God on his behalf. Sensing that he was no longer in danger, the man of God prayed. The king's arm was made whole again. In grateful appreciation—and perhaps with some ulterior motive—Jeroboam invited the prophet to the palace for refreshment (13:6-7).

The man of God refused to accept the hospitality of the apostate king. No matter what inducements might be offered, he was under orders to return immediately to Judah by a different route. Sharing in a meal would be a sign of close fellowship. This prophet was to leave no doubt that the God he served had repudiated the northern calf cult. The prophet probably returned by a different route in order to make it more difficult for his movements to be traced (13:8-10).

B. A Brazen Deception (1 Kgs 13:11-19).

While devout worshipers of Yahweh had emigrated to Judah (cf. 2 Chr 11:13-16), at least one old prophet remained in Bethel. This man's commitment level was obviously quite low; but he could not personally participate in the apostate worship in Bethel. His sons, however, had witnessed the events in the temple. The account of the fearless pronouncement of the man of God stirred the old prophet's heart. After ascertaining the route taken by the young prophet, the Bethel prophet rode off after him. The text gives no clue as to the motivation here. Did he merely crave prophetic fellowship? Or was it his intention to persuade the man of God to reverse the pronouncement he had made against the Bethel cult? (13:11-13).

The old prophet caught up with the man of God taking a brief respite under an oak along the road to Judah. When he invited the man to his home in Bethel, the old prophet was rebuffed with the same words used in response to Jeroboam's invitation. He then fabricated a story about an angelic visitation in which he was told to bring the man of God back to Bethel.[10] The motives of the old prophet are not clear. Putting his actions in the best possible light, his lie was born out of an ardent desire for fellowship with the man of God. On the other hand, he may have been acting on behalf of his king (13:14-19).[11]

C. An Ominous Prediction (1 Kgs 13:20-26).

The man of God believed the lie. He returned to Bethel to share the hospitality of the old prophet. During the meal the old prophet received a genuine revelation from God. The Holy Spirit compelled him to cry out against the man of God. He who denounced disobedience in Jeroboam is now himself denounced. The rebuke was followed by a devastating announcement: "Your body shall not come to the grave of your fathers." Part of the punishment of the old prophet was that he was forced (1) to admit that he had told a lie; and (2) to pronounce the doom of a godly man (13:20-22).

The gloomy meal at an end, the Bethel prophet saddled his donkey for the man of God who seems to have been traveling on foot. As he was making his way south toward Judah, a lion pounced upon the man of God and slew him. That this death was no accident is indicated by the peculiar behavior of the donkey and the lion, both of which simply stood near the corpse of the fallen prophet. Those who traveled that highway reported in Bethel the corpse and the strange behavior of the two animals. The old prophet knew instantly the identity of the corpse and the reason for the tragedy (13:23-26).

D. A Bitter Lamentation (1 Kgs 13:27-32).

Immediately the old prophet went to the spot where the man of God had fallen. He found the scene just as the travelers had reported it. Both the lion and the donkey were still there. With great sorrow the old prophet brought the corpse back to Bethel. There he bestowed profound respect upon that corpse by burying it in his own grave. He mourned for the young man with the customary lamentation formula: *"Alas, my brother!"* He instructed his sons to bury him beside the man of God. The old prophet was now convinced that the predictions regarding the Bethel altar and other sanctuaries in the north would come to pass.[12]

E. A Defiant Reaction (1 Kgs 13:33-34).

The dramatic demonstration at the Bethel temple and the subsequent death of the man of God for disobeying the word of God failed to make any lasting impression on the apostate Jeroboam. Shortly after these events the king returned to his policy of appointing priests from the population in general rather than restricting that high privilege, as the law required, to the sons of Aaron. Because of his contemptuous defiance of the law of God, Jeroboam forfeited his claims to all promises made to him by Ahijah the prophet (cf. 1 Kgs 11:37f.). From the moment he introduced the religious schism into Israel, his dynasty was doomed to destruction.

ADJUSTMENTS IN JUDAH
2 Chronicles 11:5-23

At the time of the schism of 930 BC Judah had several advantages over her sister kingdom to the north. Rehoboam had the privilege and advantage of ruling in Jerusalem, the city which God had chosen for his temple. The population of Judah was more heterogeneous. Furthermore, an influx of pious priests and Levites from the northern kingdom strengthened Judah in its earliest years (2 Chr 11:13-17).

Rehoboam faced some major adjustments as king of Judah. In the schism he had lost well over half the territory which his father had ruled. No longer was the Jerusalem government able to control the trade routes. The loss in revenues would be enormous. A hostile sister kingdom forced Judah to undertake emergency military construction. Rehoboam built fifteen fortified cities to protect his tiny country from any attempted invasion by Jeroboam. He stored food and weapons in each of these cities and stationed officers over them. Only in this way was he able to hold Judah and Benjamin in the face of the superior forces of his northern rival (2 Chr 11:5-12).

Though his kingdom was in the throes of poverty, Rehoboam still attempted to live in the grand style of his father Solomon. He followed his father down the path of polygamy. He had eighteen wives and sixty concubines. By these women he fathered twenty-eight sons and sixty daughters. Three of his wives (Mahalath, Abihail and Maacah) are named (2 Chr 11:18-21).[13]

Rehoboam is said to have dealt wisely with his sons. He scattered them throughout the land so as to weaken them by division. Yet he kept them all content by giving them responsibilities, abundant food, and many wives. Rehoboam designated Abijah (Abijam) as crown prince (2 Chr 11:22-23).

Rehoboam was forty-one when he began to reign. He ruled Judah seventeen years (930-913 BC).

APOSTASY IN THE SOUTH
1 Kings 14:21-31

For three years Judah walked in the way of David and Solomon. Then the southern kingdom also became involved in a great apostasy in the early years of Rehoboam. In large measure this may be attributed to the influence of Naamah, the Ammonite mother of Rehoboam (1 Kgs 14:21).[14]

A. Apostasy Described (1 Kgs 14:22-24//2 Chr 12:1).

When the kingdom of Rehoboam was secure, Judah forsook the law of Yahweh (cf. 1 Chr 12:1). The people built high places where they could worship the astral deities. They erected the pillars which symbolized Baal and the poles which were symbols of Asherah. These abominations were found throughout the land *"on every high hill and under every green tree."* Such shady spots were ideal for the immoral rites associated with the Baal cult. Most shocking of all, male cult prostitutes sprang up around the land. Whether these were homosexual or heterosexual prostitutes is uncertain. That people whom the Lord had called to holiness had adopted all of the corrupt practices of the Canaanites which God had driven out before them. They provoked the Lord to jealousy with their attachment to idols. Israel was the bride of God. Whenever the nation engaged in the worship of other gods, Scripture speaks anthropomorphically of God's jealousy.

B. Apostasy Punished (1 Kgs 14:25-28// 2 Chr 12:2-16).

Judah's apostasy was punished swiftly. In the fifth year of Rehoboam (926 BC), Pharaoh Shishak invaded the land. With Israel divided into two quarreling kingdoms, the ambitions of the Egyptians to control Palestine could be realized. A record of this invasion is inscribed on one of the pylons of the great Amon temple at Karnak (Thebes) in lower Egypt. This inscription contains the names of between fifty and sixty localities in Israel and about a hundred in Judah which were captured on this expedition (14:25).

At the approach of Shishak, Rehoboam and his people repented of their transgressions. They begged for God's mercy. God heard that prayer and spared Jerusalem from destruction at the hands of Shishak (2 Chr 12:5-8). Nevertheless, to teach his people a lesson, God permitted them to be brought under tributary obligation to Shishak. The Pharaoh took away all the treasures of the house of God and the king's palace, including the beautiful shields of gold which Solomon had hung in the house of the forest of Lebanon (14:26).

Rehoboam could do no better than to replace the golden shields with shields of bronze. These were carried by royal bodyguards whenever the king made an official visit to the temple. After the parade the shields were immediately returned to guard chambers so as to conceal from the people the humiliating fact that bronze had been substituted for gold. What a contrast! Solomon's golden shields were put on public display; but the shields of bronze were of so little value that they were stored in a guard chamber. Those bronze shields bear eloquent testimony that Rehoboam was but a pale imitation of his father (14:27-28).

A state of war existed between the sister kingdoms throughout the seventeen years in which Rehoboam and Jeroboam simultaneously reigned. Border clashes must have occurred regularly. No massive invasions, however, are reported. Rehoboam died a peaceful death. He was buried with his fathers in the city of David. He was succeeded by his son Abijah, or Abijam as it is spelled in Chronicles (14:29-31).

C. Apostasy Continued (1 Kgs 15:1-5).

Although Abijah was a worshiper of Yahweh, he continued the policy of toleration of idolatry during his three years of rule (913-910 BC). Abijah's heart *"was not perfect with Yahweh his God."* Nevertheless, God gave him a *"lamp,"* i.e., progeny, and a successor on the throne of Judah for the sake of David. For four hundred years the descendants of David continued to sit on the throne of Judah. Thus did God demonstrate his faithfulness to David, the man after God's own heart, who had observed the commandments of God except in the matter of Uriah the Hittite.

CONFLICT BETWEEN THE KINGDOMS
1 Kgs 15:7 //2 Chr 13:2-20

The state of hostilities between Israel and Judah erupted into open warfare during the days of Abijah. He invaded the northern kingdom with 400,000 men. In spite of the size of his force, Abijah was outnumbered two to one (2 Chr 13:1-3).

A. Abijah's Sermon (2 Chr 13:4-12).
The king of Judah stood on Mt. Zemaraim and preached a sermon to Jeroboam and his troops. Abijah defended the right of the house of David to rule over all Israel. He belittled Jeroboam and the *"scoundrels"* who had helped him intimidate *"the young and timid"* Rehoboam. He pointed out that Mosaic worship was being faithfully conducted in Judah, while the northern tribes were following the calf cult created by Jeroboam. He warned the northern troops that they were fighting against Yahweh. They could not possibly succeed.

B. Abijah's Victory (2 Chr 13:13-20).
While Abijah continued to ramble on with his hypocritical discourse, Jeroboam's troops were encircling the army of Judah. When the army of Judah realized it had been surrounded, the soldiers cried to Yahweh. The priests blew the sacred trumpets. Abijah's army fought with such valor that the sons of Israel fled before Judah. *"God gave them into their hand."* Israel's army suffered 500,000 casualties. *"The sons of Judah conquered because they trusted in Yahweh."* Several northern towns, including Bethel, were (temporarily) captured by Abijah. Jeroboam was not able to recover strength during the rest of the reign of Abijah.

C. Abijah's Death (2 Chr 13:21-22).

This military victory is the only distinctive accomplishment of Abijah's reign. The only other information related about this lackluster monarch is that he married fourteen wives and begat thirty-eight sons and daughters. Abijah was succeeded by his son Asa.

ENDNOTES

1. Sheba used these same words (cf. 2 Sam 20:1) to lead a rebellion against David, but the circumstances were quite different from those which launched this rebellion. Sheba believed in the dynastic principle. He believed that the scepter should remain in the house of Saul. In this case the northern representatives rejected the dynastic principle. They believed that the right to bestow sovereignty rested with the people.

2. Adoram is usually identified with Adoniram who served as superintendent of forced labor under Solomon. Cf. 1 Kgs 4:6. Rehoboam could not have chosen anyone who would have been as obnoxious to the citizens of the north.

3. The size of the force is not an overstatement in view of the fact that David's census found some 500,000 eligible for military service in Judah alone (2 Sam 24:9).

4. W.F. Albright, *From the Stone Age to Christianity* (2nd ed.; Garden City, NY: Doubleday, 1957), pp. 299f. Albright assumed that the Biblical cherubim, which were so prominent in the decorations of the temple, were winged bulls. If that is the case, Solomon's cherubim would look very much like Jeroboam's calves. Cf.1 Kgs 6:23.

5. That Jeroboam altered the month of the harvest festival merely for the sake of creating a distinction between his religion and that of Judah is not likely. The switch would make this festival more convenient for the farmers in the north where the harvest or vintage was a month later than in Judah.

6. The audacity of Jeroboam's ministering at the altar in person is underscored by the threefold repetition of the fact that he did so officiate (1 Kgs 12:32,33).

7. Josephus (*Ant.* 6.9.1) gives the name of this prophet as Yodon. The Iddo of 2 Chr 13:22 has also been nominated.

8. In Isa 44:28 and 45:1 Cyrus, the Persian king who would deliver the Jews from Babylonian exile, is named about 150 years before his birth.

9. No valid reason can be advanced for eliminating the name Josiah from this text (as proposed by Hammond), or for regarding Josiah as merely an appellation (*"he whom Yahweh sustains"*) rather than as a proper name (as Keil proposes).

10. Hammond (*op. cit.,* p. 296) argues that a communication through a celestial messenger may have been regarded as a higher form of revelation than a subjective communication to the mind of the prophet. Slotki (*op. cit.*, p. 101) argues just the opposite. Gray (*op. cit.* p. 330) suggests that the angel was mentioned in order to avoid telling a deliberate lie in the name of God, an action which might have called down immediate wrath.

11. Two more sinister interpretations have been put on the actions of the old prophet. (1) If the man of God could be lured back to Bethel to break bread, that action would in effect cancel the implied curse which he had placed on the city by refusing to eat with the king. (2) If the young prophet survived an act of direct disobedience to a command of God, the threats which he had recently made would not need to be taken seriously.

12. The mention of *"the cities of Samaria"* in 13:32 is proleptical. The city of Samaria owes its existence and name to King Omri (1 Kgs 16:24).

13. Mahalath was the cousin of the king. Her father was Jerimoth who was the son of David, probably by one of his concubines. Abihail was the daughter (or possibly granddaughter) of Eliab, David's brother. Maacah was the granddaughter of Absalom (cf. 2 Chr 13:2; 1 Kgs 15:2).

14. The name of the mother is given with every king in Judah, probably because of the position of influence which the queen mother occupied in the southern kingdom.

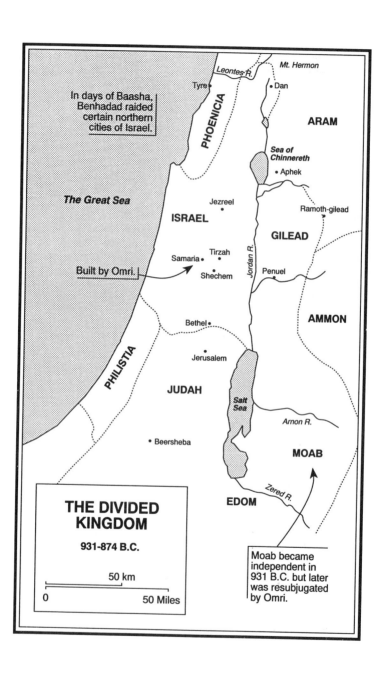

In days of Baasha, Benhadad raided certain northern cities of Israel.

Mt. Hermon

Leontes R.

Tyre

Dan

PHOENICIA

ARAM

Sea of Chinnereth

Aphek

The Great Sea

Jezreel

ISRAEL

Ramoth-gilead

GILEAD

Tirzah

Samaria

Built by Omri.

Shechem

Jordan R.

Penuel

Bethel

AMMON

Jerusalem

PHILISTIA

JUDAH

Salt Sea

Arnon R.

Beersheba

MOAB

Zered R.

EDOM

THE DIVIDED KINGDOM

931-874 B.C.

50 km

0   50 Miles

Moab became independent in 931 B.C. but later was resubjugated by Omri.

CHAPTER TWENTY-NINE

From Conflict to Cooperation
1 Kings 14-16

The political and spiritual conditions in the northern kingdom continued to worsen. In Judah, however, a valiant effort was made to bring the nation back to the Lord. A radical change in the relationship between the two kingdoms occurred sometime during the reign of Omri or Ahab. After nearly fifty years of conflict, Israel and Judah entered into a covenant of peace. Hostility gave way to harmony between the two sisters.

JUDGMENT ON JEROBOAM
1 Kings 14:1-20

Nearly the entire reign of Jeroboam is passed over in silence. At some point he had moved his capital from Penuel (12:25) to Tirzah west of the Jordan. Toward the end of his reign a crisis arose in the royal family which brought Ahijah the prophet back into the picture. The same prophet who foretold Jeroboam's reign over Israel now issued a decree of judgment against his dynasty.

A. Jeroboam's Son (1 Kgs 14:1-6).

The crown prince Abijah[1] fell desperately sick. Suspecting that the illness of his son was punitive, Jeroboam determined to secure from Ahijah some word as to the prognosis for the lad. The king's decision to seek help from Ahijah was based on the prophet's support of him in the past. He realized, however, that his own religious activities would bring only censure and perhaps an unfavorable prediction. Therefore he determined to send his wife to seek the oracle. Even she had to disguise herself so that neither the prophet nor the populace[2] would recognize her (14:1-2).

The queen was to take with her gifts to bestow on the prophet—ten loaves, some cakes, a leather bottle of honey. The present was purposely a poor one for the sake of maintaining the deception. Probably Jeroboam hoped for more than just information; he may have hoped to trick the old prophet into a declaration that the son would recover. In godless superstition he apparently believed that whatever the prophet said would come to pass even if he were tricked into saying it (14:3).

The queen hastened toward Shiloh, some thirty difficult miles from Tirzah. Ahijah spent his days there in darkness because his eyes "had set," his pupils would not adjust to the light. Probably because of his advanced age Ahijah had not followed other godly Israelites in emigrating to Judah. In any case, the attempted deception was frustrated by a direct revelation from the Lord of the blind prophet. Ahijah was told who was coming to his house and for what purpose she was coming (15:4-5).

When the queen stood at the door, the prophet ripped away the deception. He identified the queen, and asked why she had attempted to perpetrate the masquerade. No favorable oracle would fall from the lips of the prophet, for he had been instructed by God to bring to her heavy tidings (14:6).

B. Jeroboam's Sin (1 Kgs 14:7-9).

Before pronouncing sentence, the prophet briefly stated the divine case against Jeroboam. God had raised the lowly Jeroboam to the throne. The king was but God's vice-regent ruling over God's people. God had torn away a large part of the kingdom from the house of

David and had given it to Jeroboam. Yet the northern king had not walked the paths of spiritual fidelity which David had trod. In fact, Jeroboam had committed a more grievous sin than any of his predecessors whether kings or judges. In defiance of the Decalogue (Exod 20:4), Jeroboam had made *"other gods"* which were merely *"molten images,"* i.e., the calves of Bethel and Dan. God did not accept whatever theological explanation Jeroboam might have used to justify his golden calves. The king had pushed Yahweh behind his back, i.e., had contemptuously disregarded divine revelation. He thus had aroused the anger of God (14:7-9).

C. Jeroboam's House (1 Kgs 14:10-14).

The judgment which Ahijah pronounced against the house of Jeroboam would be swift and thorough. Every male of his house would be cut off. The expression *"as one takes away dung"* indicates the contempt with which the members of the royal house would be treated in that day of judgment. The corpses of those pathetic princes would be left unburied. Those who fell in the city would be eaten by roving packs of savage dogs, those who fell in the open field, by birds of prey. To the eastern mind, to be left unburied was the ultimate disgrace. Yet this is exactly what would take place because *"Yahweh has spoken"* (14:10-11).

As a sign that the long-range prediction concerning the dynasty of Jeroboam would come to pass, Ahijah gave a prediction which could be verified within a matter of hours. At the precise moment that the queen arrived back at the palace, her son would die. The entire nation would mourn for the crown prince and they would bury him. He would be the one exception to the previous prediction that the sons of Jeroboam would be left unburied. Of all the members of the royal household, this young prince alone had lived a life deserving divine recognition. These words almost suggest that Abijah dissented from his father's religious policies (14:12-13).

To accomplish his divine purposes against the house of Jeroboam, Yahweh would raise up a king which later history reveals to be Baasha (cf. 15:29). Judgment would begin that very day with the death of Abijah (14:14).

485

D. Jeroboam's Kingdom (1 Kgs 14:15-16).

The people of Israel as well as their king would taste of divine judgment. They had joined in the calf worship. Thus God would smite Israel and sweep it away as easily and swiftly as a reed might be swept down a turbulent stream. Israel would be removed from the Promised Land and carried into captivity beyond the Euphrates. This terrible fate would befall the nation because they had provoked Yahweh by making their Asherim, i.e., wooden poles representing the female deity Asherah. The old Canaanite cult flourished alongside Jeroboam's recently established calf worship in the northern kingdom. So because of all the sins inaugurated and tolerated during the reign of Jeroboam, God was forced to simply give up Israel to her enemies (14:15-16).

E. Judgment Administered (1 Kgs 14:17-18; 15:25-31).

With sad heart the queen made the long trek back to Tirzah. When the distraught lady entered the threshold of the palace, her son died.[3] The prince was buried and mourned just as Ahijah had prophesied.

Jeroboam ruled Israel for twenty-two years (930-909 BC). His son Nadab succeeded him on the throne (1 Kgs 14:20). Nadab was only able to hold the throne for parts of two years.[4] He continued the schismatic religious policies of his father. An upstart from the tribe of Issachar conspired against him. When the plot unfolded, Nadab was leading a campaign to recover Gibbethon, a Levitical city on the frontier of Dan, from Philistine control (1 Kgs 15:25-27).

Upon assuming the throne, Baasha launched a bloody purge that utterly wiped out the house of Jeroboam. By thus eliminating all potential rivals, Baasha was unconsciously fulfilling the prophecies of Ahijah the Shilonite. The massacre of Jeroboam's descendants is regarded by the author of Kings as being divine retribution for the sins of the first king of Israel (1 Kgs 15:28-31).

FIRST GREAT REFORMATION
1 Kings 15:9-24

After some two decades of apostasy in Judah, a dedicated worshiper of Yahweh took the throne. King Asa led the first of five great reformations in Judah. Unfortunately, toward the end of his reign this good king experienced a failure of faith.

A. Initial Efforts (1 Kgs 15:9-15//2 Chr 14:1-8).

In spite of the fact that he grew up in a palace dominated by an idolatrous grandmother and a hypocritical father, Asa did that which was right in the eyes of Yahweh. He removed the cult prostitutes and wooden idols from the land (1 Kgs 15:9-13).

God blessed Judah with ten years of peace and prosperity which Asa attributed to the reformation. During these years Asa built fortified cities and strengthened his army. Spearmen from Judah numbered 300,000, while bowmen from Benjamin numbered 280,000 (2 Chr 14:1-8).

B. Victory of Faith (2 Chr 14:9-15).

About 900 BC Judah was invaded by a vast host[5] led by Zerah the Ethiopian. Asa met the invaders in the valley of Zephathah at Mareshah. Prior to battle the king prayed one of the greatest prayers of Scripture. He confessed total dependence on Yahweh. He asked for help because *"we trust in you, and in your name we have come against this multitude."* The prayer concluded with the appeal *"let not man prevail against you"* (2 Chr 14:9-11).

Yahweh routed the Ethiopians before Asa. The armies of Judah pursued them as far as Gerar, five miles south of Gaza. Much plunder was carried away. Several cities in the vicinity of Gerar were sacked as well (2 Chr 14:12-15).

C. Prophetic Warning (2 Chr 15:1-7).

The Spirit of God directed Azariah to go out and meet Asa as he returned from the victory over Zerah. This prophet reminded the victorious host that *"Yahweh is with you when you are with him."* Azariah rehearsed what happened during the period of the Judges when the people forsook Yahweh. Those priestless, kingless and lawless days were full of internal strife and external oppression. *"God troubled them with every kind of distress."* For Asa, however, Azariah had a word of encouragement. If he was strong and courageous, there would be reward for his work (2 Chr 15:1-7).

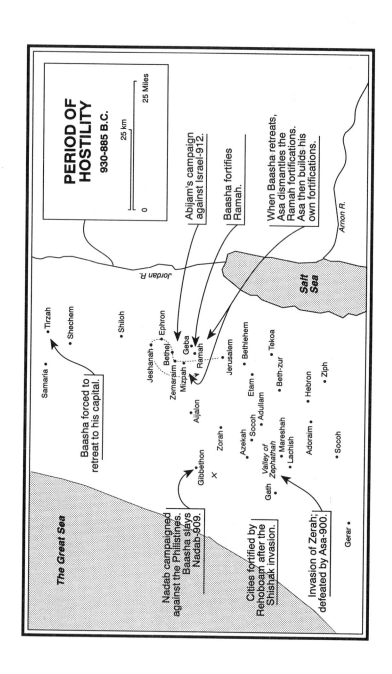

PERIOD OF HOSTILITY
930-885 B.C.

0 25 km

0 25 Miles

Abijam's campaign against Israel-912.

Baasha fortifies Ramah.

When Baasha retreats, Asa dismantles the Ramah fortifications. Asa then builds his own fortifications.

Jordan R.

Arnon R.

Salt Sea

Samaria

Tirzah

Shechem

Shiloh

Baasha forced to retreat to his capital.

Ephron

Jeshanah

Bethel

Geba

Zemaraim

Mizpah

Ramah

Aijalon

Jerusalem

Bethlehem

Tekoa

Zorah

Azekah

Socoh

Etam

Adullam

Beth-zur

Valley of Zephathah

Mareshah

Lachish

Adoraim

Hebron

Ziph

Gibbethon

X

Gath

Socoh

The Great Sea

Nadab campaigned against the Philistines. Baasha slays Nadab-909.

Cities fortified by Rehoboam after the Shishak invasion.

Invasion of Zerah; defeated by Asa-900.

Gerar

D. Renewed Revival (2 Chr 15:8-15).

The words of Azariah encouraged Asa in his reformation. He extended to the newly captured territories his efforts to remove the paraphernalia of idolatry. He restored the altar of Yahweh at the temple. Many of the pious citizens of the northern kingdom defected to Asa when they saw that he was making a sincere effort to restore the true faith (2 Chr 15:8-9).

In his fifteenth year Asa orchestrated a covenant renewal ceremony in Jerusalem. Some 700 oxen and 7,000 sheep were sacrificed to Yahweh. The people entered into a covenant to seek the Lord with all their heart. They agreed that whoever would not seek Yahweh should be executed. All present rejoiced at the renewal of the ancient covenant. They sought the Lord earnestly, *"and he let them find him."* The result was that God gave them rest on every side (2 Chr 15:10-15).

Asa continued his reform efforts. He removed his grandmother from her powerful position as principal lady because she had made an idol (lit., a horrible thing) to Asherah. He burned that idol at the brook Kidron (2 Chr 15:16).

A problem arises in reference to what Asa did to the high places, the unauthorized shrines scattered throughout the land. Did he remove those high places (2 Chr 14:3), or did he not (1 Kgs 15:14; 2 Chr 15:17)? The answer is that Asa removed the pagan high places, but did not remove the high places which were devoted to Yahweh. In spite of this defect in the devotion of Asa, his heart was *"blameless"* with the Lord. All of the valuables captured in wars fought by his father and by himself, Asa dedicated to Yahweh and placed in the house of God (2 Chr 15:17-18).

Chart No. 42

DIVIDED MONARCHY: HOSTILITY PHASE
(Sisters Quarreling)
930-885 BC

489

THE THREAT FROM BAASHA
1 Kgs 15:16-24//2 Chr 16:1-6

The second dynasty in the northern kingdom was founded by Baasha ben Ahijah. He killed the son of Jeroboam about 908 BC and exterminated all other relatives of that first dynasty. This change of dynasty in the north, however, did not induce Asa of Judah to change his attitude toward the sister kingdom. Twice the author of Kings states that a state of hostilities existed between the two kingdoms throughout the twenty-four years in which Baasha and Asa simultaneously ruled (2 Kgs 15:16,32). In the thirty-sixth year of the kingdom of Judah (894 BC)[6] the northern king committed an overt act of aggression which could not be ignored by Asa.

A. Lapse of Faith (1 Kgs 15:16-24//2 Chr 16:1-6).

Baasha attacked Judah in an effort to reconquer the territories lost to Abijah and Asa. At Ramah, only five miles north of Jerusalem, he began to build a fortress by which he intended to seal off the northern approaches of Judah (1 Kgs 15:16-17).

Asa was alarmed by this turn of events, yet for some unexplained reason he did not undertake an attack against Baasha. He resorted to political strategy. He sent an enormous gift to Ben-hadad of Damascus with a request that he attack Israel from the north. Ben-hadad gladly complied with Asa's request. He attacked several northern cities of Israel. The invasion forced Baasha to withdraw to his capital at Tirzah. Asa then dismantled the fortifications which Baasha had started. The confiscated materials were used to build two prominent Judean fortresses, one at Geba and one at Mizpah (1 Kgs 15:18-22).

B. Prophetic Warning (2 Chr 16:7-12).

Hanani the seer (prophet) condemned Asa for his failure of faith in this crisis. He asserted that Asa could have defeated Baasha just as he had earlier defeated the Ethiopians when he had relied upon Yahweh. *"For the eyes of Yahweh move to and fro throughout the earth that he may strongly support those whose heart is completely his."* In choosing to bribe Ben-hadad, Asa had acted foolishly. From this point on he would experience war (16:7-9).

490

Asa was enraged at the seer for this forthright condemnation. Hanani was thrown into prison. Asa oppressed some of the people—presumably pious souls like Hanani—at the same time. In his final years Asa was diseased in his feet. Yet in his disease he did not seek Yahweh, but only the physicians. This man who had begun as such a dynamo of faith had forgotten the God who had made him strong (16:10-12).

TURBULENCE IN THE NORTH
1 Kings 15:33-16:22

Following Ben-hadad's invasion of the northern kingdom in 895 BC the reign of Baasha of Israel rapidly deteriorated. The text briefly narrates the sad account of the turbulence surrounding Baasha's last years and those of his immediate successors.

A. The Doom of Baasha Predicted (1 Kgs 16:1-7).

Most likely the prophets had encouraged Baasha to take the initiative against the house of Jeroboam in 908 BC. When it became apparent, however, that Baasha intended to follow in the same spiritual path as his two predecessors (Jeroboam and Nadab) he lost prophetic support. Yahweh eventually dispatched a prophet from Judah,[7] Jehu, the son of the prophet Hanani,[8] to publicly proclaim in Israel the doom of Baasha (16:1).

Yahweh had used Baasha as a tool to punish the Jeroboam dynasty. For this purpose he had been elevated from the lowliest ranks to the highest position in the land. Yet Baasha had not proved faithful to Yahweh. In words almost identical to those used by Ahijah against Jeroboam (cf. 1 Kgs 14:6-16), Jehu pronounced the doom of Baasha's dynasty. The relatives of Baasha would fall in the city and in the field. Their corpses would be left unburied to be eaten by beast and bird (16:2-4).

B. The End of the Baasha Dynasty (1 Kgs 16:5-14).

The sacred historian speaks of Baasha's *"might."* That he was able to fortify Ramah just five miles from Jerusalem, and that Asa dared not directly challenge him are two indications of that "might."

Baasha died a natural death. He was buried at Tirzah. His son Elah tried to succeed him. The hand of divine destruction, however, fell swiftly on the family of Baasha just as the prophet Jehu had predicted. The judgment fell on Elah for two reasons. First, he continued to *"provoke Yahweh with the deeds of his hands,"* i.e., he participated in the calf worship. Second, Baasha was guilty of murdering his predecessor. Had Baasha been a righteous man, his destruction of the house of Jeroboam would have been regarded as a divine mission; but since he was just as evil as the man he had killed, his act was only motivated by personal ambition. For this reason he stood condemned for the murder.

Jehu's prophecy was fulfilled in this manner. When Elah had reigned two years, one of his military officers, Zimri, the commander of half of the Israelite chariot force, conspired against him. Elah seems to have been a dissolute and drunken incompetent. As king, he should have been with the army, which was engaged in a campaign at Gibbethon. Instead the king was in the house of one of his attendants participating in a drunken orgy. Perhaps Elah remained in Tirzah because he remembered the fate of Nadab, who had been assassinated at Gibbethon (cf. 1 Kgs 15:27). In any case for a king to accept the hospitality of one of his subjects was a serious breach of monarchical etiquette. Arza, the steward or attendant, may have been a part of the conspiracy, in which case Elah is made to look all the more naive. In any case, it was during this drinking party that Zimri assassinated his king (16:8-9).[9]

As soon as Zimri had been enthroned in 885 BC, he ordered all male relatives of Baasha to be executed. Thus he followed the precedent established in the first dynastic upheaval. This action would eliminate all potential rivals to the throne as well as all those who might feel obligated to avenge the blood of their relative. Zimri went a step beyond what Baasha had done back in 908 BC. He also executed the friends of the royal house, any who might be sympathetic to Elah. The bloodshed fulfilled the predictions made against the Baasha dynasty by the prophet Jehu. This dynasty had incurred the wrath of God because of its commitment to *"vanities,"* i.e., the golden calves (16:8-14).

C. Zimri's Seven-day Reign (1 Kgs 16:15-20).

Zimri was only able to hold the throne of Israel for one week. Upon hearing that Zimri had assassinated the king, the army in the field immediately declared their general, Omri, to be king. That the troops refused to recognize Zimri is not surprising. First, he was an inferior officer who was not even present on the great campaign at Gibbethon. Second, by murdering Elah's friends, Zimri doubtless made many enemies throughout the army (16:15-16).

Omri was not hesitant about accepting the office thrust upon him by his troops. He immediately broke off the siege of Gibbethon and led the army back up through the mountain passes to Tirzah. In a show of force he deployed his troops about the capital. Omri no doubt ordered Zimri to surrender. Seeing that his position was hopeless, Zimri went into the fortress of the palace—one of the innermost rooms—and committed suicide by setting the place on fire (16:17-18).

Even though Zimri died by his own hand, the Bible regards his death as being the result of divine retribution *"because of the sins which he had committed."* He is said to have walked *"in the way of Jeroboam,"* i.e., he continued to condone the calf worship in the north. Perhaps even before his seven-day rule Zimri had demonstrated his zeal for the counterfeit religion introduced by Jeroboam. On the other hand, the author may mean no more than that Zimri's revolt was not religiously motivated. In any case, the text is certainly making the point that the anarchy in the north was the bitter fruit of Jeroboam's apostasy (16:19-20).

D. A Civil War (1 Kgs 16:21-22).

The entire nation did not rally to the standard of Omri. For some unexplained reason, a rival emerged to challenge Omri's claim to the throne. Perhaps this counter-movement was the protest of the religious community against the power of the army.[10] In any case, Tibni was probably the favorite of that part of the army which was not involved in the encampment at Gibbethon (16:21).

Once the hereditary principle was overthrown, the crown in the north became a prize to be possessed by the strongest. Tibni determined that Omri would not have the throne uncontested. A fierce civil war erupted between the two factions. The text suggests that this struggle lasted about four or five years. Finally Omri was able to subdue the forces of Tibni and slay the rival (16:22).

A CHANGE IN FOREIGN POLICY
1 Kings 16:23-34

In the thirty-first year of Asa of Judah (880 BC), Omri won the civil war and became sole king in the north.[11] This dynasty—the fourth in Israel—became one of the most important because of a new religious policy and a new foreign policy.

A. The Reign of Omri (1 Kgs 16:23-28).

For the first six years of his reign Omri resided in Tirzah. During that time he was building a new capital. He chose a strategic location, a large oblong mound which dominated two main highways. Samaria, as the new city was named, was forty-two miles north of Jerusalem and twenty-five miles inland. The name was derived from that of its former owner, Shemer. Omri paid Shemer two talents of silver (about $4,250 BV) for the ground. Subsequent history proves the wisdom of Omri's choice of Samaria. The city remained the capital of Israel until the fall of the northern kingdom in 722 BC (16:23-24).[12]

Chart No. 43

DIVIDED MONARCHY: HARMONY PHASE
(Sisters Embracing)
885-841 BC

The religious situation continued to deteriorate under Omri. The prophet Micah (6:16) refers derogatorily to the *"statutes of Omri"* which may suggest some new development in the calf worship. Perhaps the calf worship was organized into a formal system at this time.

Another possibility is that Omri took additional measures to prevent those living in the north from attending the temple in Jerusalem. In any case, the practices of this king angered Yahweh even more than those of his five predecessors (16:25).

In sources outside the Bible Omri appears as one of the most prominent kings of Israel. Two other significant accomplishments of Omri can be deduced from subsequent narrative. First, he reestablished David's policy of friendly relations with Tyre. Second, he (or his son) brought to an end the era of confrontation with Judah. The old general appears to have been a very capable diplomat! The Biblical writer, interested as he was in the religious history of the kingdoms, saw little that was significant in his reign.

B. The Early Years of Ahab (1 Kgs 16:29-34).

Ahab succeeded his father Omri on the throne of Israel in 874 BC. He did evil in the eyes of Yahweh *"more than all who were before him."* The worship of Yahweh under the image of the calf continued to be the official state religion. Under Ahab, however, Canaanite idolatry was tolerated, even encouraged, due to the influence of the Phoenician princess Jezebel, Ahab's wife (16:29-31).

Jezebel was the daughter of Ethbaal, the ruler of Sidon. Tradition identifies him as the priest of Astarte who assassinated the king and usurped the throne.[13] This tradition would account for Jezebel's fierce character and her fanatical devotion to the gods of her country. This woman was a pagan missionary. She came to Israel with the avowed purpose of making her god Baal Melqart the supreme god in the land.

From the political and commercial point of view the alliance between Israel and Sidon was wise and necessary. The rising power of Aram made such an alliance desirable from the military standpoint. The Phoenicians needed the agricultural products of Israel, and landlocked Israel needed the markets available to the wide-ranging fleets of the Phoenicians. Thus, to the secular historian the marriage of Ahab and Jezebel would be a brilliant diplomatic coup. From a religious point of view, however, the marriage was disastrous.

King Ahab was led into the corruption of Canaanite idolatry. He apparently served and worshiped Baal as well as Yahweh. For Jezebel's god Ahab erected a temple, an altar and a pillar or image in

Samaria. In addition the king made an Asherah, i.e., a wooden pillar symbolizing the goddess Asherah. In Canaanite theology Asherah was the consort of Baal. Ahab was following the dictates of international courtesy which demanded that a foreign queen should have a sanctuary of her own religion in her adopted land. No less a king than Solomon could be cited as a precedent for such a policy among the Israelites (16:31-33).

A concrete example of the effects of counterfeit calf worship and Phoenician idolatry is cited at the end of 1 Kings 16. Hiel, a Bethelite, undertook what no one had dared to do for five centuries, viz., to rebuild the walls of Jericho.[14] These efforts at Jericho were probably part of Ahab's program to provide better protection on his southern border. Hiel may have been superintendent for a royal project.

Joshua's curse rested on anyone who would undertake rebuilding Jericho. The daring impiety of Hiel was punished swiftly and severely. His eldest son died when the foundations of Jericho were laid. By the time he rebuilt the gates, the last of his sons died. The swift and exact fulfillment of the prophetic threats made through Joshua was a forceful witness to the fact that the law of God could not be violated with impunity (16:34).

The closing verses of 1 Kings 16 which describe the gross degeneracy of Ahab's reign are an appropriate prelude to the account of the ministry of the great prophet Elijah. The unprecedented corruption of that age necessitated the unprecedented outpouring of divine power.

ENDNOTES

1. *Abijah* means *"Yahweh is my father."* Apparently Jeroboam regarded himself as a loyal worshiper of Yahweh or else he would never have given his son this name. Rehoboam's son and successor in the south wore the same name (cf. 2 Chr 12:16).

2. The disguise may have been intended to be a protection against the king's personal enemies rather than as a deception of the prophet. See Slotki, *op. cit.*, p. 104.

3. Some see a discrepancy between the prediction that the child would die as the queen entered *the city* and this statement. The palace, however, may have been on the edge of the city, or the city may have been little more than the palace itself.

4. Nadab succeeded to the throne in the second year of Asa (1 Kgs 15:25). He died in the third year of Asa (1 Kgs 15:28). He, therefore, could not have reigned two full years. This is a clear instance of the Hebrew habit of counting parts of years as entire years.

5. Literally, the Hebrew reads *"a thousand thousand."* This appears to be a round number implying a vast host, too large to be counted. Zerah also brought with him three hundred chariots.

6. Baasha could not have fortified Ramah in the thirty-sixth year of the reign of Asa since he died in the twenty-seventh year of that reign (1 Kgs 15:33). The text probably refers to the thirty-sixth year of the *kingdom* of Asa (i.e., the kingdom of Judah) which would have been the fifteenth or sixteenth *year* of Asa's reign.

7. Jehu wrote the history of the reign of Jehoshaphat (2 Chr 20:34). This suggests that he was a prophet of Judah who, like Amos, came north to denounce the northern king. Others have suggested, however, that Jehu was a northern prophet who took refuge in Judah during the Jezebel persecution.

8. Hanani was the prophet who admonished Asa of Judah and was thrown into prison for doing so (2 Chr 16:7).

9. Special odium seems to be attached to the action of Zimri (cf. 2 Kgs 9:31). Probably this was the case because the deed was not committed in open revolt, but stealthily after his victim had been reduced to a drunken stupor. In Jewish, and even English literature, the name of Zimri became a term of opprobrium.

10. A suggestion made by John Gray, *I & II Kings* in "The Old Testament Library" (Philadelphia: Westminster, 1970), p. 366.

11. Though he did not become sole king until 880 BC, Omri's reign of twelve years is counted from 885 BC when he was proclaimed king by the field army. Hence Omri's rule ended in 874 BC.

12. Archaeological excavations confirm the Biblical statement with regard to Omri's founding of the city of Samaria. Remains of three palaces have been found there, the earliest of which dates to the time of Omri-Ahab. The site shows no signs of occupation earlier than 900 BC.

13. Josephus, *Antiquities* 8.13.1.

14. The curse of Joshua seems to have applied only to the *walls* and *fortifications* of Jericho. The area around Jericho had been occupied long before the time of Ahab (cf. 2 Sam 10:5; Judg 3:13).

CHAPTER THIRTY

The Battle Against Baal
1 Kings 17-19

The concluding chapters of 1 Kings and the opening chapters of 2 Kings focus, not upon the king, but rather upon the king's prophetic opponents—Elijah, Micaiah and Elisha. The sacred historian here traces the efforts of Israel's spiritual leaders to help their people emerge triumphant from the spiritual crisis precipitated by governmental policy.

If there ever was a time when God needed to intervene in a mighty way in the stream of human history, it was in the time of Ahab. In that dark hour a determined effort was being made to stamp out faith in Yahweh. Only mighty miracles such as were performed by Elijah and Elisha could have been sufficient to counteract the influence of Jezebel and her 850 priests and prophets. The greatest prophet is reserved for the worst age. Israel had never had such an impious king as Ahab, nor such a miraculous prophet as Elijah.

DROUGHT IN ISRAEL
1 Kings 17:1-7

Since the founding of the kingdom of Israel in 930 BC the prophets and the kings had been at odds with one another. The king had as his primary goals military security, economic expansion and a higher standard of living for his people. The prophets, on the other hand, were concerned first and foremost about fidelity to Yahweh. They viewed with suspicion the foreign treaties negotiated by the government. The antagonism between the government and prophets reached its climax in the Ahab-Elijah clash.

A. Elijah at the Court (1 Kgs 17:1).

Elijah ("my God is Yahweh") came from the town of Tishbe, about eight miles north of the Jabbok river in the rugged region of Gilead. Because his manner matched the terrain from which he came, Elijah was frequently called simply *"the Tishbite."*

The abrupt way in which Elijah appears on the scene without a word of introduction or explanation is certainly remarkable. Elijah's sudden appearances and disappearances gave birth to the belief of his contemporaries that he was borne hither and yon by the Spirit of God.

The ministry of Elijah began with an announcement of judgment upon wayward Israel. This pronouncement is introduced with an oath formula which was appropriate for the situation: *"As Yahweh God of Israel lives."* By these words Elijah was asserting that Yahweh, not Baal, was the God of Israel. Furthermore, Yahweh was a living God, not a figment of vain imagination as was Baal.

Slaves normally stood to wait upon their masters. Therefore the words *"before whom I stand"* serve to identify Elijah as the ambassador or spokesman for Yahweh.

The judgment announced by Elijah is one that was threatened by Moses if the covenant people should fall into idolatry (cf. Deut 11:16; 17:18-23). Neither dew nor rain would fall in Israel. The normal rainy season in Palestine is from December to March. The rest of the year the earth received moisture from the dew which at times could be as heavy as a drizzle.

The duration of the drought would depend upon Elijah's word, and the prophet's word depended on some evidence of repentance from the people. The prophets of Baal would not be able to remove the curse though they claimed that their god controlled the elements of nature. Thus the drought served a polemical as well as a judicial function.

B. Elijah at Cherith (1 Kgs 17:2-7).

Shortly after Elijah announced the drought in Israel, he was directed by Yahweh to proceed eastward to the brook Cherith in some secluded area of Gilead. There he was to hide himself both to escape royal punishment and to avoid the importunity of his countrymen who would no doubt cry out to him because of the drought (17:2-3).

At the Brook Cherith God provided for Elijah in a miraculous manner. The Lord of nature commanded the ravens to bring his food to him. With unfailing regularity the birds brought bread and meat to the prophet until the brook dried up (17:4-7).[1]

MIRACLES IN PHOENICIA
1 Kings 17:8-24

When the water supply at Cherith failed, God instructed Elijah to leave the land of Israel and journey to the Sidonian village of Zarephath. This would be the very heart of the dominions of Ethbaal, the fanatical father of Jezebel. There God had commanded a widow to feed Elijah. Two great miraculous occurrences are connected with the prophet's sojourn there (17:8-9).

A. Multiplication of Food (1 Kgs 17:8-16).

Always obedient to the voice of God, Elijah hastened to Zarephath, probably taking the indirect route east of Jordan to avoid any contacts with agents of the king. At the gate of the city Elijah providentially met the very woman for whom he was looking, though he did not at first realize it. The woman was gathering sticks—a sign of her poverty—when the weary prophet approached her and requested that she secure for him a cup of water. Because Phoenicia is watered by the fresh streams from the Lebanon mountains, the drought does not seem to have affected that area so much as Israel. Supplying water to the thirsty in that region is considered a duty almost sacred. So the woman scurried off in the direction of the well or water pot (17:10).

As the woman was going to fetch the water the prophet also mentioned that he would like *"a morsel of bread."* The woman burst forth in an oath in the name of Yahweh. She apparently recognized Elijah, either by his features or dress, as an Israelite. Hence she referred to Yahweh as *"your God."* With this oath she indicated that she did not have so much as one small cake of bread. All she had was a handful of meal in a jar and a little oil. Even as Elijah approached she was gathering sticks to make a fire to prepare a final meal for herself and her son. Since the Phoenicians were in large measure dependent upon Israel for foodstuffs, the drought to the south would have created great scarcity of grain in Phoenicia. The poor would have been the hardest hit. This widow was evidently reduced to the greatest extremity (17:11-12).

Now the faith of the Phoenician woman was put to the test. Elijah challenged the woman to feed him first, then she and her son could eat. To this outlandish request the prophet added a precious promise. If the woman would put God's servant first, her jar of meal and flask of cooking oil would be miraculously preserved until the rains returned to the land (17:13-14).

Perhaps it was the authoritative manner of the man, or his prophetic garb, or the fact that he had spoken an oracle in the name of Yahweh which caused this heathen woman to believe and obey. In any case, her faith was rewarded. For many days she, her son, Elijah and *"her house,"* i.e., poor relatives, ate of that meal. All attempts to rule out the miraculous in this passage fail.[2] God was doing more for that widow than merely sustaining her providentially by natural means. God was supernaturally multiplying the woman's food supplies (17:15-16). This widow received a prophet in the name of a prophet, and she received a prophet's reward (cf. Matt 10:41).

B. Resurrection from the Dead (1 Kgs 17:17-24).

While Elijah was in residence at the widow's home, her son fell ill and died.[3] The woman immediately jumped to the conclusion that the prophet's presence had drawn the attention of God to the sinfulness of her house. She interpreted the death of the child as retribution for sins which would never would have been noticed had Elijah left her alone (17:17-18).

With calm confidence Elijah asked the desperate woman to give him the limp corpse of her son. He took the child into his chamber where he laid him on his own bed. In mighty intercessory prayer the prophet cried out to God with a question. Had God repaid the kindness of this widow with such a blow? Then in an "action prayer" the prophet stretched himself upon the child in order to keep the body warm for the expected return of life. Three times Elijah repeated this "action prayer." Each time he accompanied it with earnest entreaty that God would permit the child's life to be restored. Yahweh heard that prayer of faith. The lad revived (17:19-24).

A CHALLENGE TO BAAL
1 Kings 18:1-19

In the third year,[4] Yahweh ordered his prophet back to Israel. He was to show himself to Ahab, and then Yahweh would again send the rains (18:1). Undoubtedly the Lord also gave the prophet instructions to challenge the Phoenician prophets to a showdown on Mt. Carmel.

A. Elijah and Obadiah (1 Kgs 18:2-16).

Obadiah ("the servant of Yahweh") was the governor of Ahab's palace in Samaria, a position of no little importance. He was a god-fearing man. He risked the wrath of Jezebel by hiding a hundred prophets in caves by fifties. The division of the prophets into two companies was partly for the sake of security and partly for the sake of convenience. The greater the number to be fed, the greater the chance of detection. Throughout the period of Jezebel's ruthless persecution, Obadiah took care of these men of God by supplying them with food and water. In view of the severity of the famine, this was truly an amazing feat (18:2-4).

While Obadiah was on an errand for his king, he encountered Elijah. Ahab had sent his steward throughout the land in search of water near which grass might still be growing. The king was facing the unpleasant prospects of having to slaughter a portion of his livestock if fodder was not soon located. The king and Obadiah divided the land between them to facilitate the search. This personal inspection by the king and one of his chief officers indicates the extreme straits to which the Israelites were now reduced. Whether or not the two men were accompanied by a retinue is uncertain (18:5-6).

His humble obeisance and the terms in which he addressed the prophet reveal the profound reverence with which Obadiah regarded Elijah. The question "Is this you?" expressed the surprise of Obadiah at seeing Elijah, not any uncertainty about his identity. Elijah acknowledged that he was the long-missing prophet. He ordered Obadiah to go and inform the king that he was back (18:7-8).

Obadiah was horrified at the thought of announcing to Ahab that Elijah had returned, because he knew the dispositon of his master. Ahab had communicated with all neighboring courts in search for Elijah. He even had made foreign kings swear that they were not harboring the prophet. Obadiah was afraid that when he went to inform the king of Elijah's whereabouts, the prophet would disappear. If such should happen, then Ahab would feel that his steward had lied to him or trifled with him. In either case, he surely would have ordered his steward executed. Obadiah pled that Elijah would take note of his lifetime commitment to Yahweh and his compassion for the prophets. He begged that the prophet would not give him such a dangerous assignment (18:9-14).

Elijah set the mind of Obadiah at ease when he swore an oath in the name of "Yahweh of hosts"[5] that he would appear to Ahab that very day. Obadiah then went to find his king. Ahab in turn hastened to confront the prophet (18:15-16).

B. Elijah and Ahab (1 Kgs 18:17-20).

Ahab did not meet the prophet with a humble and contrite heart, but with sarcasm and belligerence. By means of a rhetorical question the king expressed his amazement that Elijah had ventured back into his presence. He addressed the prophet as the "troubler of Israel." This noun is derived from a verb which is used to denote alienation from society or from God which results from some heinous crime or act. Ahab thus charged Elijah with being the one who by his actions had alienated the deity (Baal?) so that the rains had been withheld (18:17).

In words seething with defiance, the Tishbite hurled the epithet back into the teeth of the king. *"It is you and your father's house who have brought the trouble on Israel!"* Elijah accused the Israelites of having *"forsaken the commandments of Yahweh;"* he accused Ahab of having *"walked after the Baalim"* (18:18).[6]

The text does not indicate how Ahab reacted to the defiant response of Elijah. The unexpected calmness and boldness of the prophet may have completely unnerved the king so that he could make no reply. In any case, Elijah hurled a challenge at the king. Let all Israel, i.e., the representatives of the nation, gather to Mt. Carmel along with the 450 prophets of Baal and 400 prophets of Asherah. These Asherah *"prophets"* were Jezebel's ministers, probably imported from Sidon. They were fed from the bounty of the queen (18:19).

Mt. Carmel was the site for the prophetic showdown. Carmel is a ridge some twelve miles in length. Near the summit is a plateau where the contest might well have taken place. A spring of water is close at hand which is said to flow even in the driest seasons. The selection of Carmel as the site of the confrontation was also dictated by the fact (1) that it had a central and convenient location; (2) that it was near the sea, from whence the rain clouds would come; and (3) that an altar of Yahweh had once been located here.

CONFRONTATION ON CARMEL
1 Kings 18:20-40

Ahab immediately complied with the demands of Elijah. He summoned the nation and the prophets of Baal to Mt. Carmel. The king *"sent unto the people,"* i.e., invited the people to attend the contest. He *"gathered"* the prophets of Baal, perhaps implying that they were unwilling to come and were forced to do so by the king. The prophets of Asherah probably did not attend the convocation because they were under the personal control of the queen. She would not allow their participation (18:20).

A. Contest Preliminaries (1 Kgs 18:21-24).

No indication is given of the size of the crowd which assembled on Mt. Carmel. No doubt the dramatic confrontation attracted hundreds, if not thousands. Elijah hoped to reach these masses. To them he directed his rhetorical question: *"How long are you going to hobble upon two crutches,"* i.e., seek the support of both Yahweh and Baal simultaneously.[7] Elijah was calling for a clear-cut decision. Let the people choose between Baal or Yahweh, then let them commit themselves wholeheartedly to that deity who was truly God. Awed by the presence of the king and the prophets, the people answered not a word. Perhaps also they were convicted in their own consciences and were consequently speechless (18:21).

To set the stage for the contest Elijah called the attention of the people to the fact that he stood alone that day as sole representative of Yahweh. On the other hand, Baal's prophets numbered 450. Thus did Elijah underscore the fact of his absolute confidence even though outnumbered. Certainly he was trying to stress the fact that truth is not determined by numbers (18:22).

Since his opponents were so numerous, and since they were supported by the crown, Elijah proposed that they supply the two sacrificial bullocks. One was to be selected and prepared by the Baal prophets, the other by God's prophet. Elijah offered his rivals their choice of the oxen as a guarantee that they would have no excuse that their animal was less fit for sacrifice. The bullocks were to be placed on the altar wood, but no fire was to be set to the wood (18:23).

Once the sacrificial animal was in place, the people were told to call on the name of their god Baal. The failure of the people to take a clear-cut stand for Yahweh was tantamount to their choosing Baal as their god. Elijah, on the other hand, would call on the name of Yahweh. The deity who responded to the prayers of his worshipers and consumed the sacrificial bullock with fire from heaven would be recognized as the true God (18:24).

The Baal sympathizers agreed to Elijah's challenge. As they saw it, the advantage was with Baal. He was the god of storm and lightning. Furthermore, the Baal prophets were allowed to select the sacrificial animal of their choice, go first, and use as much time as they needed for their incantations.

B. Efforts of the Baal Prophets (1 Kgs 18:25-29).

Having gained the assent of the people, Elijah repeated the proposal to the splendiferously clad prophets of Baal. They had been put in a position in which they could hardly refuse the test and still retain the respect of their constituents. Because the prophets of Baal were so numerous, Elijah suggested that they go first in the contest. He was anxious that the impotency of Baal be fully manifested before Yahweh demonstrated his power (18:25).

The prophets of Baal declined the opportunity to select the bullock. They took the one which was given them by representatives of the people or by Elijah himself. They then prepared the animal in the prescribed manner, and began to call on the name of Baal. From morning until noon they continued to cry out that Baal might hearken to their prayers. They then began to limp, i.e., dance about the altar, in an attempt to attract the attention of their mute master (18:26).

At noon Elijah began to ridicule his opponents. He urged them to cry louder. In condescending tones Elijah offered some possible explanations for Baal's lack of response. Perhaps he was meditating or talking; or maybe he was on a trip; or then again, maybe he was just a late sleeper and needed to be awakened! (18:27).

Elijah's barbs stirred the Baal prophets to renewed vigor as if to testify to their undying faith in their god. Grabbing the swords and spears of soldiers standing nearby they began to cut themselves, hoping by acts of self-mutilation to attract the attention of their god. This fanatical *"prophesying"* continued for some six hours—from early morning to the time of the offering of the evening sacrifice about three in the afternoon. Without question, these men were absolutely sincere in their faith (18:28-29).

C. Efforts of Elijah (1 Kgs 18:30-38).

When the Baal prophets retired from the field exhausted, Elijah called the people to him. He wanted them to have a good view of all he was about to do so that there would be no suspicion of hoax or magic. The prophet began his demonstration by rebuilding the altar of Yahweh. This altar may have been one of the high places where Israelites worshiped prior to the establishment of the temple in Jerusalem. On the other hand, this altar may have been built by some of the faithful Yahweh worshipers in the north who would not bow the knee to Baal or to the golden calf. Scarcely any doubt can exist that this was one of the altars which the government had ordered torn down (cf. 19:10). By repairing the altar, Elijah was casting himself in the role of the restorer of the law and true faith (18:30).

Twelve stones were used to restore the altar, symbolizing the twelve tribes of Israel. By this action Elijah was silently protesting the schism in the north. With the twelve stones from the old altar, Elijah built a new one *"in the name of Yahweh,"* i.e., by his authority and for his glory. A trench was dug about the altar as deep as the grain measure containing two seahs (about thirteen quarts) of seed. The sacrificial bullock was cut in pieces and laid on the altar wood. The prophet then ordered four pitchers of water to be poured on the sacrificial animal and on the wood beneath. Then he ordered for this drenching to be repeated two more times. So much water was poured over the altar that it ran down and filled the trench around the altar.[8] Apparently these actions were taken to exclude all suspicion of fraud (18:31-35).[9]

At about three o'clock in the afternoon (cf. v. 29) Elijah drew near his water-drenched altar. He lifted his eyes heavenward and began to pray. He addressed Yahweh as the God of Abraham, Isaac and Israel. He prayed that God would vindicate himself and his prophet there on that mount. Fire from heaven would prove that all which Elijah had said with regard to the famine three years earlier, and all that he had done with regard to organizing the confrontation with the Baal prophets, had been done through the word of Yahweh (18:36).

Earnestly Elijah called upon Yahweh to hearken to his prayer that the people might be convinced that he alone was God, and being thus persuaded, might turn back to the God of their fathers. This dramatic prayer had no sooner fallen from the lips of Elijah when *"fire from heaven"* (lightning)[10] fell upon the altar. The tongues of fire not only consumed (lit., *ate up*) the sacrificial animal and wood, they also disintegrated the stones, scorched the dust about the altar, and even licked up the water in the trench (18:37-38).

D. Execution of the Baal Prophets (1 Kgs 18:39-49).

The people reacted to the divine demonstration instantly and decisively. Recognizing in the fire the token of the divine presence, they fell on their faces and continued to shout in unison, *"Yahweh is*

God, Yahweh is God. " Seizing the initiative of that emotion-packed moment, Elijah ordered the Baal prophets to be apprehended. He then led the throng down to the base of the hill where he slew, i.e., ordered to be slain, the pagan prophets. Apparently this was done beside the river Kishon so that the corpses could be flushed out of the land into the sea.

The slaughter of the Baal prophets has been called an act of gross fanaticism and cruelty by some; others have seen in it a wild and terrible *vendetta* for Jezebel's persecutions of Yahweh's prophets. The following considerations may help to put this incident in proper perspective.

1. The law required the execution of those who worshiped false gods, and especially those who taught others in Israel to so worship (Exod 22:20; Deut 13; 17:2-7). However repugnant this slaughter may have been to Elijah personally, he was under obligation to carry out the law.

2. Whereas it was normally the duty of the theocratic ruler to carry out such executions, in Elijah's day the king was corrupt, powerless, and himself an idol worshiper.

3. Elijah had just proved that Yahweh was God; now he must likewise prove the the law of God was not dead.

4. These prophets had been instrumental in corrupting the people of God. They thus had threatened the very existence of true religion.

5. The action was allowed and approved by God who otherwise would hardly have answered the prayer which Elijah offered following the massacre.

6. Idolatry and irreligion are not today to be avenged by sword or fire, not because these sins are any less grievous, but because the duty of punishing these crimes has been reserved for God himself.

7. Whereas the law specified stoning as the punishment for idolatry (Deut 13:10; 17:5), the sword was used in this instance because of the numbers involved and the lateness of the afternoon hour.

INTERCESSION BY ELIJAH
1 Kings 18:41-46

King Ahab was wise enough to realize that he could not intervene to rescue the condemned prophets from the angry throng. Apparently he accompanied the crowd to the Kishon. In the excitement of the day the king had had nothing to eat or drink. Elijah therefore instructed Ahab to go up and have a meal. The king's attendants must have spread a tent for him upon the higher plateau. They had brought food for their master, but until now he had not cared to eat. By encouraging the king to eat, Elijah was suggesting that there was no longer any cause for anxiety or alarm on his part. Since the people had repented, and the wicked had been cut off from the land, the drought could now be removed. In Elijah's prophetic mind he could already hear the sound of a great rain (18:41).

Elijah then made his way to one of the prominent knolls of Carmel where he could enter into earnest intercession. The prayer posture of the prophet was somewhat peculiar. He seems to have been squatting with his head between his knees. The purpose here was to induce concentration. After some moments of petition, Elijah dispatched his servant to a higher elevation from which the Mediterranean Sea could be clearly viewed. His concentration in prayer was so intense that Elijah could not stop to scan the sky to see if his prayer had been answered (18:42).

Seven times the servant was instructed to return to his observation post. God had promised rain (cf. v. 1), and Elijah was confident that he would keep that promise. Without murmur the devoted servant executed the prophet's orders. On his seventh trip to the summit, he spotted a small cloud no bigger than the palm of a man's hand. Such small clouds were harbingers of rain in Palestine (cf. Luke 12:54). Elijah then dispatched his servant to the plateau where Ahab was dining to announce to the king that he should make haste to go to Jezreel lest he be caught in the downpour and be unable to cross the flood-swollen Kishon (18:43-44).

Shortly the sky blackened, a wind arose, and a great rain swept across the plain of Esdraelon. Ahab made his way toward Jezreel as fast as he could. The hand of Yahweh came upon Elijah giving him supernatural strength. Girding up his loins, i.e., gathering about his waist his long flowing robe, Elijah set out running toward Jezreel. He actually arrived at the gate of the city prior to Ahab and his chariot. Over this distance it would not be impossible for a man to outstrip a horse and chariot, especially since the man would run cross-country while the chariot would have to stick to the now muddy roadbed (18:45-46).

Elijah believed he had struck the death blow to the pagan practices promoted by the royal court. He wished to be in Jezreel to further any reformation efforts that the hapless Ahab might inaugurate. He knew Ahab would need all the help he could get to bolster his courage as he came face to face with his domineering wife.

CRISIS IN THE DESERT
1 Kings 19:1-8

Elijah expected that the triumph on Carmel would be followed by a great religious reformation in Israel. Such was not the case. Elijah had won a battle, but the outcome of the war against Baal was still in question.

A. Elijah's Flight (1 Kgs 19:1-4).

Upon learning of the defeat of her god and the death of her prophets, Jezebel publicly vowed that she would see Elijah dead. A messenger was dispatched to the city gate to find the prophet and to convey to him the queen's solemn vow in the name of the gods she revered that she would have his life within twenty-four hours. If, however, she meant to slay Elijah, why did Jezebel forewarn him by means of this messenger? Perhaps she felt that she would find no one that night who would be willing to carry out the execution order against a man whose supernatural powers had been so widely heralded. The dispatching of the messenger was more an act of rage than of rationality. In her exasperation she had to give vent to her impotent wrath. Her husband may have been convinced and even converted by what he had seen, but *she* was unconquered and unrelenting (19:1-2).

This unexpected turn of events caused the prophet great discouragement. In a moment of spiritual weakness he resigned as it were from his prophetic ministry, and fled the country. Profound depression mingled with fear in the heart of this man of God. He had expected the contest on Carmel to settle the Baal issue once and for all. His dream of Israel in the fold of fidelity was smashed by the defiant declaration of the queen (19:3).

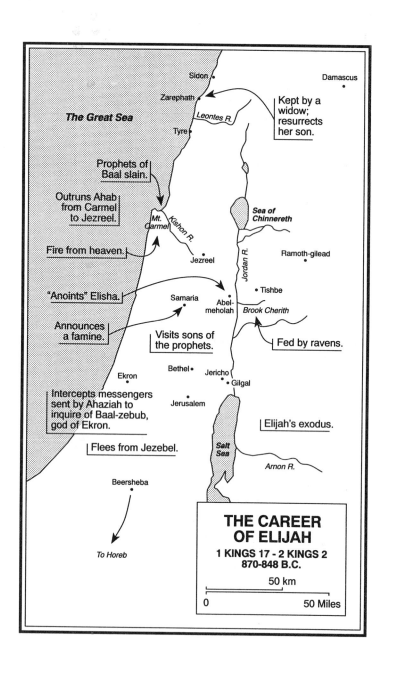

Sidon

Damascus

Zarephath

Leontes R.

The Great Sea

Tyre

Kept by a widow; resurrects her son.

Prophets of Baal slain.

Outruns Ahab from Carmel to Jezreel.

Mt. Carmel

Sea of Chinnereth

Kishon R.

Fire from heaven.

Jezreel

Jordan R.

Ramoth-gilead

"Anoints" Elisha.

Samaria

Abel-meholah

Tishbe

Announces a famine.

Visits sons of the prophets.

Brook Cherith

Fed by ravens.

Bethel

Jericho

Ekron

Gilgal

Intercepts messengers sent by Ahaziah to inquire of Baal-zebub, god of Ekron.

Jerusalem

Elijah's exodus.

Flees from Jezebel.

Salt Sea

Arnon R.

Beersheba

To Horeb

THE CAREER OF ELIJAH
1 KINGS 17 - 2 KINGS 2
870-848 B.C.

50 km

0   50 Miles

At Beersheba, ninety-five miles south of Jezreel on the southern boundary of Judah, the prophet dismissed his faithful servant. The journey to that point must have occupied at least three days. The lad was probably too exhausted to go any farther. There was no reason why this faithful servant should be subjected to the uncertainties and privations of desert travel. Besides, Elijah wanted to be alone in his depression.

When Elijah came upon a juniper (broom) tree, he sat down to rest beneath its bushy branches. There he sat alone, exhausted physically and depressed psychologically. He requested that he might die.[12] In agonizing lament he cried, *"I am no better than my fathers."* He had thought himself to be a special messenger of God, raised up mightily to bring the people of God to repentance. So long as he had a ray of hope that he might influence the moral and religious life in Israel, nothing was too difficult for him. Under that juniper tree, however, Elijah came to feel that his life was fruitless, that he had failed in his mission. He had accomplished no more than those prophets who had preceded him in the task of preaching (19:4).

B. An Angel's Assistance (1 Kgs 19:5-8).

The pathetic prophet closed his eyes and prayed that he would never open them again. God, however, had other plans for this man. An angel awakened him and directed him to arise and eat. Elijah probably had eaten little or nothing during his journey from Jezreel. His profound depression may have been due partly to physical weakness. Therefore before God could deal with his spiritual problem he had to take care of the man's physical needs (19:5).

Opening his eyes, Elijah found near his head a cake of bread and a cruse of water. After partaking, the prophet again dozed off. Once again the angel awakened him and bade him partake of the food because he yet had a long journey before him (19:6-7).

DEMONSTRATION AT HOREB
1 Kings 19:9-12

From that meal Elijah gained enough strength to sustain himself for several days. Like Moses before him and Jesus after him, Elijah fasted for forty days. These three great fasters would one day meet gloriously on the Mt. of Transfiguration. The journey from Beersheba to Mt. Horeb is about one hundred miles. Obviously Elijah did not spent the entire forty days traveling. Rather his total time in the wilderness was forty days (19:7).

A. Yahweh's Censure (1 Kgs 19:9-10).

At Horeb Elijah took up residence in a cave.[13] There the word of Yahweh came to him in the form of a question designed at once to reprove Elijah and to make him analyze his situation. At every other point in the ministry of this prophet, the Lord had been sending him to his destinations; Elijah, however, had left Jezreel without such a word. He had left in fear and distrust of God. So God asked the probing question, *"What are you doing here?"* The implication is that he had deserted his post (19:9).

Elijah did not accept censure without some self-justification. In the face of the terrible apostasy in Israel, Elijah had been very zealous for Yahweh. On the other hand, the children of Israel had broken the covenant with God, thrown down his altars, and had slain his prophets. Yet Elijah had stood firm and, so it seemed to his despondent mind, had stood alone. Now Elijah's own life was in jeopardy even though he had won a mighty victory on Carmel (19:10).

In these words there is tacit reproof of God. Why had the Lord looked upon the deterioration in the northern kingdom for so long without intervening? Elijah resented the growing corruption of the age and the frustration of his efforts to reverse it. Here is the old cry found throughout the Old Testament, the complaint that God is silent and indifferent, that the righteous are persecuted while the wicked prosper.

B. Elijah's Instruction (1 Kgs 19:11-12).

If Elijah thought his depression and his desertion of the field of battle were justified, he was mistaken. He was about to experience a theophany, a manifestation of the power and presence of God, through which he would learn a very important lesson. The Lord directed the prophet to stand at the entrance of the cave. As soon as he stepped from the cave, Elijah was confronted with a veritable tempest which ripped rocks loose from the mountain and sent them crashing to the valley below. Yahweh, however, was not in the wind. Shortly after the wind subsided, the earth began to shake. Once again the Lord was not present in the earthquake. Next came fire—perhaps a thunderstorm with bolts of lightning the likes of which the prophet never had seen before. Yahweh, however, was not in the fire. Then came the still small voice (lit., a sound of gentle silence). Elijah then knew that he was standing in the presence of God (19:11-12).

Through the Horeb signs God taught Elijah an important lesson. The spectacular and dramatic have their place in God's order of things. Most often, however, the divine program is carried forward through the still small voice which speaks to the hearts of people. While Yahweh is a God of judgment, he is also the God of mercy and grace. Elijah needed to be reminded of that fact. He needed to see that the time of fire, sword and slaughter had passed. Now the time had come to proclaim the word of Yahweh in gentle silence. The still small voice of protest would become in the course of time a powerful force; it must not be allowed to die! A successor must be chosen to carry on the work.

COMMISSION OF ELIJAH
1 Kings 19:13-18

Wrapping his sheepskin mantle about his face lest he look upon God, Elijah stepped forth from his cave into which apparently he retreated during the manifestations of divine power. Again Elijah heard the voice of God raising the same embarrassing question which was asked previously: *"What are you doing here, Elijah?"* Elijah repeated verbatim the answer he had given God earlier. The tone of his voice, however, must surely have changed. Formerly defiant, loud, belligerent, he now spoke with the still small voice, the voice of self-abasement. The facts had not changed. He knew of no other way to respond to the divine query. Now, however, he had reservations about his course of conduct. Elijah thought he knew best how God's work should be done. The theophany taught him that he had a faulty understanding of God's goals and methods. That Elijah had indeed repented is indicated by the fact that he was given a new commission by the Lord (19:14).

515

Elijah was commissioned to *"anoint,"* i.e., appoint or call, Hazael, Jehu and Elisha. Elijah was to see to it that these three individuals were made aware of their divinely appointed destiny. Hazael would be king of Damascus, Jehu would be king of Israel, and Elisha would be Elijah's successor. The three would be God's agents of judgment upon apostate Israel. Jehu would slay those who escaped the sword of Hazael; Elisha, by the sword of the spirit, would *"slay"* those who escaped the physical judgment of Jehu. The two kings would create in Israel tumultuous upheavals just like the wind, earthquake and fire did at Horeb. The word of God spoken by Elisha, however, would be that which constrained men to humble themselves before the Lord. Rightly understood, the commission to Elijah is a concrete application of the great spiritual lesson which he learned through the theophany at Horeb (19:15-17).

The Horeb commission answered Elijah's implicit criticism that God was not doing enough to thwart the sinners in Israel. God was suggesting that bold action was about to be taken against the ruling dynasty and the religion which it fostered. A ruthless foreign invader and a dynastic upheaval would be necessary to root out Baalism in Israel.

In a final note, Yahweh refuted Elijah's twice-stated allegation that he alone had remained faithful to the Lord in Israel. God revealed that seven thousand still had not bowed the knee to Baal. The figure is not only a round number, it is a symbolic one as well. The still small voice had been at work in Israel; a faithful remnant was still to be found there (cf. Rom 11:5) who had not *"kissed"* Baal.[14]

CALL OF ELISHA
1 Kings 19:19-21

Upon returning to Israel, Elijah set about to carry out the duty which God had assigned him at Horeb. He came upon Elisha plowing in a field. Elisha must have come from an affluent family for twelve yoke of oxen were working the field. Elijah passed by Elisha and cast his mantle upon the young man. This rough hairy garment had become the trademark of Elijah and the symbol of his prophetic office. To cast the cloak to or upon Elisha was therefore an appropriate way of calling him to be his successor (19:19).

After casting his mantle upon Elisha, Elijah strode on. He left it for the young man to take or reject this call as he saw fit. Elisha made up his mind at once. He ran after his new master. His request to be allowed to give his mother and father a parting embrace is altogether fitting, even touching. Had he asked permission to stay and *bury* his parents he would have merited rebuke (cf. Luke 9:59-61). Consequently Elijah granted the reasonable request. The call to be his servant did not require a repudiation of his own flesh and blood (19:20).

Elisha bade farewell to his parents and friends at a hastily prepared meal. He slew a yoke of oxen and boiled the meat thereof over a fire he had built with the wood of his plow. He may have meant this to be symbolic of his repudiation of his secular calling. The farewell feast completed, Elisha arose and went after Elijah. The young man became Elijah's attendant.

ENDNOTES

1. Josephus (*Ant.* 8.13.2). Some have argued that the vowels of the word traditionally rendered *"ravens"* can be altered to produce the word *"Arabs."* According to this view Elijah was cared for by some Bedouins who lived in the region of Cherith. Since the vowel points were not part of the inspired consonantal Hebrew, this suggestion cannot be ruled out. All ancient versions, however, attest the reading *"ravens."*

2. Gray (*op. cit.,* p. 381) offers the feeble explanation that the generosity of the widow touched the conscience of her better-provided neighbors.

3. The phrase *"there did not remain any breath in him"* (17:17) does not in itself prove the boy was dead (cf. Dan 10:17). For this reason some have suggested that no more than a coma is intended. However vv. 18, 20-21 certainly point in the direction that the child was actually dead.

4. The famine lasted a total of three years and six months (Luke 4:25; Jas 5:17). *"In the third year"* (1 Kgs 18:1) probably refers to the third year of Elijah's stay with the widow.

5. The designation *"Yahweh of hosts"* was first used by Hannah (1 Sam 1:11). The "hosts" include the armies of Israel, the stars of the heavens, and the angelic legions.

6. The plural *"Baalim"* (1 Kgs 18:18) probably refers to the various images or statues of the god Baal Melqart which had been set up in the land of Israel.

7. This translation was proposed by Fohrer and followed by Gray (*op. cit.*

517

396). The KJV, RSV, NIV and NASB render *"two opinions"* rather than *"two crutches."*

8. The Hebrew could also be translated, *"he* (Elijah) *filled the trench"* which would imply that additional water besides the twelve pitchers was used to fill the trench.

9. Possibly the pouring out of the water also had symbolic significance. It may have been a symbolic petition for rain, or a symbol of repentance (cf. 1 Sam 7:3-14).

10. Jon Ruthven argues persuasively for the likelihood that lightning is meant. He demonstrates that the absence of clouds in the sky need not preclude the possibility of a lightning strike. Jon Ruthven "A Note on Elijah's 'Fire from Yahweh'"*Bulletin of the Evangelical Theological Society* 12 (Spring 1969): 111-115.

11. Elijah might have sought asylum with good king Jehoshaphat of Judah. Some think that the cordial relations between Jehoshaphat and the northern kingdom might have included an extradition provision. More likely, however, Elijah left Judah and went out in the wilderness to die alone in his depression.

12. Literally, *"he requested his life to die."* In this expression is reflected the conception that life proceeds directly from God and consequently belongs to him. A person might wish to die, but he was not at liberty to commit suicide. See Gray, *op. cit.,* p. 408.

13. The Hebrew reads *"the cave."* Montgomery takes this to be a generic article meaning the cave region. *The Books of Kings* in "The International Critical Commentary" (New York: Scribners, 1951), p. 317. Gray (*op. cit.,* p. 409) thinks the article points to a particular cave, possibly that from which Moses saw the back of Yahweh (Exod 33:21ff.).

14. The reference is probably to kissing the hand toward the idol, a practice which was a widespread custom in the ancient world (cf. Job 31:26f.; Hos 13:2). See Leo L. Honor, *Book of Kings 1* in "The Jewish Commentary for Bible Readers" (New York: Union of American Hebrew Congregations, 1955), p. 279.

CHAPTER THIRTY-ONE

The Prophets in the Ahab Era
1 Kings 20-22

The reign of Ahab (874-853 BC) was crucial in the religious history of Israel. Through several prophets Yahweh continued to demonstrate his superiority to the gods of surrounding nations.

A SIEGE OF SAMARIA
1 Kings 20:1-22

The policy of harassment had characterized Ben-hadad's dealings with Israel in the days of Baasha (cf. 1 Kgs 15:18). Now the Aramean king determined that he would subdue Israel totally. About 860 BC Ben-hadad of Damascus went up and besieged Samaria with thirty-two "kings," i.e., heads of tiny allied principalities. This invasion may have been prompted by Omri's conquest of Moab[1] and consequent control of the Transjordan trade route, the famous King's Highway (20:1).

A. Initial Demands (1 Kgs 20:2-4).

Aramean messengers were sent to Ahab with the demands of Ben-hadad. The demands were excessive; they were designed to provoke all-out war. Ben-hadad wanted silver and gold; but also he wanted Ahab's harem and the best of his children as hostages. Surrender of the harem would be tantamount to surrendering the throne itself (cf. 2 Sam 16:21), not to mention all manhood and self-respect (20:2).

Faced with an overwhelming Aramean host, Ahab deemed it advisable to make every concession, to cast himself, as it were, on the mercy of Ben-hadad. He may have hoped that a soft answer would turn away the wrath of his adversary. He may have assumed that a verbal acknowledgment of the claims of Ben-hadad would be sufficient to placate the foe thus eliminating the necessity of having actually to hand over his family as hostages (20:4).

B. Additional Demands (1 Kgs 20:5-9).

Since Ahab had yielded so easily to his initial ultimatum, Ben-hadad made yet further demands. The initial proposal was vague and allowed Ahab to select what he would deliver over to the Aramean; the second proposal was definite and immediate. It provided for Ben-hadad's servants to pass through the palaces of Samaria seizing whatever appeared to be valuable. Realizing that his previous conciliatory submission had only stirred the Aramean braggart to make greater demands, Ahab called the elders of the land together to seek advice. They urged the king to resist these latest demands. Total capitulation was unthinkable (20:5-8).

Ahab sent word back to Ben-hadad that whereas he had been willing to comply with the initial demands, he could not permit enemy soldiers to pillage his palaces (20:9).

C. An Empty Boast (1 Kgs 20:10-12).

Infuriated by this response, Ben-hadad fired back a blustering reply. He vowed that he would make Samaria a heap of dust. He boasted that his troops were so numerous that this dust would be insufficient to fill the hands of each of his soldiers (20:9-10).

Ahab's third response to the king was a pithy and incisive proverb which consists of only four words in the Hebrew: *"It is not the one who girds on his harness who should boast, but he who survives to remove it."* When this curt reply was reported to Ben-hadad, the king and his vassals were drinking in their campaign huts. In furious rage the king issued the command—one word in the Hebrew—to commence the siege (20:11-12).

D. A Prophetic Word (1 Kgs 20:13-14).

God dispatched an unnamed prophet to offer encouragement to Ahab in this national crisis. The prophet promised that Ben-hadad and his host would be delivered into the hand of Ahab that very day. Whatever other reasons God may have had for intervention on behalf of Israel, the supreme purpose of this divine help was that Ahab might know assuredly that Yahweh was God. On Carmel Yahweh had appeared as a God of fire, wrath and judgment; now he was about to reveal himself as God of redemption. On Carmel he had shown himself to be superior to the idols of Phoenicia; now he would demonstrate his power over the gods of Aram (20:13).

Ahab welcomed this word from Yahweh, but he was puzzled by it. So the king inquired further of the prophet. Who would secure the victory? Which side would commence the hostilities? In the name of Yahweh the prophet related the strategy. The *"young men"* or servants of the district governors would gain the victory. Just who these young men were is not clear. Probably God selected an agency which was purposely weak and feeble in order that the victory might be attributed to him. This band of young men, whoever they may have been, was to commence the attack against the Arameans (20:14).

E. The Deliverance (1 Kgs 20:15-21).

Ahab found only 232 of the *"young men"* in the capital. The rest of his army numbered only seven thousand. At noon, when normally people of the Near East take a lengthy respite from all activity, the tiny force of Ahab marched forth from Samaria. Ben-hadad and his vassals were carousing and giving little thought to their military endeavors. The camp sentries immediately reported the troop movements out of the gate of Samaria. Ben-hadad gave the orders that the Israelites were to be taken alive, no doubt so that he might torture them and mock them before they were executed (20:15-18).

521

The 232 *"young men"* may have been used as a decoy to lull the Aramean troops into a false sense of security. When the Arameans came forward to take them into custody, the seven thousand troops poured forth from the city to engage the enemy. When several Arameans fell in battle, panic seized the rest. They fled for their lives with Israel in hot pursuit. Ben-hadad himself fled by horse in the company of some of his cavalry. Thus did Israel defeat the Aramean host, including cavalry and chariotry, with a great slaughter (20:19-21).

F. The Warning (1 Kgs 20:22).

Shortly after the victory over the Arameans, the unnamed prophet came to Ahab again, this time with a warning. The danger was not over. At the turn of the year, i.e., in the spring of the following year, when military campaigns were normally launched, Ben-hadad would return. Therefore Ahab should take every military precaution by strengthening both his army and the fortification of his capital (20:22).

CONFRONTATION AT APHEK
1 Kings 20:23-43

Ben-hadad's advisers were not long coming up with an explanation for the humiliating defeat at Samaria. They suggested that the Israelites had been successful because their gods were gods of the hills, whereas the Aramean gods were gods of the plains. If the armies of Israel could be lured out of the hilly terrain of Samaria and into the plains, the Arameans were convinced that they would prove to have the stronger army. In addition to suggesting that the king pick his battlefield more carefully, the advisers also suggested that the thirty-two kings, with their diverse interests and lack of military expertise, be replaced with professional officers over the host. Finally, they suggested that Ben-hadad, if he would be assured of victory, would need to have an army at least as large as the one he had lost at Samaria. The king listened to this advice and implemented it at the appropriate time (20:23-25).

A. The Battle (1 Kgs 20:26-29).

In the spring of the year Ben-hadad mustered his troops and went up against the Israelite fortress of Aphek.[3] Emboldened by their previous victory, the Israelites went out to challenge the invaders. They found the whole plain swarming with Aramean legions. In comparison the Israelites appeared like two bands of stragglers separated from the main body of the flock (20:26-27).

Under these circumstances Ahab was more than cheered by the appearance of a man of God—perhaps the same prophet who had brought news of victory a year earlier. Once again the message from the Lord was positive. Because the Arameans had relegated the Creator God to the level of a tribal deity, because they had said Yahweh was only a god of the hills, therefore he would intervene again on behalf of his people. Neighboring nations would learn of the power of the living God through this deliverance, and wavering Israel would be provided with yet another incontrovertible proof of Yahweh's divinity (20:28).

For seven days the two armies camped opposite one another. The Arameans waited for the Israelites to descend from the mountains; but Israel was reluctant to attack such a great host. On the seventh day the army of Israel charged down the hillsides and into the plains. The reason for the delay of seven days is not stated, but it is entirely possible that the sacred number seven had come to be regarded superstitiously as the most advantageous time for attack. In any case, the historian reports that the men of Israel smote a hundred thousand Aramean infantry in that one day of battle. The term *"smote"* may include wounded as well as slain (20:29).

B. Covenant with Aram (1 Kgs 20:30-34).

Those who survived the slaughter took refuge in the fortress at Aphek, which at the time would appear to have been in the control of the Arameans. There a second tragedy befell the invading host. A city wall collapsed killing 27,000 men.[4] Probably these soldiers were manning the defenses of the city when an earthquake threw down the walls (20:30b).[5]

Following the defeat in the plains about Aphek, Ben-hadad had fled into an inner chamber of the fortress (lit., *chamber within a chamber*). There his counselors advised that he surrender to Ahab because, they argued, the kings of Israel had a reputation for showing mercy[6] to their enemies. If the king and his staff were to put on sackcloth as a token of humility and ropes on their heads, i.e., around their necks, to demonstrate complete submission, there was a good chance that Ahab would allow them all to live (20:30b-31).

Ben-hadad had no alternative but to acquiesce in this suggestion. The counselors were dispatched so garbed to plead for the life of their master. Ahab seemed surprised to hear that Ben-hadad was alive. Upon receiving the news he immediately declared his willingness to enter into a peace treaty with the Aramean by declaring, *"He is my brother."* Seizing upon this favorable word, the messengers replied, *"Ben-hadad is your brother,"* by which they declared their willingness to accept the generous offer of a covenant. Then Ahab ordered that Ben-hadad be brought to him. When the Aramean king came forth from his place of hiding, Ahab invited him to come up with him into the royal chariot. This signaled great favor and reconciliation (20:32-33).

All of the details of the covenant worked out between Ahab and Ben-hadad are not recorded. The Aramean agreed to return to Israelite control the territories his father had taken from Ahab's *"father,"* i.e., predecessor, Baasha[7] (cf. 15:20). Furthermore, Ben-hadad conceded to Ahab the right to establish Israelite bazaars or quarters in Damascus in which Israelites might live and trade. Ahab was pleased with these concessions. After formalizing the agreement, the Israelite king dismissed his enemy (20:34).

Ahab had good reason for being lenient with Ben-hadad. A new power was rising in the east. Assyrian texts state that both Ahab and Ben-hadad contributed troops to a coalition army which successfully withstood the Assyrian advances in the famous battle of Qarqar in 853 BC. In the face of the rising power of Assyria, Ahab probably thought it would be better to have a friend and ally to the north than a belligerent. Others, however, think Ahab was motivated by purely commercial considerations.

C. Ahab Condemned (1 Kgs 20:35-43).

The prophets were not happy with the actions of Ahab. A certain member of the *"sons of the prophets"* went about to bring rebuke to the king. He directed his companion, i.e., one of his fellow prophets, to smite him, i.e., bruise and wound him. When the companion refused to comply, the prophet pronounced a severe judgment against him. As soon as the two parted, a lion slew the companion (20:35-36). This now is the second account of a prophet who violated an explicit commandment of God and paid for it with his life, in both cases by being slain by a lion (cf. 1 Kgs 13:24).

The great lesson which this prophet would try to illustrate to the king was that of unquestioning obedience to the commandments of Yahweh. Ahab had just transgressed the law of God by allowing one to escape whom God had appointed to destruction. He had to be taught that he had no right to be generous at the expense of others, that God's will must be done even when it goes against the grain and seems to contradict impulses of kindness. A prophet required to smite a brother, and that for no apparent reason, would no doubt find it repugnant to do so. That prophet who followed his benevolent impulses instead of the command of God forfeited his own life. The duty of unquestioning obedience was thus emphatically taught.

When the prophet gave the command to wound him to another man, he instantly complied. He probably had seen or heard what had happened to the first man who rejected that command. The prophet next put bandages over his head wound to conceal his identity. Then he went to wait for the return of the king (20:38).

As he passed by, the prophet, playing the role of a wounded soldier, cried out to the king to render a royal judgment. He pretended to be the victim of an unjust penalty assessed against him by a superior officer. He told the king that during the battle he had been ordered to guard a prisoner. If that prisoner escaped, he would forfeit his life or else pay a talent of silver (about 75 lbs.). Since common soldiers would never have so much money, the penalty for allowing escape of the prisoner would be death. The prisoner did in fact escape *"while I was busy with other duties."* Upon hearing these circumstances, Ahab declared the death penalty to be fair and just. A soldier who allowed a prisoner to escape should be executed (20:39-40).

The prophet then ripped away his bandage disguise. Ahab recognized him immediately as one of the prophets. Slowly the prophet pronounced the doom of the king. God had appointed Ben-hadad to utter destruction; he was a condemned man. Yet the king to whom

God had granted the victory had dismissed Ben-hadad instead of executing him. Therefore Ahab would forfeit his life for that of Benhadad. By means of his parable the prophet had succeeded in getting Ahab to pronounce judgment upon himself (20:41-42).

In spite of the clear condemnation of Ahab's conduct, some commentators seek to commend him on his merciful dealings with Benhadad. An assessment of his conduct must be made in the light of three facts. (1) Ahab was not free to do as he pleased with Benhadad. This was God's war and God's victory. Yahweh should have been consulted through priestly or prophetic oracle before disposing of the prisoners. (2) Ahab's previous dealings with Ben-hadad (cf. 20:6) should have indicated to him the character of this king. In the interest of future peace and security, Ahab should have executed the Aramean. (3) Surely the fate of Agag, Oreb and Zeeb as well as other aggressors against Israel should have signaled Ahab as to how to deal with Ben-hadad.

Under the divine threat and rebuke, Ahab returned to his campaign quarters sullen and angry. He realized that the prophet's prediction regarding the outcome of the battle had been fulfilled; he was therefore filled with apprehension that this new prediction would also prove true. With all the joy of victory removed, Ahab returned to the capital in Samaria (20:43).

ELIJAH AND AHAB
1 Kings 21:1-16

Shortly after the battle of Aphek, another incident transpired which brought further prophetic condemnation to Ahab. This time the bearer of bad news was Ahab's bitter enemy Elijah.

A. Covetousness of the King (1 Kgs 21:1-7).

Near Ahab's second palace in Jezreel was a vineyard possessed by a man named Naboth. This plot of ground Ahab dearly coveted. The vineyard was not required for the public welfare, but to satisfy a purely selfish personal whim. Ahab tried to induce Naboth to sell the vineyard, or to exchange it for one the king already owned. He, however, would not sell his property to one outside his family. Rebuffed by

Naboth, Ahab returned to the palace to give vent to childish grief. Sullen and angry he pouted in his private chambers, refusing to partake of food (21:1-4).

Jezebel went to Ahab's room to inquire as to the reason for the king's loss of appetite. The queen was shocked when she heard what triggered her husband's depression. She did not even bother to ask why Naboth had refused to sell his property. This queen came from a royal family that was accustomed to get whatever it wanted. She urged Ahab to arise and eat. She would see to it that he got his vineyard (21:5-7).

B. Conspiracy against Naboth (1 Kgs 21:8-16).

In short order Jezebel set in motion a plot to eliminate Naboth. Letters, written in the name of the king and sealed with the royal seal, were sent to the elders and judges of Jezreel. Jezebel's plan was simple. A fast was to be proclaimed in Jezreel, as though the city had come under a curse because of some undisclosed sin. Naboth was to be accorded his usual seat of honor. During the assembly two "sons of Belial," i.e., worthless men, publicly were to accuse Naboth of having cursed both God and the king. Such cursing, according to the law, was a capital crime (cf. Exod 22:28; Deut 13:11). Naboth then would be stoned. Because the alleged crime was treason, all of Naboth's property would be forfeited to the crown (21:8-10).

The elders of Jezreel must have been as wicked as their queen. Their ready compliance with the directive of Jezebel shows not only the moral degradation of the day, but also the terror which the name of Jezebel inspired. The crowd believed the testimony of the two witness over the protests of Naboth. Convinced that this man had brought down the curse of God on their city, the crowd shoved Naboth outside the city walls where they stoned him to death. The elders returned their word to Jezebel in Samaria that the dastardly deed had been done (21:11-14).

Jezebel immediately informed Ahab that the way was now clear for him to claim the property of Naboth. The queen's words were full of irony. Naboth had refused to sell his property; now he had lost his life and his property. The moody Ahab was jubilant when he heard that Naboth was dead. He arose immediately to go down to Jezreel to take possession of the vineyard (21:15-16).

C. Condemnation by Elijah (1 Kgs 21:17-26).

God would not allow the ruthless murder of Naboth to go unrebuked. Elijah was dispatched to meet Ahab in the vineyard which he had confiscated. That Ahab might realize the full impact of what he had done, the prophet opened the conversation with a penetrating rhetorical question: *"Have you murdered and also taken possession?"* This indictment was followed by a pronouncement of doom on Ahab. In the place where the dogs licked Naboth's blood, dogs would lick the blood of Ahab! (21:17-19).

Ahab was shocked at the sudden appearance of Elijah whom he had not seen since the Carmel contest. The conscience-stricken king could only mutter, *"Have you found me out, O my enemy?"* Ahab considered Elijah his enemy because it seemed that this prophet always had been opposed to him. Yet it was not because of personal animosity that Elijah had sought out Ahab, but because the king had *"sold himself,"* i.e., completely surrendered himself, to do what was evil in the eyes of Yahweh (21:20).

Ahab, the supreme magistrate of the land, may have been ignorant of the tactics by which Jezebel had procured the vineyard for him; but he had acquiesced in her infamous crime after its accomplishment, and he was anxious to reap the benefits of it. Thus instead of punishing his guilty wife and those who had carried out her instructions, the king, by his actions, had sanctioned the crime. Therefore, the prophetic pronouncement was directed against Ahab.

After he explained the reason for the sentence, Elijah elaborated upon it. The judgment would involve every male descendant of Ahab. Just as the royal houses of Jeroboam and Baasha had been exterminated, so now the house of Ahab would be wiped out. By his actions Ahab had provoked God to anger. He had also encouraged Israel to sin; therefore he must be punished. Furthermore, the queen must also taste the wrath of God. The dogs would eat Jezebel beside the wall of Jezreel, the scene of her latest crime. Dogs and birds would devour the unburied corpses of Ahab's family (21:21-24).[8]

The Naboth incident clearly reveals the social breakdown of Ahab's kingdom and the extent to which Jezebel's Phoenicianization had succeeded. Years of flirtation with pagan practices were taking their toil. The rights of individuals guaranteed in the Sinai covenant were being ignored. The king was no longer under the law, but was superior to it. No predecessor had so completely abandoned the ways of Yahweh. Through Jezebel, Canaanite Baal worship had been reintroduced in the northern kingdom (21:25-26).

D. Contrition of Ahab (1 Kgs 21:27-29).

Ahab was deeply affected by the dire predictions of Elijah. By several outward signs he manifested his inward repentance for the crimes he had condoned. He rent his garments, put on sackcloth, fasted and even slept in his sackcloth. He also "went about softly," i.e., humbly, contritely. Taking note of this royal repentance, Yahweh sent an important word to Elijah which in effect deferred the threatened judgment until the days of his son. This is no example of the innocent suffering for the guilty. God knew in advance that the son would be worse than his father. Furthermore, the son would also have the option of repentance by which still further reprieve could be granted. Judgment was deferred to give the house of Ahab another chance. How marvelous is the divine patience! (21:27-29).

MICAIAH AND AHAB
1 Kings 22:1-40

Another great prophet had a confrontation with Ahab over a proposed military campaign to recover a border city from the Arameans.

A. The Proposal (1 Kgs 22:1-5// 2 Chr 18:2-3).

Following the second defeat of Ben-hadad, the Arameans and Israelites remained at peace for over two years.[9] At that time Ahab received a state visit from King Jehoshaphat of Judah, a king with considerable military strength (2 Chr 17:10-19). The northern king needed the help of his southern ally to help recover territory which Ben-hadad had failed to return to Israel in compliance with the treaty of Aphek (cf.1 Kgs 20:34).

The focal point of Ahab's concern was the fortress of Ramoth-gilead which was located east of the sea of Galilee on the frontier with Aram. During the course of Jehoshaphat's visit, Ahab broached the question of a possible joint campaign to recapture the city. The alliance between Israel and Judah was new. Ahab probably wondered how this proposal would strike the pious prince of Judah (22:1-3).

Jehoshaphat should have forthrightly refused aid to Ahab (cf. 2 Chr 19:2). Instead, however, he expressed his enthusiastic interest in engaging in this war. Probably Jehoshaphat feared the growing power of Damascus and considered that it would be in his own best interest to dislodge Ben-hadad from his stronghold in Gilead. Being the godly man that he was, Jehoshaphat insisted that the will of Yahweh be sought regarding the proposed campaign (22:4-5).

B. The Court Prophets (1 Kgs 22:6-12 // 2 Chr 18:4-11).

Having primed his court prophets earlier, Ahab was not unwilling to comply with the request of Jehoshaphat. When the king put the question of the campaign to the four hundred prophets, they dutifully and unanimously urged Ahab to go up to Ramoth-gilead. They promised that the Lord (*'adonai*) would give the city into the hands of the king. These four hundred were not the prophets of Baal or Asherah. They were renegade prophets of Yahweh who were part of the apostate official calf worship of the northern kingdom.[10] They were king-appointed rather than God-called prophets (22:6).

Jehoshaphat was suspicious of the four hundred. He asked if there might yet be another prophet of Yahweh whose advice could be solicited. Indeed Micaiah the son of Imlah could be consulted. Ahab, however, admitted that he hated this man of God because he consistently had prophesied evil concerning the royal family. Jehoshaphat then administered a mild rebuke to Ahab for insinuating that a prophet of God could be motivated by personal dislike for the king. Under the circumstances Ahab could hardly refuse to permit his guest to hear what Micaiah might have to say. So he dispatched an officer to fetch the man of God (22:7-9).

The four hundred continued their prophesying even while Micaiah was being summoned. In order to convince the dubious Jehoshaphat that the campaign was safe, Zedekiah, the leader of the four hundred, constructed *"horns of iron."* These symbols of power may have been nothing more than two iron spikes held on the forehead. *"With these you shall thrust through Aram until you have consumed them."* This dramatic prediction was made in the form of a *"thus says Yah-*

weh." The rest of the four hundred continued to repeat their initial promises of success except that they followed the lead of Zedekiah in using the name Yahweh in this utterance (22:10-12).

C. Micaiah's Prophecy (1 Kgs 22:13-28//2 Chr 18:6-27).

The messenger sent to fetch Micaiah knew that Ahab needed to secure an endorsement of the proposed campaign from all the prophets. Any negative note might cause the pious Jehoshaphat to withdraw from the venture. So the messenger pled with the man of God to join the four hundred in approving the campaign. The messenger, however, misunderstood this man of God as much as did his king. Micaiah could not be intimidated or bribed. He was not afraid to stand alone. He would speak only what Yahweh revealed to him (22:13-14).

Ahab put to Micaiah the same question which he had put to the four hundred. The prophet responded with the identical answer which the court prophets had given. Ahab's hollow tone had revealed the insincerity of his question. He really did not want to know the will of God; he wanted to be deceived. No doubt Micaiah's mocking tone showed that his words were sarcastic. In an effort to impress Jehoshaphat, Ahab pretended to be greatly distressed over the prophet's manifest insincerity. Before he realized what he was saying, Ahab blurted out that what he wanted to hear was the word of Yahweh. This was a tacit admission that what he had heard from the four hundred was not the word of the Lord (22:15-16).

At this juncture the tone and demeanor of Micaiah suddenly changed. The man of God became deadly serious. He had seen a vision of Israel scattered upon the hills with no shepherd; he heard the voice of God directing those scattered ones to return to their homes in peace. No one in the royal assembly failed to see that Micaiah was foretelling the dispersion of the Israelite army as a result of the death of their king. Ahab certainly understood the thrust of these words. He had demanded the word of Yahweh and had received it. Lest Jehoshaphat be unduly influenced by this dire prediction, Ahab quickly suggested that these words were but further evidence of the prophet's prejudice toward the king (22:17-18).

The insinuation that Micaiah spoke out of malice brought forth a vigorous rebuttal from the man of God. At sometime in the past Micaiah had seen another vision relating to Ahab. He had seen Yahweh on his heavenly throne surrounded by all the hosts of heaven, i.e., angels. Yahweh asked for suggestions as to how Ahab might be enticed to go up to Ramoth-gilead that he might be slain there. Various schemes were suggested. Finally *"the spirit,"* i.e., the evil spirit, affirmed that he would be able to entice Ahab. The plan was that this spirit would take control of the mouths of Ahab's prophets and *they* would persuade the king to go up against Ramoth-gilead. Yahweh then granted to this spirit permission to so entice Ahab. Thus, declared Micaiah, Yahweh had put a lying spirit in the mouths of all Ahab's prophets; they had spoken falsehood. Furthermore, the prediction of calamity against Ahab had not just come from Micaiah, but from Yahweh who spoke through him (22:19-23).

Several important questions remain to be answered concerning Micaiah's vision.

1. How can it be that Yahweh would find it necessary to take counsel of the angelic hosts? Prophetic visions are anthropomorphic. They do not always correspond to reality. Such visions are the vehicle used to convey a cardinal truth to the mind of the prophet. In this case the truth is that Ahab's death in battle had been foreordained in the counsels of God, and that divine wisdom had devised a means for accomplishing this goal.

2. Who was the spirit who volunteered to entice Ahab? Keil and others see the spirit as a personification of the spirit of prophecy which takes hold of a man and makes him a prophet. Other commentators, however, are probably correct when they identify the spirit as Satan. That Satan has or at least did have access to the heavenly council chambers is attested by the opening chapters of the Book of Job.

3. How can the all Holy One give his sanction to deceit and lying for the purpose of tempting Ahab to his death? Here one must distinguish between the permissive and the positive will of God. Yahweh permitted the evil spirit to do his evil work. The same thought is expressed in Ezekiel 14:9 *"If the prophet be deceived . . . I, Yahweh, have deceived that prophet."* Ahab *wished* to be guided by false prophets. The justice of God permitted him to be so guided.

Zedekiah, one of the four hundred, bristled at the charge that he and his cohorts had been possessed by a spirit of lies. Without warning he stepped forward and smote Micaiah on the cheek. At the same time Zedekiah shouted, *"Where did the spirit of Yahweh pass over from me to speak to you?"* Zedekiah was conscious of some force beyond himself which compelled him to speak his prophetic word. How could the Spirit of Yahweh speak one message through Zedekiah, and something quite different through Micaiah? This scoffing question was intended to counter the story Micaiah had related so dramatically. Ridicule is one of the most effective ways of countering the arguments of an opponent (22:24).

Micaiah was not intimidated by the bombastic Zedekiah. He did not answer directly the insolent question. Rather he confidently affirmed that one day Zedekiah would *see,* i.e., perceive the truth. Only then would Zedekiah have the prophetic vision to correctly assess the political situation. In that day when Micaiah's predictions concerning the defeat of the armies of Israel were fulfilled, Zedekiah would hasten into hiding out of shame and perhaps fear of reprisals at the hand of the queen (22:25).

The two kings seem to have looked on the assault of Micaiah without protest. When the brief prophetic confrontation was over, Ahab ordered Micaiah returned to his prison cell. There he was to remain under the watchful eye of Amon the governor of the city and Joash, one of Ahab's own sons. Instructions were given that Micaiah was to receive only bread and water until the king returned from Ramoth-gilead in peace (22:26-27).

Probably owing to the presence of Jehoshaphat, Micaiah escaped with no more severe punishment. Still the man of God was undaunted. He was willing to stake his prophetic reputation on the fulfillment of this one prediction. If Ahab returned in peace, then Yahweh truly had not spoken to him. He was willing to face the capital punishment to which he was liable in that case. Before being dragged from the place, Micaiah shouted forth a call for all peoples to take note of the predictions which he had just made (22:28).

D. The Death of Ahab (1 Kgs 22:29-40// 2 Chr 18:28-34).

The two kings were not deterred by the ominous predictions of

Micaiah. They proceeded immediately to Ramoth-gilead. Ahab's action is in character; that of Jehoshaphat is more difficult to explain. Why did the godly king of Judah reject the advice of God's prophet? Some (or all) of the following considerations may help to explain his actions. (1) Jehoshaphat already had committed himself to the war effort (cf. v. 4). (2) The hospitality extended by his host may have obligated Jehoshaphat to acquiesce. (3) He may have feared being labeled a coward. (4) Those present in the assembly were treating Micaiah's prophecy with disdain. (5) Ahab may have convinced Jehoshaphat to dismiss the threats of Micaiah in view of the longstanding animosity which existed between the king and this prophet. (6) Jehoshaphat's own interests were threatened by the rising Aramean power.

On the eve of battle Ahab came up with what he thought was an ingenious plan to frustrate the dire predictions which had been made against him. Micaiah had seen *Israel* scattered as sheep having no master. To thwart this prediction, Ahab decided in effect to relinquish his role of leader of the host. He decided not to lead the army, as kings were accustomed to do, in his royal robes. Rather he would disguise himself as a lesser officer. Since Jehoshaphat's life had not been threatened by the prophet, it would be unnecessary for him to take similar precautions (22:29-30).

Ben-hadad directed his thirty-two chariot officers to concentrate their attack on the king of Israel. The Aramean rightly reasoned that the death of the king would terminate the war. Seeing the royal robes of Jehoshaphat, the chariot captains pressed in that direction. When the king of Judah realized he had been singled out for concentrated attack, he cried out in desperation to God. Yahweh intervened on his behalf (2 Chr 18:31). The charioteers recognized that it was not Ahab that they were pursuing. So they turned away from Jehoshaphat (22: 31-33).

Ahab's disguise could not avert the judgment of God. During the course of the battle, an Aramean soldier launched an arrow that was destined to find its mark in the breast of the king. Ahab knew he had been mortally wounded. He ordered his chariot driver to wheel about and carry him away from the scene of battle. Ahab did not want the army to discover what had happened lest they become discouraged and abandon the field. The fury of the battle, however, did not allow the chariot driver to comply with his king's order. To maintain a facade of normality, Ahab's servants propped him up in the chariot. Unable to attend to his wound, the king slowly bled to death (22:34). At evening Ahab died. His blood poured out into the floor of the chariot. When the army saw that their king had fallen, a shout went up among the troops. They urged one another to terminate the battle and make their way to their homes (22:35-36).

What a sad sight that must have been as the battle-weary, leaderless troops made their way back to Samaria. There they buried their fallen king. At the city pool, where harlots customarily bathed, they washed the chariot of the king. Packs of scavenger dogs licked up the blood that had been flushed from the chariot. This fulfilled the word which Yahweh had spoken concerning him through Micaiah and, in essence, through Elijah as well (22:37-38).[11]

As the account of Ahab's long reign concludes, two other brief notices about his accomplishments are given. He, like his father, was a city builder. Ahab built several towns. He was perhaps most famous for his ivory palace, i.e., a house with ivory inlays. His son Ahaziah ("whom Yahweh upholds") succeeded him as king. This name perhaps suggests that, notwithstanding his flirtations with Baal worship, Ahab remained a believer in Yahweh (22:39-40).

THE PROPHETS AND JEHOSHAPHAT
2 Chronicles 17:1-19:11

Jehoshaphat began his sole reign in 869 BC.[12] Like his father Asa, he followed Yahweh. Unlike his father, his commitment did not wane in his later years. Four chapters in Chronicles shed light on why Ahab had cultivated an alliance with Jehoshaphat.

A. The Strength of Jehoshaphat (2 Chr 17:1-19).

The strength of Jehoshaphat was manifested in two ways. First, the king of Judah was militarily strong. He stationed troops in fortified cities throughout Judah. He had garrisons in the towns of Ephraim which his father Asa had captured (2 Chr 17:1-2). He had a huge army of experienced men numbering in the hundreds of thousands (2 Chr 17:12-18).

Second, Jehoshaphat was enormously wealthy. Because he followed the Lord he had *"great wealth and honor"* (2 Chr 17:3-6). The fear of Yahweh fell on the surrounding kingdoms so that they, for the most part, did not make war with Judah. The Philistines rendered tribute in silver to him, the Arabs in thousands of rams and goats (2 Chr 17:10-11).

The source of Jehoshaphat's strength was Yahweh. The Lord was with this king because he followed the example of David. He did not seek after the Baals as did his counterparts in the northern kingdom. So Yahweh *"established the kingdom in his control."* Jehoshaphat took great pride in the ways of Yahweh. He continued the efforts of his father to remove the high places and the Asherim from Judah. He even dispatched government officials and Levites throughout the land to instruct his people in the book of the law (2 Chr 17:3-9).

B. The Prophet Jehu (2 Chr 19:1-11).

The prophets had two main criticisms of Jehoshaphat. First, he did not remove the high places outside Jerusalem. These were shrines where Yahweh was worshiped illegally. Second, he made peace with Ahab of Israel. To seal this alliance, Jehoshaphat arranged a marriage between his son Jehoram, and Athaliah the daughter of Jezebel (2 Chr 18:1). Probably the mutual fear of the rising power of Damascus forced the rival kingdoms to seek reconciliation (1 Kgs 22:41-44).

When Jehoshaphat returned to Jerusalem after his narrow escape at Ramoth-gilead, Jehu the prophet went to see him. Jehu was the son of Hanani the seer who had condemned Asa for his alliance with Ben-hadad (cf. 2 Chr 16:7). He rebuked the king for entering an alliance with those *"who hate Yahweh."* Jehu warned that compromise with the enemies of the Lord could bring the wrath of God against the king. Because of his reform efforts and his personal efforts to seek God, however, Yahweh would be lenient with Jehoshaphat (2 Chr 19:1-3).

Jehoshaphat responded to this criticism with yet other reform efforts. He appointed judges in the land in each city. An appellate system brought difficult cases to one of two supreme courts in Jerusalem. One court, presided over by the high priest, considered religious questions. A government official was supreme judge over the civil court (2 Chr 19:5-11).

ENDNOTES

1. The Moabite stone, discovered in 1868, documents that Omri of Israel conquered Moab at some point during his independent reign of six years (880-874 BC).

2. The traditional view is that the young men were the sons of vassal princes left as hostages as an assurance that they would not rebel. Modern commentators prefer the view that the *princes* were were governors of various districts of Israel. The *young men* were cadets who were recruited by these princes and sent to the capital for special training. John Gray, depicts the young men as "shock troops" or "commandos." *I & II Kings* in "The Old Testament Library" (Philadelphia: Westminster, 1970), p. 424.

3. Which of several Old Testament Apheks is meant is not clear. Probably it was to Aphek located about six miles east of Galilee that Ben-hadad gathered his forces. Keil, however, opts for the Aphek located in the great plain of Esdraelon.

4. Leo Honor thinks the meaning is that the Aramean survivors who fled to the city perished when the wall was captured. Another interpretation is that when the wall fell the escape of the survivors was cut off. *Book of Kings 1* (New York: UAHC, 1956), p. 290.

5. Less likely is the proposal of Gray (*op. cit.*, p. 429) that the wall collapsed because of undermining by the Israelites.

6. In its primary meaning *chesed* refers to loyalty to a covenant. The secondary meaning embraces the idea of mercy or humane treatment. Either meaning would be appropriate in this context.

7. Baasha was not the father or even the ancestor of Ahab, but belonged to a separate dynasty. Ben-hadad is using the term *"father"* in the sense of predecessor. Others think the reference is to Ahab's literal father, Omri.

8. The formula regarding the dogs and birds was used earlier by the prophet Ahijah against Jeroboam (14:11) and by the prophet Jehu against Baasha (16:4).

9. According to the Hebrew system of time reckoning, any time over two years would be called "three years" as in 22:1. The following verse clearly indicates that the events in 1 Kgs 22 took place in the third year and thus before the completion of that year.

10. Jezebel's persecution of the prophets must have been limited to prophets of Yahweh who were not amenable to her purposes. The prophets called in by Ahab were those who had saved their lives by compromising with the crown.

11. By his arrogant disregard for the word of God spoken by Micaiah, Ahab brought back upon himself the penalty which Elijah had foreseen, but which had been set aside as a result of Ahab's repentance (cf. 1 Kgs 21:29).

12. According to Thiele, Jehoshaphat was coregent with Asa from 872-869 BC. His "official" reign of twenty-five years was counted from 872 BC, but his sole reign began in 869 BC. Edwin R. Thiele, *A Chronology of the Hebrew Kings* (Grand Rapids: Zondervan, 1977), p. 77.

CHAPTER THIRTY-TWO

The Sons of Jezebel
2 Kings 1-3

For over three decades (874-841 BC) Jezebel was the most powerful figure in the northern kingdom. She dominated her husband Ahab, and her two sons Ahaziah and Jehoram. To a certain extent her influence reached Judah. In that southern kingdom Jezebel's son-in-law and grandson ruled as legitimate monarchs. In the year Jezebel died her daughter Athaliah seized the throne of Judah and ruled for seven years.

JEZEBEL'S SON AHAZIAH
1 Kings 22:47-2 Kings 1:18

When Ahab fell at Ramoth-gilead in 853 BC, he was succeeded on the throne of Israel by his son Ahaziah. This king, like his father, did evil in the eyes of Yahweh. He tolerated the calf worship which Jeroboam had instituted. In addition he served Baal. The sacred historian points the finger at Jezebel as being one of the reasons for the evil direction of this eighth king of Israel.

539

A. Alliance with Judah (1 Kgs 22:47-49//2 Chr 20:35-37).

Ahaziah joined Jehoshaphat of Judah in attempting to revive the maritime enterprise of Solomon. The two kings had *"Tarshish ships,"* i.e., large sea-going vessels, which they intended to sail to Ophir and Tarshish (cf. 2 Chr 20:36). These ships were launched from the Red Sea port of Ezion-geber. A tremendous storm, however, dashed the ships to pieces before they got out of the harbor (1 Kgs 22:48).

The prophet Eliezer appeared on the scene to *"prophesy"* against Jehoshaphat. He explained the disaster at Ezion-geber as being the results of the alliance with the ungodly Ahaziah (2 Chr 20:37). The northern king attributed the smashing of the ships to the inexperience of Jehoshaphat's sailors. He proposed a second venture in which his servants would join the seamen from Judah. Because of their close association with the Phoenicians, some subjects of the northern kingdom may have been highly skilled sailors. Jehoshaphat, however, accepted the explanation of the prophet. He refused any further commercial alliance with Ahaziah (1 Kgs 22:49).

B. An Accident (2 Kgs 1:2).

In his second year of rule, Ahaziah accidentally fell through the lattice which enclosed his upper chamber. As a result of this fall, the king was so injured that he lingered upon his bed hovering between life and death. In this desperate condition, Ahaziah dispatched messengers to Baal-zebub, the god of the Philistine city of Ekron, to inquire as to his prognosis. The king, of course, wanted more than just information; a favorable oracle from a deity would mean that the god would intervene on his behalf.

That a son of Jezebel would prefer to consult Baal rather than Yahweh is not surprising. Why he chose this particular Baal god, however, is far from clear. Perhaps Baal-zebub had a reputation for granting favorable oracular verdicts. On the other hand, perhaps Ekron was the nearest of the ancient Baal shrines. The name Baal-zebub means "lord of flies." Apparently this particular Baal was thought to prevent plagues of flies, or else was thought to send such plagues against his enemies.[1]

C. An Announcement (2 Kgs 1:3-8).

For the second time (cf. 1 Kgs 19:5,7) an angel of God visited Elijah the prophet, instructing him to intercept the delegation which had been dispatched to Ekron. The actions of Ahaziah were a complete denial of the lordship of Yahweh. To consult a foreign oracle was tantamount to saying that the voice of God was wholly silent. The God of Israel did have a word for Ahaziah, albeit an unsolicited one. Because he had so grievously apostatized, God sentenced this king to die from the effects of his fall (1:3-4).

Ahaziah inquired as to the reason for the hasty return of his messengers. They reported the message which the prophet had delivered. They described the man of God as being a hairy man (lit., a lord of hair) who was wearing a leather girdle. Normally the girdle was of soft material. From this description Ahaziah knew immediately that the message of doom had come from the same man who had predicted the death of his father. Some take the description of Elijah to mean that he was rough and unkempt with his hair and beard long. Others think the reference is to a shaggy garment which Elijah wore. In any case, Ahaziah realized that the dreaded adversary of his father and mother had suddenly reappeared (1:5-8).

D. An Attempted Arrest (2 Kgs 1:9-15).

No doubt Ahaziah had been instructed by his wicked mother to take strong action against Elijah should this religious radical reappear. Though lying on his bed of affliction under the divine sentence of death, this king was so hardened, unrepentant and defiant that he ordered a unit of fifty soldiers to arrest Elijah. The size of this arrest force suggests that Ahaziah was challenging directly the power of the prophet and his God. Meanwhile, Elijah had positioned himself on a hill where he calmly awaited the showdown with the king.

The captain of fifty approached the prophet, addressed him by his customary title, and ordered him to surrender. Elijah then prayed that God would vindicate his prophetic authority by destroying this band of soldiers. God heard that prayer. Fire (lightning?) came down from heaven to consume the captain and his fifty. Ahaziah sent another fifty to demand that Elijah come down *quickly*. The king apparently had grown impatient. Again the prophet prayed. Again fire from

541

heaven consumed his adversaries (1:9-12).

A third captain dispatched by the king escaped with his life because he humbled himself before God's prophet. He ascended the hill on which Elijah was still seated. He bowed himself before the prophet to beseech his compassion. Having heard of the fate of the previous units, he acknowledged that this man of God held his life and the lives of his men in his hand. He begged that Elijah might spare these men. The battle was now won. The honor of Elijah and the God he represented had been vindicated. An angel of God intervened at this point, directing the prophet to go with this captain (1:13-15).

E. Ahaziah's Death (2 Kgs 1:16).

Elijah did not change his message once he came face to face with this bitter antagonist. Boldly in the name of his God he repeated the message which he had originally sent to the king by his messengers. Because of his gross apostasy, Ahaziah would die from his injuries. Shortly thereafter the king expired. Ahaziah's official reign is said to have been two years, but in actual time he reigned about a year overlapping 853-852 BC (1 Kgs 22:51).

JEZEBEL'S SON JEHORAM
2 Kings 3:1-27

Because he had no son, Ahaziah's brother Jehoram ruled in his stead. Thus a Jehoram ruled in Israel simultaneously with a Jehoram in Judah who in fact was his brother-in-law (1 Kgs 1:17).[2] While Jehoram of Israel was evil, he was not as bad as his father and brother. Perhaps he had taken warning from the fates of his two predecessors. In any case, he "put away" the image of Baal which Ahab had erected in Samaria. This may indicate that he abolished the official status of Baalism in the northern kingdom. Jehoram's wickedness was that he continued the apostate calf worship introduced by Jeroboam back in 930 BC (2 Kgs 3:2-3).

A. Moab Campaign (2 Kgs 3:4-15a).

For some years the Moabites were put under oppressive tribute by the Omri dynasty. They was forced to send to Samaria the wool of a hundred thousand sheep and goats. This extraordinarily heavy tribute drove the Moabites to rebellion at the first opportunity which, as it turned out, was the death of the powerful Ahab (2 Kgs 3:4-5).

Jehoram mobilized his forces for an invasion of Moab. In this effort Jehoshaphat of Judah was again an ally. The good king does not seem to have learned anything from his disastrous military alliance with Ahab (1 Kgs 22) and his equally disastrous commercial alliance with Ahaziah (2 Chr 20:35f.).

The plan suggested by Jehoshaphat called for the combined forces to take the circuitous route around the southern tip of the Dead Sea to attack Moab from the south. Two reasons dictated this decision. First, the king of Edom, currently a vassal of Judah, could contribute a contingent of troops if the expedition took the southern route. Second, Moab was probably less fortified on the southern frontier (2 Kgs 3:6-8).

The torturous trip of a hundred miles through the barren wilderness of Judah took the allies seven days. What was thought to be a perennial stream in that region had failed due to a lengthy drought. The allies found themselves facing a desperate situation. The impious Jehoram was ready to blame their plight upon Yahweh. Yet no prophet of God had ever encouraged this campaign. The allies had come together on their own accord, guided strictly by political interests. In despair born of unbelief, Jehoram assumed that Yahweh meant to deliver this host into the hands of the king of Moab (2 Kgs 3:9-10).

Being a man of faith, Jehoshaphat was not ready to throw up his hands in despair. In this desperate hour he wanted to confer with a prophet of God. How relieved he must have been to learn that Elisha had accompanied the expedition, apparently without the knowledge of Jehoram. In time past Elisha had been known as the one who *"poured water on the hands of Elijah,"* i.e., had been his servant. Now God would demonstrate his power through this man for the first time before the kings of both Israel and Judah (2 Kgs 3:11).

Jehoshaphat was delighted to learn that Elisha was present. He was convinced that *"the word of Yahweh is with him."* Just how Jehoshaphat had come to have such regard for Elisha is uncertain. Perhaps it was the fact of Elisha's close association with Elijah which led Jehoshaphat enthusiastically to endorse him as an authorized exponent of God's will. In any case, the allied kings were so desperate that *they* sought out Elisha rather than merely summoning him to their pavilion (2 Kgs 3:12).

When the three supplicants approached, Elisha unleashed a sarcastic verbal barrage against Jehoram. The halfhearted repentance of this monarch had not ingratiated him to this uncompromising man of God. Jehoram had no ground of appeal to the prophet. If this son of Jezebel wanted prophetic counsel, he should seek out the prophets of his father or mother.

Jehoram responded to the prophetic sarcasm with meek deportment. In effect he begged the prophet that his initial response not be his final response. After all, it was not just the king of Israel who was in desperate straits. *Three* kings were in danger of falling to the king of Moab. To this Elisha responded with solemn adjuration that it was only because of the presence of the godly Jehoshaphat that he would condescend to help the expedition. The prophet then called for a musician to play some soothing song so that he could bring himself into the proper frame of mind to receive the divine revelation (2 Kgs 3:13-15a).

B. Prophecy of Elisha (2 Kgs 3:15b-25).

While the musician played, the *"hand of Yahweh,"* the power of the Spirit of God, came upon Elisha. He was able to reveal to the royal petitioners the means by which Yahweh would deliver them from their plight. The kings were to have pits dug in the valley by means of which the precious water which they needed might be retained. A great storm would arise many miles from the camp of the allies. The parched valley would shortly be filled with the runoff of that storm. Not only would Yahweh deliver the allies from their present danger, he would also deliver Moab into their hands (2 Kgs 3:15b-18).

True to the word of the prophet, the next morning about sunrise (*"when the meal offering was offered"*) a mighty stream of water filled the pits dug the day before. The Moabite army saw the reddish early morning sun reflecting off the water. Since there had been no rain during the night, the Moabites never suspected that the wadi near the allied camp was full of water. The confused movement of men and beasts about the trenches seen from a distance suggested hostili-

544

ties. The Moabite officers concluded that the three invading armies
had turned against one another in a bloody slaughter. Nothing
remained to do but to gather the spoil from the camp of the allies.
For this purpose the hosts of Moab surged forward in a disorderly
rush (2 Kgs 3:19-23).

The allies had anticipated the onrush of Moabites. They kept the
main body of their men concealed within the camp as an ambush.
When the first wave of greedy Moabites reached the camp, the allies
rose up to smite and completely rout them. True to the prediction of
Elisha, the allies destroyed the cities of Moab, spread stones over the
fields, stopped up the wells, and felled the fruit trees. This devastation
continued until finally only the stronghold of Kir-hareseth remained
untouched. Allied slingers began to hurl their missiles over the wall of
Kir-hareseth, thus grievously harassing the defenders (2 Kgs 3:24-25).

C. Siege of Kir-hareseth (2 Kgs 3:26-27).

The fortunes of Moab continued to decline. The king then decided
on a desperate gamble. Gathering seven hundred expert swordsmen,
he attempted to break through the allied lines to reach the king of
Edom. Perhaps he regarded the king of Edom as the weakest member of the coalition, the least likely to offer effective resistance.[3] This
attempt failed. The Moabites were again forced back into their belea-
guered fortress (2 Kgs 3:26).

The Moabite king then tried to appeal to his deity Chemosh for a
miraculous deliverance. He took the crown prince and offered him up
as a burnt offering upon the city wall in full view of both the defenders
and the attackers. The sight of their king sacrificing his own firstborn
son so stirred up the fury of the Moabites against Israel that they fought
with almost superhuman strength. In the face of this determined opposition the allies began to weaken. Finally, the campaign was called off.
Each of the confederates returned to his own land (2 Kgs 3:27).

DELIVERANCE IN JUDAH
2 Chronicles 20:1-30

In retaliation for assisting Jehoram in his effort to resubjugate
Moab, Judah itself experienced an invasion.[4] The Moabites,

Ammonites and the Meunites came to make war against Jehoshaphat (2 Chr 20:1).

A. Judah's Plight (2 Chr 20:2-4).

The invasion of the army from beyond the Dead Sea caught Jehoshaphat by surprise. By the time he got the word the enemy was at Engedi on the western bank of the Dead Sea well within the territory of Judah. The king was afraid. He *"turned his attention to seek Yahweh."* He proclaimed a fast. Citizens from throughout Judah gathered to seek the Lord.

B. Jehoshaphat's Prayer (2 Chr 20:5-13).

The king stood before the assembly of his people in the court of the temple and led in a wonderful prayer. He acknowledged the great and irresistible power of Yahweh. He expressed confidence that the Lord would hear the cries of distress which might come to him from before his temple. In narrative prayer the king described how Judah had been invaded by a force determined to drive God's people out of their inheritance. He closed the prayer by admitting powerlessness and ignorance in the face of this invasion. In this situation Judah was dependent upon Yahweh totally.

C. Jahaziel's Prophecy (2 Chr 20:14-19).

In the midst of that assembly the Spirit of Yahweh came upon a Levitical singer named Jahaziel. He urged the nation not to fear before the invaders. *"The battle is not yours, but God's."* Tomorrow they should march against the enemy, but they would not need to fight. They would *"stand and see the salvation of Yahweh"* (2 Chr 20:14-17).

In response to this encouraging word, Jehoshaphat bowed his face to the ground. All his subjects joined their king in worshiping Yahweh. The Levitical singers stood up to praise the Lord *"with a very loud voice"* (2 Chr 20:18-19).

D. Confident Praise (2 Chr 20:20-23).

In the morning Jehoshaphat addressed his troops as they prepared to march against the enemy. He urged them to put their trust in Yah-

weh and his prophets. He ordered the Levitical choir, dressed in their
holy attire, to lead the military procession (2 Chr 20:20-21).

Even as the army of Judah marched toward the confrontation
singing praises, God *"set ambushes"* among the invaders. The
Ammonites and Moabites destroyed those from Mt. Seir (Edom).
Then they turned on one another. So the entire invading force was
routed before the army of Judah even arrived at the scene (2 Chr
20:22).

E. Abundant Plunder (2 Chr 20:24-30).

Gathering the spoils from the camp of the invaders took three
days. On the fourth day the jubilant army of Jehoshaphat assembled
publicly to bless the Lord. They named the spot the Valley of Berac-
ah, i.e., "blessing" (2 Chr 20:24-26).

The army returned to Jerusalem triumphantly to the sound of various musical instruments. A joyous throng filled the courts of the temple
where only days before they had stood trembling. News of the miraculous deliverance put the dread of Judah's God in surrounding nations.
From that day forward *"the kingdom of Jehoshaphat was at peace,
for his God gave him rest on every side"* (2 Chr 20:27-30).

JEZEBEL'S SON-IN-LAW
2 Kings 8:16-24// 2 Chr 21:1-20

Jezebel's son-in-law Jehoram reigned as a coregent with
Jehoshaphat from 853 BC until the death of his father in 848 BC.
The independent reign of Jehoram lasted eight years (848-841 BC).
Influenced by his evil wife Athaliah—Jezebel's daughter[5]—Jehoram
departed from the righteous course of his father. Shortly after taking
the throne he put to death his six brothers in order to solidify his position. At the same time he executed many princes, no doubt for the
same reason. Soon afterwards he *"made high places in the mountains of Judah, and caused the inhabitants of Jerusalem to commit fornication,"* i.e., become idolaters (2 Chr 21:11).

A. God's Grace (2 Kgs 8:18-19).

The apostasy of Jehoram of Judah merited national destruction.

God, however, had made promises to David and to his seed after him. These promises would not be fulfilled if Judah's lamp of national existence were now removed. The long-suffering of God with respect to David's dynasty was demonstrated in that he bore with Judah for about three centuries longer until at last their cup of iniquity was full (2 Kgs 8:18-19). Though he could not yet destroy Judah, the Lord did bring certain chastisements upon Jehoram.

B. Prophetic Warning (2 Chr 21:12-15).

Jehoram received a letter from Elijah who, as of 848 BC had not yet been translated to heaven. The prophet condemned the king of Judah for (1) rejecting the ways of his father Jehoshaphat and his grandfather Asa; (2) walking in the ways of the kings of Israel; (3) leading his people to prostitute themselves in idolatrous worship; and (4) slaying his brothers who were better than he (2 Chr 21:12-13).

Because of his wickedness, Yahweh would strike Judah, the royal family and the king himself with a heavy blow. Jehoram would experience a slow and painful disease of his bowels (2 Chr 21:14-15).

C. Political Chastisements (2 Kgs 8:20-22//2 Chr 21:8-10).

Judah experienced two major political setbacks during the reign of Jehoram. First, the Edomites revolted and appointed for themselves an independent king. Jehoram tried to crush this rebellion, but his efforts were almost disastrous. Edomites surrounded his position at Zair near the southern tip of the Dead Sea. Only by a daring night attack was Jehoram able to break through the enemy lines and thus prevent annihilation. His army was so unnerved by this experience that they dispersed to their homes. Jehoram was never in a position to make any further invasion of Edom (2 Kgs 8:20-21).

Second, the Philistines invaded Judah in the days of Jehoram (2 Chr 21:16). Probably in connection with this invasion Libnah, located in the lowlands of Judah on the edge of Philistia, also revolted (2 Kgs 8:22).

D. Illness and Death (2 Kgs 8:23-24//2 Chr 21:18-20).

For two years Jehoram suffered with an incurable disease of his bowels. The king was buried in that portion of Jerusalem built by

David but not in the royal tombs there (2 Chr 21:20). He was followed on the throne by his son Ahaziah, who is also called Jehoahaz (2 Chr 21:17) and Azariah (2 Chr 22:6).

JEZEBEL'S GRANDSON
2 Kings 8:24-28// 2 Chr 22:1-6

Ahaziah began to reign in the twelfth year[6] of Joram of Israel (841 BC). He was twenty-two when his father died.[7] His mother was Athaliah, the Jezebel of Judah. She influenced him to follow the religious policy of the house of Ahab (2 Kgs 8:25-27).

Following the example of his grandfather Jehoshaphat, Ahaziah joined in a military alliance with his uncle, Jehoram of Israel. The objective of the alliance was to go to the relief of Ramoth-gilead which was under attack by Hazael, the new Aramean king. During the course of the defense of the city, Jehoram was severely, but not fatally, wounded. Leaving a strong garrison under general Jehu to defend the city, the two kings retired to their capitals (2 Kgs 8:28).

King Joram stopped off at the royal retreat in Jezreel in the plains to recuperate rather than make the more arduous ascent back to Samaria. After some time passed, Ahaziah of Judah made a trip to Jezreel to visit his convalescing relative. As things turned out, Ahaziah never returned from that fateful visit (2 Kgs 8:29).

THE TRANSLATION OF ELIJAH
2 Kings 2:1-12

Elijah continued as the leader of the prophetic opposition to the house of Ahab until about 848 BC. When he was translated into heaven, his assistant Elisha became the leader of the prophets.

A. Final Visits (2 Kgs 2:1-5).
After his call at Abel-meholah (cf. 1 Kgs 19:21), Elisha had become the constant companion and faithful attendant of Elijah. The latter had no fixed residence, but wandered from place to place as the Spirit of God led him (2 Kgs 2:1).

In the course of their travels the two prophets arrived at Gilgal.

Three times Elijah asked his attendant to remain behind. He knew his days on earth were numbered, and he wished to spend these final days in solitude. Under ordinary circumstances Elisha would have complied with the request of his master. The younger prophet had a premonition if not a revelation that Elijah shortly would be departing from the earth. He would not allow himself to be deprived of those final hours of fellowship and instruction. Three times in this narrative Elisha took a double oath that he would not leave the side of Elijah (2 Kgs 2:2).

From Gilgal the two men of God proceeded to Bethel, the religious capital of the northern kingdom. Elijah may have had instructions for the prophets there. The student prophets called Elisha aside and warned him that he was about to lose his master and teacher. Elisha answered the students curtly. He knew what was about to transpire without being forewarned by this band of students. *"Keep still,"* he instructed them. Such a solemn event should not be the subject of idle chatter (2 Kgs 2:3).

At Bethel Elijah again instructed Elisha to tarry at that place. The old prophet had yet another journey to take, down the rugged descent from the mountains of Ephraim to Jericho in the Jordan valley. Again Elisha would not be turned aside. He repeated the same oath he had earlier taken. Once again his master yielded. So the two men of God came to Jericho twenty miles distant. Once again the sons of the prophets called Elisha aside and shared with him their prophetic premonition. Once again Elisha administered a gentle rebuke to these impetuous students (2 Kgs 2:4-5).

B. Final Words (2 Kgs 2:6-10).

At Jericho, Elijah made his third and final attempt to separate himself from his faithful attendant. Yahweh had directed the grand old prophet to go to the Jordan. Perhaps Elisha should remain at Jericho where there was food and fellowship and shelter. Elisha, however, was staunch in his insistence that he would spend these last hours with his master regardless of where the Lord might lead.

Fifty prophetic students followed Elijah and Elisha from Jericho. Out of respect for Elijah's desire for solitude at this moment, these students hung back and finally stopped altogether on a little hill where they had a commanding view of the Jordan valley. They watched with eager curiosity as the two prophets reached the bank of Jordan. There Elijah took his mantle, rolled it up so that it resembled a rod, and smote the waters with it. Instantly the waters parted so that the two men walked across on dry land (2 Kgs 2:7-8).

With his time on earth very short, Elijah wished to leave his faithful follower some parting gift as a sign of his love. Whatever Elisha desired, if it were within his power, the older prophet would grant. Elisha requested a double portion of Elijah's spirit. The *"double portion"* was the right of the eldest son who also had authority over members of the family once the father was gone. Asking for the *"double portion"* was equivalent to asking that he be regarded as Elijah's successor (2 Kgs 2:9).

Granting such a request was not directly within the power of Elijah. Only God could designate a man as spiritual leader of the nation. Elijah could do no more than leave the matter in the hands of God. If God should grant to Elisha the privilege of actually witnessing the translation of Elijah into heaven, this would be the sign that his request had been granted. From this it would appear that the chariot and horses which Elijah saw were not ordinarily visible to the physical eye (2 Kgs 2:10).

C. Final Moments (2 Kgs 2:11-12).

The conversation of the two men of God was interrupted by the appearance of a chariot of fire pulled by horses of fire. The *"fire"* here is probably an earthly description of celestial glory. The atmosphere was in turbulence at the moment the chariot whisked Elijah away up into the heavens. Elisha saw this stupendous sight. He knew that his request for a double portion of Elijah's spirit had been granted (2:11).

At first sight of that heavenly chariot, Elisha cried out in dazed wonder, *"My father, my father! The chariot of Israel and its horses!"* The term *"father"* suggests that Elisha regarded Elijah as his teacher. Perhaps he even felt like Elisha's adopted son. Elijah himself was the chariot of Israel and its horsemen. He was the great protector of the nation. Later this same figurative form of address would be used of Elisha (cf. 13:14).

THE RECOGNITION OF ELISHA
2 Kings 2:13-25

When his friend and spiritual father disappeared into the clouds, Elisha tore his clothes in grief. Sadly Elisha picked up the mantle that had fallen from the shoulders of Elijah and walked back to the edge of Jordan (2:12).

A. Miracle at the Jordan (2 Kgs 2:13-15).

In imitation of the actions of his master, Elisha smote the waters of the river with the mantle. At the same time he cried, "Where is Yahweh God of Elijah?" Elisha wondered if the all-powerful God who had so blessed the ministry his master was still with his people now that Elijah had departed. When the waters instantly parted, Elisha knew the answer to that question. By enabling him to repeat Elijah's last miracle, Yahweh gave assurance to Elisha that the divine power would be available to him throughout his prophetic ministry (2:13-14).

When the sons of the prophets saw Elisha returning form the Jordan alone they concluded that the spirit of Elijah rested upon him. On what basis they reached this conclusion is not clear. Perhaps they had witnessed the miracle which Elisha had performed at the river; or they may have inferred that the leadership had passed to Elisha because he was now wearing the mantle of his master. In any case, they came forth and bowed before him. Thus the student prophets accorded to Elisha the recognition which they previously had given to Elijah (2:15).

B. Request of the Students (2 Kgs 2:16-18).

The sons of the prophets, having been informed of the ascension of Elijah, were quite concerned about the well-being of their former master. They assumed that the Spirit of God had whisked him away only to cast him down in some remote place. So they requested that Elisha give permission for fifty of the more robust men among them to make a thorough search of the rocky ridges and ravines of the Transjordan territory. They could not bear the thought of leaving the old prophet in such a barren spot. Elisha knew that the effort would be futile. So he rejected the first petition made of him as leader of the prophetic band (2 Kgs 2:16).

The sons of the prophets, however, continued to urge Elisha to permit them to undertake the search until he was ashamed to refuse them any longer. He reluctantly gave them the permission which they sought. Fifty men searched for three days, and of course found nothing. Elisha waited patiently at Jericho for the zealous young men to return from their futile mission. Because his veracity and wisdom to some extent had been questioned, Elisha reminded these young men of his previous advice to them (2:17-18).

C. Healing Noxious Waters (2 Kgs 2:19-22).

Having heard of the recent miracle performed by Elisha at the Jordan, the civic authorities of Jericho came to the prophet to seek his aid in removing the one unfortunate drawback to their otherwise pleasant community. A bitter spring of water gushed forth near Jericho which sent its waters in rivulets across the plain to the Jordan. Nothing could grow near this water; cattle drinking this water would abort (2 Kgs 2:19).[8]

Elisha called for a new vase filled with salt. As he poured the salt into the spring, he uttered a pronouncement in the name of Yahweh to the effect that never again would that spring produce death and miscarrying among people and stock. The waters were instantly and permanently made whole. The so-called Spring of the Sultan near the ancient ruins of Jericho may be the very spring referred to in this passage. The salt and the new vase were intended to teach that impurity can only be cleansed by what is wholly pure (2 Kgs 2:20-22).

D. Cursing the Bethel Youth (2 Kgs 2:23-25).

After a brief stay at Jericho, Elisha visited Bethel, probably to inform the sons of the prophets there about what had transpired in Transjordan. On the outskirts of the city the prophet was confronted by a gang of ruffians[9] who viciously mocked him. They jeered, "Go up, O baldhead!" This may be an allusion to the recent rumor that Elijah had ascended to heaven. These unbelieving urchins were urging the prematurely bald Elisha to imitate his master (2 Kgs 2:23).

The juvenile delinquents continued to follow behind, hooting and jeering at this man of God who now was the official representative of God on earth. Having endured this mockery and potential personal danger as long as he could, Elisha turned and calmly "cursed" these hoodlums in the name of Yahweh. This cursing consisted of pronouncing a negative prophecy against them. He may have said something like this: May evil and calamity fall upon you (2 Kgs 2:24a). Under the law of Moses, God's ministers were required to "curse" the disobedient (Deut 27:14-26).

In order to teach these young men a lesson and at the same time vindicate his prophet in Bethel, God stirred up two she-bears to come out of a nearby woods and attack the offenders. These angry bears "tore" forty-two of these fellows. The text does not indicate to what extent these young men were injured. This frightening example of God's wrath was no doubt intended to serve as an unforgettable lesson to a new generation which was growing up in contempt of God and true religion (2 Kgs 2:24).

From Bethel, Elisha went up to Mt. Carmel where presumably another group of the sons of the prophets was located. The purpose of his trip was doubtlessly the same as for his trip to Bethel, viz., to share with these men of God his firsthand knowledge of the exodus of Elijah. This trip also might have been to commemorate the great victory over Baal which had been won at that place. Having completed this mission, Elisha returned to the capital at Samaria. This prophet did not choose to imitate the semi-ascetic lifestyle of his master. He stayed for the most part in the capital working with and through the various kings.

ENDNOTES

1. John Gray thinks that the proper name of the deity was Baal-zebul—"Baal the Prince"—and that the orthodox Israelite author deliberately changed the spelling to ridicule this deity. *I & II Kings* in "The Old Testament Library" (Philadelphia: Westminster, 1970), p. 463.

2. That Jehoshaphat and Ahab both named their sons Jehoram may have been intended as a symbol of the friendship between the two kingdoms. 2 Kgs 1:17 states that the northern Jehoram came to the throne in the second year of the reign of the southern Jehoram. On the other hand, 2 Kgs 3:1 states that the northern Jehoram came to the throne in the eighteenth year of Jehoshaphat. Experts in Biblical chronology conclude that Jehoshaphat and his son Jehoram had a coregency which began in 853 BC.

3. By a very slight emendation in the text another reconstruction is possible. In Hebrew the words Edom and Aram are quite similar. It is possible that originally the text read *"break through to the king of Aram,"* in which case the text would be pointing to a desperate effort on the part of the king of Moab to break through the allied lines to safety in the territories of Aram. See note on 2 Sam 8:13f.

4. Some scholars think this invasion of Judah preceded the campaign of the allies against Moab. The text gives no clue as to the precise chronological placement of this event.

5. In 2 Kgs 8:18 Athaliah is called Ahab's daughter, but in 2 Kgs 8:26 she is called Omri's daughter. In the latter verse *"daughter"* is used in the sense of female descendant.

6. According to 2 Kgs 9:29 it was the eleventh year of Joram of Israel when Ahaziah began to reign. Such one year discrepancies result from two different systems of counting the regnal years of kings, one of which did not count the months of the accession year.

7. According to 2 Chr 22:2 Ahaziah was forty-two when he came to the throne. The scribal copying of Chronicles must be at fault here for the figure is manifestly incorrect. Ahaziah's father was only forty years old when he died, so his son could not be forty-two in that same year.

8. Gray (*op. cit.,* p. 477) takes note of a recent hydrological survey in Israel in which certain springs were discovered to be radioactive. Laboratory tests have demonstrated that water from these springs causes sterility.

9. The unfortunate translation *"little children"* (KJV) has given a very wrong impression of this passage. The Hebrew literally means *"young men."*

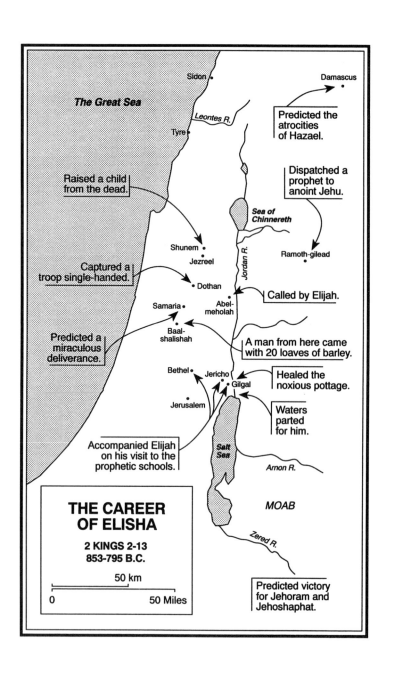

Sidon

Damascus

The Great Sea

Leontes R.

Predicted the
atrocities
of Hazael.

Tyre

Dispatched a
prophet to
anoint Jehu.

*Sea of
Chinnereth*

Raised a child
from the dead.

Shunem

Jezreel

Ramoth-gilead

Jordan R.

Captured a
troop single-handed.

Dothan

Called by Elijah.

Samaria

Abel-
meholah

Baal-
shalishah

A man from here came
with 20 loaves of barley.

Predicted a
miraculous
deliverance.

Bethel

Jericho

Healed the
noxious pottage.

Gilgal

Jerusalem

Waters
parted
for him.

Accompanied Elijah
on his visit to the
prophetic schools.

*Salt
Sea*

Arnon R.

THE CAREER
OF ELISHA

2 KINGS 2-13
853-795 B.C.

MOAB

Zered R.

50 km

0   50 Miles

Predicted victory
for Jehoram and
Jehoshaphat.

CHAPTER THIRTY-THREE

The Elisha Era
2 Kings 4-8

Elisha became leader of the prophetic schools in Israel about the year 848 BC. He lived into the reign of Jehoash who came to the throne of Israel in 798 BC. Thus for half a century Elisha led the sons of the prophets. During those years Baalism finally was defeated in the northern kingdom.

ELISHA'S PRIVATE MIRACLES
2 Kings 4:1-6:7

Elisha's ministry was undergirded by a large number and wide variety of miracles. Four miracles were performed for two faithful female disciples.

A. The Widow's Oil (2 Kgs 4:1-7).

A destitute widow did not hesitate to ask Elisha for assistance because (1) her husband had been a member of the prophetic order over which Elisha presided; and (2) because he was a God-fearing man. When her husband died, some creditor demanded immediate payment of a family debt. Since the widow could not pay off the loan, the creditor had taken her two sons into slavery as payment for the loan (4:1).

Elisha instructed the woman to secure from all her neighbors empty vessels of every size and description. This not only would test her faith, but would undergird the eternal principle that God helps him who helps himself. She was told to take those empty vessels into the privacy of her home and pour into them the small amount of oil which she possessed. As each vessel became full it was set aside and replaced by another empty vessel in order that the pouring might be continuous. When every last vessel in the house was filled, the oil ceased flowing. God would not permit waste. The miracle was performed inconspicuously lest the prophet be overwhelmed with applications for similar aid to others. The prophet directed her then to sell the oil and pay off the debt. After satisfying the claims of her creditor with part of the money, she would be able to support herself and her sons on the remainder (4:2-7).

B. A Birth Prediction (2 Kgs 4:8-17).

On his travels about the country, Elisha was accustomed to take his meals with *"a great woman,"* i.e., a woman of means, when in the town of Shunem. With the passage of time, the wealthy Shunammite became convinced that Elisha was truly worthy of the title he bore, *"man of God."* She and her husband built a special room for the prophet to use both as a sleeping chamber and as a study (4:8-10).

Elisha wished to repay his Shunammite hosts in some way. At the suggestion of his servant Gehazi—here mentioned for the first time—Elisha announced to the childless woman that within a year she would be embracing a son. Like Sarah before her, the Shunammite was incredulous in the face of this shocking announcement. Nevertheless, at that very season a year later the woman gave birth to a son just as the prophet had predicted (4:11-17).

C. A Resurrection (2 Kgs 4:18-37).

Some years later the Shunammite's son died as a result of a sunstroke. The woman put the lifeless corpse on the bed in the prophet's chamber. She then set out for Mt. Carmel some fifteen miles distant where the Elisha was ministering. She believed that the prophet would be able to duplicate the resurrection performed by Elijah in Zarephath some years earlier (4:18-21).

Elisha responded to the emergency in two ways. First, he dispatched Gehazi immediately to the Shunammite's house. Gehazi was to lay Elisha's staff upon the lad's face. This action was designed to comfort the mother and to raise in her a firm expectation of a resurrection. Second, as soon as he was able Elisha set out for Shunem along with his friend. En route they were met by Gehazi returning from carrying out his master's directions. He reported that the lad was showing no signs of life in spite of the prophet's staff (4:22-31).

Elisha entered the chamber where the dead child lay. He closed the door in order that he might not be disturbed during his efforts to revive the body. Falling to his knees, the inarticulate prayer that had been upon his heart from the moment he left Carmel was verbalized. Following the example of his master Elijah (cf. 1 Kgs 17:21), Elisha stretched himself upon the lad and brought his flesh as close as he could to that of the lad. The idea in this seems to be to prepare the body for reinhabitation of the soul or spirit by restoring warmth to it. Aside from this practical purpose, the act would also demonstrate the faith of the prophet that God would permit this great miracle to take place. Elisha's efforts accomplished their purpose; the child's body was actually warmed (4:32-34).

Still no signs of life appeared. The prophet, somewhat perplexed, got up from his prone position and paced in the room, doubtlessly analyzing the situation, praying as he did so. Then he again stretched himself upon the child. Shortly the child sneezed seven times—showing the recovery of his suspended respiration—and opened his eyes. The Shunammite was summoned, no doubt from the lower story of the house. She was instructed to take up her restored child. As anxious as the woman was to once again embrace her son, she first bowed before the prophet in humble gratitude; then she took up her son and went out to spend those precious first moments alone with the lad (4:35-37).

D. A Famine Prediction (2 Kgs 8:1-6).

A great famine had occurred during the reign of Jehoram (cf. 2 Kgs 4:38). Prior to the approach of that famine Elisha had warned his wealthy Shunammite friend to leave her home and take up residence wherever she might choose. God had determined to bring a famine upon the land which would last for seven years. The faithful woman regarded the prophet as a spokesman for God. She accepted his advice as equivalent to a divine command. She and her household migrated to the fertile Philistine plain which, though not totally exempt from famine, did not suffer from such natural calamities nearly as much as did Samaria or Judah. For seven years the Shunammite resided in that foreign land (2 Kgs 8:1-2).

When the famine abated, the woman returned to her native land to discover that some neighbor had seized her unoccupied house and land. The woman had no recourse but to appeal to the king that her properties be restored. The king happened to be talking to Gehazi when the woman came into his presence to plead her case. It would seem that Jehoram had sent for Gehazi to satisfy his curiosity with regard to the miraculous deeds of Elisha. This king and the prophet had never been on particularly friendly terms, hence the best source for accurate information about the deeds of this man of God was his servant (2 Kgs 8:3-4).[1]

Just as Gehazi was relating the most stupendous of all of Elisha's miracles—the resurrection of the Shunammite's son—this woman began to cry for the attention of the king. Divine providence so ordered matters that just when the king's interest in the woman was warmest, the woman appeared to press her claim. Gehazi was pleased to point out his old friend and her son, who by this time must have been a lad of ten years or more. The king made inquiry of the woman, not only about the miracle which had been wrought in her house, but also about her property claims. Convinced that her cause was just, the king appointed an officer of the court to expedite the return of all the woman's property. In addition, he awarded her all the profits which the land had produced during the seven years of her absence (2 Kgs 8:5-6).

ELISHA AND THE SONS OF THE PROPHETS
2 Kings 4:38-44

Three more miracles were performed by Elisha on behalf of the sons of the prophets—those students who looked to him as their mentor.

A. Healing Noxious Pottage (2 Kgs 4:38-41).

During a famine Elisha visited the prophetic school at Gilgal. He ordered that the large communal pot be put on the fire, and pottage or vegetable stew be prepared. Then students fanned out in the neighborhood to look for wild fruits or vegetables which might be put into the stew. Perhaps because of the famine the men could not be as selective as they normally were. One young fellow brought back as many "gourds" as he could carry.[2] He sliced them up into the stew. None of the more experienced students were paying attention to what he was doing (2 Kgs 4:38-39).

As the students were eating the vegetable stew, they realized, either by the bitter taste or nauseous effects, that they were eating unwholesome food. They cried out to Elisha, "O man of God, there is death in the pot!" No one was able to continue eating the stew (2 Kgs 4:40).

Elisha took prompt action. He called for some meal and cast it into the pot. Meal, of course, has no power in itself to neutralize poison any more than salt has to purify bitter waters (cf. 2 Kgs 2:19-21). While it is possible that this action might have modified some of the bitterness of the brew, the primary purpose of the meal was to symbolize purification. In any case, the pottage was served anew, and those who had faith in Elisha and continued to eat of it were in no way harmed (2 Kgs 4:41).

B. Food Multiplication (2 Kgs 4:42-44).

A man came from Baal-shalisha near Gilgal to bring Elisha twenty cakes of bread made from the firstfruits of his harvest.[3] Each loaf was the equivalent of what one person would eat at one meal. Along with these cakes, the man brought a few ripe stalks of grain which were a token of his gratitude (cf. Lev 23:10) for God's harvest mercies (2 Kgs 4:42).

Elisha ordered that the loaves be placed before the sons of the prophets who resided at Gilgal. Elisha's servant—presumably Gehazi—was incredulous. The amount of food was scarcely sufficient to suffice for a fifth of the hundred men living at Gilgal! In the face of the objection, the prophet repeated his instructions, and added an explanation in the form of a prophetic oracle. God had revealed to him that the quantity of food would prove ample for the hundred men, and that they would show that they had had enough by leaving some of it. The result was as the prophet had predicted (2 Kgs 4:43-44).[4]

C. Recovering a Lost Axe (2 Kgs 6:1-7).

The school of the prophets at Jericho had outgrown its facilities. When Elisha next visited Jericho, the students proposed to him that a new dwelling be constructed a few miles from Jericho near the Jordan where trees for such a purpose would be readily available. To this proposal Elisha gave his encouragement. Upon their insistance, he agreed also to supervise their work (2 Kgs 5:1-3).

As the men were working an ax head flew from one man's shaft into the murky waters of the river. The man was distraught. He cried out to Elisha, *"Alas, my master, for it was a borrowed one!"* The man made no direct request for assistance, but the tone of his exclamation constituted an oblique call for help (2 Kgs 5:4-5).

Elisha, being always interested in the personal problems of his disciples, asked to be shown the spot where the ax head entered the stream. The prophet then cut off a branch and cast it upon the water at that spot. The ax head miraculously was caused to rise to the surface of the water.[5] In order to test the faith of the student, Elisha then ordered him to take up the ax head. He must show that he really believed that the ax head was floating on the surface, and that he was not merely experiencing an optical illusion (2 Kgs 5:6-7).

THE HEALING OF NAAMAN
2 Kings 5:1-27

Elisha performed two great miracles which resulted in greater respect for Yahweh among Israel's neighbors. The first of these miracles involved the healing of an Aramean officer.

A. Naaman's Condition (2 Kgs 5:1-7).

As captain of the Aramean host, Naaman had achieved honor and wealth. He was *"a mighty man of valor,"* i.e., a good soldier; but he was a leper.[6] A maid, captured on a raid into Israel, became distressed over the grievous affliction of Naaman. One day she expressed her sentiment that he might be brought into contact with the powerful prophet in Samaria. She was confident that Elisha could cure him of his leprosy (2 Kgs 5:1-3).

Convinced by his wife's persistence to pursue the matter, Naaman reported the suggestion of the Israelite maid to the king. Much to his surprise, the king took the whole matter seriously. He indicated that he would send a letter by Naaman's hand to the king of Israel urging that he do what he could for the captain (2 Kgs 5:4).

So Naaman departed, taking with him an enormous treasure with which he thought he could pay for his cleansing. Ten talents of silver would be roughly equivalent to $20,000. The unit of measure is omitted for the gold, but it is likely that the amount would be six thousand shekels' weight which would roughly be equivalent to $60,000. Finally, in addition to the silver and gold, Naaman took ten changes of garments to bestow upon his benefactor. Naaman's first mistake is that he thought he could purchase his cleansing (2 Kgs 5:5).

Naaman went straight to the palace of the king of Israel. He presented the letter from Ben-hadad which, when stripped of diplomatic niceties, demanded that his general be healed. Naturally the king of Israel was upset by the letter. He tore his clothes and cried, *"Am I God, to kill and make alive?"* i.e., am I omnipotent? He did not think of Elisha, probably because he gave no credence to the reports circulating about him. The only conclusion he could reach was that Ben-hadad was making these extravagant demands as a pretext for more hostility. Here was Naaman's second mistake: he went to the wrong place in search of his cleansing (2 Kgs 5:6-7).

B. Naaman's Cleansing (2 Kgs 5:8-14).

News of the king's distress reached Elisha. He sent word to the palace inviting the king to send the foreign dignitary to his house. The Aramean would then be convinced that Yahweh had a prophet in the land (2 Kgs 5:8).

Soon Naaman and his entourage arrived at the humble abode of Elisha in the city of Samaria. A man of his station was not about to enter such humble quarters, and so he simply waited impatiently at the door of the house. Regarding the pride of his visitor as worthy of rebuke, Elisha remained within the house and sent his servant out to communicate with the dignitary (2 Kgs 5:9).

If the actions of the prophet insulted the inflated ego of Naaman, his instruction did even more, *"Go wash in the Jordan seven times."* The nearest point of the Jordan river from Samaria was some twenty miles distant. If Naaman had the faith to go to the river, and there persisted in the formal act of dipping in the river seven times, the scaly leprous skin would disappear (2 Kgs 5:10).

Naaman was angered by the treatment he had received from the unseen prophet. He had expected to have received every possible attention; but the prophet had not even greeted him at the door. The captain had expected an instantaneous cure. Instead he was told that *he* must do something—dip in the muddy Jordan. The rivers of Damascus—Abanah and Pharpar—were fresh, clear and beautiful.[7] If the leprous taint was to be *washed* away, would not the crystal clear waters of his native land have more cleansing power than the clay-colored waters of Jordan? Disgusted and perturbed, Naaman wheeled his chariot around and departed in a cloud of dust. Here were Naaman's third and fourth mistakes: he had a preconceived notion of how cleansing should be effected; and he got angry with the prophet who told him how to achieve cleansing (2 Kgs 5:11-12).

Fortunately for Naaman, his servants did not share in his wild indignation. When their master had cooled somewhat, one of his servants reasoned with Naaman. He suggested that if Elisha had directed Naaman to do some difficult thing, the captain would have attempted to do it. How much more should he be willing to do the simple, if somewhat silly, thing which the man of God had designated. The irresistible logic persuaded Naaman. At the first opportunity, he turned his chariot eastward and began to make his way through the rapidly descending valleys toward the Jordan. When he exactly complied with the prophet's instructions, the miracle occurred. Not only was the leprosy removed, Naaman's flesh became as soft as that of a little baby (2 Kgs 13-14).

C. Naaman's Conversion (2 Kgs 5:15-19).

A number of facts indicate that at the Jordan, Naaman's heart was transformed as well as his flesh. First, he was determined to express his appreciation to the man of God even though the return trip to Samaria would take him at least forty miles out of his way and delay his return to Damascus by at least one day. Second, the once pompous Aramean was now contrite. He descended from his chariot, went into the prophet's abode, and stood before him. Third, Naaman confessed faith in the supremacy of Yahweh. Fourth, he was anxious that Elisha should accept a *"blessing,"* i.e., a present, in appreciation for what he had done. Elisha thought it best, however, to decline the gift. Naaman needed to learn that Yahweh was his true healer, Elisha but his representative (2 Kgs 5:15-16).

Fifth, Naaman took two mule loads of soil back to Aram with him. Commentators conjecture that he intended to use it to consecrate a plot of ground and make it a suitable place upon which to worship Yahweh. In the mind of this newly converted heathen, the ground of Israel would be more holy, more appropriate for the worship of the God of Israel. Sixth, Naaman declared his intention to cease offering sacrifice to any god other than Yahweh. Seventh, he indicated as captain of the host he would be required to attend the temple of Rimmon with his king. He would there be compelled to bow before the image of that god. He therefore expressed the hope that Yahweh would pardon him of this wrong (2 Kgs 5:17-18).

Elisha did not declare that God would or would not overlook this departure from strict monotheism. He was not called upon to give an answer since Naaman had not asked a question but had only expressed a wish. Elisha's *"Go in peace"* should be taken simply as wishing the peace of God to be on the departing Aramean (2 Kgs 5:19).

D. The Aftermath (2 Kgs 5:20-27).

Gehazi could not bear the thought of the Aramean going home with all his treasure. He convinced himself that this foreigner deserved to bo spoiled because he was an enemy of Israel. He swore an oath using the name of God that he could run after the captain and take *something* of him. *"As Yahweh lives"* are strange words in the mouth of one who has set his mind on a course of lying and stealing (2 Kgs 5:20).

Naaman's entourage, traveling at a leisurely pace so as not to exhaust those servants who might have been on foot, was easily overtaken by the fleet-footed Gehazi. He told Naaman that Elisha had changed his mind regarding the gifts which had been offered. Two needy sons of the prophets from Mt. Ephraim had happened along, and Elisha would like Naaman to donate to them a talent of silver ($2,000) and two changes of garments. Naaman believed the story of Gehazi and wanted to do even more than the servant had requested. He suggested that two talents ($4,000) be taken, probably because the strangers who had arrived were two. Following the conventions of the Near East, Gehazi pretended to decline the more generous offer (2 Kgs 5:21-23).

Naaman took the two talents and, along with the changes of garments, put them upon the shoulders of two of his servants. At a hill just outside Samaria, Gehazi took the money from Naaman's slaves, and dismissed them. He could not run the risk of having these foreigners seen entering Samaria again. Gehazi took the bags of money and hid them in the house of his master, probably in the courtyard thereof (2 Kgs 5:24).

The sins of Gehazi escalated when he lied to his master regarding his whereabouts. Elisha then claimed that he had been with Gehazi in prophetic spirit. The prophet then reflected back to Gehazi his inner thoughts about what he would do with the newly acquired wealth, viz., purchase olive groves and vineyards, as well as sheep and oxen. Those desperate days were no time to think of acquiring property and luxury for oneself! Such actions could bring the prophetic office into contempt with unbelievers and undermine the credibility of Elisha's ministry (2 Kgs 5:25-26).

Elisha pronounced sentence against his servant. Since Gehazi had taken of Naaman's goods, he would also partake of his leprosy. Should this servant decide to marry and father children, they too would be lepers. In that instant the plague fell on Gehazi. His skin turned white as snow. Gehazi departed from the presence of Elisha to spend his remaining days with the outcast lepers (2 Kgs 5:27).

ELISHA AND THE ARAMEANS
2 Kings 5:1-6:23

The Arameans again began to assert their power against Israel in the days of Jehoram the son of Ahab. Two miracles of Elisha demonstrated God's compassion for Israel and his superiority over the gods of Aram.

A. Aramean Plans Revealed (2 Kgs 6:8-12).

Through his supernatural insight, Elisha was able to reveal to the king of Israel the secret military plans of the Arameans. The prophet had a strong personal dislike for King Jehoram, but he did not allow these personal feelings to interfere with his patriotism. The king of Israel learned to avoid those spots where Elisha indicated he would encounter an Aramean ambush (2 Kgs 6:8-10).

The king of Aram became greatly concerned at the repeated failure of his best laid plans. One officer—perhaps Naaman—suggested that the plans were being revealed by the Israelite prophet. Perhaps the Aramean had learned this through intelligence agencies in Israel. On the other hand, perhaps this official was merely surmising that a man who could heal the dreaded leprosy would have no difficulty reading the secret thoughts of a man (2 Kgs 6:11-12).

B. Aramean Troops Captured (2 Kgs 6:13-23).

Aramean spies ascertained that Elisha was currently residing in Dothan, a village about twelve miles north of Samaria. A strong force was dispatched with orders to kidnap the prophet. In order to take Elisha by surprise, the Arameans marched by night and encompassed the city (2 Kgs 6:13-14).

Elisha's new servant arose early in the morning to discover the city surrounded by a force which included infantry, cavalry, and even a chariot force. Faced with the prospect of capture and consequent slavery, the young servant rushed to his master to report his alarming discovery. *"How shall we do?"* he cried, i.e., is there any way we can save ourselves? (2 Kgs 6:15).

Elisha was quite calm in the face of this serious threat. He knew that God was with him, and it mattered not how many might be

567

arrayed against him outside the walls of Dothan. The servant, however, needed reassurance. So Elisha prayed that the servant's eyes might be permitted to see that great angelic host that hovers just beyond the realm of sight and sound. The prophet's prayer was answered. The eyes of the servant were opened, and he beheld round about the hill of Dothan a heavenly force—chariots and horses *"of fire,"* i.e., glowing with an unearthly brightness (2 Kgs 6:16-17).

Rather than waiting for the Arameans to come up the slopes of Dothan to arrest him, Elisha and his servant went down to the attacking host. As they approached the enemy, Elisha prayed that God would smite the Arameans with blindness, i.e., a state of confusion in which they would willingly follow the directions of the prophet. As a result of that prayer, the soldiers allowed Elisha to convince them that they had attacked the wrong city. Under this miraculous delusion, the soldiers allowed Elisha to lead them into Samaria. The behavior of these soldiers is absolutely inexplicable apart from direct working of God in their mental processes (2 Kgs 6:18-19).

Once inside Samaria, Elisha prayed that God would *"open their eyes,"* i.e., remove the bewilderment which had seized them at Dothan. The soldiers awoke from their delusion to realize that they were surrounded by a great throng of Israelite soldiers. King Jehoram, though not on the most cordial terms with Elisha (cf. 3:11-14), addressed the prophet by the honorable title *"father."* The king was eager to slay these helpless invaders, but he felt compelled to seek the permission of the one who had delivered them into his hand (2 Kgs 6:20-21).

Elisha declined permission to slay these men. They were not prisoners of war in the usual sense. The ultimate purpose of the miracle at Dothan was to teach these foreigners and their king to fear the God of Israel, and to respect his people and prophet in particular. Therefore, instead of slaying the Arameans, the prophet directed that they be treated hospitably and then be sent back to their own land. As a result of this episode, the Aramean raiders, who had heretofore harassed the Israelite countryside, suspended their activities for a time, and Israel had a respite (2 Kgs 6:22-23).

ELISHA DURING THE SIEGE OF SAMARIA
2 Kings 6:24-33

The kind treatment of the Aramean troop was soon forgotten. Ben-hadad gathered his entire force and invaded Israel. Realizing that he was no match for the invaders in the field, King Jehoram withdrew to his capital at Samaria and prepared for a long siege.

A. Plight of Samaria (2 Kgs 6:24-29).

Ben-hadad blockaded the city and attempted to starve its inhabitants into submission. The situation in the city deteriorated to such a degree that an ass head, the worst part of of an unclean animal, which would normally never be eaten, sold for eighty pieces of silver ($50), and a *qab* (pint) of dove's dung for five pieces of silver ($3). "*Dove's dung*" may have been the popular name for some food such as roasted chickpeas. If actual dove's dung is intended, it was probably sold as fuel (2 Kgs 6:24-25).[8]

King Jehoram[9] made regular inspections of the fortifications and guard posts on the broad walls of Samaria. On one such tour a woman cried out to the king for a judicial decision. She and a neighbor had entered a pact to eat their two sons on two successive days. Her boy had been boiled and eaten the appointed day. The following day the neighbor had reneged on the agreement and had hidden her son to avoid the ordeal of seeing him killed and eaten (2 Kgs 6:26-29).

B. Peril of Elisha (2 Kgs 6:30-33).

The king was horrified to learn how deplorable the conditions had become within the city. He tore open his clothes in anguish. Beneath his robes he was wearing sackcloth. In his distress the king swore an oath that he would have Elisha decapitated that very day. Why the king blamed Elisha for the horrors of the famine is not clear. Perhaps he felt that the prophet should work some mighty miracle to relieve the city of its suffering (2 Kgs 6:30-31).

Elisha was sitting in his home in Samaria with the elders of the land sitting before him at the time the king dispatched the prophet's executioner. Their conversation was interrupted when Elisha received a supernatural revelation of what was about to take place. The prophet called upon those present with him to resist the royal messenger and bar the door to him, because the king himself would shortly arrive. He would either confirm or countermand that original order (2 Kgs 6:32).

The messenger of the king arrived at that very moment. The elders barred the door as Elisha suggested. Then the king himself appeared on the scene. He was immediately admitted into the presence of the prophet. Jehoram seems to have repented of his hasty order to slay the prophet. He had hurried after his own messengers in order to give the prophet a final opportunity to live. The question of the king— *"Why should I wait for Yahweh any longer?"*—implies that Elisha had previously urged Jehoram to wait for divine interposition. The king interpreted the calamity as being from Yahweh. Why should he try to hold out any longer? Why should he not break with God, slay his lying prophet, and surrender the city to the Arameans? (2 Kgs 6:33).

C. Elisha's Prediction (2 Kgs 7:1-2).

Elisha responded to the king in the most solemn manner. He made such a precise prediction that within a short period of time the whole nation would know whether or not he was a true spokesman for the living God. Within twenty-four hours such a quantity of grain would be available to the inhabitants of Samaria that barley and fine flour would again be bought and sold at the pre-siege prices (2 Kgs 7:1).

The king's personal attendant was vocally incredulous. With scoffing sarcasm he insisted that the prediction was utterly impossible of fulfillment. Even if the Lord were to make windows in the heavens, and pour down through them grain instead of rain, this prediction could not come to pass. Since the disdain of the officer was directed not only at Elisha but at the power of God, the prophet answered him sternly. *"You shall see with your eyes, but you shall not eat!"* By these words the officer, if he was wise enough to discern it, was forewarned of his imminent death (2 Kgs 7:2).

D. A Joyous Discovery (2 Kgs 7:3-11).

Four lepers were on the verge of perishing at the gate of Samaria.

Friends within the city no longer had food to share with them. The only hope of survival was to desert to the Arameans. At twilight they approached the enemy camp only to find it totally deserted. Yahweh had caused the Arameans to hear what they thought was the sound of an enormous army sweeping down upon them. They jumped to the illogical conclusion that Jehoram had hired Hittite and Egyptian mercenaries to attack them from opposite directions. The Arameans fled for their lives (2 Kgs 7:3-7)

The lepers first satisfied their hunger. Then they began hiding the valuables left by the enemy. They wanted to make sure they got their share of the spoils of war. During the process of plundering, however, their consciences began to bother them. Many were perishing within Samaria while they were enjoying their good fortune. To withhold such good tidings from their desperate countrymen must surely be a criminal act for which God would punish them. So, belatedly the lepers determined to carry the news to the *"king's house,"* i.e., his officers and court (2 Kgs 7:8-11).

E. A Literal Fulfillment (2 Kgs 7:12-20).

Aroused from his sleep, the king greeted the news of the Aramean retreat with incredulity. He suspected some kind of trick. Two chariots were dispatched to check out the report. This patrol followed the main road to the Jordan. All along the way they saw the garments, weapons, and baggage discarded by the fleeing troops. Convinced that the Arameans had fled, the patrol reported back to the king (2 Kgs 7:12-15).

News of the good fortune spread through Samaria that morning like wildfire. The whole population *en masse* descended on the Aramean camp to feast and take spoil. The officer who the previous day had scoffed at the predictions of Elisha was trampled by the mob in the gate of the city (2 Kgs 7:16-20).

ENDNOTES

1. This episode involving Gehazi must be chronologically prior to 2 Kgs 5 where the servant was smitten with leprosy because of theft and lying.

2. Gustaf Dalman attempts to identify the particular plant here involved.

He points to a vine which grows in the vicinity of Jericho which produces yellow fruit like melons. These melons have powerful laxative properties. If eaten in great quantity they indeed can be fatal. See *Sacred Sites and Ways,*Trans. P. Levertoff (New York: Macmillan, 1935) p. 81ff.

3. According to the law, the firstfruits of grain, wine and oil were to be given to the priests (cf. Num 18:13; Deut 18:4,5). Apparently the more pious among the Israelites regarded the prophets as having inherited the position of the Levitical priests in the northern kingdom.

4. To speculate how this miracle was wrought, whether by an augmentation of the quantity of the food supernaturally produced, or by a lessening of the appetites of the men, is useless. A study of the feeding miracles of Jesus would suggest that the former explanation is the correct one.

5. Naturalistic explanations of this miracle—that Elisha used the stick to pry the ax head from the bottom of the stream—do violence to the account. G. Rawlinson rightly comments: "The sacred writers are not concerned to put on record mere acts of manual dexterity." *II Kings* in "The Pulpit Commentary" (New York: Funk and Wagnalls, 1909), p. 120.

6. Leprosy had many degrees. Some of the lighter kinds would not incapacitate a man for military service or make him unfit for official court duties. Naaman's "leprosy" (*tsara'at*) may have been more in the nature of an embarrassing skin disease.

7. Precise location of these rivers is uncertain. It has been suggested that they are the modern Barada river and one of its tributaries.

8. John Gray, *I & II Kings* in "The Old Testament Library" (Philadelphia: Westminster, 1970), p. 522. Josephus, however, relates that during the Roman siege of Jerusalem people ate dung. *Antiquities* 9.4.4.

9. Others think the unnamed king was Jehoahaz or Joash. In this case, the Ben-hadad of 6:24 would be Ben-hadad II, the son of Hazael.

CHAPTER THIRTY-FOUR

Three Swords of Divine Retribution
2 Kings 9:1-13:9

At Mt. Horeb God had told Elijah that the day of retribution for the Baal worshipers in the northern kingdom would surely come. The judgment would be administered by three men: Hazael, Jehu and Elisha. *"The one who escapes the sword of Hazael, Jehu shall put to death, and the one who escapes the sword of Jehu, Elisha shall put to death"* (1 Kgs 19:17). That program of divine retribution began to unfold in the closing years of the reign of Ahab's son Jehoram.

THE ANOINTING OF JEHU
2 Kings 9:1-13

When the time was right, Elisha carried out the divine commission to anoint Jehu to execute the divine wrath against the Omri dynasty. The prophet dispatched one of the prophetical students to Ramothgilead where Jehu was the commander. The young man took Jehu behind closed doors and anointed him to be king of Israel. Along with the anointing came a commission. Jehu was to smite the house of Ahab in order that God might avenge the deaths of the prophets at the hands of Jezebel. The house of Ahab should be made like the houses of Jeroboam and Baasha. The corpse of Jezebel herself was to be left for the dogs to devour. Having completed his mission, the young prophet hastily departed. Secrecy was of extreme importance.

When Jehu emerged from the house, his colleagues quizzed him about the crazy-acting messenger who had disappeared almost as suddenly as he had appeared. Jehu suspected that the whole scene had been arranged beforehand by his junior officers in a effort to get him to make a move against the unpopular Jehoram. The officers firmly disavowed any knowledge of what the young man might have said. They pressed their leader to relate it to them. Jehu then reported to them all that the prophet had said (2 Kgs 9:11-12).

The military commanders at Ramoth-gilead received the news enthusiastically. They immediately began to render to Jehu royal homage by spreading their garments upon the dust for him to walk upon. They improvised an enthronement ceremony by having Jehu ascend the outside stairs which led to the upper story of the house. When he took his position on the top-most step, they blew the trumpets and proclaimed Jehu to be king (2 Kgs 9:13).

THE SWORD OF JEHU
2 Kings 9:14-37

The revolution of 841 BC may well have been the most important political development in the history of the separate monarchies since the schism of 930 BC. Both kingdoms were affected immediately by what transpired. Besides the obvious political changes brought on by the revolution, one can trace the effects of this *coup* in the religious, economic and social realms as well.

A. Death of Jehoram (2 Kgs 9:14-26).

Jehu and his supporters made their way immediately for Jezreel where King Jehoram was convalescing after being wounded defending Ramoth-gilead a short time earlier. A watchman spied the chariot

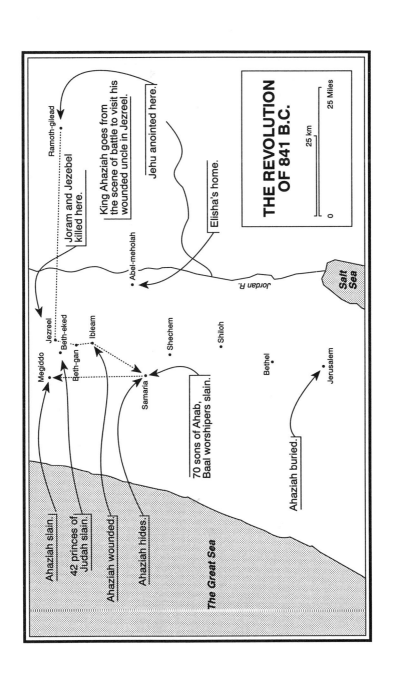

THE REVOLUTION
OF 841 B.C.

0   25 km
         25 Miles

Ramoth-gilead

Jehu anointed here.

King Ahaziah goes from
the scene of battle to visit his
wounded uncle in Jezreel.

Joram and Jezebel
killed here.

Elisha's home.

Abel-meholah

Jordan R.

Salt
Sea

Megiddo

Jezreel

Beth-eked

Ibleam

Beth-gan

Shechem

Shiloh

Samaria

70 sons of Ahab,
Baal worshipers slain.

Bethel

Jerusalem

Ahaziah slain.

42 princes of
Judah slain.

Ahaziah wounded.

Ahaziah hides.

Ahaziah buried.

The Great Sea

forces approaching. Jehoram at first thought that the small group of chariots was bringing news from the war front. The king dispatched a messenger to find out if the news was good or bad (2 Kgs 9:14-17). Jehu ordered the king's messenger to join his ranks. The royal watchmen noted this suspicious behavior and reported it at once to Jehoram. The king dispatched a second messenger with the same results. Jehoram now realized that the commander of that chariot force was acting in defiance of the crown. From the reckless pace at which the chariots were approaching Jezreel the watchman concluded that captain Jehu was leading the force (2 Kgs 9:18-20).

Since Jehu was known for his loyalty to the crown, Jehoram's apprehension disappeared. He decided to ride out with his nephew Ahaziah of Judah to meet his commander. The two kings met Jehu and his company in the portion of ground which Ahab had so ruthlessly taken from Naboth. The king greeted Jehu with the question *"Is all well?"* Jehu answered in the negative. No peace could exist between Jehu and Jehoram so long as the *"witchcrafts,"* i.e., idolatrous influence, of the queen mother Jezebel was allowed to continue in Israel (2 Kgs 9:21).

Jehoram now grasped the seriousness of the situation. He shouted a warning to his young nephew, wheeled about and attempted to flee the scene. Jehu immediately shot an arrow through the back of the king. Jehoram immediately slumped into his chariot dead. Jehu ordered the corpse to be cast into the portion of ground which once had belonged to Naboth. Thus was the house of Ahab recompensed for the murder of Naboth at the very spot announced by Elijah some fifteen years earlier (2 Kgs 9:22-26).

B. Death of Ahaziah (2 Kgs 9:27-29//2 Chr 22:7-9).

Ahaziah escaped the the scene at Jezreel unscathed. He fled southward toward the land of Judah by the way of Beth-gan, a village due south of Jezreel. Jehu ordered his men to pursue and slay Ahaziah because he was the grandson of Ahab. As Ahaziah's chariot slowed down at the steep ascent of Gur near the southern edge of the plain of Esdraelon, Jehu's archers were able to inflict a wound upon him. Ahaziah then changed directions and headed west toward Megiddo, partly because he was now in no condition to make the rugged climb back to Jerusalem, and partly because he wished to throw off his pursuers. There he died, either of the wounds he had received at the ascent of Gur, or as a result of some new violence on the part of Jehu (cf. 2 Chr 22:8,9).

C. Death of Jezebel (2 Kgs 9:30-37).

After pursuing Ahaziah as far as Ibleam, Jehu returned to Jezreel. About three hours would have elapsed since the death of King Jehoram. Jezebel was resignedly waiting for her confrontation with Jehu. When she heard he was coming, she put on eye make-up, adorned her head, and took up her position near a window. Even though she was a grandmother of at least fifty years, Jezebel still hoped to be able to capture the affections of Jehu with her beauty.[1] She attempted to flatter him by calling him *"Zimri."* This name recalled the fact that another Israelite general had revolted and slain his master and reigned as king (2 Kgs 9:30-31).

Jehu was not deterred by the wiles of Jezebel. He challenged two palace eunuchs to throw her from the window. The eunuchs grabbed the screaming queen and flung her to the courtyard below. Her falling body bounced off certain wall projections at once smearing her blood on the walls and showering it on Jehu's chariot houses as well. The captain then had his driver race over her crumpled corpse (2 Kgs 9:32-33).

Jehu was completely unaffected by the bloodshed in which he had been involved. He entered the palace and ordered a meal for himself. Not until after he had satisfied his appetite did he give any thought to the corpse of the late queen ignominiously lying untended on the ground. He then ordered this *"cursed woman"* to be given a decent burial. When the servants went to carry out these orders, all they could find of Jezebel was the skull, the feet and the palms of her hands. The scavenger dogs had eaten the rest (2 Kgs 9:34-35).

When the servants reported back to Jehu, the general remembered a prophecy delivered many years earlier by Elijah (cf. 1 Kgs 21:23). As Jehu remembered it, Elijah had said four things about the fate of Jezebel: (1) that dogs would devour her; (2) that this would take place in the *"portion"* of Jezreel, i.e., the cultivated space or portion of land outside the wall of the city; (3) that the carcass of Jezebel would be as dung upon the face of the ground; and (4) that the fragments of the body would be so scattered that it would be impossible to bury all her remains in one tomb (2 Kgs 9:36-37).

AFTERMATH OF THE REVOLUTION
In Israel
2 Kings 10:1-27

The deaths of Jehoram and Jezebel were only the start of a bloody campaign to free Israel of the influence of this ungodly family. Jehu moved quickly to eliminate all potential rivals.

A. Massacre of the Sons of Ahab (2 Kgs 10:1-11).

Jehu sent letters to the elders of the nation, those who had tutored Ahab's sons. Jehu taunted these potential adversaries. He urged them to select the boldest son of Jehoram, make him king, and come out against him with the weaponry which was stored in Samaria. Jehu was quite certain that the garrison at Samaria would not venture forth against the army of Ramoth-gilead which was backing Jehu (2 Kgs 10:1-3).

The elders of Samaria were intimidated by the scornful tone of Jehu's letters. They knew that they would not be able to muster any military support for an unpopular regime against a popular general. The elders sent back to Jehu a letter of capitulation. They placed themselves unreservedly on Jehu's side (2 Kgs 10:4-5).

Jehu immediately fired back a letter which demanded a demonstration of the professed loyalty of Samaria's leaders. He ordered them to decapitate Ahab's seventy "sons," i.e., descendants, and bring their heads the twenty miles to Jezreel within twenty-four hours. Having committed themselves in their letter to obedience, the leaders of Samaria had little choice but to allow themselves to become the tools of Jehu. Without hesitation they slew the seventy princes, put their heads in baskets, and sent them to Jezreel by messenger (2 Kgs 10:6-7).

Jehu ordered the royal heads to be put on public display in two heaps at the city gate. The next morning he addressed the spectators there. He openly admitted that he had slain his master. He feigned ignorance of how the seventy princes had died. By this time everyone knew how those men had met their death. Did this not prove that the leaders of the nation were weary of the Ahabites? Did this not clear Jehu of any private or selfish motive in what he had done? Furthermore, Jehu argued, what had transpired had been predicted by Elijah the prophet (2 Kgs 10:8-10).

Next, Jehu slew *"all that remained of the house of Ahab in Jezreel."* This probably included the princesses as well as princes. In addition he executed *"his great men,"* and the Baal priests who were on the royal payroll. Thus did Jehu destroy the entire Ahabite faction from the land (2 Kgs 10:11).

B. Massacre of Forty-two Princes (2 Kgs 10:12-14).

Having eliminated all potential opposition both in Jezreel and throughout the land, Jehu set out for Samaria. En route he happened upon a group of forty-two relatives of the deceased King Ahaziah of Judah. They were on their way to visit their northern cousins and also the queen mother Jezebel. At least that was what they claimed. Jehu realized that it was hardly possible that these men could be ignorant of recent events in the north. They must surely be coming north to give aid and assistance to their relatives of the house of Ahab. The forty-two princes of Judah who were also descendants of Ahab were taken captive and later slain.

C. Jehu and Jehonadab (2 Kgs 10:15-17).

Near Samaria Jehu happened upon Jehonadab, the founder of a remarkable sect of conservative Yahwists. He was somewhat of an ascetic who required his sons to live in tents, to possess neither house, nor field, nor vineyard, and to abstain wholly from the use of wine (cf. Jer 35:8-10). Jehu was anxious for the endorsement of this noted leader. Without a moment's hesitation Jehonadab cast his lot with Jehu. The venerable old man rode about in the new king's chariot thus giving the impression that he was in accord with the bloody anti-Ahab policy of Jehu (2 Kgs 10:15).

Jehu hinted to his new ally that further severe measures were about to be taken. When the two entered Samaria Jehu demonstrated his *"zeal for Yahweh"* by slaying all that remained of Ahab's house,

579

the wives and perhaps children of the seventy sons already slain. This action fulfilled the word which God had spoken against the house of Ahab by the mouth of Elijah (2 Kgs 10:16-17).

D. Massacre of Baal Worshipers (2 Kgs 10:18-27).

Up to this point, the revolution of 841 BC had appeared to be nothing more than a dynastic change such as had been forced upon the nation by Baasha (1 Kgs 15:27-29), Zimri (1 Kgs 16:9-12), and Omri (1 Kgs 16:17-19). No one, except a few trusted associates, as yet suspected that deep religious motives were at the root of this revolution. Publicly Jehu announced his intention to serve Baal even more zealously than had his predecessors. Consequently the prophets, priests, and worshipers of Baal were summoned to a great inaugural sacrifice. All of this Jehu did deceitfully, for his intention was to utterly destroy the Baal worshipers (2 Kgs 10:18-19).

Idolaters were liable to death under the law of Moses. Jehu would have had a perfect right to eradicate Baal worship throughout the land. The end, however, does not justify the means. To draw several hundred of his subjects by false pretenses into a trap and then slay them for doing what he had himself invited them to do, is an act wholly unjustifiable.

When the Baal worshipers assembled, Jehu followed the custom of supplying them all with proper garb. Keeping up the pretense that he was a devotee of Baal, Jehu himself entered the temple along with Jehonadab whom he wished to have as a witness to his *"zeal for Yahweh."* He urged the Baal worshipers to make sure no Yahwists were present in the building. They might have attended this festival out of curiosity, or to curry favor with the new king. Restricting sacred temple rites to true devotees would not have been thought unusual (2 Kgs 10:20-23).

When the whole multitude of Baal worshipers had entered the sacred precincts, Jehu stationed eighty of his men at the entrance. When the officiating priest had finished offering the sacrifices, Jehu ordered his men to enter the temple and slay the worshipers. All the wooden images representing deities subordinate to Baal were brought out and destroyed. The stone pillar representing Baal himself was broken in pieces. The temple of Baal was torn down. The ruins became a dump for city waste. Thus did Jehu eliminate the worship of the Tyrian Baal from Israel (2 Kgs 10:24-28).

E. A Prophetic Word (2 Kgs 10:28-31).

While Jehu was zealous for Yahweh as over against Baal, he was not of a mind to lead a reformation of Yahweh worship. The calf worship of the north had been under the curse of God from its inception (cf. 1 Kgs 13:2). Jehu never intended to reform this aspect of worship in his kingdom. His partial reformation brought no permanent blessing upon the nation (2 Kgs 10:28-29).

Through some prophet—probably Elisha—Yahweh spoke to Jehu commending him for executing the divine wrath against the house of Ahab and the Baal worshipers. Nothing is said here about the motives of Jehu. They were largely selfish. For his external obedience, God rewarded Jehu with an external earthly honor. His sons to the fourth generation would follow him on the throne of Israel. The Jehu dynasty ruled for over a century, twice as long as any other dynasty in the north (2 Kgs 10:30-31).

AFTERMATH OF THE REVOLUTION
In Judah
2 Kings 11:1-21

The revolution of 841 BC was crucial in the history of Judah as well as of Israel. The execution of the forty-two princes by Jehu (cf. 2 Kgs 10:12-14) set the stage for a usurper to take over the throne of David in Jerusalem.

A. Queen Athaliah (2 Kgs 11:1-3).

Athaliah was the daughter of Ahab and Jezebel and the wife of Jehoram of Judah. Through her influence King Jehoram had introduced the Tyrian Baal into Judah (2 Kgs 8:18; 2 Chr 21:5,11). When Ahaziah was slain by Jehu in the early hours of the revolution, the powerful position of Athaliah as queen mother was jeopardized. The regular line of succession would require the enthronement of one of her grandsons, the eldest son of Ahaziah. This would mean that the position of queen mother would pass on to the widow of Ahaziah.

For this reason Athaliah ordered all the members of the house of David put to death.[2] This would have included Athaliah's own grandsons, and probably other descendants of David belonging to branches of the house other than that of Rehoboam (2 Kgs 11:1).

Athaliah's plot to wipe out completely the house of David was frustrated by the determined efforts of Jehosheba, the sister of Ahaziah.[3] She hid the royal infant Joash in the *"chamber of mattresses,"* i.e., a storage room of the palace. After a few days she transferred him to one of the chambers of the temple. There the child remained until he was six. Jehosheba was married to Jehoiada the high priest (2 Chr 22:11). Hence she would have ready access to the temple precincts (2 Kgs 10:2).

For seven years (841-835 BC) Athaliah ruled Judah (2 Kgs 11:3). During that period Baalism was temporarily triumphant. The temple of Yahweh was allowed to fall into decay. A temple of Baal was erected in Jerusalem to rival it (cf. 2 Kgs 11:18). The usurper was held in check to some extent by the Yahwist party. She apparently was afraid openly to challenge the position of Jehoiada, and he was left in charge of the temple with its treasures and armories (cf. 2 Kgs 11:10). She allowed the temple services to continue (2 Chr 23:4-7), and permitted the priests and Levites to serve in their regular courses (2 Chr 23:8). Nonetheless, the zealous Yahwists chafed under the arrogant rule of the Jezebel of Judah.

B. Coronation of Joash (2 Kgs 11:4-12).

When Joash was seven years old, Jehoiada determined that the time had come to make the effort to restore the throne to the line of David. He summoned to the temple the five captains of the Carites, the royal guard, for a secret meeting. These men had entered the service of Athaliah under the notion that the house of David was extinct. By long standing tradition, however, the Carites were strongly attached to David and his seed[4] These men took an oath of support for the young king (2 Kgs 11:4).

The captains visited the cities of Judah and gathered a strong force of Levites, priests, and other representative men. This larger group came to the temple and also swore an oath to Joash and received a charge from Jehoiada (2 Chr 23:4-7).

582

On the fateful day three of the five companies of royal bodyguards were deployed about the palace. The other two companies, supplemented by the forces recruited from the cities of Judah, were assigned to guard the young king in the temple. To those guards Jehoiada issued shields and spears which had been captured years earlier by David in battle. Armed with these weapons the guards took up their positions in ranks stretching from one side of the temple court to the other, both before and behind the king (2 Kgs 11:5-11).

When all was ready, Jehoiada brought forth the young king and placed the crown upon his head. He then laid on the head of Joash a copy of the law of Moses to symbolize that the king must rule in accordance with the law. The priests then anointed the young prince with oil and declared him to be king (2 Chr 23:11). The crowds expressed their appreciation by clapping their hands and shouting, "May the king live!" (2 Kgs 11:12).

Chart No. 44

THE ARAMEAN KINGS OF DAMASCUS			
KINGS	**DATE BC**	**REFERENCES**	**NOTES**
Rezon	955-925	1 Kgs 11:23-24	Escaped from battle with David and founded this dynasty.
Hezion	925-913	1 Kgs 15:18	Damascus grew in prosperity.
Tabrimmon	913-890	1 Kgs 15:18	Had an alliance with Abijah of Judah.
Ben-hadad I	890-841	1 Kgs 15:18ff. 1 Kgs 20	(1) Asa of Judah sent gifts to bribe him. As a result he attacked Israel and captured certain cities; (2) Ahab twice defeated him; entered into an alliance with him. (3) His death fulfilled a prediction made by Elisha.
Hazael	841-801	1 Kgs 19:15-17 2 Kgs 8:7-15 2 Kgs 8:28-29 2 Kgs 9:14-15 2 Kgs 10:32-33 2 Kgs 13:3,22 2 Kgs 12:17,18	(1) Elijah was commissioned to anoint him. (2) Elisha prophesied his oppression of Israel. (3) Fought against Jehoram at Ramoth-gilead. (4) Reduced Jehu to a position of vassal. (5) Continued attacks in the reign of Jehoahaz. (6) Bribed by Joash of Judah to spare Jerusalem.
Ben-hadad II	801-780	2 Kgs 13:25 2 Kgs 6:24-7:20 2 Kgs 13:14-19	(1) Continued to oppress Israel; besieged Samaria. (2) Israel began to recover lost territory.
Rezin	750-735	Isa 7:1 2 Kgs 15:37 2 Chr 28:5	Joined forces with Pekah of Israel to attack Judah in 735 BC.

583

C. Death of Athaliah (2 Kgs 11:13-16).

When Athaliah heard the noise accompanying the coronation she was naturally suspicious. Though it was not her custom to enter the temple of Yahweh, she hurried next door to investigate the commotion. Entering the courtyard she was astonished to see young Joash standing upon the special platform which the king normally occupied when he attended temple services. In utter dismay Athaliah ripped her robes and shouted *"Treason!"* (2 Kgs 11:13-14).

Jehoiada ordered the soldiers to close ranks about the queen and conduct her out of the courtyard. Anyone who attempted to rescue the queen was to be slain. The queen, however, was not to be slain in the temple. Once outside the temple precincts, Athaliah was executed (2 Kgs 11:15-16).

D. Enthronement of Joash (2 Kgs 11:17-20).

Four actions were taken by Jehoiada on Joash's coronation day. First, two solemn covenants were made—one between the king and the people, and the other between the people and God. The first bound the king to govern according to the law, and the people to render allegiance to the new king. The second covenant bound the nation to maintain the worship of Yahweh (2 Kgs 11:17).

Second, the Baal temple in Jerusalem was destroyed. The altars and images of Baal were smashed. The priest of Baal was slain.

Third, officers were appointed over the temple. This included priests, Levites, singers and gatekeepers. The regular daily sacrificial ritual was re-established (2 Kgs 11:18; 2 Chr 23:18-19).

Fourth, Joash was escorted in triumphant procession from the temple to the royal palace. Once the rightful heir was seated on the throne of his ancestors the land was content. No opposition showed itself. The removal of Athaliah ended at long last the evil reign of the children of Jezebel (2 Kgs 11:19-20).

E. The Reign of Joash (2 Kgs 12:1-16//2 Chr 24:1-27).

For over half of his reign of forty years (835-796 BC) the priest Jehoiada was the counselor of King Joash. During those years Joash did right in the eyes of Yahweh. When his minority came to an end, Joash's first act was to order a restoration of the temple. All the monies collected by the priests were to be directed toward this project. The priests, however, showed no urgency about collecting these funds (12:1-6).

Together with Jehoiada, Joash worked out a new fund raising program. A public chest was set up conspicuously in the temple court near the great altar. Worshipers were encouraged to offer free will offerings for the renovation project. Periodically Jehoiada and a royal secretary would empty the chest and weigh the contents. These monies were then given to superintendents who employed the skilled laborers. Everyone had complete confidence in those overseers for they *"dealt faithfully,"* i.e., honestly. After the repair work was completed, the surplus monies were used to replace the temple vessels which had been spoiled by successive kings to bribe foreign invaders (12:7-16).[5]

Jehoiada died at the age of 130. After his death Joash followed the advice of counselors who were sympathetic to paganism. The house of Yahweh was abandoned and the nation served the Asherim and other idols. Because of this new apostasy, the wrath of Yahweh came on Judah and Jerusalem. Prophets arose to call the people back to the Lord, but they refused to listen (2 Chr 24:15-19).

The Spirit of God came upon Zechariah the son of Jehoiada the priest. He *"stood above the people"* in the court of the temple and rebuked them for having transgressed the commandments of Yahweh. At the command of King Joash they conspired against Zechariah and stoned him to death in the temple court. What an ingrate Joash turned out to be. As the prophet died he cried out *"May Yahweh see and take vengeance!"* (2 Chr 24:20-22).

Chart No. 45

DIVIDED MONARCHY: HUMILIATION PHASE
(Sisters Bowing)
841-790 BC

THE ANOINTING OF HAZAEL
2 Kings 8:7-15

For reasons not stated, Elisha at some point in his ministry made a trip to Damascus. Some have tried to link this visit to the commission given many years earlier to Elijah that he (or his surrogate) should anoint Hazael. Others speculate that Jezebel was stirring up trouble for the prophet, and so he determined to leave the country temporarily. Still another possibility is that Elisha was spending part of the time of the national famine outside the land even as his predecessor had done.[6] Whatever his reason for going to Damascus, the move was most bold. Not too long previous to this visit, the king of Damascus had made a determined effort to arrest Elisha and punish him for revealing Aramean military plans to Jehoram (cf. 2 Kgs 6:13-19). Probably Yahweh directed Elisha to make this trip, and the prophet, putting his trust in the Lord, carried out the command.

The aged Ben-hadad was quite ill at the time Elisha visited the city. Ben-hadad, knowing of the reputation of this man of God, immediately dispatched his trusted servant Hazael with presents for the prophet. He was instructed to make inquiry of Yahweh through the prophet concerning the prognosis for the king. The miracles of Elisha had convinced even these idolaters that Yahweh was a powerful God. The Aramean king paid great respect to the prophet by referring to himself in the message as *"your son"* (2 Kgs 8:7-9).

Elisha instructed Hazael to tell his master that he would surely recover from his current illness. However, God had revealed to Elisha that the king would die, not of his illness, but of another cause. After giving this answer to Hazael, the prophet fixed a hard stare upon his visitor until Hazael became uncomfortable. Hazael had already formed a plan to eliminate his master. The stare of the prophet made him realize that his plans were known (2 Kgs 8:10).

As Elisha mentally observed what lay in store for his people at the hand of Hazael, he began to weep. Hazael inquired as to the reason for this unexpected outburst. Elisha explained his actions by describing the brutal warfare which Hazael would launch against Israel—the burning of cities, slaughter of youth, dashing to pieces of little children, and ripping open of pregnant women. Hazael shrugged off the implications of this prediction by asking how he, a lowly servant—*"a contemptible dog"*—would ever be able to launch war against Israel and do the great things Elisha predicted of him. Elisha responded that Hazael would not continue in his lowly position, for Yahweh had revealed that he would one day be king of Aram (2 Kgs 8:11-13).

Hazael returned to Ben-hadad and reported only the first half of Elisha's answer to the king. He suppressed the part of the answer that announced that Ben-hadad would die, but not of the illness. On the very next day, Hazael made his move against the king. He took a thick piece of cloth, dipped it in water, and held it over the ailing king's face until Ben-hadad died of suffocation. Hazael then claimed the throne (2 Kgs 8:14-15).[7]

THE SWORD OF HAZAEL
2 Kings 10:28-36

To punish Israel for continuing in calf worship, Yahweh unleased the sword of Hazael. He began to *"cut Israel short"* by means of the king of Aram. Hazael wrested the entire Transjordan territory— Bashan and Gilead—from the control of Israel. Jehu's only consolation was that he was able to keep Hazael from crossing the Jordan (2 Kgs 10:32-33). The Aramean oppression got even worse during the reign of Jehu's son Jehoahaz.

A. Jehoahaz Punished (2 Kgs 13:1-9).

Jehoahaz succeeded his father Jehu on the throne of Israel. He ruled seventeen years (814-798 BC). Like all previous kings of Israel, he sinned by continuing to condone the calf worship at Dan and Bethel. The record also indicates that Jehoahaz did not remove the Asherah—the wooden image of the consort of Baal—from Samaria. This Asherah had been set up by Ahab at the instigation of Jezebel (cf. 1 Kgs 16:33). That Jehu had not removed this last vestige of the Ahab-Jezebel era during his long reign is surprising (2 Kgs 13:1-3,6).

Jehoahaz was punished for his sin even more severely than Jehu. God delivered Israel into the hand of the ruthless Aramean kings Hazael and his son Ben-hadad II *"all the days,"* i.e., all the days that God had appointed for the calamity. The Arameans inflicted heavy casualties upon the Israelite army. Hazael *"made them like the dust by threshing."* This may be a way of figuratively describing the utter destruction which Hazael had inflicted on the armies of Israel. On the other hand this language may be an allusion to the execution of prisoners by driving threshing implements over them—a barbaric practice known to have been practiced by the Arameans (cf. Amos 1:3). Hazael was able to limit the standing army of Israel to fifty horsemen, ten chariots, and ten thousand infantry, virtually nothing more than a police force. Jehoahaz, it would appear, was a vassal of Hazael (2 Kgs 13:1-3,7).

The oppression continued under Hazael's son Ben-hadad II who succeeded his father in 801 BC. For a time Ben-hadad was able to intensify the Aramean oppression by capturing certain unidentified cities from Jehoahaz (2 Kgs 14:25).

B. Judah Punished (2 Kgs 12:17-18//2 Chr 24:23-27).
After taking the Transjordan area from Israel, Hazael cast his eye upon the coastal plains of Palestine. The city of Gath, which may have been under control of Judah (cf. 2 Chr 11:8), fell easily to him. Encouraged by this easy victory, the Aramean king took his small army into the mountain region where he defeated the army of Joash and took much spoil (2 Chr 24:23f.). Then he commenced the siege of Jerusalem (2 Kgs 12:17). The date of this attack was about 805 BC.

Like Rehoboam and Asa before him, Joash bought off the invader with temple treasures. Valuables from the palace were also given to Hazael. The Aramean was sufficiently satisfied with the tribute rendered to him and withdrew from Judah (2 Kgs 12:18).

Shortly after the attack by Hazael, Joash was assassinated by two of his servants. Perhaps sensing his unpopularity, the king had taken refuge in *"in the house of Millo,"* a fortress built by David and Solomon. Both of the assassins had foreign mothers. No indication is given in the text as to their motive. Perhaps the humiliating capitulation to Hazael caused the people to lose all confidence in their king. Joash was forty-seven when he died.

C. The Deliverer (2 Kgs 13:4-5).
In the midst of this Aramean oppression, Jehoahaz repented and

cried out to God for deliverance. Jehoahaz did not abandon the practice of the calf worship, perhaps because he did not suspect that this was the sin which had provoked the anger of Yahweh. He did repent, however, and God accepted that repentance as imperfect as it was. God delivered his people from the destruction which they otherwise might have experienced at the hands of the Aramean kings (2 Kgs 13:4).

God raised up one who would deliver his people from their oppressors. This *"deliverer"* may have been Jehoash, the son of Jehoahaz who began to extricate Israel from the grip of the Arameans. More likely the reference is to Jeroboam II who was able to restore all the borders of Israel. Under his reign peace again returned to the northern kingdom (2 Kgs 13:5).

Chart No. 46

THE JEHU DYNASTY 841-753 BC		
KINGS	**DATES BC**	**SUMMARY**
JEHU	841-814	**REVOLUTION**
JEHOAHAZ	814-798	**RETRIBUTION**
JEHOASH	798-782	**RECOVERY**
JEROBOAM II	782-753	**RESTORATION**
ZECHARIAH	753	**RUIN**
God's promise to Jehu: "Your sons to the fourth generation shall sit on the throne of Israel" (2 Kgs 10:30).		

ENDNOTES

1. Others think Jezebel was simply preparing to meet death in a manner befitting a queen.

2. The royal house of Judah had already been greatly depleted by

Jehoram's murder of his brothers (2 Chr 21:4), by Arab marauders (2 Chr 21:17), and by Jehu's murder of the brethren of Ahaziah (2 Kgs 10:14).

3. While Jehosheba was the sister of Ahaziah, she probably was not the daughter of Athaliah. According to Josephus, she was the daughter of Jehoram by a secondary wife, and therefore actually a half-sister of Ahaziah (*Ant.* 9.7.1).

4. The Carites are probably the same of the Cherethites of earlier times. Cf. 2 Sam 8:18; 1 Kgs 1:38. They were foreign mercenary troops responsible for guarding the person of the king.

5. To this point the temple had been spoiled by Rehoboam to pay Shishak (1 Kgs 14:26), and by Asa to bribe Ben-hadad (1 Kgs 15:18).

6. Gray (*op. cit.,* p. 529) thinks Ben-hadad sent for Elisha. If this were the case, one would think that Elisha would have been taken directly into the presence of the king.

7. Hazael's usurpation is noted in Assyrian inscriptions, which refer to him as *"the son of nobody,"* the regular designation of a usurper.

CHAPTER THIRTY-FIVE

Recovery and Heyday
2 Kings 13:10-15:7

Help came to Israel in the midst of the Aramean oppression from an unexpected quarter. About 800 BC the Assyrian king Adad-nirari III attacked Damascus and inflicted serious casualties on Ben-hadad II. From that point on, Israel gradually began to recover her lost territories and to emerge from the half century of humiliating submission to Damascus.

RECOVERY FROM ARAMEAN OPPRESSION
In Israel
2 Kings 13:10-14:22

In Israel the recovery began under Jehoash (Joash) who reigned sixteen years (798-782 BC). He followed in the footsteps of his father Jehoahaz by continuing to condone and participate in the calf worship inaugurated by Jeroboam (2 Kgs 13:10-13).

A. Final Predictions of Elisha (2 Kgs 13:14-25).

The prophetic ministry of Elisha which had spanned over half a century, came to a close in the early years of Jehoash of Israel. The venerable old prophet must have been at least eighty years old. As he lay dying, the king came to his bedside. As he wept, Jehoash bestowed upon Elisha the familiar titles which were addressed to Elijah when he departed from this world. The term *"father"* recognized Elisha as the spiritual leader and teacher of Israel. The term *"chariot"* depicted him as national defender. When Elijah left this earth he left behind a capable successor; but when Elisha died, there was no one to assume spiritual leadership. King Jehoash realized that a great era of God's dealings with Israel was coming to an end (2 Kgs 13:14).

1. The first symbolic act (13:15-17). Moved by the compassion of the king, Elisha mustered his strength to give Jehoash assurance that God would still stand by his people. The old prophet instructed the king to take a bow and arrows from one of the soldiers who naturally would have accompanied the king on this visit. The prophet then instructed the king to place his hands on the bow as one would normally do when about to shoot that weapon. When the king assumed this position *"Elisha put his hands upon the king's hands"* i.e., he arose from his bed and also took the position of an archer covering the king's two hands with his own. The shooting of the arrow would then appear to be a joint act of the prophet and the king. The window shutter was then opened, and the arrow was released in the direction of Transjordan where the Arameans had won such impressive victories over the Israelites. Elisha explained that the arrow symbolized deliverance from Aramean oppression. Israel would inflict an utterly crushing defeat upon the Arameans at Aphek in Gilead.[1]

2. The second symbolic act (13:18-19). Next the king was told to take in hand the arrows remaining in the quiver and to smite them upon the ground. Jehoash smote the arrows against the floor three times. He did not enter into the spirit of the symbolic act, which represented the smiting of enemies. Elisha was angry at this evident lack of enthusiasm. If the king had been earnestly desirous of victory he would have kept striking until instructed to stop, or at least should have smitten the floor five or six times. From his prophetic perspective Elisha could see the great opportunity which was forfeited because of Jehoash's lethargic response. The Israelites would now defeat their enemies but thrice.

B. The Bones of Elisha (2 Kgs 13:20-21).

Because of the weakness of Israel at this time marauding bands of Moabites invaded Israel at the beginning of each year, i.e., in the spring of the year. Sometime after the death of Elisha, some Israelite men were carrying the corpse of a comrade for burial when the funeral party spotted one of these bands of raiders. With no time for ceremony, the burial party hastily and perhaps somewhat roughly cast the corpse into the nearest sepulcher which just happened to be the one where lay the bones of Elisha. When that corpse touched the bones of Elisha, the dead man revived and rose to his feet inside the sepulcher. God was teaching Israel respect for his prophet even after death.

C. Victories over the Arameans (2 Kgs 13:22-25).

During the Aramean oppression God had compassion upon his people. *"He turned unto them for the sake of the covenant with Abraham, Isaac and Jacob."* The time would come when he would cast off these people; but that time had not yet come (2 Kgs 13:22-23).

Though he was not able to completely extricate the nation from the Aramean grip, Jehoash was able to inflict three smashing defeats upon Ben-hadad just as Elisha had predicted.This enabled him to recover the cities which Ben-hadad had taken from his father. Much of the Transjordan territories, however, remained firmly under the control of Ben-hadad until the reign of Jeroboam II (2 Kgs 13:24-25).

RECOVERY FROM ARAMEAN OPPRESSION
In Judah
2 Kings 14:1-22

When Joash was assassinated, he was succeeded by his twenty-five year old son Amaziah. The new king ruled for twenty-nine years (796-767 BC). Amaziah, the *"thistle king,"* is another example of a good start and a tragic end.

A. Hopeful Beginning (2 Kgs 14:1-7// 2 Chr 25:1-4).

The authors of both Kings and Chronicles placed Amaziah of Judah among the good kings. Yet in his reign there was much amiss. In several respects Amaziah's reign resembles that of his father Joash. Both were zealous for Yahweh at first, but turned to idolatry at last. Both opposed prophets and treated their rebukers with scorn. Both roused conspiracy against themselves by their misconduct. Both were murdered by malcontents. Further, both were unsuccessful in war. Both had to withstand a siege on their capital. Both bought off their enemy by the surrender of the greater part of their wealth, including the treasures of the temple (2 Kgs 14:3).

Only on one score does Amaziah receive the reproof of the author of Kings: He failed to remove the high places. Not until the reign of Hezekiah was any attempt made to abolish the use of these local shrines and to enforce the law that insisted on a central sanctuary for national worship. On the other hand, the sacred historian points to one very commendable action of this king. Once he had the kingdom firmly under his control, Amaziah ordered those who had assassinated his father to be executed (cf. 2 Kgs 12:20). He refused, however, to follow what was standard policy among rulers of his time and have the sons of the assassins slain as well. Here Amaziah was submitting to the law of Moses which stipulated that sons were not to be executed for the sins of their fathers (2 Kgs 14:4-6; cf. Deut 24:16).

B. Campaign against Edom (2 Chr 25:5-16).

Subjugation of Edom was vital to the prosperity of Judah. Amaziah resolved to launch a massive effort once again to conquer that land.[2] He mustered an army of 400,000 men, which included 100,000 mercenaries from the northern kingdom. Rebuked by a prophet for lack of faith in enlisting the services of the Israelites, Amaziah dismissed the mercenaries (2 Chr 25:5-10).

Amaziah's Edom campaign met with great success. Ten thousand of the enemy fell in battle, and an equal number were captured and ruthlessly executed by being thrown from a high cliff. The climax of this campaign was the capture of the almost impregnable Edomite capital of Sela, later known as Petra. Following the lead of many great conquerors, Amaziah gave the city a new name—Joktheel, i.e., "subdued by God" (2 Chr 25:11-12; 2 Kgs 14:7).

C. War with Israel (2 Kgs 14:8-14// 2 Chr 25:17-24).

Upon returning to Judah, Amaziah discovered that the Israelite mercenaries whom he had dismissed had vented their anger by rampaging through cities of Judah killing some 3,000 men and taking much spoil (2 Chr 25:13). His confidence bolstered by his successes in Edom, Amaziah determined to avenge the actions of those Israelite soldiers by challenging the northern king, Jehoash, to a military showdown (2 Kgs 14:8).

Jehoash responded to the challenge of Amaziah by means of a fable. The thistle, the lowest and most despised plant of the forest, sent to the stately cedar to request the hand of his daughter in marriage. In antiquity such a request was tantamount to a claim to equality. A mere beast of the field happened by and trampled the thistle into the dust of the earth (2 Kgs 14:9).

The application of Jehoash's parable is obvious. Amaziah had enjoyed a measure of success against Edom. Now, like the thistle, he thought he was equal to the cedar, the mightiest of kingdoms. Amaziah had best stay at home and glory in his past triumphs. If he ventured forth against Israel he would find himself as easily crushed as the thistle beneath the feet of a wild animal. Jehoash was as confident of success as was Amaziah. His three recent triumphs over the powerful Arameans were just as impressive as Amaziah's victory over the Edomites (2 Kgs 14:10).

The message from Jehoash did not deter Amaziah. Jehoash anticipated that confrontation was inevitable. He decided that the best defense was an offense. He crossed the border and launched a sneak attack through the Philistine plain. The two forces met at Bethshemesh, which lies almost due west of Jerusalem on the western frontier of Judah (2 Kgs 14:11).

In this test of strength between the two kingdoms—the first since the days of Abijam over a hundred years earlier—the armies of Judah were utterly crushed with each soldier fleeing to his *"tent,"* i.e., home. Amaziah himself was captured and brought to Jerusalem. There under threat of death he was forced to order the gates of Jerusalem opened to Jehoash. The king of Israel broke down some six hundred feet of the northern wall of Jerusalem. The spoils of war fell to the conqueror—the objects of value which had accumulated in the temple since Joash of Judah had bribed Hazael with its treasure. The treasures of the royal palace, including all the spoils Amaziah had captured in Edom, were also taken. To discourage a retaliatory attack by Judah at a later time, hostages were taken by Jehoash (2 Kgs 14:12-14).

D. Death of Amaziah (2 Kgs 14:15-22).

Amaziah maintained himself on the throne of Judah for several years after his humiliating defeat by Jehoash of Israel. Like his father before him, Amaziah died in a conspiracy. He had aroused much dissatisfaction by his importation of foreign idols (2 Chr 25:27) and by fifteen years of inaction after his defeat by Jehoash. When he heard rumors of the conspiracy against him, Amaziah fled to Lachish on the southwestern frontier of Judah. His enemies, however, were too numerous and powerful. Amaziah was assassinated in Lachish. Though he had died in disgrace at the hands of his own servants, the conspirators were minded to treat the royal corpse with respect. The body was brought back to Jerusalem *"upon horses,"* i.e., a horse-drawn chariot, where it was buried (2 Kgs 14:15-20).

For the first time in the history of Judah *"the people"* took the initiative in determining who would rule. Azariah or Uzziah[3] was elevated to the throne. One passage suggests that this took place after the death of Amaziah (2 Kgs 14:21). Chronological considerations, however, indicate that Uzziah had been made king in place of his father some twenty-four years earlier (c. 792 BC), perhaps not long after Amaziah's ignominious defeat at the hands of Jehoash of Israel.[4] He was sixteen years old at the time. Uzziah was thirty-nine when he became sole ruler. Only after the death of his father did Uzziah achieve greatness (2 Kgs 14:21-22).

HEYDAY PERIOD
2 Kings 14:23-15:7

Israel and Judah achieved their greatest glory under the reigns of Jeroboam II in the north and Uzziah in the south. This somewhat unexpected turn of events resulted from two factors. About 800 BC, after crushing the Arameans, the Assyrians withdrew to their own territory. Then for over half a century, until 745 BC, the Assyrians remained politically dormant. This gave the states which had been oppressed by the Arameans an opportunity to recover.

A. Jeroboam in Israel (2 Kgs 14:23-29).

Jeroboam II was the greatest king of the northern kingdom, and yet his reign of forty-one years (793-753 BC) is passed over with great brevity in the Bible.[5] Like all the kings of the Jehu dynasty, Jeroboam II continued to follow the apostate calf worship, and hence he is said to have done evil in the eyes of Yahweh (2 Kgs 14:23-24).

Chart No. 47

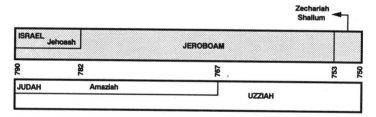

DIVIDED MONARCHY: HEYDAY PHASE
(Sisters Growing)
790-750 BC

The military successes of Jeroboam II were considerable. He was able to restore the borders of Israel as they had been in the earlier days of the northern kingdom. His kingdom stretched from the "entrance of Hamath"—the high slopes in the valley between the two ranges of the Lebanon mountains—to "the sea of the plain," i.e., the Dead Sea. The recovered territory included all of Transjordan as far south as the river Arnon, the border of Moab. Some think that Moab itself may be included in this general description of the territorial conquests of Jeroboam II.

The success of Jeroboam II is attributed to the guidance of Jonah the prophet. This is the same prophet famous for what happened to him as he tried to flee the responsibility to preach in Nineveh. The author of Kings explains the divine aid to Jeroboam II as being due to unfathomable divine compassion. God saw the extreme suffering of

HEYDAY OF THE DIVIDED KINGDOM

780-750 B.C.

50 km

0   50 Miles

The Euphrates River

Lebo-Hamath

Jeroboam conquered these areas as prophesied by Jonah-ben-Amittai.

Gebal (Byblos)

SIDONIANS

The Great Sea

Damascus

Jonah's home.

Uzziah broke down the walls of Gath, Jabneh and Ashdod.

Gath-hepher

Ramoth-gilead

Samaria

PHILISTIA

ISRAEL

Jabneh
Ashdod
Ashkelon
Gaza

Bethel
Jerusalem

Gath
Tekoa

AMMON

Home of Amos.

JUDAH

Beer-sheba

MOAB

Ammonites send tribute to Uzziah.

Gurbaal

Kadesh-barnea

EDOM

Foreigners in this region sent tribute to Uzziah.

This important seaport was recaptured by Uzziah.

Ezion-geber
Elath

his people under the Arameans and thus raised up his prophet to give inspired advice to the king in his efforts to free Israel of this oppression (2 Kgs 14:25-26).

Although the nation was deserving of judgment, Yahweh decided not to blot out the name of Israel at this time. He gave the nation a grace period, an opportunity to repent, an Indian summer before the winter of retributive judgment. He gave to Israel the deliverance promised by Elisha (cf. 2 Kgs 13:17) and later by Jonah. This deliverance which had begun under Jehoash was brought to a successful completion by Jeroboam II. Thus one Jeroboam founded the northern kingdom; another restored it to its ancient glory (2 Kgs 14:27).

One note concerning Jeroboam II has puzzled commentators for years. He is said to have recovered Hamath and Damascus *"which belonged to Judah"* (2 Kgs 14:28). These two cities north of Israel had belonged to Israel during the days of David and Solomon. How these two cities could be said to have belonged to Judah in this period has not been explained successfully. The question of the relationship between Judah and the kingdoms of Hamath and Damascus in the north must be left open.

B. Uzziah in Judah (2 Kgs 15:1-7//2 Chr 26:1-21).

Uzziah began his independent reign over Judah in 767 BC when his father and coregent of twenty-four years was assassinated.[6] Altogether Uzziah reigned fifty-two years. The author of Kings rates him as a good king with one exception, viz., that he failed to confine the worship to the place which Yahweh had designated (2 Kgs 15:1-4). The Chronicler mentions the positive influence of a prophet named Zechariah upon his life. *"As long as he sought Yahweh, God prospered him"* (2 Chr 26:5).

Judah experienced its heyday under Uzziah's reign. This king was a conqueror. He was able to recover Elath from the Edomites in the south. He captured and dismantled certain Philistine fortresses, then built his own cities in the area. He defeated the Arabians and the Maonites. Uzziah forced the Ammonites to pay him tribute. Because of his large standing army (307,500) which was both well-trained and well-armed, the power of Uzziah was feared far and wide (2 Chr 26:2-8).

Uzziah was also a builder. He refortified Jerusalem and installed catapults and other *"engines of war invented by skillful men."* He also built towers in outlying areas to protect his vast herds of cattle. He built cisterns to provide water for his vineyards and fields. He *"loved the soil."*

The marvelous prosperity which Uzziah enjoyed caused him to be filled with pride. He attempted to usurp the position and prerogatives of the priesthood, something that was forbidden to anyone who was not descended from Aaron. Uzziah took a censer, entered the temple over the protests of the priests, and burned incense on the golden altar (2 Chr 26:16-18). At that moment God struck him with leprosy. The king was forced to spend the final years of his reign in a *"house of separation"* isolated and alone. His son Jotham then assumed the royal functions of administrating the affairs of the palace and judging the people. Uzziah's sin and the beginning of Jotham's coregency took place about 750 BC (2 Kgs 15:5).[7]

C. Reign of Jotham in Judah (2 Kgs 15:32-38).

The period of independent prosperity continued in Judah for about fifteen years longer than in Israel. The southern kingdom remained strong during the sixteen year reign (750-735 BC) of Jotham, son of Uzziah.[8]

Jotham is evaluated as a good king. He is said to have done according to all that his father did except that he did not repeat the tragic mistake of attempting to enter the temple (2 Chr 27:2). Yet he made no effort to destroy the high places which were so offensive to the Lord. He did, however, build the *"high gate"* of the temple which appears to have been on the north side of that structure. This gate probably was intended to serve as further fortification against possible attack from the north (2 Kgs 15:34-35). The Chronicler relates that Jotham also restored other fortifications (2 Chr 27:3).

One of the significant accomplishments of Jotham was the subjugation of Ammon. For three years the Ammonites paid enormous annual tribute to Judah—a hundred talents of silver and 10,000 measures of both wheat and barley (2 Chr 27:5).

ENDNOTES

1. Aphek was on the direct route between Samaria and Damascus, and thus would be a likely spot for such a decisive battle. Israel had earlier inflicted a defeat upon the Arameans at this place. No record exists of the fulfillment of Elisha's prediction of an Aphek victory, but it is doubtlessly alluded to in 2 Kgs 13:25.

2. Edom had revolted against Judah and had recovered its independence during the reign of Jehoram some forty years before the time of Amaziah (cf. 2 Kgs 8:20).

3. Azariah occurs eight times in 2 Kings and once in Chronicles; Uzziah occurs four times in 2 Kings, and twelve times in Chronicles. The name Uzziah is also used by Isaiah, Hosea, Amos and Zechariah. Azariah means *"he whose help is Yahweh."* Uzziah means *"he whose strength is Yahweh."*

4. Edwin R. Thiele, *A Chronology of the Hebrew Kings* (Grand Rapids: Zondervan, 1977), p. 25.

5. A study of all the data from both kingdoms indicates that Jeroboam II served as coregent with his father Jehoash for twelve years. Thus the total of Jeroboam's reign was forty-one years (793-753 BC). He became sole ruler in 782 BC. See Thiele, *op. cit.,* pp. 25,75.

6. Thiele, *ibid.*

7. Thiele, *ibid.,* p. 78.

8. Jotham assumed control of the government when his father was banished to a *"separate house"* in 750 BC. Uzziah died in 740 BC. Jotham handed the government over to his son Ahaz in 735 BC, but he continued to serve as king emeritus for another four years (cf. 2 Kgs 15:30). See Thiele, *ibid.*

CHAPTER THIRTY-SIX

The Great Assyrian Conqueror
2 Kings 15:8-17:41

The history of Israel and Judah was radically affected by the rise of Tiglath-pileser III of Assyria. Heretofore the Assyrian military thrusts into Syria-Palestine had been merely tribute-gathering raids. A new policy, however, was inaugurated by Tiglath-pileser. This monarch was determined to build an empire. He designed the policy of massive population deportation which was so effective in holding captive peoples in check. By removing the upper classes of a conquered nation and resettling them in some remote portion of his empire, Tiglath-pileser was able to reduce the threat of local rebellions throughout his domain.

ISRAEL SUBMITS TO ASSYRIA
2 Kings 15:8-26

The heyday period for Israel ended abruptly with the death of Jeroboam II in 753 BC. In the next thirty years Israel had six kings representing five dynasties.

A. Reign of Zechariah (2 Kgs 15:8-12).

Zechariah was the last representative of the Jehu dynasty. He reigned but six months in 753 BC. The fact that he succeeded to the throne at all was a fulfillment of promises made to the founder of his dynasty (cf. 2 Kgs 10:30). God had promised Jehu that his sons would hold the throne of Israel to the fourth generation.

B. Reign of Shallum (2 Kgs 15:13-15).

Shallum, the assassin of Zechariah, was able to hold the throne for only thirty days. Hearing of his conspiracy, Menahem, an army general, marched from Tirzah to Samaria, got Shallum into his power, and put him to death.

C. Submission to Assyria (2 Kgs 15:16-22).

Zechariah had plans to continue the expansionist policies of his father Jeroboam. At the very time he was assassinated, the armies under Menahem were garrisoned at Tirzah awaiting orders to march northward to attack Tiphsah on the Euphrates River. After rather easily disposing of Shallum, the assassin of Zechariah, Menahem launched the expedition which had been previously planned. When the city of Tiphsah refused to surrender, Menahem treated it in a most cruel way. Even pregnant women were ripped open and their unborn children bandied about on the swords of his soldiers. All the territory from Tirzah in Israel to Tiphsah fell temporarily under the control of Menahem. Assyria was weak and unable to resist these incursions (2 Kgs 15:16).

Menahem's conquests in the north were short-lived. In 745 BC the mighty Tiglath-pileser, known in Babylonia as King Pul, came to the throne of Assyria. In one of his early campaigns Tiglath-pileser invaded Israel and forced Menahem to pay an enormous tribute of a thousand talents of silver ($2,000,000 BV).[1] This payment in effect made Menahem a vassal of Tiglath-pileser and placed his throne under the protection of the Assyrian monarch. To secure this tribute money, Menahem taxed the wealthy land owners fifty shekels ($2,000 BV) each.[2] Content for the moment with his take, Tiglath-pileser returned to Assyria (2 Kgs 15:19-20). Menahem reigned ten years over the northern kingdom (752-742 BC).

D. The Reign of Pekahiah (2 Kgs 15:23-26).

Menahem was succeeded by his son Pekahiah who reigned two years (742-740 BC). Nothing of significance happened during his reign. One of his captains, Pekah the son of Remaliah, conspired against him and slew him in the tower (i.e., lofty part) of the royal palace. Joining Pekah in this conspiracy were fifty Gileadites who may have been part of the royal bodyguard.

Chart No. 48

DIVIDED MONARCHY: HOMAGE PHASE
(Sisters Parting)
750-722 BC

AN ANTI-ASSYRIAN COALITION
2 Kings 15:27-16:6

Throughout the reigns of Menahem and his son Pekahiah, Pekah had maintained a rival dynasty, perhaps in Transjordan. This reconstruction is based on the statement that Pekah ruled for twenty years.[3] The independent rule of Pekah began in 740 BC and ended in 732 BC.

A. Rule of Pekah in Israel (2 Kgs 15:27-31).

Pekah was radically anti-Assyrian in his foreign policy. He joined with Rezin of Damascus in forming a coalition of western states which hoped to be able to withstand further Assyrian incursions into the area. This alliance is an extraordinary and somewhat unexpected political development. Not since the early days of Ben-hadad I had either Israel or Judah been allied with the Aramean state. For a century and a half the kings of Damascus had been bitter enemies of the people of God. The military resurgence of Assyria under the dynamic leadership of Tiglath-pileser (745-727 BC) forced the states of Syria-Palestine into a political realignment.

B. Reaction in Judah (2 Kgs 15:32-16:4).

Perhaps fearing that his father could not deal with the impending crisis created by the anti-Assyrian coalition, Ahaz seized the throne in 735 BC.[4] He rejected the overtures of the anti-Assyrian coalition. He either did not feel threatened by Assyria, or else he feared Tiglath-pileser so much that he did not wish to offend the Great King in any way.

C. Syro-Ephraimitic Invasion of Judah (2 Kgs 16:5-9).

In 734 BC Pekah and Rezin invaded Judah with the purpose of deposing Ahaz and putting someone more sympathetic to the anti-Assyrian cause on the throne.[5] Jerusalem was besieged, but did not fall. The fortifications of Uzziah (2 Chr 26:9) and Jotham (2 Chr 27:3) had, no doubt, greatly strengthened the city since the time it was captured so easily by Jehoash (cf. 2 Kgs 14:13). Frustrated at Jerusalem, the coalition roamed farther south and captured Elath driving out the garrison which had been stationed there since the days of Uzziah (cf. 2 Kgs 14:22). From that time on the Arameans (or perhaps Edomites[6]) occupied this important seaport city (2 Kgs 16:5-6).

Ahaz suffered severe casualties at the hands of the coalition. Rezin carried off a great number of captives to Damascus. Pekah is said to have inflicted 120,000 casualities in one day *"because they had forsaken Yahweh."* Several prominent members of Ahaz's administration, including one of his sons, lost their lives in this war. Some 200,000 *"women, sons and daughters"* were taken captive to Samaria (2 Chr 28:5-8). These captives were quickly released at the insistence of the prophet Oded (2 Chr 28:5-15).

At the same time Ahaz was trying to deal with the Syro-Ephraimitic invasion, the Philistines took from Judah a number of prominent villages in the lowlands and Negev. Through this combination of calamities Yahweh humbled Judah *"because of Ahaz king of*

Israel, for he had brought about a lack of restraint in Judah and was very unfaithful to Yahweh." Perhaps the Philistines were also members of the anti-Assyrian coalition (2 Chr 28:16-19).

JUDAH SUBMITS TO ASSYRIA
2 Kings 16:7-20

The Syro-Ephraimitic invasion of Judah forced Ahaz to make a crucial political decision which had religious consequences for decades to come.

A. Appeal to Assyria (2 Kgs 16:7-9).

In his extreme desperation, Ahaz turned to Tiglath-pileser of Assyria for relief from the invaders. He asked the mighty king to deliver him from the Syro-Ephraimite threat. Sacred and royal treasuries were drained in order to send to Nineveh the appropriate gift which would seal the alliance between the two countries. In 732 BC the Assyrian attacked and captured the city of Damascus. King Rezin himself was slain when the city fell. The immediate threat to Judah from Syria and Ephraim (Israel) ceased. Ahaz, however, had sold his soul for temporary security (2 Kgs 16:7-9).

B. Corruption in Judah (2 Kgs 16:10-18).

Following the conquest of Damascus, Tiglath-pileser summoned Ahaz and other vassal kings to confirm officially their submission to him through a formal treaty. While in the city, Ahaz saw an altar which struck his fancy. To curry favor with his new master, Ahaz sent back to Jerusalem to Urijah the high priest detailed instructions for making this altar. By this action he was acknowleding the superiority of the gods of Assyria (2 Kgs 16:10).[7]

Being a man with no backbone, Urijah[8] did not even remonstrate with the king, much less resist the royal orders. He did just as Ahaz ordered. When he returned from Damascus, Ahaz personally made use of the new altar for his private sacrifices. Eventually the old Solomonic altar was removed from its place of prominence, and all temple sacrifices were offered on the Assyrian altar. In the course of time temple court objects were stripped of decorative accessories probably to meet Judah's tribute obligations to Tiglath-pileser (2 Kgs 16:11-18).

Ahaz's sixteen year reign (735-720 BC; see endnote 4) was one of the most decadent on record. Of the kings of Judah, only Manasseh and Amon receive greater condemnation. Eventually Ahaz shut up the temple and suspended the sacrificial offerings and burning of incense. To replace temple worship he erected altars *"in every corner of Jerusalem"* (2 Chr 28:24; 29:7). Ahaz tolerated and participated in the corrupt worship in the high places and groves (2 Kgs 16:1-4). He reintroduced and personally participated in the worship of Canaanite deities, even to the extent of immolating his son (cf. 2 Chr 28:3).

THE FALL OF THE NORTHERN KINGDOM
2 Kings 17:1-41

The nationalist King Pekah of Israel who headed the anti-Assyrian coalition was assassinated in 732 BC. The last king of the northern kingdom, Hoshea, sought to preserve the kingdom of Israel by pledging fidelity to Tiglath-pileser.

A. The Reign of Hoshea (2 Kgs 17:1-4).
Hoshea ruled for nine years in Israel (732-723 BC). Like his predecessors in the north, Hoshea did evil in the eyes of Yahweh. He continued the apostate calf worship, leaned upon the arm of flesh, and turned a deaf ear to the voice of God's prophets. His guilt, however, did not equal that of the kings who immediately preceded him (2 Kgs 17:1-2).

When Tiglath-pileser died in 727 BC, Hoshea tried to regain his independence by withholding the annual tribute money. The new Assyrian king, Shalmaneser, came up against him and forced him to resume his position as a vassal.

Hoshea searched for some other means by which he might extricate himself from the grip of Assyria. Grasping at straws, he was persuaded to enter alliance with a certain King So of Egypt. This So is probably to be identified with Sib'e, a commander of one of the small monarchies of the Egyptian delta.[9] With this backing, the Israelite monarch tried once again to withhold tribute from Shalmaneser. This act of rebellion brought down the wrath of the Assyrian upon

Samaria. The text as it stands gives the impression that Hoshea may have gone out to meet Shalmaneser to sue for peace and pardon. He was then arrested and imprisoned (2 Kgs 17:3-4).

B. The Fall of Samaria (2 Kgs 17:5-6).

The king of Assyria came with a vast army to besiege the kingless capital of Israel. According to the Hebrew mode of reckoning parts of years as full years, the siege lasted three years. Actually the siege need not have lasted longer than one full year and parts of two other ones, i.e., a little over one year. Samaria held out as long as it could, awaiting the promised aid from Egypt. Finally in 722 BC Samaria fell to *"the king of Assyria,"* either Shalmaneser, or to Sargon who claimed the throne that same year.[10] The Assyrian records relate that 27,290 persons were carried captive from Samaria, and doubtless many others from smaller villages round about. These captives were taken and distributed in the distant eastern provinces of the Assyrian empire.

EXPLANATION OF ISRAEL'S FALL
2 Kings 17:7-23

Prophets interpreted history as well as outlined future events. The prophetic author of Kings now offers an explanation of the calamity which befell the northern kingdom. He also hints that the same fate would befall Judah.

A. Initial Apostasy in Israel (2 Kgs 17:7-12).

After God had delivered his people from the oppression in Egypt, they had taken up the worship of other gods. They followed the *"statutes of the heathen,"* i.e., their customs and religious observances, even though these were the very "statutes" which caused the Holy God to order the Canaanites expelled from the land. The kings of the northern kingdom had compounded the apostasy when they introduced into the nation the calf cult as a substitute for the pure worship ordained by Yahweh. The author of Kings regarded those calves as *"molten images"* (17:7-8, 16).

In private the Israelites participated in all kinds of rites which were not pleasing to Yahweh. High places were built throughout the land in open violation of the divine command that there be one temple and one altar. In the most insignificant locations as well as in the population centers stone pillars and the wooden Asherim were set up. The worship in the high places followed the pattern of Canaanite worship with the offering of incense. By these actions Israel indicated allegiance to the idols (17:9-12).

B. Aggravated Apostasy (2 Kgs 17:13-17).

In spite of the blatant apostasy in Israel, God graciously continued to plead with his people and warn them through *"prophets"* and *"seers."*[11] God's people responded to the prophetic efforts by continuing to *"harden their necks,"* i.e., to be obstinate, just as their *"stiff necked"* fathers who had failed God so often in the wilderness period. Rejecting the *"statutes"* of Yahweh, the people of Israel had in effect rejected the covenant with God into which they had entered at Mt. Sinai (cf. Exod 19:5-8). Yahweh's *"testimonies"*—those commandments which witness of him and reveal his nature—they also rejected. The people chose to follow *"vanity,"* the empty, futile, impotent pagan gods. As a result they themselves became vain, i.e., impotent. Whereas God had commanded and expected his people to be separate and distinct from all nations, they chose instead to follow the way of the heathen (17:13-15).

In the days of Ahab, Phoenician deities were introduced alongside the apostate calf worship. For a time both Baal and his consort Asherah had companies of prophets in Samaria. At some stage, astral deities had been introduced into Israel, the worship of the various planets. Such worship must have been imported from Mesopotamia (17:16-17a).

With the pagan deities came pagan practices such as child immolation (cf. 2 Kgs 16:3), and various magical practices (cf. 2 Kgs 9:22). The people of Israel had sold themselves to do evil with the deliberate intention, it would seem, of provoking Yahweh to wrath (17:17b).

C. Rejection of National Israel (2 Kgs 17:18-23).

When their cup of iniquity was full, God's wrath, long restrained, descended upon Israel. God removed them out of his sight. They were cast off, removed from their land. They were disowned and disinherited as the people of God (cf. Hos 1:9). Judah alone was left to carry the torch as God's peculiar people (17:18a).

By God's grace the southern kingdom was preserved for a few short years after the destruction of the northern kingdom. Judah, however, also rejected the commandments of Yahweh and embraced the *"statutes of Israel,"* i.e., the Baal worship and all the vile practices connected with it. The only sin of Israel not attested in Judah is that of the calf worship (17:19).

Since God is no respecter of persons, he rejected *"all the seed of Israel,"* i.e., Judah as well as Israel. He afflicted them by the hand of foreign oppressors—the Arameans, the Assyrians and the Babylonians. In addition to these powers, God gave his people into the hand of *"spoilers,"* i.e., neighboring nations which took advantage of the weakness of Israel and Judah to attack and plunder them. This divine program of harassment and humiliation lasted until Judah as well as Israel had been removed from God's land and God's favor (17:20).

The rejection of *"all the seed of Israel"* took place in three great stages. First, God had torn the ten northern tribes away from the house of David. By the introduction of the calf worship, Jeroboam *"drove Israel from following Yahweh."* Throughout the history of the northern kingdom, the people never turned from this great sin introduced by Jeroboam. Second, God removed Israel from his sight, i.e., from the land which was under the guardianship of Yahweh. In fulfillment of prophetic warnings dating back to Moses, Israel was carried away captive to Assyria. The third stage of the rejection of *"all the seed of Israel"* unfolds in the remaining chapters of the book of Kings (17:21-23).

A great deal of speculation has arisen about the fate of the northern tribes. At the time the Book of Kings was written, they were still scattered throughout the Assyrian empire (2 Kgs 17:23). Some of the former citizens of the northern kingdom returned to Palestine with Zerubbabel in 538 BC, and others with Ezra in 458 BC.[12] Those who remained in the lands of the captivity either united with the Jewish colonies which were later established there, or else simply adopted fully the practices of the heathen, intermarried with them, and disappeared as a distinct people. Theories of migrations of these tribes into Europe and/or the New World are spun out of fertile imaginations.

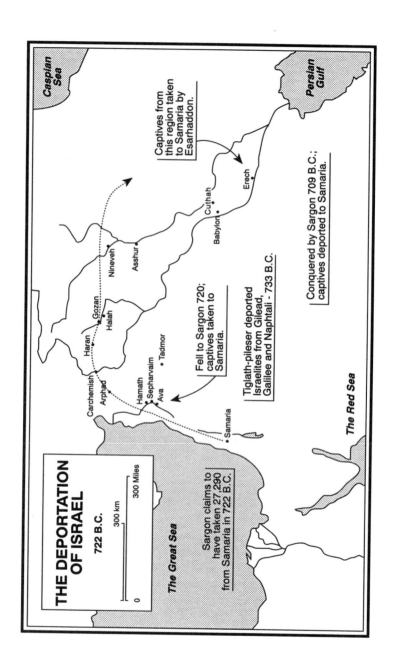

THE DEPORTATION
OF ISRAEL

722 B.C.

0   300 km

0   300 Miles

The Great Sea

Sargon claims to
have taken 27,290
from Samaria in 722 B.C.

Caspian
Sea

Persian
Gulf

Captives from
this region taken
to Samaria by
Esarhaddon.

Erech

Cuthah

Babylon

Nineveh

Asshur

Gozan

Haran

Halah

Carchemish

Arphad

Hamath

Tadmor

Sepharvaim

Ava

Samaria

Fell to Sargon 720;
captives taken to
Samaria.

Tiglath-pileser deported
Israelites from Gilead,
Galilee and Naphtali - 733 B.C.

Conquered by Sargon 709 B.C.;
captives deported to Samaria.

The Red Sea

THE REPOPULATION OF SAMARIA
2 Kings 17:24-41

Following the precedent of Tiglath-pileser, King Sargon replaced those Israelites taken into captivity with subjects from Mesopotamia and Syria.[13] By separating people from their native lands and from their leadership, the Assyrians hoped to be able to prevent rebellions from subject peoples (17:24).

The foreign colonists were ignorant of Yahweh. They therefore failed to pay the Lord proper respect. To teach them a lesson, Yahweh sent against them a plague of lions. Since rural areas of Israel were depopulated, conditions were favorable for the rapid increase of the lion population. Several of the colonists lost their lives. The situation became a matter of grave concern (17:25).

Word spread to the Assyrian king along with the suggestion that the colonists needed to learn the proper ritual to perform in order to please the God of Israel. This alone would bring about a cessation of the lion plague. The king then ordered one of the priests of Yahweh to return to Samaria to teach the colonists. While a remnant of the former citizenry of Israel remained in the land (2 Chr 34:9), they would not have been familiar with the details of the religious ritual practiced in the temples. Apparently all the priests had been deported by Sargon.

The priest and his entourage returned to dwell in Bethel, the religious capital of the old Kingdom of Israel. He taught the new settlers to *"fear Yahweh,"* i.e., the perverted form of worship once practiced in Bethel. No positive evidence exists, however, that this priest set up a new calf image to replace the one which had been carried off to Assyria (Hos 10:5).

Those who had settled in the region of Samaria were polytheists. In spite of the teaching of the priest of Yahweh, they continued to worship their native deities. They set up their idols in the high places which had been constructed by the Samaritans throughout their cities.[14] The Sepharvites were even offering up their children as sacrifices to their gods (17:29-31).

Polytheism by its very nature is syncretistic. Thus it is not strange to find that the foreign colonists in the territory of Samaria *"feared*

Yahweh and served their own gods." The Samaritans followed the apostate practice of recruiting priests from all ranks of society (cf. 1 Kgs 12:31). These priests were willing to officiate in the illegitimate high places which were maintained contrary to the law of Moses (17:32-33).

Had the Samaritans really wanted to serve Yahweh they would have attended to the *"statutes and ordinances"* which were binding upon all who would truly worship the Lord. The Sinai covenant required that God's people worship no other God. All religious devotion belonged exclusively to Yahweh who had brought these people out of the land of their bondage. God's promise of deliverance and protection for Israel was conditioned upon their faithfulness to him. All warnings about recognizing other gods were ignored by the colonists in Samaria (17:34-40).

The syncretistic worship of the Samaritans continued right down to the time of the author of Kings (17:41). By the time of Christ, however, the Samaritans had become devoted followers of Yahweh and devout followers of the law of Moses in most respects. To this day a small community of these Samaritans still can be found in Nabulus, Israel.

ENDNOTES

1. An inscription of Tiglath-pileser mentions the tribute of Menahem. See James Pritchard, *Ancient Near Eastern Texts Relating to the Old Testament,* (Princeton, NJ: University Press, 1969), pp. 282ff.

2. Fifty shekels of silver in this period was about the price of a slave. See D.J. Wiseman, *Iraq* 15 (1953): 135. Cited by John Gray, *I & II Kings* in "The Old Testament Library" (Philadelphia: Westminster, 1970).

3. Pekah began to reign in the fifty-second year of Uzziah which was 739 BC (2 Kgs 15:27). His successor, Hoshea, came to the throne in twelfth year of Ahaz of Judah or 732 BC (2 Kgs 17:1). Only a rival throne prior to the overthrow of Pekahiah can explain the twenty years of rule mentioned in 2 Kgs 15:27.

4. Ahaz had served as coregent with his father Jotham from as early as 743 BC. He was still living and occupying an emeritus position from 720-715 BC.

5. When Rezin and Pekah launched their invasion of Judah in 734 BC, Jotham was still alive (2 Kgs 15:37), but Ahaz seems to have been governing.

6. The difference in the Hebrew spelling of *"Edomites"* and *"Arameans"* is so slight that it is conceivable that a scribal error occurred here. It is difficult to imagine Arameans from Damascus remaining in far distant Elath for any length of time. It is far more reasonable to regard the capture of Elath as a blow against Judah. Once the city fell, it was returned to the native people.

7. On an earlier occasion Ahaz sacrificed to gods of Damascus because that city had proved militarily superior to Judah (2 Chr 28:23).

8. Urijah is almost certainly the Uriah of Isaiah 8:2 who earlier had served as a witness to one of Isaiah's most dramatic predictions.

9. J.A. Wilson, "So," *Interpreters' Dictionary of the Bible,* vol. R-Z, p. 394. Gray (*op. cit.*, p. 642) thinks "So" is not a person, but a place—the Egyptian capital of this period, Sais. The Hebrew text as it stands suggests that a person is intended.

10. In various texts Sargon claims to have captured Samaria. A.T. Olmstead, however, makes a strong case that Shalmaneser was still king at the time the city fell. "The Fall of Samaria," *American Journal of Semitic Languages and Literature* 21 (1904, 5) :179-82.

11. In the earliest days God's spokesmen were called *"seers"* because they foresaw the future. As time went on the preferred designation for a spokesman for God was *"prophet."* See 1 Sam 9:9.

12. On the return of individuals from the northern tribes see Ezra 2:70; 3:1; 6:16,17; 8:35; 1 Chr 9:2,3; Zech 8:13.

13. In his annals Sargon mentions deporting people from Mesopotamia to the "Hatti land" (Syria-Palestine) in the first year of his reign (721 BC). A similar repopulation of Samaria took place in Sargon's seventh year (715 BC). In the days of Esarhaddon (681-669 BC) Samaria received another infusion of foreign colonists (Ezra 4:2).

14. The Babylonians worshiped Succoth-benoth, which is generally regarded as a corruption of the name of the goddess who was the wife of Marduk, viz., Sarpanitu. The men of Cuth or Cuthah continued to honor Nergal the god of war which was the titular deity of their native city. The colonists from Hamath worshiped Ashima, a deliberate misvocalization of Asherah, the Canaanite mother goddess. Nibhaz and Tartak were purely local deities of the Avites. Adram-melech may be a special title of Shamash the sun god. Anammelech may be an intentional Hebrew corruption of the name of the goddess Anunit, the consort of Shamash (17:29-31).

CHAPTER THIRTY-SEVEN

Struggle for Independence
2 Kings 18-21

After the fall of Israel, the kingdom of Judah continued to survive for another 136 years. Hezekiah was ruling in the southern kingdom when the Assyrians captured Samaria and deported the northern tribes. Seven others followed him on the throne of David. The Judean period was characterized by two thoroughgoing revivals followed by periods of apostasy.

HEZEKIAH'S CRUSADE
2 Chronicles 29:3-31:21

Hezekiah was twenty-five when he came to the throne as a co-regent with his father in 728 BC. His father Ahaz died in 715 BC. After his father died, Hezekiah reigned twenty-nine years, until 686 BC. This king receives unqualified praise from the author of Kings (2 Kgs 18:3).[1] No other king before or after manifested such complete confidence in the Almighty. Throughout his life he faithfully observed the law of Moses. Because of his obedience, *"Yahweh was with him."* Of no other king except David is this statement made (cf. 2 Sam 5:10).

A. Clergy Commissioned (2 Chr 29:3-11).

Immediately after the death of his wicked father, Hezekiah ordered the priests and Levites to cleanse the temple of all the *"filthiness"* which Ahaz had allowed to accumulate there. During those dark days the temple doors had been locked, the lamps extinguished. No incense had been burned, no burnt offerings had been presented (2 Chr 29:3-7).

As Hezekiah assessed the situation, the deplorable political position of the nation was due to the neglect of the things of God. *"The wrath of Yahweh"* had been turned against Judah. The nation had experienced humiliating military defeats during the reign of Ahaz. Women and children had been carried into captivity. The kingdom was an object of ridicule. Only by entering into a new covenant would the burning wrath of Yahweh be turned away from the nation (2 Chr 29:8-11).

Chart No. 49

THE REIGN OF GOOD KING HEZEKIAH

B. Temple Cleansed (2 Chr 29:12-19).

Fourteen Levites representing the major branches of the tribe assumed leadership in the reformation. The cleansing of the temple precincts took eight days. For an additional eight days the priests consecrated the house itself. Every unclean thing was removed from it to the Kidron valley. On the sixteenth day of the first month the clergy reported to King Hezekiah that the cleansing of the temple was complete. Even the utensils which Ahaz had discarded had been consecrated and returned to their place beside the altar of burnt offering (2 Chr 29:12-19).

C. Worship Restored (2 Chr 29:20-36).

Early the next morning the king and princes of the city went to the temple to worship. Sacrifices were offered to purge the altar and to *"atone"* (lit., cover over) the sin of *"all Israel."* Hezekiah apparently intended to include those who had once belonged to the northern kingdom in the benefits of his sacrifice. The sacrifices were to the accompaniment of the Levitical musical arrangements of David, Gad and Nathan (2 Chr 29:20-28).

At the completion of the burnt offerings provided by the king, the assembly began to bring voluntary burnt offerings. All the while the Levites were singing praises to Yahweh *"with the words of David and Asaph the seer."* The number of priests who had consecrated themselves at this point was too small to handle the ritual slaughtering of the thousands of animals. Levites were pressed into service to assist them. On this occasion the Levites had been more conscientious to consecrate themselves than the priests. The sudden reestablishment of the divine order of worship brought joy to the heart of the king and his people (2 Chr 29:29-36).

D. Royal Proclamation (2 Chr 30:1-12).

Temple cleansing was not completed in time for the regular observance of Passover on the fifteen day of the first month. Consequently, Hezekiah, his princes and the assembly decided to celebrate the feast in the second month. Couriers carried the royal proclamation throughout all the land, and even into the region of Ephraim and Manasseh. Hezekiah particularly pled with those who had escaped the hand of the king of Assyria to come again to that sanctuary which Yahweh had consecrated forever. He urged them to serve Yahweh so that his burning wrath might be turned away from them. He assured the former citizens of the northern kingdom that they would find compassion from God (2 Chr 30:1-9).

For the most part the hardened sinners of the north were unreceptive to the gracious invitation of Hezekiah. Nevertheless, some from Asher, Manasseh and Zebulun humbled themselves and came to Jerusalem for the Passover celebration. *"The hand of God"* was on Judah. The citizens there were united to do what the king and princes commanded *"by the word of Yahweh"* (2 Chr 30:10-12).

E. Passover Celebration (2 Chr 30:13-27).

A large throng assembled in Jerusalem for the Passover. Their zeal for Yahweh was demonstrated when they removed the illegitimate altars from Jerusalem and cast them into the brook Kidron. Many in the assembly—especially those who came from the north—were not ritually consecrated. The Levites slaughtered the Passover lamb for them. Though technically in violation of the law of Moses, these people went ahead and ate the Passover. Hezekiah had prayed that the good Lord would pardon those who sincerely desired to partake even though they were ritually impure. Yahweh heard that prayer and *"healed"* the people (2 Chr 30:13-20).

Passover was followed by the week long celebration of the Feast of Unleavened Bread. Each day during the offering of the peace offerings the Levites and priests praised Yahweh with loud instruments. Hezekiah continued to encourage the Levites in these ministries. The assembly determined to extend the glorious celebration for another seven days. They had more than enough to eat. The king and his princes had contributed 2,000 bulls and 17,000 sheep. Great joy filled Jerusalem because both as to attendance and unanimity of spirit, this celebration exceeded any since the days of Solomon. The proceedings concluded with a blessing by the Levitical priests. *"Their voice was heard, and their prayer came to his holy dwelling place, even heaven."* God would bless his people once again (2 Chr 30:21-27).

F. Further Reforms (2 Chr 31:1-21).

Those who had been present at the great Passover celebration in Jerusalem returned to their cities determined to serve Yahweh alone. They removed every vestige of idolatry throughout the cities of Judah, and even in the territories of the former northern kingdom. Meanwhile the king also pressed forward in his reform efforts (2 Chr 31:1).

Even the bronze serpent which Moses had erected in the wilderness was destroyed by Hezekiah because it had become an object of worship. The people affectionately referred to it as *nehushtan*, "the little bronze thing" (2 Kgs 18:4).

Hezekiah reorganized the twenty-four courses of priests and Levites. He restored the royal subsidy so that the daily set offerings could be presented as well as the special offerings for special days. He ordered the people to give the portion due the priests and Levites so that they could devote themselves full time to the law of Yahweh. The people responded to the king's order enthusiastically. In less than four months Azariah, the high priest, reported that the priests had an overabundance of food. Hezekiah blessed Yahweh and his people (2 Chr 31:2-10).

Under royal directive, the storage rooms in the temple were prepared to house the surplus contributions and consecrated things. Levitical officers were appointed to oversee collection, storage and distribution of these gifts (2 Chr 31:11-19).

Hezekiah did what was *"good, right, and true"* before Yahweh his God. Every work he undertook he did with *"all his heart."* Consequently he prospered in his reign (2 Chr 31:20-21).

HEZEKIAH'S PERSONAL CRISIS
2 Kgs 20:1-21//2 Chr 32:24-31

Two clues aid in the chronological placement of 2 Kings 20. First, fifteen years were added to the life of King Hezekiah. Since that king died in 686 BC, his miraculous healing reported in 2 Kings 20 must have taken place in 701 BC, the very year that the Assyrians invaded Judah. Second, in 2 Kings 20 Hezekiah still had possession of his treasure (cf. vv. 13-17). Thus the illness and recovery must have taken place prior to the Assyrian invasion when the king was forced to drain his treasury to pay tribute to Sennacherib (cf. 2 Kgs 18:13-16).

A. Hezekiah's Illness (2 Kgs 20:1-4).

In those crucial days just prior to the great Assyrian invasion, Hezekiah was smitten with a life-threatening malady. To the royal chambers Isaiah the prophet was dispatched with a message of warn-

ing. *"Set your house in order[2] for you shall die and not live!"* In
the face of this shocking announcement the good king turned on his
bed away from his numerous attendants and faced the wall so that he
might pray to his God with more concentration (2 Kgs 20:1-2).

The king's prayer is a model for those who are afflicted with serious illness. He first called upon Yahweh to remember how he had
tried his very best to walk throughout life so as to meet with divine
approval. This was not presumptuous self-righteousness. Hezekiah
knew that he honestly had endeavored to serve God and do his will.
Under the old covenant, length of days was promised to the righteous
(cf. Prov 3:2; 9:11; 10:27). Hezekiah could not comprehend why he
should be cut off in middle age—he would have been thirty-nine—
when kings far less righteous had lived two and more decades
longer.[3] The king's opening statement is thus a form of expostulation
and laying hold on divine promises.

The earnestness of the king was manifested in the tears which
accompanied his prayer. Besides the natural fear of death, there were
other good reasons for Hezekiah's earnest petition. For one thing, at
this point in his life Hezekiah had no male offspring (cf. 2 Kgs 21:1).
Furthermore, Hezekiah knew that his early reformation efforts would
most surely bring upon Judah the wrath of the mighty Sennacherib.
He wished to live to see his country through this crisis (2 Kgs 20:3).

Before Isaiah had reached the second of the three courtyards
which surrounded the royal palace, God stopped him. The prophet
was ordered to retrace his steps, enter the king's bedchamber, and
reverse the thrust of the oracle he had delivered only moments before
(2 Kgs 20:4).

B. Hezekiah's Recovery (2 Kgs 20:5-11).

Hezekiah's fervent prayer was effectual. God promised the king
that within three days he would be able to worship the Lord in the
temple. God, however, did more than the king had asked. He granted
Hezekiah fifteen additional years of life which, in effect, would more
than double the length of his reign (cf. 2 Kgs 18:2). Furthermore, God
promised to deliver Hezekiah and Jerusalem from the hand of the
king of Assyria. For the sake of his reputation both in Judah and

among the heathen, and for the sake of his commitment to David, the Lord pledged himself to be Jerusalem's defender (2 Kgs 20:5-6).

Isaiah directed those present to place a lump of figs on the malignant boil. Figs were used as a remedy for such boils.[4] The prophetic order, however, seems to have been more in the nature of a symbolic act. The fig poultice underscored that from that moment forward God would gradually heal the king of his terminal malady (2 Kgs 20:7).

Even the prophet's symbolic act did not fully set the mind of Hezekiah at ease. Under the old covenant God frequently offered miraculous signs to substantiate promises which he made to people in desperate straits. That Isaiah had offered a sign to wicked Ahaz during the Syro-Ephraimitic crisis was well known (cf. Isa 7:11). Hezekiah assumed that such a sign would be granted to him. He therefore asked his friend Isaiah what the sign would be. Neither God nor the prophet was angry with this request. For Christians today to demand signs would be faithless; but in an age of miracles, when prophets were empowered to give signs, faithful people might request them without incurring God's displeasure (2 Kgs 20:8).

The sign involved the sundial, perhaps clearly visible from the window of the bedchamber. The king could indicate whether he wanted the shadow to go forward or backward on the steps. Hezekiah requested that the shadow change its direction and ascend the steps. Isaiah then prayed. God responded by bringing the shadow ten steps backward. This miracle would not necessarily involve the temporary reversal in the rotation of the earth. That the miracle was local is made clear in the parallel passage (2 Chr 32:31). Probably a very abnormal refraction of the rays of the sun caused the retreat of the shadow on the sundial (2 Kgs 2:9-11).

C. Hezekiah's Pride (2 Kgs 20:12-19//2 Chr 32:24-31).

Following his recovery, Hezekiah was visited by an embassy from Berodach-baladan.[5] For some twenty years this Babylonian king had been a thorn in the flesh of the Assyrian rulers. Scholars generally have concluded that the object of the embassy was to persuade Hezekiah to enter into an anti-Assyrian alliance with Babylon (2 Kgs 20:12).

Hezekiah was dazzled by the attention bestowed upon him by these visitors from Babylon. He *"hearkened unto them,"* i.e., listened to their suggestions of an alliance between Judah and Babylon. Hezekiah showed the Babylonian emissaries all of his treasure and armaments both in Jerusalem and in fortresses throughout Judah. He may have been trying to convince these guests that he indeed would be a valuable ally (2 Kgs 20:13).

D. Hezekiah's Rebuke (2 Kgs 20:14-19).

When the Babylonian embassy left, Isaiah appeared before Hezekiah with a message of rebuke. In order to elicit a confession about what had taken place, he interrogated the king about his visitors. The prophet's question *"What have they seen in your house?"* got to the heart of the matter. The prophet was asking whether Hezekiah had treated his guests as ordinary ambassadors, or whether instead he had courted an alliance with their master. To the credit of the king, he answered forthrightly and made no effort to conceal what had taken place. He readily acknowledged that he had shown these particular guests everything (2 Kgs 20:14-15).

The divine word of rebuke for Hezekiah was a revelation of what the future held in store for Judah. Hezekiah had gotten involved with the nation which ultimately would destroy Judah. All the treasures he boastfully had displayed to the ambassadors would one day be carried off as plunder to far-off Babylon. Hezekiah's *"sons,"* i.e., descendants, would one day become eunuchs in the court of the king of Babylon. Mere human foresight would never have suspected that within a century, insignificant Babylon would have completely turned the tables on mighty Assyria (2 Kgs 16-18).

Hezekiah accepted the prophetic rebuke. He thereby acknowledged that he had been in the wrong. As far as Hezekiah was concerned, the pronouncement was *"good"* because he himself was not personally involved. The king felt that God might have justly brought down on him personally some affliction or calamity in punishment for his political indiscretion. It was a relief to hear that the blow would not fall during his lifetime. The self-centeredness of this evaluation of the prophecy caused the attendants standing nearby to raise their eyebrows. Noticing their chagrin, Hezekiah turned to his courtiers to ask the rhetorical question, *"Is it not good, if peace and steadfastness be in my days?"* (2 Kgs 20:19).

HEZEKIAH'S POLITICAL CRISIS
2 Kings 18:13-19:37

For the king to appear so unconcerned about the future of his land was not very statesman-like. The irony, however, is that Isaiah had said nothing about *"peace and steadfastness"* in the days of Hezekiah. Shortly Hezekiah's faith was tested by a confrontation with Sennacherib.

A. Siege Preparation (2 Chr 32:1-8).

Anticipating an invasion by Sennacherib, Hezekiah took actions to make a siege of Jerusalem more difficult. Water was *"cut off"* from the springs around the city. The meaning here may be that they shut off the flow of the water in one direction, and guided it into another. A tunnel constructed in this period carried the water of the Gihon spring back into the city to the pool called Siloam. Other preparations included (1) strengthening the wall of the city; (2) building another outside wall; (3) making weapons and shields in great number; and (4) appointing military officers (2 Chr 32:1-5).

The king encouraged his people to be *"strong and courageous"* in the face of the impending Assyrian attack. He reminded them that *"the one who is with us is greater than the one with him."* The Assyrian relied upon the arm of flesh. With the Jews, however, was Yahweh. He would fight for his people. The Jews *"relied"* on the words of Hezekiah (2 Chr 32:6-8).

B. Hezekiah's Payment (2 Kgs 18:13-16).

In the fourteenth year of Hezekiah's (independent) reign (701 BC), Sennacherib attacked Judah. On the famous Taylor Prism[6] the Assyrian scribes recounted the details of this campaign. The Great King first smashed Tyre, one of the allies of Hezekiah. Most of the other anti-Assyrian confederates then capitulated, but Ashkelon, Ekron and Judah refused to submit. Sennacherib subdued the Philistine cities of the plains as well as an Egyptian relief column which attempted to come to their aid. He then launched an attack against Lachish which at this time was actually larger than Jerusalem.[7]

With his outlying fortified cities under Assyrian control, Hezekiah

decided that it was pointless to continue the rebellion. He acknowledged his transgression in rebelling against his overlord, and entreated
Sennacherib to withdraw his forces. Whatever penalty the Great King
chose to impose upon him, Hezekiah was willing to bear. Sennacherib pretended to be willing to accept Hezekiah's offer of surrender, and imposed upon his rebellious vassal the enormous tribute of
three hundred talents of silver ($600,000 BV) and thirty talents of
gold ($900,000 BV).[8] According to the Assyrian records, Hezekiah
was also compelled to (1) make certain territorial concessions; (2) surrender an Assyrian vassal king who was being detained in Jerusalem;
and (3) send two or more of his daughters to Nineveh to become part
of Sennacherib's harem.

In order to meet the tribute demands of Sennacherib, Hezekiah
emptied the treasuries of both the temple and the palace. Only some
thirty years before (cf. 2 Kgs 16:8) Ahaz had emptied these same
treasuries in order to hire the services of Tiglath-pileser. Apparently
Hezekiah had little or no gold readily available. He was forced to strip
the gold from the pillars and doors which he himself had overlaid with
the precious metal. Sennacherib relates that in addition to the two
large sums of gold and silver, Hezekiah sent to him at this time
"woven cloth, scarlet, embroidered; precious stones of large size;
skins and horns of buffaloes; and two kinds of woods."

C. Sennacherib's Demands (2 Kgs 18:17-37//2 Chr 32:9-19).

Sennacherib was not satisfied with the tribute paid by Hezekiah.
He wanted nothing less than the total surrender of Jerusalem. While
he himself was engaged in military operations in the lowland region of
Palestine, he sent an embassy to Jerusalem to demand capitulation.[9]
At the head of the contingent were three officers bearing the titles
Tartan, Rab-saris, and Rabshakeh.[10] All three titles are known from
Assyrian records. Hezekiah sent out to the wall three of his highest
officials to hear what the Assyrians had to say (2 Kgs 18:17-18).

Because he could speak fluent Hebrew, Rabshakeh acted as
spokesmen for the Assyrians. He came right to the point. Hezekiah
obviously had been making military preparations for a siege of
Jerusalem. How had he dared to take these steps? What was the
basis for his confidence? One by one Rabshakeh attempted to elimi-

nate the possible grounds upon which Hezekiah based his rebellion (2 Kgs 18:19).

First, Rabshakeh imagined Hezekiah boasting of his counsel and strength for war, i.e., of the wisdom of his advisers and his military capabilities. Such boasts were *"merely words."* Second, expectations of aid from Egypt were doomed to frustration. Egypt was nothing but a *"bruised reed"* which would snap the moment any weight was applied to it (2 Kgs 18:21).[11]

Third, Hezekiah could expect no help from Yahweh since he had been desecrating his high places. Perhaps the Assyrians had also learned that Hezekiah's reform efforts had actually angered some segments of the population. Rabshakeh may have been trying to exploit the religious unrest within Judah (2 Kgs 18:22).

Fourth, Rabshakeh resorted to ridicule. He mocked the fact that the Jewish army lacked cavalry. Hezekiah did not have enough fighting men to turn back even one unit of the Assyrian army. Finally, he argued that Yahweh himself had dispatched Sennacherib against Jerusalem. Perhaps the Assyrian had heard of the prophecies of Isaiah (Isa 7:17-24; 10:5-12) which foretold the Assyrian invasion of Judah (2 Kgs 18:23-25).

The propaganda of Rabshakeh was having its intended effect on the Jewish soldiers manning the walls. Hezekiah's officers interrupted the Assyrian at this point. They request that he speak to them in Aramaic, the diplomatic language of the day. Rabshakeh, of course, refused to comply with this request. His very purpose in coming to Jerusalem was to intimidate the soldiers and weaken the resolve of the citizens to resist. He wanted Jerusalem's defenders to realize that soon they would be brought to the last extremity of hunger and thirst. They would be forced even to consume their own excrement and drink their own urine (2 Kgs 18:26-27).

The urgent request of the Jewish diplomats only stirred Rabshakah to greater efforts. He rose and addressed himself directly to the citizens on the walls. He urged the defenders not to allow Hezekiah to deceive them, particularly with his assurances of supernatural deliverance (2 Kgs 18:28-29).

From threat Rabshakeh turned to grandiose promises. If Jerusalem would but surrender, each one in the city would be allowed to return to his own land where he might live a peaceful life. Then after a time, Sennacherib would come and transplant them to a new land. Such national deportations were so common in the Assyrian empire that Rabshakeh knew he must mention this possibility if his remarks were to enjoy any measure of credibility. So he attempted to place this practice in the best possible light. He tried to persuade the Jews that being transported hundreds of miles from their homes really would not be so bad—that they were to be envied rather than pitied for being about to experience it. The gracious Sennacherib would even try to settle them in a beautiful land just like Judah! In any case, if they followed Rabshakeh's advice they would live; if Hezekiah's, they would die (2 Kgs 18:30-32).

Rabshakeh continued by ridiculing Hezekiah's faith as fanatical and unrealistic. No local deity thus far had been able to deliver his people from the mighty Assyrian army. To make his point more emphatically, Rabshakeh ticked off the recent victories of the Assyrian war machine, including Samaria. Since the Jews could produce no example of a national god who had been able to withstand Assyria's might, they should abandon their hope of supernatural deliverance from Sennacherib (2 Kgs 18:32-35).

Rabshakeh's efforts to foment some insurrection within Jerusalem failed. The Jews on the walls strictly followed their king's orders to maintain silence. Horrified at the blasphemies of the Assyrian, Hezekiah's three ministers ripped their robes and returned to the royal palace to report all that had been said (2 Kgs 18:36-37).

D. Initial Prophecy (2 Kgs 19:1-7).

Hezekiah tore his garments and donned sackcloth when he heard the report of his ministers. He then went to the temple to seek divine counsel. At the same time the king dispatched a delegation to Isaiah the prophet. The messengers wore sackcloth to emphasize the horror which Rabshakeh's threatening boasts had engendered (2 Kgs 19:1-2).

Hezekiah's messengers described the crisis to Isaiah. The nation had no strength to face up to the impending attack. Perhaps Yahweh would take note of the contemptuous words which Rabshakeh had spoken against the living God, and then reprove those words with some mighty act of judgment. Perhaps he would intervene on behalf of the remnant of his people (2 Kgs 19:3-5).[12]

Isaiah seems to have already formulated a reply to the king even before the delegation arrived at his home. Hezekiah did not need to be afraid of the blasphemous words of the Assyrian. God would send a destructive blast against Sennacherib. He would be forced to retreat to his own land. There he would be assassinated (2 Kgs 19:6-7).

E. Sennacherib's Letter (2 Kgs 19:8-13//2 Chr 32:17).

Failing in his mission to secure the surrender of Jerusalem, Rabshakeh returned to his master. By that time Sennacherib had taken Lachish and was warring against nearby Libnah. When the Assyrian king heard that the Ethiopian general Tirhakah was marching against him, he knew that he might be forced to make a strategic retreat from Palestine. For this reason he made one last effort to secure the surrender of Hezekiah. Messengers were dispatched to Jerusalem with a letter from the Great King (2 Kgs 19:8-9).

The letter suggested that Hezekiah had been deceived by the prophets who were promising that Jerusalem would be delivered from the Assyrians. Thus far any nation which had tried to match might with Assyria had been crushed. Sennacherib documented this assertion by enumerating a number of cities which had already fallen to Assyria (2 Kgs 19:10-13).

F. Hezekiah's Prayer (2 Kgs 19:14-19// 2 Chr 32:20).

Hezekiah took the letter to the temple and spread it out before the Judge of all the earth. In mighty prayer the king called upon his God to take cognizance of this challenge by Sennacherib. He admitted that the Assyrian monarchs could boast of an impressive list of conquests. The gods of these cities had been carried off as trophies of war or burned as worthless. That, however, only proved that the gods of the nations were but the creation of man's hands. Yahweh was the living God who could not be lumped together with gods of wood and stone. Hezekiah called upon God to remember his covenant with Israel, to deliver them from this blasphemous invader in such a way as to vindicate his name among the nations of the earth (2 Kgs 19:14-19).

G. Isaiah's Oracle (2 Kgs 19:20-34).

Through Isaiah, Hezekiah received an answer to his prayer. The prophet's oracle first rhetorically addressed the Assyrian invader. By the boisterous and blasphemous conduct of Rabshakeh, Sennacherib had reviled the Holy One of Israel. Furthermore the Assyrian had offended Yahweh with his boundless self-confidence that no natural barrier could impede his conquest. Did this foreigner not realize that Yahweh determined the rise and fall of kingdoms? Yahweh had enabled Sennacherib to lay waste fortified cities. He had placed within the hearts of the nations a fear which made them wither before the armies of Assyria (2 Kgs 19:20-26).

The omniscient God of Israel knew every movement of Sennacherib and every thought of his heart. He knew of the *"rage"* of the Great King against Hezekiah and against the God in whom Hezekiah trusted. Yahweh, therefore, would take action against Sennacherib. He would treat him as Assyrian kings customarily treated their captives.[13] He would force a hook through his nose and a bridle through his lips. This wild animal would be turned back from the walls of Jerusalem. He would return home hastily along the same route by which he had entered Palestine (2 Kgs 19:27-28).

Isaiah's oracle included a sign for Hezekiah. In this case the prediction of a near event became the pledge that God would keep his word with regard to a more distant prediction. Since the Assyrians had come in the spring of the year, the Jews had not been able to plant their crops that year. They would have to eat what grew of itself. The next year—probably a sabbatical year—they would have to do the same. In the third year, however, things would return to normal. This *"sign"* had reference to the promise that Jerusalem would be free from any further attack on the part of Sennacherib (2 Kgs 19:29).

The *"remnant"* which had escaped deportation at the hands of Sennacherib would again be firmly established in their land. That remnant would once again *"bear fruit,"* i.e., exhibit all the outward signs of prosperity. From the human perspective such a prospect seemed dim indeed at the time Isaiah uttered this oracle. The *"zeal of Yahweh,"* his zealous love for his people, would bring about this restoration to prosperity and glory (2 Kgs 19:30-31).

Isaiah's oracle concludes with a forceful declaration regarding the present emergency. Sennacherib would not come to besiege Jerusalem. Rather he would be forced to leave off operations in Palestine and retrace his steps to Assyria. Yahweh would defend Jerusalem because his own honor was at stake and because of the great love which he had toward David (2 Kgs 19:32-34).

H. Judah's Deliverance (2 Kgs 19:35-37).

On the very night following Isaiah's dramatic prediction, the divine stroke fell against the armies of Sennacherib. The angel of Yahweh passed over the Assyrian camp and smote 185,000 of the enemy. When the survivors awoke in the morning they found their comrades absolutely dead, not sick or dying. Such a massive overnight catastrophe must be attributed to direct intervention by Yahweh himself (2 Kgs 20:35).

His army decimated, Sennacherib could do nothing other than beat a hasty retreat to Nineveh. Some twenty years later as he was worshiping in the temple of Nisroch he was assassinated by his own sons. Thus was fulfilled the prediction of Isaiah (cf. 2 Kgs 19:7) that Sennacherib would *"die by the sword in his own land"* (2 Kgs 20:36-37).

Chart No. 50

THE JUDEAN PERIOD: AN OVERVIEW
722-586 BC

INDEPENDENCE LOST
2 Kings 21:1-26//2 Chr 33:2-23

Good King Hezekiah was followed on the throne by the most

wicked king to ever rule in Judah. All the religious gains effected by Hezekiah were soon lost. The nation plunged anew into idolatry and all its attendant evils. Political independence, so bravely engineered by the father, was willingly surrendered by the son. Judah again fell into the orbit of Assyrian vassal kingdoms.

A. The Sin of Manasseh (2 Kgs 21:1-18//2 Chr 33:2-20).

Considering the length of his reign—fifty-five years—very little is known about the reign of Manasseh (697-642 BC). He came to the throne at the age of twelve. Wicked princes were soon able to sway the boy king to their more liberal point of view. As a result, Manasseh followed all the abominations of the heathen. High places dedicated to Canaanite deities reappeared. The worship of the Tyrian Baal, first introduced by Athaliah in Judah (cf. 2 Kgs 11:18), again made its appearance. A wooden image symbolic of the goddess Asherah was erected by the king. Worship of the heavenly bodies which had been so popular in the days of Ahaz again was tolerated. Altars to other gods were erected in both the outer and inner courts of God's temple (2 Kgs 21:1-5).

Manasseh dedicated his sons to Molech. The crown prince he offered up as a burnt offering. Manasseh superstitiously kept track of his lucky days. He resorted to enchantments, i.e., spells and the like. Necromancers (those who call up the dead) and wizards (psychics) were placed in official positions. The defilement of the temple by an Asherah image annulled God's promises to permanently abide in that sacred place (2 Kgs 21:6-9).

The national decadence culminated in a bloody persecution of the faithful. Jerusalem was filled with blood from one end to the other. A widespread ancient tradition named Isaiah as one of the victims of this persecution.

God did not leave himself without a vigorous voice of protest during the corrosive reign of Manasseh. The great prophets of that period remain anonymous; but their message was plain. Because Manasseh had done more evil than the peoples who inhabited the land before Israel, God would judge Jerusalem as he earlier had judged Samaria. The plummet which God had placed alongside the house of Ahab in the north would now be placed alongside the house of David.

Jerusalem would be emptied of its inhabitants as one empties garbage from a pan. Judah would be conquered and spoiled by her enemies (2 Kgs 21:10-15).

The Assyrian annals add one detail about the reign of Manasseh. He is mentioned as a faithful vassal of Esarhaddon (681-669 BC). He even contributed troops for the Great King's invasion of Egypt in 669 BC.

B. Manasseh's Repentance (2 Chr 33:11-17).

Toward the very end of his reign, Manasseh offended his master Ashurbanipal (669-627 BC). The Assyrians took him captive to Babylon. While in his *"affliction"* there, Manasseh repented of his sins against God and man. When the Assyrians restored him to his throne, Manasseh made a valiant effort to put away the idolatrous practices which he himself had introduced into the land. He repaired the altar of Yahweh, and re-established so far as he could the worship of the Lord.

C. Reign of Amon (2 Kgs 21:19-26//2 Chr 33:20-23).

The short two-year reign of Amon (642-640 BC) receives scant attention in Kings. Like his father in the early part of his reign, Amon *"forsook Yahweh the God of his fathers"* and embraced all the gods of neighboring nations. Amon's allegiance to Assyria aroused the indignation of many patriots who desired freedom. Some of the attendants of the king fell on him in his own house and slew him. The assassins apparently did not have the support of the powerful *"people of the land,"* the landed gentry, for those who had murdered the king were swiftly executed. If the conspirators had intended to bring about a change of dynasty, their plot failed. The people of the land sought out the rightful heir, though he was but a lad of eight, and made him king.

ENDNOTES

1. Such praise is bestowed only on two other kings of Judah—Asa (1 Kgs 15:11) and Josiah (2 Kgs 22:2). All three of these godly men had wicked fathers.

2. John Gray, I & I Kings in "The Old Testament Library" (Philadelphia: Westminster, 1970), p. 697 renders: *"Give last injunctions to your family."*

3. Uzziah lived to be sixty-eight; Rehoboam to be fifty-eight.

4. So attested by Pliny, *Hist. Nat.* 22.7 and also in the Ras Shamra texts. See Gray, *op. cit.,* p. 698.

5. The named is spelled Merodach-baladan in Isa 39:1.

6. See Pritchard, *ANET, op. cit.*, pp. 287f.

7. The Assyrian account does not actually mention the siege of Lachish, but wall reliefs depicting the conquest of this city were discovered in Sennacherib's fabulous palace-temple at Nineveh.

8. Sennacherib states that he imposed on Hezekiah a tribute of thirty talents of gold and eight hundred talents of silver. Gray (*op. cit.,* p. 674) suggests that the three hundred talents mentioned in the Bible was the amount available in stamped ingots, and the extra talents mentioned in the Assyrian inscription were obtained from other sources, such as the despoliation of the temple.

9. See Gray, *op. cit.* p. 684. The diplomatic arguments of Rabshakeh have an analogy in a siege of Babylon by Tiglath-pileser III. See B.S. Childs, *Isaiah and the Assyrian Crisis* (London: SCM, 1967), pp. 69-103.

10. The Tartan was the commander-in-chief of the field army. The Rabsaris was probably the chief of the king's bodyguard. Rabshakeh means "chief officer."

11. The Assyrians were entirely justified in their contempt for the military capabilities of Egypt in this period. Pharaoh had never yet given effective aid to any state which had come under attack by Assyria.

12. Sennacherib claims to have carried away 200,150 persons in this expedition. He already had captured all the outlying fortresses of Judah. Hence those residing in Jerusalem were truly a remnant. Stephen Stohlmann has collected the evidence, biblical and non-biblical, for a Judean exile after the 701 BC invasion. See "The Judaean Exile after 701 B.C.E." in *Scripture in Context II* (Winona Lake: Eisenbrauns, 1983), pp. 147-175.

13. Assyrian monuments depict captives being led into the king's presence by means of ropes attached to rings which had been forced through the cartilage of the nose or through the fleshy part of the lower lip.

CHAPTER THIRTY-EIGHT

The Dying Days of Judah
2 Kings 22-25

The death knell sounded for Judah during the reign of Manasseh (Jer 15:4). Because of the national reformation led by his grandson Josiah, God granted to Judah a temporary reprieve. This king, who came to the throne at the tender age of eight, determined to steer his nation out of the Assyrian orbit in which worship of pagan gods was mandatory. He led the last great reformation of the monarchy period.

FREEDOM FROM ASSYRIA
2 Kings 22:1-23:27

Josiah reigned for thirty-one years (640-609 BC). As in the case of Hezekiah, the author of Kings states that Josiah did *"that which was right in the sight of Yahweh and walked in all the ways of David his father."* This good king never deviated from the right path.

A. Initial Reforms (2 Chr 34:3-7).

Josiah began his reform movement in his eighth year when he was

635

but sixteen years old. In that year he began *"to seek the God of his father David."* The reformation gained momentum in Josiah's twelfth year (628 BC) when he began *"to purge Judah and Jerusalem from the high places, the Asherim, carved images, and molten images."* The reformation may have proceeded in stages so as to test the reaction of Assyria which doubtlessly would have regard such reform as tantamount to rebellion (2 Chr 34:1-3).

In the thirteenth year of Josiah, a young teenager named Jeremiah was called to preach (Jer 1:2). The ministry of this great prophet must have given powerful impetus to the king's reform efforts.

Chart No. 51

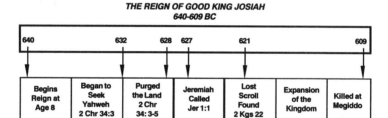

THE REIGN OF GOOD KING JOSIAH
640-609 BC

640	632	628	627	621		609
Begins Reign at Age 8	Began to Seek Yahweh 2 Chr 34:3	Purged the Land 2 Chr 34: 3-5	Jeremiah Called Jer 1:1	Lost Scroll Found 2 Kgs 22	Expansion of the Kingdom	Killed at Megiddo

B. Temple Repair (2 Kgs 22:3-20//2 Chr 34:8-30).

The reformation reached its climax in the king's eighteenth year (621 BC). Josiah dispatched a three-man committee led by Shaphan the scribe. This committee counted the monies which had been collected to pay for much needed repairs in and around the temple. The monies probably had been accumulating since the twelfth year of the king when the reformation intensified. The high priest Hilkiah distributed the monies among the Levitical superintendents who were in charge of the renovation project. These were men of impeccable honesty in whom full confidence was placed to properly administer the funds (22:3-7).

C. The Lost Scroll (2 Kgs 22:8-13//2 Chr 34:14-21).

When they were bringing out the money which had been stored in the temple, Hilkiah made a striking discovery. In one of the numerous temple storage areas he found an ancient scroll. Opinions differ as to exactly what this book was. Some think that it was only the Book of Deuteronomy or some portion thereof. Others think the entire Pentateuch was discovered.[1] Hilkiah handed the scroll over to Shaphan. He read enough of it to determine that the book was exceedingly valuable. He brought it to the attention of the king (22:8).

When Josiah heard the tone and contents of the scroll, he was quite upset. He tore his garments to demonstrate his sorrow. He recognized the language of the scroll as that of the law of God. Even though that book had for many years been lost, much of its contents had been preserved and handed down orally by the pious of the nation (22:9-11).

The king appointed a five-man committee to make further investigation regarding the scroll. Apparently Hilkiah the high priest was the chairman of this committee.[2] The committee was charged to *"inquire of Yahweh"* on behalf of the king concerning the scroll. Prior to the time of David such inquiry was made through the high priest as he utilized the Urim and Thummim. Since David's day, however, this type of revelation would be sought from a prophet of God (22:12).

The issue was not whether or not the scroll was authentic. Of this there was no doubt. Rather the king wished to ascertain whether or not the threats which the scroll contained were to have an immediate fulfillment. Josiah recognized that the nation had been doing, and to some extent continued to do, those very things which were so forthrightly condemned in the law. In view of the grave threats which Moses had made against apostasy, the king perceived that the wrath of Yahweh was about to be poured out upon his nation (22:13).

D. The Word of Huldah (2 Kgs 22:14-20//2 Chr 34:22-28).

The royal committee consulted Huldah, a prophetess who was readily available *"in the second city,"* i.e., lower district of Jerusalem. Her immediate availability seems to be the reason she was selected over Jeremiah or Zephaniah, the more prominent prophets of the period. Huldah is the only prophetess in Israel who seems to have ranked on an equal footing with the prophets (22:14).[3]

After examining the contents of the scroll, Huldah sent a prophetic oracle back to the king. Josiah's worst fears were justified. All the

threats[4] in the scroll would shortly befall Jerusalem. Such drastic punishment was justified in view of the fact that Judah had completely
turned from God. They had burned incense to other gods. They had
constructed abominable images with what appeared to be a determined effort to provoke the wrath of Yahweh. The unquenchable
wrath of God had been kindled by this apostasy. That wrath was
about to be poured out on Jerusalem (22:15-17).

Yahweh had taken note of the piety of Josiah and the determined
reformation effort which he had launched. Because the king had humbled himself when he had heard the message of the scroll, he received
prophetic assurance that the threatened destruction of Judah would
not occur during his reign. Josiah would *"die in peace,"* i.e., he
would not personally see the judgment envisioned in the scroll (22:18-
20).[5]

E. Covenant Renewal (2 Kgs 23:1-3//2 Chr 34:31-32).

After hearing the verdict of Huldah, the king's first action was to
call for a national assembly. In the courts of the temple the king read
(or caused to be read) *"all the words of the book of the covenant"*
which had just been discovered. The entire Pentateuch could scarcely
be read through in less than ten hours. For this reason many scholars
feel that the book which is referred to here is Deuteronomy. The
reading of the legal portions of the entire Pentateuch, however, cannot be ruled out entirely (23:1-2).

The king renewed the old covenant with God which had been broken during the grossly wicked reigns of Manasseh and Amon. He
pledged to obey from the heart the totality of the law of Moses. To
this commitment the representatives of the people gave their assent.
Thus they also became parties to the covenant (23:3).

F. Temple Cleansing (1 Kgs 23:4-7).

Josiah ordered the priests and Levites to remove from the house
of God all vessels that had made for and dedicated to any pagan
deity. This included the two altars which had been set up in the inner
and outer courts. In compliance with the law, Josiah burned this
pagan paraphernalia (cf. Deut 7:25; 12:3) in *"the fields of the
Kidron valley,"* i.e., the upper part of the valley to the northeast of

Jerusalem. Josiah did not want even the smoke from this fire to pol-
lute the capital. He then carried the ashes of this material to Bethel so
as to remove them completely from the vicinity of the Holy City. How
appropriate that the ashes of these pagan objects be returned to the
city in which, to large measure, the idolatrous impurities which had
corrupted both Israel and Judah had originated (23:4).

Josiah also removed the pagan priests (*kemarim*) who had been
imported during the reigns of Manasseh and Amon. These priests
offered incense to Baal, the sun, the moon and other heavenly bodies
at high places throughout the land. Josiah also destroyed the Asherah, wooden symbol of the Canaanite goddess, from the temple. Manasseh originally had set up this idol (2 Kgs 21:3). After his repentance
he had removed the Asherah (2 Chr 33:15). Later Amon had
replaced it (2 Chr 33:22). Following the example of Asa, Josiah took
this abominable image to the brook Kidron. He burned the wooden
parts to ashes and crushed the metal parts to a fine powder. This
powder was then sprinkled on the graves of the common people.
Burial places were regarded as unclean and thus fit receptacles for
any kind of impurity (23:5-6).

Josiah tore down the houses of the male temple prostitutes (lit.,
consecrated ones). These men were an essential element in the worship of Astarte. The houses of these prostitutes were in close proximi-
ty to Yahweh's temple. God's house had been defiled by the foul lust
of these "consecrated ones." The *"women who wove hangings for
Asherah"* were doubtless the priestesses of Asherah who were themselves prostitutes. The curtains which were used in the shrines where
the impure fertility rites were performed were of dainty fabrics of
many colors (23:7; cf. Ezek 16:16).

G. Reform in Judah (2 Kgs 23:8-14).

In order to prevent further illicit worship at the outlying high
places,[6] Josiah summoned to Jerusalem the Levitical priests who had
served at these shrines. He forced them to remain in the capital.
Throughout Judah, from Geba (near Bethel) to Beersheba in the
south, Josiah *"defiled"* or desecrated the high places where these
Levites had served. This action he hoped would render these shrines
permanently unsuitable for religious services. The high place type

worship had even invaded, so it seems, the city of Jerusalem. Altars and other religious paraphernalia had been set up in the large open buildings which were part of the gates of the city (23:8).

Josiah did not permit the apostate Levitical priests who had been summoned to Jerusalem to approach the altar of Yahweh or to have any part in the temple ritual. Nevertheless, they were permitted to partake of the priestly revenues. They were allowed to eat of the unleavened bread which only the priests could touch, and probably the portions of the sacrificial animals which were designated for priests (23:9).

"Topheth" was the name given to the place in the valley of Hinnom where sacrifices were offered to Molech. The exact meaning of the word is unknown. The valley of Hinnom is that depression which sweeps around the more western of the two hills whereon Jerusalem was built. This spot, sacred to Molech, was defiled by Josiah so that the abominations practiced there would forever cease (23:10).

One of the idolatries introduced during the Manasseh-Amon era was the worship of the sun. Sacred chariots and horses were stationed near one of the entrances of the temple to be ready for use in pagan processions. The sacred horses were "removed," and the wooden chariots were burned (23:11). Rooftop altars, generally associated with the host of heaven, Josiah crushed into dust and then cast that dust into the brook Kidron (23:11-12).

Josiah also destroyed the high places which Solomon had erected in the vicinity of Jerusalem for the benefit of his pagan wives. The entire ridge of hills on the east of the city came to be known as the "mount of corruption" because of the evil rites practiced there. These ancient shrines Josiah defiled by breaking their sacred pillars in pieces, cutting down the Asherim, and by filling these areas with human bones. From the earliest times bones were considered unclean (23:13-14).

Occult practices had flourished during the long reign of Manasseh. Josiah was determined to banish these devilish deeds from the land. Those with familiar spirits, i.e., mediums, and wizards who pretended to possess supernatural knowledge, were removed. The teraphim or household gods were destroyed whenever possible. Idols (gillulim—shapeless, formless things) probably again refers to objects used in private, perhaps figures used as amulets. Private superstitious practices—*"abominations"*—were uncovered and banished. Josiah conscientiously tried to fulfill all the precepts of the law of Moses with regard to these matters. In his exact obedience to the law, Josiah was without equal among the kings of Judah (2 Kgs 23:24-25).

In spite of Josiah's valiant efforts to reform the nation, the anger of Yahweh was not turned aside from Judah. At best, the reformation only gained a temporary reprieve for Judah. The sinister shadow of Manasseh still hovered over the hearts of the men of Judah in spite of all that Josiah had attempted to do. Therefore God determined to remove Judah *"from his sight"* just as he had removed Israel. Jerusalem, the city chosen by God[7] as site of his temple, would be abandoned (2 Kgs 23:26-27).

H. Reform in the North (2 Kgs 23:15-20).

When Jeroboam set up his altar at Bethel in 930 BC, he in effect made that city a high place. The buildings connected with this high place were torn down by Josiah. Whether the Bethel temple was still standing at this time is hard to determine. Probably the mixed race imported to the area by the Assyrians continued to worship at the site. The Asherah which was there Josiah crushed to powder and burned. From Israelite sepulchers Josiah ordered human bones to be brought out and burned on the Bethel altar. By this action he was unconsciously fulfilling the prophecy made by the unnamed man of God some three hundred years earlier (23:15-16; cf. 1 Kgs 13:2).

The king inquired of the local inhabitants about the significance of a pillar in the area of the tombs. He was told that this pillar marked the sepulcher of the man of God from Judah who had predicted the very things which Josiah had done to the altar. Josiah then ordered his soldiers to leave undisturbed that particular sepulcher and the bones of the two prophets buried therein (23:17-18).

Josiah's army roamed at will throughout the former territory of the northern kingdom[8] destroying and defiling the high places. This was the period of Assyrian decline, and the kings in Nineveh were no longer able to defend their outlying provinces. Taking advantage of this weakness, Josiah seems to have established his hegemony over the Assyrian provinces north of Judah. He seems to have been able to reunite under his own authority all the scattered portions of the old

Israelite kingdom, except, perhaps, the Transjordan area. He levied taxes in Samaria as freely as in Judah (2 Chr 33:9). Throughout these territories Josiah slew the pagan priests of the high places and defiled the altars of these heathen shrines by burning human bones upon them just as he had done at Bethel (23:19-20).

I. Reform Celebrated (2 Kgs 23:21-23//2 Chr 35:1-19).

The Passover feast became a focal point of Josiah's reform. The king set the priests in their offices. He *"encouraged"* them in the service of the house of God. The Levites were directed to put the ark in the temple. It would no longer be a burden upon their shoulders. This suggests that the ark had been removed from the temple and hidden by the Levites during the days of wicked Manasseh. Another suggestion is that the ark had been removed during the time of temple renovation (35:1-3).

The Levites were to organize themselves by the ancient divisions which dated back to David and Solomon. They then were to position themselves in the holy place for the slaughter of the Passover animals. All was to be done *"according to the word of Yahweh unto Moses"* (35:4-6). The parallel passage in Kings alludes to *"the book of this covenant,"* an obvious reference to the scroll recently found in the temple.[9]

The king and royal officials contributed thousands of lambs to the lay people for Passover and the feast of Unleavened Bread, which followed Passover. Priests and Levites worked together in preparing the Passover animals. After taking care of the Passover needs of the lay people, the Levites prepared the appropriate sacrifices for themselves and the priests. The singers and gatekeepers did not have to leave their posts because the Levites took care of the preparation for them (35:7-15).

Thus did Josiah orchestrate the observance of the Passover and the Feast of Unleavened bread which followed. Not since the days of Samuel had a Passover been so numerously attended and so meticulously observed. The festival was attended not only by the citizens of Judah, but by many Israelites from among the ten tribes who still remained intermixed with the Assyrian colonists in the area of Samaria (35:16-19).

SUBJECTION TO EGYPT
2 Kings 23:28-35

With the fall of Nineveh to the Medo-Babylonian coalition in 612 BC, a refugee Assyrian government was established at Haran. In 610 BC that city also fell to the Chaldean king Nabopolassar. Fearing that the international balance of power was about to be upset, Pharaoh Neco (609-593 BC) decided to intervene on behalf of the tottering Assyrian kingdom. Neco's trip to the Euphrates river took him along the coastal plain of Palestine and through the pass at Megiddo.

A. Death of Josiah (2 Kgs 23:28-30//2 Chr 35:20-27).

Why Josiah took his tiny army to Megiddo in an attempt to stop the advance of Neco is not entirely clear. The Pharaoh tried to dissuade Josiah from this foolish confrontation. Neco assured Josiah that he had no quarrel with Judah. The Egyptian even insisted that God had direct him to undertake this mission. To resist him would be to oppose God. The Chronicler seems to concur that the action of Josiah was contrary to the will of God for he declares that Josiah *"hearkened not unto the words of Neco from the mouth of God"* (2 Chr 35:22). The battle was joined and Josiah was mortally wounded (2 Kgs 23:29).

Josiah's servant put the wounded king in his *"second chariot"*—a chariot of much lighter construction and drawn by fleeter horses— and hastened toward Jerusalem. The Chronicler implies that Josiah succumbed to his wound en route to the capital. Jeremiah seems to have led the nation in lamenting the death of this good king (2 Chr 35:24-25).

B. Removal of Jehoahaz (1 Kgs 23:31-35//2 Chr 36:1-5).

After the death of Josiah, the "people of the land," i.e., the landed gentry, placed his son Shallum on the throne. On what grounds the people preferred this son to his elder brother Eliakim is not known.[10]

Upon assuming the throne, Shallum adopted the name Jehoahaz. He reigned but three months. Jehoahaz was summoned by Neco to the Egyptian military headquarters at Riblah about two hundred miles north of Jerusalem. Why Jehoahaz left the safety of Jerusalem is not clear. In any case, for him the trip was ill-fated. He was deposed and deported to Egypt. The land of Judah was put under a tribute of a hundred talents of silver ($200,000 BV) and a talent of gold ($30,000 BV) annually (2 Kgs 23:31-33).[11]

C. Jehoiakim's Enthronement (2 Kgs 23:34-35).

Neco installed his own man, Eliakim, the older son of Josiah, on the throne. Pharaoh required his vassal to take a new name as a symbol of subjection, but Eliakim himself seems to have had the right to select the new name. He chose Jehoiakim ("Yahweh will set up"). Jehoiakim was unable to meet his tribute obligations to Neco from the national treasuries which apparently were exhausted. He was forced to impose a real estate tax upon the land owners for this purpose.

During Jehoiakim's eleven years (609-598 BC) on the throne all the idolatrous practices of the Manasseh era were reintroduced. In spite of the national poverty, this petty little king spent huge sums of money on himself. In one of Jeremiah's blistering sermons he condemned Jehoiakim for building for himself a fancy new palace (Jer 22:13-14). Jehoiakim was the villain of the closing years of Judah's history. He was everything that is despicable in a national leader. He was a spendthrift, a bigot, an arrogant and irreverent tyrant who brooked no criticism, not even when that criticism came from a man of God. A prophet named Uriah was too bold in his denunciation of the king, and paid for his boldness with his life (Jer 26:21). Jeremiah was in danger on more than one occasion during those eleven years.

Jehoiakim carefully watched the political developments on the Euphrates River. From July 609 to June 605 BC the armies of the Babylonians and the Assyro-Egyptian coalition sparred. For the most part during those years the Babylonians were on the defensive. Finally, the Babylonian army under the brilliant young crown prince Nebuchadnezzar was able to launch a mighty offensive against the Egyptian stronghold at Carchemish. The Babylonians won a crushing victory. The tattered Egyptian armies fled southward from Carchemish in disarray. Nebuchadnezzar was able to roam at will through Syria-Palestine, the Hatti-land as he calls it in his annals.

SUBMISSION TO BABYLON
2 Kings 24:1-17

The battle of Carchemish changed the dynamics of the politics of the Near East. The Babylonians were now the masters of the world. Tiny Judah soon was forced to capitulate to the Babylonian juggernaut.

A. Three Years of Service (2 Kgs 24:1//2 Chr 36:6-7).

The battle of Carchemish occurred in the fourth year of the reign of Jehoiakim (Jer 46:2).[12] In that year Nebuchadnezzar came against Jerusalem. Jehoiakim was bound with bronze chains to be carried away to Babylon (2 Chr 36:6). Apparently Nebuchadnezzar changed his mind. He was content to take some hostages (e.g., Daniel) and some of the vessels of the temple (Dan 1:1-2; 2 Chr 36:6). Jehoiakim became a servant, i.e., a vassal, to Nebuchadnezzar for three years.

B. Jehoiakim's Rebellion (2 Kgs 24:2-7).

In 601 BC Nebuchadnezzar brought his army down the coastal plain of Palestine. He apparently intended to invade Egypt and destroy Neco once and for all. On the borders of Egypt, however, Nebuchadnezzar met with a stinging defeat.[13] This unexpected turn of events encouraged Jehoiakim to rebel against Nebuchadnezzar (2 Kgs 24:1).

Unable to attend to Jehoiakim personally, Nebuchadnezzar ordered bands of Edomites, Moabites and Ammonites to join local contingents of the Chaldean army in harassing Judah. Though these small units were probably unable to do much damage to the fortified cities of Judah, they did force the rural people to seek refuge in Jerusalem (Jer 35:11). In ordering these attacks on Judah, Nebuchadnezzar was really the unconscious agent of Yahweh. The prophetic threats against Judah now started to be fulfilled (2 Kgs 24:2).

The final destruction of Judah had been decreed by the mouth of Yahweh. Judah had to be removed from his sight—carried off into a foreign land—because of the sins of Manasseh which survived into the reign of Jehoiakim (2 Kgs 24:3-4).

Jehoiakim died December 9, 598 BC. The circumstances of his

645

death are not entirely clear. Jeremiah had predicted that he would be *"buried with the burial of a donkey."* His death, said the prophet, would be unlamented (Jer 22:18f.). These words suggest that Jehoiakim was assassinated, or at least that his body was dishonored after death by his own countrymen. Another possibility is that when the Chaldeans arrived in force at Jerusalem to punish the rebellious city, they disinterred the corpse and heaped indignities upon it.

Whether by violence or natural death, Jehoiakim was dead when the Chaldeans arrived. His young son Jehoiachin[14] was left to face the wrath of the mighty Nebuchadnezzar. No further aid from Egypt was forthcoming. Even though Neco had successfully defended his land in the face of the Babylonian campaign of 601 BC, the Egyptians were in no position to challenge Nebuchadnezzar's hegemony over Syria-Palestine (2 Kgs 24:6-7).

C. Jehoiachin's Deportation (2 Kgs 24:8-17).

Jehoiachin was eighteen years old when he began to reign.[15] His reign was but three months and ten days (2 Chr 36:9). During his brief reign he allowed the idolatries and superstitions which had prevailed under his father to continue. Jeremiah called this king *"a despised, broken jar"* and *"a vessel wherein is no pleasure"* (Jer 22:28).

Nebuchadnezzar's army was encamped around the walls of Jerusalem during most of the reign of Jehoiachin. The Great King himself was detained in a siege at Tyre. He had sent his servants to deal with Jerusalem. During the course of the siege Nebuchadnezzar himself appeared on the scene, probably bringing with him additional forces (2 Kgs 24:10-11).

Jerusalem was well fortified. The city could have withstood several months of siege. Jehoiachin, however, realized that further resistance would only bring upon his people incalculable hardship. Perhaps he hoped that if he surrendered Nebuchadnezzar would allow him to retain his throne as a vassal king. Whatever his motives, Jehoiachin and the leading citizens of Jerusalem walked through the gates of the city and surrendered on March 16, 597 BC.[16]

In addition to the royal captives, Nebuchadnezzar carried away from Jerusalem additional treasure from the temple. Solid gold objects were taken; gold plated furniture was stripped. Some ten thousand of the leading citizens of the nation were also deported to Babylon (2 Kgs 24:13-16).

DESTRUCTION OF JUDAH
2 Kings 24:17-25:7

Nebuchadnezzar appointed Mattaniah, another son of Josiah, to reign on the throne of David. Mattaniah took the throne name of Zedekiah ("righteousness of Yahweh"). This last king of Judah certainly made no attempt to live up to his new name (2 Kgs 24:17). He allowed the people to continue their pollutions and abominations (2 Chr 36:14).

A. Zedekiah's Rebellion (2 Kgs 24:18-20).

Zedekiah was inclined toward rebellion from the moment Nebuchadnezzar put him on the throne. Jeremiah the prophet thundered forth against the folly of resistance against Babylon, but still the political leaders clung to their suicidal course. When a new Pharaoh, Psamtik II, came to power in 594 BC Judah and neighboring countries began to make plans for a concerted effort against Babylon. Ambassadors from Edom, Moab, Ammon, Tyre and Sidon met in Jerusalem to plan the rebellion (Jer 27:3ff.). The plan must have been uncovered. That very year Zedekiah was summoned to Babylon to reaffirm his allegiance to Nebuchadnezzar (Jer 51:59ff.). Zedekiah's first major effort to break with Babylon was nipped in the bud.

A still more aggressive Pharaoh took the throne of Egypt in 588 BC. Pharaoh Apries—Hophra, as he is called in the Bible—actively encouraged a western coalition against Babylon. Zedekiah sent ambassadors to Egypt (Ezek 17:15) and entered wholeheartedly into the rebellion.

B. Siege of Jerusalem (2 Kgs 25:1-7).

The Babylonian army arrived at Jerusalem on January 4, 587 BC. They blockaded the city and began to systematically eliminate the outlying strong points. The fortified towns of Lachish and Azekah were among the last to fall (Jer 34:7).[17] The siege of Jerusalem now began in earnest. Siege towers were constructed. These movable towers

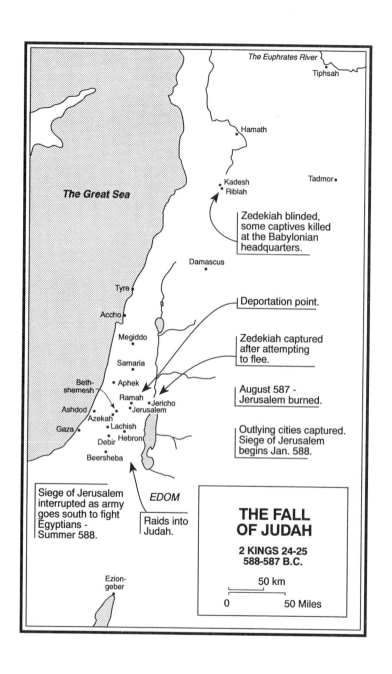

The Euphrates River

Tiphsah

Hamath

Kadesh
Riblah

Tadmor

The Great Sea

Zedekiah blinded,
some captives killed
at the Babylonian
headquarters.

Damascus

Tyre

Deportation point.

Accho

Megiddo

Zedekiah captured
after attempting
to flee.

Samaria

Beth-
shemesh

Aphek

August 587 -
Jerusalem burned.

Ramah
Jericho
Jerusalem

Ashdod

Azekah

Gaza

Lachish

Outlying cities captured.
Siege of Jerusalem
begins Jan. 588.

Debir Hebron

Beersheba

Siege of Jerusalem
interrupted as army
goes south to fight
Egyptians -
Summer 588.

EDOM

Raids into
Judah.

**THE FALL
OF JUDAH**

**2 KINGS 24-25
588-587 B.C.**

Ezion-
geber

50 km

0   50 Miles

enabled the attackers to approach the walls on the same level as the defenders. Sometimes the siege towers contained battering rams (2 Kgs 25:1).

In the summer of 587 BC an Egyptian army marched northward with the intention of relieving the pressure on Zedekiah. Nebuchadnezzar was forced temporarily to lift the siege in order to deal with this threat (Jer 37:5; Ezek 17:17). Apparently with little effort the Babylonians were able to send the Egyptians scurrying back home. Nebuchadnezzar then resumed the siege of Jerusalem (2 Kgs 25:2-3). The defenders began to suffer from famine (Jer 21:7,9; Lam 2:12,20). All the bread of the city was soon consumed. Famine was followed by pestilence (Jer 21:6-7). After a time the city was reduced to the last extremity (Lam 4:10).

On August 15, 586 BC, after a siege of eighteen months, the Babylonians were able to make a breach in the walls of Jerusalem. Zedekiah and his soldiers fled the city. Under cover of darkness the desperate king slipped past the enemy outposts and made his way toward the plains of the Jordan. He was intercepted, however, by the Babylonians. When his bodyguard deserted him, Zedekiah was helpless to defend himself (2 Kgs 25:4-5).

Zedekiah was taken captive to Riblah where Nebuchadnezzar had made his headquarters. There the rebel stood trial before the officers of the Great King. Zedekiah was forced to witness the execution of his young sons. Then the Babylonians blinded the eyes of Zedekiah, probably by means of a red-hot rod. He was then placed in fetters and carried away to Babylon (2 Kgs 25:6-7). There he remained in prison until the day of his death (Jer 52:11).

C. Destruction of Jerusalem (2 Kgs 25:8-17//2 Chr 36:17-19).

Following the capitulation of Jerusalem, the Babylonian soldiers awaited further instructions regarding the fate of the city. A month after the successful breaching of the walls, Nebuzaradan, the captain of the guard, arrived from Riblah with orders to raze Jerusalem and prepare its inhabitants for deportation. The city was burned and its massive walls were totally dismantled (2 Kgs 8-10).

Nebuzaradan ordered all Jewish hostages—those taken in the siege together with deserters—prepared for deportation. Only the very poorest of the citizens were allowed to remain in the land. The Babylonians did not wish the area to lie waste, since it could then have paid no tribute (2 Kgs 25:11-12).

Before setting fire to the temple, the Babylonians plundered that edifice of all its treasures. The giant pillars of bronze—Jachin and Boaz—were broken up to facilitate transportation to Babylon. The same applies to the ornate bases of the portable lavers and the mammoth laver called *"the sea."* All the smaller items of bronze were also carried off, along with what few vessels of gold and silver that remained from the previous despoliations of the temple in 605 and 597 BC. So much bronze was carried away by the conquerors that the scribes thought it to be an impossible task to weigh it all (2 Kgs 25:13-17).

Chart No. 52

DEPORTATIONS TO BABYLON			
DATE	REFERENCES	NUMBERS	NOTES
605 BC	Daniel 1:1 2 Chr 36:6-7		Daniel and his friends taken.
597 BC	2 Kgs 24:13-16 Jer 52:28 Ezek 1:2 2 Chr 36:10	10,000 3,023	Ezekiel and King Jehoiachin taken.
586 BC	2 Kgs 25:3-7 Jer 52:29	832	King Zedekiah blinded, taken captive.
582 BC	Jer 52:30	745	

AFTERMATH OF JERUSALEM'S FALL
2 Kings 25:18-30

The Book of Kings closes with an appendix discussing three events which transpired after the destruction of Jerusalem.

A. Execution of Leaders (2 Kgs 25:18-21).

Nebuzaradan selected the leaders most responsible for the prolonged resistance of Jerusalem to send to Riblah for execution. The

high priest Seraiah and *"the second priest"*[18] Zephaniah[19] head the
list. Three Levitical supervisors, nine state officials, and sixty *"people
of the land who were found in the midst of the city"* were also slain
there. "Keepers of the threshold," supervisors of the Levites, were also
among those executed at Riblah (2 Kgs 25:18-21; cf. Jer 52:25).

B. Assassination of Gedaliah (2 Kgs 25:22-26).

After the fall of Jerusalem, Judah became a province of the Babylonian empire. Gedaliah was appointed by Nebuchadnezzar to be governor over the poor of the land who had been left behind. He set up his
headquarters at Mizpah. Gedaliah immediately launched a campaign to
rebuild Judah. His first goal was to unite the various factions into
which the remnant of the people was divided. Once the Babylonian
army had withdrawn from the area, various guerrilla bands began to
come out of hiding. They joined Gedaliah at Mizpah (2 Kgs 25:22-23).

Gedaliah urged the captains to use their influence to secure peace
throughout the land. First, he assured them, they had no reason to
fear serving the Chaldeans. This suggests that Gedaliah had used his
influence with Nebuchadnezzar to secure amnesty for those who had
participated in the war against Babylon. Second, he called upon these
leaders to dwell peacefully in the land and render service to the king
of Babylon. If they continued to do this, he promised them a life of
peace (2 Kgs 25:24).

The tranquility of the tiny remnant of the Jews was soon shattered.
Ishmael, a member of the royal family, began plotting behind the
scenes to assassinate Gedaliah. In the seventh month,[20] Ishmael and
ten cutthroats proceeded to Mizpah. Suspecting nothing, Gedaliah
entertained these men hospitably (Jer 41:1). During the course of the
banquet, Ishmael and his men rose up and slew the governor, the
Jewish officials who served with him, and his Babylonian bodyguard.

Fearful of Babylonian retaliations, the remnant departed immediately for Egypt. At their first camping spot near Bethlehem, Jeremiah
pleaded with them to trust the Lord and remain in the land (Jer
41:17-42:22). The worldly captains, however, accused Jeremiah of
attempting to deceive them. They pushed on to Egypt (2 Kgs 25:26).
Thus two Jewish communities survived during the exile, one in Babylon, and the other in Egypt.[21]

C. Release of Jehoiachin (2 Kgs 25:27-30).

King Jehoiachin was taken captive to Babylon in 597 BC. Until the end of the reign of Nebuchadnezzar, the king of Judah was kept in prison. When the Great King died in 562 BC, his son Evil-Merodach ("stupid one of Marduk")[22] *"lifted up the head of Jehoiachin,"* i.e., restored him to royal favor. This encouraging development occurred in the last month of the thirty-seventh year of Jehoiachin's captivity. Perhaps due to the influence of Daniel, Jehoiachin's throne was placed above the thrones of the other captive kings in Babylon. The presence of these kings each on a throne of honor was thought to enhance the dignity of Evil-Merodach (2 Kgs 25:27-28).

The Babylonian king supplied suitable garments to the released monarch and invited him to dine daily at his royal table. Jehoiachin enjoyed this dignity until the day of his death. In addition, Jehoiachin received a daily allowance of all that he needed for himself and his family, besides the food which he enjoyed at the royal table.[23] The release and subsequent elevation of Jehoiachin no doubt bolstered the morale of the Jewish captives and made them ever more confident that one day God would fulfill his promise to put an end to their banishment and restore them to their native land (2 Kgs 25:29-30).

Chart No. 53

THE BABYLONIAN ERA
605-539 BC

ENDNOTES

1. It was the official temple copy of the sacred book which was found. This would not necessarily be the only existing copy of the law.

2. Shaphan the scribe and his son Ahikam served on this committee along with two others about whom nothing further is known. Ahikam once rescued Jeremiah when he was on trial for his life (Jer 26:24).

3. Miriam (Exod 15:20), Deborah (Judg 4:4), Isaiah's wife (Isa 8:2) and Anna (Luke 2:36) are called *"prophetesses,"* but in a secondary sense, as holy women, having a certain gift of song or prediction from God.

4. Chronicles uses the word *"curses."* This suggests that the passage which had most strongly affect the king was Deut 27 and 28 which contain a series of curses.

5. Josiah died in battle against Pharaoh Neco at Megiddo in 609 BC, but he was buried in peace in Jerusalem (2 Chr 35:24,25). He was the last king of Judah to be buried in peace in Jerusalem.

6. Hezekiah had *"removed the high places"* throughout Judah (2 Kgs 18:4), but under his son Manasseh the worship at these high places arose anew.

7. God *"chose"* Jerusalem when he led David to bring the ark there. He confirmed the choice when at the temple dedication fire came down and consumed the burnt offering and *"the glory of Yahweh filled the house"* (2 Chr 7:1).

8. The Chronicler gives more details. Josiah carried out his destruction of the high places, the Asherah and the images *"in the cities of Manasseh, and Ephraim, and Simeon, even unto Naphtali"* (2 Chr 34:6).

9. Since the ordinances for the observation of Passover are contained chiefly in Exodus (12:3-20; 13:5-10), it is reasonable to assume that the *"book of the covenant"* contained the text of what is presently called Exodus. Passover regulations are repeated but with much less fullness in Deut 16:1-8.

10. Jehoahaz was twenty-three when he began to reign (2 Kgs 23:31). His brother, three months later, is said to have been twenty-five (2 Kgs 23:36).

11. The tribute was very moderate compared to the three hundred talents of silver and thirty talents of gold demanded by Sennacherib (2 Kgs 18:14). Perhaps the Pharaoh was trying to be conciliatory toward Judah in anticipation of his confrontation with Babylon.

12. Using a different system of counting the regnal years of kings, Daniel 1:1 dates the coming of Nebuchadnezzar against Jerusalem to the third year of Jehoiakim. For a discussion of the two dating systems see Edwin Thiele, *The Mysterious Numbers of the Hebrew Kings* (Grand Rapids: Eerdmans, 1965), pp. 162ff.

13. James B. Pritchard, ed. *Ancient Near Eastern Texts Relating to the Old Testament* (third ed.; Princeton: University Press, 1969), p. 564.

14. Jehoiachin has two other names: Jeconiah (1 Chr 3:16,17; Jer 27:20) and Coniah (Jer 22:24,28). The two longer forms both mean "Yahweh will establish"; the shorter form means "Yahweh establishes."

15. According to 2 Chr 36:9 Jehoiachin was only eight when he began to reign. In Hebrew the number eighteen is written with two words, the word for eight and the word for ten. In the process of copying the manuscript of Chronicles, some scribe accidentally must have omitted the word for ten.

16. The date of the surrender of Jehoiachin "is undoubtedly the most precise [date] in Israelite history during the biblical period and constitutes one of the cornerstones of biblical chronology." See Gershon Galil, "The Babylonian Calendar and the Chronology of the Last Kings of Judah" *Biblica* 72 (1991) 367. The Biblical record of Jehoiachin's surrender is substantiated and supplemented by the Babylonian Chronicle. See Pritchard, *op. cit.,* p. 564.

17. In 1935 eighteen ostraca which date to the time of the siege of Jerusalem were found in the ruins of Lachish. These ostraca are military communiques between a field commander and his superior in Lachish. See Victor Matthews and Don Benjamin, eds. *Old Testament Parallels* (New York: Paulist, 1991), pp. 134-36.

18. According to 2 Kgs 23:4 several *"second"* priests served at the same time. What the office entailed is not clear.

19. This Zephaniah is probably the Zephaniah son of Maaseiah of whom so much is said in the Book of Jeremiah. See Jer 21:1; 29:25-29; 37:3.

20. The year of the assassination is not stated. If the seventh month refers to the year of Jerusalem's fall, then Gedaliah's governorship lasted only three months. Since the Babylonians came to avenge his death in 582 BC (Jer 52:30), it is more likely that Gedaliah's governorship lasted about four years, from 586-582 BC.

21. The Book of Jeremiah (chs. 41-44) expands at great length on the events associated with the death of Gedaliah and the activities of the remnant in Egypt.

22. Evil-Merodach is a parody on the actual name of this king which was Amel-Marduk ("man of Marduk").

23. Contemporary economic documents discovered in Nebuchadnezzar's palace list Jehoiachin and his five sons among those who received daily rations of food. See D. Winton Thomas, ed. *Documents from Old Testament Times* (New York: Harper and Row, 1958), pp. 84-86.

PART THREE

THE

RESTORATION PERIOD

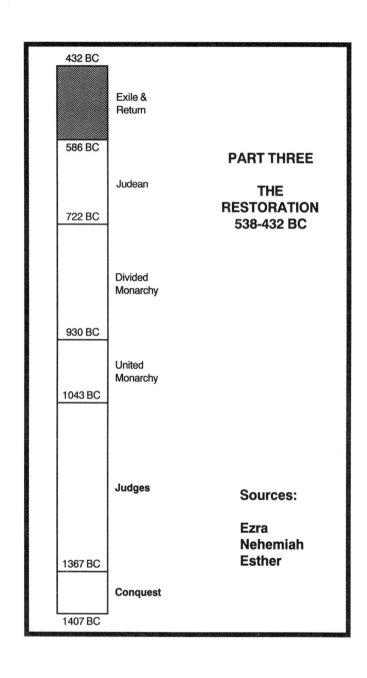

432 BC

Exile &
Return

586 BC

Judean

722 BC

Divided
Monarchy

930 BC

United
Monarchy

1043 BC

Judges

1367 BC

Conquest

1407 BC

PART THREE

**THE
RESTORATION
538-432 BC**

Sources:

**Ezra
Nehemiah
Esther**

CHAPTER THIRTY-NINE

The Post-monarchy Books
An Introduction

Ezra, Nehemiah and Esther contain the inspired record of the people of God in the postexilic or restoration period. The English Bible follows the order and placement of these books in the Septuagint version.[1] The three books are not in strict chronological sequence. The events of Esther transpired between chapters 6 and 7 of the Book of Ezra.

THE BOOK OF EZRA
The Restoration of the Nation

In both the Hebrew and Greek Bibles the books of Ezra and Nehemiah were considered one book. The separation into two distinct books came in the Latin Vulgate. This division was introduced into the Hebrew Bible in AD 1448. This literary history not withstanding, it is clear that Ezra and Nehemiah were separate literary compositions.[2]

A. Background of the Book.

The Book of Ezra is a continuation of Chronicles. The author indicates as much by repeating in the first two verses the concluding verses of the earlier book.

Babylon fell to the armies of Cyrus in 539 BC. The Persian was welcomed in the city as a liberator. The Scripture states that *"Yahweh stirred up the spirit of Cyrus"* to issue a proclamation which allowed the Jews to return to their homeland. How Yahweh stirred up Cyrus is not stated. Josephus states that the Jews showed him the prophecies of Isaiah 44-45 which named Cyrus as the one who would liberate the Jews.

B. Circumstances of Writing.

That Ezra is the author of the book which bears his name is generally conceded. As noted above, the opening verses connect this book to Chronicles. Furthermore, much of the latter part of Ezra is written in the first person (7:28-9:15). This would have to be written by one who was involved in the events he narrates. Finally, Jewish tradition assigns this book to Ezra.

Chart No. 54

CHRONOLOGY OF EZRA				
Reign of Cyrus (539-529 BC)	Reign of Cambyses (529-522 BC)	Reign of Darius (521-486 BC)	Reign of Xerxes (486-465 BC)	Reign of Artaxerxes (464-424 BC)
1st Return	Silence	Temple	Persecution	2nd Return
Chs. 1-3		Chs. 4-6	4:6-7	Chs. 7-10 4:8-23
RESTORATION DECREE (538 BC)	81 Years			SEPARATION DECREE (457 BC)

C. Chronology of the Book.

The Book of Ezra opens with the liberation decree issued by Cyrus in 538 BC. The last event of the book occurred in the first month of the eighth year of King Artaxerxes—457 BC (Ezra 10:17). Thus the book covers a period of eighty-one years.

D. Contents of the Book.

The Book of Ezra has two distinct divisions. In the first (chs. 1-6) the focus is on events surrounding the first return of the Jews to their homeland. This is sometimes called the Zerubbabel return since this prince of the house of David was the leader. The first project after returning was the reconstruction of the altar. Then immediately materials were gathered for rebuilding the temple. The foundations were laid. Opposition, however, arose. The work ceased for about sixteen years. Then due to the preaching of two prophets, Haggai and Zechariah, the work resumed. In the sixth year of Darius (516-515 BC) the temple project was completed.

A hiatus of fifty-eight years exists between Ezra 6 and 7. Nothing is known of the Jews in Judea during this period except that local enemies wrote yet another accusation to the Persian authorities concerning the activities of the Jews (Ezra 4:6). An effort to rebuild the walls of Jerusalem failed (Ezra 4:8-23). Chronologically, the events of Esther in the Persian capital of Shushan took place during this period.

Chart No. 55

CONTENTS OF EZRA		
THE FIRST RETURN **Chs. 1-6**		**THE SECOND RETURN** **Chs. 7-10**
Decree of Cyrus	**G**	Decree of Artaxerxes
Led by Zerubbabel	**A**	Led by Ezra
Main Issue: The Sanctuary	**P**	Main Issue Sanctification
Encouragers: Haggai & Zechariah	**58** **Years**	Encourager: Ezra
Outcome: Temple Built		Outcome: People Separated.

The second half of Ezra (chs. 7-10) focuses on only one year. In the year 458 BC Ezra led a group of Jews back to the homeland. He was empowered to enforce the law of God in the region beyond the river. Ezra found that many of the Jews had intermarried with pagans. Before the year was over Ezra had addressed this issue decisively.

E. Teachings of the Book.

In Ezra one sees the Master Potter at work reshaping his people. He chooses to employ human instruments to accomplish his purposes. He stirred up foreign kings like Cyrus and Darius to aid his people. Within the covenant community Yahweh worked through a dedicated governor, priest and scribe. Through the power of God opposition without and discouragement within were overcome. The book stresses the power of the word spoken by God to men through preaching, and the word spoken by men to God through prayer.

If the first half of Ezra focuses on the dedication of God's house, the second half stresses the dedication of God's people. The dramatic leadership of Ezra caused a spiritually indifferent people to realize that they needed to be separate from the peoples of the land. Ezra was not an innovator, but a reformer. He pressed for repentance, not by introducing a new legal system, but by invoking the ancient Mosaic law and the preaching of the prophets which forbade intermarriage (9:11ff.) Only through consecrated people can God's program be accomplished in this world.

THE BOOK OF NEHEMIAH
The Reconstruction of the Nation

The Book of Nehemiah is closely related to the Book of Ezra. As noted above, the two were considered one book in the Hebrew Bible until AD 1448.

A. Background of the Book.

Ezra was commissioned by King Artaxerxes in 458 BC to return to Judea to enforce the provisions of the law of God. He had wide-ranging powers, but apparently he exceeded his authority when he led an effort to rebuild the walls of Jerusalem (Ezra 4:7-23). This failed effort discredited Ezra to a certain extent. He disappeared from the history for some thirteen years.

In the Persian capital Susa, a young Jewish captive became distraught when he learned that the walls of Jerusalem had been broken down. King Artaxerxes noticed the sadness on the face of his cup-bearer. When the king learned the reason for the despondency, he commissioned Nehemiah to return to Canaan as his governor with explicit authorization to rebuild the walls of Jerusalem. The political situation in that part of the Persian empire had changed since this same king had ordered Ezra's efforts to be stopped thirteen years earlier. The king considered it now in his best interest to have a friendly province on the borders of Egypt.

B. Circumstances of Writing.

The Book of Nehemiah opens with these words: *"the words of Nehemiah, the son of Hacaliah."* The present book appears to be largely, if not entirely, based on the memoirs of this governor of Judea. Much of the book is written in the first person.

Critics point to certain notations which must be assigned to writers living after the time of Ezra or Nehemiah. For example, in a catalog of priests and Levites the name Jaddua appears (12:11,22). A Jaddua (351-331 BC) was high priest when Alexander the Great entered Jerusalem. He was the great-grandson of Eliashib, the high priest in Nehemiah's day. Could Nehemiah have known Jaddua? Nehemiah does mention a married grandson of Eliashib (13:28). If that is the case, it does not appear impossible that he may have known the future high priest Jaddua when he was a child.

Nehemiah mentions *"Darius the Persian"* (12:22). This is most likely Darius II Nothus (423-404 BC). Nehemiah's second thirteen year term as governor would have terminated during the days of this Darius. This seems to be the period during which the Book of Nehemiah was written.

C. Chronology of the Book.

The book opens with Nehemiah serving in the court of Artaxerxes I (464-423 BC) as a cupbearer. Nehemiah began his memoirs in the twentieth year of this Persian king, or 445 BC. Thus a gap of some twelve years exists between the last event in Ezra and the opening of Nehemiah.

Chart No. 56

CHRONOLOGY OF NEHEMIAH				
464	ARTAXERXES		424	DARIUS II
8th Yr. 457 **Failed Attempt to Rebuild Jerusalem's Walls** EZRA 4:8-23	20th Yr. 445 **Nehemiah Commissioned** NEHEMIAH 1-12	*FIRST GOVERNORSHIP* ◄——————► *TWELVE YEARS*	32nd Yr. 432 **Nehemiah Re-Commissioned** NEHEMIAH 13	**Book Written c. 400 BC**

In the thirty-second year of Artaxerxes (432 BC) Nehemiah returned to the Persian court to have his commission as governor renewed (13:6). He then returned to Judea to continue his work. The last events of the book are connected with the period of the second governorship. Thus the events in the book took place over a period of about fifteen years, 445-430 BC. The mention of Darius and Jaddua, however, suggests that one must extend the period covered to about 415 BC.

D. Contents of the Book.

The Book of Nehemiah relates the exciting story of how Nehemiah was able to rebuild the walls of Jerusalem in spite of opposition without and obstacles within the people of God. This is followed by an account of the reforms instituted by Ezra and Nehemiah. The book has two natural divisions: (1) the restoration of Jerusalem (chs. 1-7); and (2) the reforms among God's people (chs. 8-13).

Chart No. 57

CONTENTS OF NEHEMIAH	
RESTORATION OF JERUSALEM	**REFORMS AMONG GOD'S PEOPLE**
Rebuilding the Wall	**Reviving the People**
Chs. 1-7	**Chs. 8-13**

E. Teaching of the Book.

The overriding practical lesson of Nehemiah is that God's work demands patient endurance. The book illustrates the principle of 1 Corinthians 16:9 that where there is an open door, there are many adversaries. Baxter has captured this lesson in a series of catchy contrasts. "There is no winning without working and warring. There is no opportunity without opposition . . . no triumph without trouble . . . no victory without vigilance. There is a cross in the way to every crown that is worth wearing."[3]

Chapters 8-12 are important in understanding the teaching of the Book of Nehemiah. Following the reconstruction of the walls, Ezra was asked to read aloud the law of Moses as part of a national celebration. Ezra's work thirteen years earlier and Nehemiah's building campaign were only the prelude to full restoration. To create the ideal community of faith required the input of Ezra the priest (Ezra 9-10) and Nehemiah the governor (Neh 1-7). The sacred and the secular mingled and merged in ultimate obedience to the living Word of God. *"On that day"* the worship system was strengthened (12:44) and the purity of the people was established (13:1).[4]

THE BOOK OF ESTHER
The Preservation of the Nation

The book of Esther takes its name from its principal character. The name is Persian and means "star." The Hebrew name of Esther was Hadassah ("myrtle"). In the English Bible, as in the ancient Greek Septuagint, the book is the last of the twelve historical books. In the Hebrew Bible Esther is one of the five *Megilloth* ("scrolls") within the larger division known as the *Kethubhim* or "writings."

A. Background.

While several thousand Jews returned to Canaan in 538 BC, many more thousands remained in settlements throughout the Persian Empire. Following the reconstruction of the temple in the sixth year of Darius (515 BC) nothing more is heard of the Jews in Palestine until the return of Ezra in 458 BC. Roughly in the middle of that fifty-eight year interval a serious threat to the very survival of the Jewish people developed. The Book of Esther recounts how that threat arose and how in the providence of God the threat was squelched. Chronologically the events of the Book of Esther fit between chapters 6 and 7 of Ezra.

B. Circumstances of Writing.

The Book of Esther is anonymous. According to the Talmud, "the men of the Great Synagogue wrote . . . the roll of Esther" (Baba Bathra 15a). This probably means no more than that the book was edited under the scholars associated with Ezra. Josephus (*Ant.* 11.6.1) considered Mordecai the author. In the light of the very laudatory comments regarding Mordecai in 10:3 his authorship is most unlikely.

The author clearly demonstrates an intimate acquaintance with Persian life and customs. He probably had access to writings by Mordecai (9:20) and certain royal chronicles (2:23; 10:2). The book probably was written shortly after the assassination of Xerxes in 465 BC (cf. 10:2).[5]

In the Greek version of Esther certain additions to the book appear. These were added to the canonical book during the intertestamental period in order to supply what some Jew of that period thought was a glaring weakness. The canonical book does not mention the name of God, nor prayer, nor anything explicitly religious. The additions total 107 verses which have been inserted at six places in the book. These additions to Esther mention God's name forty-two times. These additions also allude to such standard Old Testament themes as the law, covenant, prayer, sacrifice, the temple, and Jerusalem.

C. Chronology of the Book.

The Book of Esther opens with a description of a national assembly called by the Persian king Xerxes in the third year of his reign (483 BC). Esther was selected to be part of the royal harem of Xerxes in the seventh year of his reign (479 BC). Most of the book (chs 3-10) focuses on the twelfth year of Xerxes (474 BC). That was the year in which a plot to exterminate the Jews was foiled.

Chart No. 58

CHRONOLOGY OF ESTHER		
485 BC	X E R X E S	465 BC

3rd Yr.	7th Yr.	12th Yr.
483	479	474
National	Esther	Jews
Assembly	Installed	Saved
Ch. 1	Ch. 2	Chs. 3-10

10 YEARS

D. Contents of the Book.

The Book of Esther contains historical narratives and royal decrees. The book focuses on one major crisis: the efforts of a powerful Gentile nation to exterminate the Jewish people. The material may be divided into two major divisions. In chapters 1-5 the crisis is anticipated. In chapters 6-10 the crisis is providentially alleviated. Chart 60 diagrams the contents of the book.

One curious phenomenon of the book is its omission of the name of God.[6] Various explanations have been offered for this omission. The author was certainly not a skeptic.[7] Nor does it appear likely that God withheld his name to rebuke the thousands who remained in the land of the captivity for failing to return to holy land. Probably God's name was omitted because Esther was meant to be read at Purim. The merrymaking of Purim required, according to the Mishnah, that people drink until they were no longer able to distinguish between *"Blessed be Mordecai!"* and *"Cursed be Haman!"* (cf. 9:19,22). On such occasions the name of God might be profaned if it occurred in the reading. Therefore, the author deemed it best to omit the name altogether.[8]

Esther explains the origin of the Feast of Purim. This festival is celebrated to this day on the 14th-15th days of Adar, the last month of the Jewish year (March-April). On this occasion the Book of Esther is read. Traditionally the congregation in the synagogue shouts and boos whenever the name of Haman, the major antagonist in Esther, is read. The festival takes its name from the pur or lot (3:7; 9:26). Since he was a superstitious man Haman cast lots to determine the auspicious day on which to exterminate the Jewish people.

Chart No. 59

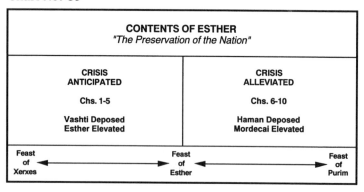

The historicity of Esther has been questioned by modern scholars. A capable defense of the accuracy of the book has been made by several evangelical scholars.[9] Even the scholars who consider Esther to be a historical novel rather than actual history list countless details of chronology, topography, palace protocol, court intrigue and Persian customs which point to the verisimilitude of the narrative. Especially striking are some thirty names of Persian and Elamite origin and twelve Persian loan-words. The Hebrew text has preserved the Persian names with amazing accuracy.

E. Teaching of the Book.

The purpose of the Book of Esther is to show how the Jews were saved from being exterminated by the hand of a Gentile antagonist. Though the name of God does not appear in this book, the providence of God is clear throughout (4:14; 5:1-6). Baxter argues that had the story explicitly explained that it was God who engineered all the recorded events, "the dramatic force and moral impact of the story would have been reduced." The author means to stress that God does not violate human free will nor interrupt the ordinary ongoing of human affairs; nonetheless his invisible hand guides all the affairs of human history.[10] Carey Moore eloquently expresses this concept: "In Esther, the God of the Jews is not seen or heard on stage but is surely standing in the wings, following the play and arranging the prospect for a successful resolution of the play."[11]

The book also has a practical significance. It contains letters by Mordecai and Esther which authorize and regulate the Feast of Purim. The time and manner for the observance of this festival are established. Purim was not to be a victory celebration, but a celebration of rest or deliverance from persecution (9:22). Choice portions of food were to be sent to one another, especially the poor (9:19,22). Every future generation of Jews was to celebrate Purim.

Another practical teaching of the book pertains to the collective self-defense of God's people. Mordecai wrote a communication to all the Jews in the Persian empire authorizing them to assemble and defend their lives against any who would attack them (8:9-12). The Jewish people in an ethnic sense were to continue to play an important role in God's program. The preservation of this people was thus extremely important. The Book of Esther has encouraged Jews to regard the preservation of their race as "a religious obligation of the first magnitude."[12]

ENDNOTES

1. Hebrew manuscripts reflect two traditions. Manuscripts from the Spanish Jewish community place Ezra and Nehemiah at the end of the third and final division of the Bible. The modern Hebrew Bible follows the order of the German and French Hebrew manuscripts which conclude the Old Testament with Ezra, Nehemiah and Chronicles (in that order).

2. The repetition of Ezra 2 in Nehemiah 7:6-70 indicates that Ezra and Nehemiah were originally distinct compositions. The two books are obviously closely related. They may have come to be considered one book in an effort to make the total number of canonical books correspond to the number of letters of the Hebrew alphabet. See E. J. Young, *An Introduction to the Old Testament* (Grand Rapids: Eerdmans, 1960), p. 400.

3. J. Sidlow Baxter, *Explore the Book,* (Grand Rapids: Zondervan, 1960), 2:230-231.

4. Brevard S. Childs, *Introduction to the Old Testament as Scripture* (Philadelphia: Fortress, 1979), pp. 636-37.

5. Robert Gordis assigns a date of 400 BC to the book. S. Talmon and E.J. Young assign the writing to the reign of Xerxes (485-465 BC).

6. In 167 verses the King of Persia is named 190 times, Persia 26 times, Ahasuerus 29 times, but Yahweh never.

7. Belief in God is implied in the fasting and wailing of 4:3,16 and in the confidence of deliverance in 4:14. The author's mention of proselytes (8:17;

9:27) shows that he was not indifferent to religion. He valued the feast of Purim which could hardly have been destitute of religious significance.

8. L.B. Paton, *A Critical and Exegetical Commentary on the Book of Esther* in "The International and Critical Commentary" (New York: Charles Scribner's Sons, 1908), p. 95.

9. E.g., W.H. Shea, "Esther and History," *Andrews University Seminary Studies* 14 (1976): 227-46; J.S. Wright, "The Historicity of the Book of Esther" in *New Perspectives on the Old Testament,* ed. J.B. Payne (Waco: Word, 1970), pp. 37-47; Edwin Yamauchi, *Persia and the Bible* (Grand Rapids: Baker, 1990), pp. 226-39.

10. Baxter, *op. cit.,* 2: 260-61.

11. Carey A. Moore, "Esther, Book of," *Doubleday Bible Dictionary;* ed. David Noel Freedman (New York: Doubleday, 1992), 2: 636.

12. Robert Gordis, *Megillat Esther* (New York: The Rabbinical Assembly, 1974), p. 13. See also Haim M. I. Gevaryahu, "Esther is a Story of Jewish Defense not a Story of Jewish Revenge," *The Jewish Bible Quarterly,* XXI (Jan 1993), 3-12.

CHAPTER FORTY

Returning from Exile
Ezra 1-6

The first six chapters of the Book of Ezra cover a single generation, 538-515 BC. The major concern of this period was the rebuilding of the house of God. For forty-nine years the ruins of that magnificent structure bore testimony to the sin which led to the destruction of Jerusalem in 586 BC.

RELEASE OF THE CAPTIVES
Ezra 1:1-11

The author of Ezra obviously envisioned his book as the continuation of the history of his people recorded in the preceding book of Chronicles. This is indicated in two ways. First, he appends to the first word the Hebrew *vav,* *"and"* (*"now"* NASB). In Semitic style, a book might begin with *"and"* especially when it was viewed as the continuation of what preceded. Second, he repeated virtually verbatim the words with which the preceding book concluded.

The focus of Ezra 1 is on an edict of emancipation by which the Jews were permitted to return to Judea. After briefly indicating the background of that decree, the author presents a synopsis of the edict itself. He then describes the response of the Jews to that edict.

Chart No. 60

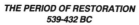

THE PERIOD OF RESTORATION
539–432 BC

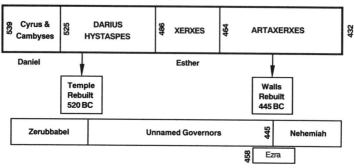

A. Background of the Edict (Ezra 1:1).

The first verse of the Book of Ezra states succinctly the facts concerning the emancipation proclamation which freed the Jews from captivity.

1. *The author of it.* The edict was issued by Cyrus king of Persia.[1] What a surprise! The ruler of the world became the agent by which exiled Jews were allowed to go home. The Cyrus Cylinder, discovered by Rassam in the nineteenth century,[2] indicates that he permitted all peoples who had been deported by the previous empires to return to their native lands.

2. *The time of it.* The edict was issued in *"the first year of Cyrus,"* i.e., the "first year" of his rule over Mesopotamia which began on New Year's Day (March 24) of 538 BC. Cyrus had become master of the world when he conquered Babylon on October 12, 539 BC.

3. *The result of it.* The edict of Cyrus had the effect of fulfilling the word of Yahweh who had spoken through the mouth of Jeremiah

seven decades earlier. The word of God cannot fail. Even before the captivity Jeremiah had predicted that Babylon's world rule would last but seventy years (cf. Jer 25:11; 29:10). Still earlier Isaiah the prophet had predicted that Cyrus, the conqueror of Babylon, would allow God's people to return to rebuild their land (Isa 44:28-45:7).

4. *The reason for it.* The edict of emancipation was issued because *"Yahweh stirred up the spirit of Cyrus."* The means by which the Lord did this is not stated. To the author of Ezra God worked in mysterious ways. Josephus *(Ant.* 11.1.2) preserves the tradition that the Jews showed Cyrus the specific prophecies of Isaiah 44-45 in which the Persian king was named as the deliverer of God's people 150 years before he was even born! This would suggest that God used Scripture to stir up the spirit of Cyrus. The important truth is that God can influence the hearts of even those who are not among his people. He is sovereign over Gentiles as well as Jews.

5. *The publication of it.* Heralds were dispatched to various Jewish communities throughout the empire to make known the decision of the king. The official written document[3] was then given to the communities to substantiate the oral proclamation. Persian custom was to translate official decrees into the language of subject peoples. Thus here the original Aramaic decree was no doubt paraphrased in Hebrew.

B. Paraphrase of the Edict (Ezra 1:2-4).

The Jewish scribe has given a Hebrew paraphrase of the official decree of Cyrus much as a news reporter might give a synopsis of a statute passed by a state legislature. First, Cyrus acknowledged that Yahweh had placed under his authority all the kingdoms of the earth. Second, the Persian realized—perhaps from prophecies of Isaiah—that Yahweh had appointed him to build his house in Jerusalem. Third, he authorized Yahweh's people to go up to Jerusalem and rebuild the house of the Lord. Fourth, those who chose not to return to Judah were encouraged to support the emigres and to make freewill offerings for the reconstruction of the temple (1:2-4).

Some see a contradiction between the religious sentiments of Cyrus represented here, and those which appear in some of the contemporary documents of his reign. Here Cyrus regards himself as the agent of Yahweh. In the Cyrus Cylinder, however, Cyrus views himself as a righteous ruler chosen by the god Marduk to restore the ancient worship in Babylon. Further, Cyrus speaks of his worship of Marduk. He also calls on other gods to intercede on his behalf before the superior gods Bel and Nebo. Actually little is known about the personal religious faith of Cyrus. If he was a polytheist, it would not be inconsistent for him to recognize Yahweh as one of many gods who assisted him in becoming world monarch. Some assume that Cyrus was a monotheistic worshiper of Ahura Mazda. In that case Cyrus might have regarded both Yahweh and Marduk as local representations of the deity which he himself worshiped. On the other hand, Cyrus may have left it up to the scribes of each ethnic group to represent his edicts in the most appropriate religious terms.

The title *"God of heaven"* occurs twenty-one times in the Hebrew Bible, twelve times in Ezra-Nehemiah. The title appears frequently in the context of Persian-Jewish communication.[4] This was a title which communicated with the pagan mind. The title stresses that Yahweh is superior to all the astral deities worshiped in Mesopotamia.

C. Response to the Edict (Ezra 1:5-11).

Those who responded to the edict of Cyrus are said to be from the tribes of Judah, Benjamin and Levi. These tribes had been carried into captivity first by the Assyrians in 701 BC, and then by the Babylonians between 605 and 582 BC. In later Old Testament history the tribes of Judah and Benjamin were closely associated.[5] Just as Yahweh stirred up the heart of Cyrus, so he also stirred up the hearts of the family heads of these tribes. These families were all motivated by spiritual concerns. Above all else, they wanted to see the house of God rebuilt (1:5).

Those who made the commitment to return to Judea were encouraged by two developments. First, the Jewish community in Babylon collected a freewill offering for the temple project and for the pilgrims. Second, Cyrus restored to the Jews the temple vessels which Nebuchadnezzar had carried away almost seventy years before (1:6-7).[6]

Mithredath the royal treasurer[7] counted out the vessels to Sheshbazzar *"the prince"* or ruler of the Jews.[8] He transported 5,400 vessels of gold and silver from Babylon to Jerusalem.[9]

THE REGISTER OF RETURNEES
Ezra 2:1-70

God honors those who pioneer in his program. Ezra 2 is an honor roll of those who accepted the challenge to rebuild a desolate land. These people did not harden their hearts to the stirring of God's Spirit. They understood that the restoration of Judea and the reconstruction of the temple were essential to the eternal purpose of God. However unappealing Ezra 2 might be to a modern reader, this chapter is "a monument to God's care and Israel's vitality."[10] Here is a people being given by a gracious God a second chance to live up to a holy calling.

A. The Leaders (Ezra 2:1-2a).

The choice of twelve senior leaders to head the group of returnees appears to have been deliberate.[11] The community they led was the reconstituted people of Israel. To this group of pilgrims now belonged all the promises given to the people of Israel in Patriarchal times.

At the head of the list is Zerubbabel, a grandson of King Jehoiachin, next to the last king of Judah. Various interpretations have been offered regarding the relationship between Zerubbabel and Sheshbazzar. Most likely Jewish tradition is correct that the leader of the returnees had both a Jewish and a Babylonian name.[12]

Second on the list of leaders is Jeshua, elsewhere called Joshua (in Greek "Jesus"). He was the high priest (Zech 3:1). His name is frequently linked with that of Zerubbabel.

Among the other leaders only two names are familiar to Bible students: Nehemiah and Mordecai. Neither, however, was the famous personage of the same name. The famous Nehemiah did not return to Judea until some nine decades later. Mordecai was an old Jew living in Susa when he was made prime minister of the Persian empire about sixty-five years after the events of Ezra 2.

B. The Pilgrims (Ezra 2:2b-35).

The sacred writer did not attempt to list every individual who returned in 538 BC. He does, however, the next best thing. He provides two groupings of the returnees. The first is by families, the second by cities. Apparently an Israelite could establish his "roots" and hence his legal right to be part of the national assembly by producing a family genealogy or village roster.

Family solidarity was very important in Israel. Eighteen prominent families supplied some 15,604 of those who made the dangerous journey home (2:2b-20).

The author next lists the returnees by their native towns.[13] Twenty-one villages are named from which 8,540 pilgrims came.

C. The Sacral Personnel (Ezra 2:36-58).

Six groups of sacral personnel are named and numbered as having participated in the return from exile.

1. The priests (2:36-39). The 4,288 priests who returned represented four different families. The priests formed about a tenth of the total of returnees. Only four of the twenty-four courses of priests organized by David were represented among the returnees.[14]

2. The Levites (2:40). Only seventy-four Levites were among the pilgrims. The Levites were to assist the priests in their ministry. The lowliness of this service perhaps explains why so few Levites chose to join the pilgrimage back to Judea.

3. The singers (2:41). The descendants of Asaph were temple singers. They numbered 128. Sometimes the signers are identified with Levites (cf. Neh 11-12), and sometimes, as here in Ezra, they are listed separately.

4. The gatekeepers (2:42). Representatives of six families of gatekeepers numbering 139 were among those who returned. The gatekeepers had the duty to lock and unlock the doors of the temple and to guard the treasury (cf. 1 Chr 9:17-29).

5. The Nethinim (2:43-54). The Nethinim (*"those given"*) or temple servants were the lowest class of sacral personnel. Thirty-five families of Nethinim were represented among the pilgrims (2:43-54). Some have traced this class back to the Gibeonites who were to be *"hewers of wood and drawers of water"* for the house of God (Josh 9:23). This group may have been supplemented from time to time by the addition of war captives who were made to serve in the sanctuary (cf. Num 31:25-47).

6. The servants of Solomon (2:55-58). A separate group within the Nethinim were *"the descendants of Solomon's servants."* Ten different families of these servants are named. The origin of this group is uncertain. Perhaps their ancestors were among certain servants given to Solomon by one of the many countries with whom he had treaty relations. These servants may have been a special scribal guild. In any case, the combined totals of the Nethinim and Solomon's servants was 392 (2:55-58).

D. Unconfirmed Claims (Ezra 2:59-63).

A number of those who wished to migrate to Judea could not verify their Israelite descent. This is not surprising. The devastation of the kingdom of Judah, the destruction of Jerusalem and the temple archives probably destroyed most of the public genealogical records. The text distinguishes two groups of those with unconfirmed ancestry.

1. The laymen (2:59-60). Family records were important for two reasons: (1) to establish ownership of property; and (2) to insure that the citizens of the restored community had an unbroken descent from the original Israel.

2. The priests (2:61-63). Only descendants of Aaron could serve as priests in Israel (Num 16:40). Some of the pilgrims claimed priestly descent but offered no documentation of that claim. The case finally was appealed to the governor. His final ruling was that these undocumented priests should have no part of priestly ministry until a high priest arose who could receive divine revelation. The implication of the governor's ruling is that (1) the Urim and Thummim were not available to the postexilic high priest; or (2) that the ability to use them had been withdrawn.[15]

E. Statistics (Ezra 2:64-70).

The entire company of pilgrims who made the journey back to Judea numbered 42,360.[16] The actual total of all the separate numbers given in Ezra 2, however, is only 29,818. Comparison with the parallel list in Nehemiah indicates that several families appearing in one list are not included in the other and vice versa. The surplus families in both lists are exactly the same figure: 1,765. Adding this 1,765 to the 29,818 yields the figure 31,583. This figure still falls short 10,777 of the grand total stated in Ezra 2:64. Obviously not all those who returned are enumerated in Ezra 2. The list contains those from Judah and Benjamin who settled in the vicinity of Jerusalem. The other 10,777 must have been from the other tribes. Though they settled outside Judea, they were still considered part of the "*assembly,*" i.e., the religious community (2:64).

Other statistics of interest include the number of servants (7,337), singers (200), horses (736), mules (245), camels (435), and donkeys (6,720). The ratio of slaves to freemen (1 to 6) indicates that those who returned were people of wealth.[17] The singing men and women mentioned here may have been the non-Levitical singers who joined the great choirs on the major festivals (2:65-67).

Upon arriving at the old site of the temple the heads of the various family groups made a substantial contribution for the work of reconstruction. In so doing they were consciously imitating their forefathers of the Exodus period who donated various precious objects to build the tabernacle (cf. Exod 25:4-7; 35:2-9). Their offering consisted of 61,000 gold drachmas (1,100 lbs.), 5,000 silver minas (3 tons), and a hundred priestly garments (2:68-69).

A chapter like Ezra 2 is regarded as boring by all but the most pedantic scholars. The believer, however, can discover even in this desert several oases of devotional stimulation. First, any effort made for God's kingdom is precious in God's sight. Though these names have long since disappeared from the face of the earth, they are known to God. Second, all people need to feel a sense of belonging, if not to family, at least to a place. Family relationships are extremely important in God's eyes. Third, every community of faith must give attention to preserving its core values or it may lose its character, even its life. For the Jews of the Restoration genealogy was a means of protecting the community from those who might be disruptive. One became a member of the covenant community by birth.

THE RECONSTRUCTION OF THE ALTAR
Ezra 3:1-13

After settling in their respective villages, the children of Israel gathered "*as one man,*" i.e., with common purpose, to Jerusalem. It was now the sacred seventh month (Tishri = Sept./Oct.)[18] presumably of the second year of the return (537 BC). The people, no doubt by pre-arrangement, were now ready to devote themselves to the restoration of proper worship. On the site of the old temple they watched Jeshua[19] the high priest and Zerubbabel the governor lead their respective families in the reconstruction of the altar of burnt offering. The new altar was set on the foundation of the old altar of Solomon's temple. These men were not religious innovators. Thus they built according to the specifications set forth in the law of Moses (Exod 27:1-8).

Because of their fear of the *"peoples of the lands"* the repatriated Jews had made the reconstruction of the altar a priority. Apparently they believed that only the faithful observance of the sacred sacrificial rituals could fortify them against the attacks of their enemies (3:1-3a).

The open-air altar became the center of the religious life of the returnees. The priests reinstituted the morning and evening regimen of burnt offerings (cf. Exod 29:38-42). The week-long Feast of Tabernacles was observed with appropriate sacrifices each day of the festival (cf. Num 29:12-38). The foundation of the temple, however, had not yet been laid (3:3b-6).

Once the altar had been restored, attention turned to the major project of rebuilding the temple of God. At that first great worship gathering in the seventh month a collection was taken. Masons and carpenters were hired. Negotiations with the Sidonians and Tyrians were completed. Like Solomon before them, the Jews would exchange agricultural products for cedar from Lebanon. The logs were transported from the mountains to the Mediterranean Sea, lashed together, and floated to the seaport at Joppa. Then those logs would be hauled by animal power up to the heights of Jerusalem. This transaction between two separate provinces of the Persian empire would not have been possible without the permission of King Cyrus (3:7)

In the second month of the second year of their return (537 BC),[20] seven months after the rebuilding of the altar, the work on the temple was ready to begin. Again Zerubbabel (representing the Davidic line) and Jeshua (representing the priestly lineage) were in the forefront. The enthusiasm of the group is indicated by the fact *"All who came from the captivity"* offered their services. The Levites as a group supervised the work of the laymen. Three families of Levites—Jeshua,[21] Kadmiel, Henadad—were appointed to supervise the Levite foremen. All of this Levitical involvement was to make sure everything was ritually correct (3:8-9).

When the foundations of the temple were in place the work stopped for a celebration. The priests wore their special garb. The Levites led in a praise service following directions which went back to David. The singing was accompanied by the clashing of cymbals and resounding trumpets. They praised Yahweh for his goodness and covenant faithfulness. All the worshipers shouted their agreement with the praises of the Levities (3:10-11).

For the younger worshipers the laying of the temple foundations was an occasion of great joy. The old men, however, wept with a loud voice. They had seen the glorious temple of Solomon which had been destroyed some fifty years earlier. The foundation before them gave little promise of duplicating the glories of the first temple. Those who listened from afar could not distinguish between the joyous shouting and the loud wailing. While young people tend to be overly exuberant, old people often miss the excitement of the present by dwelling on the past (3:12-13).

THE RESISTANCE TO THE WORK
Ezra 4:1-24

No work done for God's glory will go unchallenged. The author now documents the major efforts of the enemies of the Jews to thwart the efforts of the postexilic community. He speaks first of the efforts to stop the building of the temple. Then, parenthetically, he mentions occasions when formal objections were raised with Persian authorities about the activities of the Jews after the temple was completed.

The enemies of Judah and Benjamin approached Zerubbabel and the other leaders of the postexilic community to request permission to assist in the building project. They claimed to worship the same God. As proof they cited the fact that they had been sacrificing to this God since the days when the Assyrian king Esarhaddon (688-669 BC) had settled them in the area. God's verdict of the commitment of these people to him makes a lie of their claim (2 Kgs 17:33f.). These people were polytheists. They worshiped Yahweh only because they believed him to be the God who controlled the new land where they had settled. In no way does their worship of Yahweh indicate that they regarded him as the only God (4:1-2).

The Jewish leaders were firm in refusing the proffered aid from the surrounding peoples. They responded that ethnically, religiously, and legally these surrounding peoples had no claim in the temple which was under construction. This temple was for Yahweh who had entered into a special covenant with Abraham and his seed. He was uniquely the *"God of Israel."* Only the Jewish community had royal authorization to build this temple. Working together, they would be able to accomplish that task without outside help (4:3).

The true spirit of those who offered to *"help"* with the temple now became manifest. The people of the land discouraged (lit., weakened the hands of) the people of Judah and *"frightened"* them from building. This intimidation took the form of hiring (bribing?) royal counselors (probably Persian governors) to throw up bureaucratic road blocks to the construction effort. Among other things, they probably cut off the supplies of lumber from Phoenicia. These hostile efforts continued through the reigns of Cyrus and his son Cambyses,[22] a period of about sixteen years. As time went on the Jews became discouraged. They lost their vision. The temple project was abandoned. Not until the reign of Darius (522-486 BC) was the climate favorable for a resumption of the work (4:4-5,24).[23]

THE RESUMPTION OF THE WORK
Ezra 5:1-17

In the second year of King Darius (522-486 BC) the work of rebuilding the temple resumed after a hiatus of sixteen years. Again the work was challenged, this time with different results.

A. The Divine Catalyst (Ezra 5:1-2).

God raised up two prophets to speak to the shameful indifference which had stymied the temple project. Haggai stepped forward first. On August 29, 520 BC, he preached a powerful message in which he urged the temple work to resume (Hag 1:1-11). Temple reconstruction resumed on September 21, 520 BC (Hag 1:15). In October of that same year Zechariah delivered his first message. Stirred by the powerful preaching of these two great prophets the temple work continued apace. Every spiritual advance from Genesis to Revelation began with a word from the Lord.

Two other reminders of divine help are found in these verses. First, God was *"over them"* (NASB), i.e., it was his work that was being done. They were accountable to the Lord, and he was responsible to provide the leadership to see the job done. Second, the two prophets of God were *"with them supporting them."* The prophetic word did more than launch the new initiative. God sustains his people in their work as much as he stirs them to begin the task (5:1-2).

B. The Official Challenge (Ezra 5:3-17).

A new Persian official in the region considered it his duty to investigate what was going on in Jerusalem. Most likely this government investigation was triggered by the reports of the local enemies of the Jews. This governor, Tattenai,[24] did his duty both in making the on-site investigation, and reporting what he found to the king.

1. *The official investigation (5:3-5).* Tattenai and his lieutenant came to Jerusalem to see what authorization the Jews had for rebuilding their temple. He secured a list of the builders, in case any legal action had to be taken against them. The governor, however, elected not to stop the construction until he had time to seek direction from King Darius. The author of Ezra sees this restraint as due to the providence of God who was watching over the leaders of the Jews (5:3-5).

2. *The official report (5:6-17).* Tattenai's letter to Darius factually reported what was taking place in Jerusalem. First, he reported that he personally had observed the construction proceeding on the temple of *"the great God."* Huge stones and great beams were being put in place *"with great care."* The huge stones (lit., stones that had to be rolled) were of particular concern to the governor. They seemed larger than necessary for a worship center. Tattenai might have suspected some military fortress was being constructed. Second, Tattenai indicated that he had questioned the authorization of the project. Third, he had secured a list of the leaders of the project (5:6-10).

Tattenai went on to report how the Jews defended their actions. First, the Jews argued that they were rebuilding a temple which had been erected by a great king of Israel many years before. This construction effort was motivated by religious zeal. The builders were *"servants of the God of heaven and earth."* Second, the temple had been destroyed by Nebuchadnezzar the Chaldean because their forefathers had *"provoked"* the God of heaven. The people of Judah had then been deported to Babylon. Third, in his first year King Cyrus had issued a decree that the temple was to be rebuilt. Fourth, Cyrus had returned various temple vessels which had been confiscated by Nebuchadnezzar. He had given those valuable vessels to Sheshbazzar his governor. These were to be deposited in the rebuilt temple. Fifth, the governor Sheshbazzar had initiated the project. The present construction was but an effort to finish his work. Thus the work was proceeding under a building permit issued sixteen years earlier (5:11-16).

Tattenai concluded his letter by asking that a search be made of the *"king's treasure house"* in Babylon to see if the decree of Cyrus could be verified. In any case, Darius should send his governor directions as to how to deal with the construction effort in Jerusalem (5:17).

THE COMPLETION OF THE TASK
Ezra 6:1-22

The official inquiry of Tattenai set in motion a series of actions which gave legal authorization to the the construction work which was continuing apace in Jerusalem.

A. The Cyrus Memorandum (Ezra 6:1-5).

Darius issued a decree for a search of the royal archives to be made. The search began in Babylon and extended eventually to Ecbatana, a fortress in the province of Media. There a royal memorandum containing the seal of King Cyrus was found (6:1-2).

A Hebrew summary of Cyrus's decree appeared in Ezra 1. An excerpt from the more detailed official Aramaic version is recorded here. Because of the Jewish phraseology contained here, an older generation of scholars questioned the authenticity of one or the other or both of these proclamations. Documents from the Persian period, however, have provided convincing evidence of the authenticity of both versions.[25]

The portion of the memorandum cited here contains four points. First, Cyrus limited the size of the project. The Jerusalem temple should be rebuilt on the foundations of the first temple. The building should be sixty cubits high and sixty cubits wide.[26] Second, Cyrus prescribed the manner in which the temple should be built. The building should consist of three layers of huge stones and one layer of timber.[27] Thus the huge stones which had aroused the suspicion of Tattenai were specifically authorized in the original building permit. Third, the cost of the construction should be paid out of the royal treasury from taxes collected in the Trans-Euphrates province. Fourth, the gold and silver vessels confiscated by Nebuchadnezzar should be returned to their place in the temple (6:3-5).

B. The Edict of Darius (Ezra 6:6-13).

On the basis of this old decree by Cyrus, Darius issued his own decree. Governor Tattenai and his associates were to refrain from interfering with the work in Jerusalem. Tattenai's subordinate, the Jewish governor (Zerubbabel), was to be permitted to build the temple on its ancient foundation. Tattenai was ordered speedily to back the project financially using revenues of the Trans-Jordan province. Furthermore, whatever the priests might need to carry on the sacrificial ritual should be supplied to them. Darius desired that acceptable sacrifices be offered in that temple on behalf of the royal family. The accurate list of materials for worship suggests that Darius received advice from Jewish scholars before drafting his decree (6-10).

Darius' decree concluded with an order and a wish. First, for the person who would dare violate this decree, Darius ordered that he be impaled on a beam pulled from his own house.[28] Then the house of that man should be made a refuse heap. The ancients appreciated poetic justice in punishments. Hence it was deemed appropriate that one who hindered the building of God's house would witness his own house demolished before dying on one of its beams.

Second, the king wished that *"the God who has caused his name to dwell there,"* i.e., in Jerusalem, should overthrow any king or people who attempted to change his edict or destroy the temple. The concept that God's name, i.e., a revelation of himself, rather than his physical presence dwelled in Jerusalem also indicates Jewish influence on the contents of this decree (6:11-12).

C. The Work Completed (Ezra 6:13-15).

Tattenai the governor of the Trans-Euphrates province, and his associates, carried out the decree of Darius *"with all diligence."* Through the encouragement of the prophets Haggai and Zechariah the temple work was brought to a successful conclusion in the last month (Adar = Feb-Mar) of the sixth year of Darius (March 12, 515 BC).This was four-and-a-half years after Haggai's initial call for action (Hag 1:1).[29] In so doing the Jews were obeying the command of the God of Israel and the decrees of Cyrus, Darius, and Artaxerxes. The mention of Artaxerxes in 6:14 suggests that it was the author's purpose to lump together here the three great Persian patrons of God's people. The particular benefits bestowed by Artaxerxes will be taken up in the Book of Nehemiah (6:13-15).

D. The Temple Dedicated (Ezra 6:16-18).

The dedication of the second temple was celebrated with great joy. Some seven hundred special sacrifices were offered to mark the occasion, small in comparison to the tremendous numbers offered at the dedication of Solomon's temple.[30] Most significant was the offering of twelve goats as a sin offering for the twelve tribes of Israel. This action indicated two things: First, the sins of Israel had accumulated during the absence of the temple (586-515 BC) when no sin offering for the nation could be made. Second, this action indicates that the postexilic community considered itself as the surviving remnant of the entire covenant nation. Thus the twelve sin offerings were a confession of both failure and faith.[31] Forgiveness was still possible. The covenant with the whole people of God was still intact. In accordance with the law of Moses, priests and Levites were organized for continuing service in the new temple (6:16-18).

E. The Victory Celebrated (Ezra 6:19-22).

On the fourteenth day of the first month (515 BC) the feast of

Passover was observed by the postexilic community in their new temple. The priests and Levites had purified themselves in accordance with the law of Moses. They slaughtered the Passover lamb for themselves. They were joined in the celebration by those who had returned from exile and those who had separated themselves from the impurity of the nations of the land, i.e., proselytes or converts. In so doing, the postexilic community collectively was seeking Yahweh the God of Israel. The seven days of the Feast of Unleavened Bread which followed were celebrated with joy. They celebrated the friendly disposition of *"the king of Assyria"* which had encouraged them in rebuilding the temple. Their joy was grounded in Yahweh to whom they attributed the unexpected edict of Darius (6:19-22).

The reference to King Darius as *"king of Assyria"* is most appropriate. First, Darius now ruled the old Assyrian empire. Second, the author is attempting to make a striking point. The Lord had used the Assyrian kings to chastise his people. The long process of deportation to foreign lands had begun under the Assyrian Tiglath-pileser in 745 BC. Now the Lord had used the Assyrian king (Darius) to grant favor to the his people.[32] With the rebuilding of the temple the restoration was complete.

Thus ends the account of the first phase of the restoration of God's people. This generation witnessed anew the stirring of God's Spirit. At the beginning Yahweh stirred up the spirit of Cyrus (1:1); at the end he stirred up a complacent leadership and people (Hag 1:14). The curtain falls on Act One of the Restoration to the joyous shouts of God's people celebrating their Feast of Freedom (Passover). For almost six decades the record is silent regarding conditions in Judea, except for one hint of continued harassment by local enemies (Ezra 4:6). The spotlight now shifts to a foreign capital and a Jewish queen who saved her people from extermination.

ENDNOTES

1. The title *"king of Persia"* is used of Cyrus in the Nabonidus Chronicle, a document contemporary with the fall of Babylon. See James Pritchard, ed., *Ancient Near Eastern Texts,* 3rd ed. (Princeton: University Press, 1969), p. 306.

2. *Ibid.*, p. 315f.

3. The term *mikhtav* occurs only seven times in the Old Testament. It is a technical term meaning "inscription" or "official document." Jacob Myers, *Ezra-Nehemiah* in "The Anchor Bible" (Garden City, NY: Doubleday, 1965), p. 4.

4. The title appears frequently in the Aramaic Elephantine papyri which date to the mid-fifth century BC. See F. Charles Fensham, *The Books of Ezra and Nehemiah* in "The New International Commentary on the Old Testament" (Grand Rapids: Eerdmans, 1982), p. 43.

5. E.g., 1 Chr 6:65; 12:16; 2 Chr 11:1.

6. 2 Kgs 24:13; 25:13-16; 2 Chr 36:10,18; Jer 52:17-19.

7. Mithredath is a well-known Persian name meaning "given to (the god) Mithra." The term treasurer (Heb. *haggizbar*) is a hapax legomenon in the Old Testament. It is also of Persian origin. Fensham, *op. cit.*, p. 46.

8. The Hebrew term translated *"prince"* carries no necessary implication of royal descent. Sheshbazzar is a Babylonian name for which two interpretations have been offered: (1) "Shamash [the sun-god] protects the son;" and (2) "Sin [the moon god] protects the father." Fensham, *ibid.*

9. The list itemized in Ezra 1:9-10 adds up to 2,499. Verse 10, however, states the total as 5,400. The larger figure must have included many small pieces which were not itemized individually in the preceding verses.

10. Derek Kidner, *Ezra and Nehemiah* in "Tyndale Old Testament Commentaries" (n.p.:Intervarsity, 1979) p. 36.

11. A copy of this list in Nehemiah 7 adds one additional name, Nahamani, which evidently had dropped out of the text of Ezra in the course of copying. No evidence supports the contention of G. Coleman Luck that each of these men was a prince of one of the twelve tribes of Israel. *Ezra and Nehemiah* (Chicago: Moody, 1961), p. 16.

12. Modern scholars, however, are all but unanimous that Sheshbazzar was not the same person as Zerubbabel. The latter succeeded the former as the leader in Judea.

13. Determining in some cases whether the proper name is a personal or place name is difficult. The division of names here follows Fensham.

14. Kidner calls attention to the Tosephta which indicates that the Jews eventually reconstructed twenty-four priestly courses out of these four families. These twenty-four courses, which existed in the time of Jesus, where designated by the names of the original twenty-four of David's day. *Op. cit.,* p. 39.

15. During the intertestamental period two situations arose in which decisions had to be postponed due to lack of revelation. See 1 Maccabees 4:46; 14:41.

16. The same figure, 12,360, appears in the parallel listing in Neh 7.66.

17. The idea that the pilgrims were people of wealth is confirmed by the large freewill offering reported in 2:69. A series of bad harvests must have dissipated their wealth within the next two decades. According to Haggai (1:6,9ff), the people were in poverty at the time they undertook to rebuild the temple.

18. Three great annual festivals were scheduled in the seventh month: the Feast of Trumpets on the first day, the Day of Atonement on the tenth day, and the Feast of Tabernacles from the fifteenth to the twenty-first days.

19. In the books of Haggai and Zechariah Jeshua is called Joshua. The corresponding Greek form of the name is Jesus. Jeshua was the grandson of Seraiah (1 Chr 6:14,15) who was the high priest executed by Nebuchadnezzar in 586 BC (2 Kgs 25:18-21).

20. Coincidentally, the work on the first temple also began in the second month. This month was ideal for beginning a major construction effort. Iyyar (April-May) follows the major harvest and major festivals and comes at the beginning of the dry season.

21. The Jeshua of 3:9 is not the high priest but the Levite mentioned in 2:40.

22. Early interpreters identified the Ahasuerus of 4:6 and the Artaxerxes of 4:7 as Cambyses and Pseudo-Smerdes. The identification of Ahasuerus with Xerxes has now been established beyond question. Thus Ezra 4:6-23 must be regarded as a topical parenthesis supplementing the author's mention of the hostilities of the Samaritans during the time of the building of the temple.

23. Everything from 4:8 through 6:18 is written in the Aramaic language.

24. Kidner (*op. cit.*, p. 54) calls attention to a Babylonian record of a governor Tattenai who was serving in the Trans-Euphrates province in 502 BC. Most likely this is the same Tattenai who appears in this text.

25. See especially E. J. Bickerman, "The Edict of Cyrus in Ezra 1," JBL 65 (1946): 249-275. The Hebrew proclamation (Ezra 1) and the Aramaic memorandum (Ezra 6) represent two independent records. The former was for heralds to announce to the exiles; the latter contained the specifics and was destined for the archives. For bibliography of writers who have followed essentially the lead of Bickerman, see Edwin Yamauchi, *Persia and the Bible* (Grand Rapids: Baker, 1990), p. 90. A memorandum drafted by Persian authorities was sent to a Jewish community in Elephantine Egypt authorizing them to rebuild their temple. See Pritchard, *op. cit.,* p. 492.

26. Solomon's temple was 60 x 20 x 30 cubits (1 Kgs 6:2). Ezra 6:3 authorizes a temple sixty cubits high and sixty cubits wide. The length dimension has probably fallen from the text, or perhaps could not be read by Darius in the original memorandum. In any case, Cyrus was giving the maximum possible dimensions of the temple to ensure the building costs stayed with limits.

27. Solomon's temple was also built with one layer of timber for every three layers of stones (cf. 1 Kgs 6:36). This construction method can be documented elsewhere in the ancient Near East. The layers of timber may have minimized the damage by earthquakes. See Kidner, *op. cit.*, p. 55.

28. In impalement, the sharp end of a post was thrust through the belly, esophagus and lungs. The victim would then be left to die. Herodotus (3.159) attests that Darius impaled three thousand Babylonians when he captured the rebellious city. According to the Behistun inscription Darius impaled numerous rebels, oftentimes after mutilating them. See Yamauchi, *op. cit.*, p. 159.

29. Though nothing is said of it here, the temple was completed roughly seventy years after the destruction of Solomon's temple. Cf. Zech 1:12-17.

30. At the dedication of Solomon's temple some 22,000 oxen and 120,000 sheep were sacrificed as peace offerings (1 Kgs 8:63).

31. Kidner, *op. cit.*, p. 60.

32. Fensham, *op. cit.*, pp. 96f.

CHAPTER FORTY-ONE

Preserving the People
Esther 1-10

The Book of Esther has as its chronological setting *"the days of Ahasuerus"* who was known in secular history as Xerxes (485-465 BC).[1] This king ruled over 127 provinces[2] which stretched from India to Ethiopia.[3] Even scholars who do not advocate the historicity of Esther admit that the portrayal of Xerxes in this book corresponds to what the classical writers had to say about this monarch.[4] The geographical setting is Susa (Heb., Shushan), one of the Persian capitals.[5]

THE PROVIDENCE OF GOD
Esther 1:1-2:23

God sees the needs of his people long before those needs become a reality. He providentially places those he can use in strategic places so that they will be available when the crisis unfolds.

A. The Assembly of Ahasuerus (Esther 1:3-22).

In the third year of his reign (483 BC) King Ahasuerus made

important decisions which were to have enormous implications for God's people. The fast moving action of this crucial year began with a banquet and concluded with the demotion of the king's leading lady.

1. *A banquet for the nobles (1:3-4).* Ahasuerus gave a banquet for his princes, military leaders, and provincial officials. This banquet introduced a lengthy period of open court. For 180 days the king put all of his great wealth on display. The exact purpose of this assembly is not stated in the Bible. The gathering in Esther 1, however, seems to be the same one described by Herodotus (7.8). In order to avenge a defeat suffered by his father Darius I at Marathon in 490 BC, Xerxes was making plans for one of the greatest invasions of all time.

2. *A banquet for the citizens (1:5-9).* At the end of the planning period the king gave a seven day banquet (Heb. *mishteh* = drinking feast) for all the citizens of Susa. The banquet of Ahasuerus was held in *"the court of the garden of the king's palace,"* i.e., on the grounds surrounding the palace. The author, who describes in detail the magnificent setting, gives every impression of having been an eyewitness. Drinks were served in golden vessels of various kinds.

The royal wine was plentiful. The drinking was done *"according to the law."* Ordinarily, guests would drink together at the direction of the toastmaster. For this occasion, however, Xerxes had ordered the household servants to give to each guest whatever he desired. Such rousing Persian drinking parties are confirmed by the ancient historians.[6]

Simultaneously Queen Vashti was hosting the women at a separate banquet within the palace. Vashti is probably the same person called by Herodotus (9.108-13) Amestris.[7]

3. *The summons (1:10-12).* On the last day of the feast, the drunken Xerxes dispatched his seven harem eunuchs[8] to summon Queen Vashti to the banquet chamber. She was to appear with the royal crown. Traditional Jewish interpretation understands this to mean that Vashti was to appear wearing nothing but the crown. The king wished to put on public display the exceptional beauty of his wife. The queen refused the summons. Though she knew her modesty would cost her crown, Vashti would not compromise her moral standards.[9]

4. *The consultation (1:13-20).* Xerxes was enraged when Vashti

refused his summons. He immediately consulted with his seven advisors.[10] Four things are said about these men. (1) They were experts in Persian laws and customs. (2) Also they where men *"who knew the times."* This either means that they were astrologers or, more likely, that they were familiar with historical precedents which had the force of law. (3) They saw the face of the king. Ordinarily the Persian king was inaccessible to his subjects. These advisors, however, could personally converse with the king at any time except when he was in the presence of one of his wives. (4) They sat in first place in the kingdom, i.e., they were officials of the highest order (1:13-14).

The king could not allow the disobedience of Vashti to go unpunished. One of the counselors, Memucan, made an observation and a suggestion. Vashti's actions were an offense, not only to her own husband, but to all the princes of the realm. Those women present at Vashti's banquet would know immediately of the queen's defiance. They would thus be encouraged to treat their own husbands with contempt. Soon after the women of nobility (who apparently were not at the banquet of 1:9) would hear what the queen had done. This would result in *"plenty of contempt and anger"* (NASB). Thus actions taken against Vashti should not be considered personal revenge, but public policy benefiting the entire kingdom (1:15-18).

Therefore the council recommended that an edict be issued that would (1) banish Vashti forever from the presence of the king; and (2) give her royal position to another. These two stipulations may in reality be one. Vashti would no longer see the face of Xerxes in the sense that she would no longer appear by his side in her official capacity. This punishment, so the council reasoned, would cause all women throughout the empire to respect their husbands. The edict should be written in the laws of Persia and Media *"which cannot pass away"* (1:19-20).[11]

5. *The edict (1:21-22).* Memucan's suggestion pleased both the king and the council of seven. Letters were drafted in the language of each province, and then dispatched by swift messengers. The Persians had a communication system which was the marvel of the ancient world. It resembled the pony express system of the American west.[12]

The thrust of the Xerxes' edict was twofold. (1) Each man was to be the master in his own house. (2) The language of the husband should be the language of the household. Just how Xerxes intended to enforce his edict is not indicated.

B. The Silent Years.

The Book of Esther passes over four years—from the third to the seventh regnal years—of Xerxes. Herodotus, the Greek historian, fills in the gap. With an army of 200,000 men and a navy of hundreds of ships, Xerxes launched a massive invasion of Greece in 481 BC. At Salamis (480 BC) the Persian navy suffered a devastating defeat. A few months later the land force was defeated at Plataea, northwest of Athens (479 BC).

While Xerxes was in Sardis after the invasion of Greece he fell in love with his niece. Vashti (Amestris) waited until the king's birthday to make a request of her husband which, according to palace custom, he could not refuse. Vashti was granted the right to mutilate the mother of the king's young lover.[13] Nothing further is known of Vashti (Amestris) until she surfaced in the reign of her son Artaxerxes as a powerful figure.

C. The Selection of Esther (Esther 2:1-23).

After the war with Greece, Xerxes began to long for the company of his queen. The king's attendants suggested that he select a new queen from among the most beautiful virgins of the entire realm. This would be a bold departure from the usual procedure of taking the queen from the families of the seven senior counselors (Herodotus 3.84). Provincial overseers were to gather eligible candidates to Susa. The virgin who pleased the king should be made queen to replace Vashti. The king recognized the suggestion as sound personal and political advice. He therefore ordered its implementation (2:1-4).

Living in Susa was a Jew named Mordecai. He was a Benjamite, the great-grandson of one of those who had been taken captive in 597 BC.[14] He was raising his orphaned cousin Hadassah ("myrtle") whose Persian name was Esther ("star"). This young Jewish girl was among those taken by royal officials into the harem of Xerxes. No indication is given as to the number of virgins taken by the king. Josephus suggests that there were four hundred. The text gives no concrete indication of Esther's attitude toward the prospect of becoming a concubine of the king and potentially a queen (2:5-8).[15]

Esther found favor in the eyes of Hegai, the harem overseer. His favor was demonstrated by (1) immediately providing her with cosmetics and *"portions,"* i.e., food. Esther did not refuse to eat the food of the heathen as did Daniel. This may say something about the spiritual maturity of this Jewish maiden. (2) He assigned her seven choice maids from the king's palace. (3) He transferred her to the best place in the harem (2:9).

Following the advice of Mordecai, Esther did not reveal her ethnic origins. Mordecai must have feared for Esther's safety. Perhaps he had sensed the rise of an anti-Semitic faction within the empire. Every day Mordecai walked back and forth in front of the court of the harem. In some manner, information regarding Esther's well-being was smuggled out to him (2:10-11).

The virgin candidates went through an extensive beauty treatment. Six months they were treated with oil and myrrh and six months with spices and other feminine cosmetics (2:12). Archaeology has illuminated the particular beauty treatment involved here. Certain cosmetic "incense" burners have been found. Women of the Persian period saturated their hair and skin pores with pleasant odors from these burners.[16]

At the end of the twelve months each candidate would go into the king. She could take anything she desired—ornaments, apparel, jewels—from the harem to the palace. Having spent the night with the king, the candidate was now considered a concubine. She was assigned to *"the second harem."* She would never again enter the king's presence unless she was summoned by name (2:13-14).

When Esther's night arrived, she requested nothing except what Hegai, the king's eunuch, advised. Her natural beauty needed little enhancement from excessive ornamentation. Esther found favor with the king more than all the virgins. With Esther, Xerxes' search for a queen ended. The king elevated her to the position once occupied by Vashti. A banquet was ordered in Esther's honor and a holiday was proclaimed throughout the provinces. Esther was made queen in December 479 BC (2:15-19).

D. The Report of Mordecai (2:19-23).

At this time Mordecai was *"sitting at the king's gate."* This phrase, which appears five times in the book, has an official connotation. Mordecai had received appointment as a royal officer, perhaps a judgeship. This appointment might have been effected through the influence of Esther. In the ancient Near East the gate was a complex of buildings comparable to a modern day county courthouse.

Apparently Xerxes ordered a second gathering of virgins. This may have been a final procession honoring the unsuccessful candidates. By displaying the beauty of the runners-up the beauty of Esther was set off in more striking relief.[17]

At that time two disgruntled royal guards were plotting the assassination of Xerxes. Possibly they were seeking revenge for the deposition of Vashti. In some manner this plot became known to Mordecai. He got the word to the queen. She in turn informed the king in Mordecai's name. The plot was investigated. Those found guilty were impaled on a tree, i.e., a sharpened post. Royal scribes carefully noted this incident in the official annals of the king (2:19-23). Fourteen years later Xerxes became the victim of a similar palace conspiracy.

One of the strongest arguments for the historicity of the Book of Esther is the mention in a cuneiform tablet of a certain Marduka. He was a high official at the court of Susa during the early years of Xerxes. That this Marduka is the Biblical Mordecai is all but certain.[18]

THE PLOT OF HAMAN
Esther 3:1-4:17

Some four years after Esther became queen, King Ahasuerus promoted Haman to the position of prime minister of the realm. He is called *"the Agagite,"* i.e., from the province called Agag (3:1).[19] This Haman plotted to destroy the Jewish people.

A. The Reason for the Plot (3:1-6).

Among the king's servants only Mordecai refused to render homage to Haman. Other royal officials questioned Mordecai about his non-compliance with the royal edict to render homage to the prime minister. The old man replied only that he was a Jew. His refusal to bow to Haman was Mordecai's way of expressing Jewish national spirit and pride.[20] These officials called Haman's attention to Mordecai's disrespect. When the prime minister saw for himself the insolence of Mordecai he was filled with rage. Yet Haman did not take vengeance on Mordecai personally. Rather he determined to rid the entire kingdom of the Jewish race (3:2-6).

An accusatory letter from the enemies of the Jews in Palestine was written to the Persian court early in the reign of Ahasuerus (Ezra 4:6). This letter may have been one of the factors which made it easy for the prime minister to initiate his pogrom against the Jews.

B. The Authority for the Plot (Esther 3:7-11).

On New Years day in the year 474 BC Haman had his personal astrologers cast the *pur* (lot) *"from day to day and from month to month."* The purpose here was to determine the most propitious day for the extermination of the Jewish race. New Years day was an appropriate day for Haman's divination because in Babylonian religion that was the day when the gods came together to fix the fate of men.[21] The method employed is not clear. The lot itself may have resembled the object found by excavators in the ruins of Susa. This was a quadrangular prism which had the numbers one, two, five and six engraved on its sides.[22] The lot indicated that the thirteenth day of the twelfth month (March 7, 473 BC) was the most auspicious time to implement the attack against the Jews. Here it would seem the providence of God overruled chance (cf. Prov 16:33). The Jews would have nearly a year to take countermeasures against Haman's program of ethnic cleansing.[23]

Haman persuaded Ahasuerus that an unnamed people were dangerous to the unity of the Persian kingdom because they observed their own laws and not the laws of the realm. Haman cleverly omitted the name of the group he wished to attack for fear that the king would recall previous occasions when his predecessors had rendered favorable edicts on behalf of the Jews. He offered to reimburse the royal treasury with ten thousand talents of silver—equivalent to two-thirds of the annual income of the entire empire[24]—to pay for implementation of a decree to exterminate the Jews. Haman must have been enormously wealthy. Ahasuerus feigned lack of interest in the monetary offer. The later text, however, clearly implies that the money would go into the royal treasury (cf. 4:7; 7:4). The king so trusted Haman that he did not even inquire as to what people would be affected. He handed Haman his signet ring so that he might authorize the extermination (3:7-11).

C. The Implementation of the Plot (Esther 3:12-15).

On thirteenth day of the first month (April 17, 474 BC) the scribes penned the royal orders at the dictation of Haman. These orders, sealed with the king's seal, where dispatched to officials of various rank throughout the empire. On the thirteenth day of the twelfth month (March 7, 473 BC)[25] all Jews regardless of age or sex were to be slaughtered. Their possessions were to be seized as plunder. No doubt a portion of that plunder would be given to Haman. The Jewish population of Susa and their many friends were thrown into confusion by the edict. Meanwhile, Haman and the king callousedly celebrated the edict over drinks (3:12-15).

D. The Reaction to the Plot (Esther 4:1-8).

When Mordecai heard of the decree, he donned the garb of a mourner and went out into the city weeping loudly. He probably felt personally responsible for what had happened. By revealing his national identity he had brought this fate on his people. Mordecai stopped short of entering the king's gate because no one could enter the royal structures wearing sackcloth. Mordecai's mourning was duplicated by Jews throughout the empire when they heard the edict of the king (4:1-3).

When Esther heard of the anguish of Mordecai, she sent a change of garments to him. When he refused the gift, Esther dispatched one of her attendants to ascertain the reason for this bitter public mourning. The attendant found Mordecai in the city square in front of the king's gate. The Jew sent back to Esther (1) an account of all that had happened to him because of his refusal to honor Haman; (2) the information regarding the amount which Haman had pledged for the destruction of the Jews; (3) the text of the royal edict; and (4) an order for Esther to go to the king to plead for the deliverance of the Jewish people (4:4-8).

E. The Counterplot (Esther 4:9-17).

Esther sent her attendant to remind Mordecai that it was a capital offense to approach the king in his private residence without a summons. Only if the king raised the royal scepter would the death sentence be canceled. In the past thirty days Esther had not been summoned by Ahasuerus (4:9-12).

Mordecai sent the attendant back with an ominous message. He reminded Esther that she would not escape the general order to exterminate Jews just because she lived in the palace. He assured his adopted daughter that if she remained silent at this time, deliverance would arise for the Jews from another source. Here the faith of the old Jew in the covenantal position of the Jewish people shines through. Esther, however, should realize that Providence had placed her in her royal position for just such an emergency as this (4:13-14).

Esther was moved to action by Mordecai's words. She sent word back to him to request that all the Jews living in the capital assemble and fast—an act always accompanied by prayer—for three days on her behalf. During that same period the queen and her maidens would also fast. Fortified by this intercession, she promised to break the law and approach the king. Esther had now conquered her natural fears. She was now ready to lay her life on the line for her people. Rashness acts without fear; bravery, in spite of it (4:15-17).[26]

THE PLAN OF ESTHER
Esther 5:1-14

After the three days of fasting Esther put on her royal robes. She dared not approach the king in sackcloth. Esther stood in the inner court of the king's palace. From his throne room the king could see Esther standing in the court. He extended the royal scepter to her thus allowing her to approach. Esther drew near and touched the top of the scepter. The king inquired as to what was troubling his queen. Whatever she needed, he promised, he would give her, even to the half of his kingdom (5:1-3).[27]

Esther presented her request. She wished for the king and prime minister to come to a banquet which she had prepared. The king summoned Haman and immediately departed for the quarters of the queen. During the course of the banquet again the king repeated his willingness to grant any request which Esther might make. Esther, sensing that the time was not right to make her appeal, simply invited the king and Haman back the next day to another banquet. At that time she would make her request (5:4-8).[28]

Haman left the banquet elated that the queen had included him in her invitation. At the king's gate, however, he encountered Mordecai. Haman was enraged when the old Jew did not pay homage to him. He maintained his composure, however, and returned to his house. There he sent for some friends and his wife Zeresh (5:9-10).

Haman was bewildered by his own depression. He recited to his friends all the reasons why he should be very happy. Besides ten sons,[29] wealth, and position, he alone had been invited by Esther to attend a banquet with the king. Yet every time he happened upon Mordecai in the king's gate he became dissatisfied again. Mordecai was making his life miserable! (5:11-13).

Zeresh and his friends urged Haman to eliminate Mordecai, to make an example of him. With the king's permission the next morning he should have Mordecai impaled on a *"tree"* fifty cubits (75 feet) high. Then he could attend Esther's banquet with a joyful heart. This advice pleased Haman. He ordered the impalement *"tree"* to be erected during the night. The enormous height is probably due to the fact that the *"tree"* was erected on a high hill or on a previously existing structure (5:14).

The drama of the account should not be missed. Esther had not yet presented her petition to the king; the king did not know that Mordecai had once saved his life; and now an impalement *"tree"* had been set up for Mordecai.[30]

THE PRONOUNCEMENT OF THE KING
Esther 6:1-8:2

The king's insomnia that very night was to lead to a pronouncement which would suddenly and dramatically change the direction of the Book of Esther.

698

A. The King's Negligence (Esther 6:1-3).

Providentially that very night the king could not sleep. God accomplishes some of his greatest work during sleepless nights.[31] Xerxes ordered a scribe to read to him from the royal records. In the course of this reading the king was made aware of how Mordecai had reported the assassination plot of the two doorkeepers. The records indicated that no honor had yet been bestowed on Mordecai for his loyalty to the crown. The king desired to remedy this oversight immediately.

B. Haman's Suggestion (Esther 6:4-9).

Morning dawned. The king asked which of his counselors might be standing in the court. Haman had arrived first that morning. He was anxious to speak to the king about impaling Mordecai. As Haman entered the throne room the king posed this question: What should be done with a man whom the king desires to honor? Haman immediately assumed that the king was about to bestow another honor on him. Imagining himself as the beneficiary, Haman proposed a fourfold honor. The man whom the king wished to honor should (1) wear a robe once worn by the king; (2) ride on one of the king's own horses on whose head was a crown;[32] (3) be led by one of the king's most noble princes through the city square; and (4) the prince should proclaim before the honoree that he was being honored by the king (6:4-9).

C. Mordecai's Honor (Esther 6:10-14).

The king then ordered Haman to implement his suggestions with regard to Mordecai the Jew. The king thus knew from the royal records that Mordecai was a Jew. He did not make the connection between that fact and the ethnic cleansing which his prime minister authorized in the king's name (6:10).

What the prime minister intended for his personal honor became the greatest humiliation of his life. Haman left the court in utter shock. One can only imagine how he must have felt when he bestowed these honors on the man he had hoped to execute that very day (6:11).

After he led Mordecai on horseback through the city square, Haman returned to his home utterly humiliated. In great personal agony he related to his wife and friends what had taken place. The gloom of the moment lifted, however, when his wife and friends pointed out that Mordecai was a Jew. According to the irrevocable law of the king, all Jews would die on the thirteenth day of the twelfth month. Haman's gloom turned immediately to malicious glee. At that very moment royal servants arrived to escort the prime minister to Esther's banquet (6:12-14).

At the banquet again Ahasuerus asked Esther what her petition might be. The queen then asked for her own life and the life of her people for her request. She quickly explained that the Jewish people had *"been sold"* to be destroyed. The reference is to the price Haman had offered the king for the privilege of exterminating the Jews (7:1-4).

Ahasuerus demanded to know who would presume to do such a thing. Esther forcefully pointed to Haman as the *"foe and enemy."* At this unexpected accusation Haman trembled. The king was outraged. He stormed out into the garden to let his anger cool and to collect his thoughts. His absence permitted the incident which finally sealed Haman's fate (7:5-7a).

Haman remained in the room alone with Esther. He realized that only through Esther's intercession would his life be spared. So Haman approached the couch where Esther was reclining in true Persian fashion as she ate. There he pled for his life. Apparently in a gesture of contrition he either seized Esther's feet or perhaps even kissed them. In so doing he threw caution to the wind. No one was to come so near the wife of a Persian king! (7:7b).

The king returned to catch Haman in what could be interpreted as a compromising position. In shock the king asked if Haman was brazen enough to assault the queen with the king in the house. At that moment they *"covered Haman's face,"* i.e., put Haman under arrest. One of the king's servants pointed out that Haman had erected an impalement *"tree"* fifty cubits high where he had intended to execute Mordecai, one of the benefactors of the king. The king ordered the immediate execution of Haman. Thus did they hang Haman on the tree which he had prepared for Mordecai (7:8-10).

Ahasuerus gave the house of Haman to Esther. She in turn appointed Mordecai to manage that property. The old Jew was permitted to come before the king. He received the royal signet ring which had once been worn by Haman (8:1-2).

THE PROTECTION OF THE JEWS
Esther 8:3-9:19

Though Haman was dead, his plot was still alive. Esther fell at the feet of the king, imploring him to reverse the evil scheme of Haman. Again Ahasuerus raised the scepter to signal the attending bodyguards that the queen had the right to touch him. Encouraged by this gesture Esther stood, regained her composure, and presented her petition rationally to the king. She wanted a letter to be written to revoke the earlier letters devised by Haman. Esther pled that she personally would not be able to endure should her people be destroyed (8:3-6).

Ahasuerus first reminded Esther and Mordecai what he had already done to demonstrate sympathy for their plight. He had ordered Haman to be hung and had given his house to Esther. Now he authorized another step. Esther and Mordecai were to compose letters to be sent, under the king's seal, to the Jews throughout the realm. Technically the previous edict could not be revoked. A new decree, however, might have the desired effect. He left the matter up to Esther and Mordecai (8:7-8).

In the third month (Sivan), on the twenty-third day (June 25, 474 BC), Mordecai dispatched letters in the various languages to the officials and Jews throughout the realm. Some two months and ten days had elapsed since the earlier letters had been sent out by Haman. Under royal seal, these letters granted the Jews of the realm the right to assemble to defend their lives on the fateful thirteenth day of the twelfth month. The Jews could destroy any who came against them, and seize their spoil. They were thus given eight months to plan for their collective defense (8:9-14).

The wording in 8:11 has generally been misunderstood. Most take this verse to be an authorization by Mordecai and Esther for the Jews to go on the offensive against their enemies, killing them along with their wives and children. Another interpretation, however, is possible. The Jews were authorized to kill the entire army which might attack *"them, their children and wives, and to plunder their spoil."* These words are a citation of Haman's original edict. The exact wording of the original decree had to be cited so as to remove any ambiguity from the second edict. The Jews had a right to defend themselves against any attack against their men, women, children or possessions.[33]

Mordecai went out from the presence of the king dressed in royal robes. A large crown (i.e., headdress or turban) symbolized his office. The promotion of Mordecai was an occasion for great joy in the Jewish community. Sensing that the Jews were a people favored by the crown, many Gentiles *"became Jews"* (8:15-17).

When the thirteenth day of the twelfth month arrived the Jews were able to gain the mastery over their enemies. They assembled in their cities throughout all the provinces to lay hands on those who sought their harm. This show of strength put fear in the hearts of non-Jews. Even the government officials assisted the Jews because they feared Mordecai who had become very powerful within the kingdom (9:1-4).

Thus the Jews struck all their enemies with the sword. In the acropolis of Susa *("the capital"* NASB)—a section separated from the rest of the city—five hundred enemies were killed including the ten sons of Haman. One may assume that most of these were the cronies of the former prime minister. The Jews, however, did not lay their hands on the plunder (9:5-10).

The king was shocked at the number who were killed in Susa. Yet he did not back down on his commitment to grant Esther any request she might have regarding this crisis. Esther had two requests. First, she requested that the permission for Jewish war against their enemies be extended by one day. This request should not be viewed as vindictiveness on Esther's part but as precaution against rumored attacks upon the Jews the following day.[34] Second, she asked that the corpses of Haman's ten sons be impaled. The exposure of the bodies of these men would be a warning to all those who aimed to exterminate the Jews. The king ordered these actions to be taken. As a result, on the fourteenth day of the twelfth month the Jews defended themselves against attacks in the rest of Susa. Three hundred additional enemies were slain. Still the Jews did not plunder their enemies as they were entitled to do under the Mordecai edict (9:11-15).

Out in the provinces the casualties among those who attacked the Jews was 75,000.[35] Again no plunder was taken. The fourteenth day of the month became a holiday devoted to feasting. In Susa, however, the celebration took place on the fifteenth day. Among the Jews both days were subsequently observed as holidays (9:16-19).

AN APPENDIX
Esther 9:20-10:3

The Book of Esther closes with material which may have been added several years after that initial celebration of Purim.

A. The Letter of Mordecai (Esther 9:20-28).

At some point Mordecai determined that there should no longer be two separate holidays, the fourteenth in the provinces and the fifteenth in the capital. He authorized the annual observance of both days. The days were to be celebrated by feasting, exchanging gifts and charity to the poor. These two holidays were called Purim because Haman had decided by the *pur* or lot the month and day in which he would destroy the Jews. In this manner the feast of Purim became a universal custom among the Jews.

B. The Letter of Esther (Esther 9:29-32).

Queen Esther herself wrote letters to all the provinces concerning Purim. These letters, different from those mentioned in 9:20, were cosigned by Mordecai. Apparently some in the provinces were resisting the idea of observing both the fourteenth and fifteenth days of Adar. Esther's letter confirmed the time for the observance of Purim. It also authorized a time of fasting on the day preceding the two days of merry making. Even today some Jews still keep "Esther's fast" on the day before the celebration of Purim. The command of Esther was written in *"the book,"* i.e., the record which Mordecai was keeping of all these events (cf. 9:20). Eventually that "book" became the nucleus of the present Book of Esther.

C. The Career of Mordecai (Esther 10:1-3).

Because of his association with Mordecai, King Xerxes learned that taxation was a better way to finance his administration rather than plunder. The text suggests that the king prospered during the days of Mordecai. The old Jew was second only to the king himself in the kingdom. He was held in high regard among his own people. He was known as one who sought the good of his people and one who spoke for the welfare of his whole nation (10:1,3).

In the concluding verses of the book the author challenges his critics to check for themselves the facts he has narrated. Verification of Mordecai's advancement to prime minister could be found in the Book of the Chronicles of the kings of Media and Persia. Unfortunately this document is no longer extant. The author's words, however, leave no doubt that he intended his work to be taken as sober history (10:2).

ENDNOTES

1. The Septuagint translators thought that Ahasuerus was Xerxes' son Artaxerxes. Josephus followed the LXX in this identification. Modern scholars tend to identify Ahasuerus as Xerxes. From the liberal perspective, see L.B. Paton, *Esther,* in "International Critical Commentary" (New York: Scribner's, 1908), p. 54. From the conservative perspective see W.H. Shea, "Esther and History," *Andrews University Seminary Studies* 14 (Spring 1976): 288, n.4.

2. The Hebrew term *medina* refers to smaller governmental (or racial) units of the empire such as Judea (cf. Neh 1:3). Herodotus (3.89-94) documents that for tax purposes the empire was broken down into twenty larger areas which incorporated a number of the smaller provinces.

3. In a foundation tablet found at Persepolis Xerxes listed the countries over which he ruled. He specifically named India and Kush or Ethiopia. See James B. Pritchard, ed., *Ancient Near Eastern Texts,* 3rd ed. (Princeton: University Press, 1969), p. 316.

4. See C.A. Moore, "Archaeology and the Book of Esther," reprinted from *The Biblical Archaeologist* in *Studies in the Book of Esther* (New York: Ktav, 1982), pp. 376f.

5. Susa was one of several capitals of the Persian empire, the others being Babylon, Ecbatana, and Persepolis. Susa was an ancient capital of Elam which was rebuilt by Darius I. In about 539 BC Daniel visited Susa in a vision (Dan 8:1-8). Here also Nehemiah served as royal cupbearer in 445 BC.

6. Magnificent Persian drinking goblets such as are mentioned in Esther 1:7 have been found by archaeologists. A golden cup in the form of a winged lion dating to the fifth century BC is part of the collection of the Metropolitan

Museum of New York. A picture of such a vessel is found in Moore, *op. cit.*, p. 376.

7. Wright, *op. cit.*, pp. 40-42; Shea, *op. cit.*, pp. 235-37.

8. The names of the seven eunuchs in 1:10 and the advisers in 1:14 are Persian. The rabbis, however, attempted to give Hebrew meanings to these names.

9. Contemporary evidence does not support Josephus' explanation that Vashti's refusal was the result of a Persian law that wives should not show their faces to strangers. Goldman suggests that Vashti may have been fortified in her refusal by her own excessive use of wine. "Esther" *The Megilloth* in "Soncino Books of the Bible" ed. A. Cohen (London: Soncino Press, 1961), p. 198. Others have suggested that Vashti/Amestris was pregnant with her child Artaxerxes at the time of this drinking feast in 483 BC.

10. Seven princes figure prominently in Herodotus' discussion of Persian history. Cf. Ezra 7:14.

11. Cf. Dan 6:9,13,16. That Persian laws were irrevocable is indicated in a passage found in Diodorus Siculus (17.30). See discussion in Wright, *op. cit.*, pp. 39-40.

12. See Herodotus 8.98. R.A. Bowman reports the discovery of a leather sack in Egypt which contained sealed parchment documents written by high Persian officials in the script and language of the Egyptian Aramaic papyri. "Arameans, Aramaic, and the Bible," *Journal of Near Eastern Studies* 7 (April 1948): 65-90. Cited by John C. Whitcomb, *Esther: Triumph of God's Sovereignty* (Chicago: Moody, 1979), p. 43.

13. Yamauchi, *op. cit.*, p. 231.

14. Liberals generally make the text say that Mordecai had been deported with King Jeconiah (Jehoiachin), an event which occurred well over a century before he became Xerxes' prime minister.

15. The expression *"Esther was taken"* in Hebrew does not necessarily imply coercion. The same verb is used in 2:15 to describe Mordecai's adoption of Esther.

16. Moore, *op. cit.*, p. 385.

17. Robert Gordis, "Studies in the Esther Narrative," *Journal of Biblical Literature* 95 (March 1976): 47.

18. This cuneiform Marduka was first pointed out by A. Ungnad in 1941. The name appears in a cuneiform tablet named Amherst Tablet #258. The significance of the name has been discussed by Siegfried H. Horn, "Mordecai, a Historical Problem," *Biblical Research* 9 (1964): 14-25; Wright, *op. cit.*, p. 44.

19. J. Oppert published an inscription from the time of Sargon of Assyria (c. 725 BC) that mentions Agag as a place in Media (which later was incorporated into the Persian Empire). Gleason Archer, *A Survey of Old Testament Introduction*, rev. ed. (Chicago: Moody, 1974), p. 421. Jewish tradition considered Haman a descendant of that Amalekite king slain by Samuel some five hundred years earlier (cf. 1 Sam 15:8).

20. Moore, *op. cit.*, p. 36. The custom of falling down before a person of importance is well documented in Old Testament history. Thus it could not be religious scruples which compelled Mordecai to refuse homage to Haman.

21. Carey Moore, *Esther* in "The Anchor Bible" (Garden City, NY: Doubleday, 1981), p. 38.

22. The discovery of this "lot" is reported by Leon Wood, *A Survey of Israel's History* (Grand Rapids: Zondervan, 1970), p. 409.

23. Herodotus documents two earlier examples of Persian ethnic cleansing against the Scythians (1.106) and against the Magi (3.79). Cited by Moore, *Esther, op. cit.*, p. 43.

24. Cf. Herodotus 3.95. Cited by Whitcomb, *op. cit.*, p. 69.

25. C.F. Keil suggested a more rational basis for the long delay in the implementation of the edict. Haman anticipated that many Jews would leave their possessions and flee beyond the borders of the empire to preserve their lives. He then would be rid of the Jews. At the same time he would be able to seize their possessions with little difficulty. *The Books of Ezra, Nehemiah, and Esther* in "Biblical Commentary on the Old Testament," by C. F. Keil and F. Delitzsch. 1873. Reprint (Grand Rapids: Eerdmans, 1950), p. 348.

26. Moore, *Esther, op. cit.*, p. 53.

27. The promise is obviously a bit of royal exaggeration. It appears again in 5:6 and 7:2. Herodotus (9.109) relates a similar promise made by Xerxes to Artaynta, the bride of his son, with whom Xerxes fell in love. Cf. Luke 13:22; Mark 6:22f.

28. Moore (*Esther, op. cit.*, 87) points out the dangers of Esther's delaying tactic. The king's disposition toward her might have changed overnight. Haman might have learned of her relationship to Mordecai or the true intentions of her banquet.

29. Herodotus (1.136) observed that, next to skill with weapons, the greatest proof of manhood among the Persians was to be the father of many sons. Every year the king sent gifts to the man who could show the greatest number of sons.

30. Moore, *Esther, op. cit.*, p. 61.

31. Whitcomb, *op. cit.*, p. 87.

32. Ancient Persian sculptures represent the horses of kings and princes having on their heads ornaments resembling crowns. For an example, see plate 4 in Moore, *Esther, op. cit.*

33. Robert Gordis, "Studies in the Esther Narrative," *Journal of Biblical Literature* 95 (March 1976): 52.

34. Whitcomb, *op. cit.*, pp. 116f.

35. The figure 75,000 is supported by both Josephus and the Syriac. Modern scholars tend to accept the smaller figure of 15,000 which is found in the available manuscripts of the Septuagint.

CHAPTER FORTY-TWO

Restoring the Law
Ezra 7-10

During the reign of Cyrus (539-530 BC) the Jews had returned to Judea, rebuilt their altar, and laid the foundation of the temple. Under Darius (522-486 BC) they had completed the temple (515 BC). During the reign of Xerxes (486-465 BC) Samaritan opposition to the postexilic community continued (Ezra 4:6). Even more significantly, the Jews survived a plan to exterminate them as a people (Book of Esther). The last chapters of the story of restoration were written during the reign of the Persian King Artaxerxes (465-423 BC).

THE RETURN OF EZRA
Ezra 7:1-8:36

The second phase of the restoration began in the seventh year of King Artaxerxes (458 BC). In that year Ezra was able in some unexplained way to secure an appointment from the king to return to Jerusalem as a religious reformer. About fifty-eight years had elapsed since the completion of the temple. The godly Zerubbabel and Jeshua had died. The people in Judea were in a backslidden and despondent condition.

A. Ezra's Qualifications (Ezra 7:1-10).

Ezra was a priest. Like all priests, he could trace his ancestry back to Aaron the first high priest (7:1-5). Though he was born and raised in Babylon, he was also a *"ready"* (lit., quick) or skilled scribe or scholar with special expertise in the law of Moses (7:6a). The language suggests that he was one of those brilliant minds who could grasp with ease the complex materials found in the Mosaic law. That Ezra was so well educated is one indication that the Jews in Babylon prospered under Persian rule.

The situation in Judea, however, was a different story. Opposition from the Samaritans was a continuing problem. During the reign of Artaxerxes another effort was made to hinder the work of the postexilic community. Those behind this effort were Bishlam, Mithredath and Tabeel. Nothing further is known about the contents of this letter, the circumstances that produced it, or the results of it (4:7).

The text does not make clear how Ezra came into the favor of King Artaxerxes. What is clear is that this godly scholar requested permission to travel from the land of captivity to Judea. He also requested the authority to enforce the law of God among the Jews of that area. Because God's hand (i.e., favor) was upon him, all the efforts of this man were blessed. So it was that the king granted to Ezra all that he requested (7:6b). Perhaps the commissioning of Ezra was Artaxerxes' way of responding to the formal complaint which he had received from Bishlam and the others.

Ezra's preparation for service in God's kingdom began with his heart. *"He prepared his heart,"* i.e., he was determined, to do three things: (1) study the law of Yahweh, (2) to practice that law, and (3) to teach that law to Israel (7:10).

B. Ezra's Commission (Ezra 7:11-26).

By means of a diplomatic note King Artaxerxes granted to Ezra wide-ranging authority. In modern terminology, he might be called Secretary of State for Jewish Affairs. After a formal introduction, the king specified four areas of authority. This letter, like the others in the Book of Ezra, is given in Aramaic, the language of official correspondence in the Persian Empire.

1. Permission was granted for any of the people of Israel living in the Persian Empire to go with Ezra to Jerusalem (7:13).

2. Ezra was commissioned to *"inquire concerning Judah and Jerusalem according to the law of your God."* He was to assess the situation as to what degree the pilgrims in Judea were following God's law (7:14).[1]

3. Ezra was to carry to Jerusalem an offering for the temple. He was to supplement a gift from the royal treasury with monies secured from provincial officers and freewill offerings from Jewish exiles. The money was to be used primarily to underwrite sacrifices to be offered on the altar. Ezra was given permission to spend the balance of this fund as he saw fit (7:15-18).

4. The king sent by the hand of Ezra certain utensils which were for use in the service of the house of God. These were to be delivered to the temple authorities (7:19).

5. Ezra was authorized to tap the royal treasuries for any additional resources he might need for his work (7:20).

6. He was mandated to do zealously whatever *"the God of heaven"* might require at his temple. Artaxerxes believed that to ignore any requirement regarding temple ritual might subject the king and his sons to divine wrath (7:23).

7. Ezra was to appoint magistrates and judges for the Jews who lived throughout the Trans-Euphrates province (7:25a).

8. He was to teach any Jews who were ignorant of the laws of God (7:25b).

9. The king authorized Ezra to enforce both the law of God and the law of the king among the Jewish people. He had the authority to administer various punishments, including the execution of law breakers (7:26).[2]

A second decree (or perhaps a section within the one decree) was directed to the various royal treasurers in the Trans-Euphrates province. These officials were ordered to supply Ezra whatever he needed up to a hundred talents of silver (about 3.75 tons), a hundred kors of wheat (650 bushels), a hundred baths of wine (607 gallons), and a hundred baths of oil and salt as needed.[3] Furthermore these treasurers were ordered not to impose any form of taxation of the temple personnel (7:21,22,24).[4]

C. Praise Interlude (Ezra 7:27-28).

Ezra burst forth in praise as he contemplated the way God was working for the benefit of his people. He recognized that God had put the desire in the heart of King Artaxerxes to adorn the house of Yahweh in Jerusalem. To the Lord belonged the credit for the favorable treatment which Ezra had received from the king and his associates. The realization that God was opening doors strengthened Ezra. He realized that *"the hand of Yahweh,"* i.e., empowerment by God, was upon him. He therefore organized a group of Jewish leaders to make the trip to Jerusalem.

The words of this praise interlude are in the Hebrew language. The Hebrew continues through the end of the book.

D. Ezra's Journey (Ezra 8).

Ezra's journey to Jerusalem began on New Years day in the seventh year of Artaxerxes (April 8, 458 BC). The trip took four months (7:8-9).

1. The travelers (8:1-20). A group of 1,514 *"leading men from Israel"* and their families left Babylon with Ezra. With women and children, the group could have numbered six or seven thousand, about one sixth the size of the group which returned in 538 BC.

The emigres were honored by having their names recorded. Most of the families mentioned here were also involved in the earlier return under Zerubbabel. In this list of names the heads of two priestly families are mentioned first. They are followed by the head of the descendants of King David. The number of the men who accompanied the heads of these first three families has not been included in the text. Then follows the leaders of twelve family groups with the numbers of emigres in each group. Some think that the twelve families are representative of the twelve tribes and are another clue that the author regarded the return from Babylon as a second Exodus (8:1-14).

After traveling about nine days, Ezra and his group camped at the river of Ahava, probably one of the many canals of the Euphrates

River.[5] During the three day encampment there Ezra discovered that no Levites had joined the group. That these men should be reluctant to make the trip back to Jerusalem is understandable. They faced the a double difficulty. First, like all pilgrims, they would have to uproot their families. Second, they faced the drastic change from ordinary pursuits to the strict routines of the temple (8:15).

Ezra dispatched a delegation to nearby Casiphia (location unknown) to recruit Levites. Nine men were chosen because of their standing in the community (*"leading men"*); two for their diplomatic skills (*"teachers"*). Ezra carefully coached his emissaries about those to whom they were to appeal and what they were to say. They were to address their appeal to Iddo, the leader of the Levites, to *"bring ministers to us for the house of our God"* (8:16-17).

Again God's hand of blessing was upon the group. Two Levitical families totaling thirty-eight heads of households volunteered to return to Jerusalem. In addition 220 Nethinim or temple servants joined the travelers (8:18-20).

2. *The fast (8:21-23).* Before undertaking the trip, Ezra ordered a solemn fast. The group entreated the Lord for a safe journey. Ezra had been ashamed to request a military escort to protect the group from bandits along the way. He had assured King Artaxerxes that *"the hand of God,"* i.e., his power and blessing, was upon those who seek him, but his wrath is directed against those who forsake him. Having publicly stated his conviction regarding the protective providence of God, Ezra thought it would be inconsistent to request an armed guard. So the group resorted to prayer, and the Lord heard that entreaty.

3. *The finance committee (8:24-30).* Ezra appointed a committee of twelve leading priests and twelve leading Levites to be responsible for the transportation of the gifts for the temple. The law required priests to handle the sacred objects and the Levites to carry them (cf. Num 3:8,31; 4:5ff.).

Ezra carefully weighed out the gold, silver and other valuables which had been contributed to the work of the temple. These offerings amounted to 650 talents of silver (24.5 tons) plus silver utensils worth an additional hundred talents (3.75 tons). The gold weighed one hundred talents (3.75 tons). The contributions also included twenty bowls of gold weighing a thousand darics (19 lbs.) and two fine articles of polished bronze *"as precious as gold"* (8:24-27).

    4. *The safe arrival (8:31-36).* After twelve days of organizing at the river of Ahava, the group departed for Jerusalem. The journey of a thousand miles around the Fertile Crescent was uneventful, a circumstance attributed to the fact that *"the hand of our God was over us."* Just as God protected his people from their enemies at the Exodus from Egypt, so now he guarded these who made their exodus from Babylon. The Lord delivered them from the hand of potential enemies while en route (8:31).

    After arriving in Jerusalem the group rested for three days. On the fourth day, the committee of twenty-four publicly weighed out the gifts from Babylon and then delivered them over to the custody of the appropriate temple officials. *"Everything was numbered and weighed, and all the weight was recorded at that time"* (NASB). Both those who carried the valuables, and those who received them acted in business-like manner (8:32-34).

    The exiles who had come from captivity went to the temple to offer sacrifices. Twelve bulls and ninety-six rams (a multiple of twelve) and seventy-seven lambs[6] were offered as burnt offerings *"for all Israel."* Likewise, twelve male goats were offered as a sin offering. The inhabitants of postexilic Judea considered themselves the survivors and representatives of all the tribes of Israel. They were the covenant people (8:35).

    After religious duties had been fulfilled, Ezra's people delivered the edicts of Artaxerxes to the government officials in the Trans-Euphrates province. These officials *"supported the people and the house of God"* (NASB) as required by the royal decree (8:36).

THE WORK OF EZRA
Ezra 9:1-10:44

    Within five months (cf. 7:9 with 10:9) Ezra's efforts to teach the law of God in Judea began to bear fruit. He had pricked the conscience of the nation by his emphasis on Israel as *"the holy seed."* With no prompting from their teacher, a group of leaders approached Ezra with some bad news. The postexilic community had been unfaithful to its calling by tolerating illegal marriages with pagan women. These reports of unfaithfulness among the leaders of the Jews challenged Ezra's wisdom and courage.

A. Israel's Problem (Ezra 9:1-6).

Some *"princes"* (civil authorities) reported to Ezra that the people of Israel, including some Levites and priests, had not separated themselves from the peoples of the surrounding lands. "Abominations" (i.e., pagan worship objects) were being tolerated and even condoned. The ecumenical spirit threatened to destroy the distinctiveness of God's people! Some had even married foreign women so that *"the holy race has intermingled with the peoples of the lands"* (NASB). What was worse, this *"unfaithfulness"* was most in evidence among the princes and rulers of the people. Religiously and ethnically Israel was in danger of disappearing as a distinct people (9:1-2).

Ezra was devastated by this news. He went beyond the usual signs of mourning (tearing his garments) and plucked out some of his beard. This was a sign of indignation as well as grief. He then *"sat appalled,"* i.e., speechless with astonishment. He was astounded to think that after all the troubles of Israel and their subsequent restoration by God they should once again start down the same path of disobedience. Others who *"trembled"* over the implications of this deliberate violation of the word of God joined Ezra in his demonstration. Ezra's *"humiliation"* ended at the time of the evening sacrifice (about 3:00 P.M.). He then fell on his knees, stretched out his hands to God in a gesture of entreaty, and prayed (9:3-5).

B. Ezra's Prayer (Ezra 9:7-15).

Great revivals begin when great souls go to a great God with great fervor. Ezra's prayer is a model for revival prayer. First, he acknowledged the sinful record of his people. Ezra was ashamed to lift up his face to God. His people were drowning in a sea of guilt. That however, was nothing new. Since the days of the fathers—as long as any one could remember—the nation had been guilty before God. On account of national iniquities, Israel had been given by God into the hand of powerful kings. The people had experienced the sword (war), captivity, plunder, and open shame (lit., shame of faces). The shame continued to that very moment since Judea was but a tiny province within the vast Persian Empire (9:6-7).

Second, Ezra acknowledged the grace of God. A remnant had escaped exile to return to the Promised Land. That remnant was like a peg upon which hung all hope for the fulfillment of the glorious promises made to Israel by her prophets.[7] Through that remnant God intended to *"enlighten"* the eyes, i.e., revive the nation, in the midst of her bondage. Like Ezekiel (37:1-14), Ezra regarded the people as dead during the exile. God, however, had not forsaken them in their captivity. He had caused a trio of Persian kings—Cyrus, Darius, Artaxerxes—to show favor toward the Jews. The newly built temple bore testimony that the revival of Israel had begun. God's people had *"a wall"* (lit., a fence) in Judah and Jerusalem, i.e., a secure place (9:8-9).[8]

Third, Ezra confessed the magnitude of the present transgression. This prayer was intended for the ears of the spectators. It was a kind of sermon prayer. The confession is couched in first person (*"we"*). Great intercessors include themselves among the sinners for whom they pray. Several reasons are given as to why the intermingling with heathen peoples was such a horrendous sin.

1. Separation from the peoples of the land was commanded by God (9:10). The violation of any divine commandment is a serious matter.

2. The commandment in question was ancient (cf. Deut 7:3). It had been given before Israel ever entered Canaan (9:11).

3. The commandment had been repeated by various prophets through the ages. Thus no one could plead ignorance (9:11).

4. The commandment had been explained. God is not required to explain his commands (9:11). When he does, however, no one could plead that his directives were arbitrary or inappropriate. The words *"unclean," "uncleanness," "abominations"* and *"impurity"* describe pagan worship and those associated with it.

5. The commandment was specific (9:12a). Israelites were not to give their daughters to pagan men, nor take pagan wives for their sons. They were not to seek the peace and prosperity of the heathen in the land, i.e., they were not to have any sort of business agreement with them.

6. The commandment was accompanied by a promise and an implied threat (9:12b). By remaining separate from the heathen, Israel would be strong. God's people would continue to enjoy the land their God had given them. They would be able to leave that land to their offspring. The implication here (clearly stated in other passages) is that if they intermingled with the heathen they would lose the land. That, of course, is exactly what had happened in 586 BC.

7. The commandment had been broken in spite of the fact that this people already had been punished once for this same transgression (9:13a).

8. The commandment had been broken in spite of all the grace that God had recently shown them (9:13b). God had requited his people less than their past iniquities deserved. He had given his people *"an escaped remnant"* (NASB).

9. The violation of the commandment placed the remnant in jeopardy of total extinction (9:14).

Fourth, Ezra concluded the prayer with an acknowledgment of the righteousness of God. The remnant stood guilty before him. The righteous judgment of God would result in the total destruction of the remnant (9:15). Ezra did not ask for forgiveness. He knew that repentance which manifests itself in the removal of the sin is required before divine forgiveness can be requested.

C. Initial Steps (Ezra 10:1-8).

Ezra's actions and prayer before the house of God attracted a large crowd of men, women and children. His tears were contagious. Soon the crowd was weeping along with their leader. Finally Sechaniah[9] could stand it no longer. He publicly admitted the fact that sin had been committed through the marriages to foreign wives. Yet, in spite of this, he voiced his opinion that there was still hope. He had a plan by which he believed that the sin could be removed from the land thus making possible divine forgiveness (10:1-2).

Shecaniah's plan was bold. All of those present should make a covenant to put away their foreign wives and the children born of them. This should be carried out according to the counsel of Ezra (*"my lord"*) and *"those who tremble at the command of our God,"* i.e., those who were truly concerned over the issue. The wives should be put away legally (cf. Deut 24:1). If sending away the children seems unduly harsh, these facts must be kept in mind. First, the major problem being addressed was the religious influence of the mothers on their children. Second, sending away the children with their mothers was less cruel than forcibly separating them from their children. Third, keeping the religion of the Lord pure was the one and only aim of Ezra. Fourth, only by insulating themselves from the sea of pagan influence around them could the religious identity of God's people be maintained (10:3).

Shecaniah urged the emotionally distraught Ezra to take the lead for this was his responsibility. Shecaniah, however, promised that those present would back him. In addition he encouraged Ezra in this difficult assignment with the words *"be courageous and act"* (10:4).

To place the actions in Ezra 10 in proper perspective, several factors must be understood. First, the marriages here dissolved were illegal in the first place. Sending away the foreign wives signaled willingness to cease perpetuating an illegal act. Second, divorce was permitted in Israel, though not without some serious cause (Deut 24:1). Third, Moses permitted divorce and remarriage because of *"the hardness of heart"* of the men of Israel (Mark 10:5). Fourth, a number of Jewish wives had been divorced for no good reason in order that these heathen women might be married (Mal 2:10-16). Fifth, God hates divorce (Mal 2:16) because of what it does to individuals, families, and his cause in this world. Sixth, the situation described in Ezra 10 was one in which the lesser of two evils (divorce) had to be chosen. Seventh, "If a serious reason for divorce could ever exist, this had a better claim than most to come within that category."[10] Eighth, the problem of intermarriage with unbelievers is handled differently under the New Covenant than it was under the Old (cf. 1 Cor 7:12-14,16).

For a leader of the local community to speak up was all that Ezra needed. He immediately secured an oath from the leading priests, Levites and laymen that they would carry out the proposal of Shecaniah. Ezra then retired to one of the temple chambers to continue his prayer and fasting over the unfaithfulness of the exiles. Those who took the oath sent out a proclamation throughout Judea that all of the exiles should assemble at Jerusalem within three days. Anyone who failed to appear forfeited his possessions and his position as a member of the assembly of exiles (10:5-8).[11]

D. Actions of the Assembly (Ezra 10:9-15).

The proclamation got results. In the ninth month (December) the family heads in the regions of Judah and Benjamin appeared in Jerusalem within three days. They all sat in the open square before the house of God (i.e., in the great court).[12] As they waited for Ezra to address them, they were trembling because of (1) this matter, i.e., the potential consequences of their intermarriages; and (2) the heavy winter rain (10:9).

Finally the scribe stood up. The inclement weather prohibited a long speech. In a few carefully crafted sentences Ezra exposed the guilt of those people. He accused the assembly of being unfaithful to God because they had married foreign wives. While it is true only a fraction of those present had actually committed this trespass, the others were guilty for having tolerated it. Ezra urged the assembly to *"make confession"* to the Lord, then to separate themselves from the peoples of the land including their foreign wives (10:10-11).

A loud chorus of voices from the assembly agreed with Ezra on the action which needed to be taken. They pointed out, however, that the problem was more widespread than Ezra might realize. More than a couple of days would be needed to deal with the problem. The assembly was too large to move indoors, and the wintry rain made standing in the open square unbearable (10:12-13).

A motion was made that the sensitive issue of the foreign wives be handled by a committee of leaders. By appointment those from a given village would be required to appear before this tribunal. The testimony of the accused and the elders and judges of his village could then be heard and evaluated. The tribunal would continue to function until all alleged violations of the law had been investigated and resolved. Then the anger of God could be turned away from the postexilic community. This motion won overwhelming support of the assembly with only two negative votes. Two Levites, apparently not voting members of the assembly, supported the two men who were in opposition (10:14-15).[13]

E. The Marriage Tribunal (Ezra 10:16-17).

Ezra appointed a blue ribbon committee consisting of the heads of father's households. The group began to meet on the first day of the tenth month a bit over a week after the assembly had authorized this approach. Seventy-five days were required to make the fair investigation of all cases where men had married foreign wives. The point at issue in each case was whether or not the wife genuinely had converted to the worship of the Lord. If so, the marriage was valid; if not the marriage had to be dissolved. Less than one case per day resulted in a divorce.

The marriage tribunal found 113 cases where foreign wives had been married. Of these, seventeen cases were among priests and ten among Levites and other temple personnel. These pledged themselves (lit. "they gave their hands") to put away their wives. They offered a ram of the flock for their offense. The families affected by these actions were a small percentage of the entire population.[14] What is more alarming, however, is that some 25% of those guilty were religious leaders. Ezra could see where this trend would lead if left unchecked.

F. The Families Affected (Ezra 10:18-44).

The Book of Ezra concludes with the listing of the names of those who had married foreign wives. Nine of the thirty-three families and town groups which appeared in 2:3-35 are represented here, and two new families appear which were not in the earlier list.[15] The names of priests who had married foreign wives are given first. These priests pledged to send their illegal wives away. Each offered a ram as a guilt offering. As religious leaders the priests were setting an example for the others who were guilty.

Perhaps the author means to attach infamy to the names of those who had married foreign wives. On the other hand, he may mean to commend them for choosing to follow the difficult path of separation rather than surrender their position among God's people. In any case, the separations ordered by the marriage tribunal must have been painful, especially since in some cases children were also involved. One can assume that the court did everything in its power to see that suitable material support was provided for the women who were put away (10:18-44).

THE FAILURE OF EZRA
Ezra 4:8-23

In Ezra 4 the author gathered examples of opposition to the pos-texilic community from several different periods. One of those efforts seems to have involved Ezra.

A. The Official Complaint (Ezra 4:8-16).
A letter in the official Aramaic language was sent to Artaxerxes by Rehum *"the commander"* and Shimshai the scribe. Several groups of lesser leaders joined in support of this official complaint. These men were foreigners—Elamites, Babylonians, et al.)—who had been settled in the Trans-Euphrates province, i.e., west of the Euphrates River, by the great Osnappar, i.e., Ashurbanipal who ruled 669-626 BC (4:7-10).

The letter documents how a group of Jews had come to Jerusalem with the permission of Artaxerxes. These Jews were *"rebuilding the rebellious and evil city"* and were *"finishing the walls."* The word *"rebellious"* was an explosive word in this period, since the Persian kings were facing rebellions from one end of their empire to the other. The only group of Jews known to have come to Jerusalem with the permission of Artaxerxes was that group led by Ezra in 458 BC. Apparently this group had attempted to rebuild the walls of Jerusalem. Since they had no royal building permit, the effort was legally vulnerable. The peoples of the land were swift to exploit that vulnerability (4:11-12).

The letter charged that should the Jews succeed in their building efforts, they would declare their independence and refuse to pay taxes. The Samaritans supported their accusation with two considera-tions. First, those writing the letter *"were in the service of the king,"* (lit., "eat the salt of the palace"). They had only the best interest of Artaxerxes at heart. Second, the royal records indicated that the Jews had a history of rebellion against their foreign masters. Indeed, the city was presently in ruins because of such a rebellion. The letter con-cluded with an exaggeration. Should the construction work at Jerusalem go unchecked, the king would lose the entire Trans-Euphrates province. The insinuation is that the Jerusalem rebellion would spread through the entire province, or more preposterous, that the Jews would attempt to take over the Trans-Euphrates province (4:13-16).

B. The Official Response (Ezra 4:17-23).

In his response to the letter, Artaxerxes indicated that he had ordered a search of the royal archives. The records indicated that indeed the accusation was justified. The city in the past had a reputation for rebellion and revolt against foreign kings who tried to impose taxes on the area. For this reason, Artaxerxes directed his local representative in Samaria to issue a decree ordering the reconstruction of Jerusalem to cease until *"a decree is made by me."* This left open the possibility of a policy review at some future date. That was the possibility that Nehemiah would exploit some thirteen years later when he secured permission from this same king to return and build the walls. The king concluded his letter with a warning that his representatives in the region should not be negligent in carrying out this edict (4:17-22).

Rehum the commander and Shimshai the scribe lost no time in implementing the decree of Artaxerxes. Along with their supporters, they went to Jerusalem and stopped the rebuilding of the walls by force of arms (4:23). Rehum and his men actually went beyond the terms of this decree by demolishing and burning what had already been constructed (Neh 1:3).

ENDNOTES

1. The *"seven counselors"* of the king (Ezra 7:14) are probably members of the same group referred to in Esther 1:14—a cabinet composed of the princes of the realm. According to Xenophon (*Anabasis* 1.6.4-5), Cyrus had seven counselors.

2. The punishments were not derived from the law of God, although some of them are mentioned in the Pentateuch. These laws are state penalties. *"Banishment"* (NASB) is better understood as corporal or physical punishment. See C. Charles Fensham, *The Books of Ezra and Nehemiah* in "The New International Commentary on the Old Testament" Grand Rapids: Eerdmans, 1982), p. 108.

3. The quantities are calculated by J.M. Myers, *Ezra. Nehemiah* in "The Anchor Bible" (Garden City: Doubleday, 1965), p. 59.

4. This Persian tax exemption for Jewish clergy is paralleled by the Gadatas Inscription of Darius which prescribed tax exemption for the priests of Apollo. See Myers, *op. cit.,* p. 63.

5. The group left Babylon on the first day of the first month (7:9). They left Ahava on the twelfth day of the first month (8:31) after a stay of three days (8:15). Therefore, the trip from Babylon to the river Ahava must have taken about nine days. The location of the river Ahava is unknown.

6. The reason for the number seventy-seven lambs is not clear. Possibly 1 Esdras 8:66 is right with "seventy-two," another multiple of twelve. Others have speculated that seventy-seven was a perfect number in Hebrew numerology. In the Ugaritic language the numbers seventy and seventy-seven were used as a literary device to denote a fairly large number. See Fensham, *op. cit., p.* 122.

7. A more common explanation is that the term *"tent peg"* might be equivalent to the modern expression "foothold." Fensham (*op. cit.,* p. 129) comments: "This is language from nomadic life, and it refers to a place reached after a long journey where a tent may be pitched."

8. The term *"wall"* (*gader*) is not used for a city wall, but for an enclosure of a vineyard. The phrase *"in Judah and Jerusalem"* also is a clue that no literal wall is intended. It would be impossible to build a wall around Judah. Thus the *"wall"* mentioned in 9:9 does not refer to the wall of the city of Jerusalem which had not yet been built.

9. Because at least six other men named Shecaniah appear in Ezra-Nehemiah, it is impossible to identify this leader with certainty. Fensham, *op. cit., p.* 134.

10. Kidner, *op. cit.,* p. 71.

11. The most distant Jewish village in the province would have been no farther than forty miles.

12. An ancient authority states that the great court was 500 x 150 feet. Luck estimates that as many as 20,000 people could have assembled in that court. *Ezra and Nehemiah* (Chicago: Moody, 1961), p. 70.

13. Another view is that the four were opposed to the delay in dealing with the problem.

14. Eighty years earlier the assembly had numbered 42,360 (Ezra 2:64). Whether the membership of the assembly had increased or decreased during the eighty years is impossible to determine. If the figure remained somewhat constant, then those who intermarried would have been less than one percent of the total.

15. The two new families are a second Bani family (v. 34) and that of Binnui (v. 38).

CHAPTER FORTY-THREE

Rebuilding the City
Nehemiah 1-6

The people of God had been restored to their land in 538 BC under the leadership of Zerubbabel (Sheshbazzar). The temple had been rebuilt in 515 BC. The threat of the annihilation of the Jews was defeated by the work of Esther and Mordecai in 474-473 BC. Ezra had returned in 458 BC to restore the law to its rightful place among the people of God. Yet to be restored was Jerusalem, the holy city.

THE COMMISSION OF NEHEMIAH
Nehemiah 1:1-2:9

Just as Esther was providentially placed in the harem of King Xerxes, so Nehemiah also found himself in a position to help his people in a new crisis.

A. Nehemiah's Grief (Neh 1:1-4).

In the month of Chislev of the twentieth year of Artaxerxes

(Nov./Dec. 446 BC)[1] a delegation of Jews arrived in Susa the Persian capital. One of these men was Hanani, the brother (or kinsman) of Nehemiah the cupbearer to the king. The uppermost question in the mind of Nehemiah concerned the welfare of the Jews of the postexilic community. The news was not good. The remnant was in great distress and reproach as a result of the fact that the wall of Jerusalem was broken down, the gates burned with fire (1:1-3).

The description most likely refers to conditions following the time a few years earlier when Rehum went to Jerusalem and by force made the Jews stop rebuilding their walls (Ezra 4:23). A city without a wall was an open shame, not to mention dangerous place to live. Nehemiah was grief-stricken over this news. He fasted and mourned for days (1:4).

B. Nehemiah's Prayer (Neh 1:5-11).

Some nine prayers are attributed to Nehemiah. The prayer in chapter 1 is the longest in the book. It is directed to *"Yahweh God of heaven."* To Nehemiah Yahweh was *"the great and awesome God."* He faithfully kept his covenant with *"those who love him and keep his commandments."* Correct theology inspires bold petition. Nehemiah knew his God was great. He therefore was not afraid to make of him a bold request (1:5).

After the address, the prayer proceeds to confession. The great intercessor included himself among the sinful people for whom he prayed. He confessed that the sons of Israel had acted very corruptly against God. They had disregarded the divine commandments of the law of Moses (1:6-7).

Nehemiah next asked the Lord to remember the word he had revealed through Moses. Yahweh had threatened to scatter Israel among the people of the earth if they were unfaithful to his word. He had also promised that he would gather those who repented in those distant lands and bring them back to that land where he had chosen to reveal himself (*"cause my name to dwell"*). Those who returned to the Lord were truly his people, his servants, whom God had redeemed by his *"strong arm."* Thus God had shown his favor towards his people. Now Nehemiah was about to make a request which would ultimately benefit those same people (1:8-10).

Nehemiah asked God to be attentive to his prayer and the prayers of other faithful servants who were lifting up the postexilic community before the throne of grace. In particular, Nehemiah asked that he might be successful and find favor before "this man" (1:11a).

Not until this point in the book does Nehemiah identify himself and the king he served. He was a cupbearer to King Artaxerxes. His basic duty was to sample the wine served to the king to make sure it had not been poisoned. The position gave him frequent access to the king and made him potentially a man of great influence (1:11b).

C. Nehemiah's Appointment (Neh 2:1-8).

In the month of Nisan of the twentieth year of Artaxerxes (Mar./Apr. 445 BC), about four months after news arrived from Jerusalem, Nehemiah was scheduled for his duties in the palace. This was his opportunity. Yet Nehemiah's life was also in jeopardy because Persian kings never allowed sadness in their presence.[2] Artaxerxes soon noticed that his cupbearer was exhibiting a sadness of heart unrelated to health. Nehemiah was justifiably afraid when the king inquired about his disposition. Court etiquette would be offended if one who enjoyed the king's presence were to ask leave to depart to another place (2:1-2).

Nehemiah made no effort to evade the king's question. He told Artaxerxes that his sadness was justifiable in view of the desolate condition of Jerusalem, "the place of my fathers' tombs." The reference to the tomb was a stroke of genius. Persians were paranoid about respect for the dead and proper burial. The phrase evoked immediate sympathy from this monarch who only a few years before had order the work of rebuilding Jerusalem to cease (2:3).

In a masterpiece of diplomacy, Nehemiah avoided mentioning the word Jerusalem. That name would have reminded the king of his earlier investigation regarding the history of that city (cf. Ezra 4:8-23). Eventually, of course, the king would have ascertained the name of the city. At the outset of the negotiations, however, expediency dictated that Nehemiah not mention the name of the place.

Nehemiah had already anticipated the next question of the king, "What would you request?" He had prayed long about how he might answer that question. He requested permission to go to Judah to rebuild *"the city of my fathers' tombs."* Again the king was moved by the concern of this man for the graves of his ancestors. Artaxerxes was perfectly willing to allow Nehemiah to return to his native land. Only details regarding his time of absence from the royal court needed to be worked out.[3] The *"good hand of God"* was truly upon Nehemiah. The mention of the queen being with the king suggests (1) this was a private occasion; and (2) that she may have interceded on Nehemiah's behalf (2:4-6).

Nehemiah continued to press for concessions. He asked for passport letters which would allow him to travel without provincial interference en route to Judah. He further requested a letter to the overseer of the king's forests in the region (probably in Lebanon) authorizing a grant of timber to be used in reconstructing the gates of the city. Again the king acceded (2:7-8).

THE BEGINNING OF THE WORK
Nehemiah 2:9-3:32

The powerful leadership qualities of Nehemiah stand out in the account of how he motivated the Jews to rebuild their walls, and then organized them for this project.

A. Arrival in Jerusalem (Neh 2:9-20).

Nehemiah was accompanied by an armed Persian military escort during his journey. Not only did this provide protection, it guaranteed that Nehemiah would arrive in style. It would also render credibility to his authority and underscore the change in royal policy.

Along the way Nehemiah presented the king's letters to the various governors of the Trans-Euphrates province. Among those governors were Sanballat the Horonite[4] and Tobiah the Ammonite.[5] Tobiah was a Jew who occupied the position of *"king's servant"* in the region of Ammon. The two officials were very displeased that anyone had come to seek the welfare of the sons of Israel (2:9-10).

Upon arriving in Jerusalem, Nehemiah rested three days. Then by night he, and a few trusted associates, made a night time circuit of the walls in order to assess their condition. At one point he found it impossible for his mount to pass. The obstruction may have been the huge spill of rubble left from Nebuchadnezzar's assault 140 years earlier.[6] Nehemiah told none of the local leaders what he was doing. Apparently he did not wish to reveal his intentions until he had formulated a plan by which his mission could be concluded successfully (2:11-16).

When he had a clear concept of how the task should be approached, Nehemiah assembled the leaders of the community. First, he called attention to the obvious. Jerusalem was *"desolate,"* i.e., without walls or gates. The eyes of a stranger may see more clearly what has been made obscure by familiarity. Second, he urged them to rebuild the wall so that God's people would no longer be a reproach among the nations. Third, he encouraged them by testifying how God and King Artaxerxes had been favorably disposed to him (2:17-18a).

Nehemiah must have been a powerful motivator. The people responded, *"Let us arise and build."* The work began immediately: *"They put their hands to the good work."* Sanballat and Tobiah were joined by Geshem the Arab[7] in mocking the initial efforts (2:18b-19).

In his response to this mockery, Nehemiah did not mention his authority from the king. The enemies already knew about that. He cited higher authority, *viz., "the God of heaven."* He identified the Israelites as servants of this God. He calmly reaffirmed the intentions of the Jews to rebuild. They did not need nor want the help of these powerful officials. These antagonists had no *"portion, right, or memorial"* in Jerusalem, i.e., they had no past, present or future with the people of God.[8] These remarks had important legal ramifications. Jerusalem was the city of the Jews and the enemies had no legal authority over it (2:20).

B. Organization of the Effort (Neh 3:1-32).

Nehemiah's plan was for the entire wall to go up simultaneously. He assigned each of some forty segments of the wall to a group of builders. The list is full of heterogeneous groups working side by side for the common good of the community: families, communities, crafts (e.g., goldsmiths, and the perfumer in v. 8), and trades (merchants in v. 31). Nehemiah 3 contains another one of those honor rolls of faith which are characteristic of the postexilic literature. A few notes on this chapter are appropriate.

1. Ten gates of the city are here mentioned. The story of the wall building centers around them. In Nehemiah 12:39 two other gates are mentioned which apparently were not in need of repair. Old Jerusalem, then, had twelve gates. So also does the New Jerusalem of Revelation 21:12.

2. Among the workers was Eliashib the high priest. He led the other priests in rebuilding the Sheep Gate. Since this area of the wall was near the temple, the priests consecrated this wall (3:1).

3. Not everyone in the area supported Nehemiah's effort. The citizens of the village of Tekoa worked in the area of the Fish Gate. *"Their nobles,"* however, did not *"support"* (lit., bring their neck to) the work.

4. Women may have taken an active part in the construction. One segment of the wall was repaired by *"Shallum...and his daughters"* (3:12).

5. One worker is singled out for special commendation. Baruch *"zealously repaired"* one segment of the wall (3:20).

6. Seven work groups did double duty (vv. 11, 19-21, 24, 27, 30). Thank God for those blessed souls who do more than their share of kingdom work!

HINDRANCES WITHOUT
Nehemiah 4:1-23

As they saw the work going forward, the enemies of the Jews launched an attack to intimidate the workers.

A. Opposition by Mockery (Neh 4:1-6).

Sanballat became furious when he heard that the Jews were rebuilding the wall. Before some formal assembly of the wealthy citizens of Samaria he launched a propaganda campaign against the Jews. He used five rhetorical questions to demean the workers and question their perseverance. Tobiah spoke up to mock the quality of the work. A fox could break through their wall by merely leaping on it. Some wall! (4:1-3).

Nehemiah responded to the mockery with prayer. Undergirding the prayer is the proposition that the work being done was of God. To oppose the work, therefore, was to oppose God. Nehemiah asked that God might take their reproach and hurl it back upon the heads of the mockers, i.e., bring upon them what they had wished for the Jews. He prayed that the enemies might be removed from their land, that they might lose their wealth and their freedom. He requested the Lord not to forgive, i.e., ignore, the sins of the enemies in deriding the work of God. "The prayer was thus not vindictive because the Jews were insulted, but because God's work was ridiculed" (4:4-5).[9]

Even as the Samaritan enemies mocked, the work on the wall was progressing. Soon the walls had reached half their height. Rather than completing a number of separate sections in succession, priority was given to closing the ring at however modest a level. The progress in spite of opposition is explained by the fact that *the people had a mind to work,*" lit., "the heart of the people was to do the work" (4:6).

B. Threat of Open Attack (Neh 4:7-9).

The ranks of the enemies began to swell. Arabs from the south, Ammonites from the east, and Ashdodites from the west joined the Samaritans who lived north of Judea. God's people were encircled by enemies! The anger of these enemies increased as they witnessed the breaches of the walls being filled. A new strategy was devised to thwart the work: a swift raid which would produce disruption within the city. The builders learned of this impending attack and took appropriate precautions. First they prayed. Then they stationed a guard against such an attack night and day. Here again is the partnership between heaven and earth so evident throughout the Book of Nehemiah.

C. Discouragement of the Workers (Neh 4:10).

The Jewish work force was particularly vulnerable at this point. Because of all the debris which had to be removed and the diminished work force now that some were posted on guard duty, the strength of the burden bearers was waning. Soon everyone in Judah was repeating a couplet which reflected their doubts about the viability of the project (4:10). These were not the last builders of Zion to discover that the removal of rubbish (man-made traditions) is a necessary but discouraging work.

D. Threat of Sneak Attack (Neh 4:11-23).

The Jews who lived near the enemies heard the rumors of a massive, all-out attack. Whether they were unwitting purveyors of propaganda or useful informants is difficult to determine. They kept on warning the builders (*"ten times"*) that this attack would come from all directions. Such a prospect generated fear in Jerusalem. Nehemiah stationed guards in high spots where they could easily be seen over the low walls. This was counter intimidation. He armed all the workers and placed them with their family groups where they would have the greatest incentive to fight manfully. When he saw their fear, Nehemiah reminded the builders that God *"is great and awesome"* (4:11-14).

The Samaritans backed off when they realized the Jews were prepared for an attack. The Jews then returned to the work, but extra precautions were taken. First, Nehemiah had half of his own personal servants and bodyguards assist with the work. The other half he had ready with weapons to rush to any point where attack threatened. His servants had at their disposal swords, spears and bows which were accurate up to 300 yards.[10] Shields and breastplates are also mentioned. They were well armed! Second, the rulers remained behind the workers, both directing and encouraging them. Third, those with the job of loading and carrying materials handled them with one hand, and kept a sword in the other. Fourth, those who had to use both hands in building kept their swords at their sides. Fifth, a trumpeter stood near Nehemiah who could signal the workers where to rally in case of attack. Sixth, Nehemiah kept encouraging his subordinates with assurances that God would fight for them in any showdown with the Samaritans (4:15-20).

By taking these precautions Nehemiah thwarted the sneak attack planned by the enemy. Half of his men were on guard throughout the day. At night he encouraged his men to remain within the city. Throughout this period of danger no man removed *"his clothes,"* i.e., his military gear. Even during water breaks each man carried his weapon (4:21-23).

HINDRANCES WITHIN
Nehemiah 5:1-19

While Nehemiah dealt with a determined foe without, at the same time he had internal problems which threatened to hinder progress on the walls. Already he has mentioned the debris which was causing discouragement (cf. 4:10). Now he alludes to a serious dissension that arose among the workers.

A. The Source of the Problem (Neh 5:1-5).

Some of the Jews—especially the farmers—were poverty stricken, and their economic condition was being exploited by their brothers (5:1).

The poor families cited three reasons for their destitute condition. First, they had big families and they could not produce enough to feed their families. They, therefore, had to buy grain, and for that they had no money. Second, to secure money to buy grain they had to mortgage their real estate—fields, vineyards, even their houses. Third, the farmers had to borrow money to pay the royal tax on their estates. Perhaps these conditions had even been exacerbated by the concentrated work on the walls which pulled laborers away from their normal pursuits. Beneath the surface the cry of the populace seems to have been that the personal cost of the wall building effort was too high (5:2-4).

The destitute condition of some families had led to three unfortunate results. First, poverty stricken families were being forced to sell their sons and daughters into debtors' servitude (cf. Exod 21:1-11). Second, some of their daughters had been forced into *"bondage"* (NASB), i.e., the humiliation of undesirable marriages. Third, many of the people felt *"helpless"* (lit., "there is no power for our hands") because their property was now owned by others (5:5).

B. The Solution to the Problem (Neh 5:6-13).

Nehemiah was filled with righteous indignation when he heard the complaints of these destitute Jews. The governor met with the wealthy land owners. He accused them of violating the law of Moses (Lev 25:35-37) by exacting usury from their brothers. The lenders were acting like harsh pawnbrokers, not compassionate brothers. The depth of the poverty called for gifts, not loans. When private rebuke failed to solve the problem, Nehemiah called for a great assembly to deal with the guilty nobles (5:6-7).

Nehemiah pointed out to the assembly that efforts had been made to redeem Jewish brothers from debtors' servitude to foreign peoples. Now, however, the nobles were putting their brothers back into economic bondage. To this accusation the nobles had no reply. Nehemiah bluntly stated that what the nobles were doing was not good. In these times when God's people were a reproach among the nations, all Jews should *"walk in the fear of the Lord,"* i.e., observe the law of God (5:8-9). The law required the release of debtor slaves after six years (cf. Exod 21:2).

Nehemiah admitted that he and his associates had been guilty of lending the poor money and grain. Thus he himself had contributed to the dissatisfaction among the farmers. He pled with the nobles to join with him in (1) absolving the loans to the poor; (2) returning properties which had been seized for failure of payment; and (3) refunding *"the hundredth part of the money,"* i.e., the one percent per month charge on the unpaid balance.[11] These actions would in effect cancel the debts (5:10-11).

The nobles agreed to give back property and cancel existing debt. Nehemiah moved immediately to upgrade the commitment from promise to oath. He summoned priests and extracted an oath from these nobles that they would keep their promise. Nehemiah shook out his garment as a symbolic gesture to underscore the penalty which would befall those who reneged on the oath. The folds of garments were like pockets in which personal possessions were kept. Nehemiah emptied the pockets before the people, shaking out everything. This was symbolic of a curse. God would shake them out of their possessions if they broke their word.[12] All the assembly shouted *"Amen"* in agreement with the actions of Nehemiah and the oath of the nobles. The assembly praised the Lord. Then the people did as they had promised (5:12-13).

C. The Example of Nehemiah (Neh 5:14-19).

Nehemiah's work in Jerusalem was a labor of love. During his twelve-year tenure (445-432 BC), neither he nor his kinsmen ever ate the governor's food allowance. Former governors laid a burden on the people, requiring of them bread, wine and forty shekels of silver for food allowance. Because he feared Yahweh, Nehemiah refrained from enforcing these regulations. Furthermore, both he and his servants had worked on the wall alongside the citizens. Nor did Nehemiah use his considerable wealth to buy up land around Jerusalem. The governor fed at his table and personal expense 150 Jews and officials, not to mention *"those who came to us from the nations that were around us."* Every day an enormous quantity of food was consumed at the governor's house—an ox, six sheep, birds, wine. Yet because the servitude was heavy upon the people he did not demand the food allowance to which he was entitled (5:14-18).

In all of this Nehemiah sought the praise of God rather than man. He prayed that God would remember all the good which he had done for this people. Thus Nehemiah's actions were religiously motivated, and were not done for purely humanitarian reasons (5:19).

ATTACKS ON THE LEADER
Nehemiah 6:1-14, 17-19

The walls were now up. Only the doors of the gates remained to be set in place. Those open gateways were the enemy's last hope of regaining the upper hand without actually mounting a siege, which would be out of the question against fellow subjects of Persia. Having failed to intimidate the workers, Sanballat and Geshem now changed their tactics. Their strategy now became to eliminate Nehemiah.

A. The Lure of Compromise (Neh 6:1-4).

The enemies sent a message to Nehemiah inviting him to meet with them at Chephirim in the plain of Ono, twenty-seven miles northwest of Jerusalem and an equal distance from Samaria. This plain was outside Jewish territory.

Sanballat's plan was transparent. The plain of Ono bordered on the districts of both Samaria and Ashdod. Since both of these were hostile regions, the plan reeked of treachery. Nehemiah therefore sent word back to them that he could not come down to Ono because *"I am doing a great work."* A trip to Ono would only interrupt the work in Jerusalem. Several precious days would be wasted. So *"why should the work stop?"* Four times the invitations came to Nehemiah, and four times Nehemiah answered them in the same manner.

B. Malicious Slander (6:5-9).

Sanballat sent his messenger to Nehemiah a fifth time with an open letter. The letter reported a rumor circulating among surrounding nations, a rumor which was validated by Gashmu (Geshem the Arab). The rumor was that Nehemiah wanted to be king of the Jews, and that he would lead a rebellion against the Persians when the walls were rebuilt. Supposedly Nehemiah had authorized prophets to proclaim his kingship in Judea. Sanballat stated that he felt it his duty to inform the king of Persia about this, but wished first to confer with Nehemiah to hear his side of the matter (6:5-7).

Again the malicious intentions of Sanballat were transparent. First, he sent an *"open"* letter, one that could be read by anyone along the way. Normally the correspondence between two governors would be sealed. Second, he insisted that Nehemiah meet with him. Had he really believed that Nehemiah was involved in a rebellion against the Persians, he would never have wanted to be associated with him in any manner.

Nehemiah replied to the slander of Sanballat by simply denying that it was true. First, he exposed the source of the rumors. These rumors were only fabrications of Sanballat's mind. Second, Nehemiah exposed the real motives for such lies. The Samaritans were merely trying to frighten and discourage the wall builders. Their ultimate goal was to stop the work. Faced with this new threat, Nehemiah went again to God in prayer: *"Strengthen my hands,"* he prayed (6:8-9).

C. False Prophecy (Neh 6:10-14).

A man of God respects the word of God. Perhaps, the enemies thought, Nehemiah could be goaded into making a wrong move by the word of a prophet. So now the enemies attempted to use Nehemiah's own people against him. Obviously not all the Jews backed the wall project. Prophets, male and female, were hired to predict that Nehemiah was about to be the victim of a night time assassination. Nehemiah first heard this prediction in the house of Shemaiah who for some unexplained reason was confined at home. Perhaps his confinement was self-imposed as a kind of symbolic action to dramatize the need for precautions against the supposed assassins. Shemaiah hoped that Nehemiah's visit would be noticed by his coworkers and construed as a search for guidance and a sign of uncertainty.

Having secured his audience with Nehemiah, the prophet presented his proposal in poetic verse, a fact recognized in the Jerusalem Bible translation. Shemaiah wanted the form of his message to be as compelling as its content. He advised Nehemiah to flee behind the walls of the temple for protection. The intention here was to discredit Nehemiah in the eyes of his followers as a terrified leader who urged boldness in others while he took every precaution to save his own life. On the other hand, the intention may have been to lure this layman— and possible eunuch—into an area where only priests were permitted to go.[13] This would cause Nehemiah to lose the support of the priesthood and others who strictly followed the law of God. He might even be killed by his own people for desecrating the temple (6:10).

Nehemiah perceived immediately that God had not sent this message. The Lord never encourages cowardly acts. He reasoned that Shemaiah must be the hireling of Tobiah and Sanballat. (Tobiah was named first because he was the main instigator of this plan.) He realized that the enemies were only trying to maneuver him into a wrong move so that they might *"reproach"* him. Nehemiah prayed that God might remember in judgment these actions of Sanballat and Tobiah as well as those of Noadiah the prophetess and the others who had sold out to the enemy (6:11-14).

D. Threatening Letters (Neh 6:17-19).

During the course of the wall building effort many letters were exchanged between the nobles in Jerusalem and Tobiah the Jewish leader of Ammon. Tobiah was related by marriage to one of the leading families in Jerusalem. Several of the nobles within the city had pledged on oath their loyalty to Tobiah. These oaths were probably trading contracts. They constantly spoke of Tobiah's good deeds before Nehemiah. At the same time, these nobles were a pipeline of information to the enemies concerning every plan and action of Nehemiah. As part of the campaign to discourage and discredit Nehemiah, threatening letters were sent to him from time to time by Tobiah. Working around these fifth columnists within the community must have been very difficult for Nehemiah.

THE SUCCESS OF THE WORK
Nehemiah 6:15-16

After fifty-two hectic days, on the 25th day of Elul (Oct. 2, 445 BC) the wall was completed. Thus within ten months after he had heard of the plight of Jerusalem, Nehemiah had finished his commission to rebuild the wall (6:15). The speed with which the project was completed can be explained as a result of the following factors: (1) The people had a mind to work. (2) A large force of workmen, not only from Jerusalem, but from surrounding areas, were engaged in the task. (3) The ruins of the previous wall contained large quantities of stone which could be used in the present project. (4) God was with the workers supernaturally blessing their efforts. (5) In Nehemiah the project had a wise and energetic leader.

When the enemies saw that the wall had been completed in spite of their well orchestrated campaign to prevent it from happening, they *"lost their confidence"* (NASB), lit., "fell exceedingly in their own eyes." They no longer felt so important as they once did. They were humbled by their inability to stop the work. They recognized that the work could only have been accomplished with the help of God (6:16).

ENDNOTES

1. In the light of 2:1, one would expect the reading in 1:1 to be "nineteenth" year. Either an autumn-to-autumn reckoning of the years of Artaxerxes is being employed here, or the figure in 1:1 is the result of a scribal error. Another possibility is that "twentieth" refers, not to the regnal years of Artaxerxes, but to Nehemiah's years of service in Susa.

2. The monarchs of Persia operated on the theory that merely to be in the king's presence and enjoy his favor was sufficient to give perfect joy and happiness to the heart of any person. See G. Coleman Luck, *Ezra and*

Nehemiah (Chicago: Moody, 1961), p. 84.

3. Neh 5:14 states that Nehemiah served twelve years as governor. Most commentators assume that in this initial request a shorter period of service was mentioned. Nehemiah may have returned to Susa after the walls were completed to report to the king and to be re-commissioned.

4. In the Elephantine papyri dating some thirty-eight years after the events of Neh 2 Sanballat is named as governor of Samaria. See Pritchard, ANET, *op. cit.,* p. 492b; Thomas, DOTT, *op. cit.,* p. 264. *Horonite* is thought by some to be derived from the name of a town in Moab. Others, with more probability, trace the term to Beth-horon, a town in the in the tribal area of Ephraim which at this time was controlled by the Samaritans.

5. Tobiah is a Jewish name, not an Ammonite one. This family continued to be a powerful force in Ammon down into the third century. Some trace the hostility of Tobiah back to Ezra 2:59f. where the *"sons of Tobiah"* were not allowed to serve as priests because they could not establish their priestly pedigree. See Derek Kidner, *Ezra & Nehemiah* in "Tyndale Old Testament Commentaries" (InterVarsity, 1979), p. 82, n. 2.

6. This pile of rubble was discovered by Kenyon in 1961-63. K.M. Kenyon, *Digging up Jerusalem* (Ernest Benn, 1974), p. 18.

7. In extrabiblical sources Geshem and his son appear as rulers of a league of Arabian tribes which took control of Moab and Edom and part of Arabia in the fifth century BC. In the time of Nehemiah he may have been the commander of a band of Arab troops maintained by Sanballat.

8. Kidner, *op. cit.,* p. 84.

9. F. Charles Fensham, *The Books of Ezra and Nehemiah* in "The New International Commentary on the Old Testament" (Grand Rapids: Eerdmans, 1982), p. 182.

10. Y. Yadin as cited by Fensham, *op. cit.,* p. 186.

11. Luck, *op. cit.,* p. 102.

12. Nehemiah's action is comparable to the symbolic acts performed by prophets to announcement judgment (e.g., Jer 19:10ff.). Cf. Paul's similar gesture in Acts 18:6 and Jesus' instructions to his disciples in Matt 10:14f.

13. Fensham (*op. cit.,* 204); Kidner, *op. cit.,* p. 100.

CHAPTER FORTY-FOUR

Renewing the Commitment
Nehemiah 7-13

The building of Jerusalem's walls was the priority of Nehemiah's first months in Judea. With that task now complete, he turned to an even more formidable one, *viz.*, building a community.

PROTECTING THE CITY
Nehemiah 7:1-73

The major concerns dominating the Book of Nehemiah can be summarized in two words: community and continuity. Even while Nehemiah takes the first steps in building a community which can survive the present and live into the future, he is concerned about demonstrating that community's continuity with the past.

A. Building of Community (Neh 7:1-5).

After the wall was complete Nehemiah made various appointments of gatekeepers, singers and Levites. That the Levites are prominent in the building of the community should not be thought strange. Jerusalem was a holy city, and worship was its *raison d'être* (7:1).

Nehemiah appointed over Jerusalem his brother Hanani and Hanaiah, commander of the fortress adjoining the temple. The latter man was one local leader who could be trusted. He was *"a faithful man"* who *"feared God more than many."* Some think these appointments indicate that Nehemiah was contemplating a trip back to the Persian court to report on his progress to the king (7:2).

Precautions were to be taken to prevent infiltration of the city by the enemies during early morning or late evening darkness. The gates were to be opened late and closed early. Guards were to be stationed at each gate and at other strategic positions around the city. Residents were to be prepared to defend their own homes. Watchfulness was to be the rule of the day! (7:3-4).

Before the walls had been rebuilt few Jews had the courage to build their homes in the city limits of Jerusalem. That the population was too small to adequately defend the city on a continuing basis now became evident. Nehemiah moved decisively again. He took a census of the postexilic community. In the process he found the scroll containing the names of those who had returned to Judea back in 538 BC under Zerubbabel. He would shortly use that genealogical record to help solve the problem of the underpopulation of Jerusalem (7:5).

B. Demonstrating Continuity (Neh 7:6-73).

Nehemiah inserted a copy of this old register in the record at this point. Except for certain slight differences, the balance of Nehemiah 7 is a virtual duplicate of the list in Ezra 2. Ezra's list was prepared in Babylon. It contained a list of those who expected to return to Judea. The list given by Nehemiah contains the names of those who actually did return. This could account for the small differences between the two lists.[1] The incorporation of the list here in Nehemiah accomplishes two purposes. First, it established the city's continuity with the past. These people needed to have a sense of their inheritance and their calling. Second, it became the basis for reorganizing the population of Judea (7:5-72).

CELEBRATING THE FEAST
Nehemiah 8

The initial phase of wall building was completed on the 25th day of Elul, the sixth month (6:15). On the first day of the sacred seventh month, all those living in outlying areas gathered *"as one man"* to Jerusalem. Under the law, this day—New Years on the religious calendar—was regarded as a day of rest sacred to the Lord (cf. Lev 23:24).

A. The Law Read (Neh 8:1-12).

No mention has been made of Ezra during the days of Nehemiah's struggle to rebuild the wall.[2] For some thirteen years his godly leadership had been rejected. Now, however, the spirit of revival was sweeping over the people. They wanted to hear again the law of their God. They asked the godly old scribe to read it to them (8:1). Waiting to be asked was characteristic of the leadership style of Ezra (cf. Ezra 10:2).

What the people wanted to hear, and what Ezra presumably read to them, was ancient *("the book of the law of Moses"*) and authoritative (*"which Yahweh had commanded to Israel"*). To represent what transpired here as the earliest canonization of Scripture clearly is in error. The writings of Moses were regarded as Scripture long before Ezra read these documents to the people.

The place of assembly was the square in front of the Water Gate on the east side of the city. Unlike the earlier great assembly (Ezra 3:26), the temple court was not chosen either because it was too small, or because of the composition of the assembly. The Water Gate was one of the centers of city life. God's word cries out to be heard in the streets as well as in the sanctuaries of the land (cf. Prov 1:20f.; 8:1ff.).

The congregation consisted of men, women and *"all who could listen with understanding."* Mindless superstitution is the mark of paganism. Biblical faith requires intelligent interpretation and application of propositional truth! How much of the Pentateuch Ezra read that day is not important. What is stressed throughout the record is not the quantity of what was read, but the quality of the understanding of the auditors.

Ezra brought the scroll before the assembly and read from it from early morning until midday. He read from a platform which elevated him so that all present could see and hear. Beside him stood thirteen men, presumably leaders of the community, possibly priests. Perhaps these men assisted Ezra in the reading of the law. All the people were attentive throughout the five or six hours of reading (8:2-4).

The author delights in narrating the details of that glorious day when the people listened, for the first time in a long time, to the words of God. As Ezra opened the scroll, the people stood up as a gesture of respect for the word of the Lord. The scribe first *"blessed Yahweh."* All the people shouted a double *"Amen"* while lifting up their hands in grateful acknowledgment to the God of heaven. Then they bowed low with faces to the ground to worship the Lord. Presumably returning to a standing position, the people listened as Ezra read the Hebrew words from the scroll (8:5-6).

Thirteen Levites assisted Ezra by *"causing the people to understand the law."* Whether these men acted as translators or popular expositors is not clear.[3] G. Campbell Morgan suggested that the public reading was followed by a separation of the assembly into groups led by one of the thirteen Levites. They explained and applied the various passages which Ezra had read.[4] Merely reading the word without understanding it has no benefit for God's people (8:5-8).

The significance of this day in Jewish history should not be missed. Hereafter the Jews would be known as a people of the book. At the dedication of Solomon's temple the crowds had been overawed by the architectural beauty and supernatural glory. On this occasion attention was riveted to a man on a simple platform reading from a scroll. More specifically, attention was fixed on the words of that scroll.[5]

The people were moved to tears by the hearing of God's word. Nehemiah, Ezra and the Levites, however, kept stressing that this was a day to celebrate, not to mourn. Feasting and sharing with the less fortunate would be the appropriate way to celebrate this holy day. *"Do not be grieved, for the joy of Yahweh is your strength!"* So the people celebrated that day as a festival, not because the walls had been completed, but because they had understood the word of the Lord (8:9-12).

B. The Feast Observed (Neh 8:13-18).

On the second day the heads of families gathered to Ezra to receive further instruction from the law of God. This was a more select group than that of the previous day. In the lesson of that day they learned how they should live in booths during the feast of Tabernacles in the seventh month (8:13-14). This fresh discovery from Scripture seems to have come as a surprise to these students. This feast had been celebrated by the pioneer returnees some nine decades earlier (cf. Ezra 3:4). It seems, however, that the aspect of the feast which commemorated the wilderness wandering had been disregarded or at least reduced to tokenism.[6]

A proclamation was circulated instructing the people to go to the nearby hills and cut tree branches to make their booths according to the law. Since the feast did not begin until the fifteenth day of the month, the people had nearly two weeks in which to make their preparations (8:15).

The people complied with the directive of their leaders with enthusiasm. They brought their tree branches to Jerusalem, the proper place for the observance of the feast (cf. Deut 31:11). They erected their booths in every open place, public and private, which they could find. Some even put their booths on the flat roofs of their homes! The entire assembly lived in booths for the seven days of the feast. Not since the days of Joshua had the feast of Tabernacles been so universally and enthusiastically observed. Great rejoicing filled the land (8:16-17).

Each day of the week-long festival Ezra read to the people from the scroll of the law. He thus followed precisely the stipulations of Deuteronomy 31:11.[7]

CONFESSING TRANSGRESSION
Nehemiah 9:1-37

Fasting, repentence and confession precede forgiveness and reinstatement for God's people. The joyous festivity of Tabernacles celebration began on the eighth day to move in this direction (cf. Lev 23:27; Num 29:35).

A. Day of Fasting (Neh 9:1-4).

The day after the feast of Tabernacles was a day of fasting. The worshipers wore sackcloth, a coarse rough material made of goat's hair. The wearing of this garb symbolized mourning. Their heads were darkened by the dirt which they had thrown over themselves. The purpose of the assembly was to make a corporate confession of sin and formally pledge to separate themselves from all foreigners. The repeated readings from the law were bearing fruit! That this group confessed the sins of their ancestors as well as their own, is striking. They felt their solidarity with previous generations (9:1-2).

The format of the assembly was simple. The people stood while "*they*" (priests and/or Levites) read from the book of the law for a fourth of the day, i.e. about three hours. For an equal amount of time penitents "*confessed and worshiped*" God. Eight Levites then led the people in voicing their spiritual distress. A second group of eight Levites led a responsive prayer of praise.[8] Apparently they all recited the prayer in unison, so it must have been written beforehand. Since the language is similar to the prayer in Ezra 9, the great scribe and priest was most likely the author of the prayer (9:3-4).

B. Confession of Faith (Neh 9:5-15).

The Levites' prayer is one of the longest in the Bible. It begins with a confession of God's greatness—his glorious name, his creative works, his covenant with Abraham, and his gift of the Promised Land to Israel. The prayer shows the influence of the Scripture reading of the recent weeks. It rehearsed how God brought Israel out of Egypt with signs and wonders, dividing the sea, leading them by fiery cloud. At Sinai he gave Israel his law including the holy Sabbath. Through the wilderness period God provided manna from heaven and water from a rock. Such is the record of Yahweh's faithfulness to his people (9:5-15).

C. Confession of Transgression (Neh 9:16-31).

The Israelites, however, proved unfaithful to the gracious God who redeemed them. Within weeks they forgot the wondrous deeds he had done on their behalf. They stubbornly refused to obey his words. They made a calf idol. They appointed a leader to take them back to

Egyptian slavery. Even so, God did not forsake his people. He led them with the fiery cloud. He fed them with manna. He instructed them through his Spirit. He gave them water for their thirst. For forty years he provided for them so that *"their clothes did not wear out, nor their feet swell"* from the long marches (9:16-21).

When they left the wilderness, the Lord delivered the kingdoms of Sihon and Og into the hands of his people. He brought them into the Promised Land. There he enabled them to capture fortified cities and well-furnished houses. Fertile fields, orchards, vineyards and cisterns fell into their hands. They *"reveled"* in the good things which God had placed at their disposal (9:22-25).

Still Israel failed God. They cast his law behind their back, i.e., put it out of mind. They killed God's prophets and committed great blasphemies. To discipline them, God delivered them into the power of a series of oppressors. Each time, however, when Israel cried out to the Lord he sent a deliverer to set them free. This cycle of sin, suffering, supplication and salvation was repeated many times during the period of the Judges. Israel never seemed to learn from these experiences. Yet God continued to bear with them. He admonished them by his Spirit through the prophets. Finally God gave them into the hands of the peoples of the land, i.e., the great powers. Even then, however, he did not make a full end of them. He showed his compassion yet once more (9:26-31).

D. Appeal for Grace (Neh 9:32-37).

After this summary of the relationship of God and his people, the Levites made the only petition in this long prayer. They asked that God might note all the hardship which Israel had experienced from the days of the kings of Assyria unto that very moment. They hastened to add that their condition in no way impugned the justice of God. Israel deserved all that she had experienced, for the entire nation had not kept God's law. They had not turned from their evil ways. Thus at that moment, even though they were living in the land which God had promised their ancestors, they were slaves to a foreign power. Persian taxes required large portions of their produce and cattle. Thus the people of God were in great distress (9:32-37).

RENEWING COMMITMENT
Nehemiah 9:38-10:39

Following the acknowledgment of sin and appeal for grace, the post-Tabernacles solemn assembly began to take a more positive direction.

A. The Covenant Document (Neh 9:38-10:27).

The leaders, priests and Levites in the postexilic community agreed in writing that they would follow the law of God from that day forward. Nehemiah set the example by placing his name at the head of the list. Then followed the name of a certain Zedekiah who probably assisted Nehemiah in civil authority. Next are listed twenty-one priestly names, of which at least fifteen are the names of families. This may explain why Ezra's name does not appear in the list. He was a member of the Seriah family which heads the list (cf. Ezra 7:1; 1 Chr 6:14). Seventeen Levites and forty-four leaders of the people were also signatories. Again these lists contain both family names and individual names.

B. The Covenant Oath (Neh 10:28-29).

Following the signing of the document, the next step in renewing the covenant was the ceremony of taking an oath. The rest of the people joined their leaders in taking upon themselves *"a curse and an oath"* that they would walk by God's law. Failure to abide by the terms of the covenant would automatically trigger the implementation of the *"curse,"* i.e., stipulated penalties for disobedience.

The community was united in its commitment. Everyone, including women and children old enough to understand, joined in the oath of allegiance. The list here (priests, Levites, gatekeepers, etc.) points to an ordered community, restored to the traditional organization established centuries earlier. Furthermore, this community was sensitive to its calling to be *"separate from the peoples."*

C. The Covenant Stipulations (Neh 10:30-39).

Specific obligations were assumed by each of those who entered into the oath to walk by God's law. Seven provisions of the covenant are outlined in the closing verses of Nehemiah 10. On the negative side, this covenant involved three obligations. First, they agreed to refrain from intermarrying with the peoples of the land. Second, they would refuse to purchase any items from foreign merchants on the Sabbath or holy days. Purchasing items from foreign merchants violated the spirit if not the letter of the Sabbath law. Third, they would observe the sabbatical year (cf. Exod 23:10-11; Lev 25:2-7) by (1) not planting crops; and (2) by not making exactions on any debt, i.e., requiring payments on debt (10:30-31).

The covenant also involved four positive obligations. First, they would contribute annually one third of a shekel[9] to supply the regular sacrifices for the temple. Second, by lot families would assume for a period of time the responsibility for supplying the wood for the altar. Apparently they had discovered that everybody's business was nobody's business (10:32-34).

Third, they agreed to give the Lord his due viz., the first fruits of ground and tree and the firstborn of sons and livestock. Firstborn sons were redeemed by payment of five shekels of silver (Exod 13:13; 34:20). Firstborn livestock could also be redeemed. The first fruits and firstborn (or redemption monies) went for the maintenance of the priests who served at the temple. Tithes, on the other hand, were earmarked for Levites who lived in rural areas (Num 18:21). The Levites were then required, under priestly supervision, to bring to the temple a tenth of the tithe which they had received from the people. All temple gifts were stored in the storerooms of the temple and used for temple upkeep (10:35-39).

The final provision sums up the essence of this covenant. These re-committed servants pledged that, no matter what the cost, *"we will not neglect the house of our God"* (10:39).

The significance of what is being pledged here must not be missed. For years the Persian kings had taken responsibility for the maintenance of the temple service. Now the Jews were assuming that responsibility. This would be a heavy burden for a relatively small and poor community. The religious zeal triggered by the revival led by Ezra and Nehemiah now was being translated into concrete deeds. A faith that costs nothing is worth nothing.

REGISTERS OF NEHEMIAH'S GENERATION
Nehemiah 11:1-36

Nehemiah again records the names of various individuals and families which figured prominently in the postexilic resettlement. These lists serve (1) to give honor to whom honor is due; (2) to trace the roots of the community to the past; and (3) to stress that the community was organized to carry out its calling to be a kingdom of priests and a holy nation. As detailed as these lists are, they are not complete. Those named here come from the tribes of Judah, Benjamin and Levi. According to 1 Chronicles 9 Israelites of other tribes also took up residence in Jerusalem.

A. Residents of Jerusalem (Neh 11:1-24).

The hint in Nehemiah 7:4-5 that something was done about the sparse population of Jerusalem is now made explicit. The people cast lots to bring one out of ten families to join their leaders living in Jerusalem. All the men who volunteered to be part of this lottery were blessed by the people.[10] The willingness of many to uproot their families to repopulate Jerusalem is another indication of the eagerness to see the community of God's people restored to its former glory (11:1-2).

The register of those who came to live in Jerusalem includes sons of Judah (468), sons of Benjamin (928), priests (822), Levites (284), gatekeepers (172) and others. The temple singers had a special status in the city for they functioned under a direct commandment from King Artaxerxes (11:3-24).

The population of Jerusalem was well organized. Various overseers are mentioned (cf. vv. 9,14,22). A Benjamite named Judah was *"second in command of the city."*[11] Some of the citizens are called *"mighty men of valor"* (v. 14); others are called *"able men"* (v. 6). These expressions in Hebrew are ambiguous. They can refer to either men of wealth or men of military skill. Jerusalem is twice called *"the holy city"* (vv. 1,18). This indicates that the postexilic community saw its mission as reflecting the holiness of God.

The Persian king had a role in helping to organize the Jerusalem community. He authorized (and probably subsidized) the choirs which performed at stated times in the temple. The interests of the Jews were represented in the royal court by Pethahiah of Judah (11:22-23).

B. Residents of Villages (Neh 11:25-36).

Seventeen villages from Beersheba in the south to the valley of Hinnom in the north were occupied by sons of Judah. Fifteen villages are identified as having been occupied by the sons of Benjamin. Some of these villages (e.g., Kiriath-arba and Beersheba) clearly were outside the territorial limits of the Persian province of Judea. Yet the Jews were permitted by the government to *"encamp"* (v. 30) in these old ancestral villages. Perhaps the Jewish leaders had in mind some day reclaiming all the former territory which once had belonged to the kingdom of Judah.

REGISTERS OF PRIESTS AND LEVITES
Nehemiah 12:1-26

Again the concern of the author is continuity. The significance of the present can only be ascertained when its roots in the past are clearly understood.

A. Original Emigrés (Neh 12:1-11).

1. The priests (12:1-7). In the days of Jeshua the high priest—first generation of the Restoration—there were twenty-two heads of priestly families. Apparently two of the original twenty-four priestly divisions had not yet been restored. Fifteen of those who signed the covenant of Nehemiah 10 used their family names rather than their personal names.[12]

2. The Levites (12:8-9). Eight heads of Levitical families are named. This fills out the list found in Ezra 2:40 where only three Levitical families are mentioned. Some of these names (e.g., Sherebiah) continued to be used by Levites in Nehemiah's day. In some cases these men hold the same offices as their namesakes a century earlier (cf. Neh 8:7; 9:4; 10:12). Members of these families had been faithful to their ministries over several generations.

B. High Priestly Family (Neh 12:10-11).

Jeshua was the first high priest after the return from captivity (Ezra

3:2; Hag 1:1). That the list is probably selective is indicated by the fact that only one high priest—Joiakim—is named between Jeshua and Eliashib, the high priest of Nehemiah's day a century later. Three high priests are named as having followed Eliashib. The list terminates with those who were active in the days of Darius II (423-404 BC) during whose reign Nehemiah must have died.[13] The last name on the list is Jaddua. According to Josephus (*Ant.* 11.8.4,5) the name of the high priest who received Alexander the Great (332 BC) was Jaddua.[14]

C. Second Generation Priestly Families (Neh 12:12-21).

Joiakim was the high priest who followed Jeshua. This second generation of priests contained twenty heads of families. This list drives home once again the point that "the priestly houses held on to their traditional names, not changing them with successive leaders."[15]

D. Levitical Families in Nehemiah's Day (Neh 12:22-26).

The list of heads of Levitical families was kept in a book of chronicles (not the Biblical book by that name). This list seems to suggest that some singers were also employed as gatekeepers of the temple. The author stresses that the musical prescriptions of David were carefully followed in the postexilic community. Several of the Levitical names here appear in the list of those who signed the covenant document Nehemiah 10.

DEDICATING THE WALLS
Nehemiah 12:27-43

For the dedication of the wall all the Levites were assembled so that the event might be celebrated with great vocal and instrumental music. Purification rituals were performed both for these Levites and for the wall and its gates. On the analogy of 2 Chronicles 29:29, this probably was done by offering sin offerings and burnt offerings (12:27-30).

The highlight of the day was the walking of the walls. The leaders of the people and the musicians were divided into two groups. One group was led by Ezra. Nehemiah followed the other. The groups started in opposite directions around the circuit of the wall (12:31-42).

The procession was symmetrically arranged as can be seen in the following chart.

Chart No. 61

WALKING JERUSALEM'S WALLS	
LEFT GROUP	**RIGHT GROUP** **Led by Ezra (vv. 31-37)**
Choir (v. 38)	**Choir (v. 31)**
Nehemiah (v. 38)	**Hoshaiah (v. 32)**
Half the Officials (v. 40)	**Half the Princes (v. 32)**
Seven Priests with Trumpets Named (v. 41)	**Seven Priests with Trumpets Named (vv. 33-35)**
Eight Singers Led by Jezrabiah (v. 42)	**Eight Instrumentalists Led by Zechariah (vv. 35-36)**

The two choirs met and stood together in the house of God and sang praises to the Lord. Sacrifices followed. The city was filled with great joy (12:43).

OTHER REFORMS
Nehemiah 12:44-13:3

Certain reforms were instituted on the day Jerusalem's walls were dedicated.

A. Contributions (Neh 12:44-47).
Various officials were appointed that day to oversee the collection of temple contributions, *"the portions required by the law for the priests and Levites."* The purification rituals of the law of Moses

were performed as were the musical arrangements dating back to the days of David and Solomon. In the postexilic community from the days of Zerubbabel to the days of Nehemiah the people willingly had been paying their dues to priests and Levites because *"they rejoiced over the priests and Levites who served."*

B. Separation (13:1-3).

On wall dedication day they read aloud the Scriptures. From the book of Moses (cf. Deut 23:3-5) they learned that no Ammonite or Moabite should ever enter the assembly of God. This judgment went back to the days of Moses when these two peoples failed to aid the Israelites in their migration toward the Promised Land. In fact, the Ammonites and Moabites had attempted to curse Israel through the prophecies of Balaam. God, however, turned their curses into blessings. Having heard the verdict of Scripture, the postexilic community excluded all foreigners from Israel.

Once again the reading of Scripture had driven home to the Jews the obligation to be holy unto Yahweh. The prohibition here enjoined was not absolute. It was religious, not ethnic. Those who embraced in faith the God of Israel, like Ruth the Moabitess, could find a very different reception in Israel.

NEHEMIAH'S SECOND GOVERNORSHIP
Nehemiah 13:4-31

Nehemiah completed his first term as governor in the thirty-second year of Artaxerxes (432 BC). He returned to the Persian court to have his appointment reviewed and renewed. The record does not indicate how long he was absent from Jerusalem. During that absence, the postexilic community relapsed into some old sins. Nehemiah had been back only a short time before he once again clashed with compromise and created a spiritual earthquake.

A. Failure in Sanctity (Neh 13:4-9).

Nehemiah's archenemy Tobiah had ardent supporters in Jerusalem (cf. 6:17-19). Eliashib the high priest, being related to Tobiah by marriage, actually had prepared for Tobiah a room in one of

752

the temple chambers where contributions of the people previously had been stored. What audacity to empty a sacred chamber of that which was dedicated to God to create a warehouse for the personal possessions of any person, not to mention an enemy. From the temple, the very nerve-center of Jerusalem, Tobiah could wield his ungodly influence upon all the affairs of the Jewish people (13:4-6).

When Nehemiah returned to Jerusalem, he learned about the evil which Eliashib had done in allowing an avowed enemy of the Jews to have a room in the temple. The governor (personally?) threw Tobiah's belongings out of the room. He then gave an order for all the rooms be cleansed which had been defiled by the presence of this unbeliever. The dedicated utensils, grain offerings and frankincense were then returned to those rooms. For Nehemiah holiness was not negotiable. In this cleansing of the temple he became the forerunner of Christ (13:7-9).

B. Failure in Support (Neh 13:10-14).

If the Jews before the exile erred in thinking they could bribe God by lavish gifts (e.g., Isa 1:11), the fault of the postexilic community was in robbing God of his due (Mal 3:8). Nehemiah discovered that during his absence the Levites had not been given their due from the harvest. These servants of the Lord had been forced to leave the temple service to work the fields. The lofty commitment not to forsake the house of the God in chapter 10 had now become hollow words. Full-time servants of God cannot feed their families on rhetoric (13:10).

Nehemiah reprimanded the officials for allowing this situation to exist. He then restored the Levites to their posts. A committee of four reliable priests and Levites was appointed to distribute the tithes and offerings among their kinsmen. Nehemiah then prayed that God might remember these actions taken on behalf of his house (13:11-14).

C. Failure in Sabbath Observance (Neh 13:15-22).

Sabbath abuse was another problem which Nehemiah dealt with decisively. Some Jews were treating the Sabbath as an ordinary work day. Farmers were treading the grapes in the winepresses; others were hauling wine, grapes and figs into the city to put on sale. Nehemiah *"admonished"* these Jews (13:15).

Foreign merchants were peddling their wares in Jerusalem on the Sabbath. The nobles were reprimanded for allowing such abuse of the holy day. Nehemiah pointed out to them that this was the same sin that got their fathers in trouble with the Lord. By profaning the Sabbath they were adding to the wrath on Israel (13:16-18; cf. Jer 17:27).

Nehemiah ordered the gates of the city closed just before dark on the Sabbath. He ordered that the gates not be reopened until after the Sabbath. He stationed temporarily some of his own servants at the gates to prevent any load from entering the city on the holy day. Once or twice the foreign merchants camped outside the walls of Jerusalem on the Sabbath. They may have been trying to do business with people on the wall. Nehemiah warned these merchants that if they continued to camp in front of the wall on the Sabbath he would use force against them. He also appointed Levites to be Sabbath gate-keepers so that the holy day might be properly observed within the city. Nehemiah prayed that God would remember such good deeds and have compassion on him (13:19-22).

D. Failure in Separation (Neh 13:23-29).

During Nehemiah's absence from Jerusalem, Jews had intermarried with women from Ashdod, Ammon and Moab. Children were growing up in these homes who were unable to speak the language of Judah. Nehemiah saw clearly that religious intermarriage corrupts the second generation as well as the first. The confusion of tongues among the children signaled the erosion of Israelite identity. Nehemiah could not allow the compromise of his generation to undo the work of centuries. The situation was desperate (13:23-24).

Nehemiah contended with the men who had married these wives. He *"cursed them,"* i.e., placed a religious curse on them. He struck some of them and pulled out their hair. These were punishments which no doubt were part of the stipulated penalties in the oaths these men had taken some years before (cf. 10:30). He then made them renew their oath not to be involved in any way in intermarriage with the peoples of the land (13:25).

Nehemiah pointed out that it was marriage to foreign wives which caused Solomon, a man greatly blessed and beloved by God, to sin. In the light of the historical record of the damage done by religious intermarriage, Nehemiah expressed shock that these men had acted unfaithfully against their God in this matter (13:26-27).

In the process of his investigation, Nehemiah discovered that the grandson of the high priest had married the daughter of Sanballat the Horonite, that bitter enemy who had resisted so resolutely the building of the wall. Nehemiah *"drove him from me,"* i.e. the grandson was expelled from Jerusalem. Nehemiah called upon God to remember those who so grievously had defiled the priesthood. After doing what he could do to solve the problem, Nehemiah simply committed the whole matter to the Lord (13:28-29).

E. Other Reforms (Neh 13:30-31).

Other measures taken by Nehemiah upon his return included (1) purifying the people from everything foreign; (2) appointing specific duties for priests and Levites; (3) arranging for the wood supply for the temple; (4) arranging for the first fruits to be collected and distributed. For these reforms Nehemiah prayed that God might remember him for good. The inclusion of Nehemiah's memoirs in the sacred canon was one way Heaven answered this concluding prayer (13:30-31).

The final chapter of Nehemiah underscores the impression already created by the earlier chapters about this man. He was fervent in zeal for Yahweh. He possessed a holy boldness which made him brutally blunt with both friend and foe. Nehemiah was a masterful organizer and motivator. He was also a man of action. Even more important, he was a man of the Scriptures and a man of prayer. A man who approaches God on his knees will stand tall in any generation.

ENDNOTES

1. The differences between the lists in Ezra 2 and Nehemiah 7 are mainly in connection with numbers, the order of certain family names, the spelling of various names, and certain omissions and additions. Some of the divergences may be the result of errors in copying.

2. Luck argues that Ezra would not have allowed the spiritual conditions in Jerusalem to deteriorate so much had he been present. Therefore Luck concludes that Ezra must have been recalled to Persia shortly after the events with which his book concluded. He returned only after the walls had been completed. *Op. cit.,* pp. 110f.

3. Some think the common people did not understand Hebrew at this time. The Levites would then have translated the Hebrew words into the Aramaic which now had become the common language of the people. On the other hand, Haggai, Zechariah and Malachi all wrote during this period in Hebrew. Why would they have written in a language which was incomprehensible to the majority of the people?

4. G. Campbell Morgan, *An Exposition of the Whole Bible,* p. 194. Cited by Luck, *op. cit.,* p. 112.

5. Derek Kidner, *Ezra & Nehemiah* in "Tyndale Old Testament Commentaries" (InterVarsity, 1979), p. 106.

6. The feast of Tabernacles was a harvest festival (Exod 34:22) as well as a memorial of wilderness wandering (Lev 23:43).

7. Actually Deut 31:10-13 calls for the public reading of the law every seventh year. It is not clear whether this occasion in Nehemiah 8 coincides with the seventh year, or whether Ezra was going beyond the minimum requirement of the law and introducing an annual reading of the word.

8. The two groups of Levites (9:4 and 9:5) have five names in common, but each has three unique to itself.

9. A third of a shekel was equivalent to about one eighth of an ounce. This is not to be confused with the half shekel census tax of Exod 30:13. The annual temple tax had become a half shekel by the time of Christ (Matt 17:24).

10. Whether the volunteers of 11:2 were additional to the ones chosen by lot, or whether the verse is saying that the latter accepted the decision cheerfully, is not clear.

11. In the light of the position of Hananiah in 7:2, Judah may have been in charge of the second quarter of the city.

12. Kidner, *op. cit.,* p. 122.

13. On the identity of Darius the Persian in Neh 12:22 see E.J. Young, *An Introduction to the Old Testament* (Grand Rapids: Eerdmans, 1960), p. 409.

14. This Jaddua may not be the same individual mentioned by Josephus. On the other hand, Jaddua may have been an infant in the last days of Nehemiah. Since he was in the high priestly line of succession his name was included here.

15. Kidner, *op. cit.,* p. 124.